Handbook of Critical Theory

Handbook of Critical Theory

Edited by
David M. Rasmussen

Copyright © Blackwell Publishers Ltd 1996 except as listed on the
acknowledgments page. This arrangement and editorial matter
copyright © David M. Rasmussen 1996.

First published 1996

Blackwell Publishers Ltd
108 Cowley Road
Oxford OX4 1JF
UK

Blackwell Publishers Inc.
238 Main Street
Cambridge, Massachusetts 02142, USA

Library of Congress Cataloging-in-Publication Data

The handbook of critical theory / edited by David M. Rasmussen.
        p.   cm.
    Includes bibliographical references and index.
    ISBN 0–631–18379–5   1001 179 342
    1. Critical theory.   I. Rasmussen, David M.
    B809.3.H36   1996   95–49861
    142—dc20   CIP

British Library Cataloguing in Publication Data

A CIP catalogue record for this book is available from the British
Library.

Typeset in 10½ on 12½ pt Meridian
by Wearset, Boldon, Tyne and Wear
Printed in Great Britain by T.J. Press Limited, Padstow, Cornwall

This book is printed on acid-free paper

CONTENTS

CONTRIBUTORS

Kenneth Baynes, Associate Professor of Philosophy at The State University of New York at Stony Brook, is the author of *The Normative Grounds of Social Criticism* (1992), editor, with James Bohman and Thomas McCarthy, of *After Philosophy* (1987), and is the general editor of the *SUNY Series in Social and Political Thought*.

Seyla Benhabib is Professor of Government at Harvard University and Senior Research Associate at the Center for European Studies. She is the author of *Critique, Norm, and Utopia* (1986) and *Situating the Self* (1992); and editor of *Feminism and Critique* (with Drucilla Cornell, 1987); together with Fred Dallmayr, *The Communicative Ethics Controversy* (1990); and with John McCole, *On Max Horkheimer* (1994). Her book *The Reluctant Modernism of Hannah Arendt* is forthcoming in 1996.

James Bohman, Associate Professor of Philosophy at St. Louis University, is the author of *New Philosophy of Social Science* (1991) and editor, with Kenneth Baynes and Thomas McCarthy, of *After Philosophy* (1987) and, with David Hiley and Richard Schusterman, of *The Interpretive Turn* (1991). He also has a forthcoming book, *Public Deliberation: Democracy, Complexity and Pluralism* (1996).

Hauke Brunkhorst, a Fellow at the Kulturwissenschaftliches Institut in Essen, is the author of *Der entzauberte Intellektuelle* (1990), *Theodor W. Adorno: Dialektik du Moderne* (1990), *Demokratie und Differenz* (1994), and editor of *Gemeinschaft und Gerechtigkeit* (with Micha Brumlik, 1993).

Jodi Dean is Assistant Professor of Political Science at Hobart and William Smith Colleges. She is the author of *Solidarity of Strangers* (1996). Her book *Resiting the Political: Feminism and the New Democracy* is forthcoming in 1996.

Alessandro Ferrara, on the faculty at the Università di Roma "La Sapienza", is the author of *Modernity and Authenticity* (1993), *L'eudaimonia postmoderna* (1992), *Intendersi a Babele* (1994) and editor of *Comunitarismo e liberalismo* (1992). His book *Justice and Judgment* is forthcoming.

Rainer Forst, who teaches philosophy at the Freie Universität Berlin, is the author of *Kontexte der Gerechtigkeit. Politische Philosophie jenseits von Liberalismus und Kommunitarismus* (1994) and co-editor of *Ethos der Moderne. Foucaults Kritik der Aufklärung* (with A. Honneth and E. Erdmann, 1990).

Axel Honneth, Professor of Political Philosophy at the Freie Universität Berlin, is the author of *Social Action and Human Nature* (with Hans Joas, 1988), *Critique of Power* (1991), *The Fragmented World of the Social* (1995), and *The Struggle for Recognition* (1995).

Martin Jay is Professor of History at the University of California at Berkeley and is the author of *The Dialectical Imagination* (1973), *Adorno* (1984), *Marxism and Totality* (1984) and *Downcast Eyes: The Denigration of Vision in Twentieth-century French Thought* (1993).

Matthias Kettner, Fellow at the Kulturwissenschaftliches Institut in Essen and Lecturer in Philosophy at the Johann-Wolfgang-Goethe University in Frankfurt, is the author of *Hegels ''Sinnliche Gewißheit.'' Diskursanalytischer Kommentar* (1990) and co-editor of *Zur Anwendung der Diskursethik in Recht, Politik und Wissenschaft* (with K.-O. Apel, 1992), *Die eine Vernunft und die vielen Rationalitäten* (with K.-O. Apel, 1996) and *Transzendentalpragmatik* (with A. Dorschel, W. Kuhlmann and M. Niquet, 1993).

Thomas McCarthy is Professor of Philosophy and John Shaffer Professor in the Humanities at Northwestern University. He is the author of *The Critical Theory of Jürgen Habermas* (1978), *Ideals and Illusions* (1991), *Critical Theory* (with David Couzens Hoy, 1994), and is the general editor of the series *Studies in Contemporary German Social Thought*.

Christoph Menke, who teaches Philosophy at the Freie Universität Berlin, is the author of *Die Souveränität der Kunst. Ästhetische Erfahrung nach Adorno und Derrida* (1988; 1991) and *Tragödie im Sittlichen. Gerechtigkeit und Freiheit nach Hegel* (to appear 1996). He is editor of Paul de Man, *Die Ideologie des Ästhetischen* (1993) and co-editor of *Die Verteidigung der Vernunft gegen ihre Liebhaber und Verächter* (with Martin Seel, 1993).

David Rasmussen, Professor of Philosophy at Boston College, is founder and editor of *Philosophy and Social Criticism* (1978–), the ''Philosophy and Social Criticism'' Book Series (1995–), and *Cultural Hermeneutics* (1973–7). He is author of *Reading Habermas* (1990), *Symbol and Interpretation* (1974) and *Mythic-Symbolic Language and Philosophical Anthropology* (1971). He is editor of *Universalism vs. Communitarianism: Contemporary Debates in Ethics* (1990) and co-editor of *The Narrative Path* (with Peter Kemp, 1989) and *The Final Foucault* (with James Bernauer, 1988).

William Rehg, Assistant Professor of Philosophy at St. Louis University, is the author of *Insight and Solidarity: A Study in the Discourse Ethics of Jürgen Habermas* (1994) and the translator of *Between Facts and Norms* by Jürgen Habermas.

James Swindal is Assistant Professor of Philosophy at John Carroll University. His book *Reflection Revisited: Jürgen Habermas's Emancipative Theory of Communicative Action* is forthcoming.

Joel Whitebook, author of *Perversion and Utopia* (1995), teaches philosophy and psychoanalytic theory at The New School for Social Research. A practicing psychoanalyst, he is on the faculties of the New York Freudian Society and the Institute for Psychoanalytic Training and Research.

ACKNOWLEDGMENTS

Thanks are due for permission to reprint essays which have been previously published.

Seyla Benhabib: *"Critical Theory and Postmodernism: On the Interplay of Ethics, Aesthetics, and Utopia in Critical Legal Theory"*, reprinted by permission of the Cardozo Law Review from *Cardozo Law Review*, 11: 1435 (1990), Copyright © 1990 Cardozo Law Review.

Martin Jay: *"Urban Flights: The Institute of Social Research Between Frankfurt and New York"*, reprinted by permission of Oxford University Press, Inc. from *The University and the City: From Medieval Origins to the Present* edited by Thomas Bender, Copyright © 1989 by Oxford University Press, Inc.

Thomas McCarthy: *"Rejoinder to David Hoy"*, adapted by the author and reprinted by permission of Blackwell Publishers from *Critical Theory*, edited by David Hoy and Thomas McCarthy.

David Rasmussen: *"Critical Theory and Philosophy"*, revised by the author and reprinted by permission of Routledge from *Routledge History of Philosophy, Volume VIII*, edited by Richard Kearney.

William Rehg: *"Habermas's Discourse Theory of Law and Democracy: An Overview of the Argument"*, adapted from the translator's introduction and reprinted by permission of MIT Press from *Between Facts and Norms: Contributions to a Discourse Theory of Law and Democracy* by Jürgen Habermas.

Joel Whitebook: *"Fantasy and Critique: Some Thoughts on Freud and the Frankfurt School"*, adapted by the author and reprinted by permission of MIT Press from *Perversion and Utopia: A Study in Psychoanalysis and Critical Theory* (MIT 1995).

EDITOR'S INTRODUCTION

David M. Rasmussen

As I state in my contribution to this book, "Critical theory is a metaphor for a certain kind of theoretical orientation which owes its origin to Kant, Hegel and Marx, its systematization to Horkheimer and his associates at the Institute for Social Research in Frankfurt, and its development to successors, particularly the group led by Jürgen Habermas, who have sustained it under various redefinitions to the present day." This *Handbook of Critical Theory* attempts to present, through sixteen essays and a bibliography, analyses of the various orientations which critical theory has taken, both historically and systematically in recent years, as well as reflections on where it might be going. Although critical theory has undergone numerous transformations over the years, rest assured that it is alive and well, as is demonstrated by its practitioners, the best of whom are represented in this volume.

Critical theory has been and continues to be a powerful movement which finds representation not only in philosophy proper, but also in various branches of the social sciences and humanities. This volume offers its readers an invitation to encounter critical theory through its many and varied manifestations. Aesthetics, history, pragmatics, psychoanalysis, ethics, empirical science, the controversy over the meaning of justice, the new discussion of democracy, the discourse over civil society, the controversy over autonomy, and the most recent contributions to the philosophy and sociology of law – all these areas have found modes of expression in critical theory. At the same time, in this volume one will find the practice of critical theory as expressed through confrontation with its critics, particularly analytic philosophy and deconstruction, as it seeks to find new forms of expression forged out of a living tradition.

In Part I, *Philosophy and History*, in the chapter entitled "Critical Theory and Philosophy," I trace the notion of critique, which came to define critical theory, from its origins in Hegel's critique of Kant to its transformation into the notion of validity in the work of Jürgen Habermas. Certainly, one of the curiosities of the history of philosophy concerns the improbable institutionalization of an idea itself constructed to undermine the very institutional forms toward which it was directed. However, to the student of critical theory cognizant of its philosophical claims, it is this very attempt – to provide a living foundation for a theory which embodies a notion of critique – which stands out in a long story which began with German Enlightenment and post-Enlightenment philosophy. Martin Jay, by contrast, in the chapter entitled "Urban Flights: The Institute of Social Research between Frankfurt and New York," focuses specifically on context, on the extent to which explanations for the Institute may be said to be rooted in "the social and cultural conditions of its day." In a fascinating historical exploration of the Institute in its various locations, in Frankfurt, in New York, in California and again in Frankfurt, Jay explores the academic and urban influences which provide no "single-minded contextual account," but rather a plurality of intersecting influences which contributed to and helped define its distinctive role. Christoph Menke, turning again to philosophy in his chapter "Critical Theory and Tragic Knowledge," puts forth the thesis that critical theory as originally defined by Max Horkheimer initially presents itself as the opposite of tragic knowledge. Critical theory claims to "dissolve" necessity into freedom. Tragedy, on the contrary, considers necessity not as appearance but as "fate" which can be appropriated as affirmation. However, when reflexive reconstruction becomes interpretation, as it must later with Theodor Adorno's *Negative Dialectics*, the very process of dissolving necessity requires, Menke argues, a second step which embodies a conception of freedom which affirms necessity. Menke concludes: "A critical interpretation of social praxis which abandons the idealistic idea of reconciliation implies a tragic affirmation: it is both critical dissolving of apparent necessity and tragic affirmation of constitutive necessity." Taken together, these three chapters not only contribute to an historical understanding of the origins of critical theory but also present an insight into its philosophical meaning.

In Part II, *Social Science, Discourse Ethics, and Justice*, Hauke Brunkhorst, in the chapter entitled "Critical Theory and Empirical Research," situates critical theory's approach to empirical social research *à la* Habermas in the context of the claims and counter claims of empiricism (Popper), of hermeneutics (since Dilthey), of systems-theory (Luhmann) and functionalist reason (Parsons) as well as of Foucault's sociology of power. Brunkhorst argues that recent critical theory "renews" the Kantian point of departure in epistemology by conducting a critique of empiricism, characteristic of critical theory in its original phase (Horkheimer), which asks after the "conditions of the possibility of knowledge and its objects." Beyond that, critical theory in its most recent phase extends that point of departure by making possible a critique of functionalist reason. In Alessandro Ferrara's chapter, "The Communicative Paradigm in Moral Theory," the discussion moves to critical theory's renewal of the Kantian point of departure in moral theory. Ferarra characterizes the development of Habermas's "discourse ethics" from its original formulation in 1982 to the present. According to Ferrara, the "central intuition" upon which discourse ethics is based focuses on "ethical universalism" which in turn rests on a "dialogical revisitation of Kant's view of moral validity as generalizability." Rainer Forst, in "Justice, Reason, and Critique: Basic Concepts of Critical Theory," carries Habermasian moral theory a step further by attempting to work out a "critical theory of justice": taking up the notion of critique as it existed in early critical theory and developing a theory of justice which takes seriously the universalistic claims of reason (Habermas) and the contextual basis of social criticism (Walzer). Taken together the three chapters complement one another not only in their departure from the Kantian turn in later critical theory (Habermas) but also in their attempts to justify this turn in terms of the philosophy of the social sciences as well as the controversial field of moral theory.

In Part III, *Law and Democracy*, William Rehg, in "Habermas's Discourse Theory of Law and Democracy: An Overview of the Argument," presents the argument of Habermas's recent book, *Between Facts and Norms*, which focuses upon law as the key to an understanding of social integration in modern society. Rehg, in an analysis which highlights the link between law and deliberative democracy, shows how Habermas's new discourse on law brings law within the purview of the democratic process of public discourse. As such, Rehg, following Habermas, shows how reflection on law should not only be anchored in the "facticity" of modern experience but also is needful of justification as "valid" in the context of a democratic public will-formation, requiring a reconceptualization under a "procedural" paradigm beyond both liberal and welfare state models of understanding. James Bohman, in his chapter "Critical Theory and Democracy," focuses on critical theory's original preoccupation with democracy as it attempted in its originary phase to link Marx's concept of "radical democracy" with the idea of an "expressive totality." However, when early critical theory began to see that modern society was dominated by "instrumental reason," it turned away from democracy toward other modalities of explanation. Habermas, argues Bohman, by giving up on the idea of totality, was able to reopen the question of radical democracy ultimately severed from the "utopian legacy of holistic critical theory." Alas, in Bohman's view, Habermas, who defines himself as a radical democrat, is not radical enough in that he restricts public opinion to its ability to point "administrative power in specific directions" rather than accepting popular sovereignty for what it is, namely, the rule of the majority, to be sure with countermajoritarian institutions built in.

In Part IV, *Civil Society and Autonomy*, Jodi Dean, in "Civil Society: Beyond the Public Sphere," argues that, against the "reductionist" approach to state and society which characterized early critical theory, the concept of civil society enables critical theory to retain its emphasis on "culture" while at the same time broadening its approach to the sphere of "democratic freedom." While endorsing Jean Cohen and Andrew Arato's approach to civil society – which employs the Habermasian distinction between system and lifeworld, as well as the use of communicative action as the coordinating mechanism within civil society – Dean employs Axel Honneth's concept of "mutual recognition" to take the concept beyond the notion of the "public sphere." Cognizant of the role of "power" within civil society she conceives of that realm as the "wider terrain within which relationships of recognition are situated, institutionalized and interconnected." Kenneth Baynes, carrying on the tradition of critical theory through the practice of "immanent critique" in his "Public Reason and Personal Autonomy," argues that neither "public reason" nor "personal autonomy" can be justified independently. Rather, Baynes justifies the claim that "the two ideals mutually presuppose one another and thus acquire whatever normative weight or force they have only if they are inseparably tied to one another." Beginning with a discussion of the "public reasons" approach, Baynes finds John Rawls's appeal to "fundamental intuitive ideas" present in "political culture" unsatisfactory because it leaves this claim open to relativist interpretation. Turning to the current debate on autonomy, Baynes concludes that communicative action can not only strengthen but also be strengthened by the discourse on autonomy. The result would be a mechanism for securing the interrelationship between public reason and personal autonomy. These two essays taken together contribute to the current discourse on deliberative democracy.

In Part V, *Pragmatics, Psychoanalysis, and Aesthetics*, Matthias Kettner, in "Karl-Otto Apel's Contribution to Critical Theory," characterizes Apel's "transcendental pragmatics" as an essential contribution to critical theory. Kettner argues that Apel contributes to the program of critical theory first, like Habermas, by taking up the challenge of Horkheimer's desire for a "comprehensive program of critical reconstructive social science," and second, by providing "strong justifications for the prescriptivity . . . that ultimately propels such a program." As both "collaborator" with and "critic" of Habermas, deeply influenced by the work of Peirce and Wittgenstein, Apel's philosophical contribution to contemporary critical theory remains without equal. Joel Whitebook, in his "Fantasy and Critique: Some Thoughts on Freud and the Frankfurt School," argues, through a reconsideration of Freud, for a "rehabilitation of the psychoanalytic dimension of critical theory" which, although prominent in the thought of the early practitioners of critical theory, substantially dropped out with Habermas. By retaining only the methodological component of Freud's thinking, Whitebook suggests that Habermas "rationalistically short-circuits Reason's communication with its Other." The result is the loss of "the element of tension between Romanticism and Enlightenment that gave Freud's defense of 'the project of modernity' its complexity and appeal." Hauke Brunkhorst, in "Theodor W. Adorno: Aesthetic Constructivism and a Negative Ethic of the Non-forfeited Life," presents a biographical reflection on the aesthetic and ethical dimensions of Adorno's contribution. Accounting for the multiple influences on Adorno's life, his early family life, his experience as an exile, his early precociousness, his inclination for the aesthetic, his musical genius, and his involvement with the Institute for Social Research, Brunkhorst seeks to show how Adorno arrived at his "pessimistic diagnosis of the times" which in turn led to the sketch of "an ethic of a damaged life," and ultimately, to a philosophy of the non-identical.

In Part VI, *Postmodernism, Critique, and the Pathology of the Social*, Seyla Benhabib, in her chapter entitled "Critical Theory and Postmodernism: On the Interplay of Ethics, Aesthetics, and Utopia in Critical Theory," shows how the critique of "identity logic" embodied in the project of post-modernism is already anticipated in the work of early critical theory, partic-ularly in the work of Adorno and to some extent Horkheimer. The problematic which she seeks to elicit, by looking first at *Dialectic of Enlightenment* and later at *Negative Dialectics*, is the paradoxical phenomenon that the critique of enlightenment reason is "cursed" by the enlightenment itself. Early critical theory shares with postmodernism the "hope that the cri-tique of the Enlightenment can nonetheless evoke the utopian principle of nonidentary logic as an intimation of otherness." Benhabib concludes that critical theory attempts to "think beyond modernism while not abandoning the utopian legacy of the Enlightenment." Thomas McCarthy, in "Critical Theory and Postmodernism. A Response to David Hoy," constructs a forceful argument in defense of later critical theory around the themes of pragma-tism, genealogy, hermeneutics, and pluralism. Against Hoy's alternative explanation, McCarthy argues that critical theory conveys the "spirit" of pragmatism by incorporating not only its practical orientation but its "utopian impulse" as well. McCarthy defends Habermas's "reconstructive approach" from a critique based on Foucault's genealogical orientation by arguing that the distance between the two is not as far as is often claimed, and by suggesting that the real issue raised by the confrontation between the two theorists is "how best to write general histories." Against Hoy's defense of hermeneutics, McCarthy defends a strong use of the concept of "theory" as well as notions of validity and truth. Finally, McCarthy dissociates Habermas's notions of truth and justice from the notion of pluralism in order to show that critical theory is not opposed to pluralism. Axel Honneth, in "Pathologies of the Social: The Past and Present of Social Philosophy," argues for a reconsideration of "social philosophy," the task of which would be to define "social pathology." In a reflection on the history of social phi-losophy Honneth designates Rousseau as its founder who employed "con-cepts like 'deremption' and 'alienation' for ethical criteria by which certain modern processes of development can be conceived as pathologies." Honneth argues that because "philosophical reflection can no longer support itself upon the results of the established social sciences" – a dilemma caused in large part by the moral crises induced by "fascism" and "Stalinism" – a branch of philosophy returned to the classical themes of social philosophy.

Honneth sees the work of Hannah Arendt, Jürgen Habermas, Michel Foucault, and Charles Taylor as each contributing to this tradition. Finally, it is in Habermas's proceduralization of ethics, his attempt to "provide a critical threshold beyond which the pressures of the systems imperatives of the social lifeworld must be viewed as social pathologies," and in Taylor's notion of human beings as "self-interpreting beings" who presuppose certain "social conditions" as ethically necessary, that Honneth sees three modern strategies for developing a modern social philosophy. The three chapters in Part VI have their commonality not only in providing an elaborate defense of a living critical theory but in their construction of ever new dimensions for the future of critical theory.

The Bibliography, prepared by James Swindal, provides a comprehensive guide to both primary and secondary texts in critical theory.

Finally, allow me to thank the contributors for their fidelity to this project. To my editors, Stephan Chambers, who helped conceive the idea which led to this book, Simon Prosser, who saw the project through to its penultimate stage, and finally, Jill Landeryou, who provided the finishing touches, I express my gratitude. Special thanks go to Richard Lynch and James Boettcher, who as my graduate assistants during the final stages of the book, provided necessary editing and coordination. Thanks also to James Swindal for his prompt meeting of impossible deadlines and to Birget Jensen for assistance in translation. Finally, to Debra Matteson, who not only provided editorial competence but was able to facilitate the entire project, I owe a special debt of gratitude.

PART I

Philosophy and History

INTRODUCTION TO PART I

Philosophy and History

In Part I, *Philosophy and History*, in the chapter entitled "Critical Theory and Philosophy," David Rasmussen traces the notion of critique, which came to define critical theory from its origins in Hegel's critique of Kant to its transformation into the notion of validity in the work of Jürgen Habermas. Certainly, one of the curiosities of the history of philosophy concerns the improbable institutionalization of an idea itself constructed to undermine the very institutional forms toward which it was directed. However, to the student of critical theory cognizant of its philosophical claims, it is this very attempt – to provide a living foundation for a theory which embodies a notion of critique – which stands out in a long story which began with German Enlightenment and post-Enlightenment philosophy. Martin Jay, by contrast, in the chapter entitled "Urban Flights: The Institute of Social Research between Frankfurt and New York," focuses specifically on context, on the extent to which explanations for the Institute may be said to be rooted in "the social and cultural conditions of its day." In a fascinating historical exploration of the Institute in its various locations, in Frankfurt, in New York, in California and again in Frankfurt, Jay explores the academic and urban influences which provide no "single-minded contextual account," but rather a plurality of intersecting influences which contributed to and helped define its distinctive role. Christoph Menke, turning again to philosophy in his chapter "Critical Theory and Tragic Knowledge," puts forth the thesis that critical theory as originally defined by Max Horkheimer initially presents itself as the opposite of tragic knowledge. Critical theory claims to "dissolve" necessity into freedom. Tragedy, on the contrary, considers necessity not as appearance but as "fate" which can be appropriated as affirmation. However, when reflexive reconstruction becomes interpretation, as it must later with Theodor Adorno's *Negative Dialectics*, the very process of dissolving necessity requires, Menke argues, a second step which embodies a conception of freedom which affirms necessity. Menke concludes: "A critical interpretation of social praxis, which abandons the idealistic idea of reconciliation implies a tragic affirmation: it is both critical dissolving of apparent necessity and tragic affirmation of constitutive necessity." Taken together, these three chapters not only contribute to an historical understanding of the origins of critical theory but also present an insight into its philosophical meaning.

1 CRITICAL THEORY AND PHILOSOPHY

David M. Rasmussen

Critical theory[1] is a metaphor for a certain kind of theoretical orientation which owes its origin to Kant, Hegel and Marx, its systematization to Horkheimer and his associates at the Institute for Social Research in Frankfurt, and its development to successors, particularly to the group led by Jürgen Habermas, who have sustained it under various redefinitions to the present day. As a term, critical theory is both general and specific. In general it refers to that critical element in German philosophy which began with Hegel's critique of Kant. More specifically it is associated with a certain orientation toward philosophy which found its twentieth-century expression in Frankfurt.

What is critical theory? The term bears the stamp of the nascent optimism of the nineteenth century; a critical theory can change society. Critical theory is a tool of reason which, when properly located in an historical group, can transform the world. "Philosophers have always interpreted the world, the point is to change it." So states Marx's famous eleventh thesis on Feuerbach. Marx got this idea from Hegel who, in his *Phenomenology of Spirit*,[2] developed the concept of the moving subject who through the process of self-reflection, comes to know itself at ever higher levels of consciousness. Hegel was able to combine a philosophy of action with a philosophy of reflection in such a manner that activity or action was a necessary moment in the process of reflection. This gave rise to one of the most significant discourses in German philosophy, that of the proper relationship between theory and practice. Human practical activity, *praxis* in the sense that classical Greek philosophy had defined it, could transform theory. There are two famous instances where Hegel attempted to demonstrate the interrelationship of thought and action in his *Phenomenology of Spirit*, namely, the master–slave dialectic and the struggle between virtue and the way of the world. In the former example, which attempts to demonstrate the proposition, "Self-Consciousness exists in and for itself when, and by the fact that, it so exists for another: that is, it exists only in being acknowledged,"[3] the slave transforms his or her identity by molding and shaping the world and thus becomes something other than a slave. In the latter example, the modern way of the world (essentially Adam Smith's concept of the political economy of civil society) triumphs over the ancient classical concept of virtue as a higher form of human self-knowledge oriented toward freedom. Historical development, as the institutionalization of human action, became an element in human rationality. Critical theory derives its basic insight from the idea that thought can transform itself through a process of self-reflection in history.

Marx, early on in his development in a text that has come down to us under the title, *"Die Judenfrage,"*[4] argued from Hegel's critical insight into the context of modern society. Having already done an analysis a few months before of Hegel's *Philosophy of Right*, he turned his attention to the development of the modern state by reflecting on Bruno Bauer's essay by the same name. Here, he would come to the conclusion that the course of human freedom culminating in the modern state (which Hegel had so brilliantly documented which led from slavery to emancipation – the so-called course of human reason) was no emancipation at all. Indeed, the promised liberation of modern society from the shackles of the Middle Ages had not occurred. Hence, the task of social emancipation which could be carried on by critical reflection would lead the very agents of that reflection to a further task, namely, the transformation of society through revolution. Consequently, the promise of critical theory would be radical social transformation. The ancient assumption that the purpose of reflection was for knowledge itself, allied with the further assumption that pure contemplation was the proper end of the human subject, was replaced by another end of reflection also to be derived from classical thought, but with its own peculiarly modern twist; theory when allied with praxis has a proper political end, namely, social transformation.

However, for Marx this was not enough. Two factors remained. First, from whence was such knowledge to be derived? Second, what would be the nature of such knowledge? Between the fall of 1843 and the summer of 1844, Marx would provide answers to both questions. The answers came in the form of a class theory in which the newly emerging "proletariat" were to play the central role. For Marx, they became the concrete subject of history with the result that hopes for emancipation would be anchored in a critical theory, which would in turn be associated with the activity of a particular class. Again, Hegel had provided the groundwork for this understanding by associating the basic interest in civil society in his philosophy of law with the interest of a particular *Stände*. Of the three orders of society, the agricultural, the business, and civil service, it was only the latter which could represent the universal interests of humankind. With Marx, that latter task was transferred from the civil servants who could no longer be trusted to the proletariat, who he somewhat confidently asserted would bring about the social revolution necessary to overcome the contradictions within modern political society.

With regard to the second question, it was again Hegel, the philosopher of modernity *par excellence*, who taught Marx to look not to intuition *per se*, but to the manifestation of reason in practical institutional form for an appropriate understanding of the world. Hegel had been the first philosopher to both understand and use the work of the political economists in his work. Marx, first in a review of James Mill's *Elements of Political Economy*, and later in a much more elaborate fashion, would work out a thesis about the dynamics of history leading him to assert that economic activity had a certain priority in the development of history.

This thesis would lead Marx to assert shortly thereafter, in *The German Ideology*,[5] that for the first time real history could begin. The very assumption behind a book which had the audacity to put the term "ideology" into the title was that thought alone was ideological. There was a higher truth which Marx through his methodology would be able to attain, namely the "productive" activity of humankind. Human history would then be simultaneous with human production. The term for this new approach to the world of reflection and action would be called "historical materialism" and it would attack other more "idealistic" modes of thinking as "ideological." Hence, a critical theory would be able to unearth the false presumptions that had heretofore held humanity in its sway. Later, in *Das Kapital*, Marx would label the kind of thinking which he had characterized as "ideology" in *The German Ideology* as "fetishism." He did so in the famous last section of the first chapter of volume one, entitled "the fetishism of commodities and the secret thereof." Marx's choice and usage of metaphor is interesting, if not compelling. He uses "ideology," "fetishism," and "secret," as if there was some ominous conspiracy against humankind which a certain kind of critical and theoretical orientation could unmask. The term "fetishism" had a religious origin designating a fundamental confusion regarding perceptual orientations to the world. The very assumption that a certain theoretical orientation could unleash the "secret" behind ideology as a kind of "fetishism" represented a kind of confidence that would not only shape the historical development of critical theory in the future, but also unearth its problematic nature.

At the risk of oversimplification, one might state that there are two basic strains in the history of German philosophy. One strain argues that thought or reason is constitutive, the other, that it is transformative. The former orientation can be traced to the debate initiated by Kant over the limits of human reason, while the latter can be traced to Hegel's philosophy of history, which attempted to locate philosophical reflection in a discourse about the history of human freedom. Critical theory could be said to ally itself with this latter theme, even though the constitutive element would play an ever more significant role. In its classical, Hegelian–Marxist context critical theory rests on the nascent enlightenment assumption that reflection is emancipatory. But what is the epistemological ground for this claim? In other words, how is thought constitutive for action? Which form of action is proper, appropriate or correct? In the early writings, Marx attempted to ground the epistemological claims of transformative action in the concept of *Gattüngswesen*, i.e., species-being. This concept, taken directly from Lüdwig Feuerbach, who in turn had constructed it from both Hegel and Aristotle, affirms that in contrast to the radical individuation of the subject in modern thought, the aim or purpose of a human being is to be determined through intersubjective social action. In Hegelian terms, one constitutes valid self-knowledge through social interaction defined as human labor. According to Marx, the problem with the modern productive process is that it fails to allow the worker to constitute herself as a species-being, i.e., as a person who can function *for* another human being. Hence, the labor process reduces her to an animal, as opposed to a human, level making her autonomous, competitive and inhuman – co-operating with the productive process and not with other human beings. The point of revolution would be to bring the human being to her full and proper capacities as a being for whom the species would be the end, object and aim.

There were problems with this view. To be sure Marx represents the culmination of a certain kind of political theory that began with Hobbes, and which was in turn critical of original anthropological assumptions which saw the human being as an autonomous agent emerging from a state of nature. However, in a certain sense, the concept of species-being was as metaphysical as the Hobbesian notion of the human being in a state of nature, a view which was so aptly and appropriately criticized by Rousseau. It is my view that Marx was aware of the essentially epistemological problem that lay at the foundation of his thought. Does one ground a theory of emancipation in certain anthropological assumptions regarding the nature of the species, assumptions which were as metaphysical as those the theory was attempting to criticize? Marx attempted to overcome this dilemma by providing historical evidence. In this context his later work, the volumes of *Capital*, represent a massive attempt to give an account of human agency which was both historical and scientific. Hence the quest for a valid constitutive ground for critical theory began with Marx himself. Marx as a political economist would bring massive historical research to bear on the claim that capitalism is merely a phase in human development and not the be all and end all of history. Hence, as a true Hegelian, he would assert that, like any economic system, it bore the seeds of its own destruction. As a consequence, the metaphysical claims present in the notion of species-being would re-emerge as a claim about the implicit but incomplete socialization present in capitalism, which, when rationalized, would transform the latter into socialism. As is well known, Marx even went beyond that to attempt to develop, on the basis of his historical investigations, a scientific, predictive formula announcing the end of capitalism on the basis of the "falling rate of profit." The formula assumed that as capital advanced it would be able to generate less and less profit and so would lose its own incentive. Hence, the force of capitalism, unleashed, would lead to its own immanent self-destruction. The victor, of course, would be socialism, which would emerge from the fray, new-born and pure, the ultimate rationalization of the irrationalism implicit in capitalism. As the family would inevitably give way to the force of civil society in Hegel's philosophy of law, so capitalism would break down and re-emerge as socialism.

In 1844 the young Marx had accused his one acknowledged theoretical mentor, Hegel, of harboring a certain "latent positivism."[6] There are those who would accuse the older Marx of having done the same. If capitalism is to fall of its own weight, what is the link between thought and revolutionary action that so inspired the younger Marx? Indeed, what role would the proletariat, the heretofore messianic class of underlings, play in the transformation of society? And what of critical theory? It too would be transformed into just one more scientific, predictive positivistic model. In Marx's favor, this desire to secure the claims of a critical theory on the firm foundation of positivistic science was always in tension with the more critical claims of exhaustive historical analysis. But it was Marx himself who bequeathed to the late nineteenth century, and subsequently by implication to the twentieth century, the ambiguities of a critical theory. One could imagine the great social thinkers of the nineteenth and twentieth centuries coming together to pose a single question: upon what can we ground a critical theory? Would it be the proletariat now transformed into the working class? economic scientific analysis? the critical reflection of a specific historically chosen *noetic* agent (the vanguard)? informed individual praxis? Perhaps critical theory would produce a "dialectic of enlightenment" so cunning that its very inauguration would produce its own destruction as certain later heirs would predict. Certainly, the late nineteenth and the early twentieth centuries saw the concretization of a certain form of Marxism in a political society, not merely in the former USSR, but also in the various workers' movements in Europe and elsewhere, as well as in the founding of the International, which would raise these questions. A kind of critical theory found its apologists from Engels to Lenin, from Bernstein to Luxemburg, from Kautsky to Plekanov. Yet the systematization of critical theory as a model of reflection owes its life in the twentieth century to a group of academics who, originally inspired by the German workers' movement, attempted to give to critical theory a life in the German university.

I   BETWEEN TRADITIONAL AND CRITICAL THEORY

Although the term "critical theory" owes its definition more than anything else in the twentieth century to an essay written in 1937 by Max Horkheimer,[7] the institute which became associated with this term was founded almost two decades earlier. Certainly one of the more interesting experiments in the history of German institutional thought began when Felix Weil, the son of a German exporter of grains from Argentina, convinced his father, Hermann, to provide an endowment which would enable a yearly income of 120,000 marks to establish, in the year 1922, an Institute for Social Research in affiliation with the University of Frankfurt. Weil, inspired by the workers' movement, and having written a thesis on socialism, wanted an institute which could deal directly with the problems of Marxism on a par equal to other established disciplines in the University. The first candidate for director, Kurt Albert Gerlach, who planned a series of inaugural lectures on socialism, anarchism and Marxism, died of diabetes before he could begin. His replacement, Carl Grünberg, a professor of law and political science from the University of Vienna who had begun in the year of 1909 an "Archive for the History of Socialism and the Workers' Movement" and an avowed Marxist, was present at the official creation of the Institüt on 3 February 1922. In his opening address he indicated that Marxism would be the guiding principle of the Institüt. And so it was for a decade. To be sure, it was the kind of Marxism that was still inspired by the nineteenth century, by the idea of the proletariat, by the workers' movement, by the example of the Soviet Union and the Marx–Engels Institute in Moscow, by the conception of Marxism as a kind of science which could penetrate heretofore unknown truths which had been obscured by so-called "bourgeois" thought. Indeed, mocking Frankfurt students celebrated its orthodoxy by referring to it as "Cafe Marx."

Certainly, Marxism need not be vulgar to be orthodox. Academic problems which were standard fare for a now more or less established theoretical tradition were commonplace. Principal among them was the study of the workers' movement. Indeed, if Marxian class theory was correct the proletariat was to bear the distinctive role of being those who were able to interpret history and bring about the transformation that such insight would sustain. Praxis would then be confined to their activity. From an epistemological point of view, the problem of the relation of theory to praxis would be revealed. As Lukács would later think, there would be a certain transparent identity between Marxian social theory and the activity of the working class. Hence, academic study of the working class would be the most appropriate, indeed, the most proper subject of study for an institute which conceived itself in Marxist terms.

For the Institute for Social Research at that time, Marxism was conceived by analogy to science. Hence, the original works of the Institute were associated with capitalist accumulation and economic planning, studies of the economy in China, agricultural relations in France, imperialism, and along with this, through close collaboration with the Soviet Union, the establishment of a collection of the unpublished works of Marx and Engels. However, it wasn't until the leadership passed from Grünberg to the more able hands of one of the young assistants at the Institute, Max Horkheimer, in 1931, that the Institute was to make its mark through both productivity and its distinctive contribution to German scholarship. Although Horkheimer was never the believing Marxist Grünberg had been, certain events in Germany and the world would shape the Institute, distancing it from Marxian orthodoxy. The rise of fascism and the splintering of the workers' movement as well as the Stalinization of Russia would force the Institute to stray from the conventional Marxist wisdom about both theory and science as well as shake their confidence in the workers' movement.

During the thirties, the roster of the institute would include Theodore Adorno, Leo Lowenthal, Erich Fromm, Friedrich Pollock, Herbert Marcuse, Walter Benjamin (indirectly though, since he never became a full-fledged member) and others. Although each figure would eventually be known for independent work, and although certain members would break with the general orientation of the Institute, in retrospect, what is somewhat amazing about this illustrious group of scholars was its concern for sharing a common theoretical program under a distinctive directorship. Indeed, the two most powerful theoretical minds, Adorno and Horkheimer, continued to collaborate for their entire lifetimes. Also, it was during this period that the distinctive perspective with which this group came be identified began to be developed. Modern critical theory can be dated from this period.

The problematic which sparked a critical theory of the modern form was the demise of the working class as an organ of appropriate revolutionary knowledge and action coupled with the rise of fascism and the emergence of Stalinization. Taken together, these events would de-couple the link between theory and revolutionary practice centered in the proletariat which had become commonplace in Marxian theory. What became apparent to Horkheimer and others at the Institute was that once this link was broken, essentially the link with a certain form of ideology, it would be necessary to forge a unique theoretical perspective in the context of modern thought in general and German thought in particular. It would not be enough either to comfortably study the workers' movement or to define Marxist science. The road upon which the Institute embarked would have to bear its own distinctive stamp and character. In brief, this de-coupling would give critical theory its peculiar dynamic, not only for the thirties, but as the torch was passed in the sixties to a younger generation this same thrust would give it definition. Hence, while Grünberg's "Archive for the History of Socialism and the Workers' Movement" would define the Institute in more traditional Marxian terms, the chief organ of the Institute under Horkheimer, *The*

Journal for Social Research, would record a different purpose, namely the movement away from Marxian materialism. Writing in 1968 Jürgen Habermas would put it this way:

> Since the years after World War II the idea of the growing wretchedness of the workers, out of which Marx saw rebellion and revolution emerging as a transitional step to the reign of freedom has for long periods become abstract and illusory, and at least as out of date as the ideologies despised by the young. The living condition of laborers and employees at the time of *The Communist Manifesto* were the outcome of open oppression. Today they are instead motives for trade union organization and for discussion between dominant economic and political groups. The revolutionary thrust of the proletariat has long since become realistic action within the framework of society. In the minds of men at least, the proletariat has been integrated into society.[8]

Horkheimer's 1937 essay, which attempted to systematically define critical theory, begins not by underlining an association with the Marxist heritage that still distinguished the Institute and journal with which it was associated. Rather the essay begins by trying to answer the more general question regarding theory *per se*. "What is theory?"[9] (p. 188) In the traditional sense, theory is a kind of generalization based upon experience. From Descartes to Husserl theory has been so defined argues Horkheimer. As such, however, theory traditionally defined has a peculiar kind of prejudice which favors the natural sciences. Horkheimer, reflecting the great Diltheyian distinction between *Geisteswissenschaften* and *Naturwissenschaften* makes the appropriate criticism. Social science imitates natural science in its self-definition as theory. Put simply, the study of society must conform to the facts. But Horkheimer would argue that it is not quite so simple. Experience is said to conform to generalizations. The generalizations tend to conform to certain ideas present in the minds of the researchers. The danger is apparent: so defined, theory conforms to the ideas in the mind of the researcher and not to experience itself. The word for this phenomenon, derived from the development of the Marxist theoretical tradition following Lukács's famous characterization in 1934, is "reification." Horkheimer doesn't hesitate to use it. Regarding the development of theory he states, "But the conception of theory was absolutized, as though it were grounded in the inner nature of knowledge as such, or justified in some other ahistorical way, and thus it became a reified ideological category."[10] Although various theoretical approaches would come close to breaking out of the ideological constraints which restricted them, such as positivism, pragmatism, neo-Kantianism and phenomenology, Horkheimer would argue that they failed. Hence, all would be subject to the logico-mathematical prejudice which separates theoretical activity from actual life. The appropriate response to this dilemma is the development of a critical theory. "In fact, however, the self-knowledge of present-day man is not a mathematical knowledge of nature which claims to be the eternal logos, but a critical theory of society as it is, a theory dominated at every turn by a concern for reasonable conditions of life."[11] Of course, the construction of a critical theory won't be easy. Interestingly enough, Horkheimer defines the problem epistemologically. "What is needed is a radical reconsideration not of the scientist alone, but of the knowing individual as such."[12]

Horkheimer's decision to take critical theory in the direction of epistemology was not without significance. Critical theory, which had heretofore depended upon the Marxist tradition for its legitimation, would have to define itself by ever distancing itself from that tradition. Indeed, one of the peculiar ironies resulting from this particular turn is that the very tradition out of which critical theory comes, namely Marxism, would itself fall under the distinction between traditional and critical theory. Ultimately, in many ways the Marxist tradition was as traditional as all the other traditions. But, of course, the 1937 essay fails to recognize this. Indeed, this dilemma of recognition would play itself out in the post-1937 period. This is the very irony of the systematization of critical theory. Equally, this epistemological turn would change permanently the distinction and approach of critical theory. As I suggested earlier, critical theory found its foundation in the transformative tradition in German thought as inspired by Hegel and Marx. Now, having embarked upon an epistemological route, it would find it necessary to draw upon the constitutive dimension of German thought. If one could not ground critical theory in Marxian orthodoxy, certainly the assumption behind the 1937 essay, it would be necessary to find the constitutive point of departure for critical theory in an analysis of knowledge as such. Unfortunately, Horkheimer was unprepared to follow his own very unique insight. Instead, the constitutive elements of knowledge to which he refers are taken in a more or less unexamined form from the Marxian heritage. The distinction between individual and society, the concept of society as bourgeois, the idea that knowledge centers in production, the critique of the so-called liberal individual as autonomous, the primacy of the concept of history over logos – these so-called elements which are constitutive of a critical theory were part of the Marxist heritage.

Taken as a whole, the essay is strongly influenced by the Hegelian–Marxist idea that the individual is alienated from society, that liberal thought obscures this alienation and that the task of critical theory must be to overcome this alienation. Horkheimer put it this way:

> The separation between the individual and society in virtue of which the individual accepts as natural the limits prescribed for his activity is relativized in Critical Theory. The latter considers the overall framework which is conditioned by the blind interaction of individual activities (that is, the existent division of labor and class distinctions) to be a function which

originates in human action and therefore is a possible object of painful decision and rational determination of goals.[13]

Horkheimer is vehement in his critique of the kind of thought that characterizes so-called "bourgeois" individualism. For him, "bourgeois thought"
harbors a belief in an individual who is "autonomous" believing that it, the
autonomous ego, is the ground of reality. Horkheimer counters this view
with another, reminiscent of the early Marx. "Critical thinking is the function neither of the isolated individual nor a sum total of individuals. Its subject is rather a definite individual in his real relation to other individuals and
groups, in his conflict with a particular class, and, finally, in the resultant
web of relationships with the social totality and with nature."[14]

Of course, this view is dangerously close to traditional Marxian class theory and Horkheimer knows it. After all, who is this "definite individual"
whose "real relation" is to other individuals? Traditional Marxist theory
answered, the proletariat. Horkheimer is suspicious. "But it must be added
that even the situation of the proletariat is, in this society, no guarantee of
correct knowledge."[15] Horkheimer is hard pressed to find the appropriate
replacement of the proletariat without falling back into what he called
"bourgeois individualism." He is doubtful of the proletariat's ability to somehow "rise above . . . differentiation of social structure . . . imposed from
above." But if he wants to eliminate the proletariat as a source of truth or
correct knowledge, he doesn't quite do it. Indeed, the intellectual or critic
can proclaim her identity with the proletariat. Horkheimer is not entirely
without optimism. "The intellectual is satisfied to proclaim with relevant
admiration the creative strength of the proletariat and finds satisfaction in
adapting himself to it and canonizing it."[16] Indeed, Horkheimer is optimistic
about this identification.

> If, however, the theoretician and his specific object are seen as forming a
> dynamic unity with the oppressed class, so that his presentation of societal
> contradictions is not merely the expression of the concrete historical situa-
> tion but also a force within it to stimulate change, then his real function
> emerges.[17]

Horkheimer's reliance on Marxian doctrine as the epistemological foundation for critical theory becomes more apparent as the essay develops. Hence,
a critical theory of society will show "how an exchange economy, given the
condition of men (which, of course, changes under the very influence of
such an economy), must necessarily lead to a heightening of those social
tensions which in the present historical era lead in turn to wars and revolution."[18] As such, critical theory has a peculiar insight into the potential history of modern society. As Marx used political economy and the theory of
the primacy of production, Horkheimer will use this model of economic

determinism to predict the development of social contradictions in the modern world. Indeed, he goes so far as to state that critical theory rests upon a "single existential judgment," namely, "the basic form of the historically given commodity economy on which modern history rests contains in itself the internal and external tensions of the modern era."[19]

Equally, critical theory will be able to overcome the "Cartesian dualism" that characterized contemporary traditional theory by linking critical with practical activity, theory and praxis. Indeed, it was this belief that critical theory was somehow related to practical activity that would distinguish this kind of theoretical endeavor. "The thinker must relate all the theories which are proposed to the practical attitudes and social strata which they reflect."[20]

In retrospect, one may view this 1937 declaration as something of a *tour de force* attempting to break away from at least some of the most fundamental tenets of traditional Marxist theory, while at the same time in a curious way being caught in the very web of the system from which it was trying to escape. Hence, while dissociating itself from the assumption that truth and proper knowledge was to be rendered through the proletariat, the fundamental tenet of Marxian class theory, this treatise on Critical Theory celebrated as valid notions, concepts such as economic determinism, reification, critique of autonomy and social contradiction – assumptions derived from traditional Marxian social theory. Simultaneously, this position could not seek to justify itself independently of the events of the time. As the French Revolution determined Hegel's concept of the political end of philosophy as human freedom, and as the burgeoning industrial revolution determined Marx's thought, critical theory attempted to respond to the events of the time, the decline of the workers' movement and the rise of fascism. Hence, the indelible mark of the Institute, as well as that which distinguished the essay on Critical Theory in the decade of the thirties, was the conviction that thought was linked to social justice. The thesis, as old as the German enlightenment itself, was that thought could somehow be emancipatory. The predominance of this view gave the Institute its particular character, especially when contrasted to the other German philosophical movements of the time, phenomenology, existentialism and, to some extent, positivism. Although influenced by the same set of events as the other German philosophical movements it was critical theory that was to distinguish itself by addressing the political oppression of the day.

II   INSTRUMENTAL REASON AND THE DECLINE OF ENLIGHTENMENT

Critical theory in the post-1937 period would be characterized by two essentially related perspectives, one which broadened its critique of modes of rationality under the heading "Critique of Instrumental Reason" and the other which attempted a grand analysis of culture and civilization under the heading "Dialectic of Enlightenment." With the onslaught of World War II, Horkheimer and Adorno shared not only a deep pessimism about the future course of rationality, but also a loss of hope in the potentialities of a philosophy of history for purposes of social transformation. The confidence in the great potentialities of thought as unleashed by the German enlightenment goes underground – replaced by the pessimism of the two major thinkers of critical theory who gave up not only on being thinkers in solidarity with the proletariat, but also on the redemptive powers of rationality itself. In this sense, they not only represent a critique of what is now quite fashionably called "modernity," but they may be the harbingers of post-modernity as well.

In the course of the development of critical theory under the ever more pessimistic vision of its principal representatives, the focus would change from Hegel and Marx to Weber. Although they were never to entirely give up on the former, it was Weber who would articulate the pessimistic underside of the enlightenment which Horkheimer and Adorno would come to admire. Hegel, through his notion of reflection which made a distinction between true and false forms of externalization, between *Entaüsserung* and *Entfremdung*, always sustained the possibility of reason being able to overcome its falsifications. Marx, although less attentive to this distinction, retained the possibility of overcoming falsification or alienation through social action. Hence, whether it was through the reconciliatory power of reason in the case of Hegel, or the transformative force of social action in the case of Marx, a certain emancipatory project was held intact. Horkheimer, and eventually Adorno, initially endorsed that project. However, when Horkheimer wrote his *Critique of Instrumental Reason*,[21] it was under the influence of Weber's brilliant, sobering vision regarding reason and action forged through a comprehensive analysis of the genesis and development of western society. Weber had speculated that in the course of western history, reason, as it secularizes, frees itself from its more mythic and religious sources and becomes ever more purposive, more oriented to means to the exclusion of ends. In order to characterize this development, Weber coined the term *Zweckrationalität*, purposive, rational action. Reason, devoid of its redemptive and reconciliatory possibilities, could only be purposive, useful and calculating. Weber had used the metaphor "iron cage" as an appropriate way of designating the end, the dead-end of modern reason. Horkheimer would take the analysis one step further. His characterization of this course was designated by the term "instrumental reason." Implied in this usage is the overwhelming force of reason for purposes of social control. The combined forces of media, bureaucracy, economy and cultural life would bear down on the modern individual with an accumulated force which could only be described as instrumental. Instrumental reason would represent the ever expanding ability of those who were in positions of power in the modern world to dominate and control society for their own calculating purposes. So conceived, the kind of analysis which began with the great optimism inaugurated by the German enlightenment (which sustained the belief that reason could come to comprehend the developing principal of history and therefore society) would end with the pessimistic realization that reason functions for social control, not in the name of enlightenment or emancipation. And what then of a critical theory?

No doubt that question occurred to Horkheimer and Adorno, who, as exiles, now Southern Californians, spin out what in retrospect must be said to be one of the most fascinating books of modern times, *Dialectic of Enlightenment*.[22] Is enlightenment, the avowed aim of a critical theory, "self-destructive"? That is the question posed by the book. The thesis of the book is contained in its title. Enlightenment, which harbors the very promise of human emancipation, becomes the principle of domination, domination of nature and thus, in certain hands, the basis for the domination of other human beings. In the modern world, knowledge is power. The book begins with an analysis of Bacon's so-called "scientific attitude." The relation of "mind" and "nature" is "patriarchal";[23] "the human mind, which overcomes superstition, is to hold sway over a disenchanted nature."[24] "What men want to learn from nature is how to use it in order wholly to dominate it and other men. That is the only aim."[25] Hence, "power and knowledge" are the same. But the thesis is more complex. The term "dialectic" is used here in a form which transcends Hegel's quasi-logical usage. Here dialectic circles back upon itself in such a manner that its subject, enlightenment, both illuminates and destroys. Myth is transformed into enlightenment, but at the price of transforming "nature into mere objectivity."[26] The increment of power gained with enlightenment has as its equivalent a simultaneous alienation from nature. The circle is vicious: the greater enlightenment, the greater alienation. Magic, with its desire to control, in the pre-modern world is replaced by science, which has not only the same end but more effective means. According to this thesis, the very inner core of myth is enlightenment. "The principle of immanence, the explanation of every event as repetition, that the enlightenment upholds against mythic imagination, is the principle of myth itself."[27] Indeed, they observe, in the modern obsession with the mathematization of nature (the phenomenon so accurately observed by Edmund Husserl in his famous *The Crisis of European Science and Transcendental Phenomenology*) they find representatives of a kind of "return of the mythic" in the sense that enlightenment always "intends to secure itself against the return of the mythic." But it does so by degenerating into the "mythic cult of positivism." In this "mathematical formalism," they claim, "enlightenment returns to mythology, which it never knew how to elude."[28] Such is the peculiar character of the dialectic of enlightenment, which turns upon itself in such a way that it is subsumed by the very phenomenon it wishes to overcome.

Critical theory distinguishes itself in this period by ever distancing itself from the Marxian heritage with which it was originally associated. Some would see this as a departure from the very sources of reason from which it was so effectively nourished. Hence, a form of rationality gone wild. Others might see it from a different perspective. Perhaps the *Dialectic of Enlightenment* represents the coming of age of critical theory, as critical theory finally making the turn into the twentieth century. As such, the philosophy of history on which it so comfortably rested with its secure assumptions about the place of enlightenment in the course of western history (to say nothing of the evolution of class and economy), was undercut by their curious insight into the nature of enlightenment itself. Enlightenment is not necessarily a temporal phenomenon given its claims for a particular time and place in modern historical development. Rather, for Horkheimer and Adorno, enlightenment is itself dialectical, a curious phenomenon associated with rationality itself. In this view, the dialectic of enlightenment could be traced to the dawn of human civilization. Here we encounter a form of critical theory influenced not only by Kant, Hegel, Marx and Weber but also by Nietzsche and perhaps Kierkegaard. It would follow that texts that witnessed the evolution of human history would be placed side by side with those which gave testimony to its origin. Enlightenment can then be traced not to the so-called German enlightenment, or the Western European enlightenment, but to the original written texts of Western Civilization, which as any former Gymnasium student knows, were those of Homer. Nietzsche is credited with the insight. "Nietzsche was one of the few after Hegel who recognized the dialectic of enlightenment."[29] They credit him with the double insight that enlightenment unmasks the acts of those who govern; it is also a tool used by them under the name of progress to dupe the masses. "The revelation of these two aspects of the Enlightenment as an historic principle made it possible to trace the notion of enlightenment as progressive thought, back to the beginning of traditional history."[30]

Horkheimer and Adorno do not concentrate much on the illusory character of the enlightenment in Homer, "the basic text of European civilization" as they call it. That element has been over-emphasized by the so-called Fascist interpreters of both Homer and Nietzsche. Rather, it is the use or interpretation of myth as an instrument of domination as evidenced in this classic text that they perceive as fundamental. Here, Weber and Nietzsche complement one another. The other side of the dialectic of enlightenment is the thesis on instrumental reason. Hence, the "individuation" of self which is witnessed in the Homeric text is carried out through what seems to be the opposition of enlightenment and myth. "The opposition of enlightenment to myth is expressed in the opposition of the surviving individual ego to multifarious fate."[31] The Homeric narrative secularizes the mythic past in the name of the hero's steadfast orientation to his own "self-preservation." It secularizes it by learning to dominate it. Learning to dominate has to do with the "organization" of the self. But the very instrumentality associated with domination has its curious reverse side; something like what Marcuse would later call "the return of the repressed." As they put it regarding Homer:

> Like the heroes of all the true novels later on, Odysseus loses himself in order to find himself; the estrangement from nature that he brings about is realized in the process of the abandonment to nature he contends in each adventure; and, ironically, when he, inexorable, returns home, the inexorable force he commands itself triumphs as the judge and avenger of the legacy of the powers from which he has escaped.[32]

There is no place where this curious double thesis is more effectively borne out than in the phenomenon of sacrifice. Influenced by Ludwig Klage's contention regarding the universality of sacrifice, they observe that individuation undercuts the originary relation of the lunar being to nature which sacrifice implies. "The establishment of the self cuts through that fluctuating relation with nature that the sacrifice of the self claims to establish."[33] Sacrifice, irrational though it may be, is a kind of enabling device which allows one to tolerate life. "The venerable belief in sacrifice, however, is probably already an impressed pattern according to which the subjected repeat upon themselves the injustice that was done them, enacting it again and again in order to endure it."[34] Sacrifice, when universalized and said to apply to the experience of all of humanity, is civilizational. Its elimination would occur at enormous expense. The emergence of rationality is based on denial, the denial of the relationship between humanity and nature. "The very denial, the nucleus of all civilizing rationality, is the germ cell of a proliferating mythic irrationality: with the denial of nature in man not merely in the *telos* of the outward control of nature but the *telos* of man's own life is distorted and befogged."[35] The great loss is of course that the human being no longer is able to perceive its relationship to nature in its compulsive preoccupation with self-preservation. The dialectic of enlightenment continues to play itself out. To escape from sacrifice is to sacrifice oneself. Hence, the sub-thesis of *Dialectic of Enlightenment*: "the history of civilization is the history of the introversion of sacrifice. In other words, the history of renunciation."[36] It is this sub-thesis that they associate with the "prehistory of subjectivity."[37]

The text to which they have turned their attention is written by Homer, but the story is about the prehistory of western civilization. Odysseus is the prophetic seer who in his deeds would inform the course of action to be followed by future individuals. Odysseus is the "self who always restrains himself"; he sacrifices for the "abnegation of sacrifice" and through him we witness the "transformation of sacrifice into subjectivity." Above all, Odysseus "survives," but ironically at the "concession of one's own defeat," an acknowledgment of death. Indeed, the rationality represented by

Odysseus is that of "cunning." A necessity required by having to choose the only route between Scylla and Charybdis in which each god has the "right" to do its particular task. Together the gods represent "Olympian Justice" characterized by an "equivalence between the curse, the crime which expiates it, and the guilt arising from that, which in turn reproduces the curse."[38] This is the pattern of "all justice in history" which Odysseus opposes. But he does so by succumbing to the power of this justice. He does not find a way to escape the route charted past the Sirens. Instead, he finds a way to outwit the curse by having himself chained to the mast. As one moves from myth to enlightenment, it is cunning with its associated renunciation which characterizes reason. The great promise held by enlightenment is now seen when perceived in retrospect, from the perspective of the earlier Horkheimer and Adorno, to be domination, repression and cunning.

The thesis contained in *Dialectic of Enlightenment* can be extended beyond the origin of Western civilization. As its authors attempt to show, it can be brought back to effectively critique the eighteenth-century enlightenment as well as attempts to overcome it. As self-preservation was barely seen in Homer as the object of reason, the so-called historical enlightenment made a fetish of it. "The system the Enlightenment has in mind is the form of knowledge which copes most proficiently with the facts and supports the individual most effectively in the mastery of nature. Its principles are the principles of self-preservation." "Burger," "slave owner," "free entrepreneur" and "administrator" are its logical subjects. At its best, as represented in Kant, reason was suspended between "true universality" in which "universal subjects" can "overcome the conflict between pure and empirical reason in the conscious solidarity of the whole,"[39] and calculating rationality "which adjusts the world for the ends of self-preservation." In this view, Kant's attempt to ground morality in the law of reason came to naught. In fact, Horkheimer and Adorno find more base reasons for Kant's attempt to ground morality in the concept of "respect." "The root of Kantian optimism" is based in this view on the fear of a retreat to "barbarism." In any case, in this view the concept of respect was linked to the bourgeois, which in latter times no longer existed in the same way. Totalitarianism as represented in Fascism no longer needed such concepts nor did it respect the class that harbored them. It would be happy with science as calculation under the banner of self-preservation alone. The link between Kant and Nietzsche is said to be the Marquis de Sade. In de Sade's writings, it is argued, we find the triumph of calculating reason, totally individualized, freed from the observation of "another person." Here, we encounter a kind of modern reason devised of any "substantial goal," "wholly functionalized," a "purposeless purposiveness" totally unconcerned about effects which are dismissed as "purely natural." Hence, any social arrangement is as good as any other; and the "social necessities," including "all solidarity with society, duty and family," can be dissolved.

If anything, then, enlightenment means "mass deception" through its fundamental medium of the "culture industry" where the rationality of "technology" reigns. "A technological rationale is the rationale of domination itself."[40] In film, in music, in art, in leisure this new technology has come to dominate in such a way that the totality of life and experience have been overcome. In the end, in accord with this view, the so-called enlightenment of modern civilization is ironic, total, bitter and universal. Enlightenment as self-deception manifests itself when art and advertising become fused in an idiom of a "style" that fashions the modern experience as an ideology from which there is no escape. In the blur of modern images, all phenomena are exchangeable. Any object can be exchanged for any other in this "superstitious fusion of word and thing."[41] In such a world, fascism becomes entertainment, easily reconciled with all the other words and images and ideologies in the vast arena of modern assimilation.

In the end, *Dialectic of Enlightenment* can be viewed as a kind of crossroads for modern philosophy and social theory. On the one hand, reason can function critically, but on the other, it cannot ground itself in any one perspective. Reason under the image of self-preservation can only function for the purpose of domination. This is critical theory twice removed; removed from its foundations in the Marxism of the nineteenth century from which it attempted to establish its own independence, and removed once again from any foundation to function as a raging power of critique without foundation. In this sense, this book, more than any other to come from the so-called Frankfurt School, hailed the end of philosophy, and did so in part to usher in the era now designated as postmodernity. Thus, it was not only the successive reconstruction of phenomenology from Husserl through Heidegger that the harbingers of postmodernity could point to as legitimate forebears of their own movement, but to the voices which rang out in the *Dialectic of Enlightenment* whose prophetic rage led the way. It was left to Foucault to probe the multiple meanings of the discipline of the self and the institutional repression of the subject unleashed by the enlightenment, and to Derrida to articulate the groundlessness of a position which seeks the role of critic but cannot find the way to a privileged perspective which would enable the proper interpretation.

III   AESTHETIC RECONSTRUCTION

But if critical theory was willing, in the late forties, to partially give up on the enlightenment and the possibility of a modality of thought that harbored within it a potential for emancipation, it was not totally ready to do so. Hence, critical theory in its curious route from the early twenties to the present, would make one more turn, a turn toward aesthetics. The wager on aesthetics would keep the emancipatory hypothesis which critical theory began alive, if in muted fashion. Adorno, inspired in part by Benjamin, would lead the way out from the ashes left in the wake of an instrumental rationality whose end, as the end of philosophy, was almost apparent. If the general claims of the *Dialectic of Enlightenment* were to be sustained the theoretical consequences for critical theory would be devastating. Hence, the question regarding the manner in which a critical theory could be rehabilitated, but this time under the suspicion of a full-blown theory of rationality. In a sense, through their rather devastating analysis of rationality as fundamentally instrumental, and of enlightenment as fundamentally circular, it would have seemed that the very possibility for critique itself would be undermined. The aesthetic redemption of the claims of critical theory would have to be understood from the perspective of the framework of suspicion regarding the claims of cognition. Since cognition would result inevitably in instrumentality, it would be necessary to find a way in which critique could be legitimated without reference to cognition *per se*. Aesthetics, with which Adorno had been fascinated from the time of his earliest published work, if only provisionally, would provide a way out. If *Dialectic of Enlightenment* could be read as a critique of cognition, art represents for Adorno a way of overcoming the dilemma established by cognition. Adorno sees the capacity of a non-representation theory in the potentiality of art as manifestation. The explosive power of art remains in its representing that which cannot be represented. In this sense it is the non-identical in Art that can represent society, but only as its other. Art functions then for Adorno in the context of the program of critical theory as a kind of stand-in for a cognitive theory, which cannot be attained under the force of instrumentality.

Adorno, however, was not quite ready to give up on a philosophy of history which had informed his earlier work. Hence, under the influence of Benjamin and in direct contrast to Nietzsche and Heidegger, he was able to incorporate his understanding of art within a theory of progress. Benjamin had postulated the thesis at the end of his famous essay "The Work of Art in the Age of Mechanical Reproduction,"[42] originally published in the *Zeitschrift für Sozialforschung* in 1936,[43] that with photography, "for the first time in world history, mechanical reproduction emancipates the work of art from its parasitical dependence on ritual." As a consequence, art no longer needed to sustain a claim to authenticity. After photography, the work of art is "designed for reproducibility." From this observation, Benjamin drew the rather astonishing conclusion: "But the instant the criterion of authenticity ceases to be applicable to artistic production, the total function of art is reversed. Instead of being based on ritual, it begins to be based on another practice – politics."[44] However, it should not be assumed that the politics with which modern art was to be associated was immediately emancipatory. The thesis was as positive as it was negative. "The logical result of Fascism is the introduction of aesthetics into political life."[45] But for Benjamin this was a form of the relationship between aesthetics and politics which would attempt to rekindle the old association between art and ritual. "The violation of the masses, whom Fascism, with it the *Führer* cult, forces to their knees, has its counterpart in the violation of an apparatus which is pressed into the production of ritual values."[46] However, the tables can be turned; while fascism "equals the aestheticism of politics" Benjamin claimed, Marxist that he was, "communism responds by politicizing art."[47]

Adorno would use this insight into the nature of art and historical development freed of Benjamin's somewhat materialist orientation. While he affirmed that "modern art is different from all previous art in that its mode of negation is different" because modernism "negates tradition itself," Adorno addressed the issue of the relation of art not to Fascism but to capitalist society. Beyond that, Adorno's task was to show how art could overcome the dilemma of rationality as defined through the critique of instrumentality, while at the same time sustaining the claim that art had a kind of intelligibility. How could art be something other than a simple representation of that society? Adorno would return to the classical aesthetic idea of mimesis in order to make his point. Art has the capacity to represent, but in its very representation it can transcend that which it is representing. Art survives not by denying but by reconstructing. "The modernity of art lies in its mimetic relation to a petrified and alienated reality. This, and not the denial of that mute reality, is what makes art speak."[48] Art, in other words, represents the non-identical. "Modern art is constantly practicing the impossible trick of trying to identify the non-identical."[49]

Art then can be used to make a kind of claim about rationality. "Art's disavowal of magical practices – art's own antecedents – signifies that art shares in rationality. Its ability to hold its own *qua* mimesis in the midst of rationality, even while using the means of that rationality, is a response to the evils and irrationality of the bureaucratic world." Art then is a kind of rationality that contains a certain "non-rational" element that eludes the instrumental form. This would suggest that it is within the power of art to go beyond instrumental rationality. This is what art can do which cannot be done in capitalist society *per se*. "Capitalist society hides and disavows precisely this irrationality, whereas art does not." Art then can be related to truth. Art "represents truth in the twofold sense of preserving the image of an end smothered completely by rationality and of exposing the irrationality and absurdity of the status quo."[50]

It is Adorno's claim then that although art may be part and parcel of what Weber described as rationalization, that process of rationalization in which art partakes is not one which leads to domination. Thus, if art is part of what Weber called the "disenchantment of the world," it leads us in a direction different from that of instrumental reason. Hence, the claim that "Art mobilizes technology in a different direction than domination does."[51] And it is for this reason, thinks Adorno, that we must pay attention to the "dialectics of mimesis and rationality that is intrinsic to art."[52]

Whereas the *Dialectic of Enlightenment* could be conceived as a critique of cognition, Adorno uses art to rehabilitate a cognitive claim. "The continued existence of mimesis, understood as the non-conceptual affinity of a subjective creation with its objective and unposited other, defines art as a form of cognition and to that extent as 'rational.' "[53] Hence, in a time when reason has, in Adorno's view, degenerated to the level of instrumentality, one can turn to art as the expression of the rehabilitation of a form of rationality which can overcome the limitation of reason by expressing its non-identity with itself. In this sense, the claims of critical theory would not be lost, but transformed. Indeed, the earlier emancipatory claims of critical theory would be reappropriated at another level. Here again, Adorno's view seems to be shaped by that of his friend Walter Benjamin. For Adorno, art can reconcile us to the suffering which can never be expressed in ordinary rational terms. While "reason can subsume suffering under concepts" and while it can "furnish means to alleviate suffering," it can never "express suffering in the medium of experience." Hence, art has a unique role to play under a transformed understanding of the role of critical theory. "What recommends itself, then, is the idea that art may be the only remaining medium of truth in an age of incomprehensible terror and suffering."[54] In other words, art can anticipate emancipation, but only on the basis of a solidarity with the current state of human existence. "By cathecting the repressed, art internalizes the repressing principle, i.e. the unredeemed condition of the world, instead of merely airing futile protests against it. Art identifies and expresses that condition, thus anticipating its overcoming."[55] For Benjamin it is this view of and solidarity with suffering experienced by others in the past which has not been redeemed. For Adorno then, happiness is not simply an empty enlightenment term. It has a slightly messianic, theological twist. His fundamental thesis was "Our image of happiness is indissolubly bound up with the image of redemption."[56]

Finally, if it is possible to look at Adorno's later work on aesthetics from the perspective of the position worked out with Horkheimer in *Dialectic of Enlightenment*, it appears that a case can be made for the retrieval of the earlier emancipatory claims of critical theory on the basis of the non-identical character of the work of art. To be sure, Adorno, along with Horkheimer, had left little room to retrieve a critical theory in the wake of their devastating critique of the claims of reason. Indeed, the claims for art would have to be measured against this very critique. Yet, in a peculiar way, Adorno was consistent with the prior analysis. If reason would always lead to domination, then art would have to base its claim on the ability to express the non-identical. However, the task remained to articulate precisely those claims. In order to do so Adorno would often find himself falling back on a philosophy of history which, by the standards articulated in his earlier critique, he had already invalidated.

IV   FROM CRITIQUE TO VALIDITY

With Jürgen Habermas, Adorno's one-time student, the discourse over the rehabilitation of critical theory was taken to a higher level. Habermas's initial strategy was to rehabilitate the notion of critique in critical theory. Clearly, Habermas had long-held doubts about the way in which his philosophical mentors in Frankfurt failed to ground a critical theory in a theory of rationality which would harbor an adequate notion of critique. On this he has written eloquently in both *The Theory of Communicative Action*[57] and *The Philosophical Discourse of Modernity*.[58] What I have found interesting in studying the works of Habermas is the manner in which the argument for a critical theory of rationality began to take shape as an alternative argument to the one which Horkheimer and Adorno put forth. In this context, Habermas would avail himself of certain resources within the tradition of contemporary German philosophy which his mentors had overlooked. Earlier, I suggested that German philosophy since Kant has been shaped by the interaction between the themes of constitution and transformation. If modern critical theory began with a relatively firm belief that the grounds for the emancipatory assumptions regarding critique were clear and given in a certain orientation toward theory, in retrospect that foundation became ever less secure. Eventually, critique, as in *Dialectic of Enlightenment*, became caught in a never ending circle of internal repression and external domination. Hence, the promise of critical theory had been undermined. It was the great merit of Habermas's early work to have seen the dilemma and to have addressed it in terms of turning not to the transformative, but to the constitutive element, in the German philosophical tradition. Critical theory was for Habermas, at least originally, the problem of "valid knowledge," i.e., an epistemological problem.

It should come as no suprise then that when Habermas first juxtaposes traditional and critical theory, following in the footsteps of Horkheimer's 1937 article, he engages Edmund Husserl not only on the status of theory but also on the nature of science. By so doing, he appropriates two of the themes that were germane and of a piece in late transcendental phenomenology, namely, the association of the concept of theory with a more or less political notion of liberation or emancipation and the preoccupation of phenomenology with the status of science.

As early as the writing of *Knowledge and Human Interests*,[59] Habermas sustained the thesis that critical theory could be legitimated on the basis of making apparent the undisclosed association between knowledge and interest. This association, however, could only be specified on the basis of the clarification of theory in its more classical form. According to Habermas *theoria* was a kind of mimesis in the sense that in the contemplation of the cosmos one reproduces internally what one perceives externally. Theory then, even in its traditional form, is conceived to be related to the "conduct of

one's life." In fact, in this interpretation of the traditional view, the appropriation of a theoretical attitude creates a certain *ethos* among its practitioners. Husserl is said to have sustained this "traditional" notion of theory.
Hence, when Husserl approached the question of science he approached
it on the basis of his prior commitment to the classical understanding of
theory.

In Habermas's view, it is this commitment to theory in the classical sense
which determines Husserl's critique of science. Husserl's attack on the objectivism of the sciences led to the claim that knowledge of the objective world
has a "transcendental" basis in the pre-scientific world, that sciences,
because of their prior commitment to mundane knowledge of the world, are
unable to free themselves from interest and that phenomenology, through
its method of transcendental self-reflection, can free this association of
knowledge and mundane interest through a commitment to a theoretical
attitude which has been defined traditionally. In this view, the classical conception of theory, which phenomenology borrows, frees one from interest in
the ordinary world with the result that a certain "therapeutic power," as
well as a "practical efficacy," is claimed for phenomenology.

Habermas endorses Husserl's procedure, while at the same time pointing
out its error. Husserl is said to be correct in his critique of science, which,
because of its "objectivist illusion," embedded in a belief in a "reality-in-
itself," leaves the matter of the constitution of these facts undisclosed with
the result that one is unaware of the connection between knowledge and
interest. In Husserl's view, phenomenology, which makes this clear, can
rightfully claim for itself, against the pretensions of the sciences, the designation, "pure theory." Precisely here Husserl would bring the practical efficacy
of phenomenology to bear. Phenomenology would be said to free one from
the ordinary scientific attitude. But phenomenology is in error because of its
blind acceptance of the implicit ontology present in the classical definition of
theory. Theory in its classical form was thought to find in the structure of the
"ideal world," a prototype for the order of the human world. Habermas says
in a rather insightful manner, "Only as cosmology was *theoria* also capable of
orienting human action."[60] If that is the case, then the phenomenological
method which relied on the classical concept of theory was to have a certain
"practical efficacy," which is interpreted to mean that a certain *"pseudo-
normative power"* could be derived from the *"concealment of its actual interest."*

In the end, phenomenology, which sought to justify itself on the basis of
its freedom from interest, had instead an undisclosed interest which it
derived from a classical ontology. Habermas believes classical ontology in
turn can be characterized historically. In fact, the concept of theory is said to
be derived from a particular stage in human emancipation where "cathar-
sis," which had been engendered heretofore by the "mystery cults," was
now taken into the realm of human action by means of "theory." This in
turn would mark a new stage, but certainly not the last stage, in the deve-

lopment of human "identity." At this stage, individual identity could only be achieved through the identification with the "abstract laws of cosmic order." Hence, theory represents the achievements of a consciousness that is emancipated, but not totally. It is emancipated from certain "archaic powers," but it still requires a certain relationship to the cosmos in order to achieve its identity. Equally, although pure theory could be characterized as an "illusion," it was conceived as a "protection" from "regression to an earlier stage." And here we encounter the major point of Habermas's critique, namely, the association of the contemplative attitude, which portends to dissociate itself from any interest, and the contradictory assumption that the quest for pure knowledge is conducted in the name of a certain practical interest, namely, the emancipation from an earlier stage of human development.

The conclusion is that both Husserl and the sciences he critiques are wrong. Husserl is wrong because he believes that the move to pure theory is a step which frees knowledge from interest. In fact, as we have seen, the redeeming aspect of Husserl's phenomenology is that it does in fact have a practical intent. The sciences are wrong because although they assume the purely contemplative attitude, they use that aspect of the classical concept of theory for their own purposes. In other words, the sciences use the classical concept of pure theory to sustain an insular form of positivism while they cast off the "practical content" of that pure theory. As a consequence, they assume that their interest remains undisclosed.

Significantly, when Habermas turns to his critique of science, he sides with Husserl. This means that Husserl has rightly critiqued the false scientific assumption that "theoretical propositions" are to be correlated with "matters of fact," an "attitude" which assumes the "self-existence" of "empirical variables" as they are represented in "theoretical propositions." But not only has Husserl made the proper distinction between the theoretical and the empirical, he has appropriately shown that the scientific attitude "suppresses the transcendental framework that is the precondition of the meaning of the validity of such propositions."[61] It would follow then that if the proper distinction were to be made between the empirical and the theoretical and if the transcendental framework were made manifest, which would expose the meaning of such propositions, then the "objectivist illusion" would "dissolve" and "knowledge constitutive" interests would be made "visible." It would follow that there is nothing wrong with the theoretical attitude as long as it is united with its practical intent and there is nothing wrong with the introduction of a transcendental framework, as long as it makes apparent the heretofore undisclosed unity of knowledge and interest.

What is interesting about this analysis is that the framework for the notion of critique is not to be derived from dialectical reason as Horkheimer originally thought but from transcendental phenomenology. One must be careful here. I do not wish to claim that Habermas identifies his position with

Husserl. Rather, it can be demonstrated that he derives his position on critique from a critique of transcendental phenomenology. As such, he borrows both the transcendental framework for critique and the emphasis on theory as distinguished from empirical fact that was established by Husserl. Therefore, at that point he argues for a "critical social science" which relies on a "concept of self-reflection" which can "determine the meaning of the validity of critical propositions." Such a conception of critical theory borrows from the critique of traditional theory the idea of an "emancipatory cognitive interest" which, when properly demythologized, is based not on an emancipation from a mystical notion of universal powers of control, but rather from a more modern interest in "autonomy and responsibility." This latter interest will appear later in his thought as the basis for moral theory.

On the basis of this analysis, one might make some observations. Clearly, from the point of view of the development of critical theory, Habermas rightfully saw the necessity of rescuing the concept of critique. Implicit in that attempt is not only the rejection of *Dialectic of Enlightenment*, but also Adorno's attempt to rehabilitate critical theory on the basis of aesthetics. However, and there is considerable evidence to support this assumption, the concept of critical theory which had informed Horkheimer's early essay on that topic had fallen on hard times. As the members of the Institute for Social Research gradually withdrew from the Marxism that had originally informed their concept of critique, so the foundations upon which critical theory was built began to crumble. Habermas's reconceptualization of the notion of critique was obviously both innovative and original. It was also controversial. Critique would not be derived from a philosophy of history based on struggle but from a moment of self-reflection based on a theory of rationality. As Habermas's position developed it was that self-reflective moment which would prove to be interesting.

V   FROM THE PHILOSOPHY OF THE SUBJECT TO THE PHILOSOPHY OF LANGUAGE

Critique, which was rendered through the unmasking of an emancipatory interest *vis-à-vis* the introduction of a transcendentalized moment of self-reflection, re-emerges in the later as opposed to the earlier works of Habermas at the level of validity. The link between validity and critique can be established through the transcendentalized moment of self-reflection, which was associated with making apparent an interest in autonomy and responsibility. Later, that moment was transformed through a theory of communicative rationality to be directed to issues of consensus. Validity refers to a certain background consensus which can be attained through a process of idealization. As critique was originally intended to dissociate truth from ideology, validity distinguished between that which can be justified and that which cannot. Hence, it re-addresses the claims for autonomy and responsibility at the level of communication. It could be said that the quest for validity is superimposed upon the quest for emancipation. There are those who would argue that moral theory which finds its basis in communicative action has replaced the older critical theory with which Habermas was preoccupied in *Knowledge and Human Interests*. I would argue somewhat differently. Instead, I would argue that Habermas's more recent discourse theory of ethics and law is based on the reconstructed claims of a certain version of critical theory.

However, before justifying this claim, I will turn to the basic paradigm shift in Habermas's work from the philosophy of the subject to the philosophy of language, involving construction of a theory of communicative action on the one hand and the justification of a philosophical position anchored in modernity on the other. Both moves can be referenced to the debate between earlier and later critical theory.

If Horkheimer's, and later Adorno's, concept of "instrumental rationality" is but a reconstruction of Max Weber's concept of purposive-rational action, it would follow that a comprehensive critique of that view could be directed to Weber's theory of rationalization. In the book *The Theory of Communicative Action*, it is this theory that is under investigation as seen through the paradigm of the philosophy of consciousness. Weber's thesis can be stated quite simply: if western rationality has been reduced to its instrumental core, then it has no further prospects for regenerating itself. Habermas wants to argue that the failure of Weber's analysis, and by implication the failure of those like Horkheimer and Adorno who accepted Weber's thesis, was to conceive of processes of rationalization in terms of subject–object relations. In other words, Weber's analysis cannot be dissociated from Weber's theory of rationality. According to this analysis his theory of rationality caused him to conceive of things in terms of subject–object relations. Habermas's thesis is, against Weber, Horkheimer and Adorno, that a theory of rationality which conceives of things in terms of subject–object relations cannot conceive of those phenomena in other than instrumental terms. In other words, all subject–object formulations are instrumental. Hence, if one were to construct a theory of rationalization in non-instrumental terms, it would be necessary to construct an alternative theory of rationality. The construction of a theory of communicative action based on a philosophy of language rests on this assumption.

In Habermas's view, the way out of the dilemma of instrumentality into which earlier critical theory led us is through a philosophy of language which, through a reconstructed understanding of speech-act theory, can make a distinction between strategic and communicative action. Communicative action can be understood to be non-instrumental in this sense: "A communicatively achieved agreement has a rational basis; it cannot be imposed by either party, whether instrumentally through intervention in the situation directly or strategically through influencing decisions of the opponents."[62] It is important to note that the question of validity, which I argued a moment ago was the place where the emancipatory interest would be sustained, emerges. A communicative action has within it a claim to validity which is in principle criticizable, meaning that the person to whom such a claim is addressed can respond with either a "yes" or a "no" based, in turn, on reasons. Beyond that, if Habermas is to sustain his claim to overcoming the dilemma of instrumental reason he must argue that communicative actions are foundational. They cannot be reducible to instrumental or strategic actions. If communicative actions were reducible to instrumental or strategic actions, one would be back in the philosophy of consciousness where it was claimed by Habermas and a certain form of earlier critical theory as well that all action was reducible to strategic or instrumental action.[63]

It is Habermas's conviction that one can preserve the emancipatory thrust of modernity by appropriating the discursive structure of language at the level of communication. Hence the failure of *Dialectic of Enlightenment* was to misread modernity in an oversimplified way influenced by those who had given up on it. Here is represented a debate between a position which is anchored in a philosophy of history which can no longer sustain an emancipatory hypothesis on the basis of historical interpretation, and a position which finds emancipatory claims redeemable, but on a transcendental level. Ultimately, the rehabilitation of critical theory concerns the nature and definition of philosophy. If the claims of critical theory can be rehabilitated on a transcendental level as the claims of a philosophy of language, then it would appear that philosophy as such can be defined *vis-à-vis* a theory of communicative action. Habermas's claim that the originary mode of language is communicative presupposes a contra-factual communicative community which is by nature predisposed to refrain from instrumental forms of domination. Hence, the assertion of communicative over strategic forms of discursive interaction assumes a political form of association which is written into the nature of language as such, as the guarantor of a form of progressive emancipation. In other words, if one can claim that the original form of discourse is emancipatory, then the dilemma posed by instrumental reason has been overcome and one is secure from the seductive temptation of the dialectic of enlightenment.

NOTES

1   There are three excellent works on the origin and development of critical theory. The most comprehensive is the monumental work by Rolf Wiggershaus, The Frankfurt School: Its History, Theories, and Political Significance (Cambridge, Mass.: MIT Press, 1994). Martin Jay's historical work, *The Dialectical Imagination* (Boston: Little, Brown, 1973) introduced a whole generation of Americans to critical theory. Helmut Dubiel's *Theory and Politics: Studies in the*

Development of Critical Theory (Cambridge: MIT Press, 1985) presents the development of critical theory against the backdrop of German and international politics.

2   Hegel, *Phenomenology of Spirit* (Oxford: Oxford University Press, 1977).
3   Ibid., p. 111.
4   Karl Marx, *On the Jewish Question*, in *The Marx-Engels Reader* (New York: Norton, 1972).
5   Ibid., pp. 110–65.
6   Ibid., pp. 83–103.
7   Max Horkheimer, "Traditional and Critical Theory," in *Critical Theory* (New York: Herder and Herder, 1972).
8   Ibid., p. vi.
9   Ibid., p. 188.
10   Ibid., p. 194.
11   Ibid., p. 199.
12   Ibid.
13   Ibid., p. 207.
14   Ibid., pp. 210–11.
15   Ibid., p. 213.
16   Ibid., p. 214.
17   Ibid., p. 215.
18   Ibid., p. 266.
19   Ibid., p. 227.
20   Ibid., p. 232.
21   Max Horkheimer, *Critique of Instrumental Reason* (New York: The Seabury Press, 1974).
22   Max Horkheimer and Theodor W. Adorno, *Dialectic of Enlightenment* (New York: Herder and Herder, 1972).
23   Ibid., p. 4.
24   Ibid.
25   Ibid.
26   Ibid., p. 9.
27   Ibid., p. 12.
28   Ibid., p. 27.
29   Ibid., p. 44.
30   Ibid.
31   Ibid., p. 46.
32   Ibid., p. 48.
33   Ibid., p. 51.
34   Ibid.
35   Ibid., p. 54.
36   Ibid., p. 55.
37   Ibid., p. 54.
38   Ibid., p. 58.
39   Ibid., p. 83.
40   Ibid., p. 121.
41   Ibid., p. 164.
42   Walter Benjamin, "The Work of Art in the Age of Mechanical Reproduction" in *Illuminations* (New York: Schoken Books, 1969).
43   *Zeitschrift für Sozialforschung*, vol. 5, no. 1.
44   Walter Benjamin, "The Work of Art in the Age of Mechanical Reproduction," p. 224.
45   Ibid., p. 241.
46   Ibid.
47   Ibid., p. 242.
48   T. W. Adorno, *Aesthetic Theory* (London: Routledge and Kegan Paul, 1984), p. 31.

49   Ibid.
50   Ibid., p. 79.
51   Ibid., p. 80.
52   Ibid.
53   Ibid.
54   Ibid., p. 27.
55   Ibid., p. 26.
56   Ibid., p. 254.
57   Jürgen Habermas, *The Theory of Communicative Action* (Boston: Beacon Press, 1987), two volumes.
58   Jürgen Habermas, *The Philosophical Discourse of Modernity* (Boston: MIT Press, 1987).
59   Jürgen Habermas, *Knowledge and Human Interests* (Boston: Beacon Press, 1971).
60   Ibid., p. 306.
61   Ibid., p. 307.
62   Ibid., p. 287
63   For a more comprehensive analysis of the issues involved in this distinction see my *Reading Habermas* (Oxford: Basil Blackwell, 1990).

2 URBAN FLIGHTS: THE INSTITUTE OF SOCIAL RESEARCH BETWEEN FRANKFURT AND NEW YORK

Martin Jay

The theme of the city and the university provides a welcome opportunity to clarify an aspect of the Frankfurt School's history that has always troubled me. I refer to the vexed problem of its roots in the social and cultural conditions of its day, the link between its Critical Theory and the context which in some sense or another allowed it to emerge. As wary as I have always been of the sociology of knowledge in its more reductionist forms, I have also never felt comfortable with the school's reticence about exploring its own origins, an attitude best expressed in Theodor Adorno's remark that "a stroke of undeserved luck has kept the mental composition of some individuals not quite adjusted to the prevailing norms."[1] Even luck, deserved or not, seems to me worth trying to explain, and perhaps in the case of the Frankfurt School, looking at its relations to the cities and universities with which it was connected may provide some help. For, after all, it is not every group of intellectuals whose very name suggests both an urban and an academic link.

Even more understanding may ensue if we remember that the sobriquet "Frankfurt School" was only a late concoction of the 1960s and was never perfectly congruent with the Institute of Social Research out of which it came. The disparity between the research institute and the school of thought which emerged within its walls has, in fact, led some observers to call into question the coherence of the phenomenon as a whole. No less involved a figure than Jürgen Habermas has recently remarked that although the institute continues, "there is no longer any question of a school, and that is undoubtedly a good thing."[2]

Rather than abandoning the search for coherence because of the historical and nominal displacements of the institute and the school, it seems to me more fruitful to acknowledge the unsettled and protean nature of a cultural formation that nonetheless did retain a certain fluid identity over time. As I have tried to argue in my study of Adorno, that identity may best be understood as the product of a force field of untotalized and sometimes contesting impulses that defy any harmonious integration.[3] In that work I identified several salient forces in Adorno's personal intellectual field: Hegelian Marxism, aesthetic modernism, cultural mandarinism, a certain Jewish self-awareness, and, from the point of view of the reception rather than the generation of his ideas, poststructuralism. If we add psychoanalysis and a nuanced appreciation of Max Weber's critique of rationalization, we can perhaps see the major forces operating to constitute the intellectual field of both the institute and the school, at least until the time of Habermas's introduction of several new elements from linguistics, cognitive psychology, hermeneutics, and anthropology.[4] Now, to do justice to all of the constellations of these elements during the various phases of the group's history is obviously beyond the scope of this essay. Instead, I would prefer to focus on only a few of them and explore the possibility that their interaction may in some way reflect the school's genesis in its specific urban and academic contexts.

To make these connections will perhaps be especially revealing because the members of the school themselves rarely, if ever, thought to make them themselves. In fact, with the salient exception of Walter Benjamin, himself only obliquely related to the institute, its members never directed their attention to the important role of the city in modern society.[5] Perhaps because they knew that the critique of urban life was the stock and trade of anti-modernist, protofascist ideologies – a point clearly made in Leo Lowenthal's celebrated 1937 essay on Knut Hamsun[6] – they aimed their own critique at other targets. Georg Simmel's explorations of metropolitan life or the urban sociology of the University of Chicago's Robert Park had little resonance in their work. In fact, it was not until the institute returned to Germany after the war that it participated in an empirical community study, that of the city of Darmstadt.[7] And even then its members warned against the dangers of isolating its results from a more theoretically informed analysis of society as a whole.[8] Frankfurt itself, the environment that nurtured their own work, was never an object of systematic analysis.

No less ignored during the school's earlier history was the role of the university. Perhaps because an emphasis on education was characteristic of the revisionist Marxism they scorned, it was not one of their central preoccupations. Only after their return to Frankfurt, when Horkheimer in particular was deeply involved in the reconstitution of the German higher educational system, did a Frankfurt School member seriously ponder the importance of academic issues.[9] Far more characteristic of their first Frankfurt period is the caustic remark of the young and still militant Horkheimer in his essay collection *Dämmerung* that the absorption of Marxism into the academy as a legitimate part of the curriculum was "a step toward breaking the will of the workers to fight capitalism."[10]

What makes such a charge so ironic, of course, is that the institute itself clearly did not emerge out of the working class but rather from a particular stratum of the urban educated bourgeoisie (the *Bildungsbürgertum*) in crisis. As such, it has been seen by some observers as the first instance of an elitist Western Marxism distanced from the real concerns of the masses.[11] Whether or not this is fair to the complexities of its members' development, it does correctly register the fact that the institute must be understood as much in the context of what Fritz Ringer has called "the decline of the German mandarins"[12] as in that of the working-class struggle for socialism. However, what made the institute's unique achievement possible was the specific urban and academic situation in which its particular response to that decline was enacted. To understand that situation we will have to pause and focus on certain features of the Frankfurt am Main of their youth.

The old imperial free city had been a center of international trade and finance since the Middle Ages, even if its hegemony had been challenged by the rise of Basel, Mannheim, and especially Leipzig in the eighteenth century.[13] Along with its economic prosperity went a certain political autonomy from the larger German states, which survived until its absorption into Prussia in 1866. The ill-fated parliament in the Paulskirche in 1848 reflected the city's symbolic role as a center of liberalism as well as its earlier function as the site of the Holy Roman Emperor's election and coronation. Not surprisingly, the greatest organ of German liberalism, the *Frankfurter Zeitung*, was founded in the city by Leopold Sonnemann in 1856.

Frankfurt was also distinguished by its large and relatively thriving Jewish community, which numbered some thirty thousand members during the Weimar years and was second only to Berlin's in importance. Originally protected by both the emperor and the city council, it weathered the enmity of gentile competitors and the political reverses of the post-Napoleonic era to emerge after 1848 as an integral part of the city's economic, social, and political life.[14] Although assimilation was probably as advanced as anywhere else in Germany, Frankfurt's Jews were noted for their innovative responses to the challenges of modernity. Reform, conservative, and orthodox branches of Judaism were creatively developed within its walls.[15] It was, of course, in the Frankfurt of the 1920s that the famous Freie Jüdische Lehrhaus was organized around the charismatic rabbi Nehemiah Nobel, bringing together such powerful intellectuals as Franz Rosenzweig, Martin Buber, and Ernst Simon.

Although lacking its own university until 1914,[16] Frankfurt had enjoyed a long tradition of private support for scholarly institutions, stretching back to the efforts of Dr Johann Christian Senckenberg in the eighteenth century. When the university was founded as the amalgamation of several of these academies and institutes, it was as a so-called *Stiftungsuniversität*, funded by private contributors, often from the Jewish community, rather than by the state.[17] The philanthropist Wilhelm Merton, an assimilated Jewish director of a giant metallurgical concern, was the major benefactor. Independent of the anti-Semitic and increasingly statist university system that had long since left behind the liberal intentions of its founder Wilhelm von Humboldt,[18] the new Frankfurt University offered a radical departure in German academic life on the eve of the war. Its self-consciously modern outlook was demonstrated by its being the first German university not to have a separate theology faculty and by its express willingness to open its ranks to a broad range of students and faculty.

Before the war Merton had also funded a mercantile academy and an institute for public welfare, which have been seen as the prototype for the research institutes that were launched after 1918.[19] Included in their number was one founded in 1924 with the backing of millionaire grain merchant Hermann Weil, which chose the name Institut für Sozialforschung. This is not the place to retell the story of that founding, a task recently performed in detail by the German historian Ulrike Migdal,[20] but several points merit emphasis. First, the relative autonomy of the institute, guaranteed by Weil's largesse, was very much in the time-honored Frankfurt tradition of private, bourgeois underwriting of scholarly enterprises. Although after the war and the inflation the university itself had to call on state support to survive, Weil's continued generosity combined with his aloofness from the institute's actual work meant that it was remarkably free from political and bureaucratic pressures. Although an attenuated link with the Prussian state was forged through an arrangement that specified that the institute's director had to be a university professor, clearly something very different from a traditional academic institution was created.

The difference was manifested in several important ways. First, unlike the many seminars and institutes that proliferated during the Wilhelmian era,[21] the Institute of Social Research was not dedicated to the goal of scientific specialization and compartmentalization. Instead, it drew on the concept of totalized, integrated knowledge then recently emphasized by Georg Lukács in his influential study *History and Class Consciousness*.[22] Although the early leadership of the institute was by no means explicitly Hegelian Marxist, it nonetheless eschewed the fragmentation of knowledge characteristic of bourgeois *Wissenschaft*. Second, the institute was launched solely to foster research and without any explicit pedagogical responsibilities. This privilege meant, among other things, that the traditional mandarin function of training an educated elite designed to serve the state, a function which had become increasingly onerous during the Wilhelmian years,[23] was completely absent from the institute's agenda. That agenda, and this is the third obvious difference from normal academic institutions, included the critique and ultimate overthrow of the capitalist order.

The irony of a millionaire businessman like Hermann Weil supporting such a venture has not been lost on subsequent observers from Bertolt Brecht on.[24] Perhaps his son Felix, the disciple of Karl Korsch on whose urging the institute was created, had sugar-coated the pill by saying that it would be devoted only to the dispassionate study of the workers' movement and anti-Semitism. Perhaps, as Migdal has speculated, the senior Weil was cynically hoping for access to the Soviet grain market through the goodwill accumulated by linking his institute to the Marx–Engels Institute in Moscow. For whatever reason, the Institute of Social Research was the first unabashedly Marxist enterprise to be connected, however loosely, to a university in Germany and most likely anywhere else outside of the USSR. As such, it has led to the suspicion that the proper context in which to situate its founding is neither urban nor academic but political. One particularly wild and unsubstantiated version of this contention is Lewis Feuer's bizarre suggestion that it might well have been a Willi Münzenberg front organization that soon became a "recruiting ground...for the Soviet espionage service."[25]

Despite the absurdity of this particular charge, it is, of course, true that the institute was not founded in a political vacuum. Several of its earliest members did, in fact, have personal links to radical parties, most notably the KPD (German Communist Party).[26] And there was a friendly interchange with David Ryazanov's institute in Moscow, largely having to do with the preparation of the Marx-Engels Gesamtausgabe. The student nickname "Café Marx" was thus not unwarranted. And yet what is no less true and ultimately of more importance is that the institute was never institutionally linked with any faction, sect, or party on the left, nor did it hew to any single political or even theoretical line during its earliest years. In this sense the popular notion of a school, which was rarely applied to earlier groups of Marxist intellectuals,[27] along with that of a research institute, does capture an important truth about their status. Neither a traditional academic institution nor a party-oriented cadre of theoreticians, it presented something radically new in the history of leftist intellectuals.

The notion of a school implies not only detachment from practical concerns but also the presence of a guiding figure setting the program of inquiry. To the extent that such a master figure was able to emerge, and it was perhaps not until Horkheimer replaced Carl Grünberg as official director that one did,[28] the institute's constitution made it possible. For it gave the director explicitly "dictatorial" powers to organize research. According to the sociologist Helmut Dubiel, an elaborate interdisciplinary program was inaugurated by Horkheimer on the basis of Marx's model of dialectical *Forschung* and *Darstellung*, research and presentation, in which philosophy oriented and was in turn modified by social scientific investigation.[29] How closely the institute actually followed this model has been debated, but it is clear that for a long time the common approach known after Horkheimer's seminal 1937 essay as Critical Theory[30] did give the work of most institute members a shared perspective.

To understand its provenance, however, we cannot stay solely within the confines of academic or political life in the Weimar Republic. For the cultural milieu of Frankfurt itself also played a crucial role. Although not as stimulating an environment for nonacademic intellectual pursuits as prewar Munich or postwar Berlin,[31] Frankfurt could still boast a cultural atmosphere open to the most experimental currents of Weimar life. A rapid *tour d'horizon* reveals a variety of important innovations. Frankfurt, for example, was the locus for the great modernist workers' housing projects of Ernst May, the city's chief architect after 1925. Along with such contributions to interior design as Schütte-Lihotsky's famous "Frankfurt Kitchen," these monuments to socially conscious functionalism earned Frankfurt the honor of being called "the first twentieth-century city" by one recent observer.[32]

It was also in Frankfurt that the recent invention of the radio took on a new and powerful role as an experimental cultural medium.[33] The Süddeutsche Rundfunk was the third station in Germany to be established, after Berlin and Leipzig. Rather than pandering to the lowest common denominator of taste, Radio Frankfurt, as it was popularly known, often scheduled concerts of the most challenging modern music and broadcast innovative radio plays and serious lectures on a wide variety of subjects. The so-called wandering microphone of reporters such as Paul Lavan opened up perspectives on modern urban life that have been likened to the documentary films of William Ruttman, the director of the celebrated *Berlin: Symphony of a City*.[34]

It was in Frankfurt as well that the *Frankfurter Zeitung*, then under the direction of Sonnemann's grandson Heinrich Simon, allowed writers such as Siegfried Kracauer, Joseph Roth, Soma Morgenstern, and Benno Reifenberg to analyze a broad spectrum of cultural and social issues in its famous feuilleton section. The city was also home for one of the first German psychoanalytic institutes, established in 1929 under the direction of Heinrich Meng and Karl Landauer. No less characteristically innovative was the city's decision the following year to grant its highest honor, the Goethe Prize, to the still controversial Sigmund Freud.[35] If we add to this picture the Jewish renaissance sparked by the already mentioned Frankfurt Lehrhaus, we have a sense of how lively and progressive nonuniversity life could be in Weimar Frankfurt.

As a result, many members of the Institute of Social Research were able to leave their academic ghetto behind and enjoy intimate contact with an experimental and often modernist urban culture. At the Café Laumer on the corner of the Bockenheimer Landstrasse and the Brentanostrasse, they created an off-campus outpost which attracted many nonuniversity intellectuals. Years later the writer Ernst Erich Noth would remember the "Nachseminar" conducted there by the young Theodor Wiesengrund Adorno as far more stimulating than anything going on at the university itself.[36] Through friendships with Kracauer, closest in the cases of Lowenthal and Adorno, members of the institute had ties to the *Frankfurter Zeitung*, which also carried the work of a later colleague, Walter Benjamin. Also by way of personal ties, especially with Ernst Schoen, several institute figures were given access to Radio Frankfurt, where they held forth on cultural questions, including the modern music Adorno was so anxious to promote. In the early 1920s there were also important links between the Frankfurt Lehrhaus and future institute figures, most notably Lowenthal and Fromm.[37] Similar ties were forged with the Frankfurt psychoanalysts at the end of the decade. Not surprisingly, one institute member, Lowenthal, played an important role in initiating the city's decision to honor the founder of psychoanalysis in 1930.[38]

Even the institute's new building, a spare, fortresslike edifice built by Franz Röckle on the corner of the Bockenheimer Landstrasse and the Victoria Allee, bespoke a kinship with urban modernism. Posing a visual challenge to the ornately decorated villas in Frankfurt's fashionable West End, the Neue Sachlichkeit structure expressed the institute's defiance of the out-moded cultural ambiance of the Wilhelmian past. Although Horkheimer was later to criticize the spirit of the Neue Sachlichkeit in general as too technologically rationalist and thus complicitous with reification,[39] the institute's building was initially understood as an expression of the no-nonsense goals of a Marxist research institute dedicated to unmasking the illusory façades of bourgeois society.

If, however, the Frankfurt School's debt to the nonacademic modernist culture of their urban environment must be acknowledged, so too must its measured distance from it. As in the case of their relation to the university, most institute members maintained a certain aloofness from the urban cultural scene and the intellectual milieu it fostered. If one compares their status with that of friends such as Kracauer or Benjamin, who were entirely outside the academic hierarchy,[40] it is possible to see the effects of this distance. The latter were often dependent on the demands of the cultural marketplace in ways that influenced the form and substance of their work, which tended to be less systematic and more journalistic. Not surprisingly, Kracauer and Benjamin wrote more frequently on mass culture and urban life than institute members, and they generally did so with a more nuanced appreciation of their implications. Here the influence of Simmel's pioneering explorations of metropolitan life was clearly discernible.[41] Moreover, as demonstrated by Kracauer's 1931 essay on the economic pressure on all writers to become journalists and Benjamin's 1934 discussion of the author as producer,[42] they were far more vulnerable to the proletarianization of intellectual life than the more privileged members of the institute. The contrast is demonstrated by their differing responses to the worsening crisis of Weimar's political and cultural scene, which was already evident in ominous changes in the direction of the *Frankfurter Zeitung* and Radio Frankfurt in the last years of the republic.[43] Whereas Kracauer and Benjamin had great personal and professional difficulties in the 1930s, the institute was able to make provisions for an orderly escape from Germany in 1933 with virtually all of its resources, save its library, intact.

In short, the institute's relations with both the official university structure and the modernist urban subculture – and, one might add, the radical political parties of the day as well – were always somewhat eccentric and marginal. The phenomenon that later became known as the Frankfurt School was thus never merely a direct product of its urban or academic origins or of any organized political movement. Rather, it emerged as the dynamic nodal point of all three, suspended in the middle of a sociocultural force field without gravitating to any of its poles. Hostage to no particular defining context, it hovered in a kind of intellectual no-man's land. This ambiguous status, as might be expected, was even more strongly exacerbated after the flight from Frankfurt via Geneva to New York in 1934. For here the distance between the institute and American university life, as well as the urban culture of its adopted city, grew more attenuated than it had been in relation to its members' preexilic German counterparts. And, of course, whatever links any of its original members may have had with political praxis in Weimar were now utterly shattered.

The institute's move to Columbia University in 1934 has recently been the occasion for a polemic launched by Lewis Feuer in the English journal *Survey*.[44] Having been a participant in the exchange that followed, I don't want to rehearse all of its unpleasantness now. I would only want to emphasize that Feuer's attempt to turn the institute members into fellow-traveling crypto-Communists who duped a naive Columbia administration into welcoming them to New York is incompatible with the complicated triangulated reality of their initial Frankfurt years. As we have seen, that story cannot be flattened out into an essentially political narrative of the kind which Feuer, with his penchant for conspiracy theories, imagines.

In New York the institute's financial self-sufficiency, maintained at least until the end of the 1930s, meant that it could enjoy the luxury of relative withdrawal from all of its originally defining contexts – academic, urban, and political. Unlike other less fortunate émigrés, its members could generally avoid the compromises forced by the exigencies of their situation. Continuing to write almost exclusively in German, confining their teaching to the occasional course in the Columbia extension program, only rarely opening the pages of their journal to American authors,[45] they managed to keep the local academic world at arm's distance. Although ties with the sociology department at Columbia were slowly developed, they were as likely to be through other refugees like Paul Lazarsfeld as through native scholars like Robert Lynd or Robert MacIver. Virtually no sympathetic connections appear to have been made with the philosophers in New York. Collaborative projects with Americans did not materialize until the 1940s and then often under nonuniversity auspices, such as the American Jewish Committee, the Jewish Labor Committee, or the Central European Section of the OSS. Although some younger American scholars, later to gain prominence, such as M. I. Finley, Alvin Gouldner, C. Wright Mills, and even Daniel Bell,[46] were influenced by their fleeting contacts with the institute, it would be impossible to call them legitimate students of a school. In short, relatively secure behind the walls of the building at 429 West 117th Street provided by Columbia, the institute remained a hidden enclave of Weimar culture in exile and not in any meaningful way a part of American academic life.

If one looks at the building itself and compares it with the one the institute left behind in Frankfurt another difference from its German days can be noted. Rather than a visual provocation to the surrounding environment, a symbol of its inhabitants' defiant modernism and innovative Marxism, the building on 117th Street was merely one of a row of similarly innocuous brownstones with pseudoclassical columns and balustrades flanking the entrance. As such, it unintentionally expressed the institute's wariness about standing out in a vulnerable way in their new surroundings. Understandably anxious about their status as exiles, often reluctant to address specifically American issues out of ignorance, unsure of their own political direction, and cautious about highlighting the radicalism of their past, they remained aloof from any oppositional intellectual movement in the 1930s and early 1940s.[47]

When Horkheimer and Adorno moved to southern California in 1941 they were absorbed almost entirely into the German exile community there. They seem to have had little to do with either the academic or urban intellectual culture of Los Angeles, such as it was in those days. In fact, as the wrenchingly painful aphorisms in Adorno's *Minima Moralia* demonstrate, their alienation from any nurturing context was never as great as during these years.[48] Only the collaboration with the Berkeley Public Opinion Study Group in the late 1940s, which led to the publication of *The Authoritarian Personality*, broke this pattern. As for those institute members who remained on the East Coast, such as Neumann, Marcuse, and Lowenthal, it was only in connection with governmental service during the war that they began sustained interactions with American intellectuals.[49]

Symptomatic of their general isolation from the nonacademic intellectual urban life of their host country is the fact that in the now rapidly proliferating histories of the most important group of American cultural figures of the 1930s and 1940s, the so-called New York intellectuals, their names are rarely to be found.[50] Although they shared many of the same leftist and modernist sympathies as writers around such journals as *The Partisan Review*, there seems to have been virtually no contact between them. Only in the incipient debate over mass culture did Americans such as Dwight MacDonald find any inspiration in Frankfurt School ideas before the war's end.[51] It was not until well after the institute's return to Germany that an American oppositional culture, and then an oppositional political movement, began to recover the work done by the institute during its exile.[52]

It was, of course, only during the second Frankfurt period of the institute, begun when Horkheimer, Pollock, and Adorno returned for good in the early 1950s, that its isolation from its academic, urban, and ultimately political contexts was undone. Now for really the first time, the Frankfurt School, as it soon became known, was no longer relatively marginalized. Lured back by some of the same officials who had blithely presided over the dissolution of the institute's unrescued property during the Nazi era,[53] its leaders were feted as honored links with the Weimar past. Horkheimer was elected rector of the University of Frankfurt in 1951 and reelected the following year. He wrote and lectured on matters of educational policy and gave frequent interviews to the press on a wide variety of timely subjects.[54] The columns of the Frankfurt newspapers and the airwaves of its radio station were open to him and Adorno, who overcame their animosity to the mass media in a self-conscious effort to influence public opinion. Even the new institute building, to return to an indicator we have examined previously, bespoke a certain fit with postwar Frankfurt. Although it was similar to the Neue Sachlichkeit structure of the 1920s, it was now perfectly in accord with the International Style architecture then rising on the ruins of the bombed-out inner city. Thus, while it would certainly be overstated to say that the institute leadership had made its peace with the modern world, it was palpably less estranged from it than during either its first Frankfurt era or its exile in America.

Ironically, however, in a short time the new public for the institute's work become increasingly curious about the ideas formulated during those earlier periods. And much to the discomfort of Horkheimer in particular, it insisted on applying them to contemporary problems. Although this is not the place to analyze the Frankfurt School's complicated relationship to the German New Left, it should be noted that it was largely the ideas generated before that reception began which earned the school its reputation. It is thus appropriate to return in conclusion to the question posed earlier, of the relationship between Critical Theory and the institute's academic and urban environments during its most creative and formative years, the years before it found its audience. Can we, in other words, make sense of the force field of its intellectual impulses by situating them in their generative contexts?

The most important of those forces, it bears repeating, were Hegelian Marxism, cultural mandarinism, aesthetic modernism, Jewish self-awareness, psychoanalysis, Weberian rationalization theory, and poststructuralism. The last of these, as mentioned earlier, makes sense only from the point of view of the school's reception rather than its genesis and so cannot be meaningfully linked to the contexts we have described, even if we want to emphasize, as some commentators have recently done, the links between Jewish hermeneutic traditions and poststructuralist thought.[55] What of the others? Although a renewed interest in Hegel can be discerned in the 1920s in certain university circles,[56] Hegelian Marxism was clearly a product of the politically generated reconceptualization of Marxist theory begun by Lukács and Korsch outside the academy. During the Grünberg years the institute itself was not really beholden to a Hegelian Marxist methodology, even if, as we have seen, its program was aimed at overcoming the fragmentation of bourgeois *Wissenschaft*. Moreover, insofar as one of the chief implications of the recovery of the Hegelian dimension in Marxism was the unity of theory and practice, to the extent that the institute was a nonpolitical research enterprise, its specific institutional framework was at odds with the lessons of Lukács and Korsch.

And yet in one sense we might find a link between the Hegelian Marxist component of Critical Theory, which was especially evident in the 1930s, and the institute's peculiar academic status. By stressing the difference between appearance and essence and splitting the empirical class consciousness of the working class from its ascribed or objective class consciousness, Hegelian Marxism opened up the possibility of a vanguard speaking for the class it claimed to represent. In the case of Leninists such as Lukács and, at least for a while, Korsch, that role was played by the Communist party. For the institute members who were not able to accept that solution, it was perhaps possible to see small groups of intellectuals fulfilling a similar function. That is, without fooling themselves into thinking they were substitutes for the revolutionary meta-subject promised by Hegelian Marxism, they could at least consider themselves the temporary repositories of its totalistic epistemological vantage point. The insulated and protected quality of the institute, especially acute during its American exile, might therefore have helped sustain the assumption that the Frankfurt School, unsullied by the political and commercial compromises forced on most intellectuals, was the spokesman for the totality. Although this was a fragile hope, for reasons I want to explore shortly, it might at least be explicable in terms of the institute's peculiar academic status.

Similarly, the residues of cultural mandarinism in Critical Theory, its suspicion of technological, instrumental rationality, and its almost visceral distaste for mass culture might be explained in part by its exponents' attenuated links with the *Bildungsbürgertum* and the university system. The elitism, which Frankfurt School members often accepted as a valid description of their position, was thus not merely a function of the vanguardist implications of Hegelian Marxism; it also reflected their roots in a hierarchical academic structure. Acknowledging this possibility, however, must not blind us to the complicated relationship they had to that structure mentioned earlier. As a research institute in a privately initiated university, they were able to avoid the obligation of bureaucratic service to the state or the need to train its future leaders. Thus, they were never simply mandarins conservatively resisting challenges to the hegemony of their status group. Even though they adopted much of the pathos of Weber's theory of rationalization as an iron cage limiting the prospects of modernization, they never gave up the hope for an alternative future based on the realization of substantive reason denied by the more pessimistic mandarins.

Their refusal to follow the mandarin lesson of despair was motivated not only by their Marxist inclinations but also by their general sympathy for the creative impulses that we have seen were so prevalent in their urban environment. The messianic hopes evident in the Jewish renaissance stimulated by the Frankfurt Lehrhaus were expressed in various forms and with different degrees of intensity in the work of such institute figures as Fromm, Lowenthal, Benjamin, and Adorno.[57] So, too, the introduction of psychoanalytic themes in their work was facilitated by the hospitable climate Frankfurt provided for Freud's ideas. And finally the aesthetic modernism of Frankfurt, "the first twentieth-century city," found a ready echo in their defense of avant-garde art, even if more of the esoteric than exoteric kind represented by the Neue Sachlichkeit.[58]

Their preference for esoteric rather than exoteric modernism, the art of Schoenberg, Kafka, and Beckett rather than that of, say, the Surrealists, suggests one final observation about the institute's relation to its urban environment. As Carl Schorske has noted, the ideal of the burgher city as an ethical community had informed the neohumanism of German idealists such as Fichte.[59] Often serving as an antidote to the competing image of the modern industrial city as an inhuman locus of alienation and vice, this model emphasized the possibility of reconstituting the civic virtue of the ancient polis or Renaissance city-state. Now, although the Frankfurt of the early twentieth century may have approached this ideal in some modest respects, in the context of a national culture and polity as fragmented as that of Weimar Germany it was clear that no genuinely ethical community could arise on an urban level alone. The institute's members, with their penchant for totalistic explanations of social problems, never entertained the possibility that a renovated city life alone would make much difference. In addition, it might be speculated that the Hellenic ideal of the virtuous polis held little attraction for them because of their attenuated debt to a Hebraic tradition, whose nostalgia, as George Steiner has recently reminded us, was more for a garden than for a city.[60] Reconciliation with nature was, in fact, one of their most ardently held goals, even if they were suspicious of attempts by *völkisch* and, one might add, Zionist thinkers to realize it without radical social change. Still, reinforced by the traditional Marxist expectation that communism would mean the overcoming of the very distinction between urban and rural,[61] they never speculated on the renewal of civic virtue as an end in itself.

When the institute fled to New York this dream must have seemed even more remote from reality. Not only were they foreigners precariously situated in an alien environment, but that environment itself was even farther removed from the ethical community ideal than Frankfurt had been. For, as Thomas Bender has argued,[62] American cities like New York had long since ceased to support a vibrant metropolitan culture, and anything approaching a common intellectual life had been replaced by one-sided professional elites

incapable of talking to each other about larger problems outside their fields
of knowledge. An interdisciplinary school of thinkers, whose institute was
founded precisely to combat the specialization of apparently incommensurable discourses, could therefore only withdraw into itself under these circumstances. As a result their holistic inclinations, already called into
question by the failure of a universal class to appear, were further damaged
by the lack of a true public during their years of exile. Not surprisingly, their
very faith in the concept of totality itself was severely shaken by the time
they returned to Germany after the war. As I have tried to demonstrate elsewhere,[63] their disillusionment was a central episode in the general loss of
confidence in totality evident in the history of Western Marxism as a whole.

Even when they returned to a Frankfurt now anxious to listen to them,
they were far too chastened by their American experience to hold out any
hope for the dream of a city of virtue. Thus, as mentioned earlier, when they
did engage in a community analysis it was always with the warning that the
proper unit of analysis could not be merely urban, for the manipulation of
popular consciousness by a national and even international culture industry
precluded any purely urban renaissance of civic virtue. Although Jürgen
Habermas later introduced the notion of a resurrected public sphere as a possible antidote to the totally manipulated consciousness of one-dimensional
society, he did so with a definite awareness of the limits of the older model.
"The question that is brought to mind," he recently argued in an essay on
"Modern and Postmodern Architecture,"

> is whether the actual *notion* of the city has not itself been superseded. As a
> comprehensible habitat, the city could at one time be architecturally
> designed and mentally represented. The social functions of urban life, politi-
> cal and economic, private and public, the assignments of cultural and reli-
> gious representation, of work, habitation, recreation, and celebration could
> be *translated* into use-purposes, into functions of temporarily regulated use
> of designed spaces. However, by the nineteenth century at the latest, the
> city became the intersection point of a *different kind* of functional relation-
> ship. It was embedded in abstract systems, which could no longer be cap-
> tured aesthetically in an intelligible presence. . . . The urban agglomerations
> have outgrown the old concept of the city that people so cherish.[64]

What lessons, if any, can be gleaned from this overview of the Frankfurt
School's relations to the universities and cities with which it was associated
during its history? First, it is evident that no straightforward, reductive contextual analysis can provide a satisfactory key to explain the content of the
school's ideas. They were simply too many overlapping contexts – academic,
urban, political, and we might have added personal and intellectual as well –
to allow us to ground Critical Theory or the institute's work in any one master context. Dominick LaCapra's contention in his powerful critique of just
such an attempt, Janik and Toulmin's *Wittgenstein's Vienna*, is thus borne out

by our analysis: no single-minded contextual account can arrogate to itself the power to saturate texts or constellations of ideas with one essential meaning.[65] Indeed, if the point made earlier with reference to the importance of the poststructuralist reception of Critical Theory is taken seriously, no generative contextualism, however open to multiple dimensions, can exhaust the meaning of a cultural phenomenon for us. Its force field necessarily includes both generative and receptive movements, and it is an illusion to think we can completely bracket out the latter in the hope of merely recapturing the former.

But some limited explanatory power must nonetheless be granted to contextual analysis, if we remember the need to respect the untotalizability of multiple contexts. In the case of the Frankfurt School it was precisely the dynamic intersection and overlapping of discrete contexts that provided the stimulus to their work. Their constellation of tensely interrelated ideas, themselves never achieving a perfectly harmonious synthesis, was thus enabled by the irreducibly plural and often conflicting contexts of their lives. Without pretending that a perfect correspondence can be established between specific stars in their intellectual constellation and specific contexts out of which they emerged, I hope it has been demonstrated that some attention to their academic and urban situations helps demystify the claim of "a stroke of undeserved luck" as an explanation for their critical acumen.

One final observation is in order. It is a staple of intellectual history to credit social or cultural marginality with stimulating heterodox or innovative ideas. In the case we have been examining it would be more accurate to speak of multiple marginalities, most notably those we have identified in relation to their academic, urban, and political contexts, and conceptualize the school and the institute as nodal points (close but not precisely identical) of their intersection. Or rather in the manner of a Venn diagram we can see them occupying the overlapping area where three eccentric circles come together. The Frankfurt School's favorite phrase *nicht mitmachen*, not playing along, thus comes to mean more than just a defiance of conventionality and political camp-following; it defines instead the very conditions of their intellectual productivity, and perhaps not theirs alone.

NOTES

1   Theodor W. Adorno, *Negative Dialectics*, trans. E. B. Ashton (New York, 1973), p. 41.
2   Jürgen Habermas, *Autonomy and Solidarity: Interviews*, ed. Peter Dews (London, 1986), p. 49.
3   Martin Jay, *Adorno* (Cambridge, Mass., 1984).
4   Habermas's departures from classical Critical Theory have sometimes seemed sufficiently extensive to justify excluding him from the Frankfurt School in favor of his own "Starnberg School." See, for example, Gerhard Brandt, "Ansichten kritischer Sozialforschung

1930–1980," *Leviathan* 4 (1981): 25. For an overview of the continuities that nonetheless exist, see David Held, *Introduction to Critical Theory: Horkheimer to Habermas* (Berkeley, Calif., 1980).

5 Benjamin's work on the modern metropolis included studies of Berlin, Paris, Marseilles, Moscow, and Naples. See, in particular, *Charles Baudelaire: A Lyric Poet in the Era of High Capitalism*, trans. Harry Zohn (London, 1973); *Reflections: Essays, Aphorisms, Autobiographical Writings*, ed. Peter Demetz, trans. Edmund Jephcott (New York, 1978); and *One-Way Street and Other Writings*, trans. Edmund Jephcott and Kingsley Shorter (London, 1979). For a discussion of his work on the city, see Henning Günther, *Walter Benjamin: Zwischen Marxismus und Theologie* (Olten, 1973), pp. 165f.

6 Leo Lowenthal, *Literature and the Image of Man: Studies of the European Drama and Novel, 1600–1900* (Boston, 1957), p. 212.

7 *Gemeindestudie des Instituts für sozialwissenschaftliche Forschung* (Darmstadt, 1952–4). The institute consulted on this project. See the discussion of it in *Aspects of Sociology* by the Frankfurt Institute of Social Research, preface by Max Horkheimer and Theodor W. Adorno, trans. John Viertel (Boston, 1972), p. 156.

8 *Aspects of Sociology*, p. 163.

9 Max Horkheimer, *Gesammelte Schriften, Band 8: Vorträge und Aufzeichnungen 1949–1973*, ed. Gunzelin Schmid-Noerr (Frankfurt, 1985), pp. 361–453. See also the draft of his 1944/45 memorandum for an international academy to be set up after the war, which is included in volume 12 of the *Gesammelte Schriften: Nachgelassene Schriften*, ed. Gunzelin Schmid-Noerr (Frankfurt, 1985). It was also Horkheimer who urged Paul Kluke to write his massive history of the University of Frankfurt; see Kluke, *Die Stiftungsuniversität Frankfurt am Main 1914–1932* (Frankfurt, 1972), p. 7.

10 Max Horkheimer, *Dawn and Decline: Notes 1926–1931 and 1950–1969*, trans. Michael Shaw (New York, 1978), p. 75.

11 Perry Anderson, *Considerations on Western Marxism* (London, 1976), p. 32.

12 Fritz Ringer, *The Decline of the German Mandarins: The German Academic Community 1890–1933* (Cambridge, Mass., 1969).

13 For a history of Frankfurt in the early modern period, see Gerald Lyman Soliday, *A Community in Conflict: Frankfurt Society in the Seventeenth and Early Eighteenth Centuries* (Hanover, NH, 1974). For an account of Frankfurt in the 1920s, see Madlen Lorei and Richard Kirn, *Frankfurt und die goldenen Zwanziger Jahre* (Frankfurt, 1966).

14 The classic study of Frankfurt Jewry is Isidor Kracauer, *Geschichte der Juden in Frankfurt*, 2 vols (Frankfurt, 1927). He was Siegfried Kracauer's uncle.

15 The assimilation of Frankfurt Jews is shown by the comparatively low attendance figures for high holy day services in the 1920s: Breslau, 58 percent; Berlin, 49 percent; Frankfurt, 41 percent. Cited in Donald L. Niewyk, *The Jews in Weimar Germany* (Baton Rouge, La., 1980), p. 102. For a discussion of the creative response of Frankfurt Jews to modernization, see Jakob J. Petuchowski, "Frankfurt Jewry – A Model of Transition to Modernity," *Leo Baeck Yearbook* 29 (1984): 405–17.

16 It was one of three new universities begun in this era, along with Hamburg and Cologne founded in 1919. In 1932 it was officially named the Johann-Wolfgang-Goethe Universität in honor of Frankfurt's most illustrious citizen. For a full account, see Kluke, *Die Stiftungsuniversität*.

17 Ibid., p. 53.

18 For a history of the decline of the German university from its Humboldtian origins, see Charles E. McClelland, *State, Society and University in Germany 1700–1914* (Cambridge, 1980); for a study of the growing nationalism of students, see Konrad Jarausch, *Students, Society, and Politics in Imperial Germany* (Princeton, NJ, 1982).

19 Wolfgang Schivelbusch, *Intellektuellendämmerung: Zur Lage der Frankfurter Intelligenz in den zwanziger Jahren* (Frankfurt, 1982), p. 18.

20 Ulrike Migdal, *Die Frühgeschichte des Frankfurter Instituts für Sozialforschung* (Frankfurt, 1981).

21   McClelland, *State, Society and University*, p. 280.

22   For a discussion of the institute's holistic inclinations, see Martin Jay, *Marxism and Totality: The Adventures of a Concept from Lukács to Habermas* (Berkeley, Calif., 1984); for a different account of Horkheimer's initial attitude toward totality, see Michiel Korthals, "Die kritische Gesellschaftstheorie des frühen Horkheimer: Misverständnisse über das Verhältnis von Horkheimer, Lukács und dem Positivismus," *Zeitschrift für Soziologie* 14 (August 1985).

23   McClelland, *State, Society and University*, chap. 8.

24   Brecht's scornful discussion of the relationship appeared in his account of "Tui-intellectuals" in his *Arbeitsjournal*, ed. Werner Hecht (Frankfurt, 1973), Vol. I.

25   Lewis S. Feuer, "The Frankfurt Marxists and the Columbia Liberals," *Survey* 25 (Summer 1980): 167. Richard Sorge was later unmasked as a Soviet spy, but there is no evidence that he recruited anyone else during his brief institute stay.

26   Among the acknowledged Communists were Karl August Wittfogel, Julien Gumperz, and Richard Sorge. There has also been some speculation about the possible allegiance of others in the early 1920s. See Migdal, *Die Frühgeschichte*, p. 102.

27   One important precedent was the so-called Austro-Marxist School, which has been compared to the Frankfurt School in the introduction to *Austro-Marxism*, ed. Tom Bottomore and Patrick Goode (Oxford, 1978), p. 2. The link between the two was Carl Grünberg, who was known as the father of Austro-Marxism before he became the institute's director. Another possible model was the "Kathedersozialisten" (socialists of the lectern) around the Verein für Sozialpolitik during the Wilhelmian era, although they were very distant from Marxism *per se*.

28   Migdal claims that the institute during its Grünberg phase was more open, pluralistic, and undogmatic than later. She chides my account in *The Dialectical Imagination: The Frankfurt School and the Institute of Social Research, 1923–1950* (Boston, 1973), for failing to appreciate the virtues of Grünberg's lack of firm direction. She refers to a letter by Oscar Swede to Max Eastman (which she inadvertently attributes to "Oscar Eastman"), which I cite to make the case that Grünberg's leadership was dogmatic, but she doesn't really refute it. For a critique of her tendentious comparison between the two eras, see the review of her book by Hauke Brunkhorst in *Soziologische Revue* 3 (1982): 81.

29   Helmut Dubiel, *Theory and Politics: Studies in the Development of Critical Theory*, trans. Benjamin Gregg (Cambridge, Mass., 1985).

30   Max Horkheimer, "Traditional and Critical Theory," *Critical Theory: Selected Essays*, trans. Matthew J. O'Connell et al. (New York, 1972).

31   On prewar Munich, see Peter Jelavich, *Munich and Theatrical Modernism: Politics, Playwriting, and Performance, 1890–1914* (Cambridge, Mass., 1985). Berlin's preeminence during the Weimar Republic is discussed in such works as Peter Gay, *Weimar Culture: The Outsider as Insider* (New York, 1968); John Willett, *Art and Politics in the Weimar Period: The New Sobriety 1917–1933* (New York, 1978); and Henry Pachter, *Weimar Etudes* (New York, 1982).

32   Willett, *Art and Politics*, p. 124. For more on Frankfurt's role in modern architecture, see Kenneth Frampton, *Modern Architecture: A Critical History* (London, 1985), p. 136; and Barbara Miller Lane, "Architects in Power: Politics and Ideology in the Work of Ernst May and Albert Speer," *Journal of Interdisciplinary History* 17 (Summer 1986): 283–310.

33   For an account of Radio Frankfurt, see Schivelbusch, *Intellektuellendämmerung*, chap. 4.

34   Ibid., p. 68.

35   For an account of the decision to grant the prize, see ibid., chap. 5.

36   Ernst Erich Noth, *Errinerungen eines Deutschen* (Hamburg, 1971), p. 194.

37   For discussions of the Lehrhaus, see Schivelbusch, *Intellektuellendämmerung*, chap. 2; Nahum N. Glatzer, "The Frankfort [sic] Lehrhaus," *Leo Baeck Yearbook* I (1956); and Erich Ahrens, "Reminiscences of the Men of the Frankfurt Lehrhaus," *Leo Baeck Yearbook* 19 (1974).

38   Leo Lowenthal, *Mitmachen wollte ich nie: Ein autobiographisches Gespräch mit Helmut Dubiel* (Frankfurt, 1980), p. 61.

39   Max Horkheimer, *Dawn and Decline*, p. 96.

40   Benjamin's failure to earn his *Habilitation* in 1925 ended his hopes for an academic career. Kracauer, thwarted by a speech defect, never pursued a teaching career, moving instead from architecture to journalism.

41   For a comparison of Simmel with Kracauer and Benjamin, see David Frisby, *Fragments of Modernity: Theories of Modernity in the Work of Simmel, Kracauer and Benjamin* (Cambridge, Mass., 1986).

42   Siegfried Kracauer, "Uber den Schriftsteller," *Die Neue Rundschau* 42 (June 1931): 860–62; Walter Benjamin, "The Author as Producer," in *Reflections*. The proletarianization of intellectual life had been a preoccupation of German thinkers well before this period. See the discussion of it among the Naturalists of the 1890s in Peter Jelavich, "Popular Dimensions of Modernist Elite Culture: The Case of Theater in Fin-de-Siècle Munich," in Dominick LaCapra and Steven L. Kaplan, eds, *Modern European Intellectual History: Reappraisals and New Perspectives* (Ithaca, NY, 1982), p. 230.

43   Schivelbusch, *Intellektuellendämmerung*, chaps 3, 4.

44   See n. 25. The debate continued in *Survey* 26 (Spring 1982) with Martin Jay, "Misrepresentations of the Frankfurt School"; G. L. Ulmen, "Heresy? Yes! Conspiracy? No!"; and Lewis S. Feuer, "The Social Role of the Frankfurt Marxists."

45   During the seven years the *Zeitschrift für Sozialforschung* was published while the institute was in New York, only eight major articles were contributed by Americans; three of those were in the 1941 volume. As for the audience at the institute's extension course lectures, a letter of Karl Korsch written on 20 November 1938 may be indicative of its limits. Horkheimer's "circle of hearers," Korsch wrote, "was for the most part the people in the Institute and their wives, and a few confused students." See Douglas Kellner, ed., *Karl Korsch: Revolutionary Theory* (Austin, Texas, 1977), p. 284.

46   The connections between Finley, Gouldner, and Mills and the institute have been widely remarked in the literature on them and in their own writings. Bell's has been ignored. His essay, "The Grass Roots of American Jew Hatred," *Jewish Frontier* 11 (June 1944): 15–20, clearly displays the influence of the institute's work on anti-Semitism. Although Bell has become very critical of the Frankfurt School, he circulated this piece forty years later among his friends to warn against the neoconservative weakness for populist bedfellows.

47   See, for example, the account of an unsuccessful meeting with the editors of *The Marxist Quarterly* during the late 1930s by Sidney Hook, "The Institute for Social Research – Addendum," *Survey* 25 (1980): 177–78. Korsch's letter, cited in n. 45, also testifies to the institute's aloofness from political movements of any kind.

48   Theodor W. Adorno, *Minima Moralia: Reflections from Damaged Life*, trans. E. F. N. Jephcott (London, 1974). For an account of the general problems of life in southern California for refugees, see Anthony Heilbut, *Exiled in Paradise: German Refugee Artists and Intellectuals in America from the 1930s to the Present* (New York, 1983).

49   For an account of the institute's contribution to the war effort, see Alfons Söllner, ed., *Zur Archäologie der Demokratie in Deutschland*, 2 vols (Frankfurt, 1986). Marcuse's role is discussed in Bary Käatz, *Herbert Marcuse and the Art of Liberation* (London, 1982), p. 109.

50   See, for example, Mark Krupnick, *Lionel Trilling and the Fate of Cultural Criticism* (Evanston, Ill., 1986), in which potential comparisons with Adorno are mentioned several times (e.g., p. 110). See also James Gilbert, *Writers and Partisans: A History of Literary Radicals in America* (New York, 1968); William Barrett, *The Truants: Adventures among the Intellectuals* (Garden City, NY, 1982); Irving How, *A Margin of Hope: An Intellectual Autobiography* (San Diego, Calif., 1982). Only the last of these mentions a Frankfurt School figure, Marcuse, and then with contempt (p. 309).

51   Dwight MacDonald, "A Theory of Popular Culture," *Politics* 1 (February 1944).

52   On the reception of the Frankfurt School, see Martin Jay, "The Frankfurt School in Exile" and "Adorno and America," in *Permanent Exiles: Essays on the Intellectual Migration from Germany to America* (New York, 1985).

53   Schivelbusch, *Intellektuellendämmerung*, chap. 6.

54   Horkheimer's lectures, interviews, and articles of these years are available in the seventh and eighth volumes of his *Gesammelte Schriften*.

55   Susan Handelman, *The Slayers of Moses: The Emergence of Rabbinic Interpretation in Modern Literary Theory* (Albany, NY, 1982).

56   Heinrich Levy, *Die Hegel-Renaissance in der Deutschen Philosophie* (Charlottenburg, 1927).

57   In *Mitmachen wollte ich nie* (p. 156), Lowenthal has recently acknowledged the importance of his experience at the Lehrhaus for the development of Critical Theory.

58   For a good account of the Frankfurt School position on aesthetic modernism, see Eugene Lunn, *Marxism and Modernism: An Historical Study of Lukács, Brecht, Benjamin and Adorno* (Berkeley, Calif., 1982).

59   Carl E. Schorske, "The Idea of the City in European Thought: Voltaire to Spengler," in Oscar Handlin and John Burchard, eds, *The Historian and the City* (Cambridge, Mass., 1963), p. 60.

60   George Steiner, "The City under Attack," *Salmagundi* 24 (Fall 1973): 3–18.

61   The most important expression of this hope appeared in Friedrich Engels, "The Housing Question," in Karl Marx and Friedrich Engels, *Selected Works*, 2 vols (Moscow, 1958), I, 546–635. See also Raymond Williams, *The Country and the City* (New York, 1973).

62   Thomas Bender, "The Cultures of Intellectual Life: The City and the Professions," in John Higham and Paul K. Conklin, eds, *New Directions in American Intellectual History* (Baltimore, Md., 1979), p. 63.

63   Martin Jay, *Marxism and Totality*.

64   Jürgen Habermas, "Modern and Postmodern Architecture," in John Forester, ed., *Critical Theory and Public Life* (Cambridge, Mass., 1985), pp. 326–7.

65   Dominick LaCapra, *Rethinking Intellectual History: Texts, Contexts, Language* (Ithaca, NY, 1983), chap. 3.

3 CRITICAL THEORY AND TRAGIC KNOWLEDGE

Christoph Menke
(translated by James Swindal)

I

Horkheimer understands critical theory as a form of knowledge that is distinguished not only by a specific object – the overall process [*Gesamtprozeβ*] of society – but also by a specific relation *to* its object. This relation is a "conduct," which "aims at emancipation"[1] in order to subordinate the social formative process to "planful decision and rational determination of goals" (CT 207). Critical theory belongs to a "struggle" whose "goal" is the "rational state of society" (CT 216). Critical theory contributes to this struggle, inasmuch as it dissolves the appearance of necessity with which the existent conditions are shrouded. In this respect social praxis appears as a "fatalistic event" and

> men see themselves only as onlookers, passive participants in a mighty process which may be foreseen but not modified. Necessity for them refers not to events which man masters to his own purposes but only to events which he anticipates as probable. (CT 231)

On the contrary, critical theory describes the necessity *as* appearance in anticipation of its dissolving in freedom – "even if not as an existing" freedom. Through its method of knowledge, critical theory belongs to "the effective striving for a future condition of things in which whatever man wills is also necessary and in which the necessity of the object becomes the necessity of a rationally mastered event" (CT 230ff).

   It is the exact opposite view that is determinant for tragic experience. For "a way of affirmation" always belongs to tragic experience: "what is understood as tragic is only to be accepted."[2] Not without elitist arrogance Max Scheler designated it as the "certain coldness" by which tragic experience is characterized in contrast to critical and changeable eagerness.[3] The object of tragic experience is the failure of the realization of individual or collective purposes. This is "annihilated" (Scheler) in tragic events through an adversary, a counterforce, which opposes them *as* necessary and *with* necessity. Tragic affirmation entails the entanglement in a "contradiction" for which, on account of its necessity, it provides no solution. This unavailability designates the tragic experience as "fate." Since, or more precisely *if,* the occurrence of conflict or even of total destruction is experienced as fateful or as irresolvably necessary, it can give *to* the occurrence only a relation of acceptance.

This interrelation of affirmation and fate in tragic experience made it a key adversary of critical theory in the thirties. In fact the various wings of critical theory – the messianic critique of mythical fate (especially by Benjamin) and the Marxist critique of fetishistic reification (especially by Horkheimer) – find their points of agreement in their crusade against tragic thinking. This "critical theory versus tragic experience" paradigm reemerged, or more exactly transformed itself, in the debate regarding French Poststructuralism. For from the view of critical theory, the theoretical foundations of the conceptions of tragic thinking return in Poststructuralism. It describes an unobtainable, unavailable, objective, and necessary occurrence of self-subversion (in Derrida's *différance*) or self-struggle (in Lyotard's *différend*) of "the valuable" – and proclaims as a result an affirmative relation (indeed less a tragic than a more playful resignation) to this occurrence.

Then as now the objection of critical theory first of all concerns the political implications of the tragic discourse. Tragic discourse propagates "resignation in praxis" (Horkheimer) and promotes the "rehearsal for catastrophe" (Benjamin). This political critique centers around the theoretical implications of the concepts of necessity and unavailability that legitimates the tragic affirmation. From the viewpoint of critical theory the claim of the necessity of an occurrence is marked by a striking alternative:

> If he encounters necessity which is not mastered by man, it takes shape either as that realm of nature which despite the far-reaching conquests still to come will never wholly vanish, or as the weakness of the society of previous ages in carrying on the struggle with nature in a consciously and purposefully organized way. (CT 230)

That is the alternative by which critical theory attempts to conceive of and deal with tragic experience. Uncontrollable necessity is either predicated of nature or it is the effect of the powerlessness of a society that still has not found a "conscious and purposive organization."

In response to this objection of critical theory, I would like to show in what follows the legitimacy of a conception of tragic knowledge that consists in – but only inasmuch[4] as it consists in – articulating a *third* understanding of necessity that deviates from Horkheimer's alternative. But this alternative understanding of necessity that grounds a tragic perspective does not stand externally opposed to critical theory. For Horkheimer's alternative of natural necessity or social illusion *obstructs* – so I would like to show – its own insight in the moment of irreducible necessity that is suitable for social praxis as *praxis*. With this insight critical theory formulates the perspective out of which its alternative of natural necessity or social illusion can be recognized as a remnant of idealism: the perspective of a "materialistic" interpretation of social praxis. The external opposing of critical theory and tragic experience is a self-misunderstanding on the part of both sides. For the correctly understood concept of a materialistic interpretation of praxis implies a tragic knowledge, and the concept of such a knowledge finds an adequate grounding only in a materialistic interpretation of praxis.

II

Horkheimer understands critical theory – as I have mentioned earlier – not "as something independent," but as "an element in action leading to new social forms" (CT 216). It is part of a "struggle," whose "goal" is the "rational condition" as a "community of free persons." This entails its opposition to the "intellectual technology" that Horkheimer describes as the "traditional form of theory." He calls knowledge "traditional" if on the basis of empirical observation it arrives at causal explanation that forms part of a system of universal propositions. This knowledge has its "legitimacy" in that it serves practical purposes that are externally acquired and clearly delineated. Although strictly opposed in their "interests," traditional and critical theory thus are not polar opposites: they do not lie on the same level. This is shown in the way Horkheimer introduces the concept of critical theory: he describes critical theory not as an expression of another interest, but as the overcoming of the cognitive limits of traditional theory. The aim of critical theory is practical, but its grounds of justification are cognitive. Critical theory is superior to traditional theory *as theory*, which means superior in its knowledge.

The limits that Horkheimer sees imposed on traditional theory derive from the fact that it cannot grasp itself – its own functioning – as theory: it is not reflexive. The fact that traditional theory cannot understand itself Horkheimer shows first of all relative to its own history (cf. CT 194ff). Traditional theory describes its history as a whole, or at least in great part, according to the way it is carried out in detail: as a progressive correction of errors and as an expansion of knowledge. These are the "immanent motives" that are determinant for the theorists themselves. But from these motives one cannot conceptualize when and how historical-theoretical revolutionary establishments of "new views" emerge. For in such reorganization not only do discoveries expand, but the point of view for their assessment concerning what counts as knowledge and error also alters. But these alterations of the criteria of knowledge are not reducible to those expansions of knowledge. The alterations do not *follow* from the expansions, but must be understood on the basis of "non-scientific factors."

> In the seventeenth century, for example, men began to resolve the difficulties into which traditional astronomy had fallen no longer by supplemental constructions, but by adopting the Copernican system in its place. The change was not due to the logical properties alone of the Copernican theory, for example its greater simplicity. If these properties alone were seen as advantages, this very fact points beyond itself to the fundamental characteristics of social action at that time. (CT 195)

Fundamental transformations in the theory – both that they occurred and also how they took place – are able to be understood only on the basis of their "role in action" (CT 208). In order to be able to understand itself – initially its history – theory must enlarge itself. It must understand itself as an element of praxis, or better yet, it must understand praxis itself.

The first step that Horkheimer took in order to bring theory "to a new stage of development" (CT 199) from a traditional to a critical form was the step to a reflexive turn of theory by which it conceives itself as a moment in the "life of society." Indeed in light of the developed concept of a critical theory Horkheimer is justified in stating that the word "critical" becomes "used here less in the sense it has in the idealist critique of pure reason than in the sense it has in the dialectical critique of political economy" (CT 206 fn). But this does not work as the *first* step in the introduction and grounding of a critical theory: what critical theory should be, and above all what it is *capable* of, gains its determination on the grounds that through it "thought" succeeds to its "self-awareness" (CT 209). The Kantian idea of a self-reflection of science and knowledge always remains not just central to and exhaustive of, but *foundational* for the concept of critique in a critical theory.[5] The critical theory of Horkheimer is a specific interpretation of this reflexive turn.

In what the reflexive development of theory towards critical theory consists can be gathered from Horkheimer's critique of "ideology research and scientific sociology" in which the "investigation of social conditioning of both facts and theory" forms "a research program, indeed an entire field of theoretical work" of a traditional type. This formulation already shows that Horkheimer's 1937 distinction between traditional and critical theory also contains a critique of the program that he had outlined in his inaugural lecture of 1931 entitled "The Present Situation of Social Philosophy and the Task of an Institute for Social Research." For the project which the inaugural lecture announced was precisely that of the "investigation of social conditions of facts as well as of theory" to make a "research program of theoretical work" in a scientific spirit.[6] But in "Traditional and Critical Theory" (1937) Horkheimer insists that it is not "so much the differences of objects" from which the "opposition" between a reflexive or critical theory "to the traditional concept of theory springs" (CT 209). Rather it arises from the difference "of the subject" itself: its "conduct" or relations *to* its object. In traditional knowledge the subject stands relative to its object in a "passive" relation of "exteriority" (CT 200): the subject duplicates something that without it is already there. But in reflexive reconstruction [*Erschließen*] the object of knowledge loses "the character of pure factuality" (CT 209). Reflection, Horkheimer states, implies "activity" (CT 200). Derivable from the difference in the behavior of the subject, reflexive reconstruction turns out to be another *mode* of knowledge: a knowledge that implies an activity because it indicates a participation.

To this habitual and methodological difference – in the behavior of the knowing subject towards its object – is joined an ontological difference. It is not another "field," but another *kind* of object that the theory reconstructs in its reflexive "redevelopment." As we have seen, while Horkheimer explicitly refers to the first difference, the habitual difference, only his terminology indicates the second, the ontological difference thus linked with the first. Horkheimer uses the terminology of life philosophy [*Lebensphilosophie*], anthropology, and phenomenology that he discussed extensively in the thirties to designate the objects of his reflexive kind of cognitional theory as "praxis," "existence," and "life." Indeed Horkheimer always rejects the irrationalistic thesis that praxis, existence, and life are events that principally evade thinking (KT 1:126ff). At the same time, however, he reformulated the basic motif of an ontological difference of the "living thing," as opposed to one rendered accessible by traditional theory, by a rereading of Hegel's logic (KT 1:138ff) that repeats, though tones down the findings of, Marcuse's approach.[7]

Horkheimer also understands praxis, existence, and life as essentially "processual," which means as temporal and historical performances of an integration to (hyper-) complex unities of elements and wholes, of the objective and the subjective, and of the object and its conceptualization. The opposition between traditional and critical theory is fundamentally an ontological one: it lies between reflexively disclosed practical performances and empirically known things. To this corresponds the above mentioned methodological and habitual difference. For the difference between a "method oriented to being" and one oriented "to becoming" (CT 5) consists in the fact that the subject's knowledge of being is passive and he accepts "the basic conditions of his existence as given" (CT 207). But while the reflexive reconstruction liquifies the being in becoming, it takes part in that which it knows. If praxis becomes the object of theory, the theory becomes praxis: a comprehending and "co-performance" [*Mit-Vollzug*] achievement of praxis. Reflexive reconstruction does not just merely reveal the social "facticity" as "activity": reflexive reconstruction *is* activity.

III

The determination of theory as reflection and its object as praxis designates the first and fundamental step in the "redevelopment" from traditional to critical theory. According to Hegel, it is the step by which philosophy becomes "social philosophy." By means of this step, philosophy achieves the "knowledge of the meaning of our own being according to its true value and content" only through "the philosophical understanding of the collective whole in which we live."[8] And at the same time this is the step that Horkheimer presents (under repeated references to Heidegger) as the truth-content of historicism, *Lebensphilosophie*, and philosophical anthropology. At this point the determination of theory as reflection and its object as praxis is indeed fundamental, but still not specific, for a critical theory. The *further* step critical theory needs for its specific determination Horkheimer elucidated – so I would like to show in the following – in two opposing ways.

Horkheimer acquires the first elaboration of the program of a critical theory by way of an ideology-critical view of the understanding of praxis in positions that he summarizes as the "new philosophy of objective spirit." Under this designation Horkheimer understands conceptions that describe social praxis as an autonomous event, to which they – as much irrationally as objectivistically – ascribe a basic independence relative to the understanding and acting of the subjects (cf. KT 1:153ff). The fact that Horkheimer views these philosophical conceptions from the viewpoint of *ideology* critique means that he sets them in a direct relation – as much of symbolic expression as of effective determination – to social structures. Accordingly, the philosophically maintained independence of praxis as an autonomous object is an ideological repetition (because a naturalizing confirmation) of the independence within which society must appear as "alien" to its members (cf. CT 205).

> The world which is given to the individual and which he must accept and take into account is, in its present and continuing form, a product of the activity of society as a whole . . . This difference in the existence of man and society is an expression of the cleavage which has up to now affected the historical forms of social life. (CT 200)

The ideology-critical convergence of the philosophical and social by Horkheimer is signified by the concept of alienation. By this concept Horkheimer chose an interpretative scheme with which an entire field is at once bound in a binary and hierarchical opposition whose influence also he could not evade. The most important effect of this use of the concept of alienation was a far-reaching reinterpretation of the concept of praxis. For inasmuch as Horkheimer describes the independence of social praxis as alienating with regard to individuals, he sketches at the same time a counter-image of unalienated praxis that articulates itself in concepts and metaphors of *production* (cf. CT 200ff).[9] Unalienated praxis is production since production is an activity whose result – as Horkheimer writes in direct reference to an idealist theory of the subject – can be understood as "the result of the conscious spontaneity of free individuals." Thus what is decisive for our context – the question about the relation of critical theory and tragic knowledge – is the freedom-theoretic and reason-theoretic dimension that is linked with this action-theoretic reinterpretation of praxis as production. For the motive for this reinterpretation is the blueprint (imposed by the concept of alienation) of a model of unalienated activity as undifferentiated self-maintaining translation [*Übersetzung*]. The interpretation of social praxis as production should provide the conceptual conditions that – even if not concretely, at least as a matter of principle – can dissolve necessity into freedom: into the subject's own action without anything left over. That is the freedom-theoretic perspective within which Horkheimer – in the first variant of his elucidation – places critical theory. The description of social praxis as production suggests the image of a "rationally dominated event" since what is recognized as product can also be *re*produced by means of will and consciousness.

Let us now return to the program of critical theory, outlined at the beginning, that divests social processes that are not rationally governed and brought forth out of freedom of their appearance of necessity. This program was motivated by the demand to dissolve illusory necessity and reified objectivity. Since critical theory describes this necessity and objectivity as alienation, it confronts them with an idea of clear transparence, which in Horkheimer is expressed in the reinterpretation of social praxis in production.[10] In the ultrapure light of the concept of alienation, *all* uncontrollable necessity appears as illusory and *all* non-self-posited objectivity as false. The critique of alienation is thus uncritical: it cannot distinguish between illusory and actual necessity, or between objectivism and objectivity. But without these distinctions, the concept of praxis as *ir*reducible in free production and conscious reproduction cannot be understood. For as situated in history and in culture and realized in mediated and bodily matter, all praxis unsurpassably contains a dimension of unobtainable necessity and of irreducible objectivity. The alienation-theoretic grounds of critical theory – the *first* way of explicating we saw that Horkheimer gave to the program of a critical theory – thus circumvents its own determination as reflexive reconstruction of praxis. Yet, at the same time, Horkheimer does provide hints as to how critical theory, as a countermove to the idealism of the theory of alienation, could be grounded *as* reflexive reconstruction of praxis.

IV

The first version of Horkheimer's conception of critical theory was determined by the opposition of alienated objectivity and uncontrollable necessity to cognitive transparence and free self-activity. Horkheimer's second version circumvents this opposition by introducing the opposition of idealism and materialism, which are designated as two fundamentally different models of praxis and of its reflection. What Horkheimer understands as "idealism" reveals itself in his critique of Hegel. According to Horkheimer, Hegel represents – as we have seen – the turn to social philosophy, which at the same time designates an ontological and a methodological turn of philosophy. As social philosophy it is no longer a knowledge in the spirit of a traditional theory, merely about a "second reality," but is the reflection of present praxis.[11] Within this conception Horkheimer also sees the foundation of critical theory. But this conception became idealist in Hegel, as well as in the "most recent metaphysics" (Horkheimer specifies Jaspers and Heidegger), because Hegel interpreted the relation of reflection – the relation of a reflecting subject and a reflected praxis – as "the identity of subject and object." "Even though the most recent metaphysics expressly questions 'the solidity of a definite knowledge of being' it continues to regard absolute consciousness as the reflecting mirror of the innermost reality of being" (CT 27). Idealistically understood, reflection is the medium of a self-knowledge of reason beyond difference. That is why praxis is a reducible event beyond differentiation in reason – the reason of its (practical) producing and (theoretical) reproducing.

In contrast to this idealist conception, Horkheimer calls an understanding of reflection "materialistic" that "maintains the irreducible tension between concept and object and thus has a critical weapon of defense against belief in the infinity of mind" (CT 28). Materialism means critical consciousness of the unattainability of praxis in reflection – of the "interweaving [of spirit] in an unpenetrable 'shadowy background', in a non-conscious and non-transparent world . . . of that occurrence of the 'material existence,' of 'praxis,' of the 'lifeworld,' of the 'unconscious' and 'preconscious.' "[12] In that case, however, we can no longer insist on the idea of a dissolution of social praxis into free production. For this freedom for self-production of society could only exist if there were a transparent *self-knowledge* of society – an "absolute consciousness" of praxis. According to Horkheimer, the materialist truth beyond transcendental subjectivity *should be* the idea of a conscious and willed social self-reproduction (cf. CT 202ff), but this actually expresses only the same idealism once again. Instead materialism, when adequately understood, is the consciousness that social praxis cannot be made as a whole because it cannot be known as a whole. Thus in his materialism Horkheimer places his productionism in question.

Horkheimer set forth his insight concerning the finitude and boundedness of all reflection and production in his work on Schopenhauer in the fifties and sixties, but initially it was already in his writings in the thirties under the title of the "pessimistic trait" of materialism (CT 25). To speak of "pessimism" means to interpret only negatively the materialistic insight in the unattainability (in the difference) of praxis: as the insight into an unpreventable preventing [*unverhinderbar Verhinderndes*]. I will still try to indicate under the rubric of a "tragic knowledge" what I see as accurate in this interpretation. It seems, however, inaccurate to me insofar as the negative or pessimistic formulation of the materialistic consciousness of difference remains in the horizon of that whose impossibility it maintains. Thus, according to Horkheimer, pessimism maintains the "opposition of the world and of that which it should be." For the pessimistic "dissolving of the false trust" of the "rationalist deception" confirms that the "reconciliation, the identity of the object that the thought reaches," is "not the *actual* [emphasis mine] reconciliation."[13] In pessimism, the materialistic insight that the idealistically claimed reconciliation is impossible translated into the conclusion that the "ground of the world is evil,"[14] thus remaining under the spell of the idealist determination of the good.

In *Negative Dialectics*, which in an explicit reference to Horkheimer's program of a critical theory wants to bring "materialism to theoretical self consciousness,"[15] Adorno bestowed the experience of difference with another meaning. The materialistically revealed moments of praxis, which withdraw reflexive acquisition just as much as planned production, are not – or indeed not only – hindering, but rather enabling. For exactly that which overcomes the idealist "idea of absolute activity" and absolute consciousness is that which constitutes the reality of finite activity and of finite consciousness. Materialism – as Adorno corrects its one-sided pessimistic interpretation – discovers not only what destroys the idealist hopes, but at the same time what makes material actuality possible.

> Only if the I on its part is also not-I does it react to the not-I. Only then does it "do" something. Only then would the doing itself be thinking. Thinking, in a second reflection, breaks the supremacy of thinking over its otherness, because it always is otherness already, within itself. (ND 201)

The materialistically shown mistake of idealism consists not only in that it claims a transfiguring "meaningful totality" where in reality misery and suffering reign, but principally in the fact that the idea of meaningful totality already contradicts the conditions of possibility of all *actual* meanings, and thus of itself. "If we conceive the mind as a totality, eliminating every difference from the otherness it is to live by, according to Hegel, the mind turns for a second time into the nothingness which at the outset of dialectical logic is to reveal pure being: the total spirit would evaporate in mere entity" (ND 199).

From his *non*-pessimistic reformulation of Horkheimer's concept of materialism, in *Negative Dialectics* Adorno also draws out methodological consequences for the project of a reflective reconstruction of praxis. The materialistic insight shows difference as constitutive for praxis in two respects: as difference in praxis and thus as difference from praxis. As distinct from knowledge, social praxis contains an unattainable independence; as opposed to action, it contains an unattainable objectivity. On the basis of the same insight, Gadamer grounded his methodological demand, "to go back the path of Hegel's *Phenomenology of Spirit* insofar as one shows the determining substantiality in all subjectivity."[16] Through this move, philosophy became hermeneutics. To this Gadamerian program corresponds the methodological conclusion that Adorno drew from the unattainable otherness of "life": its reflexive reconstruction must turn into "interpretation" (ND 54). Philosophy as interpretation means a "dependence on texts" (ND 55) that understanding is never able to overcome. Unlike the project of Hegel's Logic, no "method" can be given whose compliance would allow it to bring forth "life" out of its rational self-understanding again. In order to develop the objects from their "still-positing objectivizing" in "traditional" or "identifying" understanding into their "life," philosophy must retrace through interpretation their "implicit history" and "mediation." Critical theory actualizes itself when "being is read as the text of its becoming" (ND 52). In order to reconstruct objects as "living" ones, it re-traces them as a (hyper)complex web – more precisely as a (hyper)complex interweaving. This redrawing is not a (re)producing out of oneself, but it is also not a purely passive taking up or listening; it is a reading that must always be also understood as a new and comprehensive writing. Inasmuch as it understands itself in consequence of its materialist self-reflection as interpretation – or more exactly as a specific kind of interpretation – critical theory becomes a *critical theory* in the prevailing American sense. It becomes a critique in the sense of literary and textual criticism: a (specific) theory and practice of reading.

V

My reflections up to now regarding the connection of the two foundational aspects of a critical theory have tried to make clear their ontology (the understanding of its object: social praxis) and their method (the understanding of its procedure: the reflexive reconstruction of praxis). Social praxis, as shown above, is an occurrence which neither now, owing to its present alienated form, nor in principle can be given the form of a free production, because it cannot be grasped in a totalizing knowledge. The ontological and methodological questions of a critical theory are thus immediately linked with the question posed at the beginning: the normative question about its understanding of freedom and necessity. The idea that critical knowledge of the existing necessity – as Horkheimer occasionally puts it – *implies* that the "struggle for its transformation out of a blind into a meaningful [that is a self "made" or "dominated" (KT 2:46ff)] necessity" (45 ff) cannot any longer be valid for a critical theory that understands itself as interpretation. For linked with the concept of interpretation is an understanding of praxis that contradicts the implicit idealism upon which rests the alienation-theoretic equating of unattainable necessity or exteriority with a lack of freedom.

> If a man looks upon thingness as radical evil, if he would like to dynamize all entity into pure actuality, he tends to be hostile to otherness [*das Fremde*], to the alien thing that has lent its name to alienation [*Entfremdung*], and not in vain. He tends to that nonidentity which would be the deliverance, not of consciousness alone, but of reconciled mankind. Absolute dynamics, on the other hand, would be that absolute action whose violent satisfaction lies in itself, the action in which nonidentity is abused as a mere occasion. (ND 191)

Precisely *as* interpretation, in "reading being as the text of its becoming," critical theory breaks apart from an idealist conception of freedom and wins a differentiated relation to practical necessity.[17] This relation is threefold: it consists in the dissolution of the false necessity, the demonstration of the constitutive necessity, and the maintenance of tragic necessity.

The fact that the interpretation of praxis consists, in the first place, in the dissolution of false claims of necessity determines the interpretation as dialectical. For an understanding is "dialectical" when its path to truth is the critique and the correction of the false. The conviction regarding the systematic connection between false understanding and a false life – that the false claims of necessity in whose dissolution critical theory actually consists are linked not only, as in Plato's dialectical art or in Hegel's dialectical method, with distortions of knowledge, but with social structures – defines interpretation, moreover, as not only dialectical, but critical behavior. This is the specific procedure of critical theory. Social praxis, upon which interpretation directs itself, is distorted or, more precisely, it distorts *itself* through constructions that bring to a halt the processual events of praxis in an objective way. They reduce their "texts" to "concepts" or "systems." Critical interpretation must both explain this reduction on the basis of its social function[18] and clear it up through the arrangement of "concepts" in "constellations." As a result critical interpretation opens up new spaces of freedom. For inasmuch as it reconstructs social praxis in its constellations as a textual event, it also penetrates "its hardened objects" by the "possibility of which their reality has cheated the objects and which is nonetheless visible in each one" (ND 52).

As we have seen above, one (but not *any* one) of the objectivizing representations of praxis to which the critical interpretation is aimed is the idealist exceeding of praxis in the program of its sublation beyond difference in (and reproduction through) rational knowledge. Critical interpretation shows that this idealistic representation of praxis, since it declares a false social praxis to be necessary, is not only false, but ideological. Secondly, critical interpretation can dissolve this idealistically declared *illusory* necessity only inasmuch as it shows the *constitutive* necessity and externality of praxis: insofar as it shows that the character of the external and the necessary are constitutive for praxis. Thus Adorno reformulates Horkheimer's conception of a "materialistic" interpretation as a bearing in mind [*Eingedenken*] of the external in the internal (or of the foreign in one's own), of the not-I in the I, and of the objective in activity. In its second step, critical interpretation redraws the decentration that always already carries out its work in praxis. For therein it discovers the characteristics of praxis that are the condition for praxis to occur: that precisely because they cannot be (re)produced they remain necessary. In its first step of the dissolving of apparent necessity, critical interpretation portrays freedom as the freeing *from* necessity. But in its second step, as the revealing of the constitutive necessary, critical interpretation embodies freedom as relation *to* the necessary. If critical interpretation extends to the bearing in mind of the irreducible, because constitutive, necessary, then freedom (also) becomes the performance of the necessary.

There is a necessary that cannot be reduced to an apparent one, since it is constitutive for praxis. It is such a necessary that must remain *simply* necessary and external if praxis is going to succeed. If critical interpretation is to escape from the influence of idealism, then on top of that the separation/difference [*(Unter-)Scheidung*] of critique from itself also belongs to it: the difference between the criticizable and the constitutive necessary. But there is still an idealistic residue even in the description of the irreducible necessary as constitutive of praxis. According to this description, the success of praxis lies in the failure of the translation into free and conscious (re)production. But this failure cannot be simply sublated into success. According to a formulation of Derrida,[19] the unattainable necessary is, as the condition of possibility of praxis, also the condition of the impossibility of praxis (of the impossibility of a *guarantee* of its success). What the success of praxis generally makes possible initially is also that which always further endangers, even hinders, the individual act in a praxis. Adorno has reformulated Horkheimer's materialistic insight (see §4) in such a way that the I can only "do" something "insofar as it on its part is also not-I." But the fact that the condition for the I to be is for the not-I to be does not dissolve the opposition of the not-I and I: for the not-I to be is at the same time the condition of possibility *and* limit and, as a limit, also a hindrance for the I. That is the truth of the pessimistic formulation of materialism. A tragic insight is linked with the materialistic decentering that recognizes the irreducible necessary as constitutive for freedom: the insight into the breakdown of the action at that which it makes possible.

This thesis, that critical interpretation of praxis implies a tragic insight, can be seen clearly within the formulation of the materialistic theory of freedom that Horkheimer began and Adorno carried on.[20] One of its central convictions involved the (Schopenhauerian) skepticism about the Kantian project of deriving the moral point of view out of the concept of practical reason.

> All attempts to ground . . . the moral . . . rest upon harmonious illusions . . .
> There is no grounding possible, neither through intuitions nor through arguments. Instead, it represents a psychic state of mind. (KT 1:93)

What is constitutive for morality is a "moral feeling" that can be neither reconstructed not reproduced, but that the "subject matter of psychology" is "to describe and to make understandable in [its] personal conditions and mechanisms of production from one generation to the next" (ibid).[21] Adorno had so reformulated and sharpened this objection that he referred to the principal differences of consciousness and will, and of moral reflection and praxis. According to this interpretation, Kant's concept of morality means a dissolving of the moral into consciousness, its "depracticalization (ND 236). Conversely the "transition" from moral consciousness to praxis succeeds only through an "addendum," an affective, even somatic, "impulse" (ND 228ff).

> True practice, the totality of acts that would satisfy the ideas of freedom, does indeed require full theoretical consciousness . . . But practice also needs something else, something physical which consciousness does not exhaust, something conveyed to reason and qualitatively different from it. (ND 229)

There is no moral *praxis* without an exceeding or falling short of moral *consciousness* – without the "motor form of reaction" that breaks the "mechanical autarky" (ND 230) of reflection just as much as it brings it to action.

Adorno had not only emphasized, in connection with Horkheimer, the constitutive role of pre-rational "physical impulse" (ND 241) for moral praxis, but also referred to its consequent limiting and even *hindering* role.

> In contrast to its pharisaism, the irrational moment of the will condemns all moral aspects to fallibility as a matter of principle. Moral certainty does not exist. (ND 242)

The affective, even somatic, "matter" that constitutes moral praxis also evades it. For though this matter indeed makes the morality initially possible, it *is* not moral. Through its dependence on the matter of somatic impulses, moral praxis remains dependent upon a sphere of the physical that comes under (also) its own *non*-moral laws. The impulses, without which there is no moral praxis, are subjected not even to a moral logic, but rather only to a necessity that on Horkheimer's account can be (psychologically) described. Thus moral praxis becomes principally "fallible" (Adorno) or "fragile" (Nussbaum). For thus it is not only a contingent condition, but a structurally grounded fact of moral praxis that it occurs in situations in which the somatic impulse does *not* supervene and the transition into praxis does not take place. These are situations, as Martha Nussbaum has shown in the tragedy of Hecuba,[22] in which the affective attitudes and somatic impulses which persons, on moral grounds, ought to have (in order to be able to be moral) they nevertheless cannot have on the basis of *psychological* necessity. The "material" ground [*Grund*] upon which moral praxis rests, is at the same time the abyss [*Abgrund*] which places it in question and suspends it. The materialistic theory of freedom that Horkheimer and Adorno formulate implies a tragic insight: the insight that situations necessarily belong to the actuality of moral praxis within which it conflicts with that which makes it possible.

The fragility of moral praxis is one aspect of its tragic structure that Horkheimer and even Adorno formulate as a consequence of their materialistic interpretation. How little Horkheimer and Adorno are decisive in their formulations of the tragic consequences of the materialistic interpretation and how much they always seek to avoid these consequences in favor of an idealistic perspective of reconciliation both reveal a second aspect of the tragedy of moral praxis. In contrast to the first form, its fragility, the second can be designated as the *fragmentarity* of moral praxis.[23] The *fragility* of moral praxis consists in the fact that moral demands depend for their realization upon something that is subject to its own "somatic" necessity that can turn against moral logic. The *fragmentarity* of moral praxis instead designates a tension in the normative content of moral praxis itself: between the meaning and the principle of moral praxis. The *principle* of the moral is the universal law of an equal respect for all that Kant had tried to ground from the concept of practical reason alone. But in reflection on the moral, which thus can be called "materialistic" because in it the moral is "at once comprehended and rendered final" (KT 1:88ff), the meaning of the moral does not consist in an actualization of its principles ("morality for its own sake," so to speak). The meaning of the moral is rather "the development and the happiness of life" (89) of individuals: the moral law emerges out of "care" for individuals.

Like the "addendum" somatic impulse, the reference to the development and to the happiness of the individual is a constitutive condition of moral praxis. As distinct from the "addendum" somatic impulse, it is effective not just for the actualization, but also for the emergence and the formulation of the moral principle. It is effective for the *emergence* of the moral principle, since without the precedent care for individuals there emerges no formation of the moral principle of an equal respect for all. And it is effective for the prevailing *formulation* of the moral principle, since the care for individuals develops the point of view and ways of regarding which all moral considerations of equality rely on. In both regards the reference to happiness and development of individuals is the prevailing ground of the moral law. The meaning of the moral is irreducibly presupposed in the moral principle, since this principle can be neither developed nor formulated without that meaning. From this dependence Horkheimer and Adorno established the perspective of a "sublation" (KT 1:82) or "reconciliation" (ND 271) of morality, in which the difference between the moral sense with respect to the happiness of individuals and the moral principle of universal consideration will have been dissolved. This is denied by the tragic experience that the moral sense can also stand up against the moral principle that it constitutes according to materialistic insight. The reference to individuals, to their development and happiness, is irreducibly presupposed by the moral principle and follows its own necessity that is not the logic of the moral principle: the meaning of the moral cannot be sublated into moral meaning. Moral praxis is not only made possible, but also can be hindered not only by the foreign, somatic necessity of the "addendum" impulses, but likewise by the foreign necessity of the care for the happiness and development of individuals. The equal considera-tion for all – the principle of the moral – and the care for individuals – the meaning of the moral – can interfere with one another and reciprocally hin-der or even halt their respective actualizations. If the materialistic reflection upon the somatic abyss/ground [*(Ab-)Grund*] of the moral praxis proves its tragic fragility, then materialistic reflection on the unavoidably presupposed reference to individuals proves the tragic *fragmentarity* of moral praxis.

The tragic insight – as is thus shown – does not stand, as it would have seemed at the outset, opposed to the critical attitude that is not only grounded through critical theory, but is that in which critical theory consists. On the contrary, tragic insight is a *consequence* of the understanding of critical theory as a materialistic interpretation of social praxis that Horkheimer began and Adorno further took up. In this, in its own "tragic" consequence, critical theory contradicts the remaining idealist program with which it is nevertheless still burdened in Horkheimer and Adorno. A critical interpreta-tion of social praxis, which abandons the idealistic idea of reconciliation, implies a tragic affirmation: it is both critical dissolving of apparent necessity and tragic affirmation of constitutive necessity. Only in this simultaneity can critical theory and tragic knowledge find their appropriate formulations. For without the corrective of a critical theory, tragic knowledge sees all necessity as irreducible and becomes a metaphysical transfiguration of suffering and unhappiness. And without the corrective of a tragic knowledge, critical the-ory sees all necessity as dissolvable and falls back on an idealism of transpar-ent self-knowledge and unalienated self-activity.

NOTES

1 M. Horkheimer, *Kritische Theorie der Gesellschaft* [KT], ed. A. Schmidt (Frankfurt a/M: Fischer, 1968), vol. II, p. 157 [English translations are from *Critical Theory: Selected Essays* (CT), tr. M. O'Connell (New York: Herder and Herder, 1972)].

2 H. G. Gadamer, *Wahrheit und Methode* (Tubingen: Mohr, 1975), p. 123.

3 M. Scheler, "Zum Phänomen des Tragischen," in *Die Zukunft des Kapitalismus* (Munich: Francke, 1979), pp. 91–155; here, p. 99.

4 This reservation concerns a tragic metaphysics, which derives tragic necessity out of the "essential *Seinzusammenhängen* of the world itself" (Scheler) instead of out of the structure of *this* historical world. See also C. Menke, *Tragödie im Sittlichen, Freiheit und Gerechtigkeit nach Hegel* (Frankfurt a/M: Suhrkamp, 1966), ch. 1.

5 On the concept of reflection in critical theory, see R. Geuss, *The Idea of a Critical Theory* (Cambridge: Cambridge University Press, 1981) [German pp. 67ff] and T. McCarthy, *Ideals and Illusions* (Cambridge MA: MIT Press, 1991), ch. 5.

6 See M. Horkheimer, "Die gegenwärtige Lage der Sozialphilosophie und die Aufgaben eines Instituts für Sozialforschung," in *Sozialphilosophische Studien* (Frankfurt a/M: Fischer, 1972), pp. 33–46, here pp. 40ff. H. Brunkhorst emphasizes this in "Dialektischer Positivismus des Glücks: Max Horkheimers materialistische Dekonstruktion der Philosophie," in *Zeitschrift für philosophische Forschung*, vol. 39 (1985), pp. 353–81, here pp. 378ff. In opposition to this, see A. Schmidt, *Zur Idee der kritischen Theorie* (Munich: Hanser, 1974), pp. 33ff.

7 See H. Marcuse, *Hegels Ontologie und die Theorie der Geschichtlichkeit in Schriften*, vol. 2 (Frankfurt a/M: Suhrkamp, 1989). Further, see also C. Demmerling, *Sprache und Verdinglichung: Wittgenstein, Adorno und das Projekt einer kritischen Theorie* (Frankfurt a/M: Suhrkamp, 1994), chs 1–2. On the critique of the category of reification, see para 3.

8 M. Horkheimer, "Die gegenwärtige Lage der Sozialphilosophie," p. 34.

9 For a critique of idealism, which is linked with critical theory's critique of alienation, see M. Theunissen, *Gesellschaft und Geschichte: Zur Kritik der Kritischen Theorie* (Berlin: de Gruyter, 1969). E. M. Lange has concretized this critique in an action-theoretic way in *Das Prinzip Arbeit* (Frankfurt a/M/ Berlin/ Vienna: Ullstein, 1980). See also the analysis of the critique of alienation by A. Gehlen in "Die Geburt der Freiheit aus der Entfremdung"; and J. Derrida, *"The Ends of Man,"* in *Margins of Philosophy*, trans. A. Bass (Chicago: University of Chicago Press, 1982), pp. 111–36.

10 The idea of transparence is, however, not linked to this production-oriented concept of activity. See C. Menke, "Zur Kritik der hermeneutischen Utopie," in *Ethos der Moderne: Foucaults Kritik der Aufklärung*, ed. E. Erdmann et al. (Frankfurt a/M/ New York: Campus, 1990), pp. 101–29.

11 In reference to this and for a further discussion see R. Bubner, " 'Philosophie ist ihre Zeit, in Gedanken gefaßt,' " in *Hermeneutik und Ideologiekritik*, ed. K. O. Apel et al. (Frankfurt a/M: Suhrkamp, 1971), pp. 210–43.

12 H. Brunkhorst, "Dialektischer Positivismus des Glücks," p. 358; cf. A. Schmidt, "Die geistige Physiognomie Max Horkheimers," in *Drei Studien über Materialismus* (Frankfurt a/M/ Berlin/ Vienna: Ullstein, 1979), pp. 81–134.

13 M. Horkheimer, "Die Aktualität Schopenhauers," in *Zur Kritik der instrumentellen Vernunft: Aus den Vorträgen und Aufzeichnungen seit Kriegsende*, ed. A. Schmidt (Frankfurt a/M: Athenäum Fischer, 1974), pp. 248–68, here p. 261.

14 Ibid., p. 262.

15 T. Adorno, *Negative Dialektik*, in *Gesammelte Schriften*, vol. 6 (Frankfurt a/M: Suhrkamp, 1973), pp. 197ff [English translations are from *Negative Dialectics* [ND], tr. E. B. Ashton (New York: Seabury Press, 1973)]. See also the readings of Adorno in A. Wellmer *Zur Dialektik von Moderne und Postmoderne* (Frankfurt a/M: Suhrkamp, 1985), pp. 48ff; and his *Endspiele: Die unversöhnliche Moderne* (Frankfurt a/M: Suhrkamp, 1993), pp. 178ff.

16 *Wahrheit und Methode*, p. 286; see also R. Bubner, " 'Philosophie ist ihre Zeit, in Gedeanken gefaβt,' " p. 231.

17 This also means: "textualism" means – as opposed to a widespread prejudice – not idealism, since reading does not mean dissolving into meaning.

18 This explanation remains a moment *in* interpretation. It finds no redemption in theory independent of interpretation (which it cannot give from social praxis). See Adorno's conception of an encylcopedic "Ensemble von Modellanalysen," *Negative Dialektik*, pp. 39ff.

19 J. Derrida, "Signature, Event, Context," in *Limited, Inc.* (Evanston, IL: Northwestern University Press, 1988), ch. 1.

20 See H. Schnädelbach, "Max Horkheimer und die Moralphilosophie des Deutschen Idealismus," in *Max Horkheimer heute: Werk und Wirkung*, ed. A. Schmid and N. Altwicker (Frankfurt a/M: Fischer, 1986), pp. 52–78.

21 That these descriptions must go beyond the realm of (in a narrow sense) "psychological" explanations, see A. Honneth, "Die soziale Dynamik von Miβachtung: Zur Ortsbestimmung einer kritischen Gesellschaftstheorie," in *Leviathan* (1), 1994, pp. 78–93.

22 M. Nussbaum, *The Fragility of Goodness: Luck and Ethics in Greek Tragedy* (Cambridge: Cambridge University Press, 1986), pp. 397ff.

23 In reference to T. Nagel, "The Fragmentation of Value," in *Mortal Questions* (Cambridge: Cambridge University Press, 1979), pp. 128–41 see C. Menke, *Tragödie im Sittlichen: Freiheit und Gerechtigkeit nach Hegel*, chs 5–6.

PART II

Social Science, Discourse Ethics, and Justice

Social Science, Discourse Ethics, and Justice

In Part II, *Social Science, Discourse Ethics, and Justice*, Hauke Brunkhorst, in the chapter entitled "Critical Theory and Empirical Research," situates critical theory's approach to empirical social research *à la* Habermas in the context of the claims and counter claims of empiricism (Popper), of hermeneutics (since Dilthey), of systems-theory (Luhmann) and functionalist reason (Parsons) as well as of Foucault's sociology of power. Brunkhorst argues that recent critical theory "renews" the Kantian point of departure in epistemology by conducting a critique of empiricism, characteristic of critical theory in its original phase (Horkheimer), which asks after the "conditions of the possibility of knowledge and its objects." Beyond that, critical theory in its most recent phase extends that point of departure by making possible a critique of functionalist reason. In Alessandro Ferrara's chapter, "The Communicative Paradigm in Moral Theory," the discussion moves to critical theory's renewal of the Kantian point of departure in moral theory. Ferarra characterizes the development of Habermas's "discourse ethics" from its original formulation in 1982 to the present. According to Ferrara, the "central intuition" upon which discourse ethics is based focuses on "ethical universalism" which in turn rests on a "dialogical revisitation of Kant's view of moral validity as generalizability." Rainer Forst, in "Justice, Reason, and Critique: Basic Concepts of Critical Theory," carries Habermasian moral theory a step further by attempting to work out a "critical theory of justice": taking up the notion of critique as it existed in early critical theory and developing a theory of justice which takes seriously the universalistic claims of reason (Habermas) and the contextual basis of social criticism (Walzer). Taken together the three chapters complement one another not only in their departure from the Kantian turn in later critical theory (Habermas) but also in their attempts to justify this turn in terms of the philosophy of the social sciences as well as the controversial field of moral theory.

4 CRITICAL THEORY AND EMPIRICAL RESEARCH

Hauke Brunkhorst
(translated by Stephen Findley)

INTRODUCTION

While the traditional point of departure in epistemology since Kant asks after the conditions of the possibility of knowledge and its objects, more recent theory of science limits itself to the logical analysis of scientific propositions or statements. Critical theory is the attempt to renew Kant's point of departure on the basis of empirical social research.

From this starting point we may bring some order to the manifold debates in the social sciences concerning paradigms. First of all, it is controversial whether there is a distinct logic of the social sciences over against (the logic of) the other sciences. This point is contested by, for example, analytic theory of science and the school of the Critical Rationalists. According to their views, the social sciences are, in principle, nomological sciences [*Gesetzeswissenschaften*] that proceed hypothetico-deductively like physics (I). Since Dilthey, theoreticians of a hermeneutically reflective and humanistic [*geisteswissenschaftlichen*] sociology have protested against such a view. But specifically critical, emancipatory, and dialectical approaches have also customarily distinguished themselves from the empiricist understanding of the sciences. From Horkheimer through Habermas, the unity of critical theory consists in the critique of empiricism. At the same time, however, it insists on a critical distance over against hermeneutic idealism (II). While the empiricists, who have prevailed for the most part in psychology, economics, and quantitative social research, orient themselves in their methodological self-reflection wholly in terms of analytic theory of science, theorists of hermeneutics, dialectic, and communication, as well as functionalists like Parsons or Luhmann, refer back to older epistemological points of departure that are directed towards the constitution of the realm of the social object. In universalistic systems-theory and in more recent post-structuralist thought there have been renewed attempts to elaborate a comprehensive theory of the sciences developed purely from the perspective of the observer. Such a theory would not orient itself according to the methodology of physics or of the logical analysis of its language, but according to complex concepts of system, communication, discourse, and power (III). It is here that Habermas has intervened, distinguishing between an actions-theoretical paradigm and a systems-theoretical paradigm, in order to extend critical theory's critique of empiricism to a comprehensive critique of functionalist reason (IV). The differentiation of quantitative and qualitative methods makes still more concrete the program of a materialistic social science (V).

I THE HYPOTHETICO-DEDUCTIVE PARADIGM (EMPIRICISM)

Popper's *Logic of Scientific Discovery* begins with the sentences: "A scientist, whether theorist or experimenter, puts forward statements, or systems of statements, and tests them step by step. In the field of the empirical sciences, more particularly, he contstructs hypotheses, or systems of theories, and tests them against experience by observation and experiment." The task of a logic of scientific discovery is "to give a *logical analysis* of this procedure; that is, to analyze the *method of the empirical sciences*."[1]

With that Popper has named the essential and fundamental assumptions of the *statement-view model* of the sciences.[2] This model rests upon two central premises: justification is identified with *deductive justification*, and experience with the *observation of nature*, or alternatively, with the singular propositions that describe such observations (the "basic statements" of an "observation-language"). Logical analysis restricts all connections in the system of scientific propositions to deductive ones, excluding from the realm of scientific argumentation any divergent forms (such as substantial justification, practical justification analogy construction, interpretative connections of sense, explications of context, etc.). At the same time the identification of the basis of experience with observation-reports binds science to a system of purely cognitive, representative statements and in particular excludes from all sciences, even the social sciences, any value-judgements or normative implications. "A widely accepted claim about scientific theories is this," J. P. Sneed writes: "*scientific theories are sets of statements, some of which are empirically true or false.*"[3]

Observation sentences anchor scientific systems of propositions in our sense-perception. Analytic theory of science generally assumes that we "have in sense-perceptions direct access to universally accessible objects and processes, and that we can distinguish between favorable and unfavorable circumstances for *determining through seeing, hearing, etc.* which perceptible characteristics can be attributed reliably to these objects and processes. It is customary to name these perceptible characteristics *'observable properties'* and their linguistic expression *'observation-predicates.'* "[4]

Now the *empiricist premise* of analytic theory of science implies an *assimilation of understanding to observation.* Only descriptive observation-sentences that express the direct access of sense-perception to the objective world are actually meaningful and intersubjectively fully understandable. That does not mean that the sciences could be reduced to such sentences. On the contrary, without the theoretical concepts at the heart of nomological hypotheses, there is no scientific explanation. Nonetheless the *rational, understandable, and intersubjectively verifiable* kernel of scientific explanations is the observation-statements along with the theoretical concepts that are completely defined in an observation-language. Any other theoretical concept is opaque, dark, and, insofar as it is either partially or not at all interpretable in an empirical observation-language, *irrational or extra-rational,* viz. intersubjectively *incomprehensible.* Since scientific explanations always combine *comprehensible* concepts (those referred to perception) and *incomprehensible* (theoretical) concepts (or assign them to one another with a so-called "assignment-rule"), then science, according to the analytic understanding, can be defined as *a deductive operating with networks, the threads of which are linked by means of knots of comprehensible and incomprehensible concepts.* The threads between the purely theoretical "law-cluster terms" (Putnam) are the propositions of pure theory.[4a] The threads that are held by the comprehensible observation-concepts and that are anchored to the firm ground of the facts make up the realm of the purely empirical. Finally, the threads that connect the observation knots and the opaque, "law-cluster terms" are those which Carnap names "correspondence-rules" or "assignment-rules."

According to Wolfgang Stegmüller the only language "that we perfectly understand" is observation-language. For example, the theoretical concept of intelligence is only understandable in the operational definitions of the intelligence test. "We thus concede that we have only attained a partial understanding of the terms of our theoretical language."[5] Hence only a phenomenalist language of things and events is "suited to agreement among scientists."[6] Such a language has to be nominalistic, viz., it may only refer to "concrete individuals like things, thing-moments, or events." Stegmüller justifies this claim in turn by noting that the language of the sciences should be "a comprehensible language."[7] The theoretician of science finds herself compelled "to draw the boundary [of the understandable, i.e., of the observable] quite narrowly, and to consider only that which is *sensuously perceptible* as observable."[8]

In Popper's "logic of scientific discovery" as well, the "basic statements" of the observation-language are the criterion of intersubjective meaning, or at least its fundament: "if some day it should no longer be possible for scientific observers to reach agreement about basic statements this would amount to a failure of language as a means of universal communication."[9]

This concept of understanding is intuitively unsatisfactory first of all because it declares all predicates of disposition, like, for instance, "water-soluble," but also those like "intention," "motive," "responsibility," "soundness of mind," "linguistic competence," or "intelligence" as at least partially incomprehensible. Since we successfully use them everyday, however, both in scholarly as well as in more quotidian practice, the occasion hardly ever arises, from the practical perspective, to consider them incomprehensible. From the point of view of our linguistic practice, the boundary between the intersubjectively comprehensible and incomprehensible in no way runs along the boundary between theoretical and observational language; instead, it encloses the area of the frictionless functioning of our language-games. Only where this *functioning of a normally successful praxis* bumps up against resistance does the problem of incomprehensible language force itself upon us, and indeed both in the application of theoretical concepts of disposition as well as in that language that describes concrete individuals or events (e.g., "at such and such a spatio-temporal position, an arrow fluctuates between 7.5 and 9.3").

But it is precisely with respect to the fundamental sociological concept of action that the empiricist understanding [*Verständnis*] of "intersubjective coming-to-understanding [*Verständigung*]" seems to fail. Actions are indeed spatio-temporally identifiable movements of bodies; but in order to describe them in such a way that we understand what the actor has done, we have to describe as well the opaque intentions of the actor. We *understand* the action only insofar as there is a description that specifies an intention. Thus even though actions are bodily movements, in principle they cannot be grasped in a pure observation-language. Only the fitting ascription of intention makes them comprehensible. What happened when Hamlet attempted to strike the man behind the curtains and accidentally killed Polonius must remain incomprehensible and opaque in a nominalist/phenomenalist language of things and events.[10]

Furthermore the *empiricist premises* of the analytic theory of science imply the thesis that the experiential basis of science itself fluctuates, since its language can only be *declared true* by convention in what amounts in the end to an irrational decision. According to the central thesis, perceptual experience cannot justify the basic statements, or the statements of the observation-language, but can only empirically motivate them: "I admit, again," Popper writes, "that the decision to accept a basic statement, and to be satisfied with it, is causally connected with our experiences – especially with our *perceptual experiences*. But we do not attempt to *justify* the basic statements by these experiences. Experiences can *motivate a decision*, and hence an acceptance or a rejection of a statement, but a basic statement cannot be *justified* by them – no more than by thumping the table."[11]

This is exceptionally unsatisfying, since the foundation that bears all not only fluctuates, but hangs in mid-air. Furthermore, it depends upon a dogmatically presupposed *deductivist premise*, according to which only propositions can justify other propositions, which would thus imply that every attempt to justify basic statements would have to remain circular. That is, however, pure dogma, because (1) it excludes from the outset the possibility of a *pragmatic justification* of observation-sentences; because (2) empirical *evidence* is reduced subjectivistically to evidential experience [*Evidenzerlebnissen*]; and because (3) any difference between an irrational conventionalism and a *critically constructivist conventionalism* of the elementary observation-language is made impossible.

Popper's thesis of the dependence of theory on observation-language only gets him so far, though, since he links it to his thesis concerning unproveability. For even the elementary synthetic experiences that we express in singular basic statements (e.g., "this is a bush") are due, as Peirce showed, to a complex interplay of pragmatic inferences (namely of abductive, inductive *and* deductive inferences). Thus the elementary perception of *something as something*, far from being reducible to a merely subjective experience [*Erlebnis*], has the "structure of an unconscious abductive inference." This inference leads from a (for example photographically) *ascertainable* and (linguistically) *denominable* "interpretation-free self-givenness of the phenomena" (firstness: "that over there is so and so"); through the hypothetical subsumption of a class of possible phenomena under a concept (secondness: "what is so and so, is, as a rule, a bush"); to the *interpretative* and *something-as-something*-identifying *perception* as a logical result, which would be description in an observation-language (thirdness: "thus that over there is probably a bush").[12]

Therefore it is also false "to reduce *evidence* to an "*evidence-feeling*" or "experience of certainty," without any justificatory function. "Sensuous phenomenal evidence can be made permanent in the *objective* moment of the *self-givenness of the phenomenon* in for example a photograph."[13] Different observers can then refer to the same phenomenon at different times and can correct their respective subjective "evidence-feelings" by means of the objective phenomenal evidence.

Basic statements and the judgments of experience that are justified through corrigible evidence and fallible, practico-synthetic inferences are *rationally motivated*, not merely *empirically* motivated. Hence they are no longer naturally arising facticities, but products of a directed, rationally reconstructible scientific progress that in the long run aims at the realization of an ideal consensus already assumed in every basic statement. Such a consensus would adequately present actuality.

The late Popper did recognize the subjectivist and decisionistically irrational implications of his earlier, radical fallibilism. However, in order to avoid them, he, like Frege before him, fell back into a Platonic realism, with a third world of objective Ideas and meaning. In this later phase he claims that "a theory may be true even though nobody believes it, and even though we have no reason for accepting it, or for believing that it is true; and another theory may be false, although we have comparatively good reasons for accepting it."[14] Nonetheless, with this Popper overlooks the dialectic, constitutive of true theories, between true and factical consensus, or between ideal and real communities of communication. Peirce had already pragmatistically transformed the idealistic dialectic of knowing and truth [*Wissen und Wahrheit*]) into such a dialectic. It is of course true that a theory can be true even if nobody believes in it *right now*. But the *meaning* of its truth first discloses itself when *all* good and bad reasons have been exchanged and weighed against one another. A theory is true insofar as anyone could agree to it. That is in the long run the meaning of the truth the factical acceptance of which falsification constantly prevents. In this respect the principle of falsification presupposes the concept of an absolute truth. That Popper orients [his views] according to Tarski's semanticist theory of truth leads to a neglect of pragmatics, or more precisely, to a psychologistic misinterpretation of the "assertoric powers" of speech, and to a reduction of pragmatic subjectivity to an empirico-psychological subjectivity.[15] In this connection Apel speaks of an "*abstractive fallacy* with respect to the *subject-place* of Peirce's foundational three-place relation of sign-mediated knowledge."[16] In the center of Peirce's *consensus theory of truth* thus stands the power of *rational motivation*, a power which lies within the "process of investigation" but "outside the arbitrariness" of "various heads" with their "thoroughly contradictory views," and which leads these many "heads" finally ("in the long run") "to one and the same conclusion," if only they can speak with one another long enough.[17]

In the meantime the hypothetico-deductive paradigm has also been called into question from a wholly different quarter. In his path-breaking study, *The Structure of Scientific Revolutions*, Thomas S. Kuhn was able to prove that the analytic theory of science, given its understanding of rationality as exclusively fixed on the "effects of nature and of logic," viz., on experimentally determined observations and deductive operations, not only cannot explain the factual dynamic of scientific revolutions, but cannot even rationally reconstruct them.[18] But the "metascience of science" thus threatens to degenerate into a "metascience of science fiction."[19] Beginning with Kuhn himself, many have drawn relativistic, historicist, hermeneuticist, and even scientifically an-archic conclusions in the triumphal procession which has since become the book's *Wirkungsgeschichte*. But we *only* have to share these conclusions *if* we assume, as *both* Kuhn *and* deductive empiricism do, that there is no justification and no rational discourse outside of the narrow framework of "effects of nature and logic."

If one does not share that assumption, everything actually argues for advancing from the failed scientifico-theoretical attempt to *liquidate* transcendental epistemology, to the dialectical sublation [*Aufhebung*] of it. This advance begins with the recognition of the distinct sense of the logic of the social and human sciences and (with the recognition) of the object-constituting function of their knowledge-guiding interests. Critical theory is not the scientific liquidation of, but the transcending of and preservation [*Aufhebung*] of epistemology *in* the sciences.

II   KNOWLEDGE-DIRECTING INTERESTS IN CONTROL, ORIENTATION, AND EMANCIPATION

Natural scientists have their experience with-the-world [*an-der-Welt*], human scientists *within-the-world*.[20] Whereas the investigators of nature observe their objects from the outside, the investigator into the realm of the objective spirit of a culture is already at home.[21] She moves within the "native realm of spirit" (Hegel). Indeed, in her travels through past realms or in the South Seas, she encounters foreigners and strangers, but with them she can come to an understanding [*sich . . . verständigen*], *as if* she were a native. She can learn the language and work through [*wegarbeiten*] the boundaries that exclude her from foreign forms of life. Learning to understand the foreign is both the fusion of and expansion of horizons.[22] The logic of interaction is one of understanding-in-a-situation and of "practical inference."[23] Without a foreign horizon there is no understanding. The difference from one culture to another, the distance from one time to another – these are the historical conditions of the possibility of hermeneutic experience, of humanistic and historical knowledge.[24] Mediated by language and symbols, spiritual reality [*geistige Wirklichkeit*], is a peculiar "object," into which the investigator must penetrate as it were *from the inside*, something which the investigator can only do because her temporal *Dasein* is always already in time. The investigator has to share the perspective of her object, she must take part in this perspective as an interactive-participant, if she is going to establish any "data" and gain new experience. She would not be able to understand her research-object at all, the actions and texts of foreign actors, if she were to describe them in an "observation-language" of the empiricist variety.[25]

The logic of *explanation* (in contradistinction to that of the "understanding" of the other) is the logic of the investigation of nature. The particular, as a case identical to many other cases, is subsumed under a universal law. "Theories," Popper says, "are nets cast to catch what we call 'the world': to rationalize, to explain, and to master it. We endeavor to make the mesh ever finer and finer."[26] The *interest in mastery and control* is the knowledge-guiding interest of the natural sciences.[27]

The logic of *understanding*, however, widens, deepens, alters, and secures our horizon of experience precisely when we involve ourselves with the particularity of concrete cases. The horizon of experience of the human sciences is always already fused with the experience proper to its range of objects. For

the objects of historical research are co-subjects, whose world is itself rationalized, explained, and mastered by the subjects themselves. The knowledge-guiding interest of the human sciences not only aims at understanding
the foreignness of the foreign and at making the incomprehensible comprehensible and the confused clear, but it also and especially wants to understand the alienation, meaninglessness, and hyper-complexity of our own
contemporary world so that we might find our way in this world (by orienting ourselves) according to the guiding thread of its historical being. This
interest is concerned with the restoration of security and confidence in a
world which, as a consequence of methodical thinking and of scientific-tech-
nical progress, and thanks to enlightenment, universal literacy, and industry,
is foreign, unfamiliar, and deeply unsettling with respect to the normal
unquestioning acceptance of the customary. The "native realm of spirit" is
also an "interior foreign land" (Freud), one in which modern men and
women, uncomprehending before mere road-signs ("methods"), have lost
their direction (from "true being").

The chief maxim of hermeneutics claims that "to understand something
means to understand how it became that thing."[28] Whoever knows its history or can at least make sense of one or more of its histories understands
the modern world. Narrative gives back to modern men and women their
disrupted confidence in the world and allows them to experience it genuinely as their own world. The recollective narrative achievements of the
human sciences also always attune one's understanding to an agreement
with the incomparably superior truth of history.[29] From the very beginning,
then, the human sciences' *practical interest in orientation* is not only complementary to the expansionist interest in control of the natural sciences and
technology, but is also typically defensive, aimed at the preservation of
what is tried and true, instead of at the modification of what is falsely
"known."[30] Concerned about the spiritual recompense for the consequences
and especially the unplanned side-effects of growing domination and control, the knowing of historical spirit has always been *conservative* and *compen-
satory.*[31]

Now hermeneutic experience raises the claim to be *more fundamental* than
all other sorts of experience. And it is in fact true that the mundane understanding of actions (and of symbolic expressions) is more elementary and
more comprehensive than scientific understanding [*Verstehen*] in an observation-language. The latter is not only more restrictive, but also, in comparison
with the everyday understanding of action, is completely counter-intuitive,
full of "theoretical" presuppositions, methodically derived, less "originary
[*ursprünglich*]," and secondary. By contrast hermeneutic experience makes
the abstract, methodically manipulable, and instrumental knowledge of the
physicists and engineers experiencable *as a concrete worldview.* Hermeneutics
lays bare the historical roots of an a-historical physics and of a putatively
timeless *logos*, revealing to us the domination of the analytic understanding

as a determinate and transitory "age of the world-picture,"[32] and exposing the ideal community of investigators as a concrete, social "paradigm community," the existence of which is owed not so much to the rationality of a continuous advance of science, but to a discontinuous, "irrational" power of scientific revolutions.[33] Methodical thinking has to experience its truth as a truth of its historicality [*Geschichtlichkeit*].[34] As guiding the *experience of all possible experience*, the hermeneutico-practical cognitive interest raises a reflective claim to universality.

Since the work of the late Dilthey, the *transformation of philosophy by the human sciences* moves the "historico-societal actuality" of in-formed "life" and its "context of effects" into the place of the transcendental subject of knowledge.[35] Time becomes the concrete condition for the possibility of *logos* and reverses the epistemological position of the knowing subject over against its objects. Epistemology is placed right-side up.

With this operation, the unique concept of experience of the human sciences fulfills a *double function*: it distinguishes its own type of experience, one that complements that of the natural sciences – the empirical experience within-the-world [*in-der-Welt*] versus the empirical experience with-the-world [*an-der-Welt*]. *And* it justifies the transcendental role of a kind of experience that insuperably outranks, precedes, and anticipates all other experience. Thanks to the interest in orientation of the human sciences, the interest in control of the natural sciences finds once again the furrowed and fruitful soil of life.

The weaknesses of this two-fold and universalistically over-extended concept of experience are obvious. Hermeneutics answers Popper's *abstractive fallacy* – that argues from the power of the *logos*, which explodes any merely factical acceptance, to the desubjectivized eternity of true theories[36] – with a *concretistic fallacy* – that argues from the historical self-retrieval of a limit-transcending *logos* to the inescapability of historical time and of the always temporally situated vernacular.[37] Nonetheless, we miss the *pragmatic dimension of subjectivity* in both.[38]

Thus in the end a new myth develops out of the historical Enlightenment, one no less absolutist than the scientism which has been shown its limits.[39] If the hermeneutic maxim – "to understand something is to understand how it has become" – is no longer understood as a heuristic maxim of a particular way of acquiring knowledge, but instead as an insurmountable presupposition of all experience, and if this maxim, with its sense of "temporality" and "historicality," promises an answer to the question of Being, then it implies that *every being* is *understandable*, viz., *historical*. Such a thesis is, however, a metaphysical thesis, which for precisely that reason cannot be meaningfully contested, because its negation, as a negation of a statement concerning totality, leads us to antinomies.[40]

The quasi-transcendental metaphysics of hermeneutic experience, which Heidegger had rendered at the time of *Being and Time* in the formula "Being is time," loads understanding [*Verstehen*] with a conservative prejudice and distorts the complementarity of understanding and explanation to the disadvantage of enlightenment and critique.[41]

The historical sciences are the paradigm of all the human sciences. In the *Order of Things*, Foucault has recognized the peculiarly Janus-faced role of history within the human sciences and has made it the basis of his own deconstructivist intention. The historical sciences *found* the other sciences, in that they *particularize* the universalism of the latter: "history thus offers a simultaneously privileged and dangerous area for the placement of the human sciences. To all the sciences of man it offers a background, one that constitutes it and establishes for it a fundament and, so to speak, a homeland."[42] History assigns the sciences to their transcendental region. It fulfills the Kantian function of philosophical "usher," but henceforth ironically, in that in its historical ushering it destroys the claim to truth of the sciences. History "encircles the other human sciences with a limit and from the very beginning undermines their claim to universal validity."[43] The transcendental/empirical double-status of historical experience transforms transcendental philosophy into genealogy and shatters the universality of *logos* into temporal fragments. Scientifically raised claims to *truth* are thus scaled back to the status of [claims to] merely methodological *correctness* – for Foucault no less than for Heidegger or Gadamer.

Every successful hermeneutic self-understanding within the historically produced actuality of the modern world does indeed correct the abstract, a-temporally rationalistic self-understanding of the modern world, but precisely this correction becomes assent to the historical character of the same modern world. By exposing ourselves to learning that this world (along with its science) *is* that which it has *become* and is otherwise nothing, we have gained confidence in its higher historical truth. But because of the higher authority and the insurmountable relativity of the horizon of historically pre-given meaning, the confidence-building histories of the narrative human sciences *unburden* social actors of the demands of an autonomy that *always anew* transcends any temporal context. In the realm of narrative, a realm in which fiction and reality mingle with one another in ever new descriptions,[44] the "fear of freedom" (E. Fromm) is relieved of being "condemned" (Sartre) to "self-legislating" freedom (Kant).

The bold claim to universality of hermeneutic and historical truth was first factically limited with the becoming autonomous of the social sciences, the cognitive interest of which linked up to both the natural and the human sciences, *and* related *critically* to both of the latter, demarcating the boundaries of each. In the place of the (latently absolutist) founding of the technico-scientific interest in control on the basis of the practical interest in orientation, now the *equiprimordiality of technical, practical, and emancipatory cognitive interests* steps forth, the unity of which consists in the (infinite) process of the common discovery of truth.[45] For the social sciences no less than for the natural and human sciences, reason [*Vernunft*] in this process is the respectively better argument, not the higher truth of one or more histories, and just as little the "effects of logic and nature."[46] The logic of the social sciences divests time of its superior truth, history of its power to announce definitions, and world-disclosing histories of their neutral claim to validity, and it leads the "effects of logic and nature" back to the "unforced force of the better argument."[47]

The difference between understanding and explanation separates not only the *sciences of spirit* (*Wissenschaften des Geistes*) from those of the external world, but the former, within themselves, also make use of the complementarity of understanding and explanation. As a rule they analyze the objective spirit of culture and society from both sides, from the inside and from the outside, as community and society, as life-world and as functional system. The concept of function belongs among the fundamental tools of the human sciences. Dilthey does not just distinguish nature and spirit, but he already does so recursively *within* the spirit of a historical form of life, when he immanently sets off inner and outer perspectives, namely by separating the "external organization of a society" (for example, religion as church and as association) from the "cultural systems" in need of interpretation (religion as community, fellowship of faith, "covenant," etc.).

The *critico-emancipatory social sciences* set the dissolving power of determinative reflection to work in the inner realm of spirit (Dilthey's "cultural systems") itself. They dissect the concept of understanding once again into its constitutive components, and bring the finely-honed weapons of *immanent critique* and *determinate negation* to bear on the content of tradition and on the *objectivity* of the spirit. The other side of the Hegelian legacy, from which Dilthey, moving towards the modern human sciences, only took the objective connections of function and meaning, enters with social sciences like psychoanalysis and Marxist social theory into the more sober and functional architecture of the social sciences as ideology-critical dynamite. For the reflective understanding of objective contexts of meaning does not only bump up against the functional systems of circulation of society which continue a part of natural history within social history[48] and which would mark the *limits to understanding*; within the native realm of spirit it also comes across an "interior foreign land" (Freud). This "foreign land" shows itself, "in the expressions of life that demand understanding," as the *contradictions* resulting from a "tangle of sense and nonsense."[49] The emancipatory cognitive-interest in psychoanalytically penetrating the thicket of parapraxes, split off dream-symbols, and neurotic disturbances is aimed at the dissolution of such contradictions. In the analysis of "distorted communication,"[50] understanding again detaches itself from explanation, but now however *in the interest* of cancelling and *preserving* explanation within the self-reflection common to subject and object. Psychoanalysis is still a unique model of this. For the only explanation of the fact "that men and women can react to causal-analytical explanations of their behaviour with new behaviour lies in the insight that they can translate the language of the psychologico-sociological 'explanation' through self-reflexion into the language of a deepened self-understanding."[51] The hermeneutic interest in orientation – an interest in a trusted fellowship [*Mitsein*] within a socially pre-understood world – is not, however, sufficient for a *self-understanding deepened* enough to break the latent force of the quasi-causal compulsion of split-off symbols. For this we need a post-conventional distancing from the customary and received truth of history, a truth which is warranted only by authority and tradition. The distinguishing power of critique separates *understanding* from *consent*, [merely] *lived agreement* from justified *assent*. The logic of the social sciences separates the *world-disclosive power* of a historical language from the *discursive justification* of its validity-claims, and distinguishes the new *perspective* [*Sicht*] of the social world that arises in the distance of time from the *insight* [*Einsicht*] into its structure and legitimacy. On the side of the human sciences, the emancipatory cognitive-interest differentiates *experience* and *justification*; on the side of the natural sciences, *legitimation* and *explanation*. In their interest in a "deepened self-understanding" that *dissolves* distorted forms of communication, the social sciences are *reflective sciences of crisis*, sciences that span the historical gap between the concepts of "critique" and "crisis."

In that the social sciences (as, e.g., in the work of Durkheim, Dewey, Mead, and Piaget) validate the interest in enlightenment *within* the human sciences against the totalizing claim of hermeneutic experience, and in that they hold at the same time the emancipatory interest in *inner* autonomy over against the instrumental interest of the natural sciences in external autonomy, the social sciences make the emancipatory cognitive-interest into the motor for a transformation of philosophy that does not liquidate epistemology, but sublates it. In the *social-scientific transformation of philosophy*, the concept of a "post-conventional ego-identity" (Kohlberg) grows out of the autonomous conscience of our intelligible character (Kant) by way of that strong ego which should become where the id was (Freud). Out of this *abstract and universal interior perspective*, socialization processes can not only be *analyzed from the outside* according to the criterion of the self-maintenance of complex systems (the perspective of the interest in control), and can not only be *understood from the inside* according to the criterion of historical self-understanding and of the interiorizing/recollecting power of the social collective (the perspective of the practical interest in orientation); but they also can and must be *criticized from the inside* according to the criterion of their rational identity and *conceptualized as inner processes of rationalization*.[52] Thus the critical social sciences as emancipatory sciences are the post-metaphysical heir not only of the Kantian "conscience," but also of the Hegelian "concept" as the measure of immanent critique. They dissolve the hermeneutic projection of objective truth into the always already occurring facticity of world-disclosive experience and overcome the dichotomy of truth and method. The internal dissociation of hermeneutic perspective and critical insight [*Sicht und Einsicht*] and the intra-temporal separation of time from *logos* and of history from evolution sublate, along with the totalizing hermeneutic categories "life," "spirit," and "actuality," the conservative "transfiguration of the life-world" (Apel).

III   SOCIAL SYSTEMS AND DISCOURSES OF POWER

(a)   The *radical constructivism* of more recent systems-theory[53] joins up again to the older starting-point of idealistic epistemology, and in this respect is related to the theory of the knowledge-guiding interests. It brings into sociology the phenomenologico- hermeneutical concept of the "meaning" of actions as a fundamental concept[54] and operates with a correspondingly complex concept of "communication."[55] This latter concept does in fact abstract from the participant perspective of hermeneutics and limit itself strictly to observation and the observation of observation (second-order cybernetics), but at the same time it avoids being bound to the narrow frame of reference of an empirical observation-language. Observation is situated instead on the same operating plane as the *reflecting consciousness* of transcendental and idealistic epistemologies (viz., more exactly, on the plane of the consciousness that observes as in a mirror). But in place of consciousness more general units step forward, namely *auto-poetic* or *self-referential systems*; "consciousness" is therefore only one case among many of systems that determine for themselves their difference from other systems in their environment through reflective observational achievements, through which they gain *system-autonomy*.[56] "Self-referential systems can observe themselves. They can direct their operations towards their own identity, in that they lay down a difference with the help of which their own identity can be distinguished from others."[57] This difference, which is *constitutive* for system-formation, is the difference between *system* and *environment*. It replaces the older distinction between *subject* and *object*.[58] Thus the world *is* the way we see it.[59] Luhmann writes: "radically implemented (which would even include its implementation in physics)," the concept of *auto-poesis* "requires the assumption of a being of the world that binds being and thinking."[60]

Systems actualize and generate themselves, and then can observe their self-actualizing and self-generation. "Thus in the course of history the experience which determinate societal formations can have of themselves increases."[61] Self-referential systems themselves generate their *experience* on the basis of their functional constitution. Such a self-generation of experience (the "*empirie*") is in no way willful or arbitrary, even though this self-generation remains *in itself unknown* within the system, which always and only operates with its own structures: since "no system can perform operations outside of the limits of the system, in its environment," and since "no system can connect itself through its own operations with the environment," then we can "only *assume* that reality is constantly tested through the recursivity of intellectual and communicative operations, and this successfully, because the environment of a system, while unknown and remaining unknown, does not in any case register arbitrary and discontinuous reports."[62] The world accessible to an organism "is thus its cognitive world, not a world 'as it is by itself.'"[63] Maturana writes: "therefore we literally generate the world in which we live, in that we live it."[64] Systems form themselves *in the performance* of operations that are directed towards themselves and that in this way close themselves off from their environment. Systems are no longer defined through the denseness of the object-context (which the systems themselves form), but only through their operations.[65]

We can describe on the abstract level of speech that which we (as thinking systems) observe. "So soon as a need arises to steer self-observation through pre-existing structural conditions and not to cede it completely to the relevant situation, we can speak of self-description. The description fixes a structure or a 'text' for possible observations, observations which can thereby be directed and better remembered, better passed on, and better connected to one another."[66] This is the system-theoretical concept of "objective spirit." Observation builds up observation and description, which then can be again observed and described. Auto-poetic (viz., self-referentially closed) systems form themselves through such recursive operations.[67]

The epistemological upshot is that only systems "uncoupled" from their environment and closed off through *self*-observation and *self*-description can have experience. "Knowledge is attainable only through the breaking off of operative relations to the outer world."[68] The only way to observation and description passes through the *self*, its own system, and its structural possibilities. All knowledge is self-knowledge, and every description of the world is self-description. "The question about the object of knowledge thus becomes meaningless. There are no objects of knowledge. To know means to be capable of operating adequately in an individual or social situation." We live "as thinking systems in a realm of *description*" and can, "by way of *descriptions*, increase without limit the complexity of our cognitive realm."[69] At the same time radical constructivism is a radical pragmatism that comes very close to the neopragmatism of Richard Rorty.[70] "Truth and falsehood always only exist [for radical constructivists/pragmatists] in the realm of reference that is established by an observer."[71] This perspectivism of truth means that "instead of the usual concepts that crop up in the framework of idealistic conceptions (like truth, adequacy, correspondence, actuality, etc.) [. . .] here concepts like believability, reliability, interestingness, effectivity, plausibility, compatibility, livability, survivability, advantageousness for orientation, possibility, multiplicity, exploration, responsibility, and tolerance" emerge.[72] With that, the postmodern locus at which Lyotard, Rorty, and Luhmann meet is precisely circumscribed: "objective spirit" sloughs off any claim to objectivity and truth beyond the perspectives of language-games, and the criterion for observation and description is, instead of validity and correctness, the functional need for better problem-solutions. And where there is no solution, there is also – as Marx already saw – no problem.[73]

We must first distinguish this position from that of an objective idealism which raises "reality" to "the concept" and identifies "the real" with "the rational." Radical constructivists do not deny "reality," but claim "that every single one of my assertions concerning this reality belongs to my experience. The fact that this experience then hangs together of course comes from reality."[74] If we explain the *hanging together* of multiple observations of the most diverse systems in this way, then we have again replaced the transcendental subject, which would explain the possibility of this hanging-together, with the "effects of nature,"[75] which again form only a contingent object. This epistemology is an extreme naturalism. Multiple observers agree according to such a naturalism, "because human beings as living systems are subject to the conditions that the medium, in which they live, sets to their existence."[76] Thus the epistemic relation of subject and object is here too "turned right-side up." But we would still have to wonder how we could know, in such a situation, that a "hanging-together" is possible. Kant, in fact, expressly turned himself upside down in order to *cognize* this possibility.

Therefore Luhmann, instead of replacing the transcendental and *subjective theory* of knowledge with a simple *objective theory*, starts out from the difference of "system" and "environment." As he himself sees, this of course presupposes talk of a *"world"* that "marks the unity in the difference between *system* and *environment*."[77] Now "the world" is *no object*, to which we can attribute predicates like "system" and about which we can deny other predicates like "environment," and which we could thus distinguish from *other* objects by predicative operations. It is therefore distinguishable from nothing and in this respect is the indistinguishable. For all objects always already meet us *within the world* [*in-der-Welt*].[78] And just as little as "object", and in opposition to signs (like "flower," "system," "table," "environment," "society," "nature," "red," etc.) that distinguish things or something about things, neither is "world" a predicate which we can attribute to *determinate* objects (or object-realms) precisely because we can deny it to other objects, and because we can learn its usage in an *exemplary* way through examples and counter-examples. Just as there is no counter-example to "object," there is none for "world." The "world" that "marks the unity in the difference of system and environment" is an expression, the usage and meaning of which we cannot learn through exemplary instruction with examples and counter-examples (as we do with any random predicate), but only *by the way* or "synsemantically" *within* the learning of predicative differentiation – the world is that which must accompany all our distinctions (to use Kant's language).[79] "World" and "object" are related complementarily to one another. While *objects* are those things to which we apply and deny predicates and which we denominate with names, *the world* is the insurmountable horizon in which we always already move when we describe objects, apply or deny predicates to them, and, for example, distinguish "system" and "environment" in our observing and describing.

None the less, Luhmann is of the empirico-naturalistic opinion that talk of "the world" would also be an achievement or operative practice proper to self-referential systems, exactly in the same way that the distinction of "system" and "environment" is. But this is eminently debatable. Inner-worldly "systems" generate themselves through differentiating operations (which include both simple and higher-order observation), but they perform such operations within the world that they always already have to *presuppose* as condition of possibility in every operative performance – and they must do this regardless of whether or not they speak of the world in a reifying way as object. Indeed individual systems presuppose a world for themselves, but they also *have* to presuppose one. Here the *objectivity* of the world (and of its "reality") forces itself upon them. We could not speak of "the world" without moving about in it, but we of course can talk about the stars without sitting on them. We can thus fabricate objects and ascribe to them fictive predicates (as with the famed "winged-horse" of the logicians), but we *cannot* do this with the world, the worldliness of which we presuppose along with *every* fiction. Sociological systems-theory begins not with this presupposition but with the one "that there are systems."[80] This only seems to be an ontological premise, for one has to *say that* there are systems, in order to be able to relate oneself to them *as to something.* Unless we speak of systems, or unless we at least set them off observationally from their environment, the presupposition of existence does not make the slightest bit of sense.[81]

However, the *empirical epistemology* of more recent functionalism no longer asks how it is possible *to say*, while making a claim upon truth, that there are systems; rather it merely asks how the knowing system factically organizes a thus describable self-observation (of its self as system).[82] Thus such epistemology no longer asks about the *universal* presuppositions for *adequate* knowledge of something as something; it merely asks how self-referential systems in *specific cases* of self-observation and self-description *factically behave.* Because of a radical temporalization, the paradoxes inevitably produced in every attempt at an adequate description of society as a whole are not once and for all eliminated (as they are in transcendental and idealistic epistemologies), but always only on a case by case basis, not for the long-term, but only as the occasion demands; such an occasion arises namely when a need for the resolution of paradoxes is actually registered by a system.[83] Only in the case of such need does a "creative application of paradoxes" result from a "transformation of infinite information-burdens into finite ones," namely through the case by case reduction of complexity.[84]

The empirical epistemology of the radical constructivists operates finally with a "sociological concept of knowledge" which knows only "one society"[85] – a society, viz., [that is] "only a comprehensive system of the auto-poesis of communication"; "thus the epistemologist becomes herself a rat in the maze and must simply reflect about the best place from which to observe the other rats."[86]

The methodology of functionalist and constructivist theory-formation in sociology also organizes itself according to this model of an *empiricistically oriented* Hegelian *dialectic of reflection*. Systems-theory is thus "an especially impressive super-theory." *Super-theories* "are theories that make universalistic claims (viz., claims that include themselves and their opponents)."[87] The traditional "leading differences," like those between part and whole, universal and particular, subject and object, have been replaced by the difference between *system and environment*.[88] "Totalizing super-theories" like the attempt made by systems-theory "orient learning processes not towards nature, but towards one's opponent," and raise the claim, like Hegel's immanent critique and Marx's ideology-critique, to reconstruct one's opponent with their "own concepts" and thus to explain out of the social-structural grounds of a progressive functional differentiation "why [one opponent] opposes the other."[89] To this end, of course, super-theories no longer have to enter hermeneutically and hypothetically into the perspectives of the opponent or into the internal contradictions involved in his concept-formation; instead they remain wholly within their own conceptuality of a distanced and self-enclosed observer-perspective. What matters is that "the opponent find a justified place in the theoretical framework of the super-theory."[90]

Systems-theory thus auto-poetically closes itself off from its discourse-environment and always and only gains its own experience through the "interruption of operative relations to the outer world,"[91] in which their opponents, who adhere to other paradigms of sociological theory-formation, operate. This universalism, exploding all the boundaries of sociological specialization, is the secret to the success of systems-theory, which it can then attribute to itself as a successful *completion of the system*. In such an absolutistic "closedness" (Adorno), systems-theory is "not actually sociology, but instead should be compared with metatheoretical projects that perform the function of a world-view."[92]

Systems-theory understands itself as part of the social reality to which it refers.[93] But such a reference is a pure, social contingency, not a transcendental necessity; it arises from time to time and from case to case, according to need; it is neither deduced nor disclosed, but merely observed. Thus from out of the (dialectical) "metaphysics" of spirit, an (undialectical) "metabiology" of sense-processing systems develops, as Habermas has observed.[94] *Truth* turns unexpectedly into a *mode of self-assertion* and becomes indistinguishable from the battle for existence. The *complexity and power* of this mode of self-assertion can, accordingly, through the functional differentiation of codifications of true and false in autonomous systems of knowing and of knowledge-production, be escalated in modern times to a degree completely unimaginable in pre-modern societies, the distinctions within which were limited to differences in social stratification and to a sectorial division of labor. As in the late Foucault, truth shades indistinguishably into functional power, and the power of truth-functional discourse ("the will to know") is amplified immeasurably in the transition to modernity (which Luhmann describes as functionally differentiated society).[95] None the less, it is not in a complete *dependence* upon non-discursive practices that Luhmann sees the escalation of the power of knowledge-discourses (as Foucault does), but by contrast in their *system-autonomy*.

Methodologically speaking (and in this respect Luhmann, Kuhn, and the hermeneutics of Heidegger and Gadamer all meet on common ground), this departure from the universality of truth of the European Enlightenment owes itself to a fundamental critique of Popper's thesis (cited above) to the effect that a theory can be true, even if nobody believes it and nobody has reason to accept it, and can be false, even when the best reasons speak for it and are accepted by everyone. Against this [thesis], the radical constructivism of systems-theory has devoted itself to a *consensus-theory of success*: "Consensus results only through cooperative interactions, when the behavior resulting from each organism is made serviceable to the maintenance of all organisms."[96] This theory resolves the old problem of "objective knowledge" in such a radically nominalistic way that the *distinction between objective truth and subjective knowledge disappears*. Without this distinction, however – and the elimination of this distinction is the result of radical-constructivist just as much as of neopragmatic-postmodernist epistemology[97] – there is not only no objective knowledge, *but also no subjectivist relativism*. Radical constructivism is a *perspectivism without relativism*.[98] However, in such a perspectivism we once again miss the pragmatic dimension of subjectivity, viz., intersubjectively constituted objective knowledge.

(b) That which the systems-theory of Niklas Luhmann sees as its particularly impressive achievement is precisely that to which Jürgen Habermas objects. Systems-theory no longer recognizes a region from out of which an inherently oppositional common-consciousness, one which could move the whole of society to a normative distance from itself, would still be conceivable.[99] Habermas names this position "methodological anti-humanism."[100]

Though one may not believe it about Foucault, who was throughout his life *engagé* on behalf of the oppressed rights and disregarded claims of minorities, Luhmann *is* the "happy positivist" that Foucault always wanted to be. "In the choice of its fundamental concepts," the methodological anti-humanism of Niklas Luhmann already detaches sociology from any emancipatory cognitive-interest and must therefore deny to society any possibility "of gaining as a whole and normatively a distance from itself, and any possibility of working through perceptions of crisis within the higher-level communications-processes of the public sphere."[101]

Foucault's sociology of knowledge and of power shares with Luhmann more than a neutralistic self-understanding.[102] An uncompromisingly empiricistic re-construction of Kant's transcendental epistemology and an immanently conceived "thought from outside" constitute the thread that connects both large sections of Foucault's life-work, the *archaeology of knowledge* (Foucault I) and the *genealogy of power* (Foucault II). In his "thought from outside," Foucault strives to attain a descriptive, not a normative, distance from society.

In the field of the human sciences Foucault deconstructs *first* the objectivism of the technical interest in control belonging to the social natural-sciences like medicine and psychology[103]; *then* the practical significance for orientation of the human sciences[104]; and *finally* the emancipatory cognitive-interest of the social sciences.[105] He does this, respectively, (1) by describing the historically contingent constitution, through functions of and technics of power, of the only apparently truth-functional discourse of the objective "sciences," thus destroying the "illusion of autonomous discourse";[106] (2) by forcing open the perspective of hermeneutics' "thought from inside" (see above), in order to push forward to a "thought from outside";[107] and finally (3) by radically neutralizing his own social-scientific perspective, restricting it to the cool look from the observer's perspective.[108]

All objective references, the basis in experience of thinking and of theory, must be internally constructed. As Luhmann says, only when the system closes in upon itself and breaks off its operative relations to the external world can the realm of reference of truth and falsehood be established through the observer who is constituted internally *qua* self-observation.[109] In the same vein Foucault writes: "Every discipline recognizes true and false propositions within its boundaries; beyond those boundaries, however, each allows a whole teratology of knowledge to proliferate."[110] Against Plato and Kant, Foucault expressly emphasizes that "the world is not an accomplice of our knowledge."[111] For Foucault there is no truth that transcends discourse, just as for Kuhn there is no truth beyond the historical apriori of the paradigm-community. There is always only "a language that turns in circles, referring to itself" – a self-referentially closed system.[112] In his debate with Kuhn, Popper for his part named this the myth of the "framework" (or paradigm).[113] Otherwise than for Kuhn, however, the authority [*Herrschaft*] of diverse "historical aprioris" *of purely contingent conditions of possibility* is for Foucault at the same time a discourse constituted through the *powers of instrumental* reason.[114] None the less, no discourse of knowledge and power (at least for the later Foucault) suppresses in any way a different, latent, yet objectively emancipatory discourse of oppressed classes, of repressively expelled instincts, or of any other true knowledge that is distorted through a false appearance and repression.[115]

Through a reflective move we learn to treat discourses "as regulated and discrete series of events" that contingently and discontinuously play upon the surfaces of bodies as effects without causes.[116] Thus the laboriously erected, rationalistic obstacles to and controls on discourse prove to be the illusion that through such obstacles the *productivity* (imaginative creativity) *of power*,[117] the discontinous *suddenness of the accident*, the murmuring *swarm of voices*, and the "dust of graphisms"[118] have become masterable and controllable. But they are not masterable and controllable, for the discourses of the *logos* and of knowledge are themselves nothing but the productivity of power, the suddenness of the accident, and the dust of graphisms.

From the perspective of Foucault's discourse-theory, *all* discourses are "games of signs." Even the discourse of the modern sciences, which assigns central importance to the objective reference of the neutral observation-language (the reference which Foucault names the "order of the significant"), and which would like to make reality the arbiter of its own theories – even this discourse is *possible* only by way of a radical decoupling of discourse from the things to which it refers: "Discourse loses its reality in that it subjects itself to the order of the signifier."[119] This internal construction of reality through the exclusion of any operative reference to it is the epistemological upshot of the *Archaeology of Knowledge*:[120] modern sciences, orienting themselves wholly toward an objective reference, must break off all relations to things in order to *produce* objective reference. The reflectively defamiliarized view of the archaeologist helps us to attain this insight: "archaeology is always a technique that liberates us from a deep-seated belief in the direct access to objects; in any case, the 'tyranny of the referent' must be overcome."[121] Thus has the correspondence theory of reality breathed its last.[122]

In order to break the domination of the optical metaphor of a transcendental consciousness that mirrors the real world within itself,[123] Foucault takes from Georges Bataille the image of the eye that, jerked painfully from its fixed position in the eye socket and rotated on its axis, turns towards the observer the blood-smeared white of its blind backside. With this rotation of the eyeball towards the inside of the eye-socket, the discourse-theoretician returns instantly and completely to the immanence of meaning, leaving the world of things behind himself.[124] He breaks off any operative visual contact with the outside world. But this inner voyage makes all mystery disappear. The inversion of the eye marks the collapse of the optical metaphor; it destroys itself with its violent turning towards the inner life of subjectivity. For a second all the light of the "bloodshot" pupil falls in the nocturnal world of the socket, but it henceforth discovers only the "void" "that [was] left behind by the subject fallen from the socket."[125] The subject of the look has now advanced so far into the inside of meaning that all objective reference has vanished. The light of the eye, penetrating inwards, expels both the Cartesian ghosts[126] and, from the wall of the cave, the Platonic shadows. But at the same moment [*Augenblick*], the reflective turn strikes the view [*Blick*] toward the outside with blindness: "insight *as* blindness" or, as one might put it, "blindness *as* insight."[127]

Foucault makes use of the optical metaphorics of Bataille to cancel the difference between inner and outer, between sense and meaning (reference), and between being as time and being as *logos*, in order to lead us back to the genealogical origin *prior* to such differentiation.[128] What the refracting view sees, in the moment of its collapse into the inner, is the void of the subjective world, the blank surface of the back of the skull that has become *indistinguishable* from the purely external. It is, like the world of mythology, round and hollow[129] – just as the hollows of the skull appear equally round and hollow from *both* the inside *and* the outside. In the terminology of the *Dialectic of the Enlightenment* (1955): this is the point at which the post-structuralist shape of the Enlightenment reverts back to "mythology." And in keeping with this theme of a *new mythology*,[130] Foucault can also declare that he has never written anything other than fiction.[131] "If once it was a matter of thinking the truth, today it is necessary to think occidental fiction, for the 'I speak' goes directly against the 'I think'."[132] But thus where there once was a social scientist, we now find a "founding poet".[133]

Naturally Foucault completes this turn from the objectively referred *truth-potential* of language (made possible by the "tyranny of the referent") to its *imaginative potential*, to a "discourse without reference" (the ideal of which is the "atonal logic of literary production"[134]), in a different way than Nietzsche and aesthetic modernity. He does this not *as* aesthete, nor as poet, nor as essayist on aesthetic discourse, but rather always *as an observing social-scientist*. Because Foucault plays precisely this role, his domain beyond both structuralism and hermeneutics is always bound only to *what has actually been said*.[135]

As a "theoretical" *archaeologist*, Foucault is a structuralist who has betrayed *structuralism* in that he no longer asks about meaningful regularities, but instead about their "interruption and *alteration*," about the "discontinuous *historical* conditions" of the appearance of meaning, and about the non-discursive practices of power beyond structural discourse, the practices which first endow the latter with significance. Foucault is therefore a "post-structuralist."[136] As "practical" *genealogist*, however, Foucault relates as subversively to *hermeneutics* as Nietzsche once did. This subversion of both hermeneutics and structuralism in the end allows Foucault to find his own method, which Dreyfus and Rabinow have named an *interpretative analytic*. Here the expression "analytic" connects just as deconstructively with structural archaeology as with Kant: Foucault's *archaeological analytic* is always concerned with de-subjectivized, discipline-specific and discourse-specific conditions of possibility and formation rules.[137] Both methodological aspects of Foucault's thinking run together in the expression "interpretative analytic": that of a *post-hermeneutic genealogy* (prevailing in Foucault's late work), and that of a *post-structuralist archaeology* (which serves as method). Thus Foucault's interpretative analytic leaves behind the older *hermeneutics of the everyday* (of Heidegger and Gadamer), which had still presupposed the distinction between the internal perspective of the interaction-participant, which was the perspective to be understood, on the one hand, and the external perspective of the observer, just as much as it parts company with the ideology-critical *hermeneutics of suspicion* (of Marx and Freud), which had always reckoned with a dark and rebellious subjectivity hidden behind a glittering and illusive facade.

Throughout this project Foucault starts out from two premises:

(1) In the world of the social, there are always and only practices that are the way they appear and conceal nothing behind their surfaces. There are also no constitutive rules, no "tacit knowledge," no (Chomskian) competences that would "manifest" themselves in these practices. Above all there is no subject of praxis: "Nobody is responsible for any coming into being, nobody can boast about [responsibility for] such a coming to being, it occurs in an empty in-between."[138]

(2) every practice is an interpretation (which, in turn, in an "interpretative analytic" of power and knowledge, forms a complex of practices, a "dispositive"). The "becoming of humanity [is] a series of interpretations."[139]

The last ghosts of Platonism are thereby expelled; what remains is a "pragmatically oriented historical interpretation."[140] After the internal world along with the difference between the internal and external has vanished, the actual locus for the play of power is, according to Foucault, literally the opposition-less "outside" of the human body. This separates Foucault from Max Weber and Adorno in spite of the obvious kinship among their respective projections of a dialectic of enlightenment and among their respective theories of an instrumentally centered process of rationalization. For Adorno is also always concerned with the oppression of the *inner* nature of the subject, and with the meshing of technics of power within the inner structure of personal identities, an inner structure which can *also* remove itself from these technics of power. And for Weber, the discipline by inner-worldy *askesis* – which he comes very close to describing in the words of Foucault as "unconsciously refined arrangements, invested with power, for the breeding of capitalistic individuals"[141] – is always characterized by an *intersection* of autonomous conscience-formation[142] both with a "typical narrowing of and repression of the natural life of instincts" and with the "systematic mastering of one's own inner nature, which is seen as corrupted by sin."[143] Weber and Adorno begin with the difference which Foucault will evade at any price: the difference between the subjective internal world and the objective external world.[144]

The consistent (and consistently perspectival) *thinking of the "outside"* is, therefore, the thread that unites all of Foucault's work. Another strand of this thread, at least from the time of his *Archaeology of Knowledge,* is a *monism of discourse,* for "discursive relations *comprise* both discursive and non-discursive practices." Like Luhmann from the perspective of the self-observing system, Foucault must, from the perspective of contingent discourse, thematize the unity of discursive and non-discursive practices. Later, in *Discipline and Punish,* the monism of discourse is radicalized and becomes a *monism of power:* "the *dispositive* of power *comprises* discourses and practices, knowledge and power."[145]

But according to both points of view, this radical thought from outside can no longer attain *any* normative distance to the society which this thinking observationally interprets, even if "the counterpart of the repressive order, the discourse which is to be controlled, [is still] power."[146] This is especially true of the monism of an aesthetically, politically, and economically productive and creative power: in such thinking this power "tends towards totalitarian principle."[147]

Foucault's intepretative analytic of power also remains closely related to the radical constructivism of systems-theory. Just as for systems-theory *functionally differentiated society* has become a network of loosely coupled, autopoetic systems without a center, *power,* which for the late Foucault becomes identical with socialization in general, has a similar structure. Power is no longer "what one has from time immemorial thought of it; no sovereign center of authority that imposes its law from above on those down below. It is not a property and no mere potency, nor a capacity or means allowing one to impose whatever ends she wants. Power is the war of all against all, the total context of event-like and momentary confrontations of bodies, the complex, decentered network of single, local, and antagonistic power-relations. From these power climbs upwards from below ... Everything is power. Foucault's theory is a monism of power that rests on the basis of an infinite and open pluralism of local, unequal, and unstable power-relations."[148]

If for Luhmann the unity of the world projected out of a contingent systems-perspective is always the unity in the difference between system and environment, and if in his sociological epistemology society is in the end identified with the life-world as a whole, so in the same way the late Foucault identifies the world of the social with power. In the 1940s Adorno and Horkheimer had already advanced this distanceless and one-dimensional self-description of present-day society, a description common to both Luhmann's affirmative constructivism and the paradoxical negativism of Foucault's interpretative analytic, to the concept of a world which had become a "gigantic analytic judgment."[149] Thus the subversive and ironic rehabilitation of epistemology in the social sciences, which Luhmann and Foucault have long asserted against critical rationalism, ends up with a far more radical destruction of epistemology than analytic theory of science, with its simple repression (of epistemology), delivers.

IV DISCOURSE AND EMANCIPATION: THE INNER DIFFERENTIATION OF SOCIAL-SCIENTIFIC PARADIGMS

What separates Adorno from Foucault and Luhmann – the dialectical structure of his negativism – connects him with Habermas. In contrast to the empiricistic modernists Foucault and Luhmann, Adorno has at his disposal a *normatively robust concept of modernity*, which he wields against the impenetrable structures of the administered world.[150]

In keeping with such a normative concept of modernity as *unfinished project*, Habermas supplements Foucault's theory of discourse and power with a *discourse-ethics*, and Luhmann's systems-theory with a critical and emancipatory *theory of action*.

In so doing, Habermas neither dramatizes the present-day condition of the social sciences as a heteronomy of inherited discourses, like Foucault, nor does he reduce it to a *pre-paradigmatic stage in the evolution of science*, as Thomas Kuhn did in an oft-cited marginal note in his book *The Structure of Scientific Revolutions*.

Like Luhmann, Habermas begins instead from the simple fact that there are *normal social sciences* and that we have no reason to doubt the autonomy of their discourse. This normal scientific discourse moves primarily within the framework of two competing paradigms: that of a *functionalistic systems-theory* and that of an *interactionist theory of action*. Thus the complementarity of *technical* and *practical cognitive interests*, of knowledge for the sake of control and knowledge for the sake of orientation, recurs within the social sciences.

The *action-theoretical paradigm* of sociology developed from phenomenology, hermeneutics, and symbolic interactionism into the program of a *sociology of understanding* [*verstehende Soziologie*], of which *theories of everyday-life* form the nucleus.[151] These theories begin from the view that society must be conceived *from* the perspective of the life-world, *as* life-world. The *life-world* (which is society) forms a *background* ("context") for *action* (or for the action-situation: "text") that is indeed already familiar, on the whole never explicitly known, but instead always only implicitly presupposed. Action (mostly in cooperative work) is directed either instrumentally towards objects of the external world or strategically and communicatively towards the intersection of subjective self-projections with intersubjective perspectives. For the agent, the life-world always has the self-evident character of a social apriori. Its *normative context* coordinates the individual actions through the action-*orientations* of the actors, orientations which themselves arise from the normative context, which then in turn is nourished by *cultural* traditions.

More specifically, the normative social context must be internalized in *processes of socialization* and become the core of personal ego-identity in order to become effective for coordinating action. Habermas names the paradigm of the coordination of action by the life-world "social integration."[152]

From out of the perspective of the "hermeneutic idealism of the sociology of understanding," society can of course be seen at a normative distance only selectively and sporadically – *in this respect* "the sociology of understanding" shows a kinship with the "specific *engagement*" of Foucault's post-structuralist intellectual.[153] Furthermore, hermeneutic idealism also loses itself in a micrological descriptivism of participatory observation. Field research thereby threatens to relinquish any distance to the subcultures under investigation. Sociologists of understanding find themselves confronted with a dilemma similar to that found in the study of the history of ideas, the foreignness to theory of which Luhmann has described with some irony: "The investigators that one chases into the field with the assignment to figure out how things really were – they don't come back; they don't fetch, they don't point, they just stand there, sniffing with wonder at the details."[154] But as Habermas emphasizes, the ethnomethodology and anthropological field research of the sociology of understanding sharpen the sense for the "perspectives of the conquered," for the cost of "deteriorating traditions and forms of life," and for "historical asynchronies." These sciences make one aware of the price of modernization. "Nonetheless they grant as little room to economic development and to the formation of nations and states as they do to the structurally distinct sense of rationalized life-worlds. Thus subcultural reflections, in which the sociopathologies of modernity are refracted and cast back, retain the subjectivity and contingency of *uncomprehended* events."[155]

Nourished by the traditions of orthodox Marxism, evolutionary biology (Darwinism), cybernetics, and economics (information-theory and game-theory), the *systems-theoretical paradigm* of sociology thoroughly does away with the (chief) fiction of hermeneutic idealism – the autonomy of action and of its cultural discourses within the tranquil semi-transparence of the life-world, within which one can in principle come to an understanding about *everything*. Such we have already seen in the examples of Luhmann and Foucault. With the subject, the practical autonomy of the agent disappears, and *alien* authorities together with opaque, unpredictable, and non-discursive powers overpower culture. The world now becomes recognizable in its unmastered complexity, a complexity which sets a limit to all understanding. The *explanatory systems-sciences* analyze modern society primarily from the point of view of functional differentiation and increasing complexity. They thus treat our actions as formative of *systems*, which are coordinated via the functional network of unintended *consequences* of action.

For Hegel and Marx the market is already the chief example of *systemic processes of integration* ("system integration") in developed "civil society."

However, as we have seen, a one-sided systems-functionalism is not at all in the position to find any distance, *apart from a theoretical one*, to extant society. Hence it is "insensitive to sociopathologies." Because such functionalism "assimilates, from its observer's perspective," the individual and collective fates involved in sociopathologies to mere "imbalances of inter-systemic exchange-relations," it takes from them their "meaning as identity-threatening deformations, as which they are perceived from the participant's perspective."[156]

Both paradigms of sociology thus one-sidedly absolutize one point of view: theories of action absolutize the participant's perspective and the life-world; functionalism the observer's perspective and the system.

By contrast, Habermas begins from the position that society is always both system *and* life-world. He thus defines *society* on two levels as "*systemically stabilized* contexts of action of *socially integrated* groups."[157] To this universal determination he then connects the evolution-theoretical thesis of a *de-coupling* of system and life-world at the threshold to modernity, a de-coupling which the formation of social-scientific paradigms *reactively* follows.[158] Social evolution is thereby understood as a "second-order process of differentiation: system and life-world are differentiated in that the complexity of the former and the rationality of the latter grow, not only respectively as system and as life-world – both simultaneously differentiate themselves as well from one another."[159]

While systems-theory begins with the observation that the forms of differentiation shift from the sectorial division of labor and socio-structural stratification to functional differentiation, Habermas, with the help of the de-coupling thesis, attempts to *explain* the change, empirically *presupposed* by systems-theory, in evolutionary primacy of first a segmentary differentiation, then a horizontal differentiation, and finally a functional differentiation. With this explication of the possibility of functional differentiation, Habermas approaches an equidistance from *both* the sociology of understanding *and* functionalistic sociology. More specifically, he sees in the life-world that which determines "the self-preservation of the system of society on the whole."[160] This means, however, that a *totalizing* distanciation from modern society is assumed as possible not only from the contingent perspective of a *theoretical* systems-reflection, but also from the perspective of the *practical* common-consciousness of the life-world – and even (assumed) as a condition for the possibility of the theoretical achievements of reflection.

It is precisely at this point that the *emancipatory cognitive interest* of the social sciences finds its validity: specifically, the functional differentiation of society as system has the life-world as presupposition not only as the diffuse, holistic background of the difference between system and environment, a background that moreover appears from the system-perspective as the manipulable substrate of signs and practices; this functional differentiation also presupposes the *structural differentiation* and *inner rationalization* of the life-world itself, which is what first makes possible a separating out of systems-perspectives. The core of the processes of rationalization in the life-world – for which Weber's sociology of religion as well as Parsons's thesis concerning the generalization of value provide examples – is, however, communicative reason, viz., the evolutionary redemption, "by action oriented towards understanding, of the normative contexts" of life-world habits and regularities. Communicative reason asserts itself both in the *becoming autonomous of post-traditional expert-discourses*, and in the advance of the moral consciousness, in *public discourse*, from the conventional to the *post-conventional level.*[161]

A research program is thus outlined that first makes viable a robust concept of reason (borrowed from idealistic philosophy) against the skepticism of the sociology of understanding, laying this concept as the foundation for the notion of the "life-world," in order then – in a second step – to make the latter notion the normative basis for a "critique of functionalist reason." The chief thought marshalled against functionalism (as well as against post-structuralism and hermeneutic idealism) is that of an *"immanent reference to truth"* on the part of society. With the *"facticity"* of those *validity claims* that "are posited with every form of knowing," society places itself under a *pressure for communicative rationalization.*[162] The social life-world itself rests "upon the facticity of accepted validity claims which in principle, however, can themselves become problematic."[163] Hence the *facticity* of validity claims, which accompany every earnest coming-to-an-understanding (speech-praxis), may in no way be identified with the "factuality of the *factum brutum* of something present-at-hand."[164] In opposition to the brute fact of functionally interconnected systems, of inscrutable complexity, and of the unplanned consequences of action, the facticity of validity claims is *counter-factually effective.* As a universal and rational claim of social action, this facticity transcends *every* empirical totality. None the less, in the form of the pressure for rationalization (*as well as* in the form of the compulsion of moral conscience), it also influences society empirically.

Empirical social research is of course also necessary in order that this thesis can be empirically justified.

V   SOCIOLOGY AND EMPIRICAL RESEARCH

We shall conclude by sketching the motifs and principles of a *critical research method* via a discussion of the relationship of *quantitative* and *qualitative* methods. This critical method will connect critical theory and empirical social research, and integrate the *quantitative knowledge for the sake of control* (of traditional research) with the *qualitative knowledge for the sake of orientation* (of hermeneuticist methods), according to the guiding-idea of *emancipatory cognitive-interests*, in a "post-conventional social research."[165]

So-called qualitative social research is usually exiled to the heuristic "ante-room" of "the hard empirical facts" in two respects. It belongs, according to analytic theory of science, to the "context of discovery," but has no role to play in the "context of justification," where only the "effects of logic and nature" matter.[166] Hermeneutics, phenomenology, interpretative and communicative social research are *on the one hand* historical antecedents of quantitative and statistical methods.[167] They belong to the prehistory of modern science. *On the other hand*, some qualitative method or methods, some loosely structured and more or less open investigation and evaluation procedure (e.g., the hermeneutic interpretation of texts, phenomenological description, field-research, in-depth interviews, group discussions, etc.) will always play an indispensable role in that anteroom and in the pre-test phases of social research before it moves to actual measurement and to the ascertaining of quantifiable data.

This *traditional* rank-ordering of qualitative and quantitative methods is due not only to this deductive-empirical understanding of justification, but also to the fixation on an *extensionalist concept of scaling* (measurement), a concept which is merely an explication of the analytic understanding of a scientific observation-language (developed above). According to this understanding, there is at first no opposition between quantitative and qualitative social research. Qualitative research is also "in truth" quantitative (namely, with respect to the former's non-opaque, extensionally "understandable" aspect – see above), even if it is at the lowest level of measurement, that of simple frequency-distributions. Since every qualitative investigation is based on conceptual distinctions and classifies its material – differentiating between the most distinct qualities pertaining to its objects –, then, so far as the concepts are operationally established and are defined so as to be discriminating, it fulfills the conditions of a *nominal scale*. At this level, one is merely counting and not yet measuring. Actual quantification and measurement first appear at the higher levels of scaling, when one moves from the *ordinal rank-ordering*, through the first scale that measures exactly, the *interval-scale*, up to the *rational scale* (with a fixed zero-point). Qualitative research is essentially a nominal classifying, but is, in any case, logically presupposed at all higher levels of measurement. For the axioms of the rational scale logically require those of all the lower levels, including the conceptual articulations of the nominal scale. Qualitative research is from this extensionalist point of view already logically implicit in quantitative research. Quantitative concepts – those scaled intervallically or rationally – therefore contain more information than "qualitative" concepts.[168]

The argument of the extensionalists has, for social scientists (*vis-à-vis* natural scientists), the considerable disadvantage that the concepts of the social sciences are for the most part only nominally scaled, and that exact, purely quantitative measurement in investigative practice is rare and controversial.[169] But above all, sociological extensionalism cannot do justice to the intensional structure of "meaningfully oriented" social action and to the prior understanding of the *sense of an action*, without which the social scientist has absolutely no access to his realm of objects.[170] "Interpretative comprehension," not quantitative measurement, is the methodological interest of sociology.[171] This in no way implies an exclusive disjunction between "understanding" and "explanation," nor can the social research that begins with the intensional structure of the understanding of action forego a *causal analysis* of it.[172] The reflective and meaning-like fore-structure of the social-scientific object realm is concisely expressed in Gouldner's claim that all men and women are lay sociologists. Because "sociological normativity" is unavoidable,[173] sociologists always have to deal with problems of a "double operationalization."[174] Their theoretical concepts must not only correspond to an operationally definable observation-language (as, for example, the "items" on a questionnaire would), but they must also be translated into the language of the research-objects so that the latter are, *as* co-subjects, in the position to *understand* the questions of the questionnaire.

The characteristically reflective structure of its object-realm already becomes clear with the observation that, although the social sciences can become themselves the objects of social research and a *sociology of knowledge* is possible, no physics of knowledge is, nor is any physicalist investigation of logic or of the scientific organization of physics. Moreover, social research is always objectively embedded (regardless of how appropriately) in a "value-polarized, societal, and situational consciousness."[175] Even in putting together the questions for a survey – the "royal road" of social research – the investigator is *by way of its* "doubled operationalization" referred to the "language-bound and value-related subjectness" of his object-realm: "*without* the flexible and active cooperation between researcher and research-'object', *without* the participation in interviews, experiments, and other procedures for data collection, *without* the opening up of sources of information, and without the at least tacit toleration by the public media, interested lobbies, and the leading political powers of the society under investigation – without all this, social research *is in principle impossible.*"[176]

This means, however, that not only does the investigator intervene in his object-realm as agent, "posing" and "producing" it, in that *he* becomes constructively and technically active therein; the "object-realm" of the sociologist *must* as *active agent* also come forward and be accommodating towards the investigator.

This situation differs fundamentally from that of physics or even that of biology. Not only does the research alter its object through the research (as in micro-physics), but the object "recoils" upon the subject, changing from its side the research and the researcher. For the objects of social research will not content themselves with "their service for truth and social science, unselfishly placing themselves as research material at the disposal of sociologists, like meadows for botanists."[177] Even from the perspectives of technical knowledge for the sake of control and of instrumental knowledge, the social researcher must deal with a *doubled contingency* and with an in principle symmetrical control and right to possession, if he does not want to go astray *a priori*. The observer is always already observed, a fact which he can in turn observe. The process of attaining and formulating sociological propositions is thus "always already overlaid with the 'value-premises' of the interested self-interpretations of social groups, which . . . as selection-principles exert an influence when social scientists make their methodological decisions."[178] Sociology is not only a part of social reality, and social research (is not only a part of) action – social reality is itself, in a certain respect, "sociological," and quotidian action is a pre-professional form of social research, in which gossip and rumor, as well as more sober information and observation, replace "interviews" and "experiments." "Just as the sociologist is always a social actor, so is the social actor a sociologist."[179] For, as Gouldner says, all men and women are lay-sociologists. Such is not the case in physics. "For 'the human being' is indeed as *thing* or as *body* an object of the knowledge of physics or biology, but is not *as* lay-physicist or *as* lay-biologist. The sociologist, however, typically does not have to deal with things or bodies, but with *colleagues as colleagues*. Considered thus, the difference between the sociologist and the 'object' of his investigation dwindles to the difference between a sociologist *with* and a sociologist *without* a diploma."[180]

Thus in her research as well, the sociologist bumps up against the counterfactual effectiveness of *validity claims*, whether she wants to or not. For it is not only the sociologist's "interpretative comprehension" of cases, regularities, types, and causal connections that can be *true* or *false, appropriate* or *inappropriate*; exactly the same is also true of the "interpretative comprehending" of the social world by the actors themselves. By contrast it is meaningless and false to claim that "the electron describes its own behavior in a way somehow independent of the knowledge of the physicist; thus there is no possibility at all that we *falsely* characterize the behavior of the electron in that we misunderstand, for instance, the logic of its self-description."[181] Social research is therefore *"socially investigative interaction"*: "Society can only be investigated actively, and only with and through society, viz., in social action itself."[182] In the language of systems-theory, we might say that social research is an excellent example of self-referential self-observation and self-description. But it is much more than that. Since every description *must* refer to the implicit validity claims of the "object," the social scientist cannot elude *sociological normativity*, and sociology *qua* research necessarily entails the taking of a position with respect to the questionable validity claims of the self-interpretations and "interpretative models" of its research-object.[183]

The idea of a *post-conventional social research* can now be developed in two steps. Such research (1) reverses the empiricist rank-ordering of the notions "quantitative" and "qualitative," returning with Hegel to the priority of quality over quantity, in order then (2) to relate such a hermeneutically reflective social research back to philosophically inspired research programs.

(1)   If the quantitative approach refers to an *object paradigm,* the qualitative approach refers to a *text paradigm* of the social world.[184] Along the lines of the latter paradigm, classic field research[185] and the studies that have arisen from the interactionist and phenomenological schools[186] justify an *alternative* in sociology to the empiricist-statistical research tradition, in the same way that psychology presents an alternative to behaviorism thanks to the manner in which psychoanalysis[187] and the cognitive developmental psychologies of Piaget and Kohlberg organize the relationship of the theoretical and the empirical and thereby their data. Piaget's investigations are perhaps the most prominent example of social research that both does justice to the self-referential structure of its object realm just as much as it moves the following circumstance to the center of interest: that the object realm itself raises universal validity claims in the same way that the knowledge of the psychologist postulates them. This interest is furthermore an emancipatory cognitive interest which assumes, hypothetically, the autonomy of the acting subject as goal and direction of the investigated development. Cognitive developmental psychology is the chief model of a hermeneutic *and* emancipatory science, one which nonetheless proceeds in a strictly experimental fashion, and one which, in the universality of its theoretical statements, does not compare unfavorably with physics. It can in principle be refuted through any single case, and therefore it relies secondarily (if need be) upon statistical quantifications and the usual inductive generalizations (those of empirical sociology in contrast to those of physics). Of course all of these are only true "in principle": there are always exceptions and anomalies which must be explained *ad hoc* and which disruptively and intractably accompany every normal scientific praxis (see Kuhn!). But no matter how refined, no statistical procedure can prevent this.[188]

An alternative understanding of social research, one which subordinates quantitative to interpretative methods and integrates the former with the latter instead of vice versa, was finally developed in the context of the older Frankfurt School.[189] This understanding could also be connected with the phenomenological biographies of Jean-Paul Sartre[190] in order to make the latter fruitful for the biographical research of sociology.[191] Sartre is of interest because he in no way remains ideographically stuck on the details of the single case,[192] but always aims at the analysis of an "individual universal," which must "project" itself out of a socio-structural and familio-pathological "thrownness" as an unmistakably distinct person.

(2)   A "revised empiricism" of post-conventional social research, organized according to the model of the integration of action-theory and systems-theory,[193] would, corresponding to the integration of their theory-languages, link observation-oriented and interaction-oriented languages of experience to one another and to theory. Their experiential basis would be *holistic empirical research* à la Adorno – as in, for example, the

"objective hermeneutics" of Oevermann, or the thick descriptions of Geertz.[194] But such holistic empirical research must as well always cast a "disenchanting" and "factual glance"[195] on the externally observable and extensionally measurable *consequences* and side-effects of action, in order to place the empirical research of the whole and the *empirical research of facts* in an inclusionary, not an exclusionary, relationship. Thus Wolfgang Bonß defines post-conventional social research as "combinations of quantitative and factually-referred strategies with qualitative and monographic strategies."[196] Hence a far more complex network results than the one deriving from the simple empiricist-extensionalist ordering of theory-language and observation-language (see above):[197]

Theory-language	Systems-theory	Action-theory
Observation -language	Empirical research of facts ("double contingency")	Holistic empirical research ("interaction")
Level of language / Level of Paradigm	System	Life-world

Central motifs of a *philosophical, rational universalism* can thus, by way of the theory-languages, pass into the core structure of *social-scientific research programs*.

"Materialism," Horkheimer wrote in 1933, "demands the unification of philosophy and science." Philosophy can, however, unfold a weak dialectical power *within* the sciences only in the form of *theoretical hypotheses*, hypotheses which fit together with the scientistic *and* interpretative experience-languages of sociology by way of a complex network of classification rules. *Reason* thus becomes *fallible*. Again Horkheimer: "many idealistic systems contain valuable material knowledge which, in spite of the world-view and the intentions of their founders, present important elements of scientific progress. The dialectic is itself of idealistic origin. As models for the assessment of present-day human being, as 'hypotheses' (as Dilthey himself characterized the systems of the past), many projects of modern metaphysics have the highest significance."[198] For Horkheimer, a fallibilism of practical hope in a this-worldly transcendence corresponds to this hypothetical attitude towards last principles and universal ideas: materialist knowledge "directs all energies, even the most desperate, to this world, and of course thereby exposes the single faith that it permits – the hope in the earthly possibilities of humankind – to disappointment." This "faith," however, supports itself on the *empirical* (and thus fallible) supposition that "bourgeois society along with egoism has also produced its negation, individualistic altruism."[199] This supposition attains its peculiar dialectical power from a universal hypothesis in which Horkheimer anticipates the idea of a communicative reconciliation: "many of the psychic fetters under which men and women today suffer are burst if the fitting word rings out, because this word largely annuls the violent isolation of men and women from one another, an isolation characteristic of our present. Truth possesses this power, even if it does not merely forgo all ideological consolation, but instead strives actively to eradicate it."[200]

NOTES

1   Popper (1959, p. 27) (Emphasis added).
2   Compare Sneed (1971), Stegmüller (1973), and Stegmüller (1975, pp. 483ff).
3   Sneed (1971, p. 1).
4   Sellars (1970, p. 240).
4a Putnam (1975. p. 281).
5   Stegmüller (1970, p. 293).
6   Ibid., p. 299.
7   Ibid., p. 300.
8   Ibid., p. 297.
9   Popper (1959, p. 104).
10 Cf. Davidson (1977a) and (1977b).
11 Popper (1959, p. 105).
12 Apel (1987, p. 122).
13 Ibid., p. 127.
14 Popper (1968, p. 225).
15 "Assertoric powers" is Frege's phrase. Frege had already discovered the constitutive truth-function of these "assertoric powers" of speech. Cf. Frege (1976).
16 Apel (1987, p. 133). The three-place relation comprises the semiotic, the semantic, and the pragmatic.
17 Peirce (1967, p. 349).
18 Cf. Kuhn (1967, p. 131).
19 Stegmüller (1973, p. 303).
20 Heidegger (1977, pp. 12ff).
21 Cf. Dilthey (1970).
22 Cf. Gadamer (1975, pp. 250ff, p. 284f, p. 356f, p. 375).
23 V. Wright (1974).
24 Cf. Gadamer (1975, pp. 275ff).
25 Cf. Beck (1976), von Wright (1974).
26 Popper (1959, p. 59).
27 Cf. Klüver (1971).
28 Cf. Schnädelbach (1987, pp. 125ff).
29 Gadamer (1975, pp. 250ff).

30 Cf. Ritter (1974, pp. 105ff).
31 Gadamer (1975), Ritter (1974).
32 Heidegger (1972, pp. 69ff).
33 Cf. Kuhn (1967).
34 Cf. Gadamer (1975).
35 Cf. Rothacker (1923).
36 For a critique cf. Brunkhorst (1978).
37 For a critique cf. Lorenz/Mittelstraβ (1967, pp. 198ff).
38 Cf. Lorenzen (1987, pp. 439ff).
39 On this controversy see Apel (1971).
40 Cf. Schnädelbach (1987, pp. 125ff).
41 Cf. Apel (1979).
42 Foucault (1971, p. 444).
43 Foucault (1971, p. 444).
44 Cf. Rorty (1989).
45 Cf. Apel (1971), and Habermas (1968a) and (1968b).
46 Cf. Kuhn (1967).
47 Habermas (1971).
48 Marx speaks here of "processes of metabolism" in the exchanges between nature and society.
49 Apel (1971, p. 38f).
50 Habermas (1968c).
51 Apel (1971, p. 42).
52 Cf. Lorenzen (1975).
53 Cf. Schmidt (1987); Luhmann (1988).
54 Such a [phenomenologico-hermeneutical] meaning is always anticipatory of other possibilities and is always timely [*aktuell*]. Cf. Luhmann (1971).
55 Cf. Luhmann (1982), and Luhmann (1984, pp. 191ff).
56 Cf. Luhmann 1985; toward a critique of the concept of system-autonomy cf. Brunkhorst (1983) and (1989).
57 Luhmann (1987a, p. 161).
58 Cf. Luhmann (1988, p. 10).
59 Cf. Schmidt (1987, p. 18).
60 Luhmann (1987b, p. 307).
61 Luhmann (1987a, p. 172).
62 Luhmann (1987b, p. 312f).
63 Schmidt (1987, p. 26).
64 Maturana (1987, p. 269).
65 Cf. Luhmann (1988, p. 51).
66 Luhmann (1987a, p. 161).
67 Cf. von Foerster (1987).
68 Luhmann (1988, p. 51).
69 Maturana (1982, p. 76).
70 Cf. Rorty (1989).
71 Maturana (1987, p. 108).
72 Rusch (1987, p. 202).
73 Cf. Luhmann (1988, p. 53), and Rorty (1985).
74 Von Glasersfeld (1984, p. 7).
75 See the citation from Kuhn, above.
76 Schmidt (1987, p. 35).
77 Luhmann (1988, p. 42).
78 Cf. Kamlah and Lorenzen (1967, p. 49), and Heidegger (1977, pp. 52ff).

79   Cf. Kamlah and Lorenzen (1967, pp. 39 ff).
80   Luhmann (1984, p. 30), and Luhmann (1988, p. 13).
81   Cf. Luhmann (1988, p. 16).
82   Cf. ibid., p. 22.
83   Cf. Luhmann (1987a).
84   Luhmann (1987b, p. 320).
85   This society is now of course indistinguishable from "the world"! – cf. Habermas (1981, vol. 2).
86   Luhmann (1988, p. 24), and cf. pp. 42ff as well.
87   Luhmann (1984, p. 19).
88   Cf. ibid., p. 22.
89   Cf. Luhmann (1978, pp. 17, 23).
90   Ibid., p. 18.
91   See above.
92   Habermas (1985, p. 443).
93   Cf. Luhmann (1978, p. 116).
94   Cf. Habermas (1985, p. 430).
95   Cf. Foucault (1976b, 1977b).
96   Schmidt (1987, p. 28); cf. as well Maturana (1982, p. 73), and Rusch (1985, p. 181).
97   Cf. Luhmann, Maturana, von Foerster, von Glasersfeld et al. as to the former, and Rorty and Lyotard with respect to the latter.
98   Cf. Menke (1989).
99   Cf. Habermas (1985, p. 435).
100   Ibid., p. 436.
101   Ibid., p. 436.
102   Cf. Honneth (1989, p. 392).
103   Foucault (1969), Foucault (1976a), and Foucault (1977a).
104   Cf. Foucault (1971).
105   Cf. ibid., Foucault (1976b) and Foucault (1977b).
106   Dreyfus and Rabinow (1987, pp. 27ff).
107   Cf. Foucault (1987, pp. 28ff, 46ff) and Foucault (1973).
108   Cf. Foucault (1977c).
109   I have cited Maturana to this effect above.
110   Foucault (1977c, p. 23).
111   Ibid., p. 36.
112   Foucault (1987, p. 39).
113   Cf. Popper (1970).
114   As to the "authority of historical aprioris," cf. Foucault (1987, p. 86); for the "purely contingent conditions of possibility" see Foucault (1973, pp. 184 and 289); and cf. also Foucault (1969, p. 26), where he speaks of the "concrete aprioris" of psychopathology; see as well Foucault (1971, pp. 21, 25f, 173ff, 204ff, 301ff, 411f).
115   Cf. Dreyfus and Rabinow (1987, pp. 156ff) concerning the critique of the repression-hypothesis.
116   Cf. Foucault (1977c, p. 40f).
117   Cf. Deleuze (1987).
118   Foucault (1973).
119   Ibid., p. 34.
120   Foucault (1973).
121   Dreyfus and Rabinow (1987, p. 146).
122   Ibid., p. 149.
123   Cf. Rorty (1981).
124   Cf. Foucault (1987, pp. 39ff).

125   Ibid., p. 40f.
126   Cf. Ryle (1969).
127   Cf. de Man (1983).
128   In these respects Foucault matches up with Heidegger and Luhmann. See above.
129   Cf. Godelier (1973, p. 316).
130   Cf. Frank (1982).
131   Cf. Deleuze (1987, p. 32).
132   Foucault (1987, p. 48).
133   Cf. Heidegger (1980).
134   Cf. Deleuze (1987, pp. 26, 30, 80, 88f, 92, 94).
135   Cf. Deleuze (1987, p. 27f), and Dreyfus and Rabinow (1987).
136   Fink-Eitel (1989, p. 63f).
137   See above.
138   Foucault (1987, p. 77).
139   Ibid., p. 78.
140   Dreyfus and Rabinow (1987, p. 150).
141   Weber (1969, p. 358f), and cf. Brunkhorst (1987a, pp. 164ff).
142   As in the *Protestant ethic* – "the Puritan *wanted* to be a career-man"; and as in Luther – "here I stand, *I* can do no other."
143   Weber (1920, p. 531).
144   Cf. also Honneth (1990), and Honneth (1989, pp. 391ff).
145   Fink-Eitel (1989, p. 81).
146   Ibid., p. 70.
147   Ibid., p. 78.
148   Fink-Eitel (1989, p. 88).
149   Horkheimer and Adorno (1955, p. 40).
150   Cf. Brunkhorst (1990).
151   Cf. Winch (1966); Arbeitsgruppe Bielefelder Soziologen (1973); Brumlik (1973); Schütz (1974); Cicourel (1970) and Cicourel (1975); Goffman (1982); Tenbruck (1985); Habermas (1981, vol. 2, pp. 182ff., 552ff.).
152   Cf. Habermas (1981, vol. 2, pp. 173ff).
153   Ibid., pp. 182ff.
154   Luhmann (1981a, p. 49).
155   Habermas (1981, p. 553).
156   Ibid., p. 552.
157   Ibid., p. 228.
158   Ibid., pp. 229ff.
159   Ibid., p. 230.
160   Ibid.
161   Ibid., pp. 232ff., and Apel (1988); Eder (1985).
162   Habermas (1984, p. 53).
163   Ibid., p. 43.
164   Heidegger (1977, p. 135).
165   Bonß (1983).
166   Kuhn. See above.
167   Cf., e.g., Soeffner (1979); Garz and Kraimer (1983); Berger (1974); Haag, Krüger, Schwärzel and Wildt (1972); Hopf and Weingarten (1979); and Lazarsfeld (1941).
168   Cf. Stegmüller (1970, pp. 37ff, 98ff).
169   For the empiricist-extensionalist position cf. Atteslander (1971), Schrader (1971), Fridrichs (1973), and Phillips (1970); for a critique of it cf. Cicourel (1970), Ritsert (1971), and Oevermann (1983).
170   Cf. Weber (1956, pp. 4ff), and Habermas (1982).

171   Weber (1976, p. 7).

172   Ibid., pp. 4ff, and in principle Davidson (1985); for sociology in particular see Ritsert (1975).

173   Cf. Beck (1972).

174   Ritsert/Brunkhorst (1978, pp. 26ff).

175   Beck (1972, p. 209f).

176   Ibid., p. 210.

177   Beck (1972, p. 210).

178   Ibid., p. 217.

179   Ibid., p. 203.

180   Ibid.

181   Ryan (1973, p. 185).

182   Beck (1972, p. 210).

183   Concerning interpretative models cf. Honegger (1978).

184   On this distinction cf. Taylor (1978).

185   Cf., e.g., Whyle (1955), and Wylie (1969).

186   Cf., e.g., Cicourel (1968).

187   Cf. Habermas (1968a, pp. 300ff).

188   On Piaget cf. Kesselring (1981) and (1984); on the method of Piaget and Kohlberg cf. Garz (1982).

189   Cf. Pollock (1955); Löwenthal (1975) and (1964); Ritsert (1972); and Bonß(1982).

190   Cf. Sartre (1977–80), and Brunkhorst (1980).

191   E.g. Haferkamp (1975); cf. also Kohli (1981).

192   "Sniffing with wonder" – see above on Luhmann.

193   Bonß (1983, pp. 80ff).

194   Geertz (1987).

195   Bonß (1982).

196   Bonß (1983, p. 86).

197   On the following table, cf. Brunkhorst (1983, p. 319).

198   Horkheimer (1933, p. 22f).

199   Horkheimer (1934, p. 47).

200   Ibid., p. 49f.

REFERENCES

Apel, K.-O. "Scientistik, Hermeneutik, Ideologiekritik." In *Theorie-Diskussion. Hermeneutik und Ideologie Kritik.* Edited by J. Habermas et al. Frankfurt am Main, 1971.

Apel, K.-O. *Die Erklären/Verstehen-Kontroverse in transzendental-pragmatischer Sicht.* Frankfurt am Main, 1979.

Apel, K.-O. "Fallibilismus, Konsenstheorie der Wahrheit und Letztbegründung." In *Philosophie und Begründung.* Edited by the Forum für Philosophie Bad Homburg. Frankfurt am Main, 1987.

Apel, K.-O. *Diskurs und Verantwortung.* Frankfurt am Main, 1988.

Arbeitsgruppe Bielefelder Soziologen (eds). *Alltagswissen, Interaktion und gesellschaftliche Wirklichkeit.* Reinbek bei Hamburg, 1973.

Atteslander, P. *Methoden der empirischen Sozialforschung.* Berlin, 1971.

Beck, L. W. *Akteur und Betrachter.* Freiburg, 1976.

Beck, U. "Soziologische Normativität." *Kölner Zeitschrift für Soziologie und Sozialpsychologie,* 2, 1972.

Berger, H. *Untersuchungsmethode und soziale Wirklichkeit.* Frankfurt am Main, 1974.

Bonß, W. *Die Einübung des Tatsachenblicks.* Frankfurt am Main, 1982.

Bonß, W. "Kritische Theorie als empirische Wissenschaft." *Soziale Welt,* 1, 1983.

Brumlik, M. *Der symbolische Interaktionismus und seine pädagogische Bedeutung.* Frankfurt am Main, 1973.

Brunkhorst, H. *Praxisbezug und Theoriebildung.* Frankfurt am Main, 1978.

Brunkhorst, H. "Wie man sich zu dem macht, der man ist." In *Sartres Flaubert lesen.* Edited by T. König. Reinbek bei Hamburg, 1980.

Brunkhorst, H. "Kommunikative Vernunft und rächende Gewalt." *Sozialwissenschaftliche Literatur-Rundschau,* 8/9, 1983.

Brunkhorst, H. "Die Welt als Beute." In *Vierzig Jahre Flaschenpost.* Edited by W. v. Reijen, G. Schmid, and G. Noerr. Frankfurt am Main, 1987.

Brunkhorst, H. *Theodor W. Adorno: Dialektik der Moderne.* München, 1990.

Cicourel, A. V. *Methode und Messung in der Soziologie.* Frankfurt am Main, 1970.

Cicourel, A. V. *Sprache in der sozialen Interaktion.* München, 1975.

Davidson, D. "Handeln." In *Analytische Handlungstheorie,* volume 1. Edited by G. Meggle. Frankfurt am Main, 1977a.

Davidson, D. "Die logische Form von Handlungssätzen." In *Analytische Handlungstheorie,* volume 1. Edited by G. Meggle. Frankfurt am Main, 1977b.

Davidson, D. "Handlungen, Gründe und Ursachen." In *Seminar: Freies Handeln und Determinismus.* Edited by U. Pothast. Frankfurt am Main, 1985.

Deleuze, G. *Foucault.* Frankfurt am Main, 1987.

Dilthey, W. *Der Aufbau der geschichtlichen Welt in den Geisteswissenschaften.* Frankfurt am Main, 1970.

Dreyfus, H. and P. Rabinow. *Michel Foucault. Jenseits von Strukturalismus und Hermeneutik.* Frankfurt am Main, 1987.

Eder, K. *Geschichte als Lernprozeß.* Frankfurt am Main, 1985.

Fink-Eitel, H. *Foucault zur Einführung.* Hamburg, 1989.

Foerster, H. R. v. "Erkenntnistheorien und Selbstorganisation." In *Der Diskurs des radikalen Konstruktivismus.* Edited by S. J. Schmidt. Frankfurt am Main, 1987.

Foucault, M. *Wahnsinn und Gesellschaft.* Frankfurt am Main, 1969.

Foucault, M. *Die Ordnung der Dinge.* Frankfurt am Main, 1971.

Foucault, M. *Archäologie des Wissens.* Frankfurt am Main, 1973.

Foucault, M. *Die Geburt der Klinik.* Frankfurt am Main, 1976a.

Foucault, M. *Überwachen und Strafen.* Frankfurt am Main, 1976b.

Foucault, M. *Psychologie und Geisteskrankheit.* Frankfurt am Main, 1977a.

Foucault, M. *Der Wille zum Wissen.* Frankfurt am Main, 1977b.

Foucault, M. *Die Ordnung des Diskurses.* Frankfurt am Main, 1977c.

Foucault, M. *Die Subversion des Wissens.* Frankfurt am Main, 1987.

Frank, M. *Der kommende Gott.* Frankfurt am Main, 1982.

Frege, G. *Logische Untersuchungen.* Göttingen, 1976.

Friedrichs, J. *Methoden empirischer Sozialforschung.* Reinbek, 1973.

Gadamer, H.-G. *Wahrheit und Methode.* Tübingen, 1975.

Garz, P. *Aur Bedeutung rekonstruktiver Sozialisationstheorien in der Erziehungswissenschaft.* D. Phil. Hamburg, 1982.

Garz, P. and K. Kraimer (eds). *Brauchen wir andere Forschungsmethoden?* Frankfurt am Main, 1983.

Geertz, C. *Dichte Beschreibung*. Frankfurt am Main, 1987.

Glasersfeld, E. v. "Konstruktion der Wirklichkeit und des Begriffs der Realität." In *Einführung in den Konstruktivismus*. Edited by H. Gumin and A. Mohler. München, 1984.

Godelier, M. "Mythos und Geschichte." In *Seminar: Die Entstehung von Klassengesellschaften*. Edited by K. Eder. Frankfurt am Main, 1973.

Goffman, E. *Das Individuum in öffentlichen Austausch*. Frankfurt am Main, 1982.

Haag, H., W. Krüger, L. Schwärzel and J. Wildt (editors). *Aktionsforschung*. München, 1972.

Habermas, J. *Erkenntnis und Interesse*. Frankfurt am Main, 1968a.

Habermas, J. *Technik und Wissenschaft als "Ideologie"*. Frankfurt am Main, 1968b.

Habermas, J. "Vorbereitende Bemerkungen zu einer Theorie der kommunikativen Kompetenz." In *Theorie der Gesellschaft oder Sozialtechnologie*. Edited by J. Habermas and N. Luhmann. Frankfurt am Main, 1971.

Habermas, J. *Legitimationsprobleme im Spätkapitalismus*. Frankfurt am Main, 1973.

Habermas, J. *Theorie des kommunikativen Handelns*. Two volumes. Frankfurt am Main, 1981.

Habermas, J. *Zur Logik der Sozialwissenschaften*. Frankfurt am Main, 1982.

Habermas, J. *Vorstudien und Ergänzungen zur Theorie des kommunikativen Handelns*. Frankfurt am Main, 1984.

Habermas, J. *Der Diskurs der Moderne*. Frankfurt am Main, 1985.

Haferkamp, H. *Kriminelle Karrieren*. Reinbek bei Hamburg, 1975.

Heidegger, M. *Holzwege*. Frankfurt am Main, 1972.

Heidegger, M. *Sein und Zeit*. Tübingen, 1977.

Heidegger, M. *Hölderlins Hymnen "Germanien" und "Der Rhein"*. Frankfurt am Main, 1980.

Honegger, C. *Die Hexen der Neuzeit*. Frankfurt am Main, 1978.

Honneth, A. *Kritik der Macht*. Frankfurt am Main, 1989.

Honneth, A. *Die zerrissene Welt des Sozialen*. Frankfurt am Main, 1990.

Hopf, C. and E. Weingarten (editors). *Qualitative Sozialforschung*. Stuttgart, 1979.

Horkheimer, M. "Zum Rationalismusstreit in der gegenwärtigen Philosophie." *Zeitschrift für Sozialforschung*, 2, 1933.

Horkheimer, M. "Materialismus und Moral." *Zeitschrift für Sozialforschung*, 3, 1934.

Horkheimer, M. and Th. W. Adorno. *Dialektik der Aufklärung*. Amsterdam, 1955.

Kamlah, W. and P. Lorenzen. *Logische Propädeutik*. Mannheim, 1967.

Kesselring, Th. *Entwicklung und Widerspruch*. Frankfurt am Main, 1981.

Kesselring, Th. *Die Produktivität der Antinomie*. Frankfurt am Main, 1984.

Klüver, J. *Operationalismus*. Stuttgart, 1971.

Kohli, M. "Zur Theorie der biographischen Selbst- und Fremdthematisierung." In *Lebenswelt und soziale Probleme. Verhandlungen des Deutschen Soziologentages zu Bremen 1980*. Edited by J. Matthes. Frankfurt am Main, 1981.

Kuhn, Th. *Die Struktur wissenschaftlicher Rebolutionen*. Frankfurt am Main, 1967.

Lazarsfeld, P. F. "Remarks on Administrative and Critical Communication Research." *Zeitschrift für Sozialforschung. Studies in Philosophy and Social Science*, 9, 1941.

Lorenz, K. and J. Mittelstraß. "Die Hintergehbarkeit der Sprache." *Kant-Studien*, 2, 1967.

Lorenzen, P. "Autonomie und empirische Sozialforschung." *Methodologische Probleme einer normativ-kritischen Gesellschaftstheorie.* Edited by J. Mittelstraß. Frankfurt am Main, 1975.

Lorenzen, P. "Politische Ethik." *Synthesis Philosophica*, 4, Zagreb, 1987.

Löwenthal, L. *Literatur und Gesellschaft.* Neuwied, 1964.

Löwenthal, L. *Notizen zur Literatursoziologie.* Stuttgart, 1975.

Luhmann, N. "Sinn als Grundbegriff der Soziologie." In *Theorie der Gesellschaft oder Sozialtechnologie.* Edited by N. Luhmann and J. Habermas. Frankfurt am Main, 1971.

Luhmann, N. "Soziologie der Moral." In *Theorietechnik und Moral.* Edited by N. Luhmann and St. Pfürtner. Frankfurt am Main, 1978.

Luhmann, N. "Ideengeschichte in soziologischer Perspektive." In *Lebenswelt und soziale Probleme. Verhandlungen des Deutschen Soziologentages zu Bremen 1980.* Edited by J. Matthes. Frankfurt am Main, 1981.

Luhmann, N. "Autopoiesis, Handlung und kommunikative Vernunft." *Zeitschrift für Soziologie*, 4, 1982.

Luhmann, N. *Soziale Systeme. Grundriß einer allgemeinen Theorie.* Frankfurt am Main, 1984.

Luhmann, N. "Autopoiesis des Bewußtseins." *Soziale Welt*, 36, 1985.

Luhmann, N. "Tautologie und Paradoxie in den Selbstbeschreibungen moderner Gesellschaften." *Zeitschrift für Soziologie*, 3, 1987a.

Luhmann, N. "Autopoiesis als soziologischer Begriff." In *Sinn, Kommunikation und soziale Differenzierung.* Edited by H. Haferkamp and M. Schmid. Frankfurt am Main, 1987b.

Luhmann, N. *Erkenntnis als Konstruktion.* Bern, 1988.

Man, P. de. *Blindness and Insight.* Minneapolis, 1983.

Maturana, H. R. *Erkennen.* Braunschweig, Wiesbaden 1982.

Maturana, H. R. "Kognition." In *Der Diskurs des Radikalen Konstruktivismus.* Edited by S. J. Schmidt. Frankfurt am Main, 1987.

Menke, Ch. "Relativismus und Partikularisierung." *Philosophische Rundschau*, 1/2, 1989.

Nietzsche, F. *Sämtliche Werke.* Volume 5. München, 1980.

Oevermann, U. "Zur Sache." In *Adorno-Konferenz.* Edited by L. v. Friedeburg and J. Habermas. Frankfurt am Main, 1983.

Peirce, Ch. S. *Schriften.* Volume 1. Frankfurt am Main, 1967.

Phillips, B. *Empirische Sozialforschung.* Wien, 1970.

Pollock, F. *Gruppenexperiment.* Frankfurt am Main, 1955.

Popper, Karl R. *The Logic of Scientific Discovery.* London: Hutchinson & Co., 1959.

Popper, Karl R. *Conjectures and Refutations: The Growth of Scientific Knowledge.* New York: Basic Books, 1968.

Popper, Karl R. "Eine objektive Theorie des historischen Verstehens." *Schweizer Monatshefte*, 3, 1970.

Putnam, H. *Mind, Language and Reality.* Cambridge, Mass., 1975.

Ritsert, J. *Erkenntnistheorie, Soziologie und Empirie.* Frankfurt am Main, 1971.

Ritsert, J. *Inhaltsanalyse und Ideologiekritik.* Frankfurt am Main, 1972.

Ritsert, J. (editor). *Gründe und Ursachen gesellschaftlichen Handelns.* Frankfurt am Main, 1975.

Ritsert, J. and H. Brunkhorst. *Theorie, Interesse, Forschungsstrategien.* Frankfurt am Main, 1978.

Ritter, J. *Subjektivität.* Frankfurt am Main, 1974.

Ritter, J. *Metaphysik und Politik.* Frankfurt am Main, 1977.

Rorty, R. *Der Spiegel der Natur.* Frankfurt am Main, 1981.

Rorty, R. *Kontingenz, Ironie und Solidarität.* Frankfurt am Main, 1989.

Rothacker, E. (editor). *Briefwechsel zwischen Wilhelm Dilthey und dem Grafen Paul Yorck v. Wartenburg.* Halle, 1923.

Rusch, G. *Erkenntnis, Wissenschaft, Geschichte.* Frankfurt am Main, 1987.

Ryan, A. *Die Philosophie der Sozialwissenschaften.* München, 1973.

Ryle, G. *Der Begriff des Geistes.* Stuttgart, 1969.

Sartre, J.-P. *Der Idiot der Familie.* Reinbek bei Hamburg, 1977–80.

Schmidt, S. J. "Der radikale Konstruktivismus." In *Der Diskurs des radikalen Konstruktivismus.* Edited by S. J. Schmidt. Frankfurt am Main, 1987.

Schnädelbach, H. *Vernunft und Geschichte.* Frankfurt am Main, 1987.

Schrader, A. *Einführung in die empirische Sozialforschung.* Stuttgart, 1971.

Schütz, A. *Der sinnhafte Aufbau der sozialen Welt.* Frankfurt am Main, 1974.

Sellars, W. "Theoretische Erklärungen." In *Erkenntnisprobleme der Naturwissenschaften.* Edited by L. Krüger. Köln, 1970.

Sneed, J. P. *The Logical Structure of Mathematical Physics.* Dordrecht, 1971.

Soeffner, H.-G. (editor). *Interpretative Verfahren in den Sozial- und Textwissenschaften.* Stuttgart, 1979.

Stegmüller, W. *Probleme und Resultate der Wissenschaftstheorie und analytischen Philosophie.* Volume 2: *Theorie und Erfahrung.* Berlin, 1970.

Stegmüller, W. *Probleme und Resultate der Wissenschaftstheorie und analytischen Philosophie.* Volume 2: Parts D and E. Berlin, 1973.

Stegmüller, W. *Hauptströmungen der Gegenwartsphilosophie.* Volume 2. Stuttgart, 1975.

Taylor, Ch. *Hegel.* Frankfurt am Main, 1978.

Tenbruck, F. H. "George Herbert Mead und die Ursprünge der Soziologie in Deutschland und Amerika." In *Das Problem der Intersubjektivität.* Edited by H. Joas. Frankfurt am Main, 1985.

Watzlawick, P. et al. *Menschliche Kommunikation.* Bern, 1971.

Weber, M. *Wirtschaft und Gesellschaft I.* Köln, 1956.

Weber, M. *Die protestantische Ethik und der Geist des Kapitalismus.* München, 1969.

Weber, M. *Gesammelte Aufsätze zur Religionssoziologie.* Volume 3. Tübingen, 1976.

Weber, M. *Gesammelte Aufsätze zur Religionssoziologie I.* (First published 1920.) Tübingen, 1978.

Winch, P. *Die Idee der Sozialwissenschaft und ihr Verhältnis zur Philosophie.* Frankfurt am Main, 1966.

Wright, G. H. von. *Erklären und Verstehen.* Frankfurt am Main, 1974.

5 THE COMMUNICATIVE PARADIGM IN MORAL THEORY

Alessandro Ferrara

Along with Rawls's theory of justice as fairness, Habermas's "discourse ethics" is one of the most important attempts to salvage a universalistic perspective in a historical context marked by the declining credibility of all foundational discourses. Now, after more than ten years from its beginning, Habermas's project has undergone significant modifications. The project of the "discourse ethics" in its present shape appears much more differentiated and complex than in the initial formulation, but on the other hand it must be underscored that all the subsequent modifications have adjusted, expanded, differentiated, specified the initial project in a number of respects, but certainly not as far as its central core or leading intuition is concerned. This central intuition can be captured as the proposition that ethical universalism is best understood as resting on a postmetaphysical, dialogical revisitation of Kant's view of moral validity as generalizability. I will outline the general features of the Habermasian project, will then reconstruct four stages of its development, and at the end will offer some critical considerations on one element of ambiguity that seems to persist throughout it.

THE COMMUNICATIVE PARADIGM: GENERAL PROPERTIES AND OVERALL PERIODIZATION

In a 1985 paper – "Morality and Ethical Life: Does Hegel's Critique of Kant Apply to Discourse Ethics?"[1] – Habermas characterizes the fundamental aspects of his communicative ethics on the basis of four properties. In addition to being *universalistic*, his "discourse ethics" purports to be *deontological, cognitivistic* and *formal*.

First, it is *deontological*, albeit in a peculiar sense. Habermas uses the term "deontological" not in opposition to "consequentialist" – as in the received usage – but in opposition to "comprehensive." The "discourse ethics" is deontological in that it embeds an attitude of "normative restraint," as it were. The practitioner of it permanently renounces all ambition to prescribe a philosophically correct solution to any practical problem, especially in matters concerning the good life. Rather, she understands her philosophical task as limited to the rational reconstruction of our intuitions relative to a fundamental moral phenomenon – that is, the normative force that inheres in moral norms, moral principles and especially in the so-called *moral point of view*.

Second, the "discourse ethics" is *cognitivist* not in the sense that it aspires to possess the qualities of a moral objectivism, or that it blurs the line between factual and evaluative propositions, but in the much weaker sense that it attributes to the special validity of moral utterances a status somehow "equivalent" to that usually associated to the validity of assertions. Habermas does not clarify – at least in that context – what this "equivalence" really amounts to, but on the whole it seems sensible to assume that he intends to refer to the susceptibility, on the part of a factual assertion or statement, (a) to be either valid (true) or non valid (false), and (b) to be demonstrably so.

Third, the "discourse ethics" is *formal* or *procedural* in the sense that it takes the justification of a moral principle, and not also of specific substantive tenets, as its object. Communicative ethics does not provide us with concrete precepts, but rather with a "method" for choosing in a correct, universalistically valid, way between the rival orientations that strive for our allegiance in any problematic context.

Finally, the "discourse ethics" purports to be *universalistic* in the sense that the principle of dialogical generalization underlying it is understood not as a reflection of the moral intuitions of a concrete historical epoch or culture, but as a principle "valid in general."[2]

The seminal essays collected in the volume *Moral Consciousness and Communicative Action*[3] appeared in 1983, but the development of Habermas's ethical thought spans over a period of over two decades. We can trace some constitutive aspects of it back to the 1972 essay "Wahrheitstheorien" and, at the other extreme, it is not unsound to say that the most original of Habermas's contributions to moral philosophy are to be found in his 1992 volume *Faktizität und Geltung*.[4] For clarity's sake, we can divide this intellectual development up into four major phases: (a) an initial stage, spanning from the early seventies up until 1981; (b) the 1982–3 stage; (c) the years between 1984 and 1991; and (d) the new stage inaugurated by the publication of *Faktizität und Geltung*.

THE PREPARATORY STAGE: 1972–1981

I will not spend much time on the first stage, because at that time Habermas was not interested in moral philosophy except occasionally – his investigations focused mainly on the theory of knowledge, on social theory and on the theory of moral development. Habermas has concerned himself with ethical issues during this first stage mainly in connection with the fact that some of the central concepts of his position – for instance, the notions of "ideal speech situation," of "interaction," of "communicative action" and of "presuppositions of argumentation" – do possess an ethical dimension and, at the same time, are of crucial importance for the task of grounding a universalistic standpoint in philosophy in general, and in the theory of knowledge in particular. It is possible to find embryonic references to a so-called "universal ethic of speech" and to "comunicative ethics" in the 1972 essay "Wahrheitstheorien" and in the 1973 volume *Legitimation Crisis*, as well as in several of the essays collected in the volume *Communication and the Evolution of Society*.[5] In Habermas's main work – *The Theory of Communicative Action* (1981) – we find the most articulate formulation of the notion of "communicative *action*," its presuppositions, its genesis, its function within the process of social reproduction, but we do not find any specific attempt to develop a *moral-theoretical* perspective based on that notion – with the exception of a few remarks offered by Habermas mainly in the context of his discussion of Mead and Durkheim.

Typical of this stage of Habermas's ethical thought is the absence of a systematic formulation of the main concepts. No mention is yet made of any *principle of universalization*. "Communicative ethics" still revolves around the idea that "just" is any maxim on whose "normative rightness" (*Richtigkeit* – Habermas does not yet make use of the term *Gerechtigkeit*) a "rational consensus" arises among all the potentially affected actors, where the rational quality of "rational consensus" is understood as the quality of emerging as the outcome of a debate conducted in the "ideal speech situation." As in Apel's dialogical ethics, also in Habermas's "communicative ethics" of the first stage we find no distinction between the right and the good and no restriction imposed on the object of moral-practical discourse. It seems as though all practical conflicts can in principle be submitted to the test of the ideal speech situation with equal probability – actually, with equal *certainty* – of being solved. Finally, we find no formulation of a specific *moral* principle that might guide our assessment of the validity of moral norms.

THE CLASSICAL FORMULATION OF THE COMMUNICATIVE PARADIGM: 1982–1983

The years 1982–3 – when essays such as "A Reply to my Critics," "Discourse ethics," "Moral Consciousness and Communicative Action," and "Was macht eine Lebensform rational?" are published – correspond to a stage in Habermas's intellectual development in which the project of grounding the "discourse ethics" is given a high, if not exclusive, priority. These are also the years in which the *Philosophical Discourse of Modernity* is conceived.[6] Of this Habermasian project I will highlight only one point – one, however, which will remain substantially unchanged up until the present time. Habermas suggests that moral discourse can indeed lead to rational consensus only if we evaluate the contending alternatives in light of an impartial moral principle. This principle – called "U" – is a universalization test, a kind of categorical imperative reformulated along dialogical lines. It purports to be sensible reconstruction of the meaning of the term "fair" or "just," as it occurs in an expression like "This norm is fair (or just)." In *Moral Consciousness and Communicative Action* Habermas defines "U" as the principle according to which a moral norm is valid, "fair" or "impartial," when:

> *All* affected can accept the consequences and side effects its *general* observance can be anticipated to have for the satisfaction of *everyone's* interests . . .[7]

How does Habermas argue the case for "U"? He grounds "U" by means of a "quasi-transcendental" argument which in turn pivots around the notion of *performative contradiction*. A *performative*, as opposed to *semantic*, contradiction arises when what is asserted by the speaker in the propositional content is implicitly denied by the pragmatic presuppositions of his utterance. Utterances that embed performative contradictions are, for example, "It rains, but I don't believe that it rains," "Tell me what time it is, but I know it," "I promise I will come to see you, but I don't intend to leave home." A skeptical opponent – argues Habermas along lines not dissimilar, at this point, from those followed by Karl-Otto Apel – who wished to refute the universal validity of "U", would, by the very fact of trying to establish his point *through an argument*, presuppose among other things the validity of "U", and would thereby entangle herself in a performative contradiction. In fact, do we not detect a performative contradiction in a sentence like "After having excluded A, B, and C from our discussion (or having silenced them up, or having forced our interpretation on them) we have finally been able to convince ourselves that *p*"? After this juncture, however, Habermas's and Apel's versions of the "discourse ethics" part ways. For Habermas takes up a further skeptical objection which leads him to open up a whole new terrain for the grounding of his moral theory. The objection is the following: the presuppositions of argumentation and the performative contradictions in which we entangle ourselves when violating them, as well as the justification of "U" which can be thereby derived, are binding only insofar as we move within the circle of the language game called "philosophical argumentation." Should the skeptical opponent opt for total silence, irony, aesthetic provocation or any other language game other than "philosphical argumentation," the normative cogency of these presuppositions would instantly evaporate as the rules of chess lose all relevance when we set ourselves to play checkers.

Apel responds to this challenge by a kind of "prepostmetaphysical" transcendentalization of his argument – basically, he claims for the language game "argumentation" a special status, the status of being the one language game which must be presupposed in order for all the other games to make sense. Habermas, in a more interesting way, responds to the same challenge by turning toward a social-theoretical completion of the argument. Only in an "abstract" sense can the skeptic decide to withdraw from argumentation. In any event his decision can only be limited to the "here and now." For no form of association, no social union can be stabilized and reproduced without a sizeable amount of that "communicative action" of which the activity of arguing constitutes an important subset.

This is the conceptual entry point at which the theory of social reproduction developed in *The Theory of Communicative Action* – and especially the outline of the reproduction of the life-world – becomes relevant to the foundations of Habermasian moral theory. The concept of "communicative action" becomes the interface which allows the *social*-theoretical and the *moral*-theoretical argument to run together. One the one hand "communicative action" is a kind of conduct, and a mode of action coordination, that no society can dispense with, under penalty of suffering severe and possibly destructive consequences at the level of its own reproduction processes, and, on the other hand, communicative action is a larger category in which "argumentation" belongs as a special case. Hence Habermas's point that no form of social life could survive in the long run without some of its participants' engaging some of the time in the activity called argumentation. In order to better secure the relevance of the "presuppositions of argumentation" even outside the practice of argumentation, however, Habermas introduces a second premise in his vindication of "U" which with good reasons has been considered problematical by a number of critics. According to this additional premise we normally consider fair or just those norms which regulate social interaction in the equal interest of all those concerned. Habermas's 1983 argument for grounding "U" consists then of the following two premises and one conclusion. If (1) whoever argues inevitably presupposes that (a) "no concerned person should be excluded from the deliberative discourse," that (b) "all the participants in discourse must be offered equal chances of expressing their point of view" and of "challenging the point of view of others"; and if (2) we consider valid only those norms which regulate social interaction in the equal interest of everyone; then the conclusion follows that whoever evaluates the fairness, impartiality or normative validity of a rule, norm or maxim of action, must evaluate it according to the principle "U".[8]

Finally, in *Moral Consciousness and Communicative Action* Habermas tries for the first time to demarcate more clearly the subdomain of the moral-practical realm over which "U" extends its jurisdiction. The differentiation, brought about by the process of cultural modernization, of the expert-knowledge typical of the various domains of high culture from the relatively unreflexive and commonsensical mode of knowledge characteristic of the life-world is reflected, within the moral-practical realm, as a differentiation of "decontextualized" *questions of justice* – which in principle can always receive a rational answer if addressed from the standpoint of the universalization test[9] – from the larger set of *questions concerning the good life* – which remain amenable to a rational answer only *from within* the momentarily unproblematical horizon of a concrete historical life-form or individual life-project.[10] "U" is relevant only as far as *questions of justice* are concerned. This means that only when *questions of justice* are concerned there exists an "a priori guarantee" to the effect that, if we assume that the ideal conditions of communication hold, then for each and any specific conflict a solution can be found that meets with the "rational," not just factual, consensus of all those concerned.

This is the point, within the development of Habermas's ethical thought, where a certain way of understanding the distinction between the right and the good has its beginning – an understanding of these two moral-practical notions that contrasts them in terms of the four dichotomies of *universalism* and *particularism, context-transcending abstractness* and *concrete context-bound concreteness, dialogical* as opposed to *"monological"* types of rationality, *demonstrability* and *undemonstrability*.

From the moment he formulated his first comprehensive outline of the "discourse ethics" Habermas has had to face objections often raised in a constructive and sympathetic vein, for example motivated by the intent to eliminate the unnecessary formalistic bent that he seemed to have impressed onto the initial intuition of an ethic of communication. Let me briefly recall four points raised by Albrecht Wellmer.

First, by introducing his second premise – according to which "we deem valid those norms which regulate social interaction in the equal interest of everybody" – Habermas also introduces a *petitio principii* in the justification of "U". Such premise, in fact, links the validity of a norm with the generalizability of the interest underlying it *through a definition*, whereas such linkage strictly speaking could only emerge *after* or *in consequence* of applying the "U"-test, and thus should not concur in its justification.[11]

Second, the expression "generalized observance of a norm" – which plays an important role in the formulation of "U" – is ambiguous. If taken as equivalent to "without exception," it would generate counterintuitive results. For one thing, no rule or norm could possibly pass the test. If we take it in a looser sense, i.e., as including the implicit clause "with all the due exceptions," then we thereby introduce a moment of judgment or *phronesis* right into the grounding of "U" – in fact, the assessment of the acceptability of exceptions cannot itself be brought under the scope of principles for the reason that, by definition, "exceptions" are courses of conduct that we consider *just but not generalizable.*[12]

Third, the generalization test is practically, and most likely also in principle, inapplicable. To assess the acceptability of all the consequences and side-effects of the observance of a norm may prove an impossible feat. Wellmer suggests then to reformulate "U" in a fallibilistic direction, as a test aimed at ascertaining that there are no reasons, on the part of each concerned person, *not to accept* even one of the main or secondary consequences of the observance of the norm. The fairness of a norm would then have to be conceived in negative terms, as its *non-nongeneralizability*, or, in simpler terms, as the impossibility of imagining anyone who might object against even one of its remotest consequences.[13]

Finally, in the 1983 version of the "discourse ethics" we find no distinction between the validity of a *moral* norm and the validity or legitimacy of a *legal* norm. Habermas understands his work as a reconstruction of a kind of normative validity which inheres in both cases alike. He thereby obscures three fundamental differences – continues Wellmer – which set moral precepts apart from legal norms. First, while legal norms must be promulgated by someone entitled to do so, moral precepts are binding *independently* of any formal act of instatement. Second, legal norms may have a *constitutive* role for some practices, and are usually grouped in juridical corpuses. Moral norms, instead, only *regulate* practices which pre-exist them and only rarely are articulated in the form of systems. Third, while legal norms usually have external sanctions attached to them, moral norms are linked to "internal" sanctions only – the rise of feelings of guilt and the loss of one's own self-esteem.[14] Now, according to Wellmer this conflation of moral and legal norms leads Habermas to overlook the different way in which a universalistic moral principle and a democratic principle of legitimation respectively work. In the case of moral judgment only a negative answer to the question whether we can genuinely will that a given course of conduct be generalized constitutes an "ought." In the case of a legal norm, instead, the existence of an "ought" presupposes the "communal *positive* intention of all the concerned ones to live together under certain rules."[15] In sum, at this stage Habermas conflates the two types of moral-practical argumentation, thereby causing his formulation of the "discourse ethics" to fall behind the level of differentiation that moral discourse had already attained with Kant.

THE ADJUSTMENT STAGE: 1984–1991

The attempt to respond to these and other criticisms marks the beginning of a third stage in the development of Habermas's ethical thought – a stage which extends roughly between 1984 and 1991. Typical of this stage is the attempt to finetune the distinction between the right and the good, to introduce a new distinction between moral and legal discourse, and to engage in a fruitful dialogue with the proponents of other models of procedural universalism: mainly Rawls and Dworkin.

These adjustments and corrections are to be found in the essays collected under the title *Justification and Application* and in the *Tanner Lectures*.[16] To the first among the criticisms raised by Wellmer, Habermas responds by practically abandoning the quasi-transcendental derivation of "U" from the above-mentioned premises. In a way not dissimilar from the path followed by Rawls during the eighties, Habermas now presents the principle of universalization as the expression, within a controlled vocabulary, of our intuitions *qua* participants in the culture of modernity. This process of revision finds its completion in *Beyond Facts and Norms*, the text which actually opens the *next* stage, where Habermas admits that in complex societies a given norm may clash *also under ideal conditions* with interests so diverse and irreconcilable that no unique general interest, and therefore unique solution on which it is rational to consent, can be identified. To account for our intuitions concerning fairness in these cases it becomes necessary, from the standpoint of the late Habermas, to supplement the discourse-theoretical approach with a theory of "fair compromise." A *compromise* is fair if: (a) its being established is more advantageous for all the parties than the absence of any negotiated arrangement; (b) it effectively excludes the possibility of "free-riding," and (c) it puts no one in the position of contributing more than one receives from the deal. Interesting is the fact that Habermas distinguishes compromise from "rational consensus" on the basis of the sameness or dissimilarity of the motivations with which the contending parties accept it. While in the case of moral consensus the parties agree to the fairness of a norm on the basis of the *same* considerations, in the case of a compromise each participant, like in a contract, may agree out of the most diverse reasons.[17] This adjustment of the "discourse ethics" is not without problems, however. First, if we can legitimately resort to compromise in all those contexts in which no generalizable interest exists, how are we to solve those cases – and they may well be the majority of cases, in our pluralistic societies – in which what is under dispute is precisely the existence of a generalizable interest? Second, how can any norm satisfy the new standard – introduced for distinguishing rational consensus and compromise – of being accepted on the basis of *exactly the same* reason? Doesn't this new standard commit Habermas to the dubious thesis of the universal translatability of all vocabularies into each other or into a metavocabulary? In what vocabulary are we to ascertain whether the reasons why the parties accept a norm are the same?

Wellmer's second criticism is avoided with a reformulation of "U", which we will have occasion to examine below. On the third point Habermas has never offered an exhaustive answer to my knowledge. Finally, the fourth criticism has been fully accepted: during the third stage Habermas develops a finegrained distinction between the legal, moral and political varieties of normative validity.

Above all, characteristic of this phase is an increasing legitimation of the realm of the good as a domain of moral-philosophical relevance. In the texts of the 1982–3 period questions about the good life were understood as a residual area on which practical reason, if conceived postmetaphysically, has little to say. They constitute the object of a "critique" of values or, better said, the subject matter of a reflexive articulation of the eudaimonistic intuitions inherent in a given culture. From this initial dichotomous understanding of the moral-practical realm Habermas moves soon to a tripartite model, first outlined in the section of the (1988) Howison Lecture *On the Concept of Practical Reason*, which bears the subtitle "Individual Will Formation in terms of what is Expedient, what is Good and what is Just."[18] To these three moments or vantage points of practical will correspond three distinct kinds of *discourse*: *pragmatic*, *ethical* and *moral* discourse. These three kinds of discourse address different understandings of the same question: "What should I do?" *Pragmatic* discourses – the moral-practical reflection of *instrumental* and *strategic* action – address this question from the perspective of the best way of attaining what is *useful*. For example, what should I do in order to repair a broken car or to recover from a disease? *Ethical* discourses address the question "What should I do?" from the perspective of a life-project oriented to one's own *good*. For example, given my abilities and weaknesses what career should I choose? Given a certain dilemma, to which values should I accord priority in shaping my conduct? Differently than in the previous case, at the center of my consideration are not hypothetical, but unconditional imperatives, such as: "You ought to undertake a career which makes you feel you are helping other people." These are imperatives which are relatively independent of *individual* goals and preferences.[19] Finally, *moral* discourses begin when my actions happen to violate the interests of others and to lead to conflicts which stand in need of a consensual regulation. At the center of these discourses is yet another sense of the question "What should I do?" Now I have to determine for myself whether also others – indeed, *everybody else* – would agree on my choosing a certain course of action.

To contrast these three points of view, let us take the example of a taxpayer confronted with the task of filling out his income tax return form. Suppose I have the possibility of hiding a certain revenue. From a *pragmatic* standpoint the question is whether the benefit of paying less outweighs the risk of being caught and the sanctions attached to tax cheating. From an *ethical* standpoint, the question is whether I would like to see myself as the kind of person whom we call a tax-cheater. From a *moral* point of view, finally, the question is whether everybody else could want that whoever finds himself in my situation tries to hide a source of income. The watershed between ethical and moral discourse consists then in the difference between assessing the competing lines of conduct in "egocentric" terms and assessing them from the standpoint of their generalizability.[20]

The tripartition of the moral-practical sphere outlined by Habermas at this time is in fact a *twofold tripartition* – the two tiers being disposed along the opposition of *individual* and *collective* will. Thus far we have considered only the formation of an *individual* will. When we move on to the level of collective will things get more complicated. In fact, if we conjugate the practical question *par excellence* in the plural – "What should we do?" – it appears that it can receive three different kinds of answers, in which three different processes of collective will-formation are reflected: namely, the formation of a *political*, a *moral* and a *juridical* will.

Politics is understood by Habermas as a pragmatic discourse on the means and strategies most conducive to the attainment of communally pursued goals. But this is not the only meaning of politics for him. Where an agreement on the ends of action or on the way of assigning priorities to preferences cannot be reached, we can either negotiate a compromise or accede to a second level of political will-formation – the level at which we reassess our communal identity – and enter a kind of discourse centered around the question "Who are we and who do we want to be?" Politics breaks down, then, in pragmatic discourses about means and strategies on the one hand, and practices of negotiation and ethical-political discourse on the other. Hence Habermas's definition of the *rationality* of a policy as the quality of being both instrumentally expedient and "good for us." At this point, however, Habermas introduces the dimension of justice, understood as *political justice*. Beyond being expedient and fit to who we are, a program or a policy is *just* if the outcome of its implementation is *equally good for each of us*.[21]

The question "What should we do?" can be understood also in *moral* terms. Then it means something like "According to which rules do we want to live together and regulate our conflicts?" This is the theoretical locus of universalistic moral discourse proper, of a public morality centered on the assessment of the fairness of norms. This is also the domain of politics understood as a process of legislation. The application of legal norms falls within the third domain of collective practical discourse, i.e., within the domain of *juridical* discourse – the kind of discourse entered by courts and judges, when they are required to establish whether and how a fact can be said to fall under the heading of a given norm. This third type of discourse of collective will-formation rests, according to Habermas, on a so-called "principle of impartial application."

Finally, it must be noticed that while in Habermas's early ethical writings the distinction between "grounding" and "application" seemed to overlap with the distinction between "questions of justice" and "questions concerning the good life," in the context of the Howison Lecture the relation between the two distinctions becomes much clearer. Both moral discourse and ethical discourse have a separate moment of grounding and one of application. The grounding dimension of *moral* discourse resides in the testing of the generalizability of a maxim. The "application" of the norm or maxim thus grounded requires an "additional" argumentation, which has to be conducted under the aegis of a "principle of appropriateness" (or of "impartial application") which constitutes the "applicative" equivalent of the notion of impartiality in "grounding" discourses. Also in the *ethical* realm a grounding and an applicative moment can be found. Habermas conceives of the process of existential deliberation as a discourse which embeds a moment of grounding. For example, he refers to the existence of "better reasons," in abstract and general terms, for deciding in favor of a life-plan over another and to ethical imperatives of a non-hypothetical kind. Then their ethical discourse would have an applicative moment, in which general maxims concerning the good life are brought into a relation with one's own case.

THE PRESENT STAGE: 1992 AND AFTER

We have thus reached the fourth stage of the development of Habermas's communicative approach to moral theory. In *Between Facts and Norms* the process of upgrading and integrating the ethical realm within Habermasian moral theory finds its completion. It is possible to find a systematic niche for what is now termed ethical *discourse*, as well as a systematic role assigned to *pragmatic* discourses and *moral* discourses. Not only does ethical discourse concerning the good cease to be a mere residual category, but we find an attempt to go beyond a mere analytic distinction between moral and ethical discourse – namely the attempt to trace genealogically the realm of *"das Ethische"* back to a tradition of authenticity and self-realization, which until now Habermas had hesitated to recognize as a distinct strand in the development of the modern practical sphere. *"Das Ethische"* has its source in the tradition that expresses itself mainly through the autobiographical literature of the "confessions" and "self-examinations" inaugurated by Rousseau and carried on by Kierkegaard and Sartre. At the center of this tradition we find a fully modern question on the nature of the good life, in response to which these authors do not bring up models of the good life to be imitated but rather put forward the proposal – abstract and formal as any – that the moral actor reflexively appropriate the uniqueness, irreplaceability and contingency of his or her life history. The moral-practical discourse of modernity, in this new interpretation advanced in Habermas's latest text, appears to be a kind of discourse "always already" fractured in two competing traditions which pivot around the two concepts, non-reconcilable and thus in tension, of autonomy (Selbstbestimmung) and authenticity (Selbstverwirklichung).[22] Finally, Habermas must be credited for having contributed to further differentiate our perception of the extramoral moment of the practical sphere. Not only have we a clear perception that the moral-practical realm cannot be reduced to the narrow boundaries of moral discourse understood as a generalization test, but we also can better discern the other components that compose it. Beyond ethical discourse, we now can identify pragmatic discourse, discourses of application, discourses of legitimation, and political discourses as distinct components of the practical.[23] Also, the legitimacy of legal norms is now carefully distinguished from the validity of moral norms. While the latter only need to satisfy the principle of dialogical universalization, positive legal norms must satisfy three distinct standards of validity: they must be morally just, ethically appropriate to who we are and want to be, and pragmatically expedient.

This process whereby the account of the moral point of view has over the years been purified of all the spurious elements and functions which at the beginning Habermas conflated with it, is not without problems. In my opinion the discourse-theoretic reconstruction of the moral point of view continues to be affected by an ambiguity which has not yet been removed or even addressed by Habermas. However, before elucidating this ambiguity in the last section of this chapter, let me briefly update the reconstruction of the Habermasian principle of universalization "U", which we have left to its 1983 formulation.

In Between Facts and Norms Habermas conceives the principle of universalization which guides our assessment of moral norms – the principle "U" of 1983 – as a special case of a broader principle of discourse "D". The principle of discourse "D" runs:

> Just those norms are valid to which all those possibly affected could agree as participants in rational discourses.[24]

This principle is understood by Habermas as a reconstruction of the intuitions of postconventional actors regarding what it means both for a moral and a legal norm to be justified. The specification of "D" for the moral realm – which I will call hereinafter "Dm" – is formulated by Habermas in the following form:

> A norm is just if all can will that it be obeyed by each in comparable situations.[25]

As with the 1983 principle "U", also in this case Habermas does not give us any clear argument as to why this way of summing up our intuitions as to what renders a norm just ought to be preferred over Rawls's two principles of justice, over utilitarian principles, over the principle of egalitarian impartiality suggested by Nagel, and several other competing accounts.

The ambiguity in question is part and parcel both of the principle "D" and of its moral specification, but for simplicity's sake I will develop the argument mainly with reference to "D".

THE AMBIGUITY UNDERLYING THE COMMUNICATIVE PARADIGM

Let us consider each of the terms used by Habermas in the "moral" version of the principle "D". We must note that "all" here takes on the broadest possible meaning: "humanity or a supposed republic of world citizens." No narrower frame of reference is appropriate for the purpose of determining if the adoption of a norm lies "in the equal interest of all." By "norm" it must be here understood a general expectation concerning a specific course of conduct. The clause "in comparable situations" responds to Wellmer's objection concerning the status of exceptions. While the 1983 formula "general observance of a norm" was unclear, the new formulation eliminates the problem of exceptions, even though it introduces an element of *phronesis* or judgment right at the core of the "grounding" discourse: in fact, it requires us to assess the *comparability* of situations given that by definition no two situations can be identical. But let me leave aside also this point. For the point in which the ambiguity resides is Habermas's use of the key term "will" and, in his formulation of "D", of the term "agree."

What does it really mean that everyone can *will* or *agree* that a norm be generally observed by everybody in comparable situations? Does it mean that everyone can *tolerate* that everybody else observes the norm in comparable contexts? Does it mean that everyone can *accept*, consistently with all her preferences, that the norm be observed by everybody else? Does it mean that the general observance of the norm is compatible with everyone's maintaining his self respect? Does it mean that everyone can *authentically* – i.e., as part and parcel of her vision of the good life – will that the norm be universally observed? The list of questions could be extended further. The absence of whatever indication leaves the meaning of the terms "will" and "agree" open almost to *any* interpretation. Two of these readings, however, stand out as more plausible than any other. Unfortunately, there is no clear indication that Habermas has chosen one over the other, and there is also reason to believe that were he to choose between these two meanings of "D" and of "Dm" (the moral specification of "D"), the whole edifice of the communicative paradigm would suffer severe damage – so much it depends, for its stability, on exploiting this ambiguity.

While one of these two interpretations does support the sharp distinctions that Habermas wants to draw between *grounding* and *applying* norms, the *right* and the *good, moral* and *legal* norms, *morality* and *ethics*, but is almost indefensible, the other conversely appears a much more plausible reconstruction of our intuitions concerning the generalizing moment in moral validity, but actually undermines the dichotomous understanding of the moral-practical realm that Habermas feels inclined to defend. It is a kind of theoretical *double bind* that in my opinion explains the peculiar silence that Habermas has maintained on the meaning of the term "will" and "agree" in his initial formulation of "U" and now in his specification of "D" and "Dm". Let us consider these two interpretations.

In the first case the terms "will" and "agree" can be interpreted as meaning "to wish or to consent to, on the basis of the totality of one's volitions and preferences." The universalization test then takes on the features of a *consistency* test. When we assess the fairness or moral validity of a norm, according to this first interpretation, we try to determine – in a dialogical context that satisfies certain ideal conditions – whether everyone can reasonably be said to will, *on the basis of his present volitions*, the state of affairs that presumably, to the best of our empirical knowledge, will result from the general observance of the given norm in comparable situations. We could introduce further restrictions, for example to the effect that the preferences and volitions that we take into account be not precipitous and formed on the basis of impressions, but preferences and volitions submitted to critical scrutiny and formulated in a state of "reflective equilibrium." The problematic quality of this interpretation of "D" and "Dm" would not be thereby significantly changed. Incidentally, this is the interpretation of the universalization principle which Wellmer has in mind when, after objecting that such a test would be nearly impossible to carry out, he suggests to modify it along fallibilistic lines.

The good news is that both in the Habermasian and in the Wellmerian formulation the principle of universalization thus interpreted fully supports the sharp distinction that Habermas wants to draw between ethics and morality. In fact, the universalism of *moral* validity, impartiality, fairness or justice remains solidly anchored to the consistency of the consequences of the norm and the preferences, taken in equal consideration, of everyone concerned. The kind of universalism implicit in this first interpretation of the generalization test is indeed radically discontinuous with the "softer" normativity implicit in our "clinical intuitions" concerning the state of an identity. In principle – no matter how distant "principle" in this case is from "reality" – one can always imagine a state of the world, considered from the perspective of the preferences and volitions entertained by its inhabitants, such that the universal validity of a given norm would be inconfutable.

The bad news is that there is a price, in my opinion unsustainable, to be paid for purchasing this strong, "context-transcending" view of moral validity that Habermas sees as an indispensable ingredient of his critical enterprise. The price consists in the fact that the adoption of this interpretation of "D" and "Dm" would implicitly undermine the *intersubjective* and *communicative* dimension of what would then remain a "*discourse* ethics" only by virtue of its name. If we read "D" and "Dm" in this way we could run the generalization test in terms of formal logics, as the search for inconsistencies that arise *between two lists of propositions*: (a) the list of the propositions which specify, to the best of our present knowledge, the foreseeable consequences and side-effects of the observance of a given norm, and (b) the list of the propositions which specify, to the best of our present knowledge, the volitions and preferences that everyone brings into the deliberative process. This interpretation not only would require that we bring the cultural plurality of the preferences of the members of humanity down to the unity of one language of universal commensuration without any significant loss of meaning. It would also render discourse *superfluous* for moral purposes. Discourse could still keep a form of relevance as a heuristic tool for better compiling the two lists and possibly for revising them in light of critical considerations, but not for actually comparing the two lists. It would be useful for operating *within* each list, useless for operating *between* lists. In fact, it is hard to see what the *discursive, communicative* or *dialogical* quality of the comparison between the list of the consequences and the list of the preferences would or could add to the factual presence or absence of semantic inconsistencies between them. Rational consensus on the examined norm would not *constitute* its validity, but would merely *follow* from the fact that the effects of the norm do not actually contradict any volition or preference of those concerned.

The second interpretation of "D" and "Dm" that I am going to outline avoids these difficulties. According to this alternative reading, to say that a norm is fair, impartial or just means that it has passed a generalization test conceived as the mental experiment of aggregating the foreseeable consequences and side-effects of the general observance of the norm into a synthetic and holistic image of "the way the world would look like" and then asking each and every moral actor whether the way in which things would go, the state of the world, would be such that all of us – *qua* citizens of a hypothetic world-republic – would still recognize in it the image of who we want to be, of the life that we want to lead together. To affirm that a norm is valid means, from the standpoint of a principle of generalization reinterpreted along these lines, that everyone can want to live in a world shaped, among other things, by the norm in question – that we all would still recognize this world as "our own" and not as an "alien" one.

The good news now is that under this interpretation "D" and "Dm" become genuinely dialogical or intersubjective. Insofar as they embed also a project-constitutive and "evaluative" moment concerning who we want to be, the outcome of the test really depends on the outcome of discourse. There is no way in which one could claim to know the outcome of such discourse – a discourse which, of course, could be envisaged as being conducted hypothetically or counterfactually – in the same way as one could claim to know antecedently to any real discourse whether the two lists which record the effects of a norm and of the parties' preferences are consistent with one another. While – on the first reading of "D" and "Dm" – knowing the contents of the two lists would be strictly equivalent to knowing whether they are mutually consistent, in the holistic reading of the generalization test knowing what the world would look like and knowing the preferences of people would not put us in the position of knowing whether starting from "these" preferences everyone would want to live "there," in "that" world.

The bad news, however, is that the greater plausibility of this version of the principles "D" and "Dm", as well as their truly intersubjective quality, are not without costs. By adopting it we could no longer consistently subscribe to the distinctions between the logic of moral discourse and that of ethical discourse, between the universalism of the former and the contextboundness of the latter – certainly not in the form in which Habermas understands such distinctions. To be sure, we could still distinguish between morality and ethics but this distinction would be different from the one proposed by Habermas. Moral discourse would appear as a special case of ethical discourse – namely, an instance of ethical discourse in which the congruence between a norm and "who we want to be" or "the world in which we would like to live" is examined from the standpoint of the largest collective identity that we can conceive of, namely the identity of humanity in its entirety. The object of moral discourse could no longer be sharply distinguished, from the standpoint of the question underlying it, from an ethical discourse concerning what is good for everyone, where "everyone" is understood as "every member of humanity." The validity, impartiality or fairness of a norm, according to this interpretation, would then be measured by its compatibility with our intuitions concerning the good for humankind.

One objection could be reasonably raised at this point: if we accept the fundamental point that morality and ethics are not the same, what difference does it make if we understand the moral justification of a norm as an elucidation of our intuitions concerning what is good for humanity or as that reciprocal role-taking with which Habermas equates it? What difference does it make, once the standpoint agreed on is that of the totality of human beings, if this "point of view" is called "moral" or the point of view of "the good for humanity"? In my opinion it makes a certain difference, which I would sum up in two points.

First, if moral discourse is but a special case of ethical discourse – i.e., ethical discourse about the good for humanity – then the form of rationality which proves crucial, in the last analysis, *also* for moral discourse, is that rationality of judgment or *phronesis* which Habermas has no trouble accepting as relevant when the good for a particular identity, individual or collective, is under scrutiny. Consequently the sharp distinction between the normative *cogency* of moral discourse on the one hand and the mere *appropriateness* of our intuitions concerning the good collapses.

Second, the Habermasian dichotomy which opposes the particularism of ethical judgment, always inextricably linked with a context and a concrete identity, to the universal or context-transcending quality of moral judgment, collapses. If we understand the validity of a moral norm as based on intuitions concerning the good for humanity, the context-transcending quality of moral judgment takes on a different meaning. It appears to be the result of responsiveness to a special context – the historically changing horizon of humanity in its entirety – which, among other things, has the unique property of being the largest conceivable context – one which cannot further be included into any broader context. The so-called "view from nowhere" reveals to be indeed a view "from somewhere." For the standpoint of the good for humankind changes. It is not a formula, an abstract principle of reciprocity or consistency, but a horizon of shared meanings that changes historically. It was substantively different in the era before nuclear weapons, in the era when the total aggregate output of the production processes still posed a limited threat to the integrity of the natural environment, or when science was in no position to interfere with genetic processes, or in the time when population growth posed no threat to the survival of the species. The moral point of view, understood as the standpoint of the good for humanity, remains anchored in history and experience, even if in a history and a collective experience incomparably larger in scope than any other. The qualitative distinction drawn by Habermas between justice and the good from this perspective becomes only a difference of degree, of scope.

To sum up, Habermas's discursive approach to morality remains one of the most important contemporary contributions to moral theory, and Habermas must be also credited with having succeeded in differentiating his original intuition in such a way as to form a dynamic framework capable of encompassing and integrating all the aspects of the practical sphere – from distributive justice to politics, from law to the notion of the good life – without betraying the deontological, cognitivistic, and procedural inspiration which informed his initial project. The suspicion remains, however, that the keystone on which the solidity of the entire construction rests – the dialogical reformulation of the Kantian test of generalization – might itself be less firm than Habermas would have us think. In fact if the distinction between morality and ethics rests on the ambiguity of the principle of universalization formulated by Habermas – a principle which exploits the respective strong points of two incompatible ways of conceiving the test – there is cause for alarm. The further clarification of the meaning of such a test seems then to constitute an urgent task.

NOTES

1   Cf. Jürgen Habermas, *"Morality and Ethical Life: Does Hegel's Critique of Kant Apply to Discourse Ethics?"* in J. Habermas, *Moral Consciousness and Communicative Action* (Cambridge, Mass.: MIT Press, 1990).

2   Cf. ibid., pp. 196–8.

3   J. Habermas, *Moral Consciousness and Communicative Action* (Cambridge, Mass.: MIT Press, 1990).

4   J. Habermas, *Faktizität und Geltung. Beiträge zur Diskurstheorie des Rechts und des demokratischen Rechtstaats* (Frankfurt: Suhrkamp, 1992). English translation, *Between Facts and Norms: Contributions to a Discourse Theory of Law and Democracy* (Cambridge Mass.: MIT Press, 1996).

5   See J. Habermas, "Wahrheitstheorien," in *Vorstudien und Ergänzungen zur Theorie des kommunikativen Handelns* (Frankfurt: Suhrkamp, 1984), pp. 127–83; *Legitimation Crisis* (Boston: Beacon Press, 1975) and *Communication and the Evolution of Society* (Boston: Beacon Press, 1979).

6   See J. Habermas, "A Reply to my Critics," in J. B. Thompson and D. Held (eds), *Habermas. Critical Debates* (London: Macmillan, 1982); and "Discourse Ethics," "Moral Consciousness and Communicative Action," in *Moral Consciousness and Communicative Action*; and "Was macht eine Lebensform rational?", in J. Habermas, Erläuterungen zur Diskursethik (Frankfurt: Suhrkamp, 1991; finally, see J. Habermas, *The Philosophical Discourse of Modernity* (Cambridge, Mass.: MIT Press, 1987).

7   J. Habermas, *Moral Consciousness and Communicative Action*, p. 65.

8   See ibid., p. 93.

9   See ibid., p. 108.

10   Ibid.

11   See Albrecht Wellmer, "Ethics and Dialogue," in Albrecht Wellmer, *The Persistence of Modernity. Essays on Aesthetics, Ethics and Postmodernism* (Cambridge, Mass.: MIT Press, 1991), p. 182.

12   See ibid., pp. 155–7.

13   See ibid., pp. 201–2. For similar considerations, though developed in a different vocabulary, see T. M. Scanlon, "Contractualism and Utilitarianism," in Amartya Sen and Bernard Williams (eds), *Utilitarianism and Beyond* (Cambridge: Cambridge University Press, 1982), pp. 103–28, and Thomas Nagel, *Equality and Partiality* (New York: Oxford University Press, 1991), pp. 36–7.

14   See Albrecht Wellmer, "Ethics and Dialogue," pp. 188–95.

15   Ibid., pp. 121–2.

16   See Jürgen Habermas, *Justification and Application. Remarks on Discourse Ethics* (Cambridge, Mass.: MIT Press, 1993) and "Law and Morality: Two Lectures," in S. McMurrin (ed.), *The Tanner Lectures on Human Values*, Vol. 8 (Salt Lake City: University of Utah Press, 1988).

17   Cf. Jürgen Habermas, *Faktizität und Geltung*, pp. 204–5.

18   See Habermas, *Justification and Application*.

19   This Howison Lecture is published as J. Habermas, "On the Pragmatic, the Ethical, and the Moral Employments of Public Reason," in J. Habermas, *Justification and Application*.

20   Between the ethical sphere and the moral point of view proper we find an intermediate area of "concrete universalism" – the universalism of the Golden Rule. The Golden Rule already represents a *moral* principle, in that it enjoins the actor to take the good for others in the same consideration as the good for herself, but still contains an egocentric residue in that the acceptability of the generalized maxim is still assessed with reference to what is acceptable to "me" and not to what is acceptable to "everyone else."

21   See J. Habermas, Faktizität und Geltung, p. 200.

22   Ibid., p. 128.

23   It must be said that the definitions provided by Habermas do not always give us a clear

or uncontroversial indication as to how to assign a given practical problem to a specific subdomain. For an example of Habermas's own way of sorting problems of collective will-formation under the two rubrics of moral and ethical discourse, see ibid., p. 204.

24   Ibid., p. 138 (German).
25   Ibid., p. 200 (German).

6   JUSTICE, REASON, AND CRITIQUE: BASIC CONCEPTS OF CRITICAL THEORY

Rainer Forst

The concepts of justice, reason, and critique pose a dilemma for a contemporary theory of social criticism. On the one hand, there is an immanent connection between them, for critique speaks in the name of reason and justice: social institutions or practices are criticized as being "unjust," judged through an appeal to "reasonable" standards. On the other hand, "justice" and especially "reason," which once used to be the weapons of critical thought, have become its targets. Not only has the conviction been lost that we could have a determinate and universally valid idea of these concepts; in addition, they themselves, in their specific modern form, are now suspected of being part of the very structures of thought and practice at which critique is aimed. Thus we find ourselves in the dilemma that we can neither rely on these concepts, nor do without them. In the following I suggest a way of avoiding this dilemma by reconstructing a positive connection between these concepts on the basis of an analysis of the normative claims of social criticism and the standards of reasonable justification it implies – that is, of the *reasons* that could *justify* social relations as *reasonable* and *just*.

The development of Critical Theory by the so-called "Frankfurt School" – primarily in the writings of Max Horkheimer and Theodor W. Adorno – serves as the starting point for my discussion. For it is here that one witnesses the turn from a theory of critique with a belief in "reason in history" to a radical critique of reason as "instrumental" and justice as dominated by the principle of (false) identity. Against that background the theories of Jürgen Habermas and Michael Walzer are analysed as two contemporary attempts to re-establish the possibility of a critical social theory (Habermas) or a theory of social criticism (Walzer), each of which tries to avoid the problems of Critical Theory (before as well as after its "turn"), yet suggests very different notions of reason and justice. Two main problems emerge: to what extent can reason be understood as "disconnected" from social contexts, and how is a concept of justice possible that does not sacrifice irreducible differences to general principles?

In the course of a discussion of the notions of critique (I), of reason as implied by (even immanent) critique (II), and of the consequences for a theory of justice (III), I attempt to show that it is possible to understand reason and justice as "situated," yet critical and transcendent with regard to concrete contexts, and to reformulate the idea of a "reasonable" and "just" reconciliation of individual particularity and universality so as to provide the grounds for a critical theory of justice.

I CRITIQUE

The critical theory of society designed by Horkheimer in the program for the Institute for Social Research in Frankfurt in the thirties had at its core the idea of an interdisciplinary theory of social developments and institutions guided by the philosophical ideal of contributing to the realization of a "reasonable social order," in fact to the realization of reason in history – an ideal that was, despite Horkheimer's materialist version, a heritage of German idealism.[1] This early version of critical theory followed Marx's notion of immanent critique: the critical standpoint was not a "dogmatic" standpoint beyond material and historical reality but a standpoint within that reality pointing out the contradictions inherent in it. As Marx wrote in 1843: "Reason has always existed, but not always in a rational form. The critic can therefore begin with any form of the theoretical and practical consciousness and develop, out of the forms *inherent* in existing actuality, that true reality which is existing actuality's ought-to-be and final aim."[2] Critique exposes the contradiction between social reality and the idealized understanding a society has of itself – yet as a "critique of political economy" this contradiction is further unmasked as a necessary one given the capitalist mode of production. A critical theory of this kind does not just criticize the existing society by its own standards; it also shows that the contradiction between bourgeois reality and the ideals of bourgeois society can only be overcome by changing its mode of production and creating a "rational" society. Humans as "species beings" would for the first time be the subjects, not the objects of history: communism, Marx says in 1844, "is the solved riddle of history,"[3] the realization of philosophy. Correspondingly, Horkheimer explains: "If we take seriously the ideas by which the bourgeoisie explains its own order – free exchange, free competition, harmony of interests, and so on – and if we follow them to their logical conclusion, they manifest their inner contradiction and therewith their real opposition to the bourgeois order."[4]

According to Horkheimer, Critical Theory is part of the "unfinished dialectics" of capitalist society; it is part of the social struggle for an emancipated, "rational" society. Its truth is at the same time a truth within history, bound to history, and a truth about history, based on a Marxist theory taken for granted by Horkheimer.[5] That critique is part of the struggle for the abolition of class domination does not, however, mean that its truth depends on historical success. Conceptual necessity does not imply historical necessity; in the programmatic essay on "Traditional and Critical Theory" (1937) Horkheimer defends Critical Theory even though it can not claim to speak for an existing class consciousness that justifies the hope for an end to the "darkest barbarity" of the present.

While this conception of Critical Theory holds onto the ideals of bourgeois society – even against this society – on the basis of a Marxist philosophy of history, Horkheimer and Adorno later criticized both these ideals and this philosophy of history. At the time they wrote the *Dialectic of Enlightenment* they questioned the idea of a reason in history that calls for an emancipated state of social organization in which the human species being truly would be its own subject, freed from natural as well as social domination. In the "totally administered society" they saw unfolding in every area of psychological, cultural, economic and political life, critique could only be total as well, questioning its own means of knowledge and its own standards of judgment. For a theory that saw reason and history as dialectically intertwined, the triumph of Nazism and Stalinism as the only alternatives to capitalism left neither the philosophical ideal nor the scientific means of that theoretical program intact.[6] The very basis of their idea of history – human beings emancipating themselves through labor (including the overcoming of the contradiction inherent in the capitalist process of production) – now seemed suspect to them: could it be that reason itself, in its attempt to dominate nature, had become, or had always been, an instrument of domination, not of liberation? It seemed that the only remaining possibility was a radical critique of "instrumental reason" and the hope for a "leap" into a different history, redeeming the lost hope of humanity.[7] As the alternative to a positive philosophy of history, only a negative philosophy seemed possible. Dialectical thought, bereft of its basis in history and society, became "negative dialectics" – a critique from the utopian standpoint of negative thought without a positive-utopian ideal of the just or rational society. It was primarily Adorno who drew this consequence; he had always been more skeptical than Horkheimer (and Marcuse) about the emancipatory potentials of modern society, because of its subsumption of cultural phenomena and thought itself under the rule of the principle of identity and exchange.

For the question of the possibility of a critical theory of society, this conclusion suffers from three central problems. First, the epistemological status of theory becomes questionable, for there seems to be no mode of systematic theoretical thought that does not subsume the "nonidentical" under the logic of identity. Second, the practical problem of an addressee of critique is left open: for whom and to whom does the critic speak once it is assumed that the logic of identity deafens the ears of those who suffer from this logic?

Third, the normative standards of critique are indeterminate: what does the critic appeal to, once the concepts of "reason" or "justice" have themselves become suspect? It seems that the failure of positive dialectics, and its transformation into negative dialectics – and, with this, the negativistic version of immanent critique and "determinate negation" – results from the idea that society is *either* determined by the central antagonism inherent in the mode of production *or* that it is "one-dimensional," i.e., lacking the contradictions, social struggles, and opposition which would require, and permit, a critical theory on behalf of those social forces whose claims can be defended on the basis of a theory of reason in history.

The reasons for this "either-or" have been analysed as stemming from the paradigm of the philosophy of the subject, a subject who appropriates objects, especially nature, liberating itself in that process (Marx) – or, as it were, ensnaring itself in the traps of "instrumental reason." This mode of thought leaves no conceptual room for the notion of "communicative rationality," a form of rationality that has a basis in everyday social life, or for the (diverse) norms and values that lie at the center of social struggles and that do not necessarily fit into the Marxist version of class struggle.[8]

Both the theories of Jürgen Habermas and of Michael Walzer can be read as answers to the three problems mentioned above. Both suggest a view of social integration (at least in part) based on shared norms, and oppose the idea of a totally administered society; both want to place social criticism within the normative contexts of a specific society. And yet their theories are very different. While Habermas's *Theory of Communicative Action* presents a critical theory that unites normative criticism with historical and social scientific reflections about the genesis of modern forms of life and thought, Walzer has proposed a theory of social criticism which he exemplifies through an interpretation of some social critics in the twentieth century, as well as through his own practice of criticizing American society, for instance, in *Spheres of Justice*. How is critique possible in their views, what are the tasks of the critic, and what are the normative standards of criticism?

Habermas's notion of Critical Theory shifts from a critique of the relations of production to a critique of the relations of communication; he questions the traditional Marxist conception of material reality as unfolding itself through the labor of the species being and suggests a different reading of the "rationalization" of the modern world. This reading follows Weber and Parsons rather than Horkheimer and Adorno who, according to Habermas, underestimated the extent to which modernity entails progress towards more rational forms of knowledge (science), law and morality, and art. The basis for the foundation of critique in a theory of communication is the idea that inherent in language lies the ideal of mutual understanding "without force," i.e., of "undistorted communication": "Reaching understanding [*Verständigung*] is the inherent telos of human speech."[9] Within a given society, it is the task of critique to identify the structures and forces that hinder the development of forms of mutual communication: critical theory is guided by an "interest" in emancipation, conceived as the enablement of reciprocal interaction in the life of the individual as well as of society as a whole (ego-development being dependent upon possibilities of reciprocal communication). This move allows Habermas (a) to ground critique in a theory of communication that is not dependent upon a philosophy of history, and (b) to work out a theory of modern society in which the two paradigmatic forms of rationality and action – communicative vs. purposive rationality and strategic action – correspond primarily (not exclusively) to two modes of social integration and communication: in the normatively integrated "lifeworld" persons communicate via the medium of speech directed towards reaching understanding; in the "systems" of state bureaucracy and economy, power and money are the dominant means of integration and communication. Critical theory then identifies – in a "critique of functionalist reason"[10] – the extent to which the "imperatives" of the system "colonize" the structures of the lifeworld and lead to a loss of social integration and communicative autonomy, whereby the latter refers to the capacity of social actors to determine their individual and collective lives according to their ideas of the good, and not according to the imperatives of the market or bureaucratic norms. The analysis of a one-sided rationalization of the lifeworld is the task of social science; yet critique has a necessary practical side when it is connected to the claims made by social groups protesting against the intrusion of system imperatives into communicatively structured realms – in fact, Habermas claims, the theory itself is in a certain sense a product of these social developments.[11] However, critique is not just committed to preserving a communicative lifeworld against intrusions by economic and administrative structures; rather, it aims at the enlargement of the "influence" of "communicative power" in political institutions.[12]

The concepts of communicative rationality and autonomy do not serve as the basis for the ideal of a self-transparent society, conceived as a self-governing macro-subject, but are used as analytic tools for different spheres of integration and action in a complex society. Nonetheless, the drawing of the legitimate border between "system" and "lifeworld" must be done in a communicative way; i.e., the mediation between systemic and normative imperatives must proceed on the basis of generally acceptable reasons (taking social complexity into account). Thus what is needed here is not just a *public sphere* of social actors[13] – this forms the political center of "civil society" – but also the *law* as the result of deliberative procedures of argumentation and will-formation that "translates" normative arguments and social values into a language that is generally binding as well as intelligible to systemic structures.[14] Law – legitimated by reasons generated in the public domain and received and "filtered" in political institutions – builds the bridge between the language of the lifeworld and the claims of different social actors, on one hand, and the "codes" of economic and bureaucratic institutions on the other (thus also, to a certain degree, influencing and changing these institutions, which are themselves regulated by legal norms). There is no "meta-discourse" beyond the multiple social and political spheres and institutions, but there is the requirement that *any* social arrangement must in principle be justifiable to all those affected. If the possibilities of an internal democratization of economic and bureaucratic systems are limited – and these limits are open to dispute – the boundaries between economic and bureaucratic power and other social interests and values still need to be drawn in a democratic way. The critical standard of communicative rationality then plays a double role: it is used to analyse the-structure of the lifeworld vs. the system and possible phenomena of "colonization," and it is the basis of the normative idea that social relations must in general be criticizable and justifiable in a discourse among free and equal participants – an idea that needs to be transposed into a theory of democracy and political (as well as social) *justice* according to which there are no social "imperatives" beyond justification.

The requirements of generality, openness and reciprocity, presupposed, for example, by a discourse among each and every person affected by a general norm that claims to be valid, correspond to the counterfactual idea of an "ideal speech situation"; this idea, however, is just a formal idealization of the conditions of reaching understanding and has no substantive implications apart from the requirement that discourses should always be kept open for further perspectives, arguments, and reasons (a point I will return to in section II). Thus it does not displace argumentation from concrete contexts, it merely leaves, so to speak, a door open for further criticism. It is not a picture of what democratic discourse or social life as such should or could look like: "What can be outlined normatively are the necessary but general conditions for the communicative practice of everyday life and for a procedure of discursive will-formation that would put participants *themselves* in a position to develop concrete possibilities for a better and less threatened life, on their own initiative and in accordance with *their own* needs and insights."[15]

As *normative theory*, Critical Theory thus argues for the integrity of a sphere of communicative, normative integration as well as for the realization of the possibility of social and political discourse; as *social-scientific theory*, it explains the factors and structures that impair the communicative social infrastructure and that hinder discourse (e.g., by the exclusion of actors from political argumentation and decision making);[16] and as *participant* in social struggles, it argues for those norms and institutions that can be defended to all those who are "subjects" of these norms and institutions. As normative theory, it claims the fallible truth of a reconstruction of the presuppositions of communicative action; as social-scientific theory, it is open to theoretical debate and revision; as participant in discourse, it is one participant among all others. A critical social theory in that sense is not just a theory *about* society, it is also one *within* society: its critical normative claims are valid if they are "reasonable" in the sense of being reciprocally and generally justifiable, i.e., with reasons that are undeniable as arguments *for* the establishment of institutions that make communicative autonomy possible, and as arguments *within* a discourse among social actors recognized as free and equal. On this basis, taking Habermas's theory one step further the possibility of constructing a theory of social justice arises that – minimally – argues for a distribution of the social resources necessary for the reproduction (and development) of lifeworld structures as well as of the establishment of fair political practices, and that – maximally – argues that any non-equal distribution of resources must still be generally and reciprocally justifiable (I will come back to this in section III).

Of the many questions this short and very general discussion of Habermas's theory leaves open, I want to focus on the following one, which is crucial for a theory of social criticism: can a theory guided by this kind of normative ideal really be "connected" with the specific practices, institutions, and self-understandings of a given society? Can it build a bridge to the experiences and values of particular social actors, as Habermas would like to think? Contrasting Habermas's theory with Michael Walzer's conception of social criticism can help to find an answer to this problem.

In the eyes of Walzer, the normative idea of unrestricted discourse and the formal concept of communicative rationality are not compatible with a notion of immanent criticism that cannot but be part of the social and historical processes it criticizes. For Walzer, critique is a social practice within particular normative contexts; the critic speaks the language of his or her society in accepting social standards of rationality and the normative ideals inherent in that society. The contradictions the critic points out are differences between accepted social norms and current social practices. Following Gramsci, Walzer asserts that "what makes criticism a permanent possibility . . . is the fact that every ruling class is compelled to present itself as a universal class."[17] The "connected critic" does not have to be loyal to the community he criticizes for the reason that he wants to be heard and taken seriously – that would be a functionalist argument; rather, Walzer claims that criticism runs the risk of becoming blind to the needs and values of communities when it is detached from a specific social context. The Bolshevik leaders are the example Walzer cites: they tried to model their society according to what they thought were scientifically authoritative principles, yet they failed to connect their ideas with the values held in their society and with the historical conditions of their country. There is no standpoint from which the critic can call the existing consciousness of her addressees "false"; if she does not succeed in connecting her arguments with their existing consciousness, she is a bad social critic.[18]

Methodologically, the important point about Walzer's theory of social criticism is that it relies neither on a specific reading of history and the human potential developing in it nor on a universal idea of reason: rather, criticism is localized and contextualized. Thus he is critical of the "older" Frankfurt School as well as of Habermas's version of Critical Theory. For, following Raymond Geuss,[19] he criticizes Habermas's notion of an "ideal speech situation" as detached from "actual debate" – as a "dream of a community of reason," to use a phrase of Bernard Williams,[20] removed from "real talk" in order to guarantee an ideal consensus on those principles the Platonic philosopher thinks right.[21] Ideal speech serves for the "invention" of norms that are detached from social contexts. Real discourse, according to Walzer, "is always inconclusive; it has no authoritative moments" – philosophy and truth are one thing, democracy and debate another.[22]

By using Walzer's own method of immanent critique one can, however, show in how far his critique of Habermas is a misunderstanding of the idea of "ideal" speech. For once we accept that Walzer's theory of criticism does not rest either upon a teleological idea of reason in history or upon an "ideal" notion of reason, we are left with the only "banister" (to use a phrase of Hannah Arendt) of critique he suggests: the moral self-understanding of specific communities. But then we may ask: *why* should one appeal to immanent standards (a), *when* can one appeal to them (b), and *what* is the *criterion* for a morally "right" interpretation of these principles (c)?[23]

As an answer to (a) it seems that Walzer wants to say that the loyal and connected critic thinks he should criticize his community for its own sake, because he wants the community to live up to its own standards, or to what he thinks these standards truly entail. Yet that is only half of the story, for Walzer says that criticism starts as an opposition to forms of oppression and subjugation: hence the critic takes the side of the oppressed, of the *victims* of a community. True, the community will respond to critique more receptively if they regard the critic as "one of their own," so to speak, but that plays a secondary role; primary is his defense of the victims of "injustice." That becomes clear in one of Walzer's favorite examples, Breyten Breytenbach, the South African poet. For it is obvious that the "injustice" of the society Breytenbach wants to overcome stems from his recognition of, as Walzer himself says, the "universal value in opposing oppression,"[24] and furthermore the main reason for accepting his identity as an "Afrikaner" is a negative loyalty, the acceptance of the responsibility of his people for its history of oppressing the black population. Being "prepared to share its shame," he is an Afrikaner, but criticizing his people harshly he can at the same time say "I am not an Afrikaner."[25] True, Breytenbach tries to give a "sense-making interpretation" of the "social realities" of his country, and he tries to appeal to moral "aspirations" within his own community; but there can be no doubt that he speaks in favor of universal moral values, of human rights that *should* be realized in his country – on behalf of those who hitherto did not fully belong to the South African community. We could speak here not just of a "connected," but of a "connecting" critic: he or she tries to connect shared understandings with universal moral norms.

This example shows that the answer to (b) – when can one appeal to immanent values? – cannot do without certain moral standards that *every* society must live up to: it must accept a "minimal and universal moral code" of human respect. Every person at least deserves the shelter of a simple hotel room – a moral standard that must not be violated by all those historically grown "moral homes" communities inhabit.[26] This idea of moral rights forms the basis of Walzer's "contextualized universalism," as I would call it; "reiterative universalism" or "moral minimalism" are his words. It also plays a crucial role in his theory of the "just war."[27] Walzer makes no "foundational" claim that these moral rights are inherent in reason: yet he is convinced that a "moral minimum" of respect for persons is a universal moral fact regarded in almost every human society. Whatever the particular outlook of a society is, criticism of it is justified when it violates these basic moral rules. Seen the other way round, this implies that only those standards of a society can serve as the basis of critique that do not violate these moral precepts.[28] This is an *external* criterion for the validity of critical standards that serves as the basis for moral criticism of a society's treatment of "strangers" as well as of "members."

But there is also an *internal* criterion for the standards the critic can appeal to: they must be *shared*, i.e., they must be justifiable in the general interest of the society without exclusion. For otherwise the critic would just replace the values of one ruling class with that of another that wants to rule. Thus the critic must appeal to the general values which the rulers fail to live up to. The contradiction between practice and principle is used by the critic to show that the principles that supposedly serve the general interest in fact serve particular interests. The standards of critique may be local with respect to a society – with the qualification of the external criterion of basic rights – yet they must still be general, or, as Walzer puts it, following Thomas Scanlon, "not reasonable to reject," i.e., generally justifiable.[29] If one appeals to "shared understandings" in the name of the general good, then these understandings must, if questioned, be generally justifiable and really be shared. One possible form of social criticism thus is not primarily directed at institutions but at the norms that fall short of these two (internal and external) criteria.[30] The critic then does not criticize institutions in the light of shared understandings, but these understandings themselves.

That leads to the answer to (c). If the critic suggests a specific practical interpretation of (externally and internally justifiable) principles, then what is the criterion for right and valid criticism? What social critics question in that case is the "fit" between social practices and the norms used to justify them: critique exposes the exclusion and domination within practices that belie that fit. "The critic starts, say, from the views of justice embedded in the covenantal code or from the bourgeois idea of freedom, on the assumption that what is actual in consciousness is possible in practice, and then he challenges the practices that fall short of these possibilities."[31] To be sure: these "views of justice" are the right standards of critique because they conform to a universal code of human rights and because they are shared and accepted within a society as expressing the general interest – *only* then can the critic point to social phenomena that cannot be justified in terms of these shared norms of justice, i.e., that cannot generally be justified. The critic appeals to the general public for the sake of those who only ideally, but not in practice, belong to that public. Hence the standard of critique is what is generally justifiable to *all* the members of a community without the exclusion of some; and hence valid criticism must in principle be non-rejectable by a general, nonexclusive social consensus. That, however, does not mean that there can be no valid criticism unless a general consensus on the reinterpretation of that "fit" has been reached. Rather, the critical argument that existing institutions falsely claim to be generally justified is put forward by a group that finds itself excluded from that "generality";[32] and this criticism is valid until the defense of actual practices can show that they can be justified reciprocally to everybody including those who raised their criticism. The burden of proof shifts to those who argue that the critics have in fact no real claim.

We find the deeper reason for Walzer's insistence on immanent criticism (including his critique of decontextualized ideas of reason and justice) in the general idea that human beings are "culture-producing creatures" inhabiting very different social and moral worlds, yet having the same "rights of reiteration": "the right to act autonomously and the right to form attachments in accordance with a particular understanding of the good life."[33] These rights are individual as well as collective; every commonly created world needs to be freely accepted by its members as their creation: "The theory of social construction implies (some sort of) human agency and requires the recognition of women and men as agents (of some sort). We might say, looking at the idea itself as something we have made, that the construction of social-construction-with-human-agents has certain moral entailments. Among these is the right of subjective nullification, the right of the agents to refuse any given object status – as commodities, 'hands', slaves, or whatever."[34] Criticism is directed against social relations that cannot be justified to every moral agent within a given community by standards that he or she can freely accept (or, put negatively, not reciprocally deny to others) – this is the implicit principle of criticism that Walzer affirms, and its differences to Habermas's theory are differences of emphasis, not in structure. For as long as internal criticism can only appeal to those social norms that can be shared, its vindication can only be general consensus. Within the "thick" contexts of social values, we detect a universal principle that – to express it dialectically – is sensitive to contexts precisely because it is formal and can be "reiterated" in all these contexts with different contents. The difference in emphasis is that Habermas stresses the universality of the conditions of a justified social consensus, while Walzer emphasizes the need to contextualize the normative content of what can generally be justified. Yet both insist on certain standards of human moral agency that cannot be violated with good reasons.

To this extent, the difference between "contextualist" and "universalist" criticism that, for example, Geuss explains by counterposing Adorno's notion of immanent critique and Habermas's idea of ideal speech, collapses. According to Geuss, "a critical theory is addressed to the members of *this* particular social group in the sense that it describes *their* epistemic principles and *their* ideal of the 'good life' and demonstrates that some belief they hold is reflectively unacceptable for agents who hold their epistemic principles and a source of frustration for agents who are trying to realize this particular kind of 'good life'."[35] If that is the principle of internal criticism, as Geuss suggests, he can counterpose it to Habermas's view only because he interprets Habermas's insistence on a universal notion of idealized presuppositions of social consensus not as a formal but as a substantive idealization. On the contrary, however, what is consensually justified by agents in contexts is not preconditioned by the idea of ideal speech; the latter merely explicates what it means – in a formal sense – to speak of a consensus that can claim to be legitimate, i.e., that can claim to have resulted from an argumentative procedure without delusion, exclusion, or pressure. Obviously, it is "the agents themselves" who "must be the final judges of whether or not they are being coerced and whether or not they are free,"[36] as Geuss asserts, but that "must" is grounded in a principle of free and equal justification of generally binding norms that conforms to Habermas's idea of "uncoerced consensus." The participants do not leave their contexts for a transcendental heaven of ideal speech; yet as participants they must have equal opportunities to question the claims of norms and practices of being in the general interest. That is the idea of justification on which "immanent criticism" rests – an idea of *reasonable* justification, of reciprocal and general justification *with reasons* acceptable to the "interpretive community" without exception.[37] Hence if we inquire about the notion of "reasons" implied by social criticism (the reasons for criticizing a society in the first place and the reasons that count as good reasons in critical argumentation), we find a conception of *reason* inherent in critique.

II   REASON

I consider this conception of reason – according to which generally binding norms have to be reciprocally and generally justifiable – to inhere in the idea of a critical theory.[38] Reason has to be understood in a formal sense, leaving room for the content to be given by the participants in social contexts but making sure that the general normative claims of what is considered "just" or "reasonable" are in fact justified, i.e., are in the general interest. "Reason" refers to the idea of a reasonable, uncoerced compatibility – or "rational identity" (Adorno) – of the individual (or particular) and the general: and it is the critical task to find modes of thought and action that succeed in bringing about this connection. That means that nothing can count as reasonable that cannot be justified *generally* as well as reciprocally to *every single agent*. Critique then is the medium of "reconciling" the individual and the general without subsuming the individual under false generalities. This central idea unites the concepts of *critique, reason* and *justice*: the idea of uncoerced generality that does justice to singularity. In the following I will try to outline this notion of reason which has its roots in German idealism, especially in Kant's philosophy of the critique of reason through reason.

The notion of reason as the quest for general principles can in a certain sense be found in older Critical Theory, whose idea of a "rational" organization of society was guided by the materialist vision of an organization of labor that would liberate human beings by making them the subjects, not the objects, of the process of production. This rational society would be one in which the "particular interests and the needs of the generality" would "necessarily intersect," in which "the individual" would be part of the "rational organization of the social whole."[39] These passages of an early discussion of Kant by Horkheimer, as well as the following passage on Kant in the *Dialectic of Enlightenment*, reveal the extent to which his materialist idea of reason in history was indebted to the idea of the "reasonable" as that which can be generally justified, i.e., justified to every individual as the nonrepressed part of generality: "As the transcendental, supraindividual self, reason comprises the idea of a free, human social life in which men organize themselves as the universal subject and overcome the conflict between pure and empirical reason in the conscious solidarity of the whole. This represents the idea of true universality: utopia."[40] This idea of reason – as the uncoerced integration of the individual and the whole – lies at the basis of the critique of society and constitutes the formal kernel of the dialectical view of reason unfolding itself in history – or better: which should unfold itself in history.[41]

Horkheimer's and Adorno's arrival at the conclusion that the idea of reason, once a concept used by critique, had become a means of domination, was a result of their view that the emancipatory potential of reason could only unfold itself materially through the labor of the species being of humanity, mastering nature and creating a society in which the process of production would be a conscious collective deed by all subjects. If, so they thought following Hegel and Marx rather than Kant, reason could become practical at all, then it would be only through the realization of a rational society, i.e., one without class domination. In the end of the thirties, however, they found that the increased development of the forces of production led to an ever increasing domination of nature without at the same time liberating human subjects. In fact, the "instrumental reason" employed for the domination of nature became an instrument for the domination of human beings as well; and the conclusion they drew from this development was a radical questioning of the very concept of reason and its attempt to dominate by subsuming individuals and singularity under the principle of identity and generality. Reason seemed to be an instrument for conceptual *and* practical domination. This is why, following their reference to the utopian idea of "true generality" and reason cited above, they assert: "At the same time, however, reason constitutes the authority [*Instanz*] of calculating thought, which adjusts [*zurichten*] the world for the ends of self-preservation and recognizes no function other than the preparation of the object from mere sensory material in order to make it the material of subjugation. The true nature of schematism, which reconciles the general and the particular, concept and individual case from the outside, is ultimately revealed in contemporary science as the interest of industrial society. Being is apprehended under the aspect of manufacture and administration. Everything – even the human individual, not to speak of the animal – is converted into the repeatable, replaceable process, into a mere example for the conceptual models of the system."[42] Reason – identity thinking – in both its Kantian and Hegelian form had revealed its inherent affinity to the system of exchange, which does not value singularity but subsumes everything under fixed categories.

The *Dialectic of Enlightenment* and Horkheimer's *Critique of Instrumental Reason* were the diagnosis of this failure of modern culture; while Adorno's *Negative Dialectics* was the philosophic consequence. In fact, it is again a critique of reason through reason, but a negative one: its own idea of a non-repressive relation between the singular and the general could no longer be thought of in terms of the compromised concept of "reason." Yet negative dialectics continues to fulfil the task of critical reason: criticizing false generalities and "saving" the particular, calling for a synthesis that does not violate the specific, the "non-identical." "Dialectics unfolds the difference between the particular and the universal, dictated by the universal. As it – being the break between subject and object brought to mind – is inescapable for the subject, furrowing whatever the subject thinks, even objectively, it would come to an end in reconciliation. Reconciliation would release the nonidentical, would rid it even of spiritualised coercion; it would open up the multiplicity of the different [*die Vielheit des Verschiedenen*] over which dialectics had no longer any power. Reconciliation would be the thought of the many as no longer inimical, a thought that is anathema to subjective reason . . . None of the reconciliations claimed by absolute idealism – and no other kind remained consistent – has stood up, from the logical to the political-historical."[43] Adorno thinks that reason as identity thinking betrayed the particular, the nonidentical, in the name of false reconciliation. Negative dialectics breaks with that false unity without claiming to build a new one. It starts from the suffering of the particular: "The need to lend a voice to suffering is a condition of all truth" (*Negative Dialectics*, p. 17). Against the violence of conceptual and identifying thought, and the violence of "blackmailed reconciliation" in practice, negative dialectics is solidarity with victims whose pain resists conceptualization. The utopia of thought and of practice – both domains being dialectically intertwined – would be real reconciliation: "The reconciled condition would not annex the alien in a kind of philosophical imperialism; instead, its happiness would lie in the fact that the alien, in the proximity it is granted, remains what is distant and different, beyond the heterogeneous and that which is one's own" (*Negative Dialectics*, p. 191). These sentences express visions of subject–object relations that are at the same time visions of social[44] and individual life free – or freer – from the force of identity, though not without identity, for then the idea of difference would lose its meaning. In fact there are passages in *Negative Dialectics* in which we find a positive notion of identity, sentences that remind one of the older Critical Theory: "The critique of the principle of exchange as the identifying principle of thought wants that this ideal of free and just exchange – up until today only a pretext – will be realized. . . . If no man had part of his labor withheld from him any more, rational identity would have been reached, and society would have transcended the identifying mode of thinking" (*Negative Dialectics*, 147).[45] There still is the possibility of a positive idea of reasonable reconciliation – although a possibility that constantly falls prey to Adorno's paradoxical, radical critique of that concept.[46]

Nonetheless, some characteristics of such an idea can be extracted. First, it should enable a noncoercive reconciliation of the nonidentical and the identical, of the singular and the general, the individual and the collective; second, it has to be sensitive to the victims of social domination, it has to give their suffering a voice, enable them to speak against the identity and totality of "closed" systems; third, it remains committed to the idea of general validity by general consensus, yet this "rational identity" must be achieved through a process that ensures that individual voices are not silenced; it should "lend a voice to suffering." Hence reason must be context-sensitive and at the same time strive towards true generality and reconciliation without force or power; it must be constantly self-critical in relation to its own generalizations and speak against false claims to totality and identity. As Adorno says: "Reciprocal criticism of the universal and of the particular; identifying acts of judgment whether the concept does justice to what it covers, and whether the particular fulfills its concept – these constitute the medium of thinking about the nonidentity of particular and concept" (*Negative Dialectics*, p. 146).[47] The central aim of reason is to find a reasonable unity based on reasons that are generally justifiable.

According to Habermas, only the postmetaphysical concept of communicative reason can satisfy these demands. On the one hand it is local: situated within everyday contexts of communicative action in which speakers raise certain validity claims with specific contents. But on the other hand the conditions of the "redemption" of these validity claims as "true" or morally "right" (depending on the kind of validity claim raised) transcend the contexts in which they are raised: validity must be "generally justifiable validity" – and this excludes the restriction of possible counter-arguments to a specific community of argumentation. The "ideal communication community," to use a phrase of Karl-Otto Apel,[48] does not invalidate specific communal contexts, but it denies them the right to restrict what can count as "true" or morally "right" to what they think true and right should mean. In the context of social criticism this means that all those affected by norms claiming general validity should have equal chances of participation in a legitimation-discourse. This, however, is only true for norms with a *general* form, not for "ethical" values that only claim to be valid for "me" as the person I am or for "us" as the particular community we are.[49] Only those validity claims are context-transcendent that claim to be so; yet even if some restrict themselves to particular "ways of life," one can still question whether all members of that way of life can agree and, furthermore, whether there are others affected by that life-form that need to be taken into account. It is a principle of reason that the possibility of better counter-arguments must always be kept open. As Habermas puts it: "The ideal moment of unconditionality is deeply rooted in factual processes of understanding because validity claims are Janus faced: as universal, they outstrip every given context; at the same time, they must be raised and gain acceptance here and now if they are to sustain an agreement capable of coordinating action."[50]

Communicative reason seeks to establish "the unity of reason in the diversity of its voices";[51] in being formal it leaves the content of what can be justified as reasonable to the contexts in which validity claims are being raised, yet this formality denies the possibility of drawing final boundaries as to what can count as "reasonable": reason has to keep itself open for critique.[52] This is the meaning of the "idealized" notions of truth and rightness Habermas insists on. It does not mean that there is no truth or rightness except in a transcendental heaven of ideal speakers, it just places principled doubt over all claims to have found the final answer to what is true or just. This reveals how much this notion of reason is indebted to Kant's idea of enlightenment while at the same time trying to avoid the development of reason into subsuming, instrumental reason.

Onora O'Neill has reinterpreted Kant's conception of reason as the attempt to establish a systematic unity of principles of reason within a plurality of ways of thinking and acting through a constant, "recursive" questioning of itself. Kant describes reason with the help of the metaphor of "debate," thereby indicating the internal relation between critique, reason, and communication: "Reason must in all its undertakings subject itself to criticism; should it limit freedom of criticism by any prohibitions, it must harm itself, drawing upon itself a damaging suspicion. Nothing is so important through its usefulness, nothing so sacred, that it may be exempted from this searching examination, which knows no special respect for persons [*die kein Ansehen der Person kennt*]. Reason depends on this freedom for its very existence. For reason has no dictatorial authority; its verdict is always simply the agreement of free citizens, of whom each one must be permitted to express, without let or hindrance, his objection or even his veto."[53] O'Neill comments: "A debate between citizens can serve as an image for reason, not because it follows given (hence 'alien') rules of procedure or order, or because it relies on common presuppositions, but because both are processes with a plurality of participants, whose coordination is not guaranteed or imposed by a ruler or other powers. . . . Thoughts and action that depend on unvindicated authorities will hold only where this authority is accepted, so cannot produce general understanding or agreement or resolve all conflicts of belief and action."[54] Reason thus has no authority if it cannot be vindicated "recursively" and "discursively" in a process of the unrestricted communicative "public use of reason": "Either there is unimpeded communication between all, and authoritative standards of reasoning can emerge, or there are impediments to communication and no universally shared standards of reasoning can emerge, and what passes for private reasoning lacks authority."[55] Principles of reason are principles acceptable by a plurality of actors on the basis of "reasonable" reasons, i.e., reasons that can reciprocally and generally be shared or, to use Scanlon's[56] phrase: that cannot reciprocally and generally be rejected. This latter, negative formulation is important, for it allows a critique of arguments that violate the criteria of reciprocity and generality in raising certain claims or denying those of others – so that in the face of disagreement, statements about the "reasonableness" of arguments and claims can still be made.[57] In the present context, it needs to be stressed that the "reasonable" unity established on the basis of reasons does not sacrifice the singular and particular, for every *general* consensus must, in order to be legitimate, also pay tribute to the criterion of *reciprocity*. (I will come back to this in section III.)

This conception of reason, then, can be called "post-metaphysical," for it is precisely the lack of ultimate metaphysical reasons that grounds it – its critical character derives from its being finite, lacking final reasons. Thus it is neither "foundationalist" nor "decontextualized": it consists in its constant self-questioning within contexts of argumentation. It is a critical, pluralistic, and intersubjective conception of reason.

III   JUSTICE

Habermas and O'Neill maintain an explicit relation between this notion of reason and the concept of justice, for "[p]rinciples that cannot be acted on by all must be rejected by any plurality for whom the problem of justice arises. . . . [J]ustice demands (at least) that action and institutions not be based on principles of victimization (deception, coercion, violence)."

Principles of justice have to be justifiable by the "possible consent of actual agents" after a process of undistorted discourse, and they have to be applied in a way that pays special respect to the most vulnerable. "Idealized accounts of justice tend to ignore actual vulnerabilities, and relativized accounts tend to legitimate them."[58]

Habermas's reformulation of Critical Theory and of reason based on a theory of communication has led him to a discourse theory of morality that starts from an analysis of what it means to redeem a moral claim to general validity. The principle of universalization implicit in the presuppositions of moral argumentation says that a norm can find assent in practical discourse if "all affected can *freely* accept the consequences and side-effects that the *general* observance of a controversial norm can be expected to have for the satisfaction of the interests of *each individual*."[59] The principle of discourse ethics thus says "that only those norms can claim to be valid that meet (or could meet) with the approval of all affected in their capacity as participants in a practical discourse." Reasonable principles of justice, then, would be based on reasons that can reciprocally and generally be accepted by all those for whom these principles claim to be valid. This formal definition of practical validity Habermas understands as an intersubjective version of Kant's categorical imperative avoiding Kant's metaphysical theory of two worlds; yet in the difference between facticity and validity the difference between the existing and the reasonable is preserved. It is, however, intersubjective practice that can achieve an at least partial and provisional convergence between principles that can be justified and social practices and institutions. These practices and institutions can be called *just* to the extent that they can be generally *justified* by those subject to them.

One can find a similar idea of justice in some of Horkheimer's early writings. The "universal content of the concept of justice" is that "the social inequality prevailing at any given time requires a rational foundation. It ceases to be considered as a good, and becomes something that should be overcome."[60] The reasonable and just society would be one in which the organization of the whole and the life of the individuals would be reconciled – social and individual autonomy would coincide.

Yet as Adorno reminds us, such a conception of reason and justice faces the danger of subsuming the particular, the vulnerable, the nonidentical, or the "different" under the identity of the unity established in this way – even if it is a communicative unity. Formulated and "rationalized" as abstract principles, moral norms too often constitute a false universality that negates that for which it stands. Utopia thus can be described only in the negative, as "the subject's non-identity without sacrifice."[61] In her attempt to recover a utopian dimension for Critical Theory, Seyla Benhabib has argued that Hegel's and Adorno's critique of Kantian ideas of reason and morality still teach us the need to recognize the "concrete other" in the construction of a theory of justice as opposed to the "generalized other" that serves as the paradigm for Kantian-inspired philosophies such as Rawls's.[62] While the standpoint of the "generalized other" regards every person as basically the same subject entitled to an equal share of rights and goods that can be justified from an impartial viewpoint, the standpoint of the "concrete other" regards the other "as an individual with a concrete history, identity and affective-emotional constitution".[63] Leaving aside the question of whether her critique of Rawls is justified,[64] Benhabib makes an important point about the concept of justice; in fact, she reformulates a classic problem: how can justice be "blind to difference" (treating every person equally) and at the same time not be blind to difference (taking special care of those persons and groups who are not yet equal or who have a right not to be equal in all respects, say, for example, native minority cultures)? Feminist theory has shown that equal treatment can – if it ignores the differences between the social standing and the needs of particular persons – lead to inequalities. Justice thus requires the recognition of sameness as well as of difference: every concrete person must have the equal opportunity to speak up against false generalizations about his or her needs, claims, and entitlements, exposing false claims to equality and requiring justifications of relations of inequality.[65]

Discourse theory seems to be the most appropriate theory from this point of view, for it leaves the determination of the validity of normative claims up to all the participants without exception or exclusion. In this respect, it is an advantage that the idea of reciprocal recognition inherent in free and equal discourse is a formal idea and not a positive utopia. That, it seems to me, is the lesson to be drawn from Adorno's negative dialectics[66] and from Walzer's critique of "Platonic" political philosophy: how social institutions have to be arranged can only be determined in a self-correcting, open process by those who are the members of a certain society. Furthermore, this openness in principle as to what can be thematized and discussed critically in discourse makes it possible for hitherto subordinate social groups to give voice to their concerns; and it is precisely the criteria of *generality* and *reciprocity* that make it illegitimate for dominant interests to silence dissenting, *different* voices. "Thus," says Nancy Fraser, "a discourse ethic permits the thematization and critique of interpretations of needs, of definitions of situations and of the social conditions of dialogue, instead of establishing a privileged model of moral deliberation which effectively shields such matters from scrutiny."[67]

The internal relation between justice, reason, and critique thus needs to be redefined. The claim of reason to establish a just (i.e., justified) reconciliation of particularity and generality can only be redeemed recursively and discursively[68] – on the basis of the principle of the lack of ultimate, and the need for intersubjectively valid, reasons. Institutions that enable such discourses are institutions of social self-criticism; in this respect they can be called more or less reasonable. Reason, conceptualized in a formal and procedural way, does not, as Horkheimer and Adorno thought in their critique of the formalization of reason, lose touch with the idea of justice: it requires that no false substantive principles silence the claims made by social actors and that the possibility of critique and correction must be made an integral part of a just "basic structure" (to use Rawls's term).

A just basic structure thus faces the practical task that the conception of reason faces on a theoretical level: establishing a unity within the diversity of concrete particular "phenomena," or, let us say, "identity" in the face of "difference."[69] An important lesson to be drawn from the discussion of critical theory, therefore, is the following: a conception of justice should incorporate possibilities for the recognition of persons as *particular* individuals and as citizens with *equal* rights. Social norms have to "do justice" to the needs of "concrete," "different" persons. My thesis is that a conception of justice based on a critical conception of reason as formulated above is best suited to the task of reconciling universality and particularity, by using the justificatory criteria of generality and reciprocity. For treating the other simply as like me, as a "generalized other," without recognizing his or her difference, i.e., his or her not being like me and his or her special claims to recognition, does not deserve to be called *justice*. Apart from a merely formal and stereotypical idea of equal justice (which would have to be corrected by other forms of moral concern),[70] the basic principle of justification implies that norms – and their realization in social institutions – have to be justified generally and reciprocally taking every concrete person into account. Persons are equal citizens, yet as individualized persons they have different interests and needs – and the criteria of generality and reciprocity do not exclude claims based on these differences. All it requires is that such claims be put forward with arguments that all others cannot reasonably reject in an argumentation about what justice demands. Justice, like reason, is a "recursive," self-questioning concept: its standards of generality have constantly to be kept open for dissenting claims that criticize this generality as false.

Any theory of justice would thus have to be based on the *principle of reciprocal and general justification* and the *principle of the full recognition of persons;* and any concrete endeavour to suggest such a theory would have to include universal principles as well as substantive considerations of justice in social contexts. Both the theories of John Rawls and Michael Walzer, just to name the two most prominent ones, fulfill that demand. Despite their methodological and substantive differences, both distinguish between basic moral rights which every person has, and principles of social justice which must be justified and realized in a more contextual manner.[71] Both agree that the aim of social justice is the establishment of an inclusive political community enabling the self-respect of citizens; and both agree that social inequalities stand in need of being justified to those who are least advantaged (or, as Rawls's "difference principle" says, to the "worst off") – that is implied by the idea of political membership, i.e., equal citizenship.[72] Walzer, to be sure, provides a more "immanent" critique of the social institutions of the

American welfare state; and his idea of strengthening the walls between distributive spheres to prevent a "colonization"[73] is an important critical principle, yet it also relies on the general and overarching idea of an integrated, just society. As Walzer makes clear, the main principle of social justice is not the integrity of the different "spheres of justice," rather, it is the "creation of an inclusive society": "All the people, every man and woman, are or are supposed to be equal participants in all the spheres of justice, sharing, as members, in the distribution of welfare, security, wealth, education, office, political power, and so on – and also joining in the debates about what that sharing involves and how it ought to be managed." And he concludes: "Inclusion begins with citizenship, which then serves as a value reiterated through democratic political activity in all the spheres of justice."[74] The task of a critical theory of justice then is the analysis of legal, political, and social forms of exclusion (in whatever social sphere) and the analysis of the contexts of justice, so to speak, necessary for a just society – a society in which persons are recognized as persons with different concrete ethical identities and as equal members of the political community.[75] The center of a critical theory of justice is the analysis of contexts of inclusion and exclusion.

A theory that integrates both the principle of reason according to which general norms must be reciprocally and generally justifiable and the connected principle of the full recognition of persons as "concrete equals," so to speak, can avoid the difficulties of starting with a substantive (empirical or anthropological) theory of personal self-realization – or of the good – and then constructing a social and political structure necessary for the realization of that ideal.[76] Rather, a pragmatic analysis of different (general and nongeneral) validity claims – about what is good and what is right or just – opens up the possibility of distinguishing values and norms that belong to different "contexts of justification" in which different communities (ethical, legal and political, moral) are the addressees of the respective normative claims. Consequently, four "contexts of recognition" can be analysed: of ethical persons, legal persons, citizens, and moral persons in the domains of ethics (regarding the question of the good life), law (regarding the legal standing of persons), democracy (regarding the self-government of citizens as fully participating members of political and social life), and morality (as the domain of basic human relations and mutual respect). In this way the principle of reasonable justification leads to a multidimensional perspective on the recognition that is due to persons as individuals and as members of different communities – and thereby it leads to a differentiated view of a just basic structure (that cannot be spelled out here).

This enlarged focus, then, makes a critical theory of justice possible that connects up with different experiences of injustice which, following Axel Honneth, can be understood and analysed as experiences of misrecognition.[77] The *criteria*, however, for judging which critical claims can be mutually justified as claims to justice, can neither be drawn from these experiences themselves[78] nor from a general theory of the good, for the latter would lack the specificity needed in such contexts of argumentation; rather, the criteria must be those of reciprocal and general justification. Experiences of disrespect and exclusion need to be transformed into generally and reciprocally *justifiable* claims to legal, political or social respect and inclusion. Thus the allegedly abstract theory of reason and justification appears to be more in line with the call for a criticism "connected" with particular contexts. In this respect the language of social criticism remains open toward hitherto unheard voices and perspectives and avoids the use of reified general concepts of the good or the reasonable. Seen in this light, every challenge to existing social and political relations and institutions calls into question the reasons that justify these relations and confronts them with an analysis that points out that either the normative justification for existing practices and institutions is flawed (i.e., cannot stand the test of reciprocity and generality) or that the practices and institutions do not conform to justified norms. More specifically, with the help of social analyses it can be shown how certain practices and institutions hinder the development of justifiable relations of recognition and/or communication. Critical theory in this sense is a critique of existing "relations of justification" as the presupposition for establishing and developing a justified basic structure of society.

NOTES

1   Cf. Max Horkheimer, "The State of Contemporary Social Philosophy and the Tasks of an Institute for Social Research" (1931), in *Critical Theory and Society*, ed. Stephen Eric Bronner and Douglas MacKay Kellner (New York and London: Routledge, 1989); "Traditional and Critical Theory" (1937), in *Critical Theory* (New York: Herder and Herder, 1972).

2   In a letter to Ruge (1844), in *The Portable Marx*, ed. Eugene Kamenka (New York: Penguin, 1983), p. 95.

3   "Nationalökonomie und Philosophie" (1844), in *Die Frühschriften*, ed. Siegfried Landshut (Stuttgart: Kröner, 1971), p. 235.

4   "Traditional and Critical Theory," p. 215.

5   Cf. his essay "On the Problem of Truth" (1935), in Andrew Arato and Eike Gebhardt (eds), *The Essential Frankfurt School Reader* (Oxford: Basil Blackwell, 1978).

6   Cf. Helmut Dubiel, *Theory and Politics: Studies in the Development of Critical Theory* (Cambridge, Mass.: MIT, 1985).

7   *Dialectic of Enlightenment* (New York: Herder and Herder, 1972), p. xv.

8   Cf. Jürgen Habermas, *The Theory of Communicative Action*, 2 vols (Boston: Beacon Press, 1984, 1987), esp. vol. 1, ch. IV. Habermas, *The Philosophical Discourse of Modernity* (Cambridge, Mass.: MIT, 1987), ch. V. Axel Honneth, *Critique of Power: Reflective Stages in a Critical Social Theory* (Cambridge, Mass.: MIT, 1991), chs 1–3. Seyla Benhabib, *Critique, Norm, and Utopia. A Study of the Foundations of Critical Theory* (New York: Columbia Press, 1986).

9   *Theory of Communicative Action*, vol. 1, p. 287.

10   On the difference between a critique of "instrumental" and "functionalist" reason, see ibid., vol. 1, p. 398 and Habermas, "A Reply," in Axel Honneth and Hans Joas (eds), *Communicative Action* (Cambridge, Mass.: MIT, 1991), p. 258; cf. also the discussion by Maeve

Cooke, *Language and Reason. A Study of Habermas's Pragmatics* (Cambridge, Mass.: MIT, 1994), pp. 145ff.

11   *Theory of Communicative Action*, vol. 2, pp. 402ff.

12   Cf. Habermas's answer to criticisms by Hans Joas and Thomas McCarthy in "A Reply," in Honneth and Joas (eds), *Communicative Action*.

13   On this, see esp. Habermas, *The Structural Transformation of the Public Sphere* (Cambridge, Mass.: MIT, 1990).

14   This is one of the main points of Habermas's analysis of law; cf. his *Faktizität und Geltung, Beiträge zur Diskurstheorie des Rechts und des demokratischen Rechtsstaats* (Frankfurt am Main: Suhrkamp, 1992), esp. pp. 108, 386f, 429. English translation, *Between Facts and Norms: Contributions to a Discourse Theory of Law and Democracy*, trans. William Rehg (Cambridge, Mass.: MIT Press, 1996).

15   J. Habermas, "The New Obscurity: The Crisis of the Welfare State and the Exhaustion of Utopian Energies," in *The New Conservatism. Cultural Criticism and the Historians' Debate* (Cambridge, Mass.: MIT, 1989), p. 69 (translation changed).

16   Cf., in addition to the works cited above, Habermas's *Legitimation Crisis* (Boston: Beacon, 1975).

17   Michael Walzer, *Interpretation and Social Criticism* (Cambridge, Mass.: Harvard University Press, 1987), p. 40.

18   One of Walzer's (cf. *The Company of Critics*, New York: Basic Books, 1988, ch. 10) examples for that form of criticism is Herbert Marcuse's *One-Dimensional Man*. While Walzer rightly criticizes Marcuse's one-dimensional view of the totally manipulated society guided by the idea of a radically different society with "new" human beings, his account does not do justice to Marcuse's claim that traces of a better society were not just to be found in art but also in the everyday protest of marginalized groups. Furthermore, Walzer cannot account for the fact that Marcuse's criticism proved itself quite "connected" to the cultural and political dissatisfaction of a great many people in the late sixties.

19   Cf. R. Geuss, *The Idea of a Critical Theory* (Cambridge: Cambridge University Press, 1981).

20   Bernard Williams, *Ethics and the Limits of Philosophy* (Cambridge, Mass.: Harvard University Press, 1985), p. 197.

21   See the reference to Geuss in *Interpretation and Social Criticism*, p. 11, fn. 9; and Walzer's essay "A Critique of Philosophical Conversation," in Michael Kelly (ed.), *Hermeneutics and Critical Theory in Ethics and Politics* (Cambridge, Mass.: MIT, 1990).

22   Ibid., p. 194; cf. Walzer, "Philosophy and Democracy," in *Political Theory*, 12:3 (1981).

23   In the following, I draw on my *Kontexte der Gerechtigkeit. Politische Philosophie jenseits von Liberalismus und Kommunitarismus* (Frankfurt am Main: Suhrkamp, 1994), ch. IV.1.

24   *The Company of Critics*, pp. 216, 227.

25   Ibid., p. 219.

26   *Interpretation and Social Criticism*, p. 24.

27   Cf. his *Tanner Lectures* on "Two Kinds of Universalism" and on "The National Question Revisited," ed. Grethe B. Peterson (Salt Lake City: University of Utah Press, 1990); see also "Moral Minimalism", in William R. Shea and Antonio Spadafora (eds), *From the Twilight of Probability* (Canton, Mass.: Science History Publications, 1992), now ch. 1 of *Thick and Thin. Moral Argument at Home and Abroad* (Notre Dame: University of Notre Dame Press, 1994); and *Just and Unjust Wars*, new edition (New York: Basic Books, 1992), esp. part two.

28   *Interpretation and Social Criticism*, p. 45.

29   Ibid., p. 46. Cf. Thomas M. Scanlon, "Contractualism and utilitarianism," in Amartya Sen and Bernard Williams (eds), *Utilitarianism and Beyond* (Cambridge: Cambridge University Press, 1982).

30   In his recent *Thick and Thin*, ch. 2, Walzer acknowledges the two criteria of critical standards that I called (a) "external" and (b) "internal" (although the latter in a weak sense). On the problem of the relativity of social meanings, he adds that the "maximalist morality" of

distributive justice (a) "takes shape along with, constrained by, a reiterated minimalism – the very idea of 'justice', which provides a critical perspective and a negative doctrine" (p. 26); and, furthermore, (b) that social meanings "must meet certain criteria – non-substantive but not merely formal. They must actually be shared across a society, among a group of people with a common life; and the sharing cannot be the result of radical coercion" (pp. 26f).

31   *The Company of Critics*, p. 19.

32   Nancy Fraser's theory of critical feminist discourse is exemplary for this form of critique, cf. "Struggle over Needs: Outline of a Socialist-Feminist Critical Theory of Late Capitalist Political Culture," in *Unruly Practices* (Minneapolis: University of Minnesota Press, 1989).

33   Walzer, *Spheres of Justice* (New York: Basic Books, 1983), p. 314; *Tanner Lectures*, p. 535.

34   Walzer, "Objectivity and Social Meaning," in Martha Nussbaum and Amartya Sen (eds), *The Quality of Life* (Oxford: Clarendon Press, 1993), p. 173.

35   Raymond Geuss, *The Idea of a Critical Theory*, p. 63.

36   Ibid., p. 78.

37   Cf. Walzer, *Interpretation and Social Criticism*, p. 30.

38   It should be kept in mind that the conception of reason discussed in this section is the one implied by and necessary for normative social criticism and does not exhaust the meaning of the concept of reason in general.

39   Max Horkheimer, "Materialism and Morality" (1933), in *Telos*, No. 69 (Fall 1986), p. 91f. On the concept of reason in early Critical Theory see Thomas McCarthy, "On the Idea of a Critical Theory and Its Relation to Philosophy," in McCarthy and David Couzens Hoy, *Critical Theory* (Cambridge, Mass.: Blackwell, 1994), part I, ch. 1.

40   *Dialectic of Enlightenment*, p. 83.

41   Cf. Albrecht Wellmer, "Reason, Utopia, and the Dialectic of Enlightenment," in Richard J. Bernstein (ed.), *Habermas and Modernity* (Cambridge, Mass.: MIT, 1985), p. 45f.

42   *Dialectic of Enlightenment*, p. 83f (translation altered).

43   Theodor W. Adorno, *Negative Dialectics* (New York: Continuum, 1973), p. 6f. The following page numbers refer to this text, the translation has been changed in a few passages.

44   This is how Habermas interprets this passage. Cf. his essay "Theodor W. Adorno: The Primal History of Subjectivity – Self-Affirmation Gone Wild," in *Philosophical-Political Profiles* (Cambridge, Mass: MIT, 1983), p. 107. (Partly) critical of that view are Albrecht Wellmer, "Die Bedeutung der Frankfurter Schule heute," in Axel Honneth and Albrecht Wellmer (eds), *Die Frankfurter Schule und die Folgen* (Berlin: de Gruyter, 1986), pp. 32ff, and Michael Theunissen, *Kritische Theorie der Gesellschaft* (Berlin: de Gruyter, 1981), pp. 51ff.

45   On "rational identity" see David Held, *Introduction to Critical Theory* (Berkeley and Los Angeles: University of California Press, 1980), pp. 212ff; Hauke Brunkhorst, *Theodor W. Adorno. Dialektik der Moderne* (München: Piper, 1990), pp. 299ff.

46   It should, however, be noted that, despite Adorno's strong and general critique of conceptual systems, in many critical statements about the "objective falsity" of the "totally administered world," basic concepts of Marxist social analysis serve as the (unquestioned) framework; see, e.g., *Negative Dialectics*, pp. 37, 166ff.

47   Cf. Adorno's discussion of the relation of universality and individual in moral philosophy, *Negative Dialectics*, pp. 281ff.

48   Karl-Otto Apel, "The a priori of the Communication Community and the Foundations of Ethics," in *Towards a Transformation of Philosophy* (London: Routledge, 1980).

49   I have argued for this important differentiation of "contexts of justification" in my *Kontexte der Gerechtigkeit*, chs IV.2 and v.2.

50   Jürgen Habermas, "To Seek to Salvage an Unconditional Meaning Without God Is a Futile Undertaking: Reflections on a Remark of Max Horkheimer," in *Justification and Application: Remarks on Discourse Ethics* (Cambridge, Mass.: MIT, 1993), p. 146 (translation changed).

This notion of reason also corresponds to Putnam's "internal realism": "Reason is, in this sense, both immanent (not to be found outside of concrete language games and institutions) and transcendent (a regulative idea that we use to criticize the conduct of all activities and institutions)." Hilary Putnam, "Why Reason Can't Be Naturalized," in K. Baynes, J. Bohman, T. McCarthy (eds), *After Philosophy: End or Transformation?* (Cambridge, Mass.: MIT, 1987), p. 228.

51   Jürgen Habermas, "The Unity of Reason in the Diversity of Its Voices," in *Postmetaphysical Thinking: Philosophical Essays* (Cambridge: Polity, 1992).

52   Cf. Thomas McCarthy's defense of a self-critical concept of communicative reason in McCarthy and Hoy, *Critical Theory*, part I, chs 1–3.

53   Immanuel Kant, *Critique of Pure Reason*, A 738f./B 766f., trans. Norman Kemp Smith, 2nd edn. (London: Macmillan, 1933, translation slightly changed.)

54   Onora O'Neill, "Vindicating Reason," in P. Guyer (ed.), *The Cambridge Companion to Kant* (Cambridge: Cambridge University Press, 1992), p. 293f.

55   O'Neill, *Constructions of Reason* (Cambridge: Cambridge University Press, 1989), p. 37.

56   Cf. Th. Scanlon, "Contractualism and utilitarianism."

57   I have dealt with this in more detail in my *Kontexte der Gerechtigkeit*, pp. 63–81, 289–304.

58   O'Neill, *Constructions of Reason*, p. 216f.

59   Jürgen Habermas, "Discourse Ethics: Notes on a Program of Philosophical Justification," in J. Habermas, *Moral Consciousness and Communicative Action* (Cambridge, Mass.: MIT, 1990), p. 93.

60   Horkheimer, "Materialism and Morality," p. 111 (translation altered).

61   Adorno, *Negative Dialectics*, p. 281.

62   Cf. S. Benhabib, *Critique, Norm, and Utopia*, pp. 211, 335ff; and her "The Generalized and the Concrete Other," in S. Benhabib, *Situating the Self. Gender, Community and Postmodernism in Contemporary Ethics* (New York: Routledge, 1992).

63   Benhabib, "The Generalized and the Concrete Other," p. 159.

64   See my criticism in "How (Not) to Speak About Identity: The Concept of the Person in a Theory of Justice," in *Philosophy and Social Criticism*, 18:3/4 (1992), esp. pp. 300f.

65   I discuss this is more detail in *Kontexte der Gerechtigkeit*, ch. II.3.

66   Cf. Klaus Günther, "Dialektik der Aufklärung in der Idee der Freiheit. Zur Kritik des Freiheitsbegriffs bei Adorno", in *Zeitschrift für philosophische Forschung*, vol. 39 (1985), esp. pp. 253ff.

67   N. Fraser, "Toward a Discourse Ethic of Solidarity," in *Praxis International*, 5:4 (1986), p. 426.

68   Cf. Kenneth Baynes, *The Normative Grounds of Social Criticism: Kant, Rawls, and Habermas* (Albany, NY: SUNY, 1992).

69   This, it seems to me, is the problem Derrida deals with in his reading of Benjamin's text "Zur Kritik der Gewalt," where he discusses the force inherent in general, positive law and the question of a "higher" justice. Cf. Jacques Derrida, "The Force of Law: The 'Mystical Foundation of Authority'," in *The Cardozo Law Review*, 11:5–6 (1990).

70   This is the idea behind Lutz Wingert's distinction between the principles of "justice" and "solidarity" in his *Gemeinsinn und Moral. Grundzüge einer intersubjektivistischen Moralkonzeption* (Frankfurt am Main: Suhrkamp, 1993), p. 202f. For a different interpretation of Habermas's conception of solidarity as the "other" of justice – which he clarifies in adding that it is not something different from justice but "an aspect of the same thing," namely taking moral responsibility for the preservation of a common form of life (cf. J. Habermas, "Justice and Solidarity: On the Discussion Concerning Stage 6," in Thomas E. Wren (ed.), *The Moral Domain. Essays in the Ongoing Discussion between Philosophy and the Social Sciences*, Cambridge, Mass.: MIT, 1990, p. 240f.) – see William Rehg, *Insight and Solidarity. The Discourse Ethics of Jürgen Habermas* (Berkeley: University of California Press, 1994). In Rehg's view, "rational human solidarity" is a necessary presupposition of moral insight not bound to specific forms of solidarity based on shared conceptions of the good (cf. esp. pp. 167ff). However, if this basic form of moral sensitivity refers to the moral recognition of persons as concrete persons with

specific needs and equal rights to "concern and respect" (to use Dworkin's phrase), the term "moral respect" seems to be more appropriate, as distinguished from other forms of mutual recognition – like mutual esteem and solidarity – based on the membership in ethical and political, particular communities. Cf. my discussion of "contexts of recognition" in *Kontexte der Gerechtigkeit*, ch. V.3.

71   Cf. Rawls's two principles of justice, of which the second is in need of a more contextual interpretation of "citizen's needs" and justifiable social inequalities; see John Rawls, *Political Liberalism* (New York: Columbia University Press, 1993), esp. pp. 178ff, 227ff. On Walzer's distinction between minimalist and maximalist morality cf. Michael Walzer, *Thick and Thin*, chs 1 and 2.

72   Cf. Rawls, *Political Liberalism*, pp. 180ff, and Walzer, *Spheres of Justice*, pp. 277ff on the relation of social membership and self-respect.

73   Cf. *Spheres of Justice*, p. 282. At this point I cannot go into a comparison between this and Habermas's concept of the "colonization" of the life-world (cf. section I above).

74   M. Walzer, "Exclusion, Injustice, and the Democratic State," in *Dissent* (Winter 1993), pp. 55, 64.

75   I have tried to spell out these contexts in my *Kontexte der Gerechtigkeit*; for the present context of social justice see esp. ch. III.4.

76   Cf. Axel Honneth, *The Struggle for Recognition. The Moral Grammar of Social Conflicts* (Oxford: Polity Press, 1995), esp. ch. 9 and his "The Social Dynamics of Disrespect: On the Location of Critical Theory Today," in *Constellations*, 1:2 (1994). The difficulties of such a theory I can only hint at here, which concern its normative foundations as well as its application in social contexts. For a more detailed discussion, see my *Kontexte der Gerechtigkeit*, ch. V.3.

77   Cf. his "Integrity and Disrespect: Principles of a Conception of Morality Based on the Theory of Recognition," in *Political Theory*, 20:2 (1992).

78   Honneth draws attention to this problem in his "The Social Dynamics of Disrespect," p. 268f.

ACKNOWLEDGMENT

I wish to thank Maeve Cooke for her critical reading of this text and her valuable suggestions for its improvement. For any remaining lack of clarity, responsibility is mine.

PART III

Law and Democracy

Law and Democracy

In Part III, *Law and Democracy*, William Rehg, in "Habermas's Discourse Theory of Law and Democracy: An Overview of the Argument," presents the argument of Habermas's recent book, *Between Facts and Norms*, which focuses upon law as the key to an understanding of social integration in modern society. Rehg, in an analysis which highlights the link between law and deliberative democracy, shows how Habermas's new discourse on law brings law within the purview of the democratic process of public discourse. As such, Rehg, following Habermas, shows how reflection on law should not only be anchored in the "facticity" of modern experience but also is needful of justification as "valid" in the context of a democratic public will-formation, requiring a reconceptualization under a "procedural" paradigm beyond both liberal and welfare state models of understanding. James Bohman, in his chapter "Critical Theory and Democracy," focuses on critical theory's original preoccupation with democracy as it attempted in its originary phase to link Marx's concept of "radical democracy" with the idea of an "expressive totality." However, when early critical theory began to see that modern society was dominated by "instrumental reason," it turned away from democracy toward other modalities of explanation. Habermas, argues Bohman, by giving up on the idea of totality, was able to reopen the question of radical democracy ultimately severed from the "utopian legacy of holistic critical theory." Alas, in Bohman's view, Habermas, who defines himself as a radical democrat, is not radical enough in that he restricts public opinion to its ability to point "administrative power in specific directions" rather than accepting popular sovereignty for what it is, namely, the rule of the majority, to be sure with countermajoritarian institutions built in.

7 HABERMAS'S DISCOURSE THEORY OF LAW AND DEMOCRACY: AN OVERVIEW OF THE ARGUMENT

William Rehg

Both legal theory and the theory of democracy stand at a crossroads today. In the longstanding democratic regimes of the postindustrial west, problems of social complexity, pluralism, and the welfare state have been putting aged constitutional frameworks under tremendous stress. Such challenges are only intensified with the spread of democratic impulses across the globe, to areas where the cultural and infrastructural conditions for democracy and the rule of law must still be consciously constructed. In this context, one of the more fertile and optimistic theoretical developments has been associated with ideas of "deliberative democracy." These ideas reflect a concern that citizens' participation in the democratic process have a rational character – that voting, for example, should not simply aggregate given preferences but rather follow upon a process of "thoughtful interaction and opinion formation" in which citizens become informed of the better arguments and more general interests.[1] Jürgen Habermas's *Between Facts and Norms,* with its emphasis on the role of public discourse in democracy, certainly contributes to this intellectual trend. But it would be wrong to view it simply as one more argument for deliberative democracy. In many respects the culminating effort in a project that was first announced with the 1962 publication of his *Strukturwandel der Öffentlichkeit;*[2] *Between Facts and Norms* offers a sweeping, sociologically informed conceptualization of law and basic rights, a normative account of the rule of law and the constitutional state, an attempt to bridge normative and empirical approaches to democracy, and an account of the social context required for democracy. Finally, it frames and caps these arguments with a bold proposal for a new paradigm of law that goes beyond the dichotomies that have afflicted modern political theory from its inception and that still underlie current controversies between so-called "liberals" and "civic republicans."

An undertaking of such scope, which pulls together three decades of reflection and interdisciplinary research, which is immersed in both German and American debates, and which moves at a number of different levels, places considerable demands on its readers. The primary aim of this chapter is to lighten that burden. Toward this end I survey the argument of the book in three stages. In the first section I delineate the broader considerations informing Habermas's particular approach to law: the tension between the normative and factual dimensions of law; Habermas's basic conceptual framework and methodology; and the features of modernity that are in his view decisive for modern law. With this background available, I then go on in the second section to develop the core philosophical account of rights and the constitutional state, which makes up chapters three and four of the book. Finally, in the last section I provide at least a rough sketch of Habermas's further argument in chapters five through nine, which test out the discourse theory of law in jurisprudential and sociological contexts of debate.

I

Anglo-American philosophical treatises on law often begin with a definition of the concept of law itself. In *Between Facts and Norms*, the basic concept of law as a system of rights does not make its full appearance until chapter 3. The ambitious scale of Habermas's undertaking requires considerable preparation, and thus the first two chapters set a rather elaborate stage that features both his own conceptual architectonic and the surrounding landscape of debate. The conceptual apparatus was most fully expounded in his two-volume *Theory of Communicative Action*,[3] and one might read the present work as drawing out the legal, political, and institutional implications of this earlier endeavor. In this first section I want to introduce the reader to the broader conceptual apparatus and motivate its appropriateness for the analysis of modern law and democracy. I begin by saying something about the puzzle that Habermas starts with, the paradoxical duality of modern law. We can then understand the theory of communicative action as particularly well suited to acknowledge this tension and deal with it constructively.

The Duality of Modern Law

To approach the analysis of modern law in terms of a tension "between facts and norms" – or between "facticity and validity," to translate the German title of the book more literally – is not so surprising. The legal sphere has long been characterized by theorists in terms of a duality of this sort. As we shall see, this tension resides at several levels, but at each level we find a social reality on the one side and a claim of reason (which is sometimes belied by the reality) on the other. Consider, for example, compulsory laws backed by sanctions. On the one hand, such laws appear as the will of a lawgiver with the power to punish those who do not comply; to the extent that they are actually enforced and followed, they have an existence somewhat akin to social facts. On the other hand, compulsory laws are not simply commands backed by threats but embody a claim to legitimacy. Oliver Wendell Holmes's insistence that we must understand law as the "bad man" does – i.e., look at laws only in view of the possible negative consequences of being caught at lawbreaking – cannot be the whole story. In fact, many citizens are not consistently "bad" in this sense, and it is doubtful whether a system of law could long endure if everyone took this external approach all the time. At least some portion of a population, indeed the majority, must look at legal rules as standards that everyone *ought* to follow, whether because they reflect the ways of ancestors, the structure of the cosmos or the will of God, or because they have been democratically approved or simply enacted according to established procedures. What H. L. A. Hart has termed the "internal aspect" of law is a function of its legitimacy or social recognition.[4] Exactly how such legitimacy should be construed is a further question, of course. The important point is this: law is a system of coercible rules and impersonal procedures that also involves an appeal to reasons that all citizens should, at least ideally, find acceptable.

Habermas is heavily indebted to Immanuel Kant's concept of legitimacy, which brings out this tension in law particularly well. Consider, for example, the basic equal rights of individual liberty, such as property and contract rights. Kant grounded their legitimacy in a universal principle of law (the *Rechtsprinzip*, often translated as "principle of right"), which can be interpreted as summarizing the conditions under which it is possible for a morally oriented subject to universalize coercible limits upon the external behavior of strategically oriented individuals. According to Kant, the "moral conception" of law is "the sum of those conditions under which the free choice (*Willkür*) of one person can be conjoined with the free choice of another in accordance with a universal law of freedom."[5] This analysis of rights brings out the *internal tension* between facticity and validity inhabiting law in general: As actionable and enforced, such rights (and legal norms in general) represent social facts demarcating areas within which success-oriented individuals can choose and act as they wish; as linked with a universalizable freedom, rights deserve the respect of moral subjects, and thus carry a claim to legitimacy.

However, Kant's account of legitimacy (as Habermas reads it) ultimately subordinates law to morality. Kant also relied on a metaphysical framework that is no longer plausible: on his account, the possibility of universal rational acceptability depends on a preestablished harmony of reason beyond the empirical world. Whereas subordinating law to morality oversimplifies the rational bases of legitimacy, invoking a transcendentally unified reason presumes consensus prior to actual public discourse. Nonetheless, Kant's appeal to rational consensus as a regulative ideal captures an important part of the tension in law. If law is essentially constituted by a tension between facticity and validity – between its factual generation, administration, and enforcement in social institutions on the one hand and its claim to deserve general recognition on the other – then a theory that *situates* the idealizing character of validity claims *in* concrete social contexts recommends itself for the analysis of law. This is just what the theory of communicative action allows, without the metaphysical pretensions and moralistic oversimplification we find in Kant.

A Postmetaphysical Theory of Reason

The theory of communicative action is primarily a theory of rationality, an attempt to rescue the claims of reason that were once advanced within encompassing metaphysical systems (such as that of Thomas Aquinas), philosophies of history (such as G. W. F. Hegel's), or philosophies of consciousness (such as Kant's). According to Habermas, the growth of empirical science, the pluralization of worldviews, and other developments have rendered such grand philosophical approaches generally implausible – and have in the process given rise to impoverished views of reason as merely instrumental. Hence if one is to salvage a comprehensive concept of reason today, one must take a "postmetaphysical" approach. As Habermas uses it, the term "postmetaphysical" – which should not be confused with "postmodern" – covers a number of different philosophical theories. As specific examples one might point to John Rawls's "political not metaphysical" theory of justice and Ronald Dworkin's theory of "law as integrity."[6] In any case, for Habermas a postmetaphysical vindication of reason is possible only insofar as philosophy – in an interdisciplinary cooperation with empirical inquiries of various sorts – can show how the use of language and social interaction in general necessarily rely on notions of validity such as truth, normative rightness, sincerity, and authenticity.[7] This necessitates not only a philosophical analysis of communication but also an attention to debates within a range of disciplines.

Postmetaphysical philosophy thus need not surrender all ambitions of its own. This is already evident in the focus on validity. For, on Habermas's view, claims to validity involve an idealizing moment of unconditionality that takes them beyond the immediate context in which they are raised. This is clearest with certain types of truth claims, as they are commonly understood. For example, when we assert today that the earth is a sphere (approximately), we do not simply mean that it is "true for us" that the earth is spherical. Rather, we are also saying that anyone – of whatever generation or culture – that believes otherwise is mistaken. Of course, the universalist understanding of truth has come under fire even in the philosophy of the natural sciences, and thus it should be no surprise that a philosopher who defends a universalist concept of normative validity in the practical domain – the domain of morality, politics, and law – faces rather imposing hurdles.

The crux of the challenge is constructively to maintain the tension between the strongly idealizing, context-transcending claims of reason and the always limited contexts in which human reason must ply its trade. It is thus quite understandable that the tension "between facts and norms" should stand at the very center of Habermas's attempt to bring his theory of communicative action to bear on the existing institutions of law and democracy. A legal-political theory based on a theory of communicative action cannot avoid this tension, which in fact appears at every level of the analysis, as Habermas takes pains to demonstrate in the first chapter: within the use of language itself, within modern law, and between law and social reality. I turn now to Habermas's application of the theory of communicative action, first to social coordination in general and then to modern law.

The Communicative Structures of Social Coordination

The first chapter can be read as Habermas's own highly theoretical reconstruction of the paradoxical character of law and the special role of law in modern society. This reconstruction has a number of densely interwoven strands: not just an abstract theory of validity but an ambitious theory of modernity as well, it attempts to reconstruct the rise of modern law with its dual structure. Rather than trace its intricacies step-by-step, in what follows I will illustrate the basic categories necessary to follow Habermas's account.

One should first be aware that the theory of communicative action involves a particular view about how social coordination is effected through language. Drawing on insights from American pragmatism and the speech-act theories of J. L. Austin and John Searle, Habermas considers a "formal-pragmatic" approach to language as most adequate for social theory. This approach goes beyond semantic and syntactic analyses of meaning and grammar to examine the general structures that enable competent speakers actually to engage in successful interaction, which involves more than simply knowing how to form grammatical sentences.[8] Specifically, competent speakers know how to base their interactions on validity claims that their hearers will accept or that could, if necessary, be redeemed with good reasons. As already mentioned, this involves a tension between facticity and validity insofar as a claim to validity raised here and now, and perhaps justified according to local standards, ultimately overshoots a particular community. At least this is the case with truth claims and moral claims. As understood by participants engaged in interaction and discourse, truth claims are claims about the objective world that all human beings share, and moral claims have to do with norms for interpersonal relationships that any autonomous adult should find rationally acceptable from the standpoint of justice and respect for persons. If such claims are valid, then any competent speaker of goodwill should, under suitable conditions, be able to accept the claim on the basis of good reasons. When a claim is contested, actually bringing about such rational acceptance requires actors to shift into a *discourse* in which, the pressures of action more or less neutralized, they can isolate and test the disputed claim solely on the basis of arguments.[9]

To be sure, not all types of claims anticipate the agreement of a universal audience. The differences between types of discourse can be quite important in this regard. For example, claims about what is good for a particular group (or person), or about a particular group's authentic self-understanding, may be addressed only to the individuals concerned and those who know them well. Such discourses, which Habermas labels "ethical," differ both in theme and scope of audience from the "moral" discourse concerned with universal norms of justice.[10] But even these more limited ethical claims presuppose an orientation to mutual understanding, which for Habermas is constitutive of communicative action. The orientation to reaching understanding about validity claims serves as a mechanism for social integration inasmuch as it grounds shared expectations, ways of interpreting situations, and so forth.

To illustrate Habermas's approach further, imagine that a dispute arises within a group and that its members wish to resolve it consensually on the basis of validity claims. According to Habermas, conflict resolution on the basis of reasoned agreement involves at least three idealizing assumptions: members must assume they mean the same thing by the same words and expressions; they must consider themselves as rationally accountable; and they must suppose that, when they do arrive at a mutually acceptable resolution, the supporting arguments sufficiently justify a (defeasible) confidence that any claims to truth, justice, and so forth that underlie their consensus will not subsequently prove false or mistaken. No local, spatiotemporally finite consensus can fully realize these idealizations; yet if they should subsequently prove false – if members discover that a crucial term was understood in two different ways, or that they were seriously self-deceived, or that they were mistaken about certain facts or norms – then there are grounds for questioning the original agreement and reopening the discussion. That is, these idealizations imply a tension between the de facto social acceptance (*soziale Geltung*) of a group consensus and the idealized validity (*Gültigkeit*) that such a consensus must claim for itself if members are to accept it as reasonable. Communicatively achieved agreements are in principle always open to challenge, and thus are at best a precarious source of social integration. If a community is to be a stable one, then, it requires more than explicit agreement as a basis for social cooperation.

Conflict resolution will be rendered easier the more the members of the group can limit their discursive efforts to a few problematic validity claims. For example, if they are at odds over how best to manage a particular environmental threat – one might imagine a city council debating how to deal with an imminent flood – they have a better chance of reaching agreement if they only have to resolve an empirical question about the effectiveness of two competing strategies, and do not also have to argue over fairness criteria, or what would count as a successful outcome. In short, reaching agreement communicatively requires a large background consensus on matters that are unproblematic for group members.

The implicit agreement represented by such a *lifeworld* background stabilizes a communicatively integrated group insofar as it removes a large body of assumptions from challenge – as it were fusing validity with the facticity of a given cultural background. For the background not only provides its members with shared resources for managing conflict; as a source of shared identities, it also lessens the number of issues that are likely to be contested at any given time, so that large areas of social interaction rest on a stable basis of unquestioned consensus.[11]

If members cannot agree upon how to resolve a specific conflict, say on the aforementioned question of how to deal with an impending flood, they may attempt to bargain. As Habermas understands this mode of conflict resolution, it involves a certain shift in perspective on the part of the conflicting parties from communicative to *strategic action*. Rather than attempting to convince one another of a validity claim regarding the intrinsically better strategy, each party begins to bargain with threats and promises in the hope of inducing the other to cooperate with it in pursuing a given flood policy. In more general terms, an actor who adopts a strategic attitude is primarily concerned with individual (or group) success in a social environment that includes other actors (and groups). In many contexts it is understood by those involved that such an attitude is appropriate. In fact, the need for modern law partly arises because, with the growth of capitalist market economies, contexts dominated by strategic action become increasingly important for social coordination.

The Need for Positive Law

To understand modern law within the framework provided by Habermas's theory of communicative action, we need to introduce some complications that the above illustration provisionally set aside for the sake of clarity. First, because modern societies are pluralistic, conflict resolution must occur across a number of subgroups, each of which has a somewhat different self-understanding and set of shared background assumptions. Second, modern pluralization has engendered a process that Max Weber called the "disenchantment of the world." For our purposes, this refers to the loss of the "sacred canopy," the fact that pluralization has undermined – or at least fragmented – common religious authorities and worldviews.[12] Third, modern societies have developed a complex differentiation of functional spheres defined by specific tasks of social reproduction (economy, educational system, politics, and so on).

Pluralization and disenchantment undermine the ways in which communities can stabilize themselves against shared backgrounds and authorities that removed certain issues and assumptions from challenge. Modern societies witness an increasing variety of groups and subcultures, each having its own distinct traditions, values, and worldview. As a result, more and more conflicts must be settled by reaching explicit agreement on a greater range of contestable matters, under conditions in which the shared basis for reaching such agreement is diminishing. Areas of life in which facticity and validity were once fused come under increasing critical scrutiny – facticity and validity increasingly split apart, as it were – setting in motion a process of societal rationalization. That is, members are increasingly forced to separate different spheres of validity, for example, to distinguish scientific questions from questions of faith, questions of justice and morality from aesthetic judgments, and so forth, a development that Weber attempted to capture with his concept of the differentiation of "value spheres."

This increasingly differentiated use of communicative reason at the level of the lifeworld is associated with the third of the above aspects of modernity, the functional differentiation of semi-independent subsystems in which strategic action acquires greater importance for social coordination.[13] The capitalist economy is perhaps the most obvious example of this. Buyers and sellers act "strategically" rather than communicatively inasmuch as they make decisions according to their own interests and external market conditions. Social coordination is achieved, not by reaching agreement on validity claims but "behind the actors' backs," through anonymous market mechanisms created by the intermeshing of largely unintended consequences of action. In functionalist parlance, the economy represents a level of social integration that occurs through the "nonlinguistic steering medium" of money. This medium relieves market participants of the need to reach a substantive consensus, so that – in theory, at least – they can simply pursue their own personal advantage and trust to the overall aggregate effect of the market to distribute goods and services evenly and efficiently.[14]

Besides money and the economic reproduction it steers, "system integration" is also effected through the medium of power in formally structured organizations. In bureaucratic administrations, for example, the hierarchically stratified power of superiors over subordinates effects a coordinated realization of collective goals. The authority to issue binding commands means that the superior does not have to convince subordinates of the advisability of each task assigned to them, thus reducing the need for explicit consensus. While this is by no means the whole story of how bureaucratic organizations actually function,[15] it does indicate how hierarchical organization at least reduces *some* of the burdens involved in reaching explicit agreement.

Modern law is meant to solve social coordination problems that arise under the above conditions, i.e., where, on the one hand, societal pluralization has fragmented shared identities and eroded the substantive lifeworld resources for consensus and, on the other, functional demands of material reproduction call for an increasing number of areas in which individuals are left free to pursue their own ends according to the dictates of purposive rationality. The solution is to confine the need for agreement to general norms that demarcate and regulate areas of free choice. Hence the dual character of law: on the one hand, legal rights and statutes must provide something like a stable social environment in which persons can form their own identities as members of different traditions and can strategically pursue their own interests as individuals; on the other hand, these laws must issue from a discursive process that makes them rationally acceptable for persons oriented toward reaching an understanding on the basis of validity claims.

We now have the basic elements in Habermas's concept of modern law: (a) an account of certain features of modern societies; (b) a distinction between communicative and strategic action; and (c) an account of communicative action in terms of validity claims that must be vindicated in discourses of different types. Note how this last feature goes beyond Kant's account, which ultimately subordinated law to morality. Whereas Kant took universalizable moral validity as the model for legitimate law, Habermas proposes a more complex set of discourses that underlie legitimate lawmaking. In fact, this discourse approach is the key to his argument that democracy and the rule of law are internally related.

Before taking up this argument in the next section, though, we should note that there is also an *external tension* between facticity and validity, specifically a tension between the claims of the constitutional-democratic legal order and the ways in which forms of social power actually intrude upon and undermine the conditions for legitimate lawmaking. For theorists with Habermas's sociological awareness, no plausible concept of modern law can ignore this external tension between facts and norms, and it is precisely the failure to appreciate this tension that leads to a certain onesidedness in many contemporary political theories. The second chapter gives us a sense of Habermas's course by charting the shoals on which some leading alternatives have run aground. To close this first section, then, I briefly indicate Habermas's path between the two main alternatives.

Between Rawls and Luhmann

Many Anglo-American readers will already be familiar with one of these alternatives, John Rawls's theory of justice.[16] As much as he agrees with Rawls, Habermas finds that the highly normative theory of justice does not sufficiently appreciate the social facticity confronting constitutional ideals. To be sure, Rawls's concern with overlapping consensus and the social stability of his conception of justice does attempt to show how this conception can find acceptance within a particular *cultural* context. Rawls's theory can plausibly appeal to the fact that constitutional democracies have flourished in societies in which certain political traditions and ideas of fairness are widely shared. But this still ignores the problem of how legal *institutions* can realize such ideals in contexts shaped by powerful interests and complex functional requirements. And, to judge from the pessimism of many sociological observers of democracy, appeals to cultural ideals alone will not answer the problems posed by welfarism, bureaucratization, powerful corporate interests, an apathetic citizenry, and so forth.

The other main alternative, the systems theory of Niklas Luhmann, will probably be less familiar to English-speaking readers. In fact, Luhmann is one of the most influential social theorists in Germany today (along with Habermas himself) and, judging by translations of his work, he is not completely unknown to English-speaking audiences.[17] Nonetheless, a lengthier introduction to his approach, beginning with some historical background, is called for.

In the social contract tradition going back to Thomas Hobbes – which Habermas also refers to under the umbrella of "rational" or "modern" natural law[18] – the legal constitution of society on the basis of individual rights appeared as a plausible extension of the contract relationship that governed the bourgeois economy. The economic institutions of contract and ownership already entailed a view of legal persons as free and equal, and thus as bearers of equal rights. Karl Marx's critique of capitalism turned this normative intuition inside out. Marx viewed the economy as a system of anonymous relations oriented, not toward the freedom and equality proclaimed in 1789, but toward a humanly alienating self-reproduction of capital. Law – and more generally, the consciously accepted norms and ideals behind law – was no longer seen as the key element in social coordination; the focal point of social analysis shifted to the depersonalizing economic system whose integrating achievements proceeded behind the participants' backs. Coming out of the tradition of political economy (Adam Smith, David Ricardo, James Mill, etc.), this theoretical approach requires one to adopt an external observer perspective, or what Habermas calls an "objectivating perspective" on social relations. The "performative perspective" of the participants themselves tends to be viewed with some suspicion, as subject to illusions, and it may even be dismissed as irrelevant. For Marx, the participant perspective still retained theoretical relevance inasmuch as the awareness of systemic mechanisms of capitalist integration had a critical, revolutionary power: even as he relied on an observer perspective, he addressed his theoretical analysis to participants who took the bourgeois norms of freedom and equality seriously. Contemporary systems theory, however, drops this normative involvement altogether for a thoroughly objectivating, technocratic approach to society. With its rigorous restriction to the observer perspective, systems theory takes an approach the very opposite from that of Rawls, with his commitment to the normative self-understanding of constitutional democracy.

In broad terms, systems theory has a certain appeal because of its ability to conceptualize forms of complex social organization that are effected more at an anonymous macrolevel than through the direct intentions of individual participants. I have already briefly described two such forms of organization, the market economy and bureaucratic organizations. As a "system," society (or its subsystems, such as the political system or economy) is not just the sum of individual beliefs and decisions, but a set of functionally interdependent elements whose coordinated operation maintains the whole system or subsystem. Which elements are selected and how their functioning is conceived varies with the particular version of systems theory, but mechanistic equilibrium models and biological homeostasis models have provided two of the more influential metaphors for early systems theory.[19] Though heavily indebted to Talcott Parsons, Luhmann has radicalized systems theory by drawing upon a concept of "autopoiesis" that was originally intended for living organisms.[20] Such systems are "autopoietic" in the sense that:

> the states of the system are exclusively determined by its own operations. The environment can eventually destroy the system, but it contributes neither operations nor structures. The structures of the system condense and are confirmed as a result of the system's own operations, and the operations are in turn recursively reproduced by structural mediation.[21]

This implies that systems are "operationally closed." One should not confuse this with causal independence from the outside world. The legal system, for example, could not exist without the psychological systems of its judges, lawyers, clients, and so forth. Rather, systems are operationally closed in the sense that the communication of meaning within the system is defined solely in terms of the system's own language. As a result, a system can register events outside itself only insofar as they can be "translated" into its own language. An exchange of property, for example, can be "observed" by the legal system only insofar as it is mediated by an appropriate legal mechanism such as a deed or valid will. Conversely, legal actions, for example a suit for damages to property, only have meaning in the economic system insofar as they impinge on monetary transactions. Inasmuch as the system's language, or "code and programming," determine what, and how, external events are observed, a system reproduces not only itself, but its environment as well. Conversely, there is no central overarching perspective on society as a whole, but only a multiplicity of perspectives corresponding to the different subsystems. On Luhmann's systems approach, society is "polycentric."

If we examine the structure of the systemic language of law, however, we can see that such closure is compatible with a certain kind of "cognitive openness." Programs and codes are the means by which a system solves its basic problem, that of selecting possibilities in environments that are both complex and contingent.[22] In virtue of its binary code of legal vs. illegal (where "illegal" has a broad sense that includes "not legally binding") law selects certain actions and omissions as expectable within the legal community. Thus actors can expect that others will expect them to do action A in situations of type X, or not to do B in situations of type Y, and so forth.[23] To handle disappointments of these expectations, the law attaches sanctions to their violation. Normative expectations thus have the property that disappointments of the expectation do not lead to "learning," i.e., one does not adjust one's expectation as one does in the case of a disappointed cognitive expectation, say about how nature will behave. Rather, one punishes the violator so as to reinforce the original expectation. Learning, or development in law, occurs in virtue of its "programming," which allows the legal system to adapt to new situations by developing new "programs," i.e., by creating new norms. In this way, law is "cognitively open" to its environment.

Since the environment is itself an internal construct of the system, however, cognitive openness does not break social subsystems out of their operational self-enclosure. The turn to autopoiesis has thus forced systems theorists to search for ways to account for intersystemic effects.[24] This problem also turns up in Gunther Teubner's modifications of systems theory, modifications that in Habermas's view either are empirically untenable or tacitly presuppose the very kind of communicative action that systems theory must exclude. Habermas argues that such problems cannot be resolved if theory is closed to the participant perspective that governs the everyday use of language. It is from the perspective taken in communicative action, and thus through the flexibility provided by ordinary language, that legal "communications" are able to mediate between functional subsystems and the lifeworld.

The lesson of Habermas's reading of Rawls and Luhmann is this: if an account of modern law is to be neither sociologically empty nor normatively blind, then it must incorporate a dual perspective. The theorist of law can ignore neither the participants' own normative understanding of their legal system, nor those external mechanisms and processes that are accessible to the sociological observer. The need for this dual perspective explains Habermas's continuing respect for thinkers such as Weber and Parsons, who attempted to combine internal and external perspectives in their analyses. To be sure, neither thinker succeeded in consistently maintaining both perspectives. But their failures are at least instructive, and in fact lie behind the complexity and multi-perspectival character of Habermas's own analyses. More specifically, to do justice to the dual character of law, Habermas proposes to examine it from *both* normative and empirical perspectives – *both* as a "system of knowledge" (or set of public norms) and as a "system of action" (or set of institutions) embedded in a societal context. He thus devotes chapters three through six to the normative self-understanding of constitutional democracies, whereas chapters seven and eight take up issues connected with empirical sociology: how the normative model relates to empirical investigations of democracy, and how it must be situated in regard to social power processes. Chapter nine then caps off the investigation by proposing a new paradigm for approaching the rule of law and democracy.

II

Having set forth the basic parameters of modern law in chapter one and charted various theoretical pitfalls in chapter two, Habermas is ready to reconstruct the normative understanding of the modern rule of law in chapters three and four. In analyzing modern law as a system of rights, chapter three supplies the basis for the central thesis of the book – that the rule of law, or constitutional state, is internally related to deliberative democracy.[25] Since some of the most important debates in political and legal theory arise between these two conceptual poles, showing how they are internally linked together promises to represent a considerable theoretical advance. To see what Habermas is up to, it helps to position his thesis between two opposed views, which are admittedly somewhat stylized for purposes of presentation.

On the one side are classical "liberal" views. Stemming from thinkers such as John Locke, this approach emphasizes the impersonal rule of law and the protection of individual freedom; democratic process is constrained by, and in the service of, personal rights that guarantee individuals the freedom to pursue their own goals and happiness.[26] On the other side one finds traditions of "civic republicanism" stemming from Plato and Aristotle and later reshaped by, among others, Jean-Jacques Rousseau. This approach gives pride of place to the democratic process as a collective deliberation that, at least ideally, leads citizens to reach agreement on the common good. On this view, human freedom has its summit, not in the pursuit of private preferences, but in self-governance through political participation.[27] Consequently, republican views tend to ground the legitimacy of laws and policies in notions of "popular sovereignty," whereas liberal views tend to define legitimate government in relation to the protection of individual liberty, often specified in terms of human rights.

This split is not entirely surprising if one recalls the features of modern law noted in Section I above. Modern legal norms require only outward compliance regardless of individual motivation, but they should, at the same time, have a rational basis that also makes it possible for persons to accept them as legitimate and thus deserving obedience. The need for legitimation is acute because such norms must be positively enacted without appeal to a higher source of justification such as a shared religious worldview. In view of this duality one can see that coercible law can be accepted as legitimate insofar as it guarantees two things at once. On the one hand, as demarcating areas in which private individuals can exercise their free choice as they desire, law must guarantee the *private autonomy* of individuals pursuing their personal success and happiness. On the other hand, because its enactment must be such that reasonable individuals could always assent to its constraints rationally, legitimate law must also secure the *public autonomy* of those subject to it, so that the legal order can be seen as issuing from the citizens' rational self-legislation, as it were. The two broadly construed approaches, liberal and republican, tend to stress either one side of autonomy or the other as the basis of legitimacy.

In arguing for an "internal relation" between private and public autonomy, Habermas wants to do justice to both sides – that is, provide an account of legitimate law in which both human rights and popular sovereignty play distinct, irreducible roles. Before giving this account, it helps to note the twin pitfalls Habermas wants to avoid: one must be careful to locate the legitimacy of law at the proper level, neither subordinating law to morality nor conflating it with a community's assertion of shared values and traditions of the good life. This is not to deny that both moral considerations and "ethical" reflection on substantive values are pertinent to law: laws regulate interpersonal relations in a manner similar to moral norms, but they do so only within a concrete community having a particular history and, pluralization notwithstanding, probably at least some shared understanding of the common good. Moreover, both issues of justice and the determination of policies and collective goals form important parts of law and politics. It is not surprising, then, that attempts to explain legitimacy often turn to one type of discourse or the other, depending on whether private or public autonomy receives greater emphasis.

Habermas sees a general tendency in modern natural-law theory, Kant's included, to understand basic liberties in overly moralistic terms, merely as the legal expression of the mutual respect that persons ought to show one another as morally autonomous agents. By contrast, Rousseauian civic republican accounts, by emphasizing the importance of shared traditions, civic virtue, and agreement on the common good, run the risk of reducing deliberative democracy to the ethical discourse in which a concrete community reflects on its substantive values and traditions in order to determine what course of action is good for it in a given social situation. Neither moral respect nor ethical reflection, however, can by itself account for the legitimacy of law in complex pluralistic societies.

To deal with these problems, Habermas centers his account of legitimacy on a discourse principle "D" that lies at a different level than the distinction between moral and ethical discourse. As a principle for the impartial justification of norms in general, "D" also underlies both morality and law: "Only those norms are valid to which all affected persons could agree as participants in rational discourses."[28] By anchoring the legitimacy of law in a discourse principle that is conceptually prior to the distinction between law and morality, Habermas hopes to avoid a moralistic interpretation of law and consequent favouring of private autonomy in the form of human rights. At the same time, the discourse principle points to a model of legitimation that undercuts the liberal–republican split. Legitimate law must pass a discursive test that potentially engages the entire range of different types of discourse. These include not only moral and ethical discourses, but also "pragmatic" discourses in which alternative strategies for achieving a given aim are assessed; in addition, insofar as an issue involves conflicting particular interests and values that do not permit consensus, a legitimate legal regulation of the issue must involve fair compromise.

With this framework in place, Habermas can argue that the internal relation between private and public autonomy requires a set of abstract rights that citizens must recognize if they want to regulate their life together by means of legitimate positive law. This "system of rights" – which each concrete democratic regime must appropriately elaborate and specify – delineates the general necessary conditions for institutionalizing democratic processes of discourse in law and politics. To summarize, these rights fall into five broad categories. The first three categories are the negative liberties, along with membership rights and due process rights, that guarantee individual freedom of choice, and thus private autonomy. The fourth category, rights of political participation, guarantees public autonomy. Habermas argues that each side is indispensable and cannot simply be reduced to the other: without the first three sets of rights, there is no private autonomy (and thus no free and equal subjects of law), but without the fourth set the laws and rights guaranteeing private autonomy are merely paternalistic impositions rather than expressions of self-governance. Rights of political participation, that is, enable citizens themselves to shape and further define the rights they enjoy as "privately autonomous," and thus to become "the authors of the laws to which they are subject as addressees." Finally, a fifth category of social-welfare rights becomes necessary insofar as the effective exercise of civil and political rights depends upon certain social and material conditions, e.g., that citizens can meet their basic material needs.

As conceived so far, the system of rights regulates only the interactions among equal citizens; it is only in chapter four that Habermas introduces the role of state authority, whose police power is necessary to enforce and thus stabilize the system of rights. This introduces a further step in the institutionalization of discourse, and with it, a further dimension of the tension between facticity and validity internal to the rule of law – namely, the tension between state power and legitimate law. To capture this tension, one must keep two things in view at once. On the one side, law and political power fulfill certain systemic functions for each other: the law authorizes some exercises of power and disallows others and, in addition, provides the procedures and forms that define various governmental powers and competences to begin with; government power, meanwhile, provides a threat of sanctions that makes law socially effective. On the other side, the law employed by the state in its various offices and activities must itself be legitimated through a broader discourse of citizens and their representatives. Hence, pace Luhmann, a functionalist analysis of bureaucratic power and legal procedures cannot stand on its own but must be tied to an account of public reason. For Habermas, this latter account must ultimately refer to democratic processes of "opinion- and will-formation" in the public sphere. As a formation of opinion *and* will, public discourse is not merely a cognitive exercise, but mobilizes reasons and arguments that draw upon citizens' interests, values, and identities. Political discourse thus brings in the citizens' actual sources of motivation and volition. It thereby generates a "communicative power" that has a real impact on the formal decision-making and action that represent the final institutional expression of political "will."

In this further step in his analysis of law, then, Habermas is concerned to link the informal discursive sources of democracy with the formal decision-making institutions that are required for an effective rule of law in complex societies. The constitutional state represents the crucial set of legal institutions and mechanisms that govern the conversion of the citizenry's communicative power into efficacious and legitimate administrative activity: law "represents . . . the medium for transforming communicative power into administrative power."[29] It is from this perspective that one must account for the various principles, tasks, and institutions of the constitutional state, such as the separation of powers, majority rule, statutory controls on administration, and so forth.

III

In the remainder of the book Habermas attempts to test his abstract account of law against the more concrete and empirical considerations that are relevant for understanding the actual functioning of particular legal systems. Thus, having sketched a philosophy of law in chapters three and four, he turns in chapters five and six to jurisprudence proper, or legal theory. These chapters should be of special interest to jurisprudential and constitutional scholars. There Habermas tests the philosophical analysis of the previous two chapters against specific legal theories that are (or have been) influential in two particular legal systems, those of the United States and Germany. The argument thus represents a further step toward actual legal practice, for now the self-understandings of two existing legal orders are at issue. Once again, further dimensions of the internal tension between facticity and validity organize the presentation, which is now primarily focused on judicial decision-making and the role of the Supreme Court (in Germany, the Federal Constitutional Court). In chapter five, the major concern is the jurisprudential tension between, on the one hand, the need for judicial decisions to conform to existing statutes and precedents and, on the other, the demand that decisions be right or just in light of moral standards, social welfare, and so forth. This tension has long been felt in American jurisprudence, as shown by the early critique of "mechanical jurisprudence" by theorists such as Roscoe Pound, and it defined the context for Hart's influential *Concept of Law*.[30] In developing his own position on this issue, Habermas not only surveys legal realism, legal hermeneutics, and positivism but also devotes considerable attention to Ronald Dworkin's theory of judicial decision-making.

Chapter six takes up issues involved in the separation of powers and the role of constitutional courts. Specifically, Habermas examines the apparent competition between legislature and judiciary in the welfare state; the "value jurisprudence" of the German high court (which tends to dissolve the difference between collective goods and constitutional rights); he also treats American debates over the nature of constitutional review. In the course of this last mentioned discussion he takes up John Hart Ely's proceduralism, Frank Michelman's and Cass Sunstein's civic-republican proposals, and Bruce Ackerman's distinction between "normal politics" and "higher" constitutional lawmaking.[31] In his treatment of these issues in chapters five and six, various features of a new kind of proceduralist understanding of law and democracy begin to emerge. These features are, inter alia, the intersubjective, dialogical aspect of judicial legal argumentation; the deontological character of basic rights in contrast to other values; and a nonpaternalistic understanding of the role of the Supreme Court in safeguarding the discursive quality of legislative decision-making. The end result is a proceduralist conception that incorporates the insights of the aforementioned theorists but also criticizes and attempts to go beyond them.

Before elaborating this proceduralist understanding of law more completely, Habermas shifts his perspective in the next two chapters. The account of democracy and law thus far has been normative in character. It will be empirically plausible, however, only if it confronts the challenges posed by social power and societal complexity. Thus, having dealt in chapters three through six with tensions between validity and facticity internal to constitutional democracy, in chapters seven and eight Habermas takes up issues bearing on the external tension between social facts and law. The central question is whether one can still meaningfully speak of constitutional democracies in light of rather disheartening empirical studies of power and complexity. Sociological theories of law and politics draw attention to the multifarious ways in which various social interests and powerful organizations attempt to instrumentalize the political process for strategic purposes; or else they point out how the functional complexity of contemporary societies no longer permits direct democratic control, but rather requires indirect administrative measures guided by expert knowledge. In either case, the normative ideal of a self-organizing society, with law and politics as the site of an encompassing social integration, can appear hopelessly out of touch.

As one might anticipate from chapter two, Habermas's response employs a dual theoretical perspective. Specifically, his new "proceduralist concept of democracy" acknowledges how the constitutional state is subject to social forces and functional demands most evident to the sociological observer. At the same time, it insists on the empirical relevance of deliberative democratic ideals accepted by the citizens themselves as engaged participants. This dual perspective thus enables one to spot the deficiencies in onesidedly empiricist conceptions. In addition, it provides a standpoint from which to criticize overly narrow interpretations of democratic participation (as found, for example, in rational choice theory).

Habermas's proceduralist view is also predicated on the rejection of two opposed conceptions that can be stylized, once again, as "liberal" and "civic republican." In this context, the important question is how one should understand the roles of state and society in political action. On the one hand, politics must involve more than the minimal government of liberalism, for which politics primarily is the state's preservation of an unencumbered market economy under the rule of law. On the other hand, it must be less than the collective action of a homogeneous political society – the community envisioned by classical republicanism. Whereas the liberal view overlooks the public, deliberative side of democratic institutions, the republican view suggests an overly unitary "popular will" inhering in the citizenry as a subject writ large. On a proceduralist view, only the state, as a political system invested with decision-making powers, can "act." But its action is legitimate only if the formal decision-making procedures within the constitutional state have a discursive character that preserves, under conditions of complexity, the democratic sources of legitimacy in the public at large.

In chapter seven Habermas both draws upon and criticizes different sociological theories of democracy in order to outline, in broad terms, a proceduralist approach that can handle societal complexity. In chapter eight he then goes on to examine the central challenges of social power and systemic complexity. The unsuccessful attempts to account for democratic politics solely in terms either of rational self-interest or of functional systems show that an empirically viable theory of democracy cannot dispense with the communicative sources of legitimacy. Thus Habermas's proceduralist account must show how the political system, though one functional subsystem among many, can nonetheless be tied to broader communicative processes throughout society that have a democratic, legitimating quality.

More specifically, in this "two-track" view of democratic lawmaking, formally institutionalized deliberation and decision must be open to inputs from informal public spheres. This means that the political system (and the administration in particular) must not become an *independent* system operating solely according to its own criteria of efficiency and unresponsive to citizens' concerns; nor must it become too subservient to particular interests that have access to administrative power through unofficial paths of influence that bypass the democratic process. Conversely, the public sphere must not itself be "subverted by power," whether that of large organizations or of the mass media. Habermas's model places considerable normative responsibility for the democratic process on those public forums, informal associations, and social movements in which citizens can effectively voice their concerns. Chapter eight closes with an analysis of the various conditions under which the public sphere can fulfill its democratic function. These conditions include channels of communication linking the public sphere to a robust civil society in which citizens first perceive and identify social issues; a broad range of informal associations; responsible mass media; and agenda-setting avenues that allow broader social concerns to receive formal consideration within the political system.

In the final chapter, Habermas undergirds his theory with a fuller account of the proceduralist paradigm that was adumbrated in earlier chapters. His argument thus moves to a deeper level, that of competing "paradigms of law and democracy." Here "paradigm" refers to the basic assumptions about society that inform efforts to realize constitutional-democratic ideals. Precisely because such efforts must come to grips with real social contexts, they presuppose some idea, even if a tacit one, of a historically specific social facticity. Not only judges, lawyers, and legislators, but citizens in general tend to share broad background assumptions about their society, its challenges and possibilities, and how the law should respond to these. Such assumptions can be loosely organized around different legal paradigms. In chapter nine, then, Habermas argues for the superiority of the "proceduralist paradigm" over two inherited paradigms whose opposition has stalemated a number of current discussions. The liberal paradigm of "bourgeois formal law," which dominated the nineteenth century, privileges individual freedom under the banner of minimal government, formal equality before the law, and legal certainty. Meanwhile, however, social inequalities and other problems related to complexity and unrestrained capitalism have, especially in the twentieth century, motivated attempts to instrumentalize law for substantive purposes of social utility. Behind such attempts one can discern a social-welfare paradigm of "materialized" law, so called because of its emphasis on the realization of substantive social goals and values (such as welfare provisions, social security, regulation of commerce, etc.). The problems arising from this paradigm – such as unchecked administrative discretion and intrusive welfare bureaucracies – are also quite familiar by now.[32]

The women's struggle for equality illustrates these paradigmatic issues quite well. The call for equal voting rights, demands for equal access to education, and so on, rest on notions of formal equality emphasized by the liberal paradigm. By contrast, efforts to accord specific benefits to women, such as provisions for maternity leave, special aid to women with children, childcare services, and the like, embody the social-welfare paradigm. As feminist critics have noted, a concern simply with formal legal equality ignores the real inequalities that can arise from contingent social conditions and gender differences, whereas government aid programs often define such differences inappropriately, besides fostering welfare dependency and overintrusive bureaucracies. On a proceduralist approach, the legitimate regulation of such issues requires that women themselves take part in public discussions that determine which gender differences are relevant to definitions of equality. The proceduralist paradigm thereby imparts a dynamic quality to the idea of equal rights.

Habermas's proceduralist approach also demonstrates its usefulness for other issues as well, such as the regulation of the workplace and labor politics. The general lesson, however, is this: the proceduralist paradigm allows one to see further implications of the internal relation between private and public autonomy – thus between equal individual liberties and political self-determination – that was first proposed in chapter three. One thereby gains a better handle on the difficult notion of equal treatment. In addition, one sees how administrations can meet the demands of complexity and social welfare without undermining constitutional democracy. Here Habermas, going beyond his earlier critique of the welfare state,[33] suggests that a proceduralist approach demands a new way of thinking about the separation of powers – that it requires, for example, a more democratic, participatory form of administration.

The argument of *Between Facts and Norms* is both lengthy and complex. Moreover, the philosophical component is pitched at a very abstract level.[34] However, precisely these features are what constitute the usefulness of this book for critical social theory. That is, the complexity, scope, and sophistication of Habermas's analyses – his endeavor to listen to, and combine the insights of, a variety of theoretical approaches, both normative and empirical – make this book a rich and suggestive source for social criticism and reflection on the problems facing contemporary constitutional democracies. At a time when political discourse tends to be skewed by simplistic assumptions and riven by competing ideologies, *Between Facts and Norms* provides a critique of simplistic dichotomies, on the one hand, and it offers fresh theoretical perspectives, on the other. It thus promises to advance our understanding of democracy and thereby enhance the quality of civic discourse and political decision-making.

ACKNOWLEDGMENT

This essay is a somewhat revised and shortened version of the Translator's Introduction to Jürgen Habermas, *Between Facts and Norms: Contributions to a Discourse Theory of Law and Democracy*, trans. William Rehg (Cambridge, Mass.: MIT Press, 1996). I am grateful to MIT Press for permission to reprint this in the present collection. I also thank the following persons for their willingness to read and comment on earlier versions of this essay: Thomas McCarthy, James Bohman, Jürgen Habermas, Larry May, Michel Rosenfeld, R. Randall Rainey, John Griesbach, Pauline Kleingeld, William O'Neill, Mark Burke, and Timothy Clancy.

NOTES

1 James S. Fishkin, *Democracy and Deliberation: New Directions for Democratic Reform* (New Haven: Yale University Press, 1991), p. 4; see also, for example, Joshua Cohen, "Deliberation and Democratic Legitimacy," in *The Good Polity*, ed. Alan Hamlin and Philip Pettit (Oxford: Blackwell, 1989), pp. 17–34; Cass R. Sunstein, "Interest Groups in American Public Law," *Stanford Law Review* 38 (1985): 29–87; John S. Dryzek, *Discursive Democracy: Politics, Policy, and Political Science* (Cambridge: Cambridge University Press, 1990); cf. also Benjamin Barber, *Strong Democracy: Participatory Politics for a New Age* (Berkeley: University of California Press, 1984).

2 *Strukturwandel der Öffentlichkeit: Untersuchungen zu einer Kategorie der bürgerlichen Gesellschaft* (Darmstadt: Luchterhand, 1962); the English translation appeared only recently: *The Structural Transformation of the Public Sphere: An Inquiry into a Category of Bourgeois Society*, trans. Thomas Burger with the assistance of Frederick Lawrence (Cambridge, Mass.: MIT Press, 1989).

3 *The Theory of Communicative Action*, trans. Thomas McCarthy, 2 vols (Boston: Beacon, 1984, 1987); hereafter cited as *TCA*. The German edition first appeared in 1981. For important qualifications, see his "A Reply," in Axel Honneth and Hans Joas (eds), *Communicative Action: Essays on Jürgen Habermas's "The Theory of Communicative Action,"* trans. Jeremy Gaines and Doris L. Jones (Cambridge: Polity, 1991), pp. 214–64. For an introduction, see Maeve Cooke, *Language and Reason: A Study of Habermas's Pragmatics* (Cambridge, Mass.: MIT Press, 1994).

4 H.L.A. Hart provides a good twentieth-century statement of the duality of law in *The Concept of Law* (Oxford: Clarendon, 1961). The well-known image of the "bad man's" view of law is from Oliver Wendell Holmes, "The Path of the Law," in Holmes, *Collected Legal Papers* (New York: P. Smith, 1952), pp. 167–202, here p. 171.

5 Immanuel Kant, *The Metaphysical Elements of Justice*, trans. John Ladd (New York: Macmillan, 1965), p. 34; also p. 35 (translation slightly altered); see also his "On the Proverb: That May Be True in Theory, But Is of No Practical Use," in Kant, *Perpetual Peace and Other Essays*, trans. Ted Humphrey (Indianapolis: Hackett, 1983), esp. pp. 71ff. The exact relation between Kant's principle of law and his moral principle is not entirely clear; see the discussion in Kenneth Baynes, *The Normative Grounds of Social Criticism: Kant, Rawls, and Habermas* (Albany: SUNY Press, 1992), chap. 1.

6 See John Rawls, "Justice as Fairness: Political not Metaphysical," *Philosophy and Public Affairs* 14 (1985): 223–51, and his more recent *Political Liberalism* (New York: Columbia University Press, 1993); Ronald Dworkin, *Law's Empire* (Cambridge, Mass.: Harvard University Press, 1986). There have been some recent attempts to revive a metaphysical approach in legal philosophy, but whether they can have the same scale and confidence as did ancient and medieval systems is a further question; cf., for example, John Finnis, *Natural Law and Natural Rights* (New York: Oxford University Press, 1980); for a critical assessment, see Raymond A. Belliotti, *Justifying Law: The Debate over Foundations, Goals, and Methods* (Philadelphia: Temple University Press, 1992), chap. 1.

7 For Habermas's elaboration on this, see his *Postmetaphysical Thinking*, trans. William Mark Hohengarten (Cambridge, Mass.: MIT Press, 1992) and *Moral Consciousness and Communicative Action*, trans. Christian Lenhardt and Shierry Weber Nicholsen (Cambridge, Mass.: MIT Press, 1990), esp. the first two essays and the title essay. A prime example of such interdisciplinary cooperation is the current work being done in the psychology of moral development.

8   See Jürgen Habermas, "What Is Universal Pragmatics?" in Habermas, *Communication and the Evolution of Society*, trans. Thomas McCarthy (Boston: Beacon, 1979), pp. 1–68; also *TCA* 1: 273–337; and the Christian Gauss Lectures, "Vorlesungen zu einer sprachtheoretischen Grundlegung der Soziologie," in Habermas, *Vorstudien und Ergänzungen zur Theorie des Kommunikativen Handelns*, 2nd edn (Frankfurt: Suhrkamp, 1986), pp. 11–126; English translation forthcoming, MIT Press.

9   For a fuller account of Habermas's concept of discourse, see Thomas McCarthy, *The Critical Theory of Jürgen Habermas* (Cambridge, Mass.: MIT Press, 1978), chap. 4; on moral discourse, see William Rehg, *Insight and Solidarity* (Berkeley: University of California Press, 1994).

10   For the most important distinctions, see Jürgen Habermas, "On the Pragmatic, the Ethical, and the Moral Employments of Practical Reason," in his *Justification and Application: Remarks on Discourse Ethics*, trans. Ciaran P. Cronin (Cambridge, Mass.: MIT Press, 1993), pp. 1–18; also in *Between Facts and Norms*, chap. 3, excursus, and chap. 4, part II.

11   On Habermas's concept of lifeworld, see *TCA* 2: 119–52. [hereafter, *TCA*]. Although for the members themselves the background remains largely unthematized, the theorist can differentiate its resources into three broad components: the stock of taken-for-granted certitudes and ideas ("culture"); the norms, loyalties, institutions, and so forth that secure group cohesion or solidarity ("society"); and the competences and skills that members have internalized ("personality"). A viable lifeworld is reproduced, then, through the cultural transmission of ideas, through forms of social integration, and through the socialization of its members.

12   See Peter L. Berger, *The Sacred Canopy: Elements of a Sociological Theory of Religion* (Garden City, NY: Anchor-Doubleday, 1969).

13   On the development of subsystems, see Habermas, *TCA* 2: 153–97. For helpful summaries of Habermas's account of societal rationalization, see Jane Braaten, *Habermas's Critical Theory of Society* (Albany: SUNY Press, 1991), chap. 5; and Stephen K. White, *The Recent Work of Jürgen Habermas: Reason, Justice, and Modernity* (Cambridge: Cambridge University Press, 1988), chap. 5.

14   Habermas develops his concept of media by way of a critical appropriation of Talcott Parsons; see *TCA* 2: 199–299; here esp. 256–70ff. For Parsons' account, see "On the Concept of Political Power," in Parsons, *Sociological Theory and Modern Society* (New York: Free Press, 1967), pp. 297–354. One should note here that Habermas does not simply accept the development of such systems of money and power uncritically, as is shown by his concern with the intrusion of systemic imperatives into the lifeworld; see *TCA* 2: 332–73 on the notion of "colonization." But he is also dubious of utopias that suggest one can dispense with the contribution of systemic integration in complex societies.

15   For the complications, see Thomas McCarthy, "Complexity and Democracy: The Seducements of Systems Theory," in McCarthy, *Ideals and Illusions: On Reconstruction and Deconstruction in Contemporary Critical Theory* (Cambridge, Mass.: MIT Press, 1991), pp. 152–80; see also Habermas's qualifications in "Reply," pp. 250–63.

16   See John Rawls, *A Theory of Justice* (Cambridge, Mass.: Harvard University Press, 1971), and *Political Liberalism*. See also the exchange between Rawls and Habermas in *Journal of Philosophy* 92/3 (March 1995): 109–80.

17   For example, see Niklas Luhmann, *The Differentiation of Society*, trans. Stephen Holmes and Charles Larmore (New York: Columbia University Press, 1982); *A Sociological Theory of Law*, trans. Elizabeth King and Martin Albrow, ed. Martin Albrow (London: Routledge, 1985); *Essays on Self-Reference* (New York: Columbia University Press, 1990); *Political Theory in the Welfare State*, trans. John Bednarz Jr. (Berlin/New York: de Gruyter, 1990); for a recent overview of Luhmann's approach, see his *Ecological Communication*, trans. John Bednarz Jr. (Chicago: University of Chicago Press, 1989).

18   On the association between "modern natural law" and social contract theory, see A. P. d'Entrèves, *Natural Law: An Historical Survey* (New York: Harper, 1965), chap. 3; for an influential critique of this version of "natural law," see G.W.F. Hegel, *Natural Law*, trans. T. M. Knox

(Philadelphia: University of Pennsylvania Press, 1975).

19   For a helpful introduction, see Walter Buckley, *Sociology and Modern Systems Theory* (Englewood Cliffs, NJ: Prentice-Hall, 1967); Buckley distinguishes a "process" model as well, which avoids the static implications associated with equilibrium and homeostasis.

20   Humberto R. Maturana and others contributed the seminal ideas in the theory of self-organization or "autopoiesis"; see Milan Zeleny (ed.), *Autopoiesis: A Theory of Living Organization* (New York: North Holland, 1981). For applications to law, see Gunther Teubner (ed.), *Autopoietic Law: A New Approach to Law and Society* (Berlin: de Gruyter, 1988).

21   Niklas Luhmann, "Operational Closure and Structural Coupling: The Differentiation of the Legal System" *Cardozo Law Review* 13 (1992): 1419–41; here p. 1424.

22   See Luhmann, *Sociological Theory of Law*, for a fuller explication. Note that this book preceded Luhmann's turn to autopoiesis; nonetheless, he still employs the distinction between operational closure and cognitive openness; see, for example, "Operational Closure," p. 1427; also the "Author's Preface to the Second Edition" of *Sociological Theory*, pp. xii–xiii.

23   More specifically, Luhmann points out that law stabilizes behavioral expectations across three dimensions: temporally, by holding them constant across time; socially, in that all members of the group hold the same expectations; and substantively, in that the abstract meanings contained in legal norms (role definitions, situational features, etc.) hold across sufficiently similar situations; see *Sociological Theory of Law*, pp. 41–82.

24   This is the point of Luhmann's concept of "structural coupling." The difficulties that autopoiesis creates for a systems analysis of regulatory law, for example, are discussed by Gunther Teubner, *Law as an Autopoietic System*, trans. Anne Bankowska and Ruth Adler, ed. Zenon Bankowski (Oxford: Blackwell, 1993), chap. 5. For Habermas's earlier critique of systems theory, see his *On the Logic of the Social Sciences*, trans. Shierry Weber Nicholsen and Jerry A. Stark (Cambridge, Mass.: MIT Press, 1988), chap. 5; and *Legitimation Crisis*, trans. Thomas McCarthy (Boston: Beacon, 1975), chap. 1.

25   For a summary of the central arguments of the book, see the Postscript; here I also draw upon his "On the Internal Relation between the Rule of Law and Democracy," *European Journal of Philosophy* 3 (1995): 12–20.

26   For a brief introduction, see John Gray, *Liberalism* (Minneapolis: University of Minnesota Press, 1986); for the classic statement of twentieth-century liberalism, see F. A. Hayek, *The Constitution of Liberty* (Chicago: University of Chicago Press, 1960); for an overview of approaches to the concept of the "rule of law," see Geoffrey de Q. Walker, *The Rule of Law: Foundation of Constitutional Democracy* (Carlton: Melbourne University Press, 1988), chap. 1; for an influential formulation of the liberal view of the rule of law, see F. A. Hayek, *The Road to Serfdom* (Chicago: University of Chicago Press, 1944), chap. 6; also Joseph Raz, "The Rule of Law and Its Virtue," in Raz, *The Authority of Law* (Oxford: Clarendon, 1979), pp. 210–29.

27   See, for example, Frank I. Michelman, "The Supreme Court 1985 Term – Foreword: Traces of Self-Government," *Harvard Law Review* 100 (1986): 4–77; also his "Political Truth and the Rule of Law," *Tel Aviv University Studies in Law* 8 (1988): 281–91; and Sunstein, "Interest Groups."

28   *Between Facts and Norms*, p. 107; Habermas's interpretation of "D" corrects his earlier view, which identified (D) simply as a principle of morality; see his "Discourse Ethics: Notes on a Program of Philosophical Justification," in *Moral Consciousness*, pp. 43–115, esp. pp. 66, 93.

29   *Between Facts and Norms*, p. 169.

30   See Roscoe Pound, "The Need of a Sociological Jurisprudence," *The Green Bag* 19 (1907): 607–15, and his "Mechanical Jurisprudence," *Columbia Law Review* 8 (1908): 605–10. Subsequent to Pound and prior to Hart, this issue received considerable attention in the Legal Realist movement; for an historical overview, see William Twining, *Karl Llewellyn and the Realist Movement* (London: Weidenfeld and Nicolson, 1973). Since Hart it has been the focus of debates involving the Critical Legal Studies movement; see Andrew Altman, *Critical Legal Studies: A Liberal Critique* (Princeton: Princeton University Press, 1990).

31   See the references to Michelman in note 27 above; also his "Law's Republic," *Yale Law Journal* 97 (1988): 1493–537; Cass Sunstein, "Interest Groups" (note 1) and *After the Rights Revolution* (Cambridge: Harvard University Press, 1990); John Hart Ely, *Democracy and Distrust: A Theory of Judicial Review* (Cambridge, Mass.: Harvard University Press, 1980); and Bruce Ackerman, *We the People*, vol. 1 (Cambridge, Mass.: Harvard University Press, 1991).
32   In the American jurisprudential tradition, one finds a parallel to the European development of "materialized law" in the call for "sociological jurisprudence"; see note 30 above. The classic liberal argument against the welfare state is Hayek's *Road to Serfdom*; for a response, see Harry W. Jones, "The Rule of Law and the Welfare State," in *Essays on Jurisprudence from the Columbia Law Review* (New York: Columbia University Press, 1963), pp. 400–13.
33   His earlier critique relied more heavily on the lifeworld as the source of resistance against bureaucratic intrusion or "colonization"; see *TCA*, vol. 2, chap. 8; on this point, cf. Dryzek, *Discursive Democracy*, p. 20; Amy Bartholomew, "Democratic Citizenship, Social Rights and the 'Reflexive Continuation' of the Welfare State," *Studies in Political Economy* 42 (1993): 141–56.
34   Habermas's lengthy reply to the participants in a symposium on the book provides still further elaboration of his central arguments and assumptions; see the *Cardozo Law Review* 17 (1995). For further succinct overviews of the book, see, for example, David M. Rasmussen, "How Is Valid Law Possible?" *Philosophy and Social Criticism* 20 (1994): 21–44; Kenneth Baynes, "Democracy and the *Rechtsstaat*: Habermas's *Faktizität und Geltung*," in Stephen K. White (ed.), *The Cambridge Companion to Habermas* (Cambridge: Cambridge University Press, 1995), pp. 201–32; and James Bohman, "Complexity, Pluralism, and the Constitutional State: On Habermas's *Faktizität und Geltung*," *Law and Society Review* 28 (1994): 897–930.

8 CRITICAL THEORY AND DEMOCRACY
James Bohman

According to Max Horkheimer's well-known definition, a theory is critical only if it meets three criteria: it must be explanatory, practical, and normative, all at the same time. That is, it must explain what is wrong with current social reality, identify actors to change it, and provide clear norms for criticism and practical goals for the future. Horkheimer holds that these features distinguish "critical" theory from those "traditional" theories which only seek to mirror reality as it is. The critical theory of society, as Horkheimer defined it in his programmatic writings as Director of the Frankfurt School's Institute for Social Research, "has as its object human beings as producers of their own historical form of life"; its goal is "the emancipation of human beings from the circumstances that enslave them."[1] These same criteria apply to the theory of democracy. But democratic practice has a special place in Horkheimer's program for critical reflection, since he believed that the goal of emancipation requires that human beings consensually choose and control the conditions of their lives to the greatest extent possible.

The Institute's members intended for their interdisciplinary research to identify *all* circumstances that limit human emancipation. The varied objects and dimensions of their work included psychological, cultural, political, economic and social-structural limits on human emancipation and forms of domination. Nonetheless, they were sufficiently neo-Marxist to claim that human beings are now enslaved primarily as self-creating producers of their own history. This characterization suggests that contemporary social change has a *unique* goal: to transform capitalism into a consensual form of social life. For Horkheimer, such a society is emancipated to the extent that it is democratic, that is, to the extent that it makes "all conditions controllable by human beings depend on real consensus." The political orientation of critical theory is therefore towards consensus and autonomy, towards the transformation of capitalism and its cultural forms into what Horkheimer in this essay calls "real democracy."

The term "real democracy" derives, of course, from Marx, as does linking democracy to the goal of the emancipation of self-creating and self-constituting humanity. Democracy is for Marx the political form of socialism and justified primarily through the philosophy of history. The main contribution of critical theory has been to extend this radical and anti-individualist tradition of democratic theory further, by correcting its normative deficits and incorporating the best current social research at all levels of analysis. Like Marx, critical theory seeks to replace liberal possessive individualism as the basis for a democratic polity. Orthodox Marxism, however, turned this criticism into a complete negation of liberalism, a problem of empirical overgeneralization that often continues even in the first generation of the Frankfurt School. The more balanced and democratic critique of liberalism in critical theory still accepts some liberal norms: while rejecting individualism, most critical theorists have accepted modern, liberal ideals of universal freedom and equality as constitutive of genuine political consensus. But even then they did not leave liberal institutions intact: democratic institutions on this view should no longer be aggregative or based on rational self-interest; rather, they should be participatory and based on richer notions of reason and solidarity. More importantly, the underpinnings of such a notion of democracy are no longer in economic theory; rather, they are to be found in a holistic social theory and an historical notion of universal reason. A consensual social whole replaces the fragmented and ultimately anonymous order of the market in civil society as the basis for broader political freedom. In fact, the very conditions of civil society that many liberals thought could ensure freedom now are the basis for increasing reification of social life beyond our control. As individuals become objects in a system of antagonism and necessity, they are also subjected to pressures toward uniformity, homogeneity and conformity. Indeed, these reifying forces develop to such an extent that new and anti-democratic forms of political life emerge out of liberal society, which culminate in the fascist state and authoritarian personality. For Horkheimer, these anti-democratic trends meant that "the situation of the individual is hopeless," that the subjective conditions for the exercise of freedom and the achievement of solidarity are being eroded by increasingly totalizing social reification.

Built into this critique of liberalism and its reifying form of social rationalization is a two-sided conception of totality.[2] In many respects, reference to totality becomes the defining feature of the Frankfurt School theorists' analyses of contemporary society. On the one hand, they use totality in a negative sense as an explanatory basis for criticism. It is, first of all, a descriptive concept that explains existing capitalist society as a complex, relational whole, regardless of how it may appear to its members. Ultimately, the "real totality" of liberal society is economic and hence "false"; it is (and remains today) an antagonistic and inegalitarian class society, not a harmonious whole. On the other hand, they use totality in a positive sense as the normative basis for criticism, as a normative ideal and a desirable goal for social change. A "true" totality contrasts with the real totality of capitalist society; but the opposite of the "true totality" is to be found in the "wholly false" totalities of fascism with its fictions of the organic conception of the state or a *Volk* in fascism. As Marcuse notes, such antiliberalism merely gives false, if not "totalitarian," expression to the needs of a fragmented social reality increasingly outside of democratic control.[3] In contrast, the "true" totality is not only rational and consensual. It also brings the social process back under free rational control as an expressive whole. In a "true" totality the needs and interests of each will be expressed in the whole; society will be the adequate and non-antagonistic expression of its members. Given the proper social conditions, free social praxis could create such an expressive whole.[4] Democracy does not figure directly in this positive ideal, except as the means for consensual expression of goals and for genuine moral transformation. If society is to be expressive, it can only be measured by the adequacy of the whole. Even as the Frankfurt School became less and less Hegelian in its later developments, no other more directly democratic, normative ideal replaces such a rational, expressive totality until Habermas developed his positive account of the public sphere.

In what follows, I shall explore the persistent tension between critical theory's descriptive conception of totality and the ideals of democracy that it also endorses. First, I shall show how the Frankfurt School initially develops its notion of real democracy in contrast to liberalism. At the same time, I argue, it is important to show that critical theory is not antiliberal, since it shares with liberalism the commitment to rationalism and universalism. Rather, critical theorists claim that these ideals lose their reference to social reality in the course of the development of capitalism. Second, I shall turn to critical theorists' descriptive and explanatory analyses of this process of the decline of democracy. These analyses are at two quite distinct levels. The Frankfurt School develops sophisticated analyses at the micro-level of how the psychological conditions of democracy have been gradually eroded, while at the same time developing on the macro-level large-scale descriptions of historical processes of increasingly totalizing social reification. Unfortunately, there is little analysis of any intermediate levels. Until Habermas, critical theorists believed that it was sufficient to show that processes of social reification and of the destruction of individual autonomy work in complementary ways. I argue that these facts also make the idea of an expressive totality the plausible norm for their criticism. Third, I shall show that normative totality is ill-suited to democratic theory and introduces a lack of clarity about normative political ideals into the Frankfurt School writings on democracy. Finally, I shall show how Habermas develops the intermediate explanatory level and a new norm of publicity, both of which are more appropriate to emancipatory democratic theory. Nonetheless, Habermas also does not fully resolve the tensions between the explanatory implications of descriptive totality and the political goals of radical democracy in critical theory.

Given these tensions in the early Frankfurt School, Habermas's retrieval of the public sphere is important both descriptively and normatively. Descriptively, he introduces the proper level of analysis, which also permits a more balanced assessment of reification. For Habermas, it is not total reification, but "unavoidable" social complexity that is the main problematic outcome of modern social developments for democracy. With this theoretical shift from reification to complexity, the ideal of society as an expressive totality loses its plausibility, and thus the entire interpretation of radical democracy in critical theory has to be recast. Normatively, Habermas offers a more modest, and hence more liberal, democratic ideal: that of the public use of reason within the boundaries of modern complexity and differentiation. While rejecting the normative ideal of an expressive totality, he believes that the ideals of radical democracy remain vital enough to inform critical social theory. I shall then consider difficulties in Habermas's own arguments about complexity, which in turn make it difficult for him to maintain crucial aspects of radical democracy: most importantly, popular sovereignty.

THE CRITIQUE OF LIBERALISM IN CRITICAL THEORY

The initial writings of the Frankfurt School on democracy subject classical liberalism to the same sort of ideology critique that Marx employed in his political writings, such as the critique of civil rights in "On the Jewish Question." This critique shows that liberal and individualist interpretations of rights and liberties have in reality only an economic meaning. In the context of a capitalist economic order, the moral freedom of the individual is ultimately only an illusion. As Horkheimer put this criticism of bourgeois forms of negative liberty, "The limited freedom of the bourgeois individual puts on the illusory form of perfect freedom and autonomy."[5] Much like some communitarians of today, Horkheimer criticizes the modern philosophical and legal subject as abstract, detached, and ahistorical; whatever freedom and autonomy actors have it is only as "definite individuals" in relation to the freedom of others and in historically specific communities. The freedom of real individuals can only be understood in a holistic way, in terms of the complex relations of the social whole in which individuals find themselves. In contrast to the liberal individual, the subject of critical theory "is a definite individual in her relation to other individuals and groups, in her conflict with a particular class, and finally, in the resultant web of relationships with the social totality and with nature."[6] Insofar as liberal ideology is based on abstract individualism and illusory freedom, the critic of ideology replaces it with a more complete and historical conception of individuality and autonomy. Like most good ideology critique, this criticism is an immanent one. An immanent critique such as this uses the norms or values claimed for an institution in order to criticize it on its own terms. Here Horkheimer and Marcuse contrast liberal rationalist and universalist norms with their historical realization in irrational institutions to show them to be incomplete.

The main presupposition of this ideology critique is that early modern liberal theory can be criticized immanently. Liberalism is still a "rationalist theory of society," one that holds out the possibility that individuals can use their reason to criticize the heteronomous norms and laws governing society. According to Marcuse, it is not this rationalism, but instead the "exclusion of the whole from the process of rational action" that gave rise to the ideological character of bourgeois freedom. The realization of the rationalist theory of society requires extending "rational planning of the whole of the relations of production in which individuals have to live."[7] The unplanned and nature-like market processes produce a "false" totality of unified private interests and impersonal social order. Mutual antagonism and the laws of the market create a holistic order of causal relations outside the control of individuals, an order that can be overcome democratically only through rational control and planning.

For all the problems with this form of individualism, on this view the false totality of capitalism has changed for the worse since its early market forms. According to the theory of political economy which gained acceptance in the Frankfurt School, capitalism has now developed to a monopolistic stage.[8] While I will have more to say about the normative implications of this account of advanced capitalism later, it is important here to see that Frankfurt School theorists, as opposed to orthodox Marxists, no longer saw the private rationalization of economic life as the organizing principle of twentieth-century capitalism. Now a new sort of unification has emerged, with ideologies not of individualism but of irrational and fascist forms of unity that do not meet the standards of liberal rationalism. According to Marcuse, whatever form this new unity and integration takes it still "would have to prove itself before the tribunal of individuals, to show that their needs and potentialities are realized within it."[9] Antiliberal and antimodern forms of totality fail this test, including such ideologies which stress the supremacy of the nation, community, or historical destiny common to fascist and "totalitarian" political thought.[10] In the case of these false totalities, the critic does not proceed immanently but externally, armed with a holistic social theory.

But the external criticism of false totality is not confined to the fascist state. With the development of monopoly capitalism, on this account, the liberal heritage loses all of its rational potential as politics becomes increasingly functionalized and social life reified. As the Frankfurt School adopted this theoretical perspective on reification, the philosophical underpinnings of its critique of liberalism shifted away from identifying the normative potentials in current democratic practice. The objective conditions of reification also undermine the psychological and cultural conditions for democratic change or opposition at the deepest levels. Criticism of this society and its social conditions must not only be external, but totalizing. Due to the interconnections among phenomena in a "false" totality, no aspects or "moments" are rational or worthy of being preserved.

Under these historical conditions, modern reason becomes "instrumental" and "subjective" reason. Purely instrumental reason appropriates and transforms all forms of cultural life, what Adorno and Horkheimer call the "dialectic of Enlightenment." Rather than being liberating, reason turns into its opposite; rather than being progressive in developing the forces of production, instrumental reason brings about regression into barbarism. Social rationalization leads to the spread of instrumental reason based on domination and mastery, including the domination of other human beings and of inner human nature. Modern society is a "false totality" in a new sense: it is one-dimensional, tending towards "total integration" or a "wholly administered society." Liberal institutions and norms do not escape this process and indeed are part of it, with their emphasis on self-preservation and self-interest, as well as their instrumental and manipulative view of politics and the state.

In *Eclipse of Reason*, Horkheimer turns the critique of instrumental reason against liberal democracy. He argues that the same normative contents of the liberal tradition that Marcuse tried to preserve have only had force through their metaphysical foundation in "objective reason." Whether grounded in God, nature or something else, the objectivity of moral principles and values ultimately contradict the subjectivist emphasis of liberalism: while their objective content contradicts liberal self-interest, their autonomy contradicts the actual heteronomy of market relations. The inevitable tendency of liberalism to collapse into fascism "can be derived, apart from its economic causes, from the inner contradiction between the subjectivistic principle of self-interest and the idea of reason that it is alleged to express."[11] Horkheimer gives a long list of moral and political principles embodied in modern constitutions that are supposed to be founded in "objective reason," including justice, equality, truth, rights, happiness, democracy, and property. Once reason is reduced to a formal and subjective instrument of calculation, these standards do not merely change but rather disappear.

With the progressive disenchantment of these contents of objective reason, subjective reason triumphs and undermines resistance to the forces of integration; it adapts to, rather than transforms, economic laws or political organization. With this dialectic of enlightenment, the "illusory triumph of democratic progress consumes the intellectual substance upon which democracy has lived."[12] Democracy then is reduced to simple majority rule, now so standardless that it can easily dissolve into dictatorship when it fits either subjective interests or increasingly blind and functional forces. In particular, these interests themselves become subject to more and more powerful forms of instrumental control and manipulation in the culture industry, the mass media and public relations, all of which make the democratic principles of autonomy mere pretence. Public opinion loses whatever normative sense that it had in early modernity and becomes a measurable and manipulable quantity in heteronomous mass democracy. This critique of liberalism culminates in the analysis of the spread of instrumental reason. Liberalism is the cultural aspect of the process of social reification to the extent that it reduces politics to being a means to achieve subjective ends and desiccates the cultural contents of the metaphysical-religious notion of objective reason.

This criticism of the false totality of modern society becomes more radical in the later writing of the Frankfurt School. The criticism of modern society is now "totalizing"; reason is no longer divided into "subjective" and "objective" moments but rejected *tout court*. In *Dialectic of Enlightenment*, instrumental reason is not located simply in the bureaucratization of modern life or the positivism of modern culture. It is located more deeply in the archeology of Western culture (embodied in the slogan that "myth is already enlightenment"), leaving even the metaphysical and religious heritage that Horkheimer valorized in *Eclipse of Reason* as part of this same process. Adorno's later writings, particularly *Negative Dialectics*, are a sustained attempt to formulate an alternative model of critical reason not dependent on the Idealist philosophical tradition, and in this way he frees his thinking from the idea of the future society as an expressive totality.[13] Without this crucial normative concept, however, any notion of politics or political freedom drops out of Adorno's thought, except the utopian hope grounded in aesthetic experiences of non-identity and reconciliation with "the other."

Horkheimer did not take this route. As the ambiguities of several key passages in *Dialectic of Enlightenment* show, he continued to hold out for a notion of non-instrumental reason founded in the religious-metaphysical heritage of the West.[14] This turn to the background of objective reason led Horkheimer in an increasingly religious direction, seeking the "wholly other" in negative theology. More than that, he emphasized the notion of solidarity, particularly a "universal compassion among all suffering creatures."[15] Pity and compassion are the proper moral responses to beings that are more and more "mere objects of a nature-like process." For Horkheimer, such contents can be the basis for a "new conception of God" and a "genuine liberalization of religion." As opposed to any "dogmatic" interpretation of such contents, their reinterpretation emphasizes "the longing, that the reality of the world in all its horror is not ultimate or final, unites and binds all human beings who cannot come to terms with the injustice of this world."[16] In both cases, Adorno and Horkheimer place the critical theorist outside of democratic politics, since these moral demands of solidarity and reconciliation have no footing in the "false totality" of modern society. They betoken the indefinite possibility of new and more complete norms of democracy, but not what its politics might resemble.

Because of their adoption of strongly causal, historical, and genealogical accounts of the rationalization, Adorno and Horkheimer underestimate not only the normative ideals and political achievements of liberalism but also the achievements of modern emancipatory social movements. If the spread of instrumental reason is as totalizing and dialectical as they believe, the institutional achievements of the modern constitutional state and its rule of law should change little. However, if one looks outside of the philosophical writings of this period to the Frankfurt School's own empirical research, a different picture of democratic potentials emerges. While philosophical writings are totalizing in their critiques of modern culture, the empirical writings are more cautious. They outline both the macro-sociological and social psychological trends that undermined democratic ideals. But in spite of this orientation, the empirical studies point to different possibilities contained in legal institutions and in the democratic socialization of individuals.

Empirical social science concerning democracy does not disappear in the later writings of the Frankfurt School, despite this theoretical perspective. Rather, it remains at odds with their totalizing claims about reification. This disjunction between empirical criticism of anti-democratic trends and totalizing theories of reification remained the basic contradiction of much of the work on democracy of the first generation of the Frankfurt School. It is finally overcome in the works of Jürgen Habermas, who rehabilitates the liberal public sphere. Publicity, too, provides an alternative to the false dilemma of Horkheimer's analysis of mass democracy. Neither "subjective" (or purposive) nor "objective" (or metaphysical) reason exhausts the alternatives. On the normative side, Habermas replaces expressive totality with "undamaged intersubjectivity" and non-coercive communication. This turn to communication clarifies the implicit norms of solidarity and reconciliation in the later work of Adorno and Horkheimer, while preserving the connection with a sociologically useful notion of rationality.[17] On the descriptive side, totality is replaced by complexity, which is not necessarily "false" or reifying. These shifts permit a reassessment of the politics of existing liberal institutions and of the sociology of legitimation problems of the modern state.

THE EMPIRICAL ANALYSIS OF ANTI-DEMOCRATIC TRENDS AND DEMOCRATIC POTENTIALS

One of the main theses of *Dialectic of Enlightenment* is that the objective conditions of contemporary society undermine the subjective conditions of freedom. The argument is primarily genealogical and not especially grounded in social science: it is a reconstruction of the history of Western reason, in which calculative, instrumental reason drives out the utopian reason of universal solidarity (Horkheimer's ideal of identification with all suffering creatures) and mimetic reconciliation (Adorno's analysis of the capacities for a non-identical relation to otherness typical of our appreciation of art objects). One of the main problems with the analysis is precisely its genealogical form, which leaves no other option than to search outside of the Western philosophical tradition for the faint possibility of overcoming the effects of this history. But the genealogical method does not support the strong philosophical conclusions that Horkheimer and Adorno drew. Indeed, this history is somehow supposed to be the uniquely appropriate description of modernity, rather than one of many possible reconstructions of rationalization.[18] As I have noted, the empirical analyses of the Institute in this period do not support or draw such strong conclusions. Even Friedrich Pollock, for example, admits that the totalitarian form of state capitalism is "theoretically not the only possible result of the present transformation." Nonetheless, it is the one that provides the best model for current social trends. The alternative "democratic" form of state capitalism has not yet emerged, according to Pollock, and he wonders if its democratic institutions could remain stable under the increasing bureaucratic control and technical rationalization of decision-making in every aspect of life.[19] It is, however, at least an empirical question whether or not democracy may emerge even under these conditions.

Even as the critique of instrumental reason became the dominant model of social criticism in the Frankfurt School, the various empirical research projects that Institute members were conducting relevant to democracy contradicted its radical political skepticism. The central empirical question of this research was the explanation of the emergence of fascism; more precisely, the explanation of fascism at two complementary levels: in terms of the changes in the structure of the personality and the structure of society. Missing in this analysis is anything in between the individual and totality, such as the level of institutions; and it is worth noting that dissenters in the Frankfurt School to the thesis of a false totality of total reification, such as Franz Neumann, studied precisely these sorts of cultural and institutional phenomena, such as modern law.

Despite employing the basic framework of the theory of reification outlined above, there is much in these analyses that is helpful in analyzing current anti-democratic trends and democratic potentials. These explanations become significant for a critical democratic theory only if they are reconstructed within a more *complete* social and historical theory, that is, one that includes many levels of mediation between individual and social structure.[20] Indeed, incompleteness is the classical error of all theories of reification. A more complete analysis, such as that of Habermas's social theory, introduces such levels of mediation by replacing the concept of reification with one of complexity and the individual as "object" of socialization with a more nuanced account of cultural agency. Such explanations can still underwrite the critical analysis of the ways in which the modern socialization of individuals and the organization of complex societies can undermine the conditions of political and moral autonomy. While the corresponding phenomena of "overcomplexity" fall short of total reification, this revised macro-level theory of modernity performs many of the same critical functions. It also makes room for liberal political norms and institutions in the democratic ideals of a less totalizing critical theory.

The long controversy within the Institute about the political economy of fascism notwithstanding, Friedrich Pollock's analysis of the transition from private, or liberal, to monopoly, or state, capitalism came to dominate. His analysis of the prewar German economy established trends toward the concentration and centralization that were typical of the breakdown of liberal capitalism. With the emergence of fascism, these crisis tendencies were solved in an unprecedented way, with the net effect of dissolving both the unplanned, autonomous market and the neutral, liberal state. The increasing intervention of the state led to direct state planning and rational administration of more than just the economy. Rational techniques of large and small scale replace the unregulated market, including the interlocking of all enterprises, the rational planning of production unregulated by profit mechanisms and the rationalization of the production process down to the smallest detail. All these changes reduce the contradictions of liberalism and produce a political and economic system that, in principle at least, "could solve the major economic problems that caused the collapse of liberal capitalism."[21]

This analysis did not, however, find unanimous agreement in the Institute. In *Behemoth*, Franz Neumann wisely disputes the conclusion that the fascist state produces a fully integrated society and attempts to show the ways in which both economic contradictions and the potential for uncontrolled political conflict remained. In fact, Neumann argues, such a system is even more susceptible to economic crisis due to the increasing interconnection of all aspects of the economy, heightening the need for ever increasing control and political repression. But Neumann's view did not greatly influence other members' negative account of the modern rationalization of every dimension of social life. On their view, "democratic" state capitalism would be a form of democracy in which consent, too, is administered. Both state propaganda and the "culture industry" replace consent; ultimately even the functions of ideology are no longer necessary in a culture of "total delusion."[22]

History, I think, bears out Neumann's rather than Pollock's political economy. However, the deeper problem is not just empirical, but theoretical. No conceivable mechanism could ever plausibly explain how such a complex and yet non-contradictory system could maintain such control over time.

There is no actual process of planning or administration that could accomplish these 'tasks so effectively without opposition and internal problems. First, administrative and bureaucratic rationality can be neither as fine-tuned nor as widespread as Pollock suggests. Rather than spreading to all areas of life and intensifying its capacity to control, more recent studies show that administrators operate with "bounded" rather than unlimited rationality. The structure of formal organizations cannot eliminate uncertainty at the lowest level of the performance of individual tasks. Such uncertainty gives rise to unanticipated problems of coordination within bureaucracies, including redundancy, information costs, and inefficiency. Each member of a bureaucratic organization does not, as one might think on Pollock's description, optimize the efficiency and efficacy of her task. Rather than optimizing (or maximizing), administrators use "satisficing" (sufficient under the circumstances) rationality, seeking to solve problems as they go along in ways not so different than in everyday life.[23] Moreover, planning creates its own internal problems and contradictions, including incentives for inefficiency and false reporting of information that were common in the Soviet economy.[24] Further, recent analyses of popular culture do not find it as integrative and hegemonic as the culture industry hypothesis suggests.[25] Once culture becomes an industry like any other, it can be rationalized and finally lose its autonomy. In the final analysis, however, more recent theoretical work and empirical developments in political sociology do not bear out the social scientific basis for the critique of instrumental reason. Of course, the technical rationalization of many areas of social life can and does cause reification; however, it is unwarranted to see this process as totalizing.

This "totalizing" analysis of political economy spreads into every area of social life. Since the psychic structure of individuals is directly complementary to the spread of instrumental reason, the individual, too, becomes an object of control. As Horkheimer proclaimed in a 1941 essay appropriately entitled "The End of Reason": "Today the individual ego has been absorbed into the pseudo-ego of totalitarian planning."[26] Such statements make sense only in light of the spread of instrumental reason to every aspect of life, to planned work and leisure, and even to sleeping and eating. Individual ego identity becomes a matter of adaptation to these organizational and impersonal forces necessary for survival. With the end of economic exchange among individuals in competitive markets, the destruction of local political decision-making, and the end of the patriarchal family and its form of moral socialization, the social spheres for autonomous activity disappear.

This complementary analysis of personality and societal structures informed the longest and most successful interdisciplinary research project undertaken by the Institute. It dealt with the relationship between the emergence of new forms of authority and the breakdown of the patriarchal family. Its main empirical results are found in *The Authoritarian Personality*, in which members analyzed the syndrome or psychic structure that leads to submission to authority and susceptibility to fascist propaganda. What is interesting for our purposes here is not the psychoanalytic construal of the mechanisms which produce the authoritarian personality structure and its weak ego-identity and externalized super-ego,[27] but that the work still depends on the *democratic* personality as the contrasting type of psychic structure. Such personality structures have not disappeared, according to the survey and interview data of this study. Perhaps one of the more striking results is that the core of the democratic personality is emotional or affective organization and capacities. In both *The Authoritarian Personality* and *Dialectic of Enlightenment*, resistance to reification has retreated to the micro-level, in the continued capacities for the identification with others. Since there are "democratic" emotions, democratic persuasion need not appeal only to reason and constraint: "if fear and destructiveness are the major emotional sources of fascism, eros belongs mainly to democracy."[28] The mimetic capacity for recognizing otherness without projection or self-identification, too, has political implications, in that it is the opposite of the mythological fear of otherness still present in forms of instrumental rationality. Even if we reject the accompanying theory of reification and of false totality, this complementary analysis of the politics of the emotions does not depend on its assumptions. It provides a necessary supplement to the more cognitivist orientations that we will see developed by Habermas's return to political theory and could be incorporated into a complete, empirically oriented critical theory of democracy that is not based on the ideal contrast between true and false totality, but on deliberation and discourse.

DEMOCRACY WITHOUT EXPRESSIVE TOTALITY: HABERMAS ON POLITICS AND DISCURSIVE RATIONALITY

The clearest indication of Habermas's rejection of the explanatory holism of the first generation of the Frankfurt School can be found in his consistent attempt to introduce the categories of meaning and agency back into critical social theory.[29] These were absent in the macro-sociological and depth-psychological approaches favoured by descriptive theories of the "false totality" of contemporary society. Certainly, democracy has no point without these absent categories. Democracy also makes no sense apart from specific forms of interaction and association, from the public forum to various political institutions. Habermas's earliest work, *The Structural Transformation of the Public Sphere* (1961), traced the emergence of new forms of public interaction from the intimate sphere of the family, to coffee-houses and salons, and finally to parliamentary debate.[30] New norms are necessary at this level of analysis, and for Habermas they are the norms of publicity and discursive rationality which go beyond the conditions of their historical emergence.

Differentiation and pluralization are not pathological for Habermas, but positive features of complex, modern social forms. They are not just empirical limits to democratic self-determination but even enable it in certain respects. Once a positive conception of complexity plays a role in political theory, it also follows that modern society cannot be expressively unified and reintegrated without cognitive loss or political repression. The pluralism of forms of life and the differentiation of spheres of activity are now both desirable and "unavoidable" characteristics of modern society. For Habermas, expressive totality is no longer a plausible democratic ideal but needs to be replaced by publicity and mutual recognition within discursive institutions.

Habermas challenges the descriptive adequacy of the conception of false totality in his reconstruction of the transition from liberal capitalism to its contemporary state interventionist form. In many respects, Habermas returns to Neumann's view that the state cannot solve all the problems and contradictions of capitalist production. Indeed, even with state intervention this social form remains for Habermas "crisis ridden" at key points within its structure.[31] In particular, even if the burdens of the competitive market are shifted to the administrative apparatus of the state, economically generated conflicts and unintended consequences may exceed its problem-solving capacities for any number of reasons, including fiscal crises or lack of knowledge. In these cases, the social system as a whole can still suffer from a "rationality crisis." And even if the problems are effectively solved, the costs of such solutions, the distribution of benefits and burdens that result from them, and the use of explicitly political means to solve them, all undermine the nature-like and impersonal character of market processes. Once distributive outcomes are up to conscious choice and deliberation, they must meet the requirements of legitimacy; a "legitimation crisis" may occur either if solutions cannot be found or if available ones violate generalizable interests. Since administration cannot simply manufacture motives and reasons at will but is constrained by the existing pool of cultural reasons, the failure at these other levels may produce a "motivation crisis" among citizens as well. Motivation crises indicate the limits of the micro-management strategies that Horkheimer and others assumed stretched into everday life and psychic structure. With these crisis tendencies, advanced capitalist societies are neither so integrated as Pollock and others made them out to be nor independent of ideological contestation and reason-giving. Thus, there is a space for agency and deliberation of citizens, if only in the public sphere and in social movements which contest the legitimacy of administrative decisions. Rather than being fully integrated with complementary micro- and macro-structures, advanced capitalist society is a complex and multi-leveled plurality of parts, each with different forms of integration. In those parts in which public interaction and institutions still play a role in producing legitimacy, at least, the political norms of democracy have not entirely lost their relevance. Economic growth often requires unemployment and environmental destruction; but policies which promote growth with these costs have produced new social movements and even new political parties.

With this rejection of explanatory and normative holism, Habermas returns to many of the themes of the ideology critique of liberalism. In *Legitimation Crisis*, Habermas argues that the demands of advanced capitalism limit the scope and significance of democratic institutions and norms. Much like Horkheimer's analysis of majority rule, Habermas sees the exclusive emphasis of current democratic practice on periodic elections and voting as an indication of its merely "formal" character. To this reduced version of democracy, Habermas opposes "substantive" democracy, which emphasizes the "genuine participation of citizens in political will-formation."[32] Such a stronger notion of a democratic will formed by citizens' participation also requires more than a merely "formal" or self-interested notion of rationality, just as Horkheimer refers to some notion of "objective reason." However, Habermas's notion of rationality is not metaphysical but discursive and procedural; it is developed in terms of the procedural qualities of the communication necessary to make this public will formation "rational" and for it to issue in a genuine rather than merely "de facto" consensus. Habermas's defense of substantive democracy is epistemological, in that it demands an expansion of Kantian practical reason; democracy is now founded on the intersubjective structure of communication exhibited through the special form of reflective and reciprocal communication he calls "discourse."[33] Democratic institutions are therefore discursive, in that in them free and equal citizens deliberate and make decisions in such a way that all could agree to them without coercion or distorted beliefs. The core of democratic legitimacy is thus not some metaphysical foundation in "objective reason," but the creation of discursive conditions under which all can shape those decisions which affect them. The validity of a decision would be related to "rational consensus" to the extent that it passes a test of intersubjective universalization: a norm is justified only if all could agree to it under ideal conditions.

This consensus is primarily epistemological and not political; it establishes a procedural and discursive notion of rationality. The main argument here is the refutation of the value skeptic (such as Weber) who sees politics as the struggle between "gods and demons." Because of the epistemological character of this view of rationality, Habermas has been suspicious of attempts to apply it or its counterfactual constructs such as the ideal speech situation *directly* to the structure of political institutions. As early as *Theory and Practice* (1966), he distanced himself from Rousseau's claim that the general will can only be achieved in a direct republican form of democracy: by failing to see that the ideal agreement of the social contract specifies only a certain procedural and reflexive level of justification, Rousseau confused "the introduction of a new principle of legitimacy with proposals for institutionalizing just rule."[34] Habermas has also argued from the start that democratic principles need not be applied everywhere in the same way, as defenders of participatory, "council democracy" might have it.[35] Marx, too, is Rousseauian enough to have succumbed to the illusions of direct democracy, putting forth democratic ideals and forms of organization whose scope is limited to face-to-face interaction. Habermas here finds a modified version of the political skepticism of the Frankfurt School useful for dealing with this problem. He holds that the mediation of these democratic norms with social facts requires an adequate theoretical account of social rationalization. But for Habermas it is complexity, and not reification, that is the overwhelming social fact of modern society relevant to democratic theory. It is a fact that he believes neo-Rousseauian and neo-Marxist defenders of participatory democracy continue to ignore.[36] According to Habermas, no normative conception of politics or law can be developed independently of a descriptively adequate model of the complexity of contemporary society, lest it fall prey to Hegel's criticism of the impotence of the Kantian moral ought.[37] Without this descriptive component, these norms become abstract and empty ideals rather than reconstructions of the rationality of actual practices.

The main reason that Habermas is not a Rousseauian is that complexity fundamentally changes the conditions for popular sovereignty, for the unified will of the people. There are two distinct forms of complexity which work to undermine sovereignty in this sense. One internal and the other external. The first has to do with the discursive complexity of political decision-making. Political deliberation cannot be reduced to moral discourse and its extremely demanding idealizations of the ultimate unanimity of all concerned. Rather, it concerns a whole network of overlapping and interconnected discourses concerning policies, goals, and norms. The second sort of complexity is even more deflationary for the sorts of utopian claims of critical theory. Given a certain degree of differentiation in society, there are strong constraints upon the scope of a principle of democracy and the effectiveness of deliberative problem solving. In particular, popular sovereignty loses its meaning as a radical norm. The "people" remains a fiction, since complex societies do not have a political center in the nation state for collecting information or making decisions entirely by consensual means. Complex societies are "polycentric," and this fact changes the nature of democratic institutions and political participation.

In the next section, I will deal with each of these forms of complexity in turn and then consider whether or not they entirely vitiate the radical democratic ideals of critical theory. I shall argue that Habermas's telling criticisms of the notion of expressive totality through external, social complexity does not undermine a more modest version of radical democracy in the public sphere. This is because his arguments concerning internal, discursive complexity do not have all the strong consequences that he thinks they do for popular sovereignty.

THE TENSION BETWEEN PUBLICITY AND COMPLEXITY: HABERMAS AND RADICAL DEMOCRACY

Habermas's turn to communicative action was supposed to provide him with the means to answer Weberian value skepticism and to avoid its implications for the legitimacy of the modern state. Since Weber saw no alternative to instrumental reason, Habermas needed some other form of reason to describe cultural rationalization and learning in modernity. After rejecting his own attempt to formulate a theory of "cognitive interests," Habermas focused his theory of rationality on a Peircean consensus theory of truth for the sciences and a Kantian deontological ethics for the discursive justification of moral norms.[38] Initially, at least, it seemed to Habermas that the rationality of moral norms provided the key to a richer notion of "substantive" democracy that went beyond formal aggregation of self-interest. But this approach proved to be increasingly unfruitful for democratic theory, as Habermas explored the internal complexities of discursive rationality. In his most recent work, he has abandoned the analogies between the justification of moral norms and democratic decision-making so prominent in *Legitimation Crisis*. While exploring moral justification served the epistemological purpose of pointing the way beyond Weber, it proved a misleading and undercomplex model for democratic deliberation. Besides leading to the subordination of law and politics to morality, the idealizations and abstractness of moral discourse set the standard of agreement too high for democratic theory.

The reason why it set such high standards is that Habermas's moral theory is rigorously deontological. It requires that moral norms are restricted to questions of justice that can be settled impartially under a communicative procedure of universalization.[39] The moral point of view necessarily abstracts from the particular identities of persons, including their political identities, and encompasses an ideally universal audience of all humanity. Although politics and law include moral concerns within their scope of deliberation in such issues as basic human rights, they encompass both less and more: less to the extent that they aim at a limited community of associated citizens, and more to the extent that they include problems related to the practical goals and cultural identities of a specific political community. There are thus at least three aspects of practical reason relevant to democratic deliberation: pragmatic, ethical and moral uses of reason are all employed in different sorts of situations, with different objects (pragmatic ends, the interpretation of values, and the just resolution of conflicts) and thus with different forms of validity.[40] Democratic deliberation may include and mix together any of these uses of practical reason. Because of this variety, both its discourses and its claim to legitimacy are necessarily complex. Furthermore, there are unavoidable, inherent and systemic constraints on complex processes of political communication, including "inevitable" asymmetries in the distribution of resources and knowledge.[41] Thus, democratic deliberation is not a special case of moral judgment and its idealizing assumptions, but a complex discursive network which includes argumentation of various sorts, bargaining and compromise, and political communication for the purpose of the free expression of opinions.[42] What regulates their use here is a principle at another level: publicity, or that practical reason is employed publicly. If free and equal citizens use their reason autonomously, then their deliberation is democratic. According to Habermas, democratic deliberation under socially complex conditions further requires the "medium of law," that is, that the results of its deliberation be expressed in law.

For all the modesty of this proposal and its clear distinction between morality and politics, the discursive complexity of democratic deliberation introduces further complications that Habermas does not fully recognize. First, Habermas admits that political deliberation does not pick out a single aspect of validity. Since practical reason is internally diverse and all aspects come into play in politics, there is room for potential conflicts among the pragmatic, ethical and moral uses of reason. These conflicts exist even at the level of an ideal democratic theory: while the ineliminability of internal conflicts makes a discursive democracy realistic, it also eliminates the utopian possibility of a world without moral loss, in Isaiah Berlin's phrase. Second, Habermas argues that the principles of morality and of democracy are separate sub-principles of the same principle of discourse, which he calls "D". According to D, impartial justification is possible for various norms of action within the reciprocal recognition of communicative interaction. Unlike the moral principle (or "U"), the *principle of democracy* does not require that validity be based on the agreement of "all those affected." Instead, as a principle of legitimacy it requires two different features of the law-making process: (1) that laws meet the agreement of all citizens and (2) that the process of law making be discursive, that is, structured according to mutual recognition by citizens of each other as free and equal.[43] The problem with such a weakened principle of democracy is that it still sets the standard of consensus too high. Given the potential conflicts indicated by the first form of discursive complexity, it is hard to see why such procedures would necessarily lead to the agreement of *all* citizens in culturally pluralistic societies, if by this we mean unanimity about every particular law. Certainly, "ethical" and hence culturally specific elements of interpretation will enter into such processes; they do not admit of convergence towards consensus, especially as diverse and potentially conflicting cultural self-understandings enter into the debate on particular issues. They cannot be so easily abstracted from, especially if the conflict of ethical interpretations itself is precisely at stake. Simply introducing compromise as an alternative democratic outcome, as Habermas does, is not enough to solve the problem. While few fair compromises meet with the agreement of all citizens, many permit continued cooperation, despite conflicts, in the absence of any stronger consensus.

The only way out of this problem with the first half of Habermas's democratic principle is to modify the second half in a liberal direction: a law is legitimate if it is agreed to in a participatory process that is fair and open to all citizens. The difference here is that citizens will cooperate in such a process so long as they can see that it is fair, not if they agree with any particular law, goal or decision. Cooperation here is defined as the continued participation in ongoing public discourse, despite disagreement with any particular decision reached by discursive means. In my reformulation, the principle of democracy is as follows: "A law is legitimate only if it is agreed to by all citizens in a fair and open participatory process in which they may continue to cooperate freely." In this way, what citizens agree to democratically only concerns *how* they exercise their political autonomy. It is exercised in the cooperative use of practical reason among citizens within a common public sphere. However institutionalized, some common public sphere is necessary if citizens are to be equal participants in a democracy. The principle of publicity prescribes a form of cooperation that applies even if there are numerous counter- or sub-public spheres.[44] Under internal conditions of discursive complexity discussed above, the democratic principle is a regulative ideal of common citizenship in the political public sphere, not of the legitimacy of law. It is an ideal that also guides the institutionalization of discourses in institutions such as law, with their often indirect ways of distributing discursive roles and decision-making powers according to public, constitutional principles. This may include majority rule and the separation of powers, by which laws are democratically enacted and carried out, tested by the courts, and revised continuously through public opinion.

Even with this greater complexity of discourses, Habermas still does not think that the democratic principle and its criteria of public agreement can be applied directly to political institutions. As Habermas puts it, "Unavoidable social complexity makes it necessary to apply the criteria in a differentiated way."[45] Such complexity eliminates two possible conceptions of publicity that are typical of radical democratic theories: first, that it is possible for the sovereign will of the people and its decision-making power to constitute the whole of society; and, second, that a society formed out of purely communicative association is possible. Both of these mistakes have been made in the Rousseauian and Marxian variants of radical democracy. Habermas is not objecting to these ideals as such, so much as their lack of institutional mediation (although even he says little about the character of legal and political institutions) and their overburdening of public deliberation. Modern complexity is not reifying in itself, as some radical democrats make it out to be. Indeed, the differentiation of society also opens up new possibilities for both private and political autonomy, as well as the communicative and discursive structuring of many areas of life. Under these conditions, as well as cultural conditions of the pluralization of forms of life, discursive democracy requires the mediation of political and legal institutions.

Institutions and their rules can overcome the basic deficits of communicative self-organization that are empirical facts in modern societies: they compensate for "the cognitive indeterminacy, motivational insecurity and the limited coordinating power of moral norms and informal norms of action in general."[46] Under these conditions, we have to change the model for critique of democratic institutions and ideals. To the disappointment of radical democrats, it can no longer be based on the direct contrast of the ideals of communicative association with the reality of complex society. Certainly, modern societies can be overcomplex and hence reifying; but reification is now understood more restrictively as the generation of illegitimate and communicatively resistant forms of power that accumulate in complex institutions.[47] Ultimately, this means that Habermas must abandon the ideology critique of liberalism that was so central to early critical theory. Rather, Habermas tries to appropriate liberal constitutionalism and rights and combine them with radical democracy and its emphasis on self-determination. The question is whether anything remains of radical democracy if these realistic arguments about social complexity and the accompanying critique of ideals of participation are the descriptive starting point for critical theory.

For all Habermas's insistence on institutional mediation, he nonetheless attempts to preserve the radical democratic critique of current liberal practice and a weakened version of reification, now confined to political institutions. To do this, he must hold onto some stronger notion of popular sovereignty than liberalism alone provides, despite all his criticisms of unmediated versions of the unified will of the people in civic republicanism and in socialism. Law and politics must "ultimately" be under control of the people themselves. Without this notion of popular sovereignty and an active public, political will, democracy loses its point. But given his criticism of undercomplex and "direct" models of communicative association, Habermas interprets the "ultimate" role of popular sovereignty quite minimally: politics and law must remain at least open and accessible to the opinions of the general public sphere and to self-organized actors in civil society such as social movements. Whereas the informal spheres of opinion formation remain directly subject to the norms of communicative association, the formal institutions in which decisions are made are not. Social complexity thus requires a strong practical distinction between what Habermas calls "opinion" and "will formation." But such a distinction does not stand up to much scrutiny, if formal institutions are themselves democratic. The same processes that go on in the public sphere at large go on in these institutions to the extent that they may still be considered democratic. It is misleading to place much weight on this distinction, since, in Habermas's own terms, they are *procedurally* identical. It is a distinction without a difference.

Since at least a minimal popular sovereignty now resides in the complex network of communication in the public sphere, it is still possible for Habermas to speak of continuing the radical democratic project of extending democratization of the existing political system. In the final analysis, it may be that this sovereignty is too minimal and too indirect to preserve the radical contents of democracy. Kant, too, thought that the will of the people could be expressed in the public sphere and then only indirectly affect independently and monarchically preserved political power. Hegel, too, preserves complexity by sacrificing democracy: sovereignty is monarchical and not popular. Marx's criticism of the democratic deficits of Hegel's *Rechtsstatt* applies to Habermas's minimalist interpretation of the political content of popular sovereignty: "In a democracy the constitution, the law, the state, insofar as it is a political constitution, is itself only a self-determination of the people and a determinate content of the people."[48] Habermas's version of complexity is open to the same nominalist suspicion about agency that Marx raises against Hegel's highly complex and mediated constitutional state. With or without complexity, too strong a distinction between will and opinion forming institutions not only undermines any actual democratic sovereignty; will formation is entirely given over to institutional actors who are only "influenced" by the public or "open to" reasons it puts forward. It also makes it difficult to see why Habermas continues to call his democratic theory "deliberative," since the public is given only opinion forming capacity. Communicative power formed in the public sphere must continue to be sovereign, even with the mediation of constitutional state institutions and the constraints of social complexity. "Public opinion," Habermas argues, does not "by itself rule, but rather points administrative power in specific directions"; or as he sometimes puts it, it does not "steer" but "countersteers" institutional complexity.[49] But the public does rule in a democracy, in the sense that it is the majority and not administrators acting as proxies for institutions or "sub-systems" who ultimately make decisions and have power. The rule of the majority is what institutionalized popular sovereignty means, and its weaknesses need to be corrected by rational countermajoritarian institutions (such as judicial review), not by social complexity and the differentiation of sub-systems for decision making. Moreover, the majority must be an informed and rational one, in that its decisions are the outcome of fair and open public deliberation.

Without popular sovereignty in some form or another, granting too much to social complexity and its forms of power simply threatens to eliminate any vestige of radical democracy and the very meaning of democratization itself. If, as Habermas admits, democratic political power "ultimately" has to depend on the will of the people, then sovereignty cannot simply be dissolved into "anonymous" communicative networks or dispersed in civil society; it must be a political will not only with an indirect influence on institutions but also real decision-making powers. The attempt to avoid the excesses of past versions of radical democracy and majoritarian rule should not lead to the abandonment of the deliberating public itself, nor to the rejection of the democratic constitution of power by citizens. Popular sovereignty, too, must be added as the third part of the discursive principle of democracy itself: "laws are legitimate if (1) they are agreed to in a fair and open participatory process, (2) citizens agree to each law in the sense of continued cooperation, and (3) this process makes the public deliberation of the majority the source of sovereign power." Only in this way can public participation be the source of resistance to the bureaucratic tendencies that take more and more issues out of the public sphere and make them matters for administrative or economic efficiency rather than for practical reason.

CONCLUSION: RADICAL DEMOCRACY, TOTALITY AND CRITICAL THEORY

In its initial phases, critical theory developed a clear and radical orientation to democratic theory through the ideal of a self-organized, free society that is an expressive totality. The normative contrast operative here is between the real consensus of democracy and the reifying effects of capitalist rationalization. But since Frankfurt School theorists saw the spread of instrumental reason as turning modern society into a "false" totality, democracy played less and less a role in their normative thinking; they sought potentials for non-dominating social relations deeper in the psychological capacities of human beings for solidarity, compassion, and the mimetic identification with others. Habermas's analysis of the crisis tendencies of modern society once again reopened the space for democratic organization. Habermas's thinking about democracy also shows a similar development from a radical, participatory conception of democracy to one that is more indirect and procedural, mediated through legal and political institutions, and limited in scope by macro-conditions of social complexity. This conception of democracy marks the culmination of Habermas's own movement away from the diagnosis of the breakdown of late capitalism and the search for new principles of organization for society as a whole. His most recent work now entirely separates democracy from this utopian legacy of holistic critical theory.

Despite his new-found liberal modesty, Habermas calls his theory "radical," seeing himself as a "radical democrat" and developing its long tradition in modernity.[50] This tradition has provided a real alternative to liberalism and civic republicanism and incorporates the best features of both. Radical democracy is perhaps more liberal than ever before, now that its own excesses have become so clear in the spectacle of the rapid disintegration of state socialism. Radical democracy no longer means the total transformation of society, but is rather a piecemeal project of reform that builds upon the constitutional and institutional achievements of the past. In this reformist democracy, the role of critical theory is to show the potentials and limits of the public and autonomous employment of practical reason. According to the radical democratic view, public reason is not exercised in the state, but in the public sphere of free and equal citizens. In the civil rights movement, for example, citizens collectively changed the entire character of legal interpretation of political equality. To the extent that a critical social theory is defined by its link to radical democracy, it searches for the potential for more extensive democracy, that is, for increased scope for public deliberation and popular sovereignty.

It is certainly democracy that is the real "unfinished project of modernity," as Habermas has put it. Given the practical character of social scientific knowledge, critical theorists can best understand their own activity in terms of democratic ideals: as social scientists, they are reflective participant-critics in the democratic public sphere. Above all, my sketch here has shown how thoroughly democratic ideals have informed the orientation of critical theory from the start. From Horkheimer and Adorno to Marcuse and Habermas, it has sought to articulate and enlarge the possibilities of a human life that is shaped by reason and free of domination. The legacy of critical theory has been to show why radical democracy still represents a genuine and achievable goal, even in complex societies.

NOTES

1   Max Horkheimer, "Traditional and Critical Theory," in *Critical Theory* (New York: Seabury Press, 1982), p. 244.

2   For an excellent treatment of totality as the basic concept of Western European Marxism, see Martin Jay, *Marxism and Totality* (Berkeley: University of California Press, 1984); for the distinction between "normative" and "non-normative holism," see chapter 1, especially pp. 23ff.

3   Herbert Marcuse, "The Struggle Against Liberalism in Totalitarianism," in *Negations* (Boston: Beacon Press, 1968), pp. 18ff.

4   In his analysis of the Hegelian and Romantic origins of this concept of totality, Charles Taylor shows how "expressivism" is a reaction to the fragmentation, abstractness and atomism of liberal society. See his *Hegel* (Cambridge: Cambridge University Press, 1975), as well as his essays on atomism and negative freedom in his *Collected Papers* (Cambridge: Cambridge University Press, 1985).

5   Horkheimer, "Traditional and Critical Theory," p. 211.

6   Ibid.

7   Marcuse, "The Struggle Against Liberalism," pp. 20–1.

8   See Friedrich Pollock, "Is National Socialism a New Order?" in *Studies in Philosophy and Social Science* (hereafter *SPSS*) 9:3 (1941) and "State Capitalism," in *SPSS* 9:2 (1941); Franz Neumann, *Behemoth* (New York: Harper and Row, 1944) and his *The Democratic and the Authoritarian State* (Glencoe: Free Press, 1964). It is the acceptance of Pollock's descriptive totality of a society totally integrated through the state which led to a virtual abandonment of political reflection in the Frankfurt School after the early 1940s.

9   Marcuse, "The Struggle Against Liberalism," p. 7.

10   Steven Holmes's judgment of Marcuse's analysis of liberalism is clearly mistaken on this point, as Marcuse's insistence on the "tribunal of individual judgment" shows. See Stephen Holmes, "The Permanent Structure of Antiliberal Thought," in *Liberalism and the Moral Life*, ed.

N. Rosenblum (Cambridge, Mass.: Harvard University Press, 1989), p. 228. One of Marcuse's main targets here is the Romantic politics of Heidegger's Nazi writings and speeches, and Marcuse is consistently universalist and humanist in his criticism. He rightly sees close affinities between Heidegger's philosophical views and the political theory of Carl Schmitt.

11   Horkheimer, *Eclipse of Reason* (New York: Seabury Press, 1987), p. 21. This book was originally published in 1947.

12   Ibid.

13   See T. W. Adorno, *Negative Dialectics* (New York: Seabury Press, 1973), in which Adorno tries to develop a "dialectical non-identity of subjects" to replace the Marxist and neo-Marxist collective subject of history. As the criticism of Kant in this work shows, Adorno sees no place at all for negative liberties; they are internalized domination.

14   There is a rather sharp difference between the deep historical genealogy of the subject in the beginning of the book and its analysis of *The Odyssey* and the more moderate "Excursus on Enlightenment and Morality"; the latter only criticizes reason instrumentalized to self-preservation and preserves autonomous moral reason, while the former indicts all of Western reason in the same development toward reification. See Seyla Benhabib, *Critique, Norm and Utopia* (New York: Columbia University Press, 1986), p. 164. The latter view, developed by Adorno more explicitly in later writings, is self-contradictory.

15   For an analysis of these claims about religious meaning, see my "Entwertende und bewahrende Kritik: Wahrheit und Religion in Spatphilosophie Horkheimers," *Kritische Theorie und Metaphysik*, ed. M. Lutz-Bachmann (Würzburg: Echter Verlag, 1996). For a cogent criticism from the point of view of Habermas's alternative way out of social reification, see Jürgen Habermas, "To Seek to Salvage an Unconditional Meaning Without God is a Futile Undertaking: Reflections on a Remark of Max Horkheimer," in *Justification and Application* (Cambridge, Mass.: MIT Press, 1993), pp. 133–46.

16   Horkheimer, "Bemerkungen zur Liberalisierung der Religion," *Sozial-philosophische Studien* (Frankfurt: Fisher Verlag, 1972), pp. 135–6.

17   See Habermas, *The Theory of Communicative Action*, vol. I (Boston: Beacon Press, 1984), especially the treatment of Adorno's conception of mimesis and reconciliation in chapter 4.

18   Marcuse puts it this way: "Contemporary society is increasingly functioning as a rational whole which overrides the life of its parts, progresses through planned waste and destruction, and advances with the irresistible force of nature – *as if* governed by inexorable laws." See Marcuse, *Studies in Critical Philosophy* (Boston: Beacon Press, 1973), p. 208; I do not dispute Marcuse's descriptions of phenomena of reification, but only that he, like Adorno and Horkheimer, conceptualizes them falsely as non-intentional, nature-like causality.

19   Friedrich Pollock, "State Capitalism," *SPSS*, vol. 9 (1941), p. 201.

20   For an argument for the necessity of completeness as a criterion of macro-sociological explanations, see James Bohman, *New Philosophy of Social Science* (Cambridge, Mass.: MIT and Polity Press, 1991), chap. 4. It is the incompleteness of macro-sociological explanations that gives them their dramatic qualities, as in the case more recently of Foucault's claims about the spread of the panopticon into a "disciplinary society." Like the Frankfurt School, Foucault provides no mechanism for such total reification, and the causes mentioned in *Discipline and Punish* do not warrant such sweeping claims.

21   Friedrich Pollock, "Is National Socialism a New Order," *SPSS*, vol. 9 (1941), p. 201. For an excellent account of the Neumann-Pollock dispute about the significance of state capitalism, see David Held, *Introduction to Critical Theory* (Berkeley: University of California Press, 1980), chap 2. For its influence on Adorno and Horkheimer's philosophical work in the 1940s, see Seyla Benhabib, *Norm, Critique and Utopia*, chap. 5.

22   See the section on the culture industry in *Dialectic of Enlightenment*, as well as Adorno's analysis of ideology in *Aspects of Sociology* (Boston: Beacon Press, 1972). The culture industry and fascist propaganda make ideology irrelevant, to the extent that they no longer have to hide the fact that they are lies. This new situation makes modern, administrated culture a

Verblendungszusammenhang, a context of "total delusion" for Adorno and Horkheimer.

23 On the concept of bounded rationality, see Herbert Simon, *Models of Man: Social and Rational* (New York: Harper and Row, 1957), pp. 196–206; on the everyday character of even formal-administrative decisions, see Harold Garfinkel, "Good Organizational Reasons for Bad Clinical Records," *Studies in Ethnomethodology* (Englewood Cliffs: Prentice-Hall, 1967), pp. 186–207. These and other recent sociological investigations of rational organizations do not bear out Pollock's political sociology.

24 See Jon Elster and Karl Ove Moene, *Alternatives to Capitalism,* "Introduction" (Cambridge: Cambridge University Press), pp. 4–5.

25 This is true even in research on television viewing; audience reception of this and other media of popular culture is not as passive as initial (and not terribly empirical) analyses suggested. The work of Raymond Williams and Stuart Hall has been influential in showing the important role of interpretive agency in popular culture and counterculture. For an analysis of different, class-specific and often extremely skeptical audience codes of interpretation of television, see David Morley, *Family Television* (London: Comedia Press, 1986). For an alternative framework for the analysis of the mass media in Critical Theory that incorporates interpretive agency, see John Thompson, *Ideology and Modern Culture* (Stanford: Stanford University Press, 1990).

26 Horkheimer, "The End of Reason," *SPSS,* 9:2 (1941), p. 377.

27 See T. W. Adorno et al., *The Authoritarian Personality* (New York: Norton, 1953), especially part III; see also Max Horkheimer's general philosophical analysis of the project, "Authority and the Family," in *Critical Theory,* pp. 47–128.

28 Ibid., p. 480. See also Herbert Marcuse, *Eros and Civilization* (Boston: Beacon Press, 1966), for a fully developed depth-psychological account of liberation.

29 Habermas's methodological writings after the "positivism dispute" correct the micro-sociological deficits of critical theory, which focused on depth psychology and not social action. In *On the Logic of the Social Sciences,* Habermas incorporates recent accounts of social action and interpretive social science into a two-level critical theory. See Habermas, *On the Logic of the Social Sciences* (Cambridge, Mass.: MIT Press, 1988), for Habermas's discussion of intentional and meaningful action, developed into a full, alternative account of rationality in *The Theory of Communicative Action,* vol. I, chapter 1. The absence of these levels of reflection led first generation Frankfurt School theorists into systematic dead-ends in social science.

30 Habermas, *The Structural Transformation of the Public Sphere* (Cambridge: MIT Press, 1989), especially part I. This work again employs the ideology critique of liberalism, comparing the norms which emerged in the public sphere of private individuals with their actual realization and development. While these norms remained unrealized, Habermas does speak of a "propitious moment" in early modernity in which a free and open public sphere of citizens existed in some form. Similarly, the bourgeois family is seen as creating the possibility of new forms of interaction and "audience-oriented subjectivity," although in actuality it remained a "patriarchal" institution. The analysis of the decline of the public sphere in the late nineteenth century in this work is not so independent of the general theoretical orientation of the Frankfurt School after World War II. Habermas sees the public sphere as increasingly commodified, as it is transformed from a sphere of critical public discussion into a reified sphere of passive consumption of programmed cultural objects. Habermas had not yet incorporated a notion of social complexity into his account of the transformation of the public sphere, one that eventually replaces the one-sided idea of rationalization and decline.

31 See Habermas, *Legitimation Crisis* (Boston: Beacon Press, 1975), parts I and II.

32 Ibid., p. 36.

33 As Habermas puts it in his criticisms of Weber, a cognitivist ethics must show that "practical questions admit of truth." See Habermas, ibid., p. 102.

34 Habermas, "Legitimation Problems of the Modern State," in *Communication and the Evolution of Society* (Boston: Beacon Press, 1979), p. 186.

35 See, for example, Habermas's "Preface" to *Theory and Practice* (Boston: Beacon Press, 1973), "Some Difficulties in the Attempt to Link Theory and Practice," esp. 32–40.

36 See Habermas's criticisms of Joshua Cohen's otherwise similar conception of "deliberative democracy." He distances himself from Cohen in the following way: "In contrast to Cohen, I would like to understand democratic procedure as the core of a separate constitutional political system and not as a model for *all* social institutions." Habermas, *Faktizität and Geltung* (Frankfurt: Suhrkamp Verlag, 1993), p. 369; English translation, *Between Facts and Norms: Contributions to a Discourse Theory of Law and Democracy* (Cambridge, Mass.: MIT Press, 1996). Democratic procedures cannot expand to the self-organization of society as a whole and regulate its complexity, "for the simple reason that democratic procedure must be embedded in contexts it cannot itself regulate" (p. 370). Such a criticism is a self-criticism of Habermas's own view in *Legitimation Crisis* as well. Nonetheless, Habermas insists that he is still a "radical democrat." In *Civil Society and Political Theory* (Cambridge, Mass.: MIT Press, 1992), Jean Cohen and Andrew Arato argue that such a conception of differentiation and complexity requires abandoning all hopes for radical democracy. I think Habermas is correct in not drawing such a strong conclusion, but he never clearly shows why this is the case and why he is still a radical democrat, for reasons that I will outline at the end of this essay.

37 Ibid., p. 238.

38 Moral norms and cognitivist ethical theories are the focus of the discussion of the "logic of legitimation problems" in part III of *Legitimation Crisis*. The focus shifts in Habermas's recent work, *Between Facts and Norms*, in which he makes a sharp distinction between a discursive "principle of democracy" and a discursive "principle of morality." See chapter 3 in particular for an extended discussion of this distinction.

39 Habermas, "Discourse Ethics: Notes on a Program of Philosophical Justification," *Moral Consciousness and Communicative Action* (Cambridge, Mass.: MIT Press, 1990), p. 43–115.

40 Habermas, "On the Pragmatic, the Ethical and the Moral Employments of Practical Reason," in *Justification and Application*, pp. 1–18; in these different uses of practical reason, distinct discourses are employed, each with their own internal structures. These discourses are all at work in democratic deliberation and give it what I have been calling its "discursive complexity." As I noted, Habermas spends all of chapter 3 of *Faktizität und Geltung* arguing that law and morality are distinct, in that law is discursively complex in ways that morality is not; thus, political and legal discourses cannot be analyzed as "special cases" of moral discourse.

41 Habermas, *Faktizität und Geltung*, pp. 395–6. These inherent constraints on political communication are "unavoidable": experts will always have unequal expertise so long as knowledge is cooperatively organized; there will be many other inevitable asymmetries, including differences in the availability of information, access to means of production of public messages, and even time as a resource. These inherent constraints are not the same as one's produced by power of ideology or cultural prejudice.

42 Habermas, ibid., p. 286ff.

43 Habermas's formulation of the principle of democracy (as opposed to the principle of morality) is a principle of legal legitimacy: "Only those juridical statutes may claim legitimacy if they could meet with the agreement of all citizens in a discursive law-making process that is itself legally constituted." For Habermas's attempt to give a "precise and sharp" distinction between the principles of morality and democracy, see *Faktizität und Geltung*, pp. 141ff.

44 See Nancy Fraser's criticism of Habermas's *Structural Transformation of the Public Sphere*, "Rethinking the Public Sphere: A Contribution to the Critique of Actually Existing Democracy," in *Habermas and the Public Sphere*, ed. C. Calhoun (Cambridge, Mass.: MIT Press, 1992), pp. 109–42. Fraser introduces a plurality of publics, including counter-publics, as well as strong and weak publics, depending on the distribution of institutional decision-making powers. I would insist, with Habermas, that the plurality of publics can only be democratic if there is some common public sphere of all free and equal citizens.

45 Habermas, *Faktizität und Geltung*, p. 384.

46   Ibid., p. 397.

47   Ibid., chap. 7, especially section III for the distinction between internal-communicative and external-social forms of complexity.

48   Karl Marx, "Critique of Hegel's Philosophy of Right," in Marx and Engels, *Collected Writings* (London: Lawrence and Wishart, 1975), vol. I, p. 31. The problem that Marx is raising here is Hegel's tendency to think of agents as mere placeholders within an independent complex system of interdependent roles and functions; Hegel makes the converse of the liberal mistake of detaching rational action from the whole and makes the constitutional system itself solve problems of sovereignty and the irrationality of public opinion.

49   Habermas, *Faktizität und Geltung*, p. 398.

50   See Habermas, "Volkssouvernität als Verfahren," in *Die Ideen von 1789* (Frankfurt: Suhrkamp Verlag, 1989), pp. 7–38. For a different, non-skeptical treatment of democracy and complexity, see James Bohman, *Public Deliberation* (Cambridge, Mass.: MIT Press, 1996), ch. 4.

Civil Society and Autonomy

Civil Society and Autonomy

In Part IV, *Civil Society and Autonomy*, Jodi Dean, in "Civil Society: Beyond the Public Sphere," argues that, against the "reductionist" approach to state and society which characterized early critical theory, the concept of civil society enables critical theory to retain its emphasis on "culture" while at the same time broadening its approach to the sphere of "democratic freedom." While endorsing Jean Cohen and Andrew Arato's approach to civil society – which employs the Habermasian distinction between system and lifeworld, as well as the use of communicative action as the coordinating mechanism within civil society – Dean employs Axel Honneth's concept of "mutual recognition" to take the concept beyond the notion of the "public sphere." Cognizant of the role of "power" within civil society she conceives of that realm as the "wider terrain within which relationships of recognition are situated, institutionalized and interconnected." Kenneth Baynes, carrying on the tradition of critical theory through the practice of "immanent critique" in his "Public Reason and Personal Autonomy," argues that neither "public reason" nor "personal autonomy" can be justified independently. Rather, Baynes justifies the claim that "the two ideals mutually presuppose one another and thus acquire whatever normative weight or force they have only if they are inseparably tied to one another." Beginning with a discussion of the "public reasons" approach, Baynes finds John Rawls's appeal to "fundamental intuitive ideas" present in "political culture" unsatisfactory because it leaves this claim open to relativist interpretation. Turning to the current debate on autonomy, Baynes concludes that communicative action can not only strengthen but also be strengthened by the discourse on autonomy. The result would be a mechanism for securing the interrelationship between public reason and personal autonomy. These two essays taken together contribute to the current discourse on deliberative democracy.

9 CIVIL SOCIETY: BEYOND THE PUBLIC SPHERE

Jodi Dean

Civil society is a vital terrain for critical theory. As a concept, it signifies an appreciation of openness and democracy, a move away from ideas of one-dimensionality and total administration and toward notions of action, participation, and solidarity appropriate to contemporary, postconventional societies. As a location, civil society designates the network of institutions, movements, associations, and discourses in which democratic action is situated. The early Frankfurt School's approach to state and society was reductionist: prior to his pessimistic shift to negative dialectics, Horkheimer focused on the emancipatory interest of the proletariat; Marcuse hypostatized a variety of social movements into a "new revolutionary class." The concept of civil society replaces this approach with a differentiated understanding of the location of political action, enabling critical theory to retain its emphasis on culture even as it broadens it to conceive of spaces for democratic freedom. In short, the development of the concept of civil society marks critical theory's shift from totality to multiplicity, from a unified social theory to one positing a differentiated model of society and a postconventional orientation to diversity. Unfortunately, this shift to multiplicity has been obscured by contemporary critical theorists' continued reliance on a notion of the public sphere.

For many the concept "civil society" suggests Lockean liberalism, Hegelianism, or Gramscian Marxism. As formulated by Jean Cohen and Andrew Arato in their influential 1993 book *Civil Society and Political Theory*, however, the critical theory formulation of the concept breaks with the stress on the economy characteristic of these early versions to provide a more complex category befitting the differentiated societies of postmodernity. Cohen and Arato employ Habermas's system – lifeworld distinction to locate civil society "as a sphere of social interaction between economy and state, composed above all of the intimate sphere (especially the family), the sphere of associations (especially voluntary associations), social movements, and forms of public communication."[1] Civil society, then, refers to the institutionalized components of the lifeworld. Through institutions which preserve and renew cultural traditions, group solidarities, and individual and social identities, civil society mediates between the lives of social members and the state and economic systems. Further, this complex model of state, economy, and civil society depicts contemporary societies as drawing from three resources to secure integration – money, administrative power, and solidarity. Although civil society is understood as influencing the state and the economy, it does not control them. Both the state and the economy are crucial for the systemic integration, the political organization and material reproduction, of complex modern societies. So in contrast to those who challenge the continued existence of the state and the economy, Cohen and Arato argue for an extension of radical democracy that does not threaten overall social stability.

In addition to drawing from Habermas's work in *The Theory of Communicative Action*, this model of civil society reconstructs the normative dimension of traditional theories of civil society. It is based on an ideal of democratic legitimacy rooted in discourse ethics and a framework of basic rights. Accordingly, Cohen and Arato stress that the fundamental coordinating mechanism within civil society is communicative action. Of course, communicative action is not the only source of social solidarity. Instead, associations in civil society are part of a complex network of relationships. The expansion and differentiation of discursive spheres and the institutionalization of democratic decision-making procedures throughout and within these associations, then, remind us of the primacy of democratic participation and discursive questioning for a contemporary and inclusive concept of civil society.

Thus, rather than simply a descriptive category for empirical social theory, Cohen and Arato's concept of civil society presents itself as a powerful normative ideal. Added to and intertwined with their descriptive account of the concept is an emphasis on those categories of civil society with normative appeal: plurality, publicity, privacy, and legality. This last category emphasizes the role of rights in securing social members' opportunities for democratic participation and protecting the autonomy of the institutions of civil society from the state and the economy. Indeed, precisely because of the priority Cohen and Arato place on rights as guarantors of opportunities for both self-realization and self-determination we can understand civil society as the very site of difference for a complex model of postconventional, democratic societies.

None the less, for Cohen and Arato as well as Habermas and Seyla Benhabib the normativity of civil society has been limited to its constitutive categories rather than appearing as a fundamental characteristic of the concept itself. The reason for such a limitation lies in the continued emphasis on the notion of the public sphere. For Habermas, the public sphere refers to a communicatively generated space, while civil society is the institutional location which permits the creation of this space.[2] Benhabib, too, locates the public sphere in civil society, even as she sees the public sphere as one of "mutually interlocking and overlapping networks and associations of deliberation, contestation, and argumentation."[3] The notion of the public sphere, then, is normative, whereas civil society, *the normativity of whose categories structures the public sphere*, remains descriptive.

Up till now, within critical theory the concept of civil society has been understood in the context of notions of the public sphere. It has been offered as its institutionalization, as a response to particular problems plaguing the concept of the public sphere, but not as an alternative to it.[4] Once we read the contemporary reemergence of the concept of civil society in the context of the *critique* of the public sphere, however, it becomes clear that we must jettison the latter concept in favour of the former. The category of the public sphere, even when viewed in terms of a wide variety of diverse and overlapping publics and combined with a notion of civil society, blocks the move from totality to multiplicity. Thus, if civil society is to function as a site of difference within a postconventional conception of a multicultural, democratic society, it must replace the notion of the public sphere.

Briefly put, the concept of the public sphere has been important to a critical theory oriented to communicative rationality. As Axel Honneth has argued, however, the stress on communicative rationality overly narrows critical theory's ability to provide a critical diagnosis of the times.[5] Accordingly, he urges a turn to the relationships of mutual recognition in which identities and competencies develop.[6] I claim that just as the public sphere has figured as the predominant site of democratic deliberation within the proceduralism of discourse ethics, so does civil society provide the corresponding network of ties and connections in which relationships of mutual recognition are situated and upon which they depend.[7]

I   HABERMAS AND *THE STRUCTURAL TRANSFORMATION OF THE PUBLIC SPHERE*

Critical theory's sustained engagement with the notions of the public sphere and civil society began with Habermas's *Habilitationschrift, Strukturwandel der Öffentlichkeit*. Aiming to "derive the ideal type of the bourgeois public sphere from the historical context of British, French, and German developments in the eighteenth and early nineteenth centuries," Habermas attempted to give an account of the kind of social conditions conducive to a critical-rational discussion of public issues by private persons.[8] To this end, he traces the changes in what he sees as the private sphere, the conjugal family and the economy, and in the "authentic public sphere," which technically remained part of the private sphere insofar as it was separate from the realm of state authority.[9] The key components of this "authentic public sphere" were the literary public sphere and the political public sphere.

What is crucial to Habermas is the way the eighteenth century witnessed a shift in the grounds of authority in the public sphere. Whereas in the seventeenth century public authority refers to that of court and state over and against the common people, with "public" connoting the visible representation of king and nobles, in the eighteenth century the public sphere is one of the private people come together as a public. Together as a public, the private people claim the public sphere "against the public authorities themselves, to engage them in a debate over the general rules governing relations in the basically privatized but publicly relevant sphere of commodity exchange and social labor."[10] Constitutionally, the authority of the public comes to rest on the notion that all power stems from the people. Their self-legislation, their establishment of the participatory freedoms of the press, of opinion, and of assembly, of the individual freedoms of the patriarchal family, and of the economic freedoms of property and exchange, establishes the limits of state authority and institutionalizes as an organizing principle the continuing role of critical debate.

So despite the fact that this new public sphere remains fundamentally bourgeois, that is, anchored in the economic interests of a particular class of property owners, it also carries with it a set of norms which enable it both to secure itself against the state and to function as a terrain for critical-rational debate. Accordingly, Habermas finds that the salons, coffee houses and *Tischgesellschaften* (table societies) of France, England, and Germany, which function as instantiations of the literary public sphere whose ideal of critical publicity gives rise to the political public sphere, share similar institutional criteria of equality, accessibility, and inclusivity. First, they disregard status, stressing the importance of the equality of all. As Habermas explains, "The parity on whose basis alone the authority of the better argument could assert itself against that of social hierarchy and in the end carry the day meant, in the thought of the day, the parity of "common humanity."[11] Second, the discussions in the salons, coffee houses, and table societies problematize issues which had previously been unquestioningly accepted. Now non-elites could wrest public issues and cultural products from the interpretive grasp of state and clergy, claiming as their own the right and opportunity to create and challenge meaning. Third, in the same way that cultural products come under the critical scrutiny of the people, so does the notion of the people, the public, itself emerge as reflexive and inclusive, as always open to critique. "However exclusive the public might be in any given instance, it could never close itself off entirely and become consolidated as a clique; for it always understood and found itself immersed within a more inclusive public of all private people . . ."[12] Thus, for Habermas, the public institutionalized in the literary public sphere of salons, coffee houses, and table societies is always conscious of being part of yet a larger public.

Of course, the public of the world of letters is also profoundly private. The concerns it so passionately debates are deeply tied with a subjectivity rooted in the patriarchal conjugal family. Despite the family's material dependence on commodity exchange in the market, in its patriarchal form it secures an illusion of autonomy through ideals of voluntariness, a lasting community of love, and the cultivated personality. Although these ideals conflict with the actuality of bourgeois family life, for Habermas they extend beyond mere ideology insofar as they represent an ideal of humanity which, while present in the bourgeois world, nonetheless promises redemption from it. In other words, these ideals suggest the hope of purely human relationships, of the fundamental experience of humanity. These relationships take the literary forms of the letter and the diary, a letter to oneself. Because of the popular and cultural significance of letters, whether published as novels or as collections of correspondence, Habermas concludes that the subjectivity characteristic of the bourgeois public sphere is "always already oriented to an audience."[13]

Having sketched his ideal-typical model of the bourgeois public sphere and the ideals of equality, reflexivity, and inclusivity necessary for critical-rational debate, Habermas uses this model as a standpoint from which to critique the contemporary constitutional welfare state. These ideals, in other words, function as the normative basis for his analysis of the infiltration of the public sphere by power, most specifically that of a manipulative media power under the sway of commercialized economic interests and parties and political organizations preoccupied with mobilizing mass loyalty.

In *The Theory of Communicative Action*, Habermas refines this critique. First, he finds a deeper anchoring of the ideals of the public sphere in the presuppositions of the everyday communicative practices structuring the lifeworld. Second, he revises his account of the infiltration of the public sphere, linking it now with the colonization of the lifeworld by the systems of the state and economy. Together these two moves enable Habermas to explain how it is possible for the critical force of public debate to erect a dam against the colonizing encroachment of system imperatives: rationalization refers to more than a Weberian increase in instrumental rationality; communication, too, can become more rational to the extent that procedures are established which permit the realization of the norms of inclusion, equality, reflexivity, and reciprocity. To this extent, in his later work Habermas abandons the totalizing conception of a fusion between state and civil society which characterize his diagnosis in *Strukturwandel* in favor of the more differentiated system-lifeworld model.[14]

While critics have leveled a wide variety of objections against Habermas's analysis of the bourgeois public sphere, I focus on those points most relevant to later changes in the concept of the public sphere and the corresponding discussion of civil society.[15] These include the location of public authority, the normativity of the ideals of the bourgeois public sphere, and Habermas's characterizations of the private sphere and bourgeois subjectivity.

Habermas's account of the shift in public authority from king to people retains the notion of state centered power characteristic of the philosophy of the subject. In his later reflections on this account he acknowledges that

> the presumption that society as a whole can be conceived as an association writ large, directing itself via the media of law and political power, has become entirely implausible in view of the high level of complexity of functionally differentiated societies. The holistic notion of a societal totality in which the associated individuals participate like the members of an encompassing organization is particularly ill suited to provide access to the realities of an economic system regulated through market and of an administrative system regulated through power.[16]

Indeed, Habermas now views the discourse ethics conception of the democratic process as differing from its liberal and republican competitors on precisely this point. Rather than adopting a state-centered notion of society, be it one which sees the state as the guardian of a market economy or as the institutionalization of an ethical community of citizens, discourse theory relies on a decentered notion of society in which "the success of deliberative politics depends not on a collectively acting citizenry but on the institutionalization of the corresponding procedures and conditions of communication."[17]

Further, as numerous critics have pointed out, Habermas overstates the ideal of a single, unitary public sphere and the generality of its norms. For example, Elsa Barkley Brown has described the role of the church in the constitution of a black public sphere in post-slavery America. Focusing on the black community in Richmond, Virginia, she notes:

> Within black Richmonders' construction of the public sphere, the forms of discourse varied from the prayer to the stump speech to the testimonies regarding outrages against freedpeople to shouted interventions from the galleries into the debates on the legislative floor. By the very nature of their participation – the inclusion of women and children, the engagement through prayer, the disregard of formal rules for speakers and audience, the engagement of the galleries in the formal legislative sessions – Afro-Richmonders challenged liberal bourgeois notions of rational discourse. Many white observers considered their unorthodox political engagements to be signs of their unfamiliarity and perhaps unreadiness for politics.[18]

Thus, not only does Brown suggest the active presence of spheres outside the "official" public sphere, but she also points out that the norms of these "other" spheres may differ significantly from those of the bourgeois public sphere. Furthermore, drawing from work by Joan Landes, Mary Ryan and Geoff Ely, Nancy Fraser argues that the norms of the public sphere depend on the exclusion of women and the working class. She addresses the way there was never any one bourgeois public but a variety of competing and counterpublics, writing: "the problem is not only that Habermas idealizes the liberal public sphere but also that he fails to examine other, nonliberal, nonbourgeois, competing public spheres."[19] In short, he adopts an homogeneous and homogenizing conception of the public sphere.

Again, Habermas has since revised his assessment of the bourgeois public sphere, now stressing the "pluralization of the public sphere in the very process of its emergence."[20] In this context, he looks more closely at the exclusion of women from the public and the gendered nature of the public and the private spheres. Nonetheless, he rejects the notion that the exclusion of women was constitutive of the public sphere because he remains committed to the view that the bourgeois public sphere always carried with it the potential for its own self-transformation. Thus, he contrasts the position of women in regard to the masculinity of the public sphere with the relationship between traditional monarchical domination and the common people. Unlike women, the latter were "forced to move and express themselves in a universe that was different and *other*."[21] Stressing that critical self-referentiality and reflexivity were constitutive of discourse in the bourgeois public sphere, he concludes that women were not constitutively excluded. In this connection, Habermas interprets feminism as exclusively concerned with the universalization of civil rights, arguing that their emphasis on inclusion and equality represents the continuation of the self-understanding of the public sphere.

Few feminists will find this argument convincing, rightly suspecting that such a notion of the public sphere continues to repress difference, specifically sexual difference.[22] The ideals of the bourgeois public sphere, especially as they emerge out of the family and literary public sphere, require the denial not of women's dependence but of men's on the wives who look after their material and emotional needs. As Patricia Mann explains:

> Ideals of male autonomy, or freedom from dependency upon others, rested upon a denial of women's personhood such that it was possible to dismiss the social significance of male dependency upon women within the family. Ideals of male achievement under capitalism, of answering only to oneself and one's own interests, and of devoting oneself single mindedly to the pursuit of material forms of wealth, presupposed wives whose services and interests could be *wholly subsumed* within those of the liberal man.[23]

The very ideal of autonomy presupposes the exclusion of women. The rights securing this masculine autonomy in the market and in the political public sphere were rooted in an ideal of rationality. For women to claim these rights as their own, they have had to conform to a masculine standard. But, because rationality and autonomy are already masculine, women are constructed as feminine; they are defined as having their own distinct characteristics and embody those capacities viewed as masculine in a different way. They thus can neither see themselves nor be seen as bearers of rights which fundamentally deny their difference.

For example, establishing equality has required women to show that they are equal to or the same as men. The male standard is the norm against which all else is measured. So simply saying that women can challenge their exclusion is not enough when the norms that determine their inclusion are already gendered. In effect, the masculinity of the norms of the public sphere functions as a new center. Women have not had the luxury, neither now nor in the eighteenth and nineteenth centuries, of living in a decentered society. They have had to appeal to a state, a public, and a set of norms which remain fundamentally masculine.[24]

Furthermore, the gendered limits of what can be considered a public issue have been clear to women. The norms of the public sphere function to exclude certain topics from debate and to establish standards for what can be said and what must remain unsaid. In order to speak under these conditions, women have had to conform to a set of standards and expectations they did not establish. They have been "forced to move and express themselves in a universe that is different and other." Even with efforts to open up the debate as to what is legitimate and what is not, women remain excluded because of the very rules which give form to this debate. These rules have determined which topics can be seen as worthy of political debate, which themes are universal or general enough to warrant public interest.

What is striking in Habermas's denial of the constitutive aspects of women's exclusion from the bourgeois public sphere is his implicit acceptance of the gendered structure of the literary and political public spheres. Although the primary audience in the literary public sphere, women are excluded from the political sphere. Just as the family functions to create a particular type of subjectivity, so does the literary sphere help to create a normativity women could not attain. Cohen and Arato write:

> The ideal of humanity coming from the intimate sphere of the family and pervading the literary public sphere is of course moral, universalist, and antipolitical – a clear reflection of the position of women in bourgeois society. Women came to represent "morality" and the "interests of humanity" by virtue of their very powerlessness and "disinterestedness" (their supposed lack of a strong self with real particular interests), without being deemed capable of attaining a universalist, reasoned moral point of view themselves; their presence as the audience of the literary public sphere and as the symbol of moral humanity was linked to their exclusion from all the spheres of civil society and the polity, apart from the family. This is why they could symbolize rather than attain the universalist, moral point of view and why the norm of humanity itself reflected the problematic position of women: powerless humanity.

This notion of powerlessness is key. Habermas wants to deny the constitutive exclusion of women because he holds onto the notion that the public sphere, understood now in terms of the communicative spaces created by participants in discourse, is, at least in principle or in its "pure form," undistorted by the "infiltration" of power. Power comes from outside. It is not part of action oriented toward reaching understanding, which, when institutionalized in democratic procedures, yields "influence."

Finally, there are some problems with the notion of subjectivity at work in *Strukturwandel*. Even if we leave aside the obvious distortions which arise in a subjectivity developed in the context of the patriarchal family,[25] Habermas's conception of a subject who, "by communicating with itself, attained clarity about itself," belies the conflicts and multiplicities already present within any subjectivity.[26] Just as his notions of state and public in this early work remain overly totalized, so does his notion of the subject. More to the point, his account of subjectivity suggests less a communicative subject than a subjugated one, one compelled to create and present itself before a *judging and normalizing* audience of others. Interestingly, his account of audience-oriented subjectivity resembles his discussion of the traditional representative publicness of king and lord. The attention to presentation and rhetoric which characterize the sentimental and well-worded letters of the eighteenth century remind one of the concern with demeanor, rhetoric, and attire accompanying the staging of publicity in the High Middle Ages. Indeed, Habermas's description of the representation of the lord *before* the people equally describes the presentation of subjectivity in the letter: "representation pretended to make something invisible visible through the public presence of the person of the lord" – or letter.[27] In his later work, Habermas has moved away from this representational account of subjectivity in favor of a more complex understanding of an intersubjectively constituted subject, a subject who, in its dependence on relationships of mutual recognition, remains fragile and vulnerable.

II   CIVIL SOCIETY AND CHANGES IN THE NOTION OF THE PUBLIC SPHERE

The moves toward a decentered conception of society, an emphasis on the institutionalization of procedures of democratic decision-making on a variety of levels, and a stress on the relationships of mutual recognition in which fragile identities are situated have acquired conceptual coherence, at least in part, through the inclusion of the notion of civil society. Habermas's shift from the norms of the bourgeois public sphere to the presuppositions of communicative action left an institutional deficit in his critical theory of society.[28] The rules of practical discourse anchored in the presuppositions of communicative action are supposed to structure practical discourses for the justification of normative validity claims. These well known rules of universality, inclusivity, equality, and reciprocity, however, are rarely realized in practice. Since for Habermas discourses must actually be carried out if a claim is to be justified, where and how these discourses can take place is a crucial question. Similarly, although the concept of the lifeworld helps explain the possibility of increased rationality at the level of communication, it remains overly focused on the background assumptions of language and culture upon which individuals draw in everyday life. As Cohen and Arato point out:

> The institutions of social integration, institutionalized groups, collectives, and associations are omitted from this treatment, despite their obvious political and economic relevance. In their absence, the possibility that lifeworld institutions can influence "the formally organized domains of action" is not really thematized; the idea that communication between lifeworld and system could use channels other than the media of money and power is not even raised.[29]

In response to the institutional deficit in discourse ethics and the concept of the lifeworld, Cohen and Arato present their complex model of civil society in terms of a variety of institutionalized discourses and procedures of democratic decision-making, discourses and procedures which not only are communicatively structured but which allow for the critical discussion of norms and values and can be understood as providing the differentiated network of practices behind the lifeworld processes of socialization, societal integration, and cultural reproduction.

This model of civil society has influenced the concept of the public sphere in recent critical theory. In the first place, Cohen and Arato stress that, unlike traditional models of civil society which either equate it with the market, contrast it with and exclude from it the intimate or domestic sphere of the family, or overly politicize the concept itself, their model projects the ideal of "the plurality of democracies." In their words, "The legitimating principles of democracy and rights are compatible only with a model of civil society that institutionalizes democratic communication in a multiplicity of publics and defends the conditions of individual autonomy by liberating the intimate sphere from all traditional as well as modern forms of inequality and unfreedom."[30] Picking up on Cohen and Arato's emphasis on the necessity of multiplicity for contemporary understandings of democracy, Benhabib rejects the fiction of a general deliberative assembly characteristic of that early democratic theory still based in the philosophy of the subject and urges a model of democratic deliberation which privileges "a *plurality of modes of association* in which all affected can have the right to articulate their point of view."[31] These "modes of association" which Benhabib links to the public sphere are precisely the groups, discourses, and institutions Cohen and Arato find in civil society. Benhabib writes:

> These can range from political parties, to citizens' initiatives, to social movements, to voluntary associations, to consciousness-raising groups, and the like. It is through the interlocking net of these multiple forms of associations, networks, and organizations that an anonymous "public conversation" results. It is central to the model of deliberative democracy that it privileges such a public sphere of mutually interlocking and overlapping networks and associations of deliberation, contestation, and argumentation.[32]

Habermas, while stressing the distinction between civil society as the institutionalized basis of a public sphere understood in terms of the social space generated in communicative action, likewise emphasizes the plurality of publics and the network-like structure of differentiated publics which enables the public sphere to generate political influence.

In the second place, just as the concept of the civil society has drawn attention to the institutionalization of discourses and hence contributed to the shift to a decentered notion of society, so has it added to critical theory's ability to move away from the gendered opposition between public and private spheres found in *Strukturwandel* and implicit in the discourse ethics' conception of justice. This has contributed to a more diverse conception of the public sphere, one which seeks to avoid homogenization. Habermas has stressed that practical discourses concern issues of justice; questions of the good life are ethical questions which cannot be answered in the same way. Traditionally, the concerns of women have been said to be particular questions, far removed from the general issues at stake in the public sphere. As critics such as Benhabib have pointed out, it has thus appeared as if discourse ethics relies on a gendered split which cannot take into account the concerns and interests of women.[33] Once we understand discourses as institutionalized on a variety of terrains stretching throughout our social spaces, as questions of validity which can neither be determined in advance nor isolated in a pregiven domain, however, we realize that the very concept of a boundary between the public and private spheres is itself an issue to be democratically determined.[34] Habermas writes:

> The threshold separating the private sphere from the public is not marked by a fixed set of topics or relationships but by *altered conditions of communication*. These [conditions] certainly vary the accessibility [of the two spheres], safeguarding the intimacy of the one sphere and the publicity of the other. However, they do not seal off the private sphere from the public but only channel the flow of topics from one sphere into the other.[35]

Since the boundaries of public and private shift, through both the participatory communicative interactions of agents in civil society and the influence these interactions can have on the legislative process, it is no longer necessary to presume that the public sphere must repress difference, traditionally and symbolically confined to the domain of the private. Instead, difference is already assumed as an aspect of institutionalized discourses in civil society and protected via a variety of rights.

In the third place, although admittedly to a lesser extent, civil society's attention to institutions has contributed to critical theory's appreciation of the importance of relationships of mutual recognition for the protection of vulnerable identities. While these relationships are significantly thematized in Habermas's work on moral development, to the extent that the concept of civil society reminds us of the variety of types of relationships and interactions interwined throughout the social net, it draws us away from an exclusive focus on purely deliberative politics to remind us of the importance of networks of solidarity. The associations and groups of civil society enable individuals both to form identities and to participate in dialogue. Thus, ensuring that these relationships remain intact, that individuals receive the recognition necessary for the very formation of their identities, is vital to the communicative dimensions of the normative aspect of civil society.

Even as the concept of the public sphere has come under the influence of the notion of civil society, it nonetheless has remained prior to it. Despite its own move toward openness and multiplicity, and the benefits of a model which incorporates the institutional contribution of civil society, to the extent that the public sphere continues both to anchor the discussion of deliberative politics, and, consequently, to occupy the center of a critical theory of society, critical theory fails to do justice to the multiplicity and diversity of postconventional societies. The question, then, is why a notion of the public sphere is still deemed so important and useful.

There are two connected answers. Benhabib claims that "a normative theory of deliberative democracy requires a strong concept of the public sphere as its institutional correlate."[36] Leaving aside the problem that civil society has been understood as providing the institutional component of deliberative democracy, we will still want to know why a strong concept of the public sphere is required. Benhabib presents her answer in the context of a critique of Iris Marion Young, writing: "Some formula of the moral ideal of impartiality as a regulative principle which should govern not only our deliberations in public but also the articulation of reasons by public institutions is absolutely central to democratic legitimacy."[37] Her idea is that democratic legitimacy means that laws and policies must be in the equal interests of all concerned. Clearly, Benhabib is correct with respect to the articulation of reasons by public institutions. We would rightly be suspicious of laws or policies which were explicitly justified as to the benefit of the few.[38] More problematic is her notion that a moral ideal of impartiality should govern our deliberations in public. It is not at all clear how she can combine this idea with an emphasis on the plurality of discourses within the public sphere.

At issue is the site of application of the rules of discourses (summarized by Benhabib as the moral ideal of impartiality). If these rules apply to specific associations and discussions in civil society, then few discussions can be said to be aspects of a public sphere since few discussions are actually carried out in accordance with these rules. From the specialized discourses of the academy, to the commercialized discourse of the media, to the exclusive nature of groups organized by interest, ethnicity, and sexuality, to deliberately exclusionary think tanks and private clubs, the discussions institutionalized in civil society remain partial. In fact, for many who have articulated their demands under the rubric of "identity politics," the partiality of their discussions and interactions is crucial to their capacity to understand and present themselves as a group. If the rules of discourse apply to civil society as a whole, to the variety of discussions as they compete and overlap, then one set of norms has been hypostatized over others, subverting the very diversity Benhabib's conception of heterogeneous publics was supposed to provide. If the rules are supposed to apply to the products of discourse, reflecting the outcome of a diverse set of discussions, the regulative ideal of a public sphere then operates to occlude inequality. It too easily suggests that all discourses are situated at the same level, that each has an equal opportunity to participate in public debate. Finally, if the rules are understood strictly as constitutional provisions, as guarantees of the freedoms of association, opinion, and the press, then the public sphere remains tied to and dependent upon the state, reinforcing a state-centered conception of democracy. Indeed, we lose the independence and creativity of discussions such as those urged by the new social movements, relying on a top-down understanding of democratic deliberation and forfeiting our ability to conceive of the establishment of new fora and terrains of contestation and debate.

I prefer to understand the rules of discourse as the ideal presuppositions governing real practical discourses, that is, real discussions of the validity of norms, and not as indicators or determinants of what counts as a public sphere. In fact, when the issue is characterizing the variety of discussions constitutive of democratic debate, discussions which can range from those of justice, to those of the good life or our self-understanding as members of a particular community, to those pragmatic discourses in which we determine how best to realize our choices and ends, understanding them all as part of the diversity of civil society reminds us that most of our characterizations will remain both artificial and potentially dangerous to the extent that we fail to acknowledge how they are always already overlapping and interconnected. I thus agree with Judith Butler when she writes: "To set the 'norms' of political life in advance is to prefigure the kinds of practices which will qualify as the political and it is to seek to negotiate politics outside of a history which is always to a certain extent opaque to us in the moment of action."[39] Using the rules of discourse to determine the boundaries of the public sphere misdirects us into focusing on closure, answers, and categorization of discourses. A stress on civil society, however, points us toward openness, questioning, and an acceptance of the messiness of political styles and engagements.

Adding an "s" to the public sphere is not enough to move it from homo- to heterogeneity. So long as we remain limited by the notion that "the" or "a" public sphere is necessary for deliberative democracy we will reinstate a totalizing model that fails not only to allow for inclusion but to take accountability for the ways in which many are always already excluded. We will risk equating discourses and associations as if they were all equally situated. Simply stressing the multiplicity of possible publics and counterpublics does not attune us to the ways in which discourses and associations in civil society mutually and asymmetrically form and construct each other. Furthermore, we will disadvantage particular communicative relationships and participatory practices, not seeing them on their own terms, but redefining (and hence colonizing) them in accordance with one set of norms. Not all harms can be adequately conceived as violations of rules of discourse. Many, as Honneth reminds us, are violations of the identity needs of persons, of their need for sustenance, dignity, and respect. Thus, we need to recognize that insofar as participatory rights are institutionalized in a constitution they allow for the emergence and protection of a variety of differing discourses and associations in civil society, in principle privileging none as "public" while encouraging the publicity of them all. Further, we need to remain attuned to the limits of rights and discourse and seek to do justice to the depth of human needs and the multiplicity of forms of suffering. In short, the problems arising from a notion of the public sphere rooted in an ideal of moral impartiality suggest the need to move away from a strict focus on communicative rationality.

As she answers the question, "why the public sphere?" with reference to the importance of an ideal of impartiality, Benhabib points us toward yet a second answer to the question, "why the public sphere?", one articulated most forcefully by Habermas. For Habermas, the ideal of a public sphere asserts itself as a bulwark against the systematizing effects of the state and economy. Reproduced through communicative action, the public sphere "is a warning system with sensors that, though unspecialized, are sensitive to the entire gamut of society. From the perspective of democratic theory, the public sphere must, moreover, amplify the pressure of problems, i.e., . . . convincingly and *influentially* thematize them, furnish them with contributions, and dramatize them in such a way that they are taken up and dealt with by parliamentary complexes."[40] In other words, the public sphere is the primary locus of the struggle to protect the lifeworld, our private intimacies and solidarities, indeed, communicative rationality itself, against invasion. Its purpose is the critical articulation of problems in such a way that will lead to legislative results.

Habermas's assumption that the public sphere is a necessary bulwark against the encroachment of state and economy suffers from two primary oversights: an inadequate account of the role of power and a restrictive focus on communicative rationality. Habermas wants to retain the idea of the public sphere because his critique of the colonizing forces of state and economy presupposes an area immune from power. This, of course, makes sense when we recall Cohen and Arato's exposure of the institutional deficit in the notion of the lifeworld, a critique to which Habermas has responded by including the notion of civil society as the locus of a revised, multiple, and procedural notion of the public sphere.

For Habermas, power infiltrates. It comes from outside into areas previously untouched by its manipulative and regulatory forces – as if these areas were not from the outset already influenced or even constructed by a variety of processes and relationships of power. Habermas has explicitly reaffirmed the idea advanced in *Strukturwandel* "of the changed infrastructure of a public sphere infiltrated by power."[41] But such a conception of power denies the presence of power within "public" discourses, setting up the misleading notion that the fallible results of public deliberations *should* enjoy the presumption of rationality.

Furthermore, Habermas's focus on communicative rationality evokes a monolingual notion of the public sphere. As we saw with Benhabib, the stress on the public sphere ends up subordinating multiplicity and diversity to a unitary vision of what "counts" as "public," a vision measured in terms of a discourse's ability to channel itself into a predetermined conception of political influence understood along the lines of already given rules of argumentation. If we are truly to conceive of multiple discursive spheres, we must allow for a variety of types of communication and representation. Indeed, acknowledging the fallibility of discourses, of their outcomes, their institutionalizations, and of *our contemporary understanding of the very rules which underlie them* means that we have to be wary of formulations which privilege some languages and rationalities over others or which could end up damaging participants' sense of self.[42] We should not be seduced into equating "rationality" with procedural conformity, a conformity which all too often can substitute "the letter of the law" for its spirit.[43] When we do, we absolve ourselves from our accountability toward those who remain silenced, denigrated, and excluded.

Queer politics in the United States provides a practical illustration of some of the limits of a procedural focus on the public sphere. As lesbians and gay men have attempted to influence political outcomes via the established channels of the assertion of rights within a public discourse, they have encountered a particular and paradoxical set of constraints, constraints which are the products of a heterosexist society. To gain rights, they have to adopt a strategy of identity articulation which puts them at public risk. Cindy Patton writes:

> Homosexuals' attempts to gain protection to practice sex as private has produced a legal paradox: to insert privacy into the already accepted package of civil rights (to political participation, equal access, protection from discrimination) requires establishing lesbians and gay men as a publicly inscribed class. In the most immediate sense, a gay person must "come out" in order to get the right to privacy.[44]

The key issue, then, is not whether lesbians and gay men deserve rights, for of course they do, but what participating in the process of claiming and fighting for rights means in the context of a society which denies them human dignity. Patton concludes that "the crucial battle now for 'minorities' and resistant subalterns is not achieving democratic representation but wresting control over the discourse concerning identity construction. The opponent is . . . the other collectivities attempting to set the rules for identity constitution in something like a 'civil society'."[45] Procedural conformity constrains precisely what is involved in "minorities'" power and ability to claim rights.[46]

Habermas's proceduralized version of the public sphere, moreover, draws our attention away from the bodily and material influences on discourses in civil society. My point is not simply that styles of performance and presentation influence the character of discussions. Rather, discourses and systems of representation construct our understandings of our bodies, their boundaries, and their meanings. Although Habermas has tended to presume that issues such as sexism, racism, and homophobia are remnants of a traditionalism best countered through an appeal to the universal claims of modernity, both recent research and contemporary political events demonstrate the close connection between these forms of oppression and contemporary society. For example, Lillian Faderman's work demonstrates that intimate relationships between women were smiled upon in turn of the century American society, only emerging as a perceived threat to the values of the patriarchal family after the creation of the category "lesbian."[47] Additionally, the New Right in the United States has been able to increase its influence through misleading rhetorical devices which appeal to public health, support for the family, and concern with American jobs while masking the images and connotations which reveal these devices as stand-ins for the threat posed by AIDS-infected homosexuals and drug addicts, a sexist and racist preoccupation with single and/or African-American mothers, and the desire to police US borders against the "flood" of legal and illegal aliens. When a notion of a "public sphere" serves as our primary category for understanding and analyzing political contestation, we risk neglecting the impact of discourse on bodies and the role of bodies in discourse.

III   BEYOND THE PUBLIC SPHERE

I have argued that despite efforts to combine civil society's focus on the diversity and multiplicity of contemporary discourses and associations, so long as it remains either the locus of or coupled with a normatively prior conception of the public sphere we will fail to acknowledge the exclusions any public already presupposes. I have suggested further that these exclusions are the product of a restricted focus on communicative rationality understood in terms of the procedures of democratic discourse. This takes me, then, to Honneth's contention that critical theory has to move away from a strict orientation toward reaching understanding and instead turn to a theory of recognition. Accordingly, I conclude with a few remarks suggesting the potential of understanding civil society as the site of relationships of recognition, a site which, even as it includes a notion of power, is able to play a normative role in critical theory because of its attunement to difference, vulnerability, and solidarity.

Honneth points out that at the center of Habermas's theory of society is a "theory of language which can demonstrate convincingly that the endangered potential of human beings is their ability to reach understanding communicatively."[48] Habermas's reconstruction of the linguistic rules which structure action oriented toward reaching understanding is thus supposed to anchor the theory in everyday social reality. As Honneth argues, however, the social process which gives rise to these rules unfolds "behind the backs of the subjects involved"; few experience moral violations simply as transgressions of discourse rules. As a way out of this dilemma, Honneth focuses on the intersubjective premises of Habermas's theory, concluding that "the normative presupposition of all communicative action is to be seen in the acquisition of social recognition: Subjects encounter each other within the parameters of the reciprocal expectation that they receive recognition as moral persons and for their social achievement.[49]

A key benefit of this move is that it enables critical theory to diagnose social pathologies which extend beyond barriers to rational agreement. Honneth writes:

> The rational conditions of reaching understanding free from domination can no longer be employed as a criterion for what has to be regarded as a "disorder" or pathological development of social life; rather, the criterion is now the intersubjective presuppositions of human identity development. These presuppositions can be found in social forms of communication in which the individual grows up, acquires a social identity, and ultimately, has to learn to conceive of himself or herself as an equal and, at the same time, unique member of society. If these forms of communication are constituted such that they do not provide the amount of recognition necessary to accomplish these various tasks in forming an identity, then this must be taken as an indication of the pathological development of a society.[50]

With the move to a theory of recognition the discursive rationality of processes of reaching understanding is no longer the primary indicator of the validity of social practices and institutions. Now our attention moves to the suffering caused by those of forms of degradation and disrespect threatening to human identity. Not only does this expansion of the critical terrain allow for the inclusion of those bodily, psychic, and emotional harms rendered secondary by the Habermasian relegation of them to the domain of ethics, tradition, and particularistic cultural values, but it also highlights the importance of pre- or non-linguistic violations of personal and social integrity. Put somewhat differently, Honneth's focus on relationships of mutual recognition makes possible the inclusion of inexpressible harms as harms. Once these relationships are moved to the fore, that which is not yet able to be spoken can still appear as a violation, for even if the suffering itself remains unarticulated, the pain it causes and the distorted relationship in which it emerged can be singled out for critique.

Honneth develops his theory in terms of three key types of disrespect and their corresponding forms of recognition: to violations of physical integrity corresponds love, to degradations affecting a person's normative self-understanding correspond rights, and to denigrations of individual or collective styles of life corresponds solidarity.[51] What is interesting to me is less Honneth's typology of disrespect and recognition per se than the way his overall categorical framework permits the inclusion of a notion of power and draws our attention to difference, vulnerability, and solidarity. Indeed, it is precisely here where I find the points of convergence between the theory of recognition and a normative conception of civil society: civil society constitutes the wider terrain within which relationships of recognition are situated, institutionalized, and interconnected.

As I have mentioned, one of the problems with the notion of the public sphere is its externalization of power. Consequently, a conception of civil society capable of including power, of allowing for the ways in which our relationships, associations, and discourses are always to a certain extent structured in terms of power although not reducible to plays of power would be theoretically advantageous. The theory of recognition makes possible this inclusion of power because it does not presuppose that relationships of recognition are or necessarily should be fundamentally equal; it is not rooted in the ideal presupposition of a domain free from power.

First, it explicitly articulates the importance of struggles for recognition within a broader political context. This attention to struggles reminds us that political discourse is not impartial but deeply connected both to the particular identity needs of social members and those still excluded from society and to the procedures and institutions already formed in the interests of the few, those who recognize. Indeed, once we recall that for contemporary agents the very terms and symbols of recognition are themselves contested, we highlight the workings of power within democratic politics.

Second, the theory of recognition allows for the asymmetries which arise in all our social and interpersonal relationships. On the one hand, these asymmetries can be thematized. We can investigate the ways they engender forms of disrespect harmful to personal identity and integrity. Perhaps more radically we can inquire into the kinds of identities these asymmetries enable, reminding ourselves that every relationship is potentially implicated in power. On the other hand, the mere presence of symmetry in a relationship may not be enough to secure the identities of those involved. Not only may formal equality and reciprocity mask past denigrations and harms, but they could also prevent us from attending to the overall context and content of a given relationship. In other words, the mere fact that a group provides its members with recognition does not tell us anything about the political content of that group. For example, Honneth discusses the social esteem Neo-Nazi youth groups provide to their members, young people alienated and isolated from the larger society.[52] This tension in the need for recognition and the ways in which it can be found, then, places the issue of power clearly at the center of a normative conception of civil society. To be sure, it is a tension that remains unresolved, but deliberately so, preferring the complexity and messiness of politics in civil society to the homogenized discourses of the public sphere. To this extent, what is achieved in the course of political debate and struggle remains deeply connected to who we are, requiring neither the constitution of a domain of the excluded and abject nor the elevation of some transcendent conception of the rational.

The acceptance of the integral and constitutive role of power is closely tied to civil society's ability to include difference: it does not predefine political debate in terms of a given set of discursive rules (although of course it can still subject the outcomes of political debate to practical discourses). Instead, the regulative ideal of a discursive democracy comes to connote the variety of forms of political participation and types of political discourse already present in the institutions and association of civil society. We see this in Honneth in his inclusion of three different types of relationships of recognition, relationships each with their own discursive structures. Additionally, because of Honneth's focus on relationships of mutual recognition we are able to focus on the relational characteristics of difference. Differences always connote a relationship, a comparison, even when we are unsure as to whether these are differences we value or differences used to denigrate particular others.[53] Understood in the context of the differentiated discussions and associations of civil society, these relationships of difference lose that attribute of naturalness common to traditional conceptions of the public sphere to become characteristics of a variety of ties and comparisons.

Finally, Honneth's theory of recognition draws our attention to the vulnerability of both persons in civil society and the relationships upon which they depend. Unlike the disembodied agents of the public sphere, those in civil society are physically vulnerable. They can suffer physical harms and require a physical and emotional sustenance that can enable them to be secure in their own bodies. Unlike the autonomous and rational agents of the public sphere, the interconnected persons in civil society are mutually interdependent; their identities are inextricably tied together. To this extent, their mutual vulnerability necessitates common expectations of solidarity. Each must expect from the other a responsible orientation to the relationships upon which they all depend.[54] Indeed, this solidarity is a prerequisite for their ability to engage in political discourse and debate, for their capacity to turn away from violence and attempt to come to a peaceful resolution to the problems confronting them.

As developed by Cohen and Arato, the concept of civil society has pushed critical theory toward a greater appreciation of the complexity and multiplicity of the discourses and associations constitutive of contemporary postmodern societies. It stresses the importance of rights, privacy, publicity, and plurality. Once this conception of civil society is no longer subordinated to a notion of the public sphere and limited by an exlusive focus on communicative action and instead conjoined with a theory of recognition it can serve itself as a normative framework for contemporary democracies. Stressing the multiplicity of discourses understood as political, it takes seriously the notion of a decentered state. Rooted in the mutual vulnerability of persons dependent upon the recognition of others, it makes possible the thematization of needs and harms which may continue to resist or escape articulation. Indeed, to this extent it brings to light the ways in which individuals or groups may be included, enabling us to move away from an overly simplified stress on inclusion. And, it highlights our embodiedness, making our physicality a primary consideration for those senses of security and self-trust which prefigure any political or emotional relationship.

But perhaps most importantly this normative conception of civil society does not seek to establish a domain free from power. To this end, it acknowledges its own contextuality and fallibility, accepting from the outset that many will remain excluded, although we must work to find ways of including them. Such an acknowledgment, moreover, enables this version of civil society to have a more appreciative relation to difference: no discourse or discussion is excluded in advance. Judgments about the justice or rightness of any discourse or practice are part of the everyday action of politics, to be determined in process and in context. The move to a theory of recognition, anchored in civil society, then, captures the reflexive dimension promised by but absent from Habermas's conception of the bourgeois public sphere.

ACKNOWLEDGMENT

I am indebted to David Ost for his helpful comments on an earlier draft of this chapter.

NOTES

1   Jean Cohen and Andrew Arato, *Civil Society and Political Theory* (Cambridge, Mass.: MIT Press, 1992), p. ix. Although I focus on the theoretical contributions of civil society to critical theory, Cohen and Arato rightly stress the important political dimensions of the concept, especially for the new democracies of Eastern Europe. For additional accounts of civil society, see John Keane, *Democracy and Civil Society* (London: Verso, 1988), the contributions to *Civil Society and the State*, edited by John Keane (London: Verso, 1988), and, in a communitarian formulation, Michael Walzer, "The Civil Society Argument," *Dimensions of Radical Democracy*, edited by Chantal Mouffe (London: Verso, 1992). For a critical history of the politics of the emergence of the concept of civil society in the contemporary Frankfurt School, see John Ely, "The Politics of 'Civil Society'," *Telos* 93 (Fall 1992).

2   Jürgen Habermas, *Faktizität und Geltung* (Frankfurt: Suhrkamp Verlag, 1992), chapter 8.

3   Seyla Benhabib, "Deliberative Rationality and Models of Democratic Legitimacy," *Constellations* 1,1 (April 1994), p. 35.

4   See, however, Ulrich Rödel, Günter Frankenberg, and Helmut Dubiel, *Die demokratische Frage* (Frankfurt: Suhrkamp, 1989). Rödel et al. present a normative vision of civil society in the context of their discussion of post-unification German politics. See also, Jodi Dean, "Including Women: The Consequences and Side Effects of Feminist Critiques of Civil Society," *Philosophy and Social Criticism* 3/4, 18, pp. 379–406.

5   Axel Honneth, "The Social Dynamics of Disrespect," *Constellations* 1, 2 (October 1994), p. 265.

6   See Axel Honneth, *Kampf um Anerkennung. Zur moralischen Grammatik sozialer Konflikte* (Frankfurt: Suhrkamp Verlag, 1992).

7   For Honneth's own thinking on civil society, however, see Axel Honneth, "Für die Demokratisierung im Westen unbrauchbar. Thesen zur Verwendung des Civil-Society-Modells," *links* 24, 1 (January 1992).

8   Jürgen Habermas, "Further Reflections on the Public Sphere," translated by Thomas Burger, in *Habermas and the Public Sphere*, edited by Craig Calhoun (Cambridge, Mass.: MIT Press, 1992), p. 422.

9   Jürgen Habermas, *The Structural Transformation of the Public Sphere*, translated by Thomas Burger (Cambridge, Mass.: MIT Press, 1989), p. 30.

10   Ibid., p. 27.

11   Ibid., p. 36.

12   Ibid., p. 37.

13   Ibid., p. 49.

14   For a thorough discussion of the fusion argument in *Strukturwandel*, see Cohen and Arato, *Civil Society*, pp. 241–54. For Habermas's own understanding of the development of his thought see, Habermas, "Further Reflections," pp. 441–44. For an account of the connections between *Strukturwandel* and other key texts in Habermas's early work, most specifically, *Legitimation Crisis*, see Jean Cohen, "Why More Political Theory?" *Telos* 40 (Summer 1979), pp. 70–94.

15   For a collection of some of the more important English language critiques, see *Habermas and the Public Sphere*.

16   Habermas, "Further Reflections," p. 443. See also, Jürgen Habermas, "Volkssouveränität

als Verfahren. Ein normativer Begriff der Öffentlichkeit, *Die Moderne – ein unvollendetes Projekt* (Leipzig: Reclam-Verlag, 1990), pp. 180–212.

17 Jürgen Habermas, "Three Normative Models of Democracy," *Constellations* 1,1 (April 1994), p. 7.

18 Elsa Barkley Brown, "Negotiating and Transforming the Public Sphere: African American Political Life in the Transition from Slavery to Freedom," *Public Culture* 7, 1 (Fall 1994), p. 110. Other important critiques of the racial bias within and exclusions constituted by Habermas's public sphere include: Houston A. Baker, Jr., "Critical Memory and the Black Public Sphere," pp. 3–34; Michael Hanchard, "Black Cinderella?: Race and the Public Sphere in Brazil," pp. 165–85; and, Michael Dawson, "A Black Counterpublic?: Economic Earthquakes, Racial Agenda(s), and Black Politics," pp. 195–223, all in *Public Culture* 7, 1 (Fall 1994).

19 Nancy Fraser, "Rethinking the Public Sphere; A Contribution to the Critique of Actually Existing Democracy," in *Habermas and the Public Sphere*, p. 115.

20 Habermas, "Further Reflections," p. 426.

21 Ibid., p. 429.

22 For a thorough account of feminist critiques of this position, see Dean, "Including Women."

23 Patricia Mann, *Micropolitics: Agency in a Postfeminist Era* (Minneapolis: University of Minnesota Press, 1994), p. 45.

24 I am indebted to Anthony Dynkin for his insights on this issue.

25 For an excellent account of the gendered pathologies which arise when subjectivity is based on the denial of recognition to the mother, see Jessica Benjamin, *The Bonds of Love* (New York: Pantheon, 1988).

26 Habermas, *Structural Transformation*, p. 51.

27 Ibid., p. 7.

28 Cf. Cohen and Arato, *Civil Society*, pp. 389–410.

29 Ibid., p. 431.

30 Ibid., p. 455.

31 Benhabib, "Deliberative Rationality," p. 35.

32 Ibid., p. 35.

33 See Seyla Benhabib, *Situating the Self* (New York: Routledge, 1992), pp. 107–13.

34 Cf. Jean Cohen, "Discourse Ethics and Civil Society," *Philosophy and Social Criticism* 14, 3/4 (1988), p. 321; and Jodi Dean, "From Sphere to Boundary: Sexual Harassment, Identity, and the Shift in Privacy from Sphere to Boundary," *Yale Journal of Law and Feminism* 6, 2 (1994).

35 Habermas, *Faktizität und Geltung*, chapter 8. I am indebted to Bill Rehg for furnishing me with a draft of his translation of the manuscript.

36 Benhabib, "Deliberative Democracy," p. 40.

37 Ibid., p. 40.

38 It goes without saying that I do not consider affirmative action legislation, protections of the rights of lesbians and gay men, welfare entitlements, or provisions for maternity leave and day care the particular interests of the few. These sorts of enactments are remedies to the selective legislation of the past which privileged the interests of the straight, male, white, land-owning few. In fact, such benefits are in the equal interests of all as they move us toward a more just and equitable society.

39 Judith Butler, "For A Careful Reading," in *Feminist Contentions: A Philosophical Exchange*, Seyla Behabib, Judith Butler, Drucilla Cornell, and Nancy Fraser (New York: Routledge, 1994), p. 129.

40 Habermas, *Faktizität und Geltung*, chap. 8.

41 Habermas, "Further Reflections," p. 437.

42 See Thomas McCarthy, "Practical Discourse: On the Relation of Morality to Politics," *Habermas and the Public Sphere*, p. 55.

43   See Patricia Williams, *The Alchemy of Race and Rights* (Cambridge: Harvard University Press, 1991).
44   Cindy Patton, "Tremble, Hetero Swine!" *Fear of a Queer Planet*, edited by Michael Warner (Minneapolis: The University of Minnesota Press, 1993), p. 170.
45   Patton, "Tremble," p. 173.
46   There is an extenstive critical legal literature in this area. For an excellent collection of recent essays, see *After Identity*, edited by Dan Danielsen and Karen Engle (New York: Routledge, 1995).
47   Lillian Faderman, *Odd Girls and Twilight Lovers* (New York: Penguin, 1991).
48   Honneth, "Social Dynamics," p. 259.
49   Ibid., p. 262.
50   Ibid., p. 265.
51   Axel Honneth, "Integrity and Disrespect: Principles of a Conception of Morality Based on the Theory of Recognition," *Political Theory* 20, 2 (May 1992), pp. 187–201.
52   Honneth, "Social Dynamics," p. 268.
53   See also Martha Minow, *Making All the Difference* (Ithaca: Cornell University Press, 1990).
54   For a discussion of this definition of solidarity see Jodi Dean, "Reflective Solidarity, *Constellations* 2, 1 (April 1995).

10 PUBLIC REASON AND PERSONAL AUTONOMY

Kenneth Baynes

Since its beginnings critical social theory has criticized the norms and practices of existing social institutions by appeal to the ideals and values implicit in those norms and practices. By engaging in this form of "immanent critique," however, critical theorists conceded that traditional philosophical concepts – such as reason, truth, and freedom or autonomy – have a "truth-content" that is not limited to the particular theory in which they are employed.[1] Clarifying the "normative foundations" of its own critical enterprise has accordingly remained an important desideratum of critical social theory from Horkheimer to Habermas.[2]

What I would like to outline here, as a continuation of this critical enterprise, is part of a larger project on the normative foundations of democracy. This project itself has two components: On the one hand, I am interested in specifying generally the social and institutional conditions required for what has recently been described as "deliberative" or "discursive" democracy.[3] On the other hand, in what is perhaps the more strictly "philosophical" component of the project, I want to clarify some of the normative assumptions that inform this idea of a deliberative democracy.

This second component is motivated by a recognition of the fact that in modern, pluralist societies the justification of what Rawls has called the "constitutional essentials" – that is, the basic rights and liberties of citizens and the principles specifying the general structure of government – is not appropriately based on an appeal to controversial metaphysical or religious worldviews. Rather, the only acceptable justification of constitutional essentials is one that appeals to values that cannot reasonably be rejected by anyone who has an interest in justifying such essentials to others. Now there is an obvious element of circularity in this formulation. The question, however, is whether it is viciously circular or whether, as I would prefer to see it, it represents a kind of bootstrapping operation in which fundamental political values are justified via reflection on the presuppositions of (public) justification itself.

In recent literature this strategy has been pursued in what can be called a "public reasons" approach. The idea is that the principles and norms which structure the fundamental institutions of society – what Rawls calls the basic structure – should be ones based on reasons that all can affirm insofar as they regard one another as free and equal persons with certain basic moral powers (Rawls) or as co-deliberators in the practice of justification (Scanlon) or as persons capable of acting communicatively (Habermas). Thus, in his recent book *Political Liberalism*, Rawls introduces a "principle of legitimacy" which reads: "Our exercise of political power is fully proper only when it is exercised in accordance with a constitution the essentials of which all citizens as free and equal may reasonably be expected to endorse in the light of principles and ideals acceptable to their common human reason."[4] Similarly, Jeremy Waldron suggests that the fundamental commitment of liberalism is not to a notion of negative liberty but to the view that "the social order must be one that can be justified to the people who have to live under it. . . . Society should be a *transparent* order, in the sense that its workings and principles should be well-known and available for public apprehension and scrutiny."[5] Various proposals of Thomas Scanlon, Thomas Nagel, and Jürgen Habermas could be mentioned here as well.[6] The idea contained in each of these approaches is that the ideal of public reason provides a "publicity constraint" on the acceptability of norms and principles structuring institutions and governing action.

A number of questions can be raised about this appeal to "public reason." Why, to begin, should this ideal of public reason or "publicity constraint" be considered binding on moral or political deliberation and why should it outweigh other values and considerations – such as concern for the welfare of my family or friends, or the integrity of my own life projects? In a recent article, "The Limits of Public Reason," Bruce Brower suggests that Rawls's attempt to answer these questions is not only circular but "unilluminating" as well.[7] There is, he suggests, no independent argument to be found in Rawls for why it is rational to accept the ideal of public reason as normatively binding.

Moreover, Brower also claims that this publicity constraint which, as he understands it, requires us to discount any "non-public" reasons that might be offered for or against constitutional essentials, fails to show equal concern and respect for all citizens. For example, since support for a principle of religious toleration on the grounds that it is the best way to advance one's *own* faith is not a public reason, it should be discounted as an acceptable reason for the principle. From Brower's point of view, such a position amounts to a failure to show respect for someone who holds that view. Although Brower does not indicate it, this criticism of public reason parallels criticisms of impartiality and formal equality that have been made by critical theorists such as Adorno and Horkheimer as well as some more recent postmodern and feminist theorists. The claim is that the strictly formal or procedural ideals of publicity, impartiality or equality inevitably exclude differences or silence those who are deemed to be outside the "norm".[8]

A third criticism of public reason arises from a more characteristically liberal perspective. Donald Moon, for example, has expressed concern that the notion of unconstrained debate or too strong an emphasis on public justification threatens basic rights of privacy and erases any distinction between the public and private realm.[9] I will return briefly to these last two criticisms in my conclusions. Let me begin, however, with the question of the justification of the publicity constraint.

Given his method of reflective equilibrium and his constructivism, it is, I think, inevitable that there be an element of circularity in Rawls's case for public reason.[10] However, I do not think that this makes his strategy "unilluminating." Rather than attempting to ground an ideal of public reason in a minimally normative conception of rationality, Rawls appeals to what he calls the Rational *and* the Reasonable – *Verstand* and *Vernunft* – where the latter notion includes a sense of fairness and mutual recognition.[11] The ideal of public reason and the related "publicity constraint" must, accordingly, be seen as requirements of practical reason in this expanded sense.

Nonetheless, I agree with Brower that there is something unsatisfactory in Rawls's account of public reason. Rather than offering a recursive or reflexive justification that appeals to the conditions and presuppositions of the practice of justification, Rawls appeals to the "fundamental intuitive ideas" latent in our political culture. This leaves him open to more relativist interpretations such as the one offered by Richard Rorty as well as to various forms of feminist criticism.[12]

I would like to test out an alternative approach here. I propose that neither the ideal of public reason nor the more familiar liberal idea of individual or personal autonomy to which it is often opposed are justifiable as independent or free-standing ideals. Rather, the two ideals mutually presuppose one another and thus acquire whatever normative weight or force they have only if they are taken as inseparably tied to one another.[13] Thus, to state my thesis in terms of Kant's well-known formula: public reason without personal autonomy is empty and personal autonomy without public reason is blind. The ideal of public reason has normative force only if public reasons are seen as arising from the deliberations of autonomous individuals. On the other hand, the notion of individual or personal autonomy, understood as the capacity for critical or reflective self-governance, is normatively attractive only if it is taken to imply that one acts for reasons that could not reasonably be rejected by others. This view of the interdependence of public reason and personal autonomy is quite at odds, for example, with the sharp distinction Rorty draws between a public moral identity and ethical autonomy or private irony.[14] I would now like to defend this thesis through an analysis of recent work on personal autonomy.

Recent "hierarchical" accounts of freedom or autonomy have been proposed, at least in part, as a response to the perceived inadequacies in the Kantian account, especially its model of rational agency in which a (noumenal) self stands outside time, is free from the influences of socialization, and is the spontaneous cause of actions.[15] According to the alternative account, autonomy is conceived as the capacity to be motivated by first-order preferences or desires that are appropriately endorsed by higher-order preferences or values.[16] Autonomy does not require that the action be the product of a deep, noumenal self, but rather that a particular relation (in general, one of coherence) exist between the desire that is effective in action and the agent's wider motivational structure. A person acts freely if she does what she wants, and a person wills freely (autonomously) if she wills to be motivated by what (as a higher-order preference) she really wants.

This hierarchical or, more generally, "want satisfaction" account faces a central difficulty when confronted with what has been called the case of the "happy slave."[17] The mere fact that a person has a higher-order preference to be motivated by certain ground-floor desires does not seem to provide a sufficient condition for autonomy or freedom. What is so special about upper-story preferences (if they too are simply additional preferences) that enables them to endow agents and acts with autonomy?[18] If this higher-order preference is to carry such authority mustn't it too be endorsed by a still higher-order preference, and so on *ad infinitum*? One response by advocates of a hierarchical account has been to claim that the higher-order endorsement of lower-order preferences must be one which expresses the agent's "authentic self" (Dworkin) or be one with which she "decisively identifies" (Frankfurt).[19] However, apart from the vagueness which surrounds these notions, the difficulty with this approach is not merely that the possibility of infinite regress of higher-order desires seems to be rather arbitrarily cut off, but that there seems to be no reason why we should assume that such an authentic or decisive identification makes the desire one's *own*.[20]

It is not surprising, therefore, that some recent (compatibilist) critics have expressed some dissatisfaction with hierarchical accounts of autonomy.[21] Although the hierarchical account apparently rejects the idea of a noumenal self (and thus of a "causality of reason" in Kant's sense), in its own attempts to clarify the way in which higher-order preferences may be taken to reflect what the agent *really* wants or is more truly his *own* the hierarchical account also falls back on the idea of a deep self, untainted by socialization, as the source of self-creation and self-determination. According to these critics, the hierarchical account is confronted with a dilemma: either they can offer no reason for regarding second or higher-order preferences as more truly the agent's own and thus no reason for regarding action resulting from a coherent motivational structure as autonomous or, in offering such an account, they are forced back onto a model of a deep self that is somehow responsible for its higher-order preferences. Furthermore, short of positing a deep self as

the author of one's highest-order preferences, the attempt to define autonomy in connection with a structural account of motivations seems destined
to fail unless some account is also provided of the actual (historical)
sequence by which an individual comes to have the preferences that she
has.[22] Regardless of whether or not a harmony exists within the agent's
motivational structure, unless the agent's particular preference structure
could have been otherwise in the sense that it was formed in a manner that
is responsive to (good) reasons there seems little reason to regard the person
(or her motivational structure) as autonomous.

In *The Theory and Practice of Autonomy*, Gerald Dworkin attempts to address
criticisms of this sort in connection with a revised definition of autonomy.[23]
As he now defines it, "autonomy is conceived of as a second-order capacity
of persons to reflect critically upon their first-order preferences, desires,
wishes, and so forth and the capacity to accept or attempt to change these in
light of higher-order preferences and values" (p. 20). This revised account,
in which Dworkin substitutes the requirement of critical reflection for his
earlier requirement of identification (p. 15), is also accompanied by (a) an
explicit rejection of a deep self in favor of a procedural conception of the self
– "self-definition in abstraction from the self that is defined" (p. 30) – and
(b) a stated desire to develop a "constructivist" conception of practical reasoning (or critical reflection) that is finally understood in connection with
the "idea of interpersonal justification" (p. 59).

Constructivism, as introduced by Rawls, holds that the standards of moral
deliberation (or critical reflection) do not consist in whether or not the reasoning process adequately expresses or corresponds to a prior and independent moral order of values, but in whether or not the deliberative process
reflects a particular conception of the agent and his moral powers.[24] One
aspect of this conception, according to Dworkin, is the agent's capacity for
(and interest in) interpersonal justification. Other constructivist accounts
have also emphasized this notion of public justification or intersubjective
agreement as a requirement of reason.[25] The capacity for critical reflection
implies that the reasons for which one acts are reasons that one is prepared
to justify to others and that one (reasonably) believes others who share an
interest in public justification could not reasonably reject. In what follows I
will consider the significance of Scanlon's contractualist version of
Strawson's account for Dworkin's analysis of the capacity for critical
reflection.

In "Freedom and Resentment" P. F. Strawson offers an analysis of the
conditions of freedom (or moral responsibility) that seems initially to be
quite independent of hierarchical accounts.[26] Strawson suggests that the
terms of praise and blame that we apply to the behavior of others is based on
the reactive feelings and attitudes we have when we believe that behavior to
express a certain quality of the agent's will. These reactive attitudes and feelings are in turn taken by Strawson to be constitutive for certain kinds of

interpersonal relations without which, practically speaking, we cannot imagine living (pp. 68, 74). Emotions such as gratitude, resentment, and forgiveness form part of a "general framework of human life" (p. 70) that is accessible only from the participant's perspective of one who shares in these reactive feelings and attitudes, and which is itself not susceptible of further, external rational justification (p. 78).[27]

The novelty of Strawson's account is that (the value of) moral responsibility is made to depend on the presence of this sort of interpersonal relation rather than, as he puts it, on "the obscure and panicky metaphysics of libertarianism" (p. 80). Nevertheless, inadequacies have been noted in Strawson's account as well.[28] First, Strawson offers no general account of what he means by an interpersonal relation and the attitudes and feelings that serve to define it. It does not mean any sort of interaction with others, but only ones of a certain sort: Strawson describes the reactive attitudes as the "non-detached attitudes and reactions of people directly involved in transactions with each other" (p. 62), links them essentially with "involvement or participation in a human relationship," and their absence with "human isolation," and repeatedly characterizes them as "participant-related" and as "involved." But what general sort of relation or interaction does he mean? Presumably a therapist and her patient are "involved" with one another, but this does not seem to be the sort of involvement that Strawson has in mind.[29] Strawson also suggests that individuals who adopt a wholly objective attitude toward one another can no longer quarrel or reason together, but can at most pretend to quarrel or reason (p. 66). But just what is the connection between the activity of reason-giving and the participant attitude that is constitutive of interpersonal relations?

Second, Strawson offers a "non-propositional" (Bennett) or noncognitivist analysis of judgments concerning moral approbation or disapprobation. Our moral judgments are made to depend on the reactive feelings and attitudes we have toward the behavior of others rather than on the beliefs we hold about that behavior.[30] Although it may be that our moral judgments are frequently accompanied by certain attitudes or feelings toward the behavior of others, the presence of such emotions does not seem to be a necessary condition of moral judgment.[31] Rather, what is central for an account of moral responsibility is not our reaction, but the basis of our judgments concerning the character of the agent's will as it is expressed in his or her actions. Thus, rather than providing an account of the cognitive basis of our moral judgments, like the "influenceability theory" he rejects, Strawson tends to focus on what we are *doing* when we praise and blame others.[32]

In "The Significance of Choice" Scanlon goes a long way toward addressing these inadequacies by developing a specifically "contractualist" version of Strawson's account. On this version, what is central to our judgments concerning the quality of will (and thus for applying terms of praise and blame) is whether or not the agent has acted for reasons that are ". . . in

accord with standards which that agent either accepts or should accept insofar as he or she is concerned to justify his or her actions to others on ground
that they could not reasonably reject" (p. 170). According to Scanlon, this
contractualist account "gives specific content to the idea that moral judgments presuppose a form of interpersonal relationship" in that agents who
are a candidate for praise or blame are "considered as possible participants in
a system of co-deliberation" (p. 167). A centrally defining feature of the specific interpersonal relation in which terms of praise and blame acquire their
"special force" is that of participants in a process of co-deliberation. Strawson comes close to suggesting this when he suggests that adopting an objective attitude toward others precludes the possibility of reasoning with them
(p. 66). Scanlon's contractualist account thus provides a more complete
analysis of the possible link between the activity of reason-giving and the
special sort of interpersonal relation that Strawson is concerned to identify.

Scanlon's contractualist version also provides Dworkin's notion of critical
reflection with greater content. The capacity for critical reflection should
now be understood as the capacity to assess one's action in accordance with
standards that could not reasonably be rejected by others. A person is
morally autonomous insofar as she has the capacity to reflect critically on
the reasons for her action and to provide grounds for her actions that she
(reasonably) believes to be in accord with standards that no one could reasonably reject as a basis for an informed and uncoerced agreement (or that
could not reasonably be rejected by anyone who has an interest in justifying
his or her actions publicly). Moreover, if autonomy is understood as the
capacity for critical reflection defined in this way and if the self who governs
in self-governance is not identified with a deep self, but is interpreted procedurally (in relation to these capacities), then autonomy need not be set in
opposition to (certain forms of) socialization, but will in fact require the
presence of specific forms of social integration and socialization, namely
those that enhance the capacities for critical reflection and deliberation.[33]

There are, I believe, strong parallels between this account of autonomy
and Habermas's theory of communicative action.[34] The definition of autonomy as (among other things) the capacity for critical reflection upon the
reasons for action within the context of a possible public or intersubjective
agreement has much in common with Habermas's analysis of social perspective taking and the idea of a moral-practical discourse as the search for
agreement between free and equal participants. Moreover, the different sorts
of hypothetical attitudes that, according to Habermas, actors can adopt when
they acquire a decentered understanding of the world, abstract a norm from
its context of application, and enter into a discourse where reasons are
assessed, can also be seen as aspects of the capacity for critical reflection that
I have outlined above.[35] Finally, the attempt to develop a procedural conception of the self – "self-definition in abstraction from the self that is defined"
(Dworkin) – has obvious similarities with the structural component of the

lifeworld that Habermas calls "personality" whose ideal "vanishing point" is "a condition of the risk-filled self-direction of a highly abstract ego identity".[36] Here it is not a deep self that is the touchstone for (personal) autonomy, but a highly formal (and hence empty) conception of identity formation through an ongoing process of self-discovery, self-definition and self-direction.[37]

Beyond these similarities, however, the account of autonomy outlined above and Habermas's theory of communicative action may be able to supplement one another in at least two important ways. First, Habermas's analysis of communicative action and its essential connection with the internal perspective of the participant provides a basis for strengthening Strawson's (ungeneralized) account of the special sort of interpersonal relation that is crucial for his account of moral responsibility. Habermas's analysis of the intimate connection between (communicative) action, reason-giving and an orientation to validity-claims also offers support for Strawson's claim that it is (practically) inconceivable to imagine rejecting the interpersonal standpoint altogether.

On the other hand, I believe that the analysis of autonomy as a capacity for critical reflection on the reasons for action can also be used to strengthen Habermas's characterization of the Yes/No position-taking that hearers can adopt in relation to specific speech-act offers. In acting communicatively – that is, in seeking to reach a mutual understanding (*Verständigung*) with someone about something in the world – competent speaking and acting subjects mutually suppose the capacity to assess (accept or reject) the basic validity-claims that are raised with their utterances. A consensually achieved understanding about something in the (natural, social or personal) world implies that each participant attributes to others the capacity to accept or reject the offer made in his speech act and that each participant is ready to supply reasons should the utterance's validity be challenged.

But what sort of competence is it that actors attribute to one another in their communicative interactions? What does it mean to say that the hearer is "free" to accept or reject the claims presented in a speech-act offer? If any insinuation of a "Brave New World" scenario in which individuals are "socialized" in ways intended to ensure consensus or agreement is to be avoided, the analysis of the relation between reason and agreement within the model of communicative action must be supplemented with an account of the autonomy-competency that speakers and actors must possess (and which they must impute to one another).[38] Individual participants in a discourse must not only want to agree, they must also prefer to have that want, etc., and their preferences must have been formed in ways that are "reasons-responsive" (e.g., if a person had good and sufficient reason to have preferred otherwise, she would have preferred otherwise; the process of her preference-formation must not be one that impairs her deliberative capacities). Unless there is good reason to suppose that agreements are reached in ways that do not subvert or undermine the sort of autonomy-competency discussed above, then there will be little reason to attribute any (rational) validity to those agreements. A moral-practical discourse presupposes that those who participate are free and equal in the sense that each is entitled to be convinced, through the exercise of his or her autonomy-competency, that the norm in question could meet with the reasoned agreement of all affected. This delicate balance of the interconnection between reason, autonomy, and intersubjective agreement must be maintained if the normative force or validity of a consensually-achieved agreement is to have any genuine authority.

In conclusion let me return briefly to the two further criticisms of public reason I mentioned at the outset, i.e., the problem of difference and the threat to privacy. First, it has been suggested that the ideal of public reason and its accompanying "publicity constraint" fail to respect each individual in his or her uniqueness. A strong version of this objection can be found in difference critiques which claim that any attempt to specify the "limits of public reason" will incorporate more substantive values that exclude difference and silence those whose voice fails to measure up to the norms of reason.[39] One could mention, for example, the fact that the same principle of equality can, on one interpretation, deny women maternity leave and yet, on another, support laws prohibiting only women from working at certain times or in certain occupations. This is a serious objection that cannot be adequately addressed here.[40] I would like to propose, however, that ultimately two distinct notions of respect are involved: respect for others as equals and respect for others as unique.[41] While there may indeed be an inevitable tension between them, respect for others as unique need not displace the value of public reason so much as challenge us always to be open to questioning the more specific form it takes and constraints it imposes at any given time. Surely the fact that considerations which fail to satisfy the publicity constraint are not permitted to have an influence on the determination of constitutional essentials does not mean that persons who endorse those considerations have, for that reason, not been shown equal respect in either sense. They will not have been shown equal respect only if the considerations that are prohibited were prohibited because the specific form of public argumentation excluded the considerations from receiving a fair and adequate hearing at all.

Second, and even more briefly, I would like to suggest that the more traditional liberal concern that publicity may undermine privacy rights is based on a confusion of two issues: the legitimate domain of public (by which I mean primarily governmental) regulation and the obligation to provide a public justification for actions that affect others and/or principles regulating the basic structure. Neither feminist challenges to the traditional division between the public and the private nor the demand for public justification of basic norms translates *directly* into a justification of the public policing of the bedroom or family life. Whether there should be greater public regulation of traditionally private affairs and the specific form such regulation should take – indeed even what should count as a private affair – is a matter of political struggle and contestation that, in the final analysis, must be settled through dialogue and deliberation appropriately pursued in the public sphere. Though some matters are no doubt unsuited for public regulation; few, if any, are unsuitable for public debate.

NOTES

1   See, for example, Herbert Marcuse, "Philosophy and Critical Theory," in *Negations: Essays in Critical Theory* (Boston: Beacon Press, 1968), p. 148; see also Thomas McCarthy's discussion of Horkheimer's attempt to avoid the relativism of Mannheim's sociology of knowledge while at the same time resisting more traditional conceptions of truth, reason and freedom, David Hoy and Thomas McCarthy, *Critical Theory* (New York: Blackwell, 1994), chap. 1.

2   An important motivation in Habermas's break with earlier critical theory and his attempt to locate the normative foundations of critique within a theory of communicative action is his belief that "bourgeois consciousness has become cynical" and thus that the earlier form of immanent critique was no longer adequate, see *The Theory of Communicative Action*, vol. II (Boston: Beacon Press, 1987), p. 382f.

3   See, for example, Joshua Cohen, "Deliberation and Democratic Legitimacy," in *The Good Polity*, ed. A. Hamlin and P. Pettit (New York: Basil Blackwell, 1989); John Dryzek, *Discursive Democracy* (New York: Cambridge University Press, 1990); and Jürgen Habermas, *Between Facts and Norms* (Cambridge, Mass.: MIT Press, 1996).

4   *Political Liberalism* (New York: Columbia University Press, 1993), p. 137.

5   J. Waldron, "Theoretical Foundations of Liberalism," *The Philosophical Quarterly* 37 (1987): 146.

6   Most recently, see Jürgen Habermas, "Reconciliation through the Public Use of Reason: Remarks on John Rawls's Political Liberalism" and Rawls's "Reply to Habermas" in *The Journal of Philosophy* 92 (1995): 109–80.

7   "The Limits of Public Reason," *The Journal of Philosophy* 91 (1994): 6–26.

8   See my "Equality and Difference in Recent Political Theory," in *Proceedings of the 7th East–West Philosophers' Conference* (Honolulu: The University of Hawaii Press, forthcoming).

9   *Constructing Community: Moral Pluralism and Tragic Conflicts* (Princeton University Press, 1993), chap. 4.

10   For a critical discussion of Rawls's method of reflective equilibrium, see my *The Normative Grounds of Social Criticism: Kant, Rawls and Habermas* (Albany: SUNY Press, 1992), pp. 68–76.

11   *Political Liberalism*, p. 54f.

12   "The Priority of Democracy to Philosophy," in *Objectivity, Relativism, and Truth* (New York: Cambridge University Press, 1991); for an alternative, non-relativist reading of Rawls's project, see my "Constructivism and Practical Reason in Rawls," *Analyse und Kritik* 14 (1992): 18–32.

13   Jürgen Habermas defends a similar position in his claim concerning the "co-originality" of public and private autonomy in *Between Facts and Norms* (Cambridge, Mass.: MIT Press, 1995), chap. 3.

14   Rorty, "Moral Identity and Private Autonomy: The Case of Foucault," in *Essays on Heidegger and Others* (New York: Cambridge University Press, 1991), p. 196.

15   Whether Kant must be interpreted this way is a question I shall not go into here. Recently, several scholars have attempted a more charitable reading of Kant. See, for example,

Henry Allison, *Kant's Theory of Freedom* (New York: Cambridge University Press, 1990) and Onora O'Neill, *Constructions of Reason* (New York: Cambridge University Press, 1989). Much of the debate hinges on the question of how to interpret Kant's "two-standpoint" doctrine – must it be read as implying two ontologically distinct worlds or can it be taken only to imply two distinct "frameworks of thought" (O'Neill, p. 67).

16 See Harry Frankfurt, "Freedom of the Will and the Concept of a Person," *The Journal of Philosophy* (1971) [reprinted in *Moral Responsibility*, ed. Fischer (Cornell, 1986)]; Wright Neely, "Freedom and Desire," *The Philosophical Review* 83 (1974): 32–54; Gerald Dworkin, "Acting Freely," *Nous* 4 (1970): 367–83; and Charles Taylor, "Responsibility for Self," in *Free Will*, ed. G. Watson (Oxford, 1982).

17 See D. Zimmerman, "Hierarchical Motivation and Freedom of the Will," *Pacific Philosophical Quarterly* 62 (1981): 354–68 and I. Thalberg, "Hierarchical Analyses of Unfree Action," *Canadian Journal of Philosophy* 8 (1978): 211–26.

18 For this criticism, see Gary Watson, "Free Agency," in *Free Will*, ed. Watson, and "Free Action and Free Will," *Mind* (1985): 145–72.

19 Thus, Frankfurt writes, "When a person identifies himself *decisively* with one of his first-order desires, this commitment 'resounds' throughout the potentially endless array of higher orders. . . . The fact that his second-order volition to be moved by this desire is a decisive one means that there is no room for questions concerning the pertinence of volitions of higher orders," in "Freedom of the Will and the Concept of a Person," in Fischer, p. 76.

20 In a recent essay, Frankfurt seems to have adopted a position closer to the one now advocated by Gerald Dworkin discussed below (see Frankfurt, "Identification and Wholeheartedness," in *Responsibility, Character and Emotions*, ed. Schoeman (Cambridge, 1987), p. 43, where the process of deliberation or openness to reason seems to be the important factor).

21 See especially, David Schatz, "Free Will and the Structure of Motivation," *Midwest Studies in Philosophy* 10 (1986): 451–82; Susan Wolf, "Sanity and the Metaphysics of Responsibility," in *Responsibility, Character and the Emotions*, ed. F. Schoeman (Cambridge, 1987), pp. 46–62; and Diana Meyers, *Self, Society and Personal Choice* (Columbia, 1989).

22 This criticism and alternative account is developed by, among others, John Martin Fischer in "Responsiveness and Moral Responsibility," in *Responsibility, Character and Emotions*, ed. Schoeman, pp. 81–106; it resembles a conception of freedom advocated earlier by W. Neely [above] and A. MacIntyre [in "Determinism" *Mind* 56 (1957): 28–41] where what is crucial is whether the actual process through which the agent acquired the preferences she has is one that "could have been otherwise" in the sense that had she had good and sufficient reason to prefer otherwise she would have. See also, I. Thalberg, *Misconceptions of Freedom* (1983), pp. 112f.

23 *The Theory and Practice of Autonomy* (Cambridge, 1988).

24 For this view of constructivism in moral theory, see Rawls, "Kantian Constructivism in Moral Theory," *Journal of Philosophy* 77 (1980): 515–72, and Samuel Freeman, "Contractualism, Moral Motivation, and Practical Reason," *Journal of Philosophy* 88 (1991): 281–303.

25 See Scanlon, "Contractualism and Utilitarianism"; O'Neill, *Constructions of Reason*; and Samuel Freeman, "Contractualism, Moral Motivation, and Practical Reason," *The Journal of Philosophy* 88 (1991): 281–303.

26 In *Free Will*, ed. G. Watson, pp. 59–80; also, perhaps more clearly than in hierarchical accounts, Strawson is concerned with *moral* responsibility in contrast to a more general conception of personal responsibility or autonomy. Moral autonomy is also my primary concern in what follows, though it is clear that the relation between moral and personal autonomy is one of a complex interdependence, perhaps not unlike Rawls's description of the relation between the Reasonable and the Rational (see "Kantian Constructivism in Moral Theory," p. 530).

27 By contrast, in cases where we do not believe the action in question to be an expression

of the agent's will (or intention), the reactive attitudes and feelings no longer apply and the terms of praise or blame are no longer appropriate. Strawson describes the response to such behavior as one involving an objective attitude, as one that is opposed to the participant's attitude, and thus as one that lies outside the framework of interpersonal relations. The point is not that the objective attitude is never appropriate; on the contrary, it is often necessary to adopt such an attitude to explain a person's behavior and/or to gain occasional relief from "the strains of involvement" (p. 67). Nevertheless, in opposition to the skeptic's response to the "causal thesis" (which implies a world in which only the objective attitude has a place), Strawson maintains that the objective attitude is not one that can be consistently maintained in our practical lives. Its possibility cannot even be seriously entertained as a choice.

28   For interesting discussions of Strawson's position, see J. Bennett, "Accountability," in *Philosophical Subjects*, ed. Z. van Straaten (Oxford, 1980), pp. 14–47, and T. M. Scanlon, "The Significance of Choice," in *The Tanner Lectures on Human Values*, vol. 8 (Cambridge, 1988).

29   See Bennett, p. 35f.

30   See Bennett, p. 24; Scanlon, pp. 167, 169–70.

31   See Scanlon, p. 167.

32   See Scanlon, p. 165.

33   See, in general, J. Habermas, "Individuation through Socialization," in *Postmetaphysical Thinking* (Cambridge, Mass.: MIT Press, 1992), pp. 149–204.

34   For Habermas's own remarks on Strawson's account of moral responsibility, see "Discourse Ethics," in *Moral Consciousness and Communicative Action* (Boston, 1990), pp. 45f.

35   Compare *Moral Consciousness and Communicative Action*, pp. 125, 126, 138, 177; for a discussion of these attitudes and account of Habermas's model of autonomy, see my *The Normative Grounds of Social Criticism: Kant, Rawls and Habermas* (Albany: SUNY Press, 1993), p. 143f.

36   *The Theory of Communicative Action* II, p. 138, and *The Philosophical Discourse of Modernity*, pp. 343, 345.

37   Again, compare the discussion in Diana Meyers, *Self, Society and Personal Choice*, from which I draw these three terms as a description of our "autonomy-competency."

38   Of course, as with all of the accounts of autonomy discussed above, one would also need to supplement the analysis of the conditions for autonomy with an account of the different "excusing conditions" that render it inappropriate to impute autonomy to an agent (that is, when it is no longer appropriate to hold the agent morally responsible). In this chapter I am interested in what competencies actors must impute to one another if the idea of communicative action is to have the normative significance Habermas assigns to it.

39   See, for example, Iris Young, *Justice and the Politics of Difference* (Princeton: Princeton University Press, 1990), chap. 4.

40   See "Equality and Difference in Recent Political Theory" (forthcoming).

41   See, for a similar contrast, Charles Taylor's distinction between the notion of "equal respect" and the "recognition of equal value" in *Multiculturalism and the Politics of Recognition* (Princeton, NJ: Princeton University Press, 1992), and Stephen White's distinction between "the responsibility to act" and the "responsibility to otherness" in *Postmodernism and Political Theory* (New York: Cambridge University Press, 1991).

PART V

Pragmatics, Psychoanalysis, and Aesthetics

Pragmatics, Psychoanalysis, and Aesthetics

In Part V, *Pragmatics, Psychoanalysis, and Aesthetics*, Matthias Kettner, in "Karl-Otto Apel's Contribution to Critical Theory," characterizes Apel's "transcendental pragmatics" as an essential contribution to critical theory. Kettner argues that Apel contributes to the program of critical theory first, like Habermas, by taking up the challenge of Horkheimer's desire for a "comprehensive program of critical reconstructive social science," and second, by providing "strong justification for the prescriptivity . . . that ultimately propels such a program." As both "collaborator" with and "critic" of Habermas, deeply influenced by the work of Peirce and Wittgenstein, Apel's philosophical contribution to contemporary critical theory remains without equal. Joel Whitebook, in his "Fantasy and Critique: Some Thoughts on Freud and the Frankfurt School," argues, through a reconsideration of Freud, for a "rehabilitation of the psychoanalytic dimension of critical theory" which, although prominent in the thought of the early practitioners of critical theory, substantially dropped out with Habermas. By retaining only the methodological component of Freud's thinking, Whitebook suggests that Habermas "rationalistically short-circuits Reason's communication with its Other." The result is the loss of "the element of tension between Romanticism and Enlightenment that gave Freud's defense of 'the project of modernity' its complexity and appeal." Hauke Brunkhorst, in "Theodor W. Adorno: Aesthetic Constructivism and a Negative Ethic of the Non-forfeited Life," presents a biographical reflection on the aesthetic and ethical dimensions of Adorno's contribution. Accounting for the multiple influences on Adorno's life, his early family life, his experience as an exile, his early precociousness, his inclination for the aesthetic, his musical genius, and his involvement with the Institute for Social Research, Brunkhorst seeks to show how Adorno arrived at his "pessimistic diagnosis of the times" which in turn led to the sketch of "an ethic of a damaged life," and ultimately, to a philosophy of the non-identical.

11 KARL-OTTO APEL'S CONTRIBUTION TO CRITICAL THEORY

Matthias Kettner

1 INTRODUCTION

Karl-Otto Apel once characterized his position *vis-à-vis* the Frankfurt School's brand of critical theory "as one of participation (perhaps as an outsider) in the critical reconstruction of the philosophical foundations of *Critical Theory*."[1] First and foremost, this "participation" consists in clarifications of epistemological and ethical problems that are one step removed from, but inherent in, specific sociological, political and historical doctrines of (orthodox) Marxism and (unorthodox) Frankfurt School Neo-Marxism. With unswerving intellectual continuity Apel has been pursuing a project of radical transformation both in theoretical and in practical philosophy. Apel's philosophical project is one of reconstruction, not of deconstruction. Rich and variegated philosophical resources go into this reconstruction.[2] Amongst these, two prominent philosophical strands give it the determinate contours that Apel calls "transcendental pragmatic." This term denotes Apel's philosophical impulse to reframe Kantian themes in intersubjectivist terms. In order to do so, Apel draws substantially on (1) semiotic pragmaticism in a Peircean key as well as on (2) Wittgenstein's pragmatism of language games. Other major currents that flow into Apel's transcendental pragmatics are (3) continental traditions of the philosophy of language and of hermeneutics – from Humboldt to Heidegger.

Apel's transformation project is fuelled by the insight that the epistemological turn in modern philosophy from Descartes to Husserl is obsessed with a subject of knowledge that does not exist. As knowledge ties in with universal validity and universal validity in turn is inextricably linked to those rule governed communal practices which we accept as proper ways of raising, redeeming, or rejecting such validity claims, it follows that the subject of knowledge must be communal. Validity is posited in practices of intersubjectivity.[3] Yet as a posit, validity extends intersubjectivity *beyond* the actual practices of intersubjectivity in which it appears as so posited. Validity, to put it crudely, is not in the head. Validity resides neither in the mental activity of the psychological self nor in the constitutive acts of an unencumbered subject of consciousness as methodological individualism and solipsism would have it. Though Apel's critique of the metaphysics of subjectivity is radical, he does not want to dismiss the notion of subject altogether. Rather, Apel wants to debunk the veil of solipsism that surrounds it, and to diagnose the abstractive fallacies that are engrained in the myth of a prelinguistic or precommunicative subject.[4]

Apel's contribution is that of *Transcendental Pragmatics* to critical theory.[5] Two aims are salient in Apel's work as it relates to critical theory. The first is to provide a sound conceptual context for what Apel deems worth retaining from Horkheimer's seminal ideas of interdisciplinary materialism, namely (like Habermas) a comprehensive program of critical reconstructive social science. The second aim is to include (unlike both Habermas and Horkheimer[6]) in such a comprehensive program of critical reconstructive social science strong justifications for the prescriptivity (norms, values, ideals) that ultimately propel such a program. Hence one way to understand Apel's impact on other second and third generation Frankfurt School theorists is by looking at the constructive challenges and responses that have grown out of a long-standing cooperation with Habermas.

Apel was born in 1922. Habermas and Apel share a background of philosophical concerns whose roots reach back into the intellectual climate of post-war Bonn. At the University of Bonn in the fifties, eminent but conservative scholars, e.g., Erich Rothacker, were continuing the *Geisteswissenschaften* as if nothing had happened. The political and moral catastrophe of Nazi Germany and the Second World War were no themes for philosophical reflection. It took the student rebellion of the sixties to shatter this defensive complacency. Apel became acquainted with critical theory during his time as professor at Kiel (1961–69) and Saarbrücken (1969–1972). Marx, Marcuse and Horkheimer made much more of an impression on Apel than Adorno, whose penchant for a critical stance rife with self-referential inconsistencies Apel has never been prepared to accept as necessary. It is perhaps not unfair to say that Apel's access to critical theory more or less dovetails with the outlook that Habermas gave it then and later. Though there is much common ground between Apel and Habermas, important differences remain and seem to have been deepening more recently.[7] This essay will thus underscore Apel's role as a sympathetic collaborator and, as it were, an adamant critic of Habermas.

2   TOWARDS A VIABLE CONCEPTION OF CRITICAL THEORY

In one of his seminal essays, Horkheimer introduced a contrast between "traditional" and "critical" theory. In 1937 Horkheimer's distinction had the air of a promissory note. Critical theory today, its diverse ramifications notwithstanding, is still lacking an uncontroversial analysis of its very idea. As a generic description of Horkheimer's peculiar project of interdisciplinary materialism that later was to become "Kritische Theorie der Gesellschaft," it is perhaps not inappropriate to characterize critical theory by its aim to construct "a comprehensive social science (where *science* is construed non-scientistically) which integrates into a single theory the descriptive-explanatory-interpretative side of things and the normative-evaluative-emancipatory side of things."[8]

That such an endeavor must fail in its attempt to produce knowledge, not to mention *scientific* knowledge, was the common denominator of much of the criticism that came from then prevalent theories of science and rationality – theories of science and rationality that the old Frankfurt School summarily labelled "positivism," "scientism," "instrumental reason" or any combination thereof. "Positivists" assert that an empiricist account of natural science is an adequate account and, moreover, that all scientifically valid knowledge must have essentially the same cognitive structure, namely objectification of observables. Objectification of observables gives us a purchase both on prediction and on causal explanation whose abstract logical structure was spelled out in Hempel's hypothetico-deductive model of nomological explanation. Contrary to the accepted view, critical theory posits that there are kinds of inquiry that aim at meaning comprehension but not at objectification of observables and still others that aim at reflective insight, over and above objectification of observables. Critical theory maintains that such nonstandard inquiries of the latter kind can yield valid knowledge. Moreover, the systematicity of such inquiries, notwithstanding their hermeneutic underpinnings, has rational credentials as good as those with which we usually credit scientific endeavors in the very narrow sense of the word, e.g., empirical natural sciences.

2.1 Differentiated Science versus "Unified Science"

Apel has contributed more than any other critical theorist to the ongoing project of a comprehensive critical theory of science. Such a theory should fulfill three conditions. It must (1) go beyond the dogmas of empiricism (e.g., the dogma that value-free science exhausts the notion of scientific objectivity). It (2) should sublate the dichotomies of logical positivism (e.g. the dichotomy of explanation vs. understanding[9]). Furthermore, a comprehensive critical theory of science (3) must overcome the cultural-historical relativism of Gadamerian hermeneutics as well as the sociologism of Habermasian "universal pragmatics." Apel's differentiated theory of science yields important insights into the structural similarities and differences that exist between whole families of epistemic practices, e.g., standard natural sciences, biological sciences, behavioral sciences (as quasi-nomological social sciences), hermeneutic sciences, reconstructive social sciences, and post-metaphysical philosophy.

Apel has elaborated the heuristic assumption that "the different synthetic achievements of the different sciences – e.g., causal explanation, functional explanation, understanding of good reasons (sometimes called teleological or rational explanation) – are not intelligible as synthetic achievements of cognition, if they are to be reduced to a unitary logical model of deductive or inductive nomological explanation."[10] Synthetic achievements of cognition may be dependent on different categories of posing questions which in turn can be considered as expressing different cognitive interests. The plausibility of this nexus depends crucially on the notion of cognitive interests. What are cognitive interests?

For Apel cognitive interests are a topic of transcendental reflection upon certain conditions of the possibility of human knowledge to which idealism, Kantian or other, has never been prepared to accord much significance. Cognitive interests are part of a background that gives forms of inquiry their distinctive significance for human beings like us. This background does not boil down to monadic cognitive endowments and capacities of individuals. Rather, this background is present as a way in which cognitive interests of individuals are interwoven with language games and with projectable forms of ongoing practices.[11] As an epistemological notion, the concept of cognitive interests rings decidedly Kantian, but as a universal-pragmatic notion, it has at the same time a decidedly anthropological air. Instead of taking theories and the existence of theoretical knowledge for granted, Apel finds it necessary to inquire into social-anthropological conditions of the possibility of the constitution of theories as possible systematizations of synthetic achievements of cognition.

The three cognitive interests that Apel acknowledges correspond closely to the architectonics that Habermas proposed at a time when he was still convinced that a fusion of social theory and epistemology was the way to go.[12] Yet there is a significant difference in the way that Apel and Habermas conceive of that cognitive interest which is most closely associated with the endeavour of critical theory, namely the interest in self-reflection/emancipation. In the remainder of this section, I will sketch Apel's threefold scheme of cognitive interests. As it turns out, his scheme for a differentiated theory of science not only has a critical edge against logical positivism's pretense of "unified science." It moreover has a critical edge against Habermas's own conjecture of emancipatory knowledge.

As the subject of valid cognition is rooted in communicative practices, cognition must be construed as a world-involving activity that is ruled by practical interests. Cognitive interests are species of practical interests. Yet the sense in which each kind of cognitive interest respectively can be said to be of a practical nature differs. (1) There is a cognitive interest that is practical in a technical sense of praxis. This is the interest in controlling states of affairs, events and processes, and in objectifying a world of facts, in short, a *cognitive interest in objectification.*[13] (2) Moreover, there is a cognitive interest that is practical very much in the ethico-political Aristotelian sense of the term, i.e., as an interest in reaching mutual communicative understanding, or agreement, or both. This cognitive interest is perhaps best construed as an interest in disclosure and interpretation of significant meaning in a world of co-subjects and their acts and utterances, and in assessing and evaluating the reasons people have, or think they have by virtue of their particular ways of making sense of the world. In short, it is a *cognitive interest in interpretation.*[14]

Interpretation or understanding is embedded in intersubjective communication *about* something that the interlocutors take to be an objective matter, in some sense of "objective," in their common world. Interpretation or understanding cannot be replaced by descriptions and explanations of objective processes that we can observe in the behavior of our communication partners, e.g., in their verbal behavior, in their utterances, or in the texts they produce. Their actions, utterances and texts can only fulfill their function within our communication so long as we regard them as expressive vehicles, or as transparent media of the meaning-intentions that we are to understand. Against a recent tendency toward a mentalistic return in philosophy, which threatens to roll back advances towards an intersubjectivist paradigm that have been hard won through the once celebrated linguistic turn,[15] Apel thinks that even meaning-intentions should not be classified primarily as isolated psychological phenomena, but rather as meaning-*claims,* truth-*claims,* rightness-*claims,* and implicit sincerity-*claims,* in the context of communication about something, i.e., about some objective matter or topic. As soon as this embedding structure of understanding within the context of communication about something is dissolved, communicative understanding dissolves too.

Types of cognitive interests do not map directly into types of science. Rather, types of cognitive interests underlie types of science as dialectical moments, capable of being articulated and subdued in various ways. As dialectical moments they enter into complex constellations. Yet experimental physics, hermeneutic philology, and Marxist critique of ideology somewhat resemble pure ideal types (in Max Weber's sense of the term) of inquiries that are conspicuously geared to *one* essential cognitive interest. However, the vast majority of particular forms of science (e.g., political history, macro-economics, linguistics, cognitive developmental psychology, socio-biology, social systems theory, etc.)[16] draw on, and abstract from, more than one cognitive interest in different phases of their particular processes of inquiry as governed by their respective methodological canons.[17]

2.2   Against Historicist and Instrumentalist Misconstruals of Natural Science

Apel's assertion that a universal cognitive interest in objectifying and controlling world-states and processes is constitutive for the kind of knowledge that is evidently produced by standard "natural sciences" is a complex claim. It seeks to make the *claim* of such knowledge (to be "true to the facts") relative to human interests and practices – yet without relativizing the universality (of assent) and objectivity (of content) that are so characteristic of empirical truth. Apel's notion of cognitive interests precludes that we conceive of natural science as purely instrumental – as Horkheimer and Adorno were tempted to do. *Pace* Horkheimer and Adorno, social history of modern capitalism, no matter how deep and comprehensive, would not teach us all there is to know about the significance of natural science. Natural science is the rational enterprise of nomologically ordered knowledge of the empirical world. Such knowledge, *if* valid, is relevant for efficient agency in the technological sense of praxis. But its *validity* cannot be equated with the effectiveness of such agency. It cannot be justified as *knowledge* by pointing out its relevance for such agency – nor by reference to the natural history in the course of which mankind's interest in technical control and mankind's habits of thinking nomologically about the natural world were formed and refined in accordance with the evolutionary benefits that accrue to this specific kind of world-disclosure. Hence it would be a mistake to attribute to Apel the instrumentalist position that natural scientific knowledge *is* nothing but knowledge from the viewpoint of efficient technical usability. Surely empirical truth is not just practical utility for a human agent. But without some *conceptually universal* tie to human agency and to significant practices in which human agency flourishes in the actual world, the cognitive enterprise of treating the world as a source of empirical knowledge would lose its very point for us – or rather, it would never have had any point for incorporated agents like us in a world like ours. Certainly there are other human interests of a very general kind that went, and still go, into the scientific pursuit of truth, e.g., religious, speculative, narcissistic, exploitative interests. Some of them (e.g., the speculative interest in a transparent and all-encompassing world order) may even be necessary conditions of scientific inquiry. Yet none of them contributes to the idea of valid scientific knowledge in the way that the technical interest (in objectifying and controlling world-states and processes) contributes to the very idea of empirical truth. The conceptual relation between human agency and the acquisition of nomologically ordered knowledge has been historically highlighted by the rise of modern experimental science since the *renaissance* as opposed to a contemplative stance towards the *cosmos* in antiquity.[18]

2.3   Methodological Differences between Natural Sciences and Social Sciences

Total objectification is a possible cognitive stance only with regard to nature whereas the intrinsically intentional nature of the objects of social science allows for this stance only under certain methodological abstractions. Put in traditional terms: the social sciences are "confronted with a *subject–object*."[19] Apel's point sounds perhaps more familiar when expressed in less traditional language: social sciences constitute their subject matter by relying on a methodological prima facie presupposition "that there are regularities constitutive for the specific character of their objects. These regularities must be considered as rules or norms followed more or less intentionally (although not necessarily in a conscious way) by human subjects of actions."[20] Moreover social sciences as opposed to natural sciences cannot test their hypotheses by communication-free observation. For it is conceptually impossible for us to infer from an observed correspondence between a *regularity* that we ascribe to x from a third-person perspective plus our observations of x's behavior that the regularity is a *rule* for x.[21] Knowledge produced by the social sciences is mediated by a double hermeneutics. And the social scientist is potentially a participant in the very target practices of his or her methodologies. The testing of hypotheses, in this case, necessarily involves the social scientist in communicative participation. Apel substantiates this point with reference to Noam Chomsky. In Chomsky's linguistic research program for the description of a universal grammar, like in any other research program directed at the explanation of supposedly universal human competencies other than syntactical competence, normative reconstructions (e.g., of utterances as grammatically well formed) provide methodologically necessary conditions of adequacy. Apel claims that such reconstructions have to be proven as correct by communicative understanding between the social scientist and her object. Her object (which sometimes may be the scientist herself) is also a co-subject and thus a *subject–object*. Hence Apel distinguishes the subject–object relation of the natural sciences from the subject–co-subject relation of the social sciences.

The objectifying stance in the social sciences incurs further limitation by the intrinsically historical nature of their objects. Ongoing human practices are in principle non-predictable, not only due to human creativity, but also due to the self-determining capacities of human agency. Human agents are free to reflectively assimilate and *use* any socio-historical knowledge that is produced to represent human agents as predictably determined and unfree. For Apel, self-fulfilling or, as it were, self-destroying prophecies, whose ubiquity in the social sciences was forcibly pointed out by Robert K. Merton, reveal essential properties of the object of social science. They appear as methodologically vicious paradoxes only against a background-expectation of total control. However, the cognitive interest in objectification, which corresponds to the background-expectation of total control, has central significance only in the natural sciences. With regard to the social sciences, the cognitive interest in objectification cannot be central in the social sciences. It becomes constitutive only for what Apel describes as the "limiting case" of social science, namely quasi-nomological behavioral science. Such science rests on experiments and yields predictively relevant knowledge. It is the limiting case of social science in the sense of quasi-natural science where pride of place is given to the cognitive interest in objectification.

If we want knowledge to base social technology on, we have no other choice than letting other cognitive interests take the back seat to the cognitive interest in objectification. Under what conditions do we want to do this? Whose purposes are thus being furthered, whose needs forgone, and for what reasons? Apel implies that where social sciences produce knowledge fit for social technology, such epistemic activities must be "reflectively controlled by another type of social science, whose epistemological paradigm is *not* a quasi-physicalistic subject–object-relation undisturbed by Merton-effects but rather a kind of scientific mediation of society's self-reflection as a communication-community in the making."[22] Dialogical planning, sensors of civil society[23] within systemic science and technology, and deliberative procedures of public policy-making using scientific knowledge as a resource for acceptable options and decisions rather than as a stricture on such options and decisions – these are some of the things Apel has in mind. His differentiated theory of science allows him, in contrast to Horkheimer's and Adorno's wholesale rejection (from 1947 on) of science as instrumental reason, to express a qualified acceptance of scientifically informed social technology.

Social technology, according to Apel, is not intrinsically undesirable. To equate technologically useful knowledge with the power to treat people not as ends but only as means is as much of a categorical mistake as the opposite view held by technocrats, who (wrongly) believe that, in order to effect a meliorating transformation of society, only a technically applicable science is needed. Where social sciences produce knowledge aimed at instrumental use,

> we "are in fact supplementing the power of man over nature . . . by increasing the potential power of men over men, the complementary and compensatory function of hermeneutical social sciences constituted by the leading interest in communicative understanding should be directed towards the shaping and continuous reshaping of an educated, critical and competent public opinion."[24]

In his transcendental-pragmatic framework for a differentiated theory of science, Apel is able to recast the deep ambivalence in critical theory's assessment of *technomorphous* ("manipulative") uses of knowledge that are modeled on the paragon of natural science. Moreover, he can express this ambivalence without falling into an untenable paradox: the descriptive, explanatory, and predictive results of technologically relevant empirical social sciences may be *true* and *useful* within the confines of their questions and methods. Their questions and methods, on the other hand, may be found to contain presuppositions concerning human nature that are *untrue* and *illusory* if they go unchecked by questions and methods pertaining to hermeneutic science and critical reconstructive inquiries.

Apel has extensively discussed the issue of how the postulate of value-free social sciences hooks on the notion of objectivity in these sciences. For Apel, the real issue that has to be disentangled from a bundle of debates that notoriously surround Max Weber's positivistic postulate of value-free social and cultural science is how to construct evaluative forms of social sciences that we can normatively justify, rather than how to avoid constructing such forms altogether.[25] The motive that is usually considered to be the most important one for defending value-free social and cultural sciences is to secure intersubjective validity for their results. "Abstention from value-judgement is considered as the only way of securing intersubjective validity in the field of the humanities. This would indeed be true if a rational foundation of intersubjectively valid ethical norms were impossible."[26] Needless to say that for Apel this impression is spurious. Rigid abstention from value-judgments, then, is only provisionally feasible, i.e., as a controlled methodological abstraction. To make it an essential requirement is inevitably to miss an essential element in every type of social science, namely its hermeneutic dimension.

2.4   A New Epistemological Paradigm

Apel's continuing efforts toward a comprehensive critical theory of science beyond objectivism and relativism have culminated at present in the introduction of a genuinely new epistemological paradigm. For lack of a connotatively equivalent English expression, Apel calls this paradigm "Verständigung über etwas." (In German this nominalization of the verb "sich verständigen" has a product–process ambiguity. It means both (1) communicatively prompted agreement, and (2) the process of reaching an understanding about something.) This term denotes what, according to transcendental-pragmatic analysis, is the deep structure of *any* cognitively significant practice of essentially finite human beings: sign-mediated relations through which objectification can be intended (subject–object relations) that are embedded in, and complemented by, sign-mediated relations through which communicative understanding can be intended (subject–co-subject relations). It is impossible for essentially finite human beings, in those of their practices which are cognitively significant, to take a god's-eye view. To pretend otherwise marks the essence of all traditional metaphysics.[27]

Cognitively significant human endeavors aim at, or contribute to, the determination of universal validity claims. Universal validity claims, paradigmatically the claim to truth, when propositional contents are being asserted, and the claim to rightness, when normative contents are being justified, are claims that make what is being claimed susceptible to open-ended, fallibilistic, self-corrective practices of inquiry and argumentation.[28]

This post-metaphysical and post-empiricist epistemological paradigm of "Verständigung über etwas" epitomizes Apel's architectonics of cognitive interests. Notwithstanding the strong similarities in Habermas's and Apel's respective theories of science, Apel differs importantly from Habermas in his assigning to argumentative discourse an intra- and inter-theoretically privileged function as the ultimate arbiter of all universal validity claims, specifically to argumentative discourse in its most reflective forms. The generic function of argumentative discourse (as arbiter of all universal validity claims) potentially pervades any particular *"Verständigung über etwas"*: the structural possibility of argumentative discourse, in a way, accompanies "Verständigung über etwas" much like Kant's transcendental apperception would accompany thought. But unlike Kant's transcendental ego, argumentative discourse is an essentially intersubjective activity of real people. In its most reflective forms, argumentative discourse

> is not just one language game among others. It is that unique language game by which we can talk about language-games in general and can try to settle all kinds of questions about problematic validity-claims that can be raised in other language games. The function of argumentative discourse, which today must still be shared by philosophy and all of the sciences, consists in settling all kinds of problems about validity-claims by arguments alone, i.e. by providing good reasons and not e.g. by rhetorical persuasions or by negotiations using offers and threats.[29]

2.5 Reconstructive Criticial Social Science

So far we have been dealing with only two cognitive interests – an interest in objectification and an interest in interpretation. A third cognitive interest is to be found in Apel's architectonics, namely the "interest in critically-emancipatory self-reflection." Critical-reconstructive social sciences, paradigmatical examples of which are psychoanalysis and the critique of ideology, are essentially tied to this interest.

What Apel describes in transcendental-pragmatic terms as the cognitive interest "in critically-emancipatory self-reflection"[30] can be illustrated by reference to the constitutive dimension of what in more familiar Marxist terms has been programmatically proclaimed as the humanization of nature and the naturalization of man.[31]

Strategical-political praxis of changing socio-political structures may be justified as emancipatory if, and only if, it may be considered as a consequence of the overcoming of inner constraints of a pseudo-nature by critical self-reflection, in contradistinction to those types of social engineering which are based instead on a manipulative utilization of reified structures of social relations.[32]

By treating critique of ideology and psychoanalysis as two critical reconstructive projects of inquiry, both of which are obviously not value-free, Apel's differentiated theory of science avoids the pitfalls of either reducing them to hermeneutics (understanding of meaning) or of assimilating them to natural science (explanation from nomic necessities). Hence the charges that Marxism and psychoanalysis are merely pseudoscientific travesties of science (Karl Popper) are equally misplaced as are charges that psychoanalysis is a natural science but a very poor one (Adolf Grünbaum).[33]

What then *are* characteristic features of a critical reconstructive project of inquiry, besides being driven by an interest in emancipatory self-reflection? This latter cognitive interest, according to Apel, places the interest in objectification and control, and the interest in reaching communicative understanding, into a constellation such that the former serves the latter in such a way as to increase the scope of intentional human agency. Operative in this peculiar constellation is what can be termed neither a "logic of discovery" nor a "logic of justification" but rather, a logic of self-reflection.[34] By virtue of being driven by an interest in emancipatory self-reflection, the way critical reconstructive projects of inquiry work can be analyzed in four phases:

1   A *partial* and *provisional* suspension of full reciprocity of communication between co-subjects.[35]

2   *Adoption* of the objectifying stance as a methodological device that is necessary for the production of explanatory knowledge about human behavior;

3   *Reinsertion* of such knowledge into communicative exchanges so that the knowledge gained (in 2) engenders transformations in the self-understanding of the subject who (in 2) was only an object.

4   *Self-application*: The self undergoing such transformation (in 3) is thereby put into a *normatively better* position (in psychoanalysis, e.g., a "more autonomous" position) as a subject *vis-à-vis* the self's contingent determinations as an object.

Although Apel's concept of "cognitive interest in critically-emancipatory reflection" at first glance seems to parallel Habermas's concept of a "cognitive interest in emancipation," there is a crucial difference between the two.

In a brief but momentous lecture held in Kiel in 1969 during the height of the German "student revolt,"[36] Apel criticized Habermas for having introduced the concept of a cognitive interest in emancipation in such a way as to identify it by implication with *theoretical reflexion* (as telos of all reflective cognitive inquiry, including philosophy) and *political activism* (as telos of all practical engagement towards social critique). Apel concedes that, at least at the level of reflective thinking, there is an internal relation between our epistemic practices on the one hand and the advocacy for social conditions marked by an unrestricted and uncoerced communal and individual life, on the other hand. But this *a priori* justifiable partisanship of reason for forms of life in which the life of reason can flourish, which Apel will later explicate as the normative core of Discourse Ethics, does not obliterate the conceptual difference between political action ("critical engagement") backed by critical reconstructive social science and, on the other hand, the social sciences that do the backing. To collapse this conceptual difference, as Habermas tended to do, by subsuming both under a unitary concept of an interest in emancipation, misleadingly suggests that the *taking* of determinate political *action* could be described as the mere *application* of allegedly "critical" *science*.

This shortcut from reflective inquiry to politics obscures the rather complex and indirect relations that exist between the democractic legitimacy of political activism and the epistemic credentials of cognitive enterprises. This shortcut runs the whole gamut of objections that can be derived from studying the historical vicissitudes of Marx's dictum that the world must not only be interpreted, but must be changed. Praxis and theory, Apel holds, are *essentially* non-identical human endeavors. This holds true *pace* Habermas even at the level of cognitive interests with their corresponding modes of relating human agency to (subjective, objective, and intersubjective) worlds.

Moreover, by collapsing the reflective resources of philosophy into practical engagement towards social critique, Habermas obscures that logical space which his own reasoning about the general nature of cognitive interests and their relation to praxis occupies.[37] Reasoning about the general nature of cognitive interests is by implication reasoning about itself. Hence such reasoning must include considerations about its peculiarly reflective mode of thematization. The logical space of reasoning about the general nature of cognitive interests is obviously situated within the argumentative discourse of self-reflective philosophical thinking and not in the practical engagement towards social critique, although the latter might be normatively justified in view of the former. According to Apel, this non-identity indicates a kind of bifurcation, or bipolar structure, *within* that cognitive interest which Habermas termed "emancipatory." Habermas's construction (wrongly) tends to dismiss the peculiar autonomy of philosophical discourse by putting self-reflective philosophical thinking in line with other enterprises of critical reconstructive social inquiry. Habermas's tendency to deny philosophy any "privileged place" within the web of empirical social sciences[38] has been the target of Apel's criticism again and again. Habermas's attitude to the idea that philosophy has specific methodological canons and resources is deeply ambivalent.[39] Habermas readily dismisses the idea of asymmetric justificatory links that hold between parts of philosophical discourse and parts of the discourses that shape particular sciences. This quick dismissal is not based on an in-depth analysis of epistemic holism. Rather it is based on a refusal to construe asymmetric justificatory links in terms other than those of privilege, hierarchy, cultural hegemony and the gloomy specter of the "philosopher king."[40]

Apel's perhaps most important objection against Habermas's line of detranscendentalization is that Habermas is depriving *all* reconstructive social sciences of the very possibility of justifying, in normative (i.e., prescriptively universal) terms, their own evaluative import, by making philosophy merely one more reconstructive social science.

> The old Frankfurt School – and, in a sense, even Habermas before his *universal pragmatic* turn – has followed the Hegel-Marxian suggestion that the Humean/Kantian distinction between the "is" and the "ought" could be obliterated by exploiting the history-immanent dialectics of "determinate negation", i.e. – as Habermas used to explain – by normative-practical ideals that are at least implicitly manifested by the validity-claims of that society and hence are contained in the history itself as an unredeemed promise.[41]

For Apel, methodological adherence to determinate negation – gearing critique of ideology to the immanent aspirations, standards, and claims of the very practices and communities that are the target of the critique – is not a sufficient condition of adequacy for such critique. Apel points out untiringly that one of the necessary conditions of adequacy that has to be met is the condition that the deontological standards of valuation which are contained in, or in the background of, such critique be justified in ways that make these standards philosophically unassailable for skepticism, relativism, and historicism.

Securing the fragile autonomy of self-critical reason by setting limits to skepticism, relativism and historicism is for Apel no lofty concern of a minority of die-hard intellectuals who are contingently socialized in philosophical traditions meandering from Kant and Hegel to Nietzsche and Gadamer. Rather, it is a task that has a wider bearing on the good life of, and social justice in, political communities of citizens. Furthering human rights, sustaining the civil society and extending democratic pratices are all collective projects that draw support from normative infrastructures. Their authority can to some extent be strengthened or weakened depending on the rational powers of arguments available, from within particular traditions, from heterogeneous practical contexts, and from within different communities, for marshaling against those whose vested interests favour the decline and subversion of such projects. Apel's repudiation of Rortyan ironic bourgeois liberalism[42] and his intransigent criticism of thinkers who, like Nietzsche and Foucault, rage against purportedly universal claims of reason, which they view as so many forms of suppression, grow out of Apel's personal experience with Nazi communitarianism.[43] Only in a radically open community of discourse including potentially everyone, can reason contribute to life what the enlightenment had always proclaimed it should do: to help overcome unnecessary repression and to further an autonomy of difference compatible with equal respect for everyone alike. By emphatically insisting on a radically open community of discourse as the practical locus of a notion of rationality, whose non-Eurocentric validity transcends the contingencies of its European origin from within, Apel reminds critical theory that diagnosing the eclipse of reason and at the same time belittling as *prima philosophia* ("foundational," "metaphysical") any theoretic attempt at rooting its claims may, by inviting nihilism, contribute to the very eclipse one decries.[44]

2.6 Reductionism and Self-Referential Pragmatic Consistency

One of the hallmarks of critical theory has always been critique of ideological guises of metaphysics – e.g., as "subjectivism" in the dominant ideology of everyday life, as "positivism" in the sciences, as "nihilism" and "irrationalism" in moral and political philosophy, and as "first philosophy" and "system philosophy" in the foundationalist camp within theoretical philosophy. Detranscendentalization, epistemological naturalism, deconstruction, radical constructivism, social systems theory, to name but a few, all proudly wear post-metaphysical thinking on their sleeves.

Apel embraces detranscendentalization, broadly conceived, as a necessary move within a critical philosophy that struggles against its own sublime metaphysical shackles. Yet Apel insists on a condition of adequacy for any such project, namely to avoid self-referential pragmatic inconsistency with regard to the universal validity claims that are inscribed into such projects owing to their purported rational role within the web of reflective deliberations that earn the name of philosophy. Otherwise post-metaphysical thinking cannot avoid becoming entangled in the very gestures of absolutization which it rejects. According to Apel, many theoretical approaches that promise to discard metaphysical thinking covertly or overtly contain reductionisms. When we make these explicit by testing for self-referential pragmatic consistency they usually reveal metaphysical premises or metaphysical pretensions in the corresponding approach.

In this regard, it is interesting to note that Apel wishes to vindicate a notion that was first introduced by Imré Lakatos for the study of epistemic transitions from less adequate to more adequate epistemic states within scientific traditions: the primacy of "internal" over "external" reconstructions.[45] This notion has a direct bearing on critical theory's reconstructive analyses of societal rationalization processes. Giving this notion a transcendental-pragmatic reading, Apel elaborates what he calls a "principle of self-appropriation" (*Selbsteinholungsprinzip*).[46] Basically, this principle demands that any reconstructive science (RS) of some domain x be compatible in its validity claims with the view we get when we look at the very development of RS in essentially the same way that we look at x via RS.[47] The principle of self-appropriation figures prominently in Apel's vision of a comprehensive critical theory. With this principle Apel hopes to enable critical theory to retain a concern for self-justifying theory-structures (so characteristic of philosophies of history in a Hegelian key) while opening critical theory up as wide as possible to the motives of radical scepticism of reason (so characteristic of the post-metaphysical thrust in much of modern philosophy[48]).

> I believe the principle of self-appropriation shows incontrovertibly that the rational reconstruction of rationalization processes must always take precedence over strategies of external explanation and unmasking (such as externally explanatory sociology, base-superstructure theories, and other types of ideology critique; psychoanalysis; "genealogies" à la Nietzsche or Foucault; structuralistic, system-functionalistic, or Being-historical explanations of the present era; deconstruction; and so on). Naturally this in no way says that the above external explanations cannot be more or less appropriate supplements to a "maximally internal" (Lakatos) reconstruction. It does mean, though, that the *reductionism* of the "nothing but" explanations – the really influential and mostly scientistic antimetaphysics of modernity and seemingly of "postmodernity" as well – is definitively finished off by the self-appropriation principle of the reconstructive sciences. The "happy total demystifiers of human rationality" either get caught in performative self-contradictions or immunize themselves against possible criticism . . . It must also be emphasized that fully grounding the reconstruction of rationalization processes in the self-appropriation principle allows the charge of Eurocentrism to be avoided, in contrast to Max Weber's hypothetically grounded reconstruction, which has to appear obviously one-sided and incomplete" in light of the rich notion of communicative rationality that is manifested in argumentative discourse. "The Charge of Eurocentrism can be leveled only if one considers it possible to criticize the very reason one demonstrably makes use of, on the basis of the "Other of reason" or, what amounts to the same thing, "another reason" that later could become the standard.[49]

2.7   Apel's Critique of Habermas' Sociologism

Apel's pursuit of a transcendental-pragmatic turn in philosophy has many valuable spinoffs for critical theory. Not the least of which is an alertness to reductionist tendencies in Habermas's project of reformulating a critical theory of society within the formal-pragmatic framework of a theory of communicative action. In this respect, Apel is a trenchant critic of Habermas whose theoretical intentions Apel by and large shares.

In a number of writings,[50] most notably in his contribution to the "unfinished project of enlightenment" on the occasion of Habermas's sixtieth birthday,[51] Apel touched on a feature of Habermas's thinking that, Apel fears, "threatens its coherence and even its consistency"[52] – Habermas's sociologism.

Habermas's sociologism crops up in two related problems. First, there is Habermas's strained antifoundationalism. Habermas (rightly) repudiates speculative philosophy of history as a source of rational authority for the political advocacy and evaluative commitments that characterize critical theory. But Habermas (wrongly) shies away from *all* strong philosophic justificatory arguments. Confounding descriptions with prescriptions, or at least the appearance of doing so, is the price Habermas has to pay, but should not be willing to pay, for the evasion of those strong justificatory arguments Apel is after. Such justificatory arguments have a "transcendental-pragmatic" point in that the actual performance of sceptical moves in argumentative discourse yields insight into the *salva rationalitate* non-contingency of certain normative commitments.[53] The legitimate scope of the criticalness of critical theory is only as wide as the scope that can be given to the justification of the normative commitments that are built into it.

Habermas is inconsistent in that he is invoking the meta-language-game of reflective philosophical argumentation with its peculiar maximum scope validity claims[54] while at the same time denying the feasibility of that very type of argumentation. Habermas uses the expressive powers of reflective philosophical argument to deny that reflective philosophical argument can have such powers.

Second, Apel observes a tendency in Habermas towards the transfiguration of the lifeworld as a field of normative authority that, according to Apel, the lifeworld cannot have, at least not without question-begging circularity. Habermas cannot have it both ways: he cannot (1) bracket the normativity of *all* particular forms of life (so dear to neo-aristotelian advocates of "Sittlichkeit" and to communitarian zealots of "ethos") by claiming universal normative primacy for norms whose universalizability we can ascertain as soon as we adopt the peculiar moral point of view embodied in discourse, and (2) anchor the purported normative primacy of discourse ethics' peculiar moral point of view in contingent features of *our* Euro-genic ethical lifeworld – namely that our actual lifeworld empirically (and luckily) is, but could fail to be, communicatively rationalized in ways that ensure the ubiquity of discourse. That universalist morality (as specified by discourse ethics) ought to trump any particularistic ethos, is a claim that may be rationally evident against the background of a suitably shaped lifeworld (namely ours) but may fail to be evident against the background of another lifeworld that has been historically shaped in radically different ways. The alleged normative primacy of the discourse ethical moral point of view cannot be rooted in the vicissitudes of lifeworld histories. Such normative primacy neither is a social fact nor could it be one. It is a counterfactual ideal. Habermas fails to provide the strong justification one needs in order to attribute primacy to the claims of discourse ethics ranging over diverse ethical lifeworlds, or over ethical lifeworlds in which other dimensions of rationality reign supreme which challenge such primacy.[55]

3   DISCOURSE ETHICS, AND THE LIMITATIONS OF UTOPIAN THOUGHT

Like Habermas, Apel criticized the critical theory expounded by Horkheimer and Adorno for having failed to unravel the web of normative assumptions that underwrite their critical evaluations. The "old Frankfurt School had not yet completely freed itself from the Hegelian and Marxian conception of a *speculative philosophy of history* . . . as a substitute for a normative foundation of ethics."[56]

Some recent strands of theoretical work in the field of critical theory, especially Habermas's work on the democratic state and debates about civil society,[57] make ample use of an ethical framework that presents itself as an alternative to other unifying moral theories such as utilitarianism, contractualism, and Kantian deontologism. Apel's work has been pivotal for the introduction of this framework: discourse ethics.[58]

3.1   Ideological Complementarity

The main ideas of the entire framework which by now have become more familiar through Habermas's work were originally layed out in one of Apel's landmark essays:[59] *The A Priori of the Communication Community and the Foundations of Ethics: The Problem of a Rational Foundation of Ethics in the Scientific Age.* Apel starts off in this essay with a penetrating critique of selective rationalization processes that in Eastern socialist societies were tied up with communism, and that in Western capitalist societies are associated with liberalism. Both draw on strong universalist ethical intuitions whose rational authority both, though in different ways, must eventually erode. Owing to the selectivity of the rationality assumptions that prevail in these two grand rationalization processes, both are unable to refurnish with rational authority the ethical resources they deplete. The resulting paralyzation of universalist ethical resources is all the more devastating as mankind is increasingly being drawn into common problems on a planetary scale (e.g., the ecological crisis). Coping with these problems would be facilitated if universal ethical resources were available that could support an overlapping consensus of appropriate macro-ethical orientations.[60] In mainstream Western liberalism, this subversion takes the form of a denial that there is any rationally ascertainable objectivity beyond the objectivity of fact-stating discourse, ideally that of science. Ethical orientations, like previous religious beliefs, become relegated to a subjectively construed private sphere that no longer commands intersubjective assent. Hume's distinction between *is* and *ought* is acknowledged as it should be but seems to prove an insurmountable obstacle to the idea of objectively grounding normative claims. This "complementarity of existentialism and scientism," Apel observed in 1973, is one of the hallmarks of liberalism as the dominant ideology of the West. Under the ideological premises of communism, as it were, Hume's distinction between *is* and *ought* is allegedly bridged. Apel maintains that such bridging, call it dialectical or otherwise, is bound to be spurious, and moreover demands the price of rendering individual moral responsibility similarly private and impotent as is the case in Western liberalism.

> The question why someone subjectively takes up the cause of the proletariat, for example, is answered by reference to the objective results of scientific socialism whilst the understanding and acceptance of these results is made dependent upon taking up the cause of the proletariat. Here, the total mediation of subjectivity and objectivity postulated by Hegel as a speculative *ex post* reflexion is presented as the result of a scientific, objective analysis.[61]
>
> As the critically engaged "subjective practice" of revolutionaries is integrated in this manner into the dialectical concept of the objectively knowable reality (of history), the impression is created that an ethical foundation of the totally committed subjective praxis becomes superfluous for Marxism. The dialectical analysis and synthesis of the necessary course of history seems from the outset to sublate Hume's distinction between what is and what ought to be into the totality of reality that is interpreted as rational.[62]
>
> I wish to emphasize that, under the Eastern "system of integration", i.e. under the dogmatic presupposition that an elite of party philosophers guarantees the unity of scientific knowledge and morality on the basis of a dialectical "superscience", it is also impossible to speak of an ethics of collective responsibility. I believe that the difference between the insoluble ideological contradiction of the West and that of the East can be traced back to the following fact. In the former case, moral decisions of conscience by all individuals are postulated, yet an intersubjective validity of ethical norms, and consequently a moral solidarity, cannot be grounded. In the latter case, the collectivity of society's moral responsibility is postulated, but it cannot be mediated, either theoretically or in political, practical terms, by individuals' decisions of conscience. Such decisions are basically superfluous and – the practical consequence is similar to that of the Western system of complementarity – they are relegated to the private sphere.[63]

3.2   Need-claims, Validity-claims, and the Categorical Discourse Demand

In a constructive response to the diagnosed challenge, Apel then points out that the intersubjective validity of moral norms is a precondition for the very possibility and validity of science. Hence the idea of scientific objectivity poses no decisive objection against the possibility of an intersubjectively valid ethics.

Apel then gives this negative thesis a positive turn by arguing that "the *rational argumentation* that is presupposed not only in every science but also in every discussion of a problem, in itself presupposes the validity of universal, ethical norms."[64] In a complex argument whose details[65] unfortunately cannot be presented in this overview, Apel arrives at the seminal formulations of a communicative ethics ("discourse ethics", *Diskursethik*) that is undeniably part of the conceptual presuppositions of validity-oriented argumentative practices:

> The a *priori* of argumentation contains the *claim* to *justify* not only all the "assertions" of science, but also all human *claims* (including the implicit claims of human beings upon one another that are embedded in actions and institutions). Anyone who takes part in an argument implicitly acknowledges all the *potential claims* of all the members of the communication community that can be justified by rational arguments (otherwise the claim of argumentation would restrict itself in subject matter).[66]

Furthermore,

> the members of the communication community (and this implies all thinking beings) are also committed to considering all the potential claims of all the potential members – and this means all human "needs" inasmuch as they could be affected by the norms and consequently make claims on their fellow human beings. As potential "claims" that can be communicated interpersonally, all human "needs" are ethically *relevant*. They must be *acknowledged* if they can be justified interpersonally through arguments and "one should not unnecessarily sacrifice a finite, individual human interest."[67]

Turning to the particular point of discourse concerned with the resolution of moral problems ("practical discourse"), Apel specifies the following basic principle of discourse ethics:[68]

> (*U!*): "all human *needs* – as potential *claims* – i.e. which can be reconciled with the needs of all the others by argumentation, must be made the concern of the communication community."[69]

This basic principle, other than the more specific Habermasian universalization "principle U" that is often and misleadingly taken as *the* basic unifying principle of discourse ethics,[70] has the illocutionary form of an imperative. Both $U_{Habermas}$ and Apel's practical discourse demand $U!$ are dialogically reformulated successor notions of the Kantian categorical imperative. Yet $U_{Habermas}$ takes up the categorical imperative only in the sense of a universalization test thus omitting its categorical prescriptivity whereas $U!$ expresses a demand.[71]

The discourse ethical framework that Apel derives by focusing on the normative infrastructure of validity-determining argumentative practices is more general and yet more demanding than the discourse ethical framework that Habermas derives by focusing on presuppositions of generic communicative action. This difference between the "transcendental-pragmatic" (Apel) framework and the "formal-pragmatic" framework (Habermas) of discourse ethics owes much to Apel's appropriation of specifically Peircean insights into the communal nature of validity-determining argumentative practices such as, e.g., scientific inquiry. Overstating the difference, one might say that where Habermas's elaboration of discourse ethics focuses on articulating a *moral point of view* that Habermas takes to be represented in "the ideal speech situation,"[72] Apel is more radical: he goes one step further than Habermas by articulating a *moral engagement* that stems from membership in an ongoing collective project. This ongoing collective project transcends from within the epochal confines of the project that Habermas refers to as that of modernity. Rather than the more specific project of modernity, the project in which the normativity of discourse ethics is rooted is the flourishing of argumentative discourse within real communication communities that permanently fail to live up to those idealizations which they permanently project and anticipate.[73] Discourse ethics, for Apel, is rooted in a dual perspective that cannot be circumvented. This uncircumventable dual perspective can be made reflectively obvious for anyone who invokes argumentative discourse. This dual perspective is on the one hand that of a concrete individual qua member of real communication communities *vis-à-vis* other such concrete others; and on the other hand the perspective of a member among members of an "ideal" community of communication. The ideal community of communication is the idea of a community whose cognitively significant projects do not *suffer* from the pragmatic boundary conditions under which our real communication communities operate in the actual world.[74]

3.3 The Weak Utopian Vision in Discourse Ethics

This dual perspective, or rather the reflective awareness of discrepancies that is fostered by this dual perspective, obviously appears outrageously utopian if "ideal communication community" is (wrongly) identified with a straightforward goal that could be achieved by political means.[75] Argumentation holds no political blueprint for the best society. On the other hand, the dual perspective embedded in argumentation does not boil down to a Kantian regulative idea[76] that would incur Hegel's criticism of (Kant's) "powerless-ness of the moral *ought.*" We are

> not concerned with a purely *idealistic* presupposition in the sense of an *a priori* of consciousness. Nor, however, are we concerned with a purely materi-alistic presupposition – such that Kant's ideal and normative "consciousness as such" is to be replaced by the "being" of empirical society. I believe that the point of our *a priori* is that it marks the *principle of a dialectics* (on this side) *of idealism and materialism.* For anyone who engages in argument auto-matically presupposes two things: first, a *real communication community* whose member he has himself become through a process of socialization, and sec-ond, an *ideal communication community* that would basically be capable of adequately understanding the meaning of his arguments and judging their truth in a definitive manner. What is remarkable and dialectical about this situation, however, is that, to some extent, the ideal community is presup-posed and even counterfactually anticipated *in* the real one, namely, as a real possibility of the real society, although the person who engages in argu-ment is aware that (in most cases) the real community, including himself, is far removed from being similar to the ideal community. But, by virtue of its transcendental structure, argumentation is left no choice other than to face this both desperate and hopeful situation.[77]

There is then no strict disjunction between utopia, communicative reason, and discourse ethics. There is no prognostically relevant intrinsic link between them either. Concrete societies are infinitely complex historical individuals that manifest discursive openness in varying degrees and ways. No exaggerated utopian ideal of the would-be collectively good societal life can do justice to this historically evolving complexity. And no speculative philosophy of history can tell its grand tale of progress and regression with any determinate verdict on the responsibilities we now have for the shape of future social worlds, to the extent that we can influence their formation. Discourse ethics, however, does contain a weak utopian vision. *U!* demands nothing less than the permanent collective task of restructuring all institu-tions of society. The revision of a form of social life according to *U!* presup-poses carefully reviewing it in the light of critical reconstructive social sciences that give us a grip on enabling and disabling conditions for discur-sive spaces and help us recall those discursive spaces that have been estab-lished or foreclosed in the past. The practical discourse demand *U!* morally commits us to an ongoing search for forms of societal organization that would optimally enable human beings to articulate, scrutinize and coordi-nate their diverse ideas of the good life, to the maximum extent that is com-patible with the argumentative assent of everyone concerned in the consequentiality of their pursuit.

ACKNOWLEDGMENT

I thank Richard Lehun and Frederik van Gelder for language assistance.

NOTES

1 Apel (1979): Towards a Reconstruction of Critical Theory. In S. C. Brown (ed.), *Philosophical Disputes in the Social Sciences* (Sussex: Harvester Press), pp. 127–39.

2 For a sympathetic and concise portrait of Apel's intellectual development, see Eduardo Mendieta's introduction to the selection of Apel's essays he edited (Karl-Otto Apel (1993): *Selected Essays*, Volume one, *Towards a Transcendental Semiotics* (Atlantic Highlands, NJ: Humanities Press). Volume two of the *Selected Essays* (1996, forthcoming) will contain a selection of papers on "Ethics and the Theory of Rationality."

3 For an illuminating discussion of the link between symbolic interactionism and both Apel's and Habermas's notion of intersubjectivity, see Mendieta, Eduardo (1994) G. H. Mead: Linguistically Constituted Intersubjectivity and Ethics. *Transactions of the Charles S. Peirce Society*, vol. XXX no. 4, pp. 959–1000.

4 For an intellectual autobiography spanning the time from Apel's Heidegger and Wittgenstein studies in the fifties to his Peircean reading of Kant in the seventies, see Apel (1978): Transformation der Transzendentalphilosophie: Versuch einer retrospektiven Zwischenbilanz. *Philosophische Selbstbetrachtungen*, vol. 4 (Frankfurt: Peter Lang).

5 The following books contain discussions of Apel's transcendental pragmatic turn: Bleicher, Josef (1980): *Contemporary Hermeneutics: Hermeneutics as Method, Philosophy, and Critique* (London: Routledge & Kegan Paul). Dallmayr, Fred R. (1981): *Beyond Dogma and Despair: Toward a Critical Phenomenology of Politics* (Indiana: University of Notre Dame Press). Dallmayr, Fred R. (1981): *Twilight of Subjectivity: Contributions to a Post-Individualist Theory of Politics* (Amherst, Mass.: University of Massachusetts Press). See also chapter 4 in Fred R. Dallmayr (1987): *Critical Encounters: Between Philosophy and Politics* (Indiana: University of Notre Dame Press). Kuhlmann, Wolfgang and Dietrich Böhler (1982), eds: *Kommunikation und Reflexion: Zur Diskussion der Transzendentalpragmatik Antworten auf K.-O. Apel* (Frankfurt: Suhrkamp). Cortina, Adela (1985): *Razón Comunicativa y responsabilidad solidaria. Ética y política en K.-O. Apel* (Salamanca: Editiones Síqueme). Benhabib, Seyla and Fred R. Dallmayr (1992), eds: *The Communicative Ethics Controversy* (Cambridge, Mass.: MIT Press). Dorschel, A., M. Kettner, M. Niquet, W. Kuhlmann (1993), eds: *Transzendentalpragmatik* (Frankfurt: Suhrkamp).

6 For a critical assessment of Horkheimer's decisionist adoption of an ethics of compassion and solidarity among finite beings, see esp. Michiel Korthals (1985): Die kritische Gesellschaftstheorie des frühen Horkheimer, *Zeitschrift für Soziologie* 4, 315–29. Herbert Schnädelbach (1986): Max Horkheimer and the Moral Philosophy of German Idealism. *Telos* 66, Winter 1985–86, 81–101.

7 For instance, cf. section 10 (pp. 76–88) of "Remarks on discourse ethics" in Habermas (1993 [Germ.: 1991]): *Justification and Application: Remarks on Discourse Ethics* (Cambridge, Mass.: MIT Press), 19–111.

8 P. 127, Kai Nielsen (1991): The very idea of a Critical Theory. *Ratio*, IV, 124–45

9 Apel conceives of understanding and explanation as "complementary" forms of knowledge corresponding to complementary cognitive interests. Understanding and explanation supplement each other (within a cognitive context broadly conceived). They exclude each other as different intentions of asking questions (within their cognitive contexts narrowly construed). In virtue of this mutual exclusion and supplementation they are irreducible to each other. For a more elaborated account of this "complementarity" relation, cf. Apel (1979):

Towards a Reconstruction of Critical Theory. In S. C. Brown (ed.), *Philosophical Disputes in the Social Sciences*, p. 13. Apel (1984): *Understanding and Explanation. A Transcendental-Pragmatic Perspective* (Cambridge, Mass.: MIT Press), pp. 63, 243–49. Apel (1982): The "Erklären-Verstehen"-Controversy in the Philosophy of the Human and Natural Sciences. In G. Floistadt (ed.), *Contemporary Philosophy. A New Survey. Chronicles of the International Institute for Philosophy* (IIP), vol. 2 (The Hague/Boston/London: Martinus Nijhoff), 19–50. Apel (1987): Dilthey's distinction between "explanation" and "understanding" and the possibility of its "mediation". *Journal of the History of Philosophy* XXV, no. 1 (1987), 131–49.

10   Apel (1979): *Towards a Reconstruction of Critical Theory*, p. 6.

11   Cf. Apel (1984): *Understanding and Explanation. A Transcendental-Pragmatic Perspective*, esp. p. 190f.

12   Cf. Habermas (1971): *Knowledge and Human Interests* (Boston: Beacon Press).

13   "Technisches Erkenntnisinteresse" or, in the terms of a somewhat outdated Max Schelerian sociology of knowledge, "Interesse an Verfügungswissen."

14   The terms that Apel most often uses in German to denote this cognitive interest are *"Hermeneutisches Erkenntnisinteresse," "Verständigungsinteresse," "Interesse an Verständigungswissen."*

15   John Searle's suggestion to ground speech-act theory in a theory of the intentionality of the mind, and to view linguistic meaning as a derivative form of intentionality, see Apel (1991): Is Intentionality more basic than Linguistic Meaning? In E. Lepore and R. van Gulick (eds), *John Searle and his Critics* (Cambridge, Mass.: Blackwell), pp. 31–55. Apel (1993): Intentions, Conventions, and Reference to Things: Meaning in Hermeneutics and the Analytic Philosophy of Language. In Apel (1994), *Selected Essays*, vol one, *Towards a Transcendental Semiotics*, 51–82.

16   Cf. Apel (1968): Szientistik, Hermeneutik, Ideologiekritik: Entwurf einer Wissenschaftslehre in erkenntnisantropologischer Sicht. *Wiener Jahrbuch für Philosophie*, 1, 15–45. See English translation of this essay, esp. p. 72, Scientistics, hermeneutics and the critique of ideology: Outline of a theory of science from a cognitive-anthropological standpoint, in Apel (1980): *Towards a Transformation of Philosophy*. For a transcendental-pragmatic analysis of the constellation of cognitive interests that specifically underlie history as a type of social science, cf. esp. pp 259–65, Apel (1992): The hermeneutic dimension of social science and its normative foundation, *Man and World*, 25, 247–70.

17   What generically marks off the social sciences from the natural sciences is that all of the former but none of the latter have, already at the level of their objects, a hermeneutic dimension. Having such a hermeneutic dimension is, of course, not a sufficient condition for a science to be a "hermeneutic science." To think otherwise leads to a hermeneutic idealism that Apel eschews. "By social sciences I understand all those sciences that, on the one hand, are concerned with the *social reality* in space and time and thus far *share* – more or less – the cognitive interest in objectification with the natural sciences but, on the other hand, must also participate – more or less – in the cognitive interest in communicative understanding and thus far in the hermeneutic dimension of cognition – simply because they are dealing with the reality of human beings and their cultural achievements" (1992), The Hermeneutic Dimension, p. 259.

18   Cf. Apel (1968, 1980): Scientistics, hermeneutics and the critique of ideology, pp. 46–76. How intentional human agency and the concept of causality are intrinsically linked is best explained in Apel (1984): *Understanding and Explanation. A Transcendental-Pragmatic Perspective*, pp. 59–68, 192f.

19   Apel (1979): *Towards a Reconstruction of Critical Theory*, p. 17.

20   Ibid., p. 17.

21   For more on rules and rule following, see Apel (1984): *Understanding and Explanation*, esp. pp. 74–79.

22   Apel (1979): *Towards a Reconstruction of Critical Theory*. p. 23.

23 Cf. J. L. Cohen and A. Arato (1992): *Civil Society and Political Theory* (Cambridge, Mass.: MIT Press). Cohen and Arato (cf. pp. 544; 547) use the metaphor of "receptors" of civil society to describe a precondition for the formation of communicative counterforce against colonization of critical sectors of the lifeworld.

24 Ibid., p. 36

25 Cf. Apel (1973): Wissenschaft als Emanzipation? Eine kritische Würdigung der Wissenschaftskonzeption der "Kritischen Theorie," in *Transformation der· Philosophie*, vol. 2, pp. 128–54, esp. p. 145, where Apel specifies necessary and sufficient conditions for the meaning of the term "value-free" in regard to scientific inquiries: "Genau insofern und insoweit eine – oft unreflektierte – Vorverständigung darüber besteht, daß eine Wissenschaft experimentell überprüfbares und insofern auch technologisch verwertbares Verfügungswissen liefern soll, – genau insofern und insoweit kann und muß eine Wissenschaft als wertfrei aufgefaßt und praktiziert werden." Hence one of its necessary conditions makes value freedom depend on a consensus about the kind of knowledge we want the respective science to produce. On the other hand, no consensus about the kind of knowledge we want a science to produce can be a rational consensus unless it respects the seemingly ontological determinations of the object domain of the respective science. That knowledge be open to experimental corroboration ("experimentell überprüfbar") puts a strong methodological constraint on knowledge. As it turns out, this constraint cannot be met in every object domain no matter how much we might want it there to be met.

26 Apel (1979): *Towards a Reconstruction of Critical Theory*, p. 35.

27 Here Apel's critical analysis of metaphysical thinking agrees with Putnam's and Habermas's. Cf. Apel (1987): Die Herausforderung der totalen Vernunftkritik und das Programm einer philosophischen Theorie der Rationalitätstypen. *Concordia*, 11, 2–23. For a shorter version in English, cf. (Apel 1992): The challenge of totalizing critique of reason and the program of a philosophical theory of rationality types. In D. Freundlieb and H. Hudson (to appear 1993) eds, *Reason and Its Other* (Oxford: Berg Publishers), pp. 23–48. See also Transcendental Semiotics as First Philosophy. In Apel (1993): *Selected Essays*, vol. one, *Towards a Transcendental Semiotics*, 112–31. Apel (1993): The Transcendental Conception of Language Communication and the Idea of a First Philosophy: Towards a Critical Reconstruction of the History of Philosophy in the Light of Language Philosophy. In: *Selected Essays*, 83–111.

28 The pragmatic idea of validity that springs from the pragmatic conception of rationality that both Apel and Habermas share can be called "discursive cognitivism." For instance, Discourse Ethics can be correctly characterized as embodying an extended cognitivism; a cognitivism with regard to evaluative and normative statements that goes beyond the true and the false. In Discourse Ethics, such statements are supposed to be cognitive in the extended sense because it is possible to argue for or against their validity, independently of whether they are true or false in the way fact-stating assertions can be true or false. So this kind of cognitivism differs from other kinds of cognitivism in moral theory (as in e.g., "moral realism") that construe evaluative and normative statements as literally having truth values. For Apel's consensus theory of truth that goes much further than Habermas's discourse theory of truth, see Apel (1987): Fallibilismus, Konsenstheorie der Wahrheit und Letztbegründung. In: Forum für Philosophie Bad Homburg (ed.): *Philosophie und Begründung* (Frankfurt: Suhrkamp), pp. 116–211. An English translation of this important essay will soon be published as a separate book by Humanities Press (1994). Also cf. Apel (1993): C. S. Peirce and Post-Tarskian Truth. In *Selected Essays*, pp. 175–206.

29 Apel (1992): The Hermeneutic Dimension, p. 252.

30 Apel (1979): *Towards a Reconstruction of Critical Theory*, p. 6.

31 *Cf. Transformation der Philosophie*, vol. 2, p. 127.

32 Apel (1979): *Towards a Reconstruction of Critical Theory*, p. 8.

33 Cf. Adolf Grünbaum (1984): *The Foundations of Psychoanalysis. A Philosophical Critique* (Berkeley: University of California Press), esp. pp. 267–85. In contrast, Apel holds that the

"usual issue of the scientistic defences of Marxism and psychoanalysis at best represents a bad approximation to the prestige-paradigm of (quasi-natural) science at the cost of the characteristic features of a critical reconstructive project of inquiry, springing from an interest in emancipatory self-reflection," Apel (1979): *Types of Social Science*, p. 39. For some objections on Apelian lines to Grünbaum's construal of psychoanalysis, see M. Kettner (1991): Peirce's Notion of Abduction and Psychoanalytic Interpretation. In B. E. Litowitz and P. S. Epstein (eds), *Semiotic Perspectives on Clinical Theory and Practice* (Berlin/NY: Mouton de Gruyter), pp. 163–80.

34   For the notion of a logic of self-reflection, see Schnädelbach, Herbert (1977): *Reflexion und Diskurs. Fragen einer Logik der Philosophie* (Frankfurt: Suhrkamp).

35   In (1973), *Transformation der Philosophie*, vol. 2, p. 124, Apel exemplifies this point by reference to historical analyses of the onset of the First World War. A partial and provisional suspension of full communicative reciprocity is necessary in order to dig beyond what politicians said about their reasons for action and to describe the economic interests of the big industry as forces that were operative under conditions of a pervasive imperialism in the world arena around 1910.

36   An article based on that lecture first appeared as "Wissenschaft als Emanzipation?" in *Zeitschrift für Allgemeine Wissenschaftstheorie*, 1 (1970), 173–95. This article was later included in Apel (1973): *Transformation der Philosophie*, vol. 2 (Frankfurt: Suhrkamp), pp. 128–53. Unfortunately, the article is not included in the selection that has been translated into English (1980), *Towards a Transformation of Philosophy*.

37   Cf. Apel (1973): Wissenschaft als Emanzipation?, p. 153.

38   Here, strangely enough, Habermas is much in line with the kind of holistic naturalism advocated by, e.g., Donald Davidson.

39   Cf. Habermas (1990 [Germ. 1983]): Philosophy as Stand-In and Interpreter. In Habermas, Jürgen: *Moral Consciousness and Communicative Action* (Cambridge, Mass.: MIT Press), pp. 1–20.

40   Habermas's superficial discussion of Apel's position in "Remarks on Discourse Ethics" (in *Justification and Application: Remarks on Discourse Ethics*, pp. 19–111), esp. part 10, provides a good case in point.

41   Apel (1992): The Hermeneutic Dimension, p. 267.

42   Cf. Apel (1988): *Diskurs and Verantwortung* (Frankfurt: Suhrkamp), esp. pp. 395–412, for Apel's critique of Rorty and Lyotard.

43   In an essay entitled "Zurück zur Normalität? – Oder könnten wir aus der nationalen Katastrophe etwas Besonderes gelernt haben?" (in Apel (1988): *Diskurs und Verantwortung*, pp. 370–474) Apel gives a very remarkable account of personal experiences and motives that were relevant for the intellectual genesis of discourse ethics. See also Apel (1993): Das Anliegen des anglo-amerikanischen "Kommunitarismus" in der Sicht der Diskursethik. In M. Brumlik and H. Brunkhorst (eds), *Gemeinschaft und Gerechtigkeit* (Frankfurt: Fischer), pp. 149–72.

44   For Apel's treatment of Eurocentrism and the possibility of a dialogue between the third and the first world, see esp. Apel (1995): "Discourse Ethics" before the Challenge of "Liberation Philosophy": An Attempt at a Response to Enrique Dussel. First Part. (Forthcoming in *Constellations*.) See also Apel, K.-O. (1993): Do we need universalistic ethics today or is this just Eurocentric power ideology? *Universitas* 2, 79–86. Apel (1990): Diskursethik als Verantwortungsethik. Eine postmetaphysische Transformation der Ethik Kants. In P. Fornet-Betancourt (ed.): *Ethik und Befreiung* (Aachen: Concordia Verlag), pp. 10–40.

45   I. Lakatos and A. Musgrave (1970), eds: *Criticism and the Growth of Knowledge* (Cambridge: Cambridge University Press). For a reconstructive history of science, the primacy of internal over external reconstruction is a methodological principle of rationality that bears interesting similarities to the holistic "principle of charity" that Donald Davidson made familiar in rational interpretation theory. Davidson holds that this principle is constitutive for the ascription of intentions to, and by, rational actors. (Cf. D. Davidson (1984): Inquiries into Truth and

Interpretation, Oxford: Oxford University Press.) Space does not permit me to discuss how Apel's seminal thoughts on *performative self-contradictions*, and on why to avoid committing them, cohere with Lakatos's and Davidson's views.

46   An interesting application of this principle can be found in Apel's response to Enrique Dussel's critique, see note 43.

47   Sometimes Apel hints at a stronger reading of the principle of self-appropriation. On this second reading, the principle seems to require RS to contribute to an (teleological?) explanation of the emergence of those rationality presuppositions that are inherent in RS. (Cf. Apel (1988): *Diskurs und Verantwortung*, esp. pp. 50, 118, 313, 470.) Unfortunately Apel has not yet spelled out in an altogether clear way the difference between the strong and the weak reading of the above mentioned principle.

48   Cf. Richard J. Bernstein (1991): *The New Constellation. The Ethical-Political Horizons of Modernity/Postmodernity* (Cambridge: Polity Press).

49   P. 154, Apel (1992): Normative Grounding of Critical Theory through Recourse to the Lifeworld? A Transcendental-Pragmatic Attempt to Think with Habermas against Habermas. In A. Honneth et al. (1992), eds: *Philosophical Interventions in the Unfinished Project of Enlightenment* (Cambridge, Mass.: MIT Press), pp. 125–75.

50   Cf. esp. section II (pp. 103–53) in Apel (1988): Kann der postkantische Standpunkt der Moralität noch einmal in substantielle Sittlichkeit "aufgehoben" werden? Das geschichtsbezogene Anwendungsproblem der Diskursethik zwischen Utopie und Regression. In *Diskurs und Verantwortung. Das Problem des Übergangs zur postkonventionellen Moral* (Frankfurt: Suhrkamp).

51   Apel (1992): Normative Grounding of Critical Theory through Recourse to the Lifeworld? See also Schnädelbach, Herbert (1990): The Transformation of Critical Theory. In A. Honneth and H. Joas (eds): *Communicative Action: Essays on Jürgen Habermas' Theory of Communicative Action* (Cambridge, Mass.: MIT Press), pp. 7–22.

52   Ibid., p. 125.

53   "Where does the social sciences' critical-reconstructive understanding, insofar as this is to be in a position for evaluative assessment, get its standards for rationally assessing reasons, in particular, the standards of assessment for the critical reconstruction of rationalization processes assumed to correspond to the three validity claims of human speech?" Habermas's answer, much like Apel's, draws on the assumption that practices of reaching understanding ("Verständigung über etwas"), owing to the inescapable universal validity claims that are tied up with such practices, can have regulative principles of "teleological progress only in a universal consensus (or as I would put it, in the consensus of an unlimited ideal communication community). Taking Peirce and Royce as a point of departure, I proposed this myself in my contribution to the 1970 Gadamer festschrift [= Scientism or transcendental hermeneutics? On the question of the subject of the interpretation of signs in the semiotics of pragmatism. In (1990): *Towards a Transformation of Philosophy*, pp. 93–135]. The proposal was intended as a normative alternative – at that time still without an ultimate transcendental-pragmatic justification – to the Heidegger-inspired Gadamerian conception of the "happening of truth", which has it appear that only an always context-dependent "understanding otherwise" is possible. In his conception of "universal pragmatics" Habermas then fleshed out the postulate of consensus formation by partially assimilating the analyses of speech-act theory, Karl Bühler's trichotomy of linguistic functions, and the concept of validity claims redeemable, when challenged, in argumentative discourse. Yet how can this concept be grounded without giving the impression of a dogmatically posited teleological philosophy of history? By declaring the regulative idea of a required progressive rationalization to be a hypothetical goal assumption that one does not justify any further? This, in fact, is what it comes to when Habermas treats the consensus-oriented presuppositions of argumentative discourse merely as empirically testable hypotheses. If that is the case, his conception would not differ in principle from Max Weber's approach, which is ultimately considered value neutral. But then expanding the Weberian conception of the rationalization process in the direction of communicative

rationality and discourse ethics becomes especially problematic. For how is one to conceive a *deontological* ethic that supposedly traces the "unconditional moment" of its validity ultimately back to an hypothesis in need of empirical testing?" Apel (1992): Normative Grounding of Critical Theory through Recourse to the Lifeworld?, p. 148, footnotes omitted.

54   For instance, where Habermas in a reply to his critics bluntly declares that there "are no meta-discourses in the sense that a higher discourse is able to prescribe rules for a subordinate discourse. Argumentation games do not form a hierarchy" (p. 231, A. Honneth and H. Joas (1990), eds: *Communicative Action: Essays on Jürgen Habermas's "The Theory of Communicative Action"* (Cambridge, Mass.: MIT Press). Cf. also Apel (1992): Normative Grounding of Critical Theory through Recourse to the Lifeworld?, p. 163f.

55   Apel's point would still hold even if contrary to fact the lifeworlds of virtually every community or society already were rationalized in the appropriate way. A justification "is required if we want to demonstrate by compelling argument not only that universal moral validity *claims* are to be found in the ethical lifeworlds of every sociocultural variety – this much Max Weber could accept – but that these claims, rather than retreating before rational questioning (or "enlightenment") as illusions, can on the contrary be definitively justified by the reflective awareness such questioning brings to bear on its own normative conditions of possibility. In doing this, such a justification recurs not simply to the background resources of the lifeworld – precisely these have been called into question by the "enlightenment" – but to the *presuppositions of argumentation*, which are no longer rationally contestable inasmuch as the very attempt to do so actually brings them into play" (Apel 1992, p. 140).

56   P. 248, Apel (1992): The Hermeutic Dimension.

57   Cf. esp. pp. 345–420 in Jean L. Cohen and Andrew Arato (1992): *Civil Society and Political Theory* (Cambridge, Mass.: MIT Press).

58   Cf. esp. pp. 56–74 in David Rasmussen (1990): *Reading Habermas* (Oxford: Basil Blackwell); pp. 181–99 in Thomas McCarthy (1993): *Ideals and Illusions. On Reconstruction and Deconstruction in Contemporary Critical Theory* (Cambridge, Mass.: MIT Press); pp. 279–97 in Seyla Benhabib (1986): *Critique, Norm and Utopia. A Study of the Foundations of Critical Theory* (NY: Columbia). Rehg, William (1994): *Insight and Solidarity: The Discourse Ethics of Jürgen Habermas* (Berkeley: University of California Press).

59   This essay is based on a lecture Apel gave at the Institute for Philosophy of Science in 1967 at the University of Göteborg. The essay was later included as the closing chapter of the second volume of Apel's *Transformation der Philosophie* (Frankfurt, 1973). An English translation appeared as chapter 7 in Apel (1980): *Towards a Transformation of Philosophy*, pp. 225–300. A reprint of this seminal and inaugural essay will appear in volume two of Apel's selected essays, see note 2. See also Apel (1979): The Common Presuppositions of Hermeneutics and Ethics: Types of Rationality Beyond Science and Technology. In J. Sallis (ed.), *Studies in Phenomenology and the Human Sciences* (Atlantic Highlands, NJ: Humanities Press), pp. 35–53.

60   The theme of a planetary macro-ethics of mankind is a theme that Apel has copiously written about over the years, cf. esp. (1984): The Situation of Man as a Problem of Ethical Reason, *Praxis International* 4/3, 250–65; (1987): The Problem of a Macroethic of Responsibility to the Future in the Crisis of Technological Civilization: An Attempt to Come to Terms with Hans Jonas' "Principle of Responsibility", *Man and World* 20, 3–40; (1991): A Planetary Makroethics for Humankind: The Need, the Apparent Difficulty, and the Eventual Possibility, in E. Deutsch (ed.), *Culture and Modernity: East–West Philosophical Perspectives* (Honolulu: University of Hawaii Press); (1992): The Ecological Crisis as a Problem for Discourse Ethics, in A. Öfsti (ed.), *Ecology and Ethics* (Melbu: Nordland Academy Press), pp. 219–60. These essays, and others on the same topic, will appear shortly in volume two of Apel's selected essays, see note 2.

61   Apel (1980): The *a priori* of the Communication Community, p. 232.

62   Ibid., p. 231.

63   Ibid., p. 241.

64   Ibid., p. 257.

65   Interesting details are, e.g., Apel's clarification of the expression "ethics of logic" (ibid., p. 258), and the criticism of Habermas's "ideal speech situation" approach (ibid., p. 293f). Also important is the way Apel criticizes Charles S. Peirce for unduly having hypostatized the human interest in objective knowledge into a moral absolute (ibid., p. 276f).
66   Ibid., p. 277.
67   Ibid., p. 277. Note that where Apel is referring to "claims" here he is not only referring to so-called universal validity claims of speech acts (intelligibility, truth, rightness, truthfulness) but to human needs generally considered as human expressions that in the usual way of things tend to make demands on (other) human beings. That Apel is introducing discourse ethics with reference to need-claims is important, e.g., with regard to questions of the differential moral authority that goes with needs, wishes, desires, and interests respectively. Habermasian formulations of discourse ethics suffer from his exclusive reliance on the bottle-neck concept of *interests*. I have drawn attention to this difference between Apel and Habermas in Kettner (1992): Human Rights, Human Dignity, and the Object Range of Moral Concerns according to "Discourse Ethics", in Jon Wetlesen (ed.), *Menneskeverd. Humanistiske Perspektiver. Skriftserie for HFs Etikk-Seminar, vol. 1* (Oslo: Oslo University Press), pp. 128–52.
68   For the reasons given below, I will abbreviate this principle with a U followed by an exclamation mark that signifies imperative illocutionary force.
69   Pp. 277f, Apel (1980). Also cf. p. 298 where Apel points out the very limited moral authority that any merely factual account of bona fide *true* human needs can have. The same holds for certain neo-Aristotelian accounts said to pertain *essentially* to human nature. Even when psychologically or socio-historically elaborated into accounts amounting to something in the vein of a normative genesis of cultural needs from natural needs, such accounts do not yet provide overriding normative trumps for the respective need-claims. Within the scope of "*U!*" there are no privileged need-claims in the sense of need-claims exempt from critical scrutiny. Natural human needs – i.e. food, shelter, sexuality, etc. – though obviously morally relevant "can be justified only as cultural needs." This means that they can only be justified ethically as *claims* that can be satisfied in a given social situation (e.g., at a given stage in the development of the "forces of production"). I believe, however, that the normative genesis of cultural from natural needs indeed has a function within the practical discourse in terms of a critique of ideology. The justification of needs, however, also entails the confrontation of subjectively "real" needs with the "reality principle" (Freud), and this confrontation, in turn, requires a normative and empirical genesis of the social situation, e.g., of the development of the "forces of production" and the "relations of production" (Marx) and *also* of the political power situation within a given state.
70   $U_{Habermas}$ says that for a norm N to be morally right ("normative gültig") means that everyone could, in practical discourse, accept the foreseeable consequences and side-effects that the general observance of N can be expected to have for the satisfaction of each person's interests.
71   The use of the symbol "*U!*" is mine, not Apel's. This symbol conveniently expresses an important difference between the Apelian universalization principle and Habermas's principle of universalizability, *U*, which Apel also endorses. Sometimes he distinguishes *U!* from *U* by calling the former "diskursethisches Handlungsprinzip."
72   Cf. Habermas's essay "What is Universal Pragmatics?"
73   Habermas's "ideal speech situation" is an idealization that stands in complex relations to communicative action. Similarly, Apel's "ideal communication community" is an idealization that stands in complex relations to validity-determining practices of argumentation in real communication communities in today's actual world. Both idealizations are neither equivalent in content nor is their intra-theoretical role the same respectively, in Habermasian "formal pragmatics" and in Apelian "transcendental pragmatics." Unfortunately, an in-depth discussion of these differences is still lacking.
74   Note that Apel's concept of an ideal community of communication ("ideale Kommunikationsgemeinschaft") is not an idealistic abstraction as would be the idea of an

otherworldly community *not subject* to *any* pragmatic boundary conditions. Neither is it a meta-physical hypostatization: The ideal community of communication is not an alternative to any existing communication community in our actual world. Rather, it is a counterfactual projection we necessarily make from within any one of these.

75   Apel engenders such misunderstanding by sometimes speaking of the "realization of the ideal communication community in the real communication community" (e.g., 1980, p. 282). This obscures the fact that such realization is essentially a labour of determinate negation: criticizing real communication communities for unnecessary shortcomings of their discursive conditions and working towards ameliorating the conditions of discourse so diagnosed. For a precise formulation, see the concluding paragraphs of Apel's (1982) essay on utopian reason: Ist die Ethik der idealen Kommunikationsgemeinschaft eine Utopian? In W. Voßkamp (ed.), *Utopieforschung*, vol. 1 (Stuttgart: Metzler), pp. 325–55. English version in: S. Benhabib and F. R. Dallmayr (1992), eds: *The Communicative Ethics Controversy* (Cambridge, Mass.: MIT Press), pp. 23–59.

76   Cf. p. 343, Apel (1982): Ist die Ethik der idealen Kommunikationsgemeinschaft eine Utopie?

77   Apel (1980): The *a priori* of communication and the foundations of ethics, p. 280f. Apel then goes on to derive from *U!* two long-term action-guiding principles that are politically relevant especially for collective actors responsible for representatives of such actors: "First, in all actions and omissions, it should be a matter of ensuring the survival of the human species qua real communication community. Second, it should be a matter of realizing the ideal communication community in the real one. The first goal is the necessary condition for the second; and the second goal provides the first with its meaning – the meaning that is already anticipated with every argument" (p. 282). For the meaning of "realizing the ideal communication community," cf. note 74.

12 FANTASY AND CRITIQUE: SOME THOUGHTS ON FREUD AND THE FRANKFURT SCHOOL

Joel Whitebook

I

To appreciate the extent to which contemporary Critical Theory has distanced itself from psychoanalysis, one must recognize how intimate the relationship between the two fields once was. Max Horkheimer, for example, stated unequivocally to Leo Lowenthal: "We really are deeply indebted to Freud and his first collaborators. His thought is one of the *Bildungsmächte* [foundation stones] without which our own philosophy would not be what it is."[1] The natural rapport between psychoanalysis and the early Frankfurt School resulted, in part, from the fact that both movements were products of the traumatic and fertile encounter between Central European Jewry and the German Enlightenment. And perhaps nothing symbolizes the intimacy of the relationship better than the fact that the Frankfurt Psychoanalytic Institute was originally established in 1929 as a "guest institute" within the Institute for Social Research. They were literally housed in the same building, indeed shared the same classrooms, on Frankfurt's Viktoria-Alee, where, it might be added, such distinguished analysts as Paul Federn, Hanns Sachs, Siegfried Bernfeld, and Anna Freud offered lectures to the general public.

This arrangement, which at the time caused something of a sensation in proper academic circles, allowed the still disreputable discipline of psychoanalysis to establish its first official, albeit indirect, tie to the conservative German university system. Freud himself was so appreciative of this affiliation that he wrote Horkheimer two letters thanking him for his assistance.[2] The Critical Theorists, moreover, also played a crucial role in promoting Freud's candidacy for the Goethe Prize, which he received in 1930. Loewenthal recalls that "at the time, no one wanted to grant Freud an official prize; psychoanalysis was a despised and scorned science; it was anathema – extreme and avant garde. For that reason, for the city of Frankfurt to grant Sigmund Freud the Goethe Prize was quite extraordinary."[3] And, theoretically, the Frankfurt School's attempt to treat Freud on a par with such unquestionable masters of German thought as Kant, Hegel, and Nietzsche, and to effect a synthesis between Freud and Marx was no less "extreme and avant garde." Today, as Martin Jay has observed, "it is difficult to appreciate the audacity"[4] of these undertakings.

In the thirties, under the tutelage of the psychoanalyst Erich Fromm, at that time member of both institutes, the Critical Theorists turned to psycho-analysis to make up for a fundamental deficiency in Marxian Theory: namely, its lack of a psychology and its almost total disregard for the so-called subjective dimension. The turn to Freud, however, was not motivated by theoretical considerations alone. As the decade continued to unfold, the task of explaining why the proletariat had failed to fulfill its historic mission when the objective conditions were presumably ripe, and why Europe was racing headlong towards catastrophe became increasingly urgent. In an attempt to address these questions, the members of the Institute, equipped with the resources of psychoanalysis, undertook their pathbreaking investi-gations of authority, the family, the individual and culture. These inter-related studies in turn formed the empirical basis for the meta-historical analysis of the *Dialectic of Enlightenment*, which would became the *magnum opus* of the Frankfurt School.

In *The Dialectic of Enlightenment*, written in 1944, Horkheimer and Adorno undertook the radical re-evaluation of civilization from which Freud, with his stoical resignation, had always abstained. The Critical Theorists came to the conclusion that their previous position had to be radicalized to fathom "all that had happened." The question that Horkheimer and Adorno posed to themselves was the following: How was it that the process of enlighten-ment and the conquest of nature, which according to both the liberal and the Marxian tradition, were intended to emancipate humanity from cen-turies old bondage, had resulted in a new and historically unprecedented form of barbarism? They answered that while the entire modern tradition, from Bacon to Marx, agreed that the mastery of the external environment and creation of sufficient social wealth was at least a necessary precondition for the betterment of humanity's estate, it had failed to realize one crucial point: namely, that humanity had to dominate its own inner nature in order to undertake the domination of external nature. And the analysis of the domination of inner nature of course provided the point of *entrée* for the sys-tematic incorporation of Freud's thinking into Critical Theory.

To carry out the conquest of the material environment, Horkheimer and Adorno maintained that human beings had to transform themselves into dis-ciplined purposive agents, and society into a totally bureaucratized and administered system. They identified the unity of the "autocratic" ego with the unity of instrumental reason (or "Identity Thinking" as Adorno would later call it) and argued that both impose an abstract, forced unification on the heterogeneous, the different and the Other. Toward the inside, the auto-cratic ego represses the polymorphous perversity of the individual's instinctual make-up to forge a unified self. And toward the outside, the same ego imposes the grid of instrumental reason on the multifariousness and particularity of external nature to control and manipulate it. This double process of domination issues is a central thesis of the book: the reification of external nature and the reification of internal nature mutually entail each other:

> The subjective spirit which cancels the animation of nature can master a despiritualized nature only by imitating its rigidity and despiritualizing itself in turn.[5]

The problem is, then, that the entire process is self-vitiating: to the extent that the conquest of external nature has been completed – and the presumed objective conditions for human emancipation thereby created, as Horkheimer and Adorno (as well as Marcuse) rather naively assumed they had been by mid-twentieth century – the human subject has been so deformed and reified in the process that it cannot appropriate the fruits of its own labor: "With the denial of nature in man not merely the *telos* of the outward control of nature but the *telos* of man's own life is distorted and befogged."[6] The domination of inner nature, which was supposed to provide the preconditions for human emancipation, ultimately makes that emancipation impossible. Based on the logic of Horkheimer and Adorno's totalized diagnosis, then, only the utopian transfiguration of civilization could provide a solution. However, like Freud and Max Weber, they could not envision any alternatives to civilization whose regressive features were not more disturbing than the given historical prospects themselves. For the Critical Theorists the only escape from this fateful logic was to be found in esoteric works of art and philosophy – nothing with a more encompassing social trajectory could be located in the current historical setting. This was the impasse that Horkheimer and Adorno bequeathed Critical Theory, an impasse to which each subsequent Critical Theorist has had to respond in his or her own way.

II

After the Second World War, two major works dealing with Freud emerged in Critical Theory, Marcuse's *Eros and Civilization* and Habermas's *Knowledge and Human Interest*. The substantial differences separating the two books – which, among other things, mark the difference in Critical Theory before and after its encounter with the Liberal Tradition – are determined, to a large extent, by the different responses the author's give to *The Dialectic of Enlightenment*.

Marcuse accepts the fundamental premises of Horkheimer and Adorno's analysis and is therefore saddled with a radical formulation of the dilemma. He must then, of necessity, attempt to formulate an equally Radical, which is to say, utopian solution. Marcuse subscribed to the thesis that the barbaric events of this century were not transient historical aberrations but results of the internal and totalizing logic of modern civilization:

> Throughout the world of industrial civilization, the domination of man by man is growing in scope and efficiency. Nor does this trend appear as an accidental, transitory regression on the road to progress. Concentration camps, mass exterminations, world wars and atom bombs are no "relapse into barbarism," but the unrepressed implementation of the achievements of modern science, technology and domination.[7]

At the same time, however, writing in the economically booming but culturally puerile fifties, and in line with *The Dialectic of Enlightenment*, he also believed that all significant oppositional forces had been efficiently neutralized through their absorption into a seamlessly running system in which a pre-established harmony existed between artificially generated needs and the consumeristic fulfillment of those needs. Domination therefore was not even experienced as domination. Short of an economic collapse, which at the time was unforeseeable, this absorption could apparently continue indefinitely. Indeed, the fact that *Eros and Civilization*, the most utopian of Marcuse's major works, was written at a time when the possibilities of meaningful political action appeared at their lowest is one instance of the not uncommon connection between utopian speculation and political despair.

Eros and Civilization's stated intentions are purely theoretical, namely, to contribute "to the *philosophy* of psychoanalysis,"[8] by demonstrating the *theoretical* possibility of "a non-repressive civilization, based on a fundamentally different experience of being, a fundamentally different relation between man and nature, and fundamentally different existential relations."[9] Marcuse could not, however, locate any empirical dynamics moving in that direction. At most, he could only point to the tension caused by the discrepancy between the current repressive reality and the potential for "a qualitatively different, non-repressive reality principle"[10] which had been created by the scientific and technological achievements of civilization itself.

It was only after the political explosions of the sixties that *Eros and Civilization* was discovered as a major text for the self-understanding of the utopian movements that had sprung up. During the heady exuberance of those days, moreover, Marcuse himself began to treat the speculative ideas of *Eros and Civilization* as the basis for a concrete political program. Declaring that utopia had ended as a "noplace," as a mere phantasm, he argued it could now be achieved as an historical reality.[11] Using strictly Marxian arguments against the Marxian critique of utopia, he maintained that, contrary to Marx's prediction, the forces of production had matured under capitalism, rather than under socialism, to the point where an eschatological break in the continuum of history had become a possibility. What had formerly been considered a purely idealist utopian society could now be achieved as an historical reality. In language that resonated with the slogans of May '68, Marcuse called for a move from Marx back to Fourier, and from socialist realism to socialist surrealism. In one of the final paroxysms of Marxian-Enlightenment hubris, he proclaimed that "today any form of the concrete world, of human life, any transformation of the technical and natural environment is a possibility." For him, only "the total mobilization of existing society against its own potential for liberation" prevented that possibility from being actualized in a progressive direction.[12] And he derived the concrete filling for that utopia from his investigations in psychoanalysis.

Like the poststructuralist and feminist appropriators of Freud who came after him, Marcuse sought to uncover a "hidden trend in psychoanalysis"[13] that would undo Freud's pessimistic and paternalistic liberalism. In *Eros and Civilization*, he attempts to demonstrate that "Freud's own theory provides reasons for rejecting his identification of civilization with repression"[14] in the hopes of dissolving the seemingly immutable opposition between the instinctually embodied individual and society. Such a demonstration would have refuted, at least in principle, the self-vitiating logic of civilization as Freud described it in *Civilization and Its Discontents* and as Adorno and Horkheimer took it over in *The Dialectic of Enlightenment*. Marcuse's strategy is to historicize Freud's notion of the reality principle, to show that, for the most part, the reality principle, at least today, is a matter of convention. Against Freud, who maintains that the (repressive) reality principle is by *physis*, that is, transhistorical and pertaining to the human conditions as such, Marcuse argues that it is historically contingent and therefore mutable. Freud, according to Marcuse, hypostatizes a "a specific historical *form* of civilization as the *nature* of civilization."[15] Moreover, "the notion that a nonrepressive civilization is impossible is a cornerstone of Freudian theory."[16]

To make his case, Marcuse introduces two correlated sets of distinctions: between the reality principle and the performance principle, on the one hand, and between necessary repression and surplus repression, on the other. Regarding the first, Marcuse admits there is a transhistorical dimension of the human condition – a basic reality principle, as it were – but construes it in such a way as to minimize its ultimate importance. The basic reality principle refers to the renunciation that will always be necessary to negotiate the metabolism between humanity and external nature. Regardless of how thoroughly external nature may be mastered, that is, how thoroughly automated technology may become, it will always remain necessary to exert some effort, and therefore to practice some renunciation.

The performance principle, in contrast, is a term Marcuse introduces to designate "the prevailing historical form of the *reality principle*"[17] which operates in advanced societies. In such societies, where modern science and technology have the potential to create abundance, shorten the working day and pacify the struggle for existence, the extensiveness of actual renunciation is enforced not because of physical necessity, but because of the necessity to maintain a system of political and economic domination.

The point of departure for Marcuse's distinction between repression and surplus repression is Freud's Marxian observation, that "the mutual relations of men are profoundly influenced by the amount of instinctual satisfaction which the existing wealth makes possible." The distinction is meant to provide a quasi-quantitative concept for "measuring" the degree of historically unnecessary renunciation that operates in a given society. That is, it is meant to measure the difference between the "amount of instinctual gratification" that could be permitted if the existing forces of production *were utilized to their fullest* and the amount that is actually permitted on the basis of their repressive organization. Repression *simpliciter*, which pertains to the phylogenetic dimension of human existence, refers to the degree of renunciation necessitated by the basic reality principle and surplus repression refers to the superfluous renunciation imposed by the performance principle. Surplus repression, then, *obviously modelled on Marx's notion of surplus labor*, could be used as a psychoanalytic means for measuring the exploitation in a given society:

> Within the total structure of the repressed personality, surplus-repression is that portion which is the result of specific societal conditions sustained in the specific interest of domination. The extent of this surplus-repression provides the standard of measurement: the smaller it is, the less repressive is the stage of civilization. The distinction is equivalent to that between the biological and the historical sources of human suffering.[18]

Marcuse maintains – and this is one of the assumptions that undoubtedly today strikes us as utterly naive – that the forces of production have developed to the point where surplus repression constitutes by far the commanding share of renunciation exacted in modern society. If science and technology were directed to ends other than maintaining the current socioeconomic order, so the argument goes, surplus repression could be eliminated. In this "Marxification" of Freud, Marcuse is also drawing on Marx's distinction between the realm of necessity and the realm of freedom, without mentioning it by name. As Marx puts it in a famous passage:

> In fact, the realm of freedom actually begins only where labor which is determined by necessity and mundane considerations ceases; thus in the very nature of things it lies beyond the sphere of actual material production. Just as the savage must wrestle with Nature to satisfy his wants, to maintain and reproduce life, so must civilized man, and he must do so in all social formations and under all possible modes of production [in other words, the

basic reality principle]. . . . [T]he true realm of freedom, . . . can blossom forth only with this realm of necessity as its basis.[19]

Unlike Marx, however, who maintained they would only be developed in a future socialist society, Marcuse believes that the material conditions now exist to make the historical transition possible – which would amount to a rupture in the continuum of domination – from the realm of necessity to the realm of freedom, and from human pre-history to history proper. He links these Marxian themes to his Freudian categories by arguing that the scientific and technological accomplishments, which are themselves the fruits of the performance principle, already have "created the preconditions for a qualitatively different, non-repressive reality principle."[20] Moreover, as opposed to Marx – as well as Adorno and Habermas – who abstained on principle from utopian speculation, Marcuse believes it is legitimate and possible to provide positive content for that utopia. Indeed, *Eros and Civilization* can be seen as an attempt to provide psychoanalytic content for Marx's intentionally empty notion of the realm of freedom.

Marcuse sets out then to validate "the hypothesis of a non-repressive civilization" by demonstrating "the possibility of a non-repressive development of the libido under the conditions of mature civilization,"[21] that is, under conditions where surplus repression had been eliminated. If this could be done, *if he could show that the domination of internal nature was not necessary for the maintenance of mature civilization*, then the impasse articulated in *The Dialectic of Enlightenment* could be overcome. The basic conceptual move that allows his demonstration to proceed – *which is, in fact, the basic and problematic move of Marcuse's entire Marxifying reconstruction of Freud* – is the identification of materal scarcity with reality or necessity as such:

> Behind the reality principle lies the fundamental fact of Ananke [necessity] or scarcity (*Lebensnot*), which means that the struggle for existence takes place in a world too poor for the satisfaction of human needs without constant restraint, renunciation, delay.[22]

If necessity were equivalent to scarcity, and if scarcity were historically contingent and therefore eliminable, then *Ananke* itself could be averted and the "repressive modification of the instincts"[23] eliminated as well. Marcuse argues that, because Freud always assumed that the existence of material scarcity is an immutable condition, he viewed the opposition between the pleasure principle and the reality principle as an ontological fact. But for Freud, as Ricoeur has shown, there is also an essential connection between *Ananke* and temporality in the form of transience; *Ananke* presents itself to us in the figure of loss, the ineluctable result of the fleeting existence of all things, that is, *the inexorable uni-directional flow of time and the loss that inevitably results from it.*[24] And the difference between the treatment of time in Freud and Marcuse, for whom it is also a central concern, is telling.

The argument of *Eros and Civilization*, however, like the argument of Marx's *Capital*, centers on *the distribution of time* in another one of its modalities, namely, the length of the working day. For Marx, whose "guiding model," at least in his Left Aristotelian and non-technocratic vein, "was doubtless the Athens of Pericles,"[25] modern science and technology could reduce the length of the working day to an absolute minimum. This reduction could in turn qualitatively increase the amount of leisure time, which is the necessary precondition for pursing the "higher" activities beyond the struggle for existence.

In accordance with Marx's basic scheme, but now expressed in psychoanalytic terms, Marcuse attempts to show how "the general reduction of the necessary labour of society to a minimum," that is, the radical reduction of the length of the working day, could provide the basis for the "free development of individualities."[26] The quantum of instinctual energy devoted to labor, which, owing to the length of the working day, has been the largest single portion of the total available instinctual energy available under the performance principle, could be released for other purposes. In conjunction with the resexualization of the body, this quantum of liberated libido could in turn be reorganized in the non-repressive manner Marcuse is seeking to demonstrate is possible. He refers to this reorganization of the instincts as "the transformation of sexuality into Eros":

> No longer used as a full-time instrument of labor, the body would be resexualized. The regression involved in this spread of the libido would first manifest itself in a reactivation of all erotogenic zones and, consequently, in a resurgence of pregenital polymorphous sexuality and in a decline of genital supremacy. The body in its entirety would become an object of cathexis, a thing to be enjoyed – an instrument of pleasure. This change in the value and scope of libidinal relations would lead to a disintegration of the institutions in which the private interpersonal relations have been organized, particularly the monogamic and patriarchal families.[27]

And, with respect to "the quantum of instinctual energy still to be diverted into necessary labor," that is, with respect to the basic reality principle and basic repression, it would be "so small"[28] that its overall impact could be minimized and managed in such a way as not to jeopardize the larger scheme.

Marcuse is sufficiently honest in his thinking and thoroughgoing in his utopianism to confront the major obstacle opposing his program directly, namely, *transience*. "But the fatal enemy of lasting gratification is *time*, the inner finiteness, the brevity of all conditions. The idea of integral human liberation therefore necessarily contains the vision of the struggle against time."[29]

At this point, not just the banal unworkability of utopia but the profound philosophical flaws in Marcuse's position – as well as the deep differences between his project and Freud's – become fully apparent. The figure of Narcissus, whom Marcuse attempts to construe as a utopian culture hero, is relevant here: Narcissus's captivation by his immobile image in the river, the Heraclitean symbol of all becoming, *represents an attempt to arrest time and deny loss.* Marcuse, it should be stressed, intends that the struggle against time be taken *literally.* He rejects the merely aesthetic exercise of remembrance *à la* Proust as just that, "artistic and spurious." For "remembrance" to become "a real weapon" it must be "translated into history."[30] Citing Walter Benjamin to illustrate his point, Marcuse notes that, in July of 1789, revolutionaries in Paris evinced at least an intuitive grasp of the need to conquer time by "simultaneously but independently at several places" shooting "at the time pieces on the towers of Paris."[31]

But would "the struggle against time," that is, against transience – assuming, of course, that we can make sense of the notion – even be desirable? Paul Ricoeur, in his *Freud and Philosophy*, which was conceived as an implicit debate with Marcuse, understood *Ananke* not as economic scarcity but as the "inexorable" or the "ineluctable."[32] This understanding is more satisfactory than Marcuse's Marxifying account.

Ricoeur shows that as Freud initially conceptualized the reality principle it was simply understood in perceptual terms, as the principle of mental functioning introduced with the (relative) renunciation of hallucinatory wish fulfillment, the achievement of a sufficient quantum of bound cathexis for the ego to function and for the institutionalization of reality testing. Similarly, the concept of reality, prior to the introduction of narcissism, had been *neutral,* simply the opposite of the hallucination: "Reality does not pose a problem, it is assumed as known; the normal person and the psychiatrist are its measure; it is the physical and social environment of adaptation."[33] Thus far, although the order and connection of things do not necessarily correspond to the order and connection of our wishes, *they do not necessarily oppose them either.* Up to this point, "nothing in [Freud's] analysis bears a tragic accent: nothing foreshadows the world view dominated by the struggle between Eros and death."[34]

However, after the introduction of the concept of narcissism in 1914 – which provided Freud with both the motivation and the vocabulary to articulate what Kohut has called his "truth morality"[35] – the concept of reality acquires the connotation of *harshness.* As such, it becomes opposed to the nexus of our wishes and to our narcissism, *which seeks to deny that harshness by creating consoling illusions.* The most extreme formulation of this position is to be found in *Civilization and Its Discontents* where Freud states that the program of the pleasure principle "is at loggerheads with the whole world."[36] A direct line can be traced from the concept of narcissism, taken as desire's propensity to deny the harshness of reality, through the introduction of the death instinct, which represents the foremost instance of harsh reality, to the reformulation of the reality principle as *Ananke.* The reality principle develops from "a principle of mental regulation" to "the cipher of possible wisdom." "*Ananke* does not merely pertain to reality testing, but to a wisdom that dares to face the harshness of life" and is, therefore, "the symbol of disillusionment."[37]

To understand the meaning of *Ananke* as "the cipher of possible wisdom" we must, in turn, understand death as the ultimate cipher of a reality whose harshness results, in no small part, from its temporal constitution, that is to say, from transience. Death, as the primary instance of transience and loss, is the supreme barrier to our omnipotence and the ultimate reminder of our "helplessness and . . . insignificance in the machinery of the universe."[38] As such, it constitutes the principal affront to our narcissism, which consequently mobilizes the innumerable strategies of illusion to deny transience in general and death in particular. If science or wisdom, and the two are indistinguishable for Freud, comprise the apprehension of reality shorn of the consoling illusions we project onto it, then "our incorrigible narcissism"[39] is indeed the opponent of wisdom in this sense.[40] This means that science not only prescribes a cognitive task, but an affective one as well:

> Resignation to the ineluctable is not reducible to a mere knowledge of necessity, i.e. to a purely intellectual extension of what we call perceptual reality-testing; resignation is an affective task, a work of correction applied to the very core of the libido, to the heart of narcissism. Consequently, the scientific world view must be incorporated into the history of desire.[41]

A disturbing question, however, *indeed the question on which the entire Freudian enterprise turns,* must be raised at this point: Why does this "resignation to the ineluctable" result in the erotic enhancement of life rather than depressive despair in the face of a thoroughly disenchanted universe? What, in short, separates Freud's vision from Beckett's? Or, as Ricoeur puts it:

> Finally, what about the reality principle, which seems indeed to usher in a wisdom beyond illusion and consolation? How does this lucidity, with its attendant pessimistic austerity, ultimately fit in with the love of life which the drama of love and death seems to call for?[42]

Freud's answer to this question is to be found in the concepts of mourning, symbolization and the formation of psychic structure.

In "Thoughts on War and Death" Freud offers a personal observation which stuns the reader with its uncharacteristically provocative brutality. With war, he writes, "life has, indeed, become interesting again; it has recovered its full content." The reason for this is that "death will no longer be denied; we are forced to believe in it. People really die."[43] While the strident tone of this remark may result from Freud's struggle to master his own anguish and disillusionment at the time, the meaning is, nevertheless, clear.

Life is impoverished to the extent that we practice denial to narcissistically defend ourselves from loss.

Freud elaborates this idea in "On Transience," a paper which can be as philosophically serene as "Thoughts" can be brutal. During a summer walk in the Dolomites, a young poet complained to Freud that, although he recognized the beauty of the surrounding countryside, he could not enjoy it because "he was disturbed by the thought that all this beauty was fated to extinction. . . ."[44] Freud explains this condition as "a revolt . . . against mourning." Because the experience gave the poet "a foretaste of mourning" and because he lacked the confidence he could tolerate "the extraordinarily painful"[45] process of mourning – which, nevertheless, "comes to a spontaneous end" – he abstained from investing his libido in the beauty of nature in an attempt to avoid the pain at its inevitable loss.[46] *Denial, rather than insulating life from its inevitable pain, actually impoverishes it:* "Life is impoverished, it loses in interest, when the highest stake in the game of life, life itself, may not be risked."[47] For Freud, denial, which clings to the pleasure principle, is not an efficient allotment of one's resources even with respect to the calculus of pleasure and pain.

Finally, the link between mourning and "resignation to the ineluctable," goes further. Mourning, in response to loss, results in the symbolization and psychic structure which make transience, and hence reality, tolerable. Hence, the intrinsic relation between *Logos* and *Ananke*. Considerations such as these lead Ricoeur to argue

> . . . if man could be satisfied, he would be deprived of something more important than pleasure – symbolism which is the counterpart of dissatisfaction. Desire, qua insatiable demand, gives rise to speech.[48]

The elimination of the gap between the wish and its object, "integral satisfaction" in Marcuse's terms, would preclude the conditions that make possible our existence as symbolizing animals.[49] And symbolization, we must insist, does not simply belong to "the cultural household of the performance principle." Ultimately, then, the difference between Freud's skeptical realism and Marcuse's utopianism concerns the question of transience. Whereas Marcuse, who must be complimented for his speculative consistency, envisages the utopian "conquest of time," which would comprise an attempt at the omnipotent denial of *Ananke*, Freud formulates a program for the, to be sure, always relative coming to terms with transience.

III

Today, of course, it is not difficult to criticize the utopianism of *Eros and Civilization*. Indeed, I could have chosen to interrogate it on a number of grounds, for example, its search for an uncontaminated first nature, economism, naivety, sloppy argumentation and impracticality. For two reasons, however, I chose to concentrate on its attempt to devise a scheme to circumvent our finitude. The first reason is psychoanalytic: whereas earlier generations of progressive analysts had to contend with the aggressive drive as an apparent obstacle to the creation of a more humane society, today – because of everything that has been learnt about Pre-oedipal development in the last fifty years – Left Freudians must confront the problem of omnipotence as well. (The problems of aggression and omnipotence are, needless to say, closely related.) The second reason is political, for the events of the past several decades, indeed the events of the century, have chastened the utopian sensibility and engendered a suspicion of omnipotence and grandiosity in political life. The result has been a new appreciation of human finitude – of difference, particularity and plurality – and a skepticism toward grandiose political projects and the meta-narratives generally associated with them. Moreover, although it sometimes degenerates into an uncritical celebration of actually existing democracy, the demise of communism has rightfully produced a new respect for liberalism – that sober philosophy which makes no assumptions about human perfectibility but seeks to justly mediate the interactions of essentially flawed individuals whose interests and desires might be in conflict at any given moment.

Whereas the early Frankfurt School exhibited a marked antipathy toward liberalism and a dramatic underappreciation of the democratizing forces in the modern world, a centerpiece of Habermas's contribution has been to effect a necessary and salutary encounter with the liberal tradition within Critical Theory. In contrast to Marcuse, he challenges the totalizing monism of *The Dialectic of Enlightenment*. Where Horkheimer and Adorno see history developing only in the dimension of instrumentalization – the development of rationality and of the subject are two complementary aspects of that process – Habermas introduces the second dimension of intersubjective communication. This in turn enables him to elucidate the moral, legal and democratizing advances of modernity and to counteract the Weberian anti-modernism and concomitant political quietism of the Frankfurt School. It also means that he does not have to envision an eschatological break in the continuum of history to resolve the crisis of modernity.

Today, after the Habermasian turn, Critical Theory is confronted with a new question, namely: What follows the working-through of Liberalism? Or, to put it differently, is there any sense in which the distinction between Critical and Traditional Theory can still be defended? It is in this area, I would suggest, that a return to the *topoi* of psychoanalysis can be productive.

The de-utopianization of Critical Theory was concomitant with the different uses Habermas makes of – indeed, with a certain domestication of – psychoanalytic theory in *Knowledge and Human Interests*. Because his dualistic scheme allowed him to conceptualize forms of rationality and identity that were not altogether corrupt, Habermas did not have to embark on the search for the good Other of instrumental reason and the autocratic subject. The unconscious and the drives, therefore, did not have to assume the radical role in his appropriation of Freud that they did in Marcuse's. Indeed, we can observe the convergent logic of Habermas's theoretical and political positions in his interpretation of the unconscious.

Habermas's overall philosophical program, the "linguistic turn" in Critical Theory,[50] requires the emphatic rejection of a prelinguistic unconscious – or the psychic imaginary to use Castoriadis's term.[51] He must, therefore, reject Freud's distinction between word-presentations (*Wortvorstellung*) and thing-presentations (*Sach- or Dingvorstellung*) and *ipso facto* the existence of a non-linguistic unconscious consisting in a stream of pictorial representations:

> Now the distinction between word-representations and asymbolic ideas is problematic, and the assumption of a non-linguistic substratum in which these ideas are severed from language are "carried out," is unsatisfactory.[52]

By denying the distinction between word-Presentations and thing-Presentations, Habermas obeys a prohibition on images, a *Bilderverbot*, as it were, which, if it is of a somewhat different but related nature, is nevertheless as stringent as any in Benjamin and Adorno. And in so doing, he not only denies, as I will argue, a source of the political imaginary but rejects one of the fundamental tenets of Freud's metapsychology:

> The system *Ucs.* contains the thing-cathexes of the objects, the first and true object-cathexes; the system *Pcs.* comes about by this thing-representation being hypercathected through being linked with the word-presentations corresponding to it. It is these hypercathexes, we may suppose, that bring about a higher psychical organization and make it possible for the primary process to be succeeded by the secondary process which is dominant in the *Pcs.*[53]

In Freud the point is thoroughly unambiguous: the unconscious is characterized by the primary process and Thing-Representations; the pre-conscious and consciousness, by the secondary process and Word-Representations. Indeed, the border between the unconscious and the pre-conscious is traversed by the addition of word-cathexes to thing-cathexes and is, therefore, at the same time, the border between the prelinguistic and the linguistic. As Freud maintains in his discussion of the "considerations of representability" (*Rucksicht auf Darstellbarkeit*), imagistic mentation, because of its plasticity (*Bildhaftigkeit*) and fluidity, because of the fact that "concrete terms . . . are richer in associations than conceptual ones,"[54] and because it can present wishes scenically as fulfilled, is much better suited for the anarchic purposes of the primary process and the pleasure principle than the syntactically and energically bound secondary processes of linguistically mediated thought.

Thus, in denying the distinction, Habermas also neutralizes the unconscious as the radical Other of the ego and rationality. To use Adorno's terminology, Habermas loses the non-identity of the unconscious.

As Thomas McCarthy observes, the single point that perhaps most separates Habermas from that of the earlier Critical Theorists in regard to his appropriation of Freud is that "the lessons he derives from this reconstruction [of psychoanalysis] are largely methodological."[55] For Habermas "psychoanalysis is relevant . . . as the only tangible example of a science incorporating methodical self-reflection."[56] He believed that psychoanalysis provided a model of the type of methodologically legitimate, self-reflective science on which a critical theory of society should model itself.

In the seventies, the preponderance of the methodological motive in conjunction with the desire to demonstrate the progressive dynamic of modernity eventually led him away from the critique of ideology modeled on psychoanalysis to what he now called reconstructive science. As Axel Honneth points out, this move was connected with a significant shift in Habermas's analysis of rationalization, which has not always been sufficiently recognized:

> From then on he no longer interprets the process of rationalization, in which he attempts to conceive the evolution of society, as a process of the will-formation of the human species; rather, he understands them as a supra-subjective learning process carried by the social system.[57]

And the non-dynamic cognitive psychology of Piaget and Kohlberg, with its formal developmental schemas, rather than the psychoanalysis of Freud, provided him the supra-subjective and purportedly progressive learning process he needed, to defend what he came to call "the project of modernity."[58]

The transition from psychoanalysis to cognitive learning theory had another important consequence, namely, a de-corporealization of Critical Theory. The move entailed a departure from what Horkheimer and Adorno called the "underground" history of Europe, that is, the history of the body and "the fate of the human instincts and passions which are displaced and distorted by civilization."[59] This dimension had, of course, been crucial to the early Frankfurt School. Honneth observes:

> [Habermas's] investigation . . . is directed exclusively to an analysis of rules . . . so that the bodily and physical dimension of social action no longer comes into view. As a result, the human body, whose historical fate both Adorno and Foucault had drawn into the center of the investigation . . . loses all value within a critical social theory.[60]

Ironically, Critical Theory, *which had been one of the first schools to grant theoretical dignity to the question of the body*, was thus losing interest in the topic –

indeed, depriving itself of the conceptual terms to discuss it adequately – at precisely a time when it was becoming central to many other contemporary discourses, for example, feminist, gay and Foucauldian.

The *topos* of the body is one point where a renewed encounter with psychoanalysis could prove fruitful for Critical Theory. Another point, referred to above, refers to the fate of the transgressive imagos – which are an ubiquitous feature of psychic life – after Critical Theory's *Auseinandersetzung* with liberalism. Let us accept the basic thrust of Habermas's reformulation of Critical Theory, and assume that his rectification of the Frankfurt School's Weberian anti-modernism, chastening of its speculative and utopian excesses, and narrowing of its project to render its findings more secure and its political aim more accurate is essentially correct. The following question can still be raised: What is the fate of the transgressive-utopian impulse, given this new sobriety? For better or worse, that impulse will exist as long as people dream, and we can safely assume they have continued to dream even after the linguistic turn. To be sure, it was misguided in the extreme for Left Freudians – from the Surrealists to Marcuse – to call for the translation of the oneiric into social reality in a relatively unmediated fashion. It is, however, no less shortsighted to exclude it from social theory altogether. Any process of enlightenment worth its name must engage the nocturnal.[61]

The transgressive phantasms of the unconscious are not only a source of regression, but can also provide the *imagos* of a different reality. If Marcuse tended to naively idealize those imagos as such, Habermas has, for systematic reasons, denied himself access to them almost completely. This is especially unfortunate, given the fact that today we are witnessing, as Castoriadis has put it, an "atrophy of the political imagination"[62] on a massive scale. At the same time as we have, for good reasons, become reticent about utopian speculation, developments in various regions of the world – from the countries of the Southern Hemisphere to the North Atlantic Community, from the Far East to the former Soviet Union – seem to be surging ahead without a vision to inform them. At best, technocratic planners in Brussels and elsewhere try to steer the course of development to ensure the conditions of stable economic growth while avoiding crises of catastrophic proportions. At worst, the most ominous elements of the past rush in to fill the void. While it is no doubt true that the principles of liberalism constitute an unsurpassable horizon for the modern world, those principles can accommodate an indefinitely wide range of historical content, of forms of life. And since the collapse of the Berlin Wall, the public discourse in both the East and the West has exhibited a distinct paralysis of the imagination concerning that content. This is why a return to psychoanalysis could prove productive for Critical Theory after its encounter with liberalism. For decentered utopianism can most productively and legitimately be focused on that content after the end of utopia. In addition to the cultural memories sedimented in the lifeworld, the only other source for visions of a better society – which could be proposed, defended, debated, tested, discarded, amended and so on in a democratically constituted public sphere – is the radical *imaginaire*.

ACKNOWLEDGMENT

This chapter has been adapted from the Introduction, Chapter 1 and the Excursus of Joel Whitebook, *Perversion and Utopiae: A Study in Psychoanalysis and Critical Theory* (Cambridge Mass.: The MIT Press, 1995).

NOTES

1 Quoted in Martin Jay, *The Dialectical Imagination: A History of the Frankfurt School and the Institute of Social Research, 1923–1950* (New York: Little Brown, 1973), p. 102. The question had itself been put to Loewenthal by Ernst Kris, one of major émigré analysts in New York.

2 See Leo Lowenthal, *An Unmastered Past: The Autobiographical Reflections of Leo Lowenthal*, ed. Martin Jay (Berkeley: University of California Press, 1987), p. 51, Karen Brecht *et al., Here Life Goes On in a Most Peculiar Way . . .: Psychoanalysis Before and After 1933*, trans. Christine Trollope (Hamburg: Kellner Verlag, 1985), pp. 56 ff, and Martin Jay, *The Dialectical Imagination*, pp. 86ff. Horkheimer, it should be noted, was also instrumental in establishing the Sigmund Freud Institute in Frankfurt after World War II.

3 *An Unmastered Past*, p. 51.

4 *The Dialectical Imagination*, p. 87.

5 Max Horkheimer and Theodor Adorno, *The Dialectic of Enlightenment*, trans. John Cumming (New York: Herder and Herder, 1972), p. 57.

6 *The Dialectic of Enlightenment*, p. 54.

7 H. Marcuse, *Eros and Civilization: A Philosophical Inquiry into Freud* (Boston: Beacon Press, 1966), p. 4.

8 *Eros and Civilization*, p. 7.

9 *Eros and Civilization*, p. 5.

10 *Eros and Civilization*, p. 129.

11 Herbert Marcuse, "The End of Utopia," *Five Lectures*, trans. Jeremy J. Shapiro and Shierry Weber (Boston: Beacon Press, 1970), pp. 62–82.

12 "The End of Utopia," pp. 62, 64.

13 *Eros and Civilization*, chap. 1.

14 *Eros and Civilization*, p. 4.

15 *Eros and Civilization*, p. 147.

16 *Eros and Civilization*, p. 17.

17 *Eros and Civilization*, p. 35.

18 *Eros and Civilization*, p. 88.

19 Karl Marx, *Capital, vol. III*, ed. F. Engels (Moscow: Progress Publishers, 1971), p. 802.

20 *Eros and Civilization*, p. 129.

21 *Eros and Civilization*, p. 139.

22 *Eros and Civilization*, p. 35.

23 *Eros and Civilization*, p. 132.

24 See Roy Schafer, "The Psychoanalytic Vision of Reality," *A New Language for Psychoanalysis* (New Haven: Yale University Press, 1976), pp. 35ff.

25   Hannah Arendt, *The Human Condition* (Chicago: The University of Chicago Press, 1958), p. 133.

26   Karl Marx, *Grundrisse: Introduction to the Critique of Political Economy*, trans. Martin Nicolaus (Baltimore: Penguin Books, 1973), p. 706.

27   *Eros and Civilization*, p. 201.

28   *Eros and Civilization*, p. 253.

29   *Eros and Civilization*, p. 191.

30   *Eros and Civilization*, p. 231.

31   Walter Benjamin, "Theses on the Philosophy of History," *Illuminations*, trans. Harry Zohn (New York: Schocken Books, 1968), p. 262 (Marcuse's translation.)

32   Paul Ricoeur, *Freud and Philosophy* (New Haven: Yale University Press, 1970), pp. 330, 332.

33   Ricoeur, *Freud and Philosophy*, p. 263.

34   Ricoeur, *Freud and Philosophy*, pp. 324–5.

35   Heinz Kohut, *How Does Analysis Cure?*, ed. A. Goldberg (Chicago: University of Chicago Press, 1984), p. 54.

36   *Civilization and its Discontents*, Standard Edition, vol. XXI, p. 76.

37   Ricoeur, *Freud and Philosophy*, pp. 238, 327.

38   Freud, *The Future of an Illusion*, Standard Edition, vol. XXI, p. 49.

39   Ricoeur, *Freud and Philosophy*, p. 334.

40   And Kohut is consistent to simultaneously affirm the positive aspects of narcissism and challenge Freud's adherence to the scientific paradigm.

41   Ricoeur, *Freud and Philosophy*, p. 332.

42   *Freud and Philosophy*, p. 310.

43   "Thoughts for the Times on War and Death," Standard Edition, vol. XIV, p. 291.

44   Freud, "On Transience," Standard Edition, vol. XIV, p. 307.

45   "Mourning and Melancholia," p. 245.

46   "On Transience," pp. 306–7.

47   Freud, "Thoughts for the Times on War and Death," p. 290.

48   *Freud and Philosophy*, p. 322.

49   This is one of the main respects, I believe, in which Ricoeur's work can be seen as "an internal discussion or debate with Herbert Marcuse." *Freud and Philosophy*, p. 462.

50   See Albrecht Wellmer, "Communications and Emancipation: Reflections on the Linguistic Turn in Critical Theory," *On Critical Theory*, ed. John O'Neill (New York: Seabury Press, 1976).

51   See Cornelius Castoriadis, *The Imaginary Institution of Society*, trans. Kathleen Blamey (Cambridge, Mass.: MIT Press, 1987), and Joel Whitebook, *Perversion and Utopia*, chap. 4.

52   *Knowledge and Human Interests*, p. 241. This passage equates the domain of words with the domain of the symbolic as such, and thereby denies the existence of a semiotic realm which is larger than, but inclusive of, the linguistic. In contrast, the attempt to identify a signifying function that exceeds the scope of language in the strict sense is at the heart of Ricoeur's analysis of the linguisticality of the unconscious. See *Freud and Philosophy: An Essay on Interpretation*, trans. Denis Savage (New Haven: Yale University Press, 1970), pp. 398–9. See also "Image and Language in Psychoanalysis," *Psychoanalysis and Language: Psychiatry and the Humanities*, vol. 3, ed. Joseph Smith, M.D. (New Haven: Yale University Press, 1978), pp. 314ff.

53   Freud, "The Unconscious," Standard Edition, vol. XII, pp. 201–2. In this fundamental respect at least, Habermas is remarkably close to Lacan, indeed, to use Ricoeur's term, they represent the two foremost "linguistic reformulators" of Freud. Habermas and Lacan attempt to combat Freud's supposed biologism and argue that he did not have the conceptual tools available to him in his day to formulate his theory properly. As Habermas puts it, for Freud to have adequately conceptualized the phenomena he was encountering in the consulting room, "he would really have needed a theory of language, which did not exist at the time and whose outlines are only just beginning to take form today" (*Knowledge and Human Interests*, p. 238).

Both Habermas and Lacan argue, moreover, that with the development of the study of language in the twentieth century, they now possess the conceptual tools to articulate what Freud could only express inadequately and thereby to eliminate the crude biologism from psychoanalytic theory.

54   *The Interpretation of Dreams,* Standard Edition, vol. V, p. 340.

55   Thomas McCarthy, *The Critical Theory of Jürgen Habermas* (Cambridge, Mass.: MIT Press, 1978), p. 195.

56   Jürgen Habermas, *Knowledge and Human Interests,* trans. Jeremey J. Shapiro (Boston: Beacon Press, 1971), p. 214.

57   Axel Honneth, *The Critique of Power: Reflective Stages in a Critical Social Theory,* trans. Kenneth Baynes (Cambridge, Mass.: MIT Press, 1991), p. 284.

58   See especially the programmatic statement in Jürgen Habermas, "Modernity – An Incomplete Project," *The Anti-Aesthetic: Essays on Postmodern Culture,* ed. Hal Foster (Port Townsend, Washington: The Bay Press, 1983), pp. 3–15. The essay also appeared under the title of "Modernity versus Postmodernity," in *New German Critique,* vol. 22 (Winter, 1981). See also Richard J. Bernstein, "Introduction," *Habermas and Modernity,* pp. 1–34.

59   Max Horkheimer and Theodor Adorno, *The Dialectic of Enlightenment,* trans. John Cumming (New York: Herder and Herder, 1972), p. 231.

60   *The Critique of Power,* p. 281.

61   Significantly, it is in a discussion of Foucault's *Madness and Civilization* – which condemns the modern Enlightenment for constituting itself through the expulsion of the irrational – that Habermas endorses the conception of " 'reason' proper to German Idealism" which sought to enter a dialogue with its "split-off" Other, namely, madness. Foucault, of course, thought that this sort of dialogue between Reason and *folie* took place in the Renaissance before the Great Confinement. See Jürgen Habermas, *The Philosophical Discourse of Modernity,* trans. Frederick Lawrence (Cambridge, Mass.: MIT Press, 1987) p. 412, n. 3.

62   Cornelius Castoriadis, "The Retreat from Autonomy: Post-Modernism and the Generalization of Conformity," *Thesis Eleven,* vol. 13 (1992), p. 20.

63   One symptom of this atrophy of the political imagination is a comment that has surfaced not infrequently since 1989, representing Taiwan as our ideal *polis.* In fact, the suggestion has been made that a desirable outcome for Eastern Europe and the Middle East would be a society resembling this techno-capitalist wasteland.

13 THEODOR W. ADORNO: AESTHETIC CONSTRUCTIVISM AND A NEGATIVE ETHIC OF THE NON-FORFEITED LIFE

Hauke Brunkhorst
(translated by James Swindal)

In later reflections on his life Adorno noted:

> I was born in 1905 in Frankfurt. My father was a German Jew, and my mother, herself a singer, was the daughter of a French officer of Corsican – originally Genovese – origin and of a German singer. I was born and raised in an atmosphere dominated completely by theoretical (even political), artistic, and above all musical interests.[1]

The political culture of his parents' house was liberal and cosmopolitan. The close relationships with which Adorno grew up in the south of Frankfurt were well-protected and thoroughly bourgeois, like a "hothouse." He used this phrase in *Minima Moralia*, a collection of aphorisms written in America during World War II concerning the true life in the false. The autobiographical left its mark in the text, which reflected on the socializing fate of the precocious young genius that Adorno was. The precocious "are an irritation to the natural order, and spiteful health feasts on the danger threatening them, just as society mistrusts them as a visible negation of the equation of success with effort."[2]

UNDESERVED FORTUNE

One can say without exaggeration that Adorno accepted the undeserved fortune that befell him readily and without pretension. He was neither contorted nor disfigured from the burden of work or the sweat of his brow. This undeserved fortune consisted in a lightness, a playful ephemeralness, and a fortuitous coincidence that Adorno ascribed to the actual utopia of fortune, to the utopia of a "cloudless day." The "idea of the absolute," he would write later, is not the eternal, but the temporal and infinite past that is "ephemeral . . . as the aroma of wine."[3] The evil world, and with it the labors of the concept and the work of the struggle for *Dasein*, broke through late and abruptly into the artificial life of the "hothouse plant." Adorno could always justly claim to have lived a happy childhood, which helped all the dormant talents in him to emerge quickly.

Admittedly the family in which he grew up was not one of those "happy families" of which Tolstoy spoke, in which every member is so similar to each other that recounting its history is not worthwhile.[4] The relationships in Adorno's family differed much from the classical scheme of bourgeois socialization.

Adorno's father was a wine wholesaler with close relationships in Rheingau and England. At the turn of the century he converted to Protestantism, as many liberal Jews of his time did. Contrary to the Freudian scheme, he was a rather peripheral figure in the family, hardly the fear-inspiring and respect-instilling type cut from the mold of the neurotic bour-geoisie. Even more deviant from the Oedipal type was his relationship to his mother, for whom the young Adorno was allowed to experience love in duplicate. In addition to his Catholic mother, whose maiden name Adorno later took, there was also in their home her sister Agatha, herself an accom-plished pianist. She was so much present that "Teddie," as Adorno sooner or later was called even by his friends, called both of them mother. Thus Adorno, the only and much loved child of the Wiesengrunds, found in both women the dual confirmation of his early developing self-consciousness: his emotional sensibilities and his musical sense.

INDIVIDUALITY AS THE CENTER OF POWER

Since the bourgeois society of the external world regulated by the principle of exchange disrupted such a happy childhood only at a very late date, Adorno was able to oppose his own well developed ego to the surging reality principle. Adorno's deeply ambivalent relationship to institutions of modern ethical life was nourished by the background experiences of his childhood and of his own family. Against the identitarian power of thinking and of the normative that trained individuals to be "disciplinary-individuals" (Foucault) and functioning segments of the bourgeois world order, Adorno offered the rebellious power of the "non-identical," the anarchistic move-ment and impulse that always withdraws from integration. The "extremely tender and subtle layer" of the non-objectivizable, of the spontaneous, and of the instinctive was woven with the memory of the childhood of private happiness that was neither organizable nor institutionalizable. But this non-identical, as Adorno later called it, requires an institutional framework, a "fastening to organization" (Hegel). The nature of the completely socialized individual can come into its own only where there is institutional alienation. The *Dialectic of Enlightenment*, which Adorno completed in 1944 during his

Californian exile together with Max Horkheimer and with the help of Leo Löwenthal and his wife Gretel, explicitly stresses that *all* desire in human life is a product and consequence of alienation.[5] And in *Minima Moralia* he claims: "it sometimes seems as if the fatal germ-cell of society, the family, were at the same time the nurturing germ-cell of uncompromising pursuit of another."[6] "Individuality," he writes in the sixties, "is just as much the product of (social) pressures as it is that center of power that stands over against it."[7]

Fascism expelled Adorno and his friends from Germany in 1933 and forced them into exile in Switzerland, England, France, and finally in New York and the West Coast. For Adorno fascism was more than a totalitarian variant of coercive class domination and instinct repression. He was convinced that the historical singularity of its "encompassing collective order" was connected less with bourgeois institutions and expropriations than with the totalization of domination, profit, and repression *accomplished by* the liquidation of all the repressive institutions of the bourgeois order. If Adorno once said that the bourgeois is virtually the Nazi, it would be valid only in connection with the insight that the Nazi constitutes itself above all in the liquidation of the bourgeois.

From the perspective of the events of 1944, the "grassy seat" of *Minima Moralia* expresses Adorno's sadly transformed relationship to his parents, who lost not only their strength but also their "awesomeness." They became far more tragic victims than their children:

> One of the Nazi's symbolic outrages is the killing of the very old. Such a climate fosters a late and lucid understanding with our parents, as between the condemned. . . . The violence done to them makes us forget the violence they did. . . . The rising collectivistic order is a mockery of a classless one: together with the bourgeois it liquidates the Utopia that once drew sustenance from motherly love.[8]

FROM EXTREME TO EXTREME

Beginning in grammar school, Adorno took private lessons in composition and piano playing. These years were stereotypical for a precocious genius. Before his *Abitur* he skipped a grade and even was exempted from his final oral exams. When he was fifteen he met Siegfried Kracauer, the editor of the *Frankfurter Zeitung*, who was fourteen years his senior. Kracauer quickly became his intellectual and philosophical mentor. Every Saturday they would read Kant's *Critique of Pure Reason* together. This study, and the relationship with Kracauer generally, left deep philosophical traces in Adorno's work. It is no exaggeration to say that the *Critique of Pure Reason* was the key work in Adorno's intellectual development. The idea of a negative dialectic, which is Adorno's most unique philosophical contribution, owes much to it. This influence is particularly evident in Kant's antinomies, since they do not nullify contradiction, but maintain it and allow thought to move back and forth between its opposing extremes. A dialectic is a "movement between the extremes"[9] that penetrates "completely through the extremes"[10] without synthesis and middle term. Such a dialectic is for Adorno not only a source of philosophical meaning, it is also the grounding assumption of his aesthetic constructivism and his ethical theory of the non-forfeited life.

The transformation "from extreme to extreme," from expression into construction and from technical rationality into mimetic expressivity, is evident in what Adorno deeply pondered in Schönberg's music. He claims that "after his tenth work, his compositions swing between the extremes of the totally thematic and the unthematic; he sought not a balanced systematization but rather to hold both extremes in abrupt opposition."[11]

For Adorno even the idea of a non-forfeited life, in which the ego develops where the id was, always culminates in a maintenance of oppositions that threaten to destroy the ego and to shatter its stable identity. The unique achievement of a strong ego, which is meant to take the place of the free floating impulse of the id, is for Adorno in no way the repression of its impulses or the denial of its natural "bodily lust." This must be guided by a non-forfeited life, which does not retreat behind that dynamic of modern times that allows us, as Hegel says, to experience more in one day than the inhabitant of the ancient world did in his entire life. This requires us to integrate spontaneous impulses *and* our projected freedom determined both theoretically and practically by constructive rationality. Only the rational, strong, and complex ego is in itself differentiated enough to allow impulse and nature, which overpower the ego, to be what they are (or, as Adorno often says, to be what they want to be of their own accord).

CAPITALISM RATIONALIZES NOT TOO MUCH, BUT TOO LITTLE

From early on Adorno adopted a position regarding the conservative critique of rationality and enlightenment similar to his friend Siegfried Kracauer. He adopted his critique of the "action-circle" ("Tat-Kreis," whose members were, besides others, the brothers Ernst and Georg Jünger) of the "conservative revolution" developed in the twenties, according to which capitalism rationalizes not too much, but too little. "Ideals, which the intellect has not imbibed and tasted, are useless products of nature,"[12] Kracauer wrote in the twenties. Adorno would later not forgo any opportunity to crusade "without a model" against the grammar school mush of "warmed over infinite values."[13]

Despite this crusade, when studying for his *Abitur* Adorno read the *Theory of the Novel* by Georg Lukács and the *Spirit of Utopia* by Ernst Bloch. These two books fascinated him most among their works. They belong alongside the *Critique of Pure Reason* at the cornerstone of his thought.

> The dark brown four hundred page volume, printed on thick paper, promised something of what one hoped from medieval books and what I when a child felt from the leather-bound *Heroic Treasure*: a belated magic book of the eighteenth century full of obscure references, many of which I still reflect on today. The spirit of utopia appeared as if it were written by Nostradamus' own hand. The name "Bloch" also had this aura. Dark as a passageway and threateningly muted as a trumpet blast, the expectation of the dreadful he awakened was made quickly suspect as shallow and inferior to the concepts of philosophy, with which I was becoming familiar.[14]

For Adorno an essential function of aesthetic modernity is to generate meaning out of several sources: out of the ephemeral, out of what is "withdrawn from the world of appearance (Freud)," out of the subsiding form of good and long stable traditions, and even out of handed down, already existent, aging, and "used up" material. Though this modernity does not depart from the hermeneutic circle, which links what is present and future to what is past, it radically denies its own truth content for the sake of the possible new. It must allow everything it constructs to emerge out of a receding semantics of the historical.

"THE UNCULTURED MUSIC ASSAILS THE CULTURED JACOBINICALLY"

This phrase is as valid for Gustav Mahler's music as for Eichendorff's lyrics. Adorno notes that everything with which Mahler dealt,

> is already there . . . His themes are dispossessed. Here nothing sounds as one is accustomed to hear: all is diverted by a magnet . . .; precisely the misused position gains for it a second life as a variant.[15]

Just as in Hegel's philosophy of right a *second nature* is created out of spirit, in Adorno's negative dialectic a *second* immediacy emerges *after* the radical diremption of the "dull oppositionlessness" (Hegel) of the original. In modern music everything depends on the construction of a *second musical language* that sublates the false opposition of uncultured and cultured art. This in turn helps the cultural good, sunken in a false immediacy, gain a new life. Such was Mahler's achievement:

> Jacobinean, the lower music turns into the upper ... The self-righteous smoothness of the average form is demolished by the excessive sounds

> coming out of the pavilions of the military band and the palm garden orchestra . . . The symphony digs for the treasure, which still heralds only the roll of the drums out of the distant past or a surrounding of sound, since the music settles in. It would like to seize the masses, which flee from the cultured music, without conforming to them.[16]

Everything new is merely the result of experimental variation of the old and of constructive intervention in the past. When this succeeds to the extent it does in Eichendorff's poems, the "unfettered Romantic" moves "without realizing it to the threshold of modernity."[17] This is "the modern element" in Eichendorff that reaches the "most extraordinary effects with a stock of images . . . which must have been threadbare even in his day."[18] Adorno noticed that Eichendorff's poem *Sehnsucht* contained "almost no feature that is not demonstrably derivative, but each of these features is characteristically transformed through its contact with the others."[19]

When Adorno started his study of philosophy in Frankfurt with Hans Cornelius, he was already completely outside of the neo-Kantian mainstream of the Scholastic philosophy of that time that Cornelius himself represented. He concluded his study with his dissertation on Husserl, a dutiful exercise which he quickly completed. Nevertheless Cornelius exerted a lasting though indirect influence on Adorno, mediated by a young Max Horkheimer who had just finished his post-doctoral thesis and had become Cornelius's assistant. The son of an undertaker from Stuttgart, Horkheimer was no Scholastic philosopher either, but did stand closer to the traditional style of German philosophy than Adorno did. During his preparations for his doctoral exam, Adorno got to know both Horkheimer and his friend Friedrich Pollock, both of whom lived at that time in a hotel in Königstein, near Frankfurt. "Both are communists," he wrote to Leo Löwenthal on 16 July 1924, with whom he had already been a friend for some time, "and we have lengthy and passionate discussions about materialistic conceptions of history at the end of which we concede to remain much opposed."[20] A lifelong friendship between Horkheimer and Adorno developed, resulting in their collaboration on the *Dialectic of Enlightenment* and, upon their return to West Germany after their exile, their role as the most notable figures of the so-called Frankfurt School in the fifties and sixties. The very term "critical theory" refers to the thinking of the negative developed by both of them.

BETWEEN CONSCIOUSNESS RAISING AND CONSCIOUSNESS RESCUING CRITIQUE

In 1923 Adorno met Walter Benjamin. They quickly became friends. The dark and puzzling work of Benjamin, eleven years his elder, played an important role in the development of Adorno's thought. He became indebted to Benjamin not only for his "micrological" method, but most of all for his idea of a negative dialectic. Adorno's development of an outline of his negative dialectic began in his inaugural lecture of May 1931 and continued unabated for the rest of his life. He seasoned Benjamin's "arrested dialectic" with Hegel's dynamism. Moreover, Benjamin's posthumously published historical-philosophical theses and his project of an aporetic-ambivalent "domination of the domination of nature" were important influences on the *Dialectic of Enlightenment*. But Adorno distanced himself both from Benjamin's all too manifest theological impulses and from his overly forceful revolutionary hope for the utopia-breaking potential of the new art of the masses. At the end of his life Adorno would leave behind not a "theological-political" fragment as Benjamin did, but an aesthetic-theoretical one that kept a distance from both politics *and* theology. Less decisionistic than Benjamin, Adorno remained upon the comparatively surer path of German idealism, forming ideas which were not particularly modest, but far more conventional than Benjamin's. In *Negative Dialectic* he proclaims "to have consistently conceived of what dialectic means."[21] Adorno undertook a project that integrated Horkheimer's Enlightenment idea of *consciousness raising* critique with Benjamin's aesthetic theological idea of a *rescuing* critique.

Initially Adorno's study of philosophy was only a diversion for him. In the early twenties his actual area of interest was musical critique and aesthetics, and his dream was to compose. Between 1921 and 1931 he published nearly one hundred works on composition, mostly critiques written for radio. At the end of this period Adorno was a respected and feared music critic who relentlessly sided with the Schönberg school. Early in 1925 he went to Vienna as the pupil of Alban Bergs, to be trained as a composer and concert pianist. "Everything Schönbergesque is sacred," he wrote on the eighth of March to Kracauer, adding with an ominous note "otherwise only Mahler is approved of these days, and whoever opposes is derided." In the newspaper *Die Musik* he exalted Schönberg's authority in unconditional terms: "it is not proper for any critique to oppose the contemporary works of Schönberg; truth is set by them."[22]

Despite all of his irrational fascination with Schönberg, the early Adorno, who was far more successful as a critic than as a composer, remained entirely rational in his quest for an aesthetic for the new music. Schönberg's twelve-tone technique was entirely systematic and as such represented in Adorno's eyes the decisive advance from nature and immediacy to technical media-producing art in a "rationalizing process of European music." It was to him no less than art's demythologization: "the material has become clearer and freer and eradicates for all time the mythical conditions of number, as they dominate high tone lines and tonal harmony."[23]

With great enthusiasm Adorno simultaneously launched two careers after his schooling: philosopher and musician. But in the mid-twenties both came to a halt. Adorno had to give up the dream of being a composer and put his post-doctoral thesis on hold. After he was failed by Cornelius, he succeeded only in 1933 to finish his post-doctoral thesis with Paul Tillich and to teach a few semesters as a Privatdozent. In 1933 Adorno received one of the first draft orders. After futile attempts to enlist as a journalist and piano teacher, in 1934 he went to England in order to continue his studies at Oxford. Once there he came to know the analytic philosopher Gilbert Ryle, whose thought admittedly had little effect on his own. After a last visit to Frankfurt in 1937 he flew to New York, where he became a member of Horkheimer's Institute for Social Research. His first task in the Institute was to oversee the musical component of the *Radio Research Project* headed by Paul Lazarsfeld. After some initial difficulties, Adorno became a highly skilled empirical social researcher both during his subsequent years in America and after his return to postwar Germany. Benjamin's micrological method proved to be helpful in his development as a researcher. Adorno proved so successful in his social research, that long after his death an entire direction of social research in Germany, termed "objective hermeneutics," is still based on his methodology.

"PURPOSELESSNESS FOR PURPOSE"

The onesided, controversial, but brilliant account of Adorno's multifaceted and ambiguous experiences of exile is his theory of the culture industry developed in the *Dialectic of Enlightenment* and in numerous individual studies. His thesis is that in the age of Hollywood and television the enlightenment risks turning into mass deception. Kant's determination of art as "purposiveness without purpose" had become, as it was called in a polemic formulation replete with black irony, "purposelessness for purpose": the instrumental nihilation of the meaning of life. Holding to the *difference* between enlightenment and mass deception, Adorno denounced the culture industry as a betrayal of the original intentions of the enlightenment. Its consciousness raising critique undermined Benjamin's onesided favorable rescuing critique of the cinema, jazz, and of entertainment.

All in all America remained foreign to Adorno. When he returned after the war, he wrote to Horkheimer with an eye on the old Europe before his departure from Paris:

> Max. The unconditioned: there is nothing else!

He believed that America would no longer be able to conceive of the unconditioned in the European tradition of education. But that was a blindness, from which even his sense for dialectic had not been able to protect him.

During the New York years Adorno became very close to Horkheimer, who directed the Institute. Moreover, Adorno ousted other members, especially Herbert Marcuse and Leo Löwenthal, from their proximity to Horkheimer's paternal friendship. The pessimistic and misanthropic Horkheimer was fascinated by Adorno's "hate-sharpened gaze upon what exists." After the dissolution of the Institute in New York, Adorno and Horkheimer immediately went off to California alone, accompanied only by the trusted Friedrich Pollock. This same trio would also return together to Germany after the war.

Although after the war "the ruins of Europe were cleared away," in Adorno's estimation European culture was still in ruins.[24] What he found upon his return was an utterly historistic (by the "Geisteswissenshaften") stamped university milieu, and a post-war culture that was open and liberated from the pressure of the Nazi domination. But he also found a young literature "of which anything can be said, except that it is young." In its texts Adorno felt himself recalling "an army boot richly and carefully filled up with purple and golden brown foliage." This *resurrected culture* combined a depoliticized discourse, no longer left entirely as it was in the Weimar years, with a universalization of the provincial and an evident lack of "explosive force, lust for adventure, even envy." True intellectual passion corresponded to something circular, dead, rigid.[25] "My seminar," he wrote in 1949 to Leo Löwenthal,

> is like a Talmud school. As I wrote to Los Angeles, it is as if the ghosts of murdered Jewish intellectuals traveled into the German students. Completely eerie. But precisely in a true Freudian sense, it is also terribly familiar.[26]

THE DOUBLE DISTANCE OF THE EXILE

During his American exile, Adorno remained entirely a foreigner. His rigid and stable old-European distance allowed him all the more clearly to recognize the shadow side of America's apparent progress. But upon his return to Europe he began to see the old continent with American eyes and from the alienating distance of his exile he noticed all the more strongly the barbarity of its remaining conditions. Since the Frankfurt School had returned to the University of Frankfurt, Adorno rarely passed up an opportunity to emphasize that the newly opened Institute for Social Research was the university's avant-garde. He also touted the superiority of modern statistical methods and analytic techniques to the old social-scientific belief in the world-disclosing power of the understanding. As his skepticism of social-scientific empiricism steadily increased, he developed a career as a sociologist.

It was a long time before Adorno became an ordinary professor in Germany. The position he finally received in 1957 was unofficially referred to as the "consolation chair." Adorno and Horkheimer were shunned and exposed to their colleagues' anti-semitism. Adorno would never attain a "normal" position at a German university. Horkheimer bitterly noted: "the majority of Germans who sympathized with National Socialism are today better off than those who opposed Fascism."

In 1959 Adorno became Horkheimer's successor as director of the Institute and after 1965 was twice chosen as chairman of the *Deutschen Gesellschaft für Soziologie*. The positivist controversy became a key cultural-political topic. By 1968, it was evident that this controversy was an integral part of the cultural upheaval of the time. Adorno opened the Frankfurt *Soziologentage* conference that year with the brilliant paper *Late Capitalism or an Industrial Society?*

EFFECTIVE HISTORY

Adorno's message, communicated with marked success in the sixties through his ever stronger criticism of mass culture, reached a broad range of editors who published his work and listeners who greedily awaited his next radio talk. Adorno was present in the feuilletons, lecture halls, and even occasionally on the televisions of the young republic. Intellectuals like Enzensberger, even before Marcuse, strengthened Adorno's influence by popularizing some of his more esoteric critiques of culture. Adorno's friendship with cultural figures, like the Max-Planck Director Hellmut Becker, opened up access to an educational system and to a pedagogy. Moreover, the work of Jürgen Habermas secured for critical theory an academic reputation for years to come. Habermas and Oscar Negt developed new political dimensions of Adorno's economic critique, including even a radicalized form in the *German Socialistic Student Organization*. With Alexander Kluge, Adorno's ideas set in motion the beginnings of the new German films. Adorno himself published an ongoing series of short writings that appeared in the *Hessischen Rundfunk*, the *Sender Freies Berlin*, the *FAZ*, the *Frankfurter Rundschau, Die Zeit, Der Spiegel*, and the *Neue Züricher*. His work also appeared in the *Darmstädter Echo* and the *Frankfurter Neue Press*, a very local newspaper in which he patiently responded to questions about end of the year changes. He protested against the emergency laws, speaking to the organizational committee for the Christian–Jewish coalition, to conferences of the German council on architecture and functionalism, and to the European pedagogy conference on education after Auschwitz. His essays appeared in the *Neuen Rundschau*, the *Frankfurter Heften*, the *Akzenten*, in *Merkur*, in journals as diverse as the business-oriented *Deutsche Post*, the *Rundfunk und Fernsehen*, and the *Volkshochschule im Westen*. To the idiotic query, "About what did you laugh the most in 1966?," Adorno, the unrelenting critic of the German condition, reacted with his characteristic seriousness:

An elected NPD-official said in an interview: your laughter will soon disappear. For me in this year, it has already been long past. Couldn't you have expressed it better than with that ominous phrase?[27]

Shortly before the completion of *Aesthetic Theory*, Adorno died of a heart attack on 8 August 1969 while on vacation in the Swiss Valais. His wife Gretel survived him. They had no children. In his writings, which with his increasing age were frequently written on the occasions of the birthdays or deaths of close friends, Adorno not only railed against the idea of a gerontocracy, but also against the equally antiquated clandestine alliance between metaphysics and death. In the *Gratulor* on the occasion of Max Horkheimer's seventieth birthday, he recalled Kant's idea of immortality in a positive light. It gives us "strength for opposition to nature's deterioration . . ., which is united in sympathy for oppressed nature."[28] On the occasion of the death of his old friend Siegfried Kracauer he noted:

the only thing that this life of thinking did not reflect upon, truly his blind spot, was death. Since it has now overtaken him, it pays back what his own intentions struggled against: against all completive [*Abschluβhafte*] . . . Since he had to die, the most individual of all things, the universal clamors.[29]

ADVOCATE OF THE NON-IDENTICAL

The last citation crystallizes the most important themes of Adorno's negative dialectic: the emphasis on the self-reflective conscious life, the metaphysical-critical invective against all completive and against speculative systematic thinking, and the plea for the "open" and "experimental" that Adorno set against totality during his era's time of false and simple *extorted reconciliation*. The "non-identical," the guiding motive of his thought, is the individual that recoils from subsumption under universal concepts and norms. Its denials and "injury" became for Adorno a strong protest against the existent. Albrecht Wellmer correctly called Adorno an *advocate of the non-identical*. The "non-identical" is the *individual* that can never be completely fixed by any universal description; it can always be newly described. The "blinding coherence" of which Adorno speaks refers to that *blinding of the subject* that imagines itself to be in possession of absolute truth and to be able to give a *definitive* description and conception of the individual. Like Hegel, Adorno even occasionally called this individual *die Sache selbst*. The blinding of a simple "subjective" centered upon the perspective of the ego and upon a onesided projection of a limited "reason" Adorno also called *identitarian thinking*. Provided that it left its mark on a "collective consciousness" (Durkheim) or a much broader "occidental rationalism" (Weber), Adorno could speak of a "blinding coherence."

Claims about absolute or "completive" knowledge are presumptions about a human reason that is not conscious of its own limits. It itself is the reason of a finite, individual, and nature-enslaved being. In this respect human reason, if it believes to have understood the absolute truth and "the whole," is forever *not* identical with itself. It is never completely transparent to itself, for *our* reason is itself something individual, a product of a process of individualization. Completive identitarian thinking is deceived about itself and its own history. But what eludes the identitarian self-knowledge of reason is the way in which reason itself has remained an opaque and impenetrable piece of "nature." Adorno thus understands the *dialectical Enlightenment* as an "awareness of nature in a subject," that should recall for our reason the cognitively repressed "primal history of subjectivity."

Such achievements of memory in no way lead us back to the "dull oppositionlessness" (Hegel) of nature-bound individuality. In *Negative Dialectics* Adorno writes that "the illusion to get hold of the many immediately," in that we simply achieve a renunciation of reason, science, and the reflective power of the identitarian thinking, "would smack of a mimetic regression into mythology and back into the horror of the diffuse."[30] Worse than the blindness of identitarian thinking would be a regression into the barbarity of dull oppositionlessness. Therefore we can escape from the forgetfulness of our thinking and the blindness of our reason (Adorno often speaks of a "utopia of being escaped") only inasmuch as we seek to make identitarian thinking visible with the tools of constructive rationality: the self-eluding individual of our nature-bound finite existence. Adorno thus demanded not a dismissal of reflection, but a development of a *second reflection*: not a return into the immediate and undivided, but a continuation of the mediations and differentiations of thinking to the point of a *second immediacy*. This occurs inasmuch as it also demands not the romantic cessation of affirmative art, which clarifies and glorifies what exists, but the bold construction of a *second musical language*. This is gained only through *more* technique and complete domination of material, not through pre-technical expressivity.

Adorno had developed these philosophical views much earlier in several works. Most notable among them was his 1931 inaugural lecture on the *Actuality of Philosophy*. Preceding this was his never submitted post-doctoral thesis first published posthumously as the *Begriff des Unbewußten in der transzendentalen Seelenlehre*. Similar ideas were also developed in the post-doctoral thesis he did submit entitled *Kierkegaard's Construction of the Aesthetic* and published in 1931, which owed much to Kracauer and Benjamin.

EXPERIMENTAL FREEDOM

Since Adorno saw the *Actuality of Philosophy* as a practice of *thought*, he distinguished it sharply from scientific *explanation*. Philosophy is a *second reflection*, but as an interpretive activity it remains referred to the first reflection of scientific explanation. It is no less experimental and constructive than science, since it operates with "models" and develops new "orders of research." It relies not upon original forces, but only upon the science, reflection, and identitarian thinking that had long since dismantled and divided up "prefounded" actuality into its "elements." *Interpretation* always begins with the *difference* (Hegel's *Entzweiung*) between identity and non-identity or between reflection and the thing. What is in the end disclosed to interpretation as the true "by convincing evidence" is *only* the result of an experimental and operative praxis, since it takes everything that it arranges for investigation from pre-established actuality. Thus the *essay* is, in the true meaning of the term "research," the proper form of philosophical interpretation. Decades later this gave rise to the essay on the *Essay as Form* which Adorno in 1958 published in advance of his *Notes on Literature*.

The essayistic technique of exposition, which Adorno's work utilized even in his large systematic texts, meant to preclude every representation of a "second distant world developed through the analysis of the apparent world." This representation was the core of the subjectivist projection of an absolute truth in the world from without. In this scheme, the true is disclosed to us more as simply the result of our own praxis. Out of the *pre-found* elements it "crystallizes" a *new* constellation that fits exactly to our problems and inner-worldly "puzzles," like the *correct* "combination" of the lock of the "well secured safe."[31] In his inaugural lecture Adorno argued that "whoever interprets by seeking a world in itself behind appearances, which lies as a ground for them and bears them, acts as one who wants to find in a puzzle the representation of a deeper Being, which the puzzle mirrors." This is the age old Platonic method, which Adorno rejects. For the

> task of philosophy is not to research the hidden and immediate intentions of actuality, but to interpret the intentionless actuality, inasmuch as the power of the construction of figures . . . sublates the questions out of the isolated elements of the actuality. These are the questions whose pregnant composure is the task of science; a task to which philosophy always remains bound, because its illuminatory power isn't capable of illuminating anything other than those hard questions.[32]

From Adorno's earliest writings, a pragmatic theory of truth, borrowed as much from American pragmatism as from the early Heidegger, replaced the Platonic image-reproduction-representation relation of the correspondence theory of truth with an action-experience relation. *Negative Dialectics*, conceived over thirty years later, is in essence the exposition of this idea, whose seeds Adorno had already sown in his inaugural lecture.

While still in his exile in England Adorno worked on a lengthy study of Husserl, which appeared in 1956 with the title *Zur Metakritik der*

Erkenntnistheorie. It issues a clear rejection of all originary philosophical claims to final grounds.

As a colleague in the New York Institute under the direction of Horkheimer, Adorno worked primarily on his study of the culture industry and on the social psychology of prejudice. Particularly notable is his "Fetischcharakter der Musik und die Regression des Hörens," in *Zeitschrift für Sozialforschung* from the later thirties, which was his pessimistic reply to Walter Benjamin's hope-filled essay "The Work of Art in the Age of Mechanical Reproduction." The studies of the thirties ushered in those of the forties, especially his chapter on the culture industry in the *Dialectic of Enlightenment*, and then later his study of the *Authoritarian Personality*. The latter made the Frankfurt School instantly famous in the scientific world and is the reason why including the F and A scales of character types he developed is still a stable component of research on prejudice. These character types were the subjects of a whole series of research projects in America in the fifties.

Another important object of Adorno's empirical research was the mechanism of the subject-centered projection of objective truth onto the foreign and alienating world of others (races, peoples, minorities, foreigners, intellectuals, etc.). He summarizes this socio-psychological research of the Institute in a chapter in the *Dialectic of Enlightenment* co-authored with Leo Löwenthal:

> Anti-semitism is based upon a false projection.... Mimesis imitates the environment, but false projection makes the environment like itself.[33]

Horkheimer and Adorno interpreted the false projection of anti-semitism as an extreme case of identitarian thinking. While they see in "true mimesis" a strong ego's achievement of a decentering, false projection harshly turns one's ego into the center of a world that becomes either the "weak or all-powerful total concept of all that is projected onto it."[34] Thus the racist represents one crazed by the complementary drives of both greatness and success.

> The closed circle of eternal sameness becomes a substitute for omnipotence. It is as though the serpent which said to the first men "you will be as God" had redeemed its promise in the paranoiac. He makes everything in his own image.[35]

AN ETHIC OF DAMAGED LIFE

At the end of the war, Adorno finished *Minima Moralia* along with the *Dialectic of Enlightenment*. Both books contained an extremely pessimistic diagnosis of the times. The hopes provided by science and Enlightenment in the thirties appeared irrevocably dashed. But appearances deceived. Both works tried in such conditions to hold onto the Enlightenment without any idealistic illusions and metaphysical hopes, which appeared virtually to exclude an actualization of its reason. One should read them, as the subtitle of the *Dialectic of Enlightenment* reminds us, as "philosophical fragments," and neither as an ongoing history of philosophy nor as negative. For a correct understanding one must keep in mind Adorno's method, the essay as form, and read these as philosophical interpretations, models, and attempts at ordering. Then they are disclosed in their double function as *diagnoses of the times* and as radical *thought-experiments* that investigate the limits of an Enlightenment under conditions of its opposite. The dialectic of Enlightenment has to do with the historical and social conditions of the reason justified by it. Under these conditions, theory threatens to be assimilated to technique, praxis to universal accommodation, and art to industry. The aims of *Minima Moralia* are immediately practical in a similar way: the aphorisms sketch an ethic of damaged life. The question is how a correctness can possibly exist in the damaged life of modernity. The answer is apodeictic: "there is no true life in a false one." But that does not mean that there is no possibility of right *action*; the thesis confirms only that there is no *entirely* true life in a false life. But thus it is still a long way from the claim, as Nietzsche suggested, that everything is allowed. Every individual act can still be judged as to its rightness or wrongness. Moreover, the actions and characteristic traits of modern man and the various aspects and all individual moments of his lifeworld are accessible to moral evaluation. *Minima Moralia* is nothing other than a collection of such judgments as, for example, that it is an outrage when one says "I." (One thinks of a German economic minister who, opening an automotive show, declares: "everyone knows that *I* am fond of large and fast cars.") Moreover, Adorno's thesis only confirms that *no true life* would be possible in the case of a completely false life. But this does not mean that a *non-forfeited* life cannot be imagined. The *double negation*, Hegel's logical insight that always guided Adorno, is in no way identical with a simple affirmation concerning our ethical relationships. Moreover, *Minima Moralia* are "reflections from damaged life," as the subtitle confirms, and the damaged life is *not yet* the completely false life. It is similarly true of frequently cited aphorisms like: "the whole is the untrue." This phrase does not mean that there is no truth in the world, no true statements, and no right actions. The content of the sentence simply takes deadly aim at the core of Hegelian metaphysics by proclaiming truth cannot be expressed as a whole either by society or by history. Adorno thus presents first and foremost a critique of a metaphysics that represents a totalizing reason. Such a critique of totalizing reason, though it is in many ways similar to the critiques of Nietzsche, Heidegger, and the post-modern deconstructionists, is just as far from them as it is from the old transfiguring metaphysics.

The critique of metaphysics in *Negative Dialectics* is salutary, not damaging. The critique aims to determine its truth in the process of overcoming it. It "is in solidarity with metaphysics in the moment of its fall." But it wants neither an exaltation of the new nor a rehabilitation of the old. "It has to do with the absolute, but one broken and intermediate," without any claim to "completive unities."[36]

DESPIRITUALIZATION THROUGH SPIRITUALIZATION

In the light of *Negative Dialectics*, the dialectic of Enlightenment never appears so hopelessly stricken with aporias as it does in *The Dialectic of Enlightenment*. In 1949 Adorno published *Philosophy of Modern Music*, a book written during the previous nine years that he wanted to be recognized as his contribution to the theme of the *Dialectic of Enlightenment*. It postulated an open dialectic between progress and regression and separated the productive antimony of progress from the destructive contradictions of regression (although it itself remained well aware of the entwinement of both tendencies). As Adorno made clear in the example of Schönberg and Stravinsky, every progress in modernity is threatened as much from technocratic reification as from the heterogeneity of the residual immediacy of nature. But it is not only endangered by both threats, it is also in a way made possible by them, specifically through the onesidedness of identitarian thinking and the indefinability of the non-identical, the individual, the agency drive, and diffuse impulses. The difference of onesidedness and undefinability is the "entwinement turmoil" of that Poe-like maelstrom that Adorno cited beginning with his post-doctoral thesis and continuing through to *Aesthetic Theory*. It is at the same time the condition without which there is no modern freedom.

The voluminous fragment *Philosophy of Modern Music* provides an aesthetic theory for the musical monographs about Wagner, Mahler, and Berg, and an aesthetic theory for *Notes on Literature*. Its claim to be theory is meant in earnest. Its aim is not the aestheticization of theory, but a theory of the aesthetic. It has to do with the "laws of movement" of modern art, which Adorno believed he had recognized in the shattered autonomy of the constructivistic form of spirit and of a courtly-love form of expression. Abstraction, reflection, and formalistic spiritualization loosen all conventional chains from the meaningful and expressive in art. Both extremes run diametrically opposed to one another and still belong together, as did Schönberg's expressive "music style of freedom" from the early period around 1910 and his technical perfectionistic twelve-toned music of the twenties. *Spiritualization* makes *de-spiritualization* possible. This is cultural modernity's law of motion that explains how it is as full of risks as it is full of opportunity. The modernism of art and culture allows the "explosion of metaphysical meaning" to be permeated with the emancipation of the subject. The explosion, which allows the "anti-traditional energy . . . to become the entwining maelstrom,"[37] destroys metaphysics and at the same time frees its trivial and sublime meaning[38] – at least in the happy moments in which we do not pass up our life.

NOTES

1 Adorno, *Autobiographie aus Zitaten* (Frankfurt: Suhrkamp, 1978), p. 1.
2 Adorno, *Minima Moralia: Reflections from Damaged Life* (London: New Left Books, 1974), p. 161.
3 Adorno, *Noten zur Literatur* (Frankfurt: Suhrkamp, 1981), p. 72.
4 See Leo Tolstoy, *Anna Karenina*, p. 7.
5 See Horkheimer and Adorno, *The Dialectic of the Enlightenment*, tr. J. Cumming (New York: Herder and Herder, 1972).
6 Adorno, *Minima Moralia*, pp. 22–3.
7 Adorno, *Negative Dialektik* (Frankfurt: Suhrkamp, 1973), pp. 240, 244, 278ff.
8 *Minima Moralia*, pp. 22–3.
9 Cf. Martin Jay, *Marxism and Totality* (Berkeley: University of California Press, 1974), p. 250.
10 Adorno, *Nevenpunkte der Neuen Musik* (Reinbek: Rowohlt, 1969), pp. 19, 29.
11 Adorno, "Vers une musique informelle," in *Schriften*, vol. 16 (Frankfurt: Suhrkamp, 1973ff), pp. 501, 537.
12 Siegfried Kracauer, "Minimalforderungen an die Intellektuellen," in *Deutsche Intellektuelle 1910–1933*, ed. M. Stark (Heidelberg, 1984), p. 366.
13 Adorno, *Ohne Leitbild* (Frankfurt: Suhrkamp, 1967), p. 9.
14 Adorno, "Henkel, Krug und frühe Erfahrung," in *Henkel, Krug und frühe Erfahrung: Noten zur Literature* (Frankfurt: Suhrkamp, 1974), pp. 556ff.
15 Adorno, "Über den Fetischcharakter der Musik," in *Zeitschrift für Sozialforschung* (1938), p. 354.
16 Ibid.; Adorno, "Mahler," in *Schriften*, vol. 13, pp. 184ff.
17 Adorno, *Notes to Literature*, vol. I, ed. R. Tiedemann, tr. S. W. Nicholsen (New York: Columbia University Press, 1991), p. 64.
18 Adorno, *Notes to Literature*, p. 66.
19 Adorno, *Notes to Literature*, p. 71.
20 Leo Löwenthal, *Mitmachen wollte ich nie* (Frankfurt: Suhrkamp, 1980), pp. 248ff.
21 Rolf Wiggershaus, *Adorno* (Munich: Beck, 1988), p. 37.
22 See Wiggershaus, *Die Frankfurter Schule* (Munich: Hanser, 1986), pp. 88ff.
23 Adorno, "Reaktion und Fortschrit," in *Adorno Krenek, Briefwechsel* (Frankfurt: Suhrkamp, 1974), p. 180.
24 Adorno, "Vermischten Schriften II," in *Schriften*, vol. 20: 2, p. 461.
25 Ibid., pp. 453ff.
26 Leo Löwenthal, "Erinnerungen an Theodor W. Adorno," in *Adorno-Konferenz 1983* (Frankfurt: Suhrkamp, 1983), pp. 399ff.
27 Adorno, "Vermischten Schriften II," p. 737.
28 Adorno, "Vermischten Schriften I," in *Schriften*, vol. 20: 1, p. 164.
29 Ibid., p. 196.
30 Adorno, *Negative Dialektik*, p. 160.
31 Ibid., pp. 165ff.

32   Adorno, *Schriften*, vol. 1, pp. 335ff.
33   Horkheimer and Adorno, *Dialectic of Enlightenment*, p. 187.
34   Ibid., p. 190.
35   Ibid.
36   Adorno, *Noten zur Literatur*, pp. 573, 570.
37   Adorno, *Ästhetische Theorie* (Frankfurt: Suhrkamp, 1970), p. 41.
38   See Albrecht Wellmer, *Die Moderne und das Erhabene* (forthcoming).

PART VI

Postmodernism, Critique, and the Pathology of the Social

Postmodernism, Critique, and the Pathology of the Social

In Part VI, *Postmodernism, Critique, and the Pathology of the Social*, Seyla Benhabib, in her chapter entitled "Critical Theory and Postmodernism: On the Interplay of Ethics, Aesthetics, and Utopia in Critical Theory," shows how the critique of "identity logic" embodied in the project of postmodernism is already anticipated in the work of early critical theory, particularly in the work of Adorno and to some extent Horkheimer. The problematic which she seeks to elicit, by looking first at *Dialectic of Enlightenment* and later at *Negative Dialectics*, is the paradoxical phenomenon that the critique of enlightenment reason is "cursed" by the enlightenment itself. Early critical theory shares with postmodernism the "hope that the critique of the Enlightenment can nonetheless evoke the utopian principle of nonidentary logic as an intimation of otherness." Benhabib concludes that critical theory attempts to "think beyond modernism while not abandoning the utopian legacy of the Enlightenment." Thomas McCarthy, in "Critical Theory and Postmodernism: A Response to David Hoy," constructs a forceful argument in defense of later critical theory around the themes of pragmatism, genealogy, hermeneutics and pluralism. Against Hoy's alternative explanation, McCarthy argues that critical theory conveys the "spirit" of pragmatism by incorporating not only its practical orientation but its "utopian impulse" as well. McCarthy defends Habermas's "reconstructive approach" from a critique based on Foucault's genealogical orientation by arguing that the distance between the two is not as far as is often claimed, and by suggesting that the real issue raised by the confrontation between the two theorists is "how best to write general histories." Against Hoy's defense of hermeneutics, McCarthy defends a strong use of the concept of "theory" as well as notions of validity and truth. Finally, McCarthy dissociates Habermas's notions of truth and justice from the notion of pluralism in order to show that critical theory is not opposed to pluralism. Axel Honneth, in "Pathologies of the Social: The Past and Present of Social Philosophy," argues for a reconsideration of "social philosophy," the task of which would

be to define "social pathology." In a reflection on the history of social philosophy Honneth designates Rousseau as its founder who employed "concepts like 'deremption' and 'alienation' for ethical criteria by which certain
modern processes of development can be conceived as pathologies."
Honneth argues that because "philosophical reflection can no longer support
itself upon the results of the established social sciences" – a dilemma caused
in large part by the moral crises induced by "fascism" and "Stalinism" – a
branch of philosophy returned to the classical themes of social philosophy.
Honneth sees the work of Hannah Arendt, Jürgen Habermas, Michel
Foucault, and Charles Taylor as each contributing to this tradition. Finally, it
is in Habermas's proceduralization of ethics, his attempt to "provide a critical
threshold beyond which the pressures of the systems imperatives of the
social lifeworld must be viewed as social pathologies," and in Taylor's notion
of human beings as "self-interpreting beings" who presuppose certain
"social conditions" as ethically necessary, that Honneth sees three modern
strategies for developing a modern social philosophy. The three chapters in
Part VI have their commonality not only in providing an elaborate defense
of a living critical theory but in their construction of ever new dimensions
for the future of critical theory.

14 CRITICAL THEORY AND POSTMODERNISM: ON THE INTERPLAY OF ETHICS, AESTHETICS, AND UTOPIA IN CRITICAL THEORY

Seyla Benhabib

I would like to begin with a disclaimer. This chapter does not specifically deal with deconstruction, let alone with "deconstruction and the possibility of justice." I am concerned here with the general cultural *Zeitgeist* of the present, which, in the last decade has been referred to as "postmodernism."

The question of postmodernism, although at first sight only tangentially related to the theme of "deconstruction and the possibility of justice," is not without implications for it. Deconstruction, whether its defenders would also describe themselves as postmodernist or not, undoubtedly is among the most influential contemporary approaches in the human sciences which are increasingly skeptical toward modernity and the Enlightenment ideal of reason. This ideal is considered inseparable from several unsalvageable illusions like the myth of the centered, self-conscious rational subject, transparent to itself: the methodological assumption of the transparency of reference and the determinacy of meaning, and the striving for a lucid, rational mode of intersubjective communication among equal minds. Let me leave aside the skeptical question of whether anybody today subscribes to these illusions, and whether in fact the "critique of the Enlightenment" has not become a catch-phrase for obfuscating some fundamental crossroads in contemporary philosophy. These queries will be answered obliquely in this chapter, via a strategic *detour*.

The thesis is that already Adorno, who is a "high modernist," engages in a powerful critique of the "identity logic of Western reason" and of the Enlightenment, without, however, forsaking belief in the healing power of rational reflection in attaining individual autonomy and collective justice. Adorno criticizes the drive toward abstract generalizations, which is a mode of grasping the concrete only by reducing it to some replicable instance of a general rule. Adorno demystifies the ideal of rational self-identity, dominant in Kantian moral theory and psychoanalysis, as representing a repressive and rigid ego conception. Adorno also rejects the rationalist search for cognitive clarity and transparency in favour of the method of dissonance, juxtaposition, and fragmentation. A closer reading of Adorno may not only alert us to the dialectical tension between high modernism and postmodernism, it may also suggest that a dialogue between critical theory and deconstruction, which so far has been a *dialogue des sourds* (a dialogue of the deaf), must heed the mediating voice of Adorno.[1]

I MODERNISM/POSTMODERNISM

In the recent, flourishing debate on the nature and significance of postmodernism, architecture seems to occupy a special place.[2] It is tempting to describe this situation through the Hegelianism: it is as if the *Zeitgeist* of an epoch approaching its end has reached self-consciousness in those monuments of modern architecture of steel, concrete, and glass. Contemplating itself in its objectifications, Spirit has not "recognized" and "thus returned to itself," but has recoiled in horror from its own products. The visible decay of our urban environment, the uncanniness of the modern megalopolis, and the general dehumanization of space appear to prove the Faustian dream to be a nightmare. The dream of an infinitely striving self, unfolding its powers in the process of conquering externality, is one from which we have awakened. Postmodernist architecture, whatever other sources it borrows its inspiration from, is undoubtedly the messenger of the end of this Faustian dream which had accompanied the self-understanding of the moderns from the beginning.

Faust, which Pushkin had called "The Iliad of the moderns,"[3] was indeed the quintessential modernist text, interweaving the project of self-development with that of social transformation. As Marshall Berman has argued in *All That is Solid Melts into Air*,[4] it is no accident that Faust commits his first truly evil act when he orders Mephisto to burn down the cottage of the old couple, Philemon and Baucis, in order to realize his dream of drying the marshland. Faust, the modernist, is also the developer, the city-builder, the architect. Standing at the beginning of the nineteenth century, watching the glimmerings of the technological progress that the application of the modern natural sciences would make possible, Goethe is in a more realistic position than Descartes, the founder of modern philosophy, to dream of rendering ourselves "*maîtres et possesseurs de la nature.*"[5]

Almost two and a half centuries ago Descartes laid the conceptual foundations of this Faustian dream. And once more the quintessential modernist appears as the city-builder, as the architect. Here is Descartes, reflecting in his *Discours de la Méthode* on the images of two cities: the one traditional, old, obscure, chaotic, unclear, lacking symmetry, overgrown; the other transparent, precise, planned, symmetrical, organized, functional. The tradition of knowledge is like the old city; it lacks coherence, functionality, clarity, as well as symmetry. Just as the city that emerges from the plan of the single architect is the more "perfect" one, argues Descartes, so too, the system of knowledge developed by a single mind is superior to the overgrown and chaotic medieval habitat of Scholasticism. "[T]here is very often less perfection in works . . . carried out by the hands of various masters, than in those on which one individual alone has worked," writes Descartes.[6] He continues:

> Thus we see that buildings planned and carried out by one architect alone are usually more beautiful and better proportioned than those which many have tried to put in order and improve, making use of old walls which were built with other ends in view. In the same way also, those ancient cities which, originally mere villages, have become in the process of time great towns, are usually badly constructed in comparison with those which are regularly laid out on a plain by a surveyor who is free to follow his own ideas. Even though, considering their buildings each one apart, there is often as much or more display of skill in the one case than in the other, the former have large buildings and small buildings indiscriminately placed together, thus rendering the streets crooked and irregular, so that it might be said that it was chance rather than the will of men guided by reason that led to such an arrangement.[7]

Postmodernism in all fields of culture heralds the end of this Faustian-Cartesian dream. The end of this dream has brought with it a conceptual and semiotic shift in many fields. This shift is characterized by the radical questioning of the very conceptual framework that made the modernist dream possible in the first place. The following statement by Peter Eisenman, one of the key figures in the modernist/postmodernist constellation in architecture, captures the elements of this new critique quite precisely:

> Architecture since the fifteenth century has been influenced by the assumption of a set of symbolic and referential functions. These can be collectively identified as the classical. . . . "Reason," "Representation," and "History." "Reason" insists that objects be understood as rational transformations from a self-evident origin. "Representation" demands that objects refer to values or images external to themselves. . . . "History" assumes that time is made up of isolatable historical moments whose essential characteristics can and should be abstracted and represented. If these classical assumptions are taken together as imperatives they force architecture to represent the spirit of its age through a rationally motivated and comprehensible sign system . . . But if these "imperatives" are simply "fictions" then the classical can be suspended and options emerge which have been obscured by classical imperatives.[8]

The ideal of the rational, self-transparent subject of cognition, the "clarity and distinctiveness" of whose representations would serve as the foundation for a new city of knowledge, is today viewed as a fiction. The subject has been forever fractured, displaced, and decentered. Since Nietzsche and Freud, we know that "[o]f ourselves we are not 'knowers.' "[9] And since Saussure and Wittgenstein, we can no longer view reference as a clear relation between a sign, a signifier, and a signified. The relation of the sign to the signifier is what constitutes the signified, and creates the space within which reference becomes at all possible. The vision of history as a cumulative continuum, progressing toward some shared goal, and whose essential characteristics can and should be abstracted and represented, was shattered for the European intelligentsia at least since World War I. Undoubtedly, for the large masses of the population it was the Holocaust and the atomic bombs dropped on Hiroshima and Nagasaki in this century that first brought home the destructive and uncanny side of the modernist project.

Justifiable as the current postmodernist mood in the culture may be, I for one cannot avoid the sense that the postmodernist critique also flattens the internal contradictions and tensions of modernity to the point where this legacy ceases to challenge, to provoke, and to probe. From the beginning, however, the modernist dream not only contained the search for the domination of nature, but also anticipated the ethical-political utopia of a community of free and rational beings. For Kant and Rousseau, the dignity of the moral subject was defined by its capacity to act in accordance with a law of reason that all rational creatures could likewise will to be a principle for themselves. Is this utopia of an autonomous, rational community, "a kingdom of ends" as Kant might say, just as repressive as the project of the domination of nature has turned out to be? Is the rational moral utopia of modernism only possible through the repression of nature and the other within us? Should we celebrate the passing away of the modernist subject? Should we revel in that "heterogeneous presence" called the postmodernist self, lost between a system of signifiers, maybe itself a disappearing referent?"[10] What discomforting ethical thoughts must one entertain if one thinks through the postmodernist project to its end?

We must begin to probe the implications of the postmodernist project not just in aesthetics but in ethics as well. Postmodernism gestures its solidarity with the other, with the "différend," with "women, children, fools and primitives," whose discourse has never matched the grand narrative of the modern masters.[11] Yet can there be an ethic of solidarity without a self that can feel compassion and act out of principle? Can there be a struggle for justice without the possibility of justifying power by reason? What is justice if not the rational exercise of power?

I will approach these questions obliquely by examining the interplay between ethics, aesthetics, and utopia in the thoughts of Horkheimer and Adorno. My suggestion is that the philosophers of high modernism, maybe much like Picasso and Max Beckmann, Klee and Kandinsky, had a more troubled, complex and, in some cases, tortured vision of the project of the moderns. It is not obvious that their tortured questioning of modernity is still not our own. I want to begin with that text which is the pinnacle of high modernism in the European philosophical tradition, written at the time the Cartesian-Faustian dream is disclosed to be a nightmare: the *Dialectic of Enlightenment* by Adorno and Horkheimer.

II   THE NIGHTMARE OF THE ENLIGHTENMENT

As has often been remarked, the *Dialectic of Enlightenment* is an elusive text.[12] A substantial part of it was composed from notes taken by Gretel Adorno during discussions between Adorno and Horkheimer. Completed in 1944, it was published three years later in Amsterdam and reissued in Germany in 1969. More than half the text consists of an exposition of the concept of the Enlightenment, with two excursus, one authored by Adorno on the *Odyssey* and the other authored by Horkheimer on Enlightenment and morality.

In one of the notes appended to the text, "The Interest in the Body," Adorno and Horkheimer write:

> Beneath the familiar history of Europe runs another, subterranean one. It consists of the fate of those human instincts and passions repressed and displaced by civilization. From the perspective of the fascist present, in which what was hidden emerged to light, manifest history appears along with its darker side, omitted both by the legends of the national state no less than by their progressive criticisms.[13]

This interest in the subterranean history of Western civilization is no doubt the guiding thread for the subterranean history of reason which the text unfolds. The story of Odysseus and of the Holocaust, the myth which is Enlightenment and Enlightenment which becomes mythology, are milestones in Western history: the genesis of civilization and its transformation into barbarism.

The promise of the Enlightenment to free man [sic!] from his self-incurred tutelage is defeated by a form of rationality, perfected in the domination of nature. Instrumental reason and the value of the autonomous personality are irreconcilable. "The worldwide domination of nature turns against the thinking subject himself; nothing remains of him but this eternally self-identical 'I think' that should accompany all my representations."[14]

Adorno and Horkheimer read the story of Odysseus in this light. This story reveals the dark spot in the constitution of Western subjectivity: the fear of the self from the "other" – which is identified with nature in this context – is overcome in the course of civilization only by dominating the "other." Since, however, the other is not completely alien but the self as nature is also other to itself, the domination of nature means self-mastery and repression. The story of Odysseus distinguishes between the dark forces of nature and the call toward home and civilization. Odysseus again and again is threatened by engulfment and by deindividuation. The call of the Sirens, the temptations of Circe, the cave of the Cyclops beckon the hero to a state in which the line between the human and the animal, pleasure and work, the self and the other disappears. Myth relates the story of how the hero constitutes his identity by repressing these others. But this repression of otherness can only come with the internalization of sacrifice. Odysseus escapes the call of the Sirens only by subjecting himself to them. While his men, whose ears are filled with wax, row his ship away, he, the hero, tied to the mast, is subject to their irresistible charm and is yet carried away by his deaf men who cannot hear his cries. The hero overcomes nature not only by internalizing sacrifice, but also by organizing the labour of others which he can utilize to his ends.

Yet as the regression from culture to barbarism brought about by National Socialism shows, Odysseus's cunning, the origin of Western rationality, has not been able to eliminate humanity's fear of the other. The Jew is the other, the stranger, the one who is super-human and subhuman. Whereas Odysseus's cunning consists of the attempt to appease otherness via a mimetic act by becoming like it – Odysseus offers the Cyclops human blood to drink, sleeps with Circe, and listens to the Sirens' song – fascism, through projection, makes the other like itself.

> If mimesis makes itself like the surrounding world, so false projection makes the surrounding world like itself. If for the former the exterior is the model which the interior has to approximate, if for it the stranger becomes familiar, the latter [fascism] transforms the tense inside ready to snap into exteriority and stamps even the familiar as the enemy.[15]

Western reason originates in mimesis, in the act to master nature by becoming like it, but it culminates in an act of projection which, via the technology of death, succeeds in making otherness disappear. "Ratio which suppresses mimesis is not simply its opposite; it itself is mimesis – unto death."[16]

Culture is the process through which the human self acquires identity in the face of otherness. Human reason, beginning as magic, first attempts to master otherness by becoming like it. Magic develops into ratio. Ratio is the cunning of the name-giving self. Language separates the object from its concept, the self from its other. Language masters externality by reducing it to an identical substratum. Whereas in magic, the name and the thing named stand in a relationship of "kinship, not one of intention,"[17] the concept which replaces the magical symbol in the course of Western culture reduces the "manifold affinity of being" to the relation between the meaning-giving subject and the meaningless object. The transition from symbol to concept already means disenchantment, *Entzauberung* in Max Weber's sense of the term. Ratio abstracts, seeks to comprehend through concepts and names. Abstraction, which can grasp the concrete only insofar as it can reduce it to identity, also liquidates the otherness of the other. Adorno and Horkheimer, with relentless rhetoric, uncover the "structure of identitary thinking" underlying Western reason.

> When it is announced that the tree is no longer simply itself but a witness for another, the seat of mana, language expresses the contradiction that something is itself and yet at the same time another beside itself, identical and non-identical. . . . The concept, which one would like to define as the characterizing unity of what is subsumed under it, was much more from the very beginning a product of dialectical thinking, whereby each is always what it is, in that it becomes what it is not.[18]

With this step criticizing the very structure of Western reason as one of domination as such, Adorno and Horkheimer place themselves in a paradoxical spot. If the plight of the Enlightenment reveals the culmination of the identity logic, constitutive of reason, then the theory of the dialectic of the Enlightenment, which is carried out with the tools of this very same reason, perpetuates the structure of domination it condemns. The critique of the Enlightenment is cursed by the same burden as the Enlightenment itself. Adorno and Horkheimer are fully aware of this paradox and hope that the critique of the Enlightenment can nonetheless evoke the utopian principle of nonidentitary logic as an intimation of otherness. The end of the Enlightenment, of the modernist project gone wild, cannot be stated discursively. The overcoming of the compulsive logic of modernism can only be a matter of giving back to the nonidentical, the suppressed, and the dominated their right to be. Since even language itself is burdened by the curse of the concept that represses the other in the very act of naming it,[19] we can evoke the other but we cannot name it. Like the God of the Jewish tradition who must not be named but evoked, the utopian transcendence of the compulsive logic of the Enlightenment and modernism cannot be named but awakened in memory. The evocation of this memory, the "rethinking of nature in the subject" (*das Andenken der Natur im Subjekt*) is the achievement of the aesthetic.

Art and the aesthetic realm in general carry a nondiscursive moment of truth. The recovery of the nonidentical is the achievement of the true work of art.

> That moment of the art work by means of which it transcends reality . . . does not consist in the attained harmony, in the questionable unity of form and content, inner and outer, individual and society, but rather, in those traces, through which discrepancy appears, and the passionate striving towards identity is necessarily shattered.[20]

For Adorno and Horkheimer, the space occupied by the aesthetic is defined by the parameters of the critique of discursive logic. The aesthetic emerges as the only mode of expression that can challenge the compulsive drive of Western reason to comprehend the world by making it like itself, by systematizing it, by abstracting from it, or in Max Weber's terms, by "rationalizing" it. The aesthetic intimates a new mode of being, a new mode of relating to nature and to otherness in general. Insofar as the critique of identity logic is not only a cognitive critique, however, but also an ethical and political critique of a mode of world domination, the aesthetic negation of identity logic also implies an ethical and political project. The utopian content of art heals by transforming the sensibilities of the modern subject: art as utopia, art as healing, but as an ethical and political healing which teaches us to let the otherness within ourselves and outside be. Art releases the memories and intimations of otherness which the subject has had to repress to become the adult, controlled, rational, and autonomous self of the tradition.

In these reflections on art, identity, and the ethical utopia of reconciliation with otherness, we can recognize not only contemporary feminist criticisms of male subjectivity but the postmodernist critique of the autonomous self as well. Especially in Adorno's critique of Kant and of traditional psychoanalysis, we begin to see the points where high modernism and contemporary postmodernism converge.

III   ADORNO AND UTOPIA OF THE NON-IDENTICAL

The *Dialectic of Enlightenment* takes us to that point where the critique of system-building, abstracting and formalizing Western logic becomes a critique of the rational, autonomous self also cherished by this tradition. The aesthetic emerges as an ethical-political and utopian realm which negates identity logic while intimating modes of a different subjectivity. Particularly, Adorno's critique of the modern moral subject as a compulsively identitary self reveals many affinities with the feminist and postmodernist critiques of the rational, autonomous ego.

Echoing feminist and postmodernist positions already in the *Dialectic of Enlightenment*, Adorno and Horkheimer write: "Mankind had to do frightful things to itself before the self, the identical, purposeful, male character of men could be created, and something of this is reflected in every childhood."[21] The rational and autonomous subject of the Enlightenment, the quintessential modernist, is a male subject – women, children, and, we should add, nonmodern peoples are excluded from its reality, precisely because they do not exercise the power of instrumental reason. But I would like to distinguish among two very different strands of the critique of the subject before placing Adorno more explicitly in this context.

There is a postmodernist celebration of the "death of the subject." This line of interpretation begins with the critique of an intentional self, supposedly preceding language or a system of representations in general. The fiction of the intentional subject, which we can most clearly attribute to Descartes, Kant, and Husserl, is a fiction precisely because the subject cannot know itself independently of its system of representations, and if this is so, it cannot be said to precede these representations. Self-consciousness is not some originary act preceding signification and representation; only within a system of representations can the subject be present to itself. "Language speaks us" or "representations constitute us." This is an insight of the linguistic critique of the philosophy of consciousness in our century, and one that is shared by Wittgenstein, Ferdinand de Saussure, and Jacques Derrida, as well as Jürgen Habermas.

This cognitive-linguistic critique of the philosophy of consciousness as represented by Descartes, Kant, and Husserl allows several options: once the sovereign subject preceding any system of significations is displaced by the vision of the subject constituted within a system of significations, one can argue either that the autonomous subject as such disappears or that the autonomy of the subject must now be reconstituted within a heterogeneous system of representations which it can never control. Postmodernists like Lyotard follow the first option and celebrate the death of the subject as a cognitive fiction as well as a moral ideal; the early Lyotard, following Deleuze and Guattari, viewed the subject as a system of quanta of energy, a center of libidinal economy, reacting more than acting.[22]

Adorno's critique of Kant and psychoanalysis follows the second option of rethinking autonomy and subjectivity as the qualities of a subject situated within a system of heterogeneous representations. Adorno's goal is to rethink the autonomy of the self, as a being situated within nature rather than as a being that is its "master and possessor," as Descartes would have it.[23]

The gist of Adorno's critique of Kant in *Negative Dialectics* which spans some eighty pages is the following statement:

> According to the Kantian model, the subjects are free, insofar as, conscious of themselves, they are identical with themselves; and in such identity they are once more unfree, insofar as they stand under its compulsion and perpetrate it. They are unfree as non-identical, as diffuse nature, and as such free because in the stimulations that overcome them – the non-identity of the subject with itself is nothing else – they will also overcome the compulsive character of identity.[24]

In Adorno's view, insofar as the tradition identifies autonomy with a rigid and compulsive moral consciousness, one must bid farewell to this ideal. Autonomy is the capacity of the subject to let itself go, to deliver itself over to that which is not itself, but to remain "by itself in otherness." The Kantian moral ideal, by contrast, "presupposes the internalization of repression, as the I which remains self-same develops into a steady instance; Kant absolutizes this I as the necessary condition of ethical life."[25] If so, would Adorno's ideal be, like that of the postmodernists, a subjectivity without the subject, a self that was not self-same, an "I" whose pure apperception need not accompany all our representations? Yet for Adorno the dissolution of the self can only be regressive:

> If under the immeasurable pressure which weighs upon it, the subject, as schizophrenic, falls into the condition of dissociation and ambivalence, of which the historical subject has divested itself, so the dissolution of the subject is equal to the ephemeral and condemned image of a possible subject. If its freedom once demanded that myth stop, so now it emancipates itself from itself as from a final myth.[26]

Under present conditions, "ego weakness," "the transition of the subject into passive and atomistic, reflex-like behavior," is the norm. The autonomous self cannot be replaced by the reflex-like ego ideal of the present; we must think of autonomy as the condition of an ego with fluid boundaries, who does not disappear or disintegrate in the face of otherness. The rationalist utopia of the Enlightenment, the ideal of the autonomous self, is destroyed in the course of history, because such rationalism defines reason against nature, and as the repression of nature. Identitary logic, the deep structure of Western reason, denies otherness within and without. Autonomy then means self-mastery, self-repression, and self-control; but autonomy which destroys otherness is itself subject to the revenge of those forces it has eliminated. History documents this return of the "repressed." The rationalist-moral utopia of the Enlightenment is rejected by Adorno in favor of the utopia of the nonidentical; individual autonomy is now understood as the capacity of the self to let "diffuse nature be" and yet retain a coherent sense of selfhood. At the social level this would imply a form of togetherness in diversity, or unity in difference.

"Utopia," writes Adorno, "would be the nonsacrificial nonidentity of the subject" ("*Utopie wäre die opferlose Nichtidentität des Subjekts*").[27] The ability of the subject to be "by-oneself-in-otherness" is like the capacity to forget oneself in the aesthetic experience of the *Naturschoene*. The "naturally beautiful" is an allegory, a cipher, and a sign of reconciliation. One must not think of this in essentialist categories, as an eternally given and unchanging content of beauty. The "naturally beautiful" is antithesis, the antithesis of society, and as undetermined, the antithesis of determination. It is a mode in which the mediation between subject and object, humans and nature can be thought of. The "other" is that utopian longing toward the nonidentical which can only be represented as "allegory" and as "cipher."[28] The utopia of a nonsacrificial nonidentity of the subject is intimated in that noncompulsory relation to otherness which forces the subject to transcend rigid ego-boundaries.

IV   THE ETHICS AND POLITICS OF THE NON-IDENTICAL

In a wonderful article, entitled "On the Dialectic of Modernism and Postmodernism," Albrecht Wellmer has laid bare the gist of Adorno's reflections of modern art as they bear on questions of morality and politics. Wellmer writes:

> For Adorno modern art meant the farewell to a type of unity and meaningful whole, represented in the epoch of great bourgeois art by the unity of the closed work and the unity of the individual self. Aesthetic enlightenment discovers, as Adorno sees it, in the unity of the traditional work as well as in the unity of the bourgeois subject something violent, a lack of reflection and something illusory: i.e., a type of unity which was only possible at the price of the repression and exclusion of the disparate, the non-integrated, the silenced and the repressed. . . . The open forms of modern art are for Adorno the response of an emancipated aesthetic consciousness to the illusory and violent nature of such traditional totalities of meaning. . . . The "opening up" or "de-limitation" of the work is to be thought of as corollary of a progressive capacity to aesthetically *integrate* the diffused and dispersed. . . . [W]e could say that the new – i.e., open forms of aesthetic synthesis in modern art point to new forms of psychic and social "synthesis." . . . [Modern art] would suggest new types of aesthetic, psychological-moral and social "synthesis" – of "totality" – in which the diffused and the non-integrated, the senseless and the split off would be brought home to a sphere of non-violent communication . . . .[29]

The project of bringing home the diffused, the senseless, and the split off in "a sphere of non-violent communication" is how critical theory attempts to think beyond modernism while not abandoning the utopian legacy of the Enlightenment. Indeed, new options have emerged in the present with the demise of the classical episteme: we can either celebrate the death of the modernist subject or seek to transform the embattled self of modernity into a new self that can appreciate otherness without dissolving in it, that can respect heterogeneity without being overwhelmed by it. This, I think, is the only plausible ethical and political option. The first option, the celebration of the death of the subject *tout court*, transforms postmodernist thought into a "*froehliche Wissenschaft*," a gay science, in Nietzsche's terms, that affirms multiplicity and heterogeneity but can no longer criticize it. Postmodernism then becomes status quo thinking in avant-garde garb.

The joyful eclecticism and historicism of postmodernism, the savoring of the "play of surfaces," is a conciliatory impulse. Proceeding from the wrong assumption that all transformatory ethics and politics must presuppose an authoritarian vision of a future totality, the postmodernist critique of various left traditions turns into a reconciliation with the given.[30] But neither the equation of utopia with totalitarianism nor the equation of transformatory practice with authoritarianism is compelling. Surely we can think beyond the failure of the rationalist utopias of progress to a new utopia, not of appeasement and rest, but of constant integration and differentiation. "The project of bringing home the diffused, the repressed, and the marginalized" is an endless task.[31] The task of thinking through to a new model of synthesis or unity which does not flatten the unified, of abstraction which does not eviscerate the content it abstracts from, of conceptualization that does not dub irrational what it cannot find the right words for – this task need not be understood as an eschatoteleology, but can instead be viewed as a constant challenge to the imagination to transcend the rationalism of the modernist project without forsaking reason itself.

NOTES

1   See J. Habermas, *The Philosophical Discourse of Modernity* (F. Lawrence trans. 1987). Habermas's discussion of these issues, however, has not generated the kind of engagement on the part of the postmodernists which one would have wished for. See Norris, Deconstruction, Postmodernism and Philosophy: Habermas on Derrida, 8 *Praxis Int'l* 426 (1989); Hoy, Splitting the Difference: Habermas's Critique of Derrida, 8 *Praxis Int'l* 447 (1989). See generally Symposium on Jürgen Habermas's "The Philosophical Discourse of Modernity," 8 *Praxis Int'l* 377 (1989) (containing the most interesting exchanges so far on these issues). These essays forthcoming in: M. Passerin d'Entrèves and S. Benhabib eds. *Habermas and the Unfinished Project of Modernity* (1996).
2   Parts of the following discussion have appeared in S. Benhabib, Epistemologies of Postmodernism: A Rejoinder to Jean-François Lyotard, in 33 *New German Critique* 103 (1984) [hereinafter Epistemologies of Postmodernism], reprinted in *Feminism/Postmodernism* 107 (L. Nicholson ed. 1990).
3   M. Berman, *All That Is Solid Melts into Air: The Experience of Modernity* (1988).
4   Id. at 37–86.
5   R. Descartes, *Discours de la Méthode* 56 (Classiques Larousse ed. 1934).
6   R. Descartes, Discourse on the Method of Rightly Conducting the Reason, in *The Philosophical Works of Descartes* 79, 87 (E. Haldane & G. Ross trans. 1978).
7   Id. at 87–88.
8   P. Eisenman, accompanying text to exhibit piece in "*Revision der Moderne*," Deutsches Architekturmuseum, Summer 1984.
9   F. Nietzsche, *The Birth of Tragedy and The Genealogy of Morals* 149 (F. Golffing trans. 1956).
10   Kristeva, Le Sujet en procès in *Polyeoque* 55–136 (1977).
11   See J. Lyotard, *The Postmodern Condition: A Report on Knowledge* 27 (G. Bennington and B. Massumi trans. 1984).
12   Parts of this discussion have appeared previously in S. Benhabib, *Critique, Norm, and Utopia: A Study of the Foundations of Critical Theory* 163–82 (1986) [hereinafter Critique, Norm, and Utopia].

13 M. Horkheimer and T. Adorno, *Dialektik der Aufklärung* 207 (1969) [herinafter *Dialektik*]; M. Horkheimer and T. Adorno, *Dialectic of Enlightenment* 231 (J. Cumming trans. 1972) (English version of *Dialektik der Aufklärung*) [hereinafter Dialectic of Enlightenment]. All translations in the text are my own.

14 *Dialektik*, above note 13, at 27; Dialectic of Enlightenment, above note 13, at 26.

15 *Dialektik*, above note 13, at 167; Dialectic of Enlightenment, above note 13, at 187.

16 *Dialektik*, above note 13, at 57; Dialectic of Enlightenment, above note 13, at 57.

17 *Dialektik*, above note 13, at 13; Dialectic of Enlightenment, above note 13, at 11.

18 *Dialektik*, above note 13, at 17–18; Dialectic of Enlightenment, above note 13, at 15.

19 *Dialektik*, above note 13, at 16–17; Dialectic of Enlightenment, above note 13, at 10.

20 *Dialektik*, above note 13, at 117; Dialectic of Enlightenment, above note 13, at 131.

21 *Dialektik*, above note 13, at 47; Dialectic of Enlightenment, above note 13, at 40–1.

22 V. Descombes, *Modern French Philosophy* 184–5 (L. Scott-Fox and J. Harding trans. 1980) (citing J. Lyotard, *Economie Libidinale* (1974)).

23 R. Descartes, above note 5, at 56.

24 T. Adorno, *Negative Dialektik* 292 (1973) [hereinafter Negative Dialektik]; T. Adorno, *Negative Dialectics* 299 (E. Ashton trans. 1979) (English version of Negative Dialektik) [hereinafter Negative Dialectics]. All translations in the text are my own.

25 *Negative Dialektik*, above note 24, at 266; Negative Dialectics, above note 24, at 271–2.

26 *Negative Dialektik*, above note 24, at 275; Negative Dialectics, above note 24, at 281.

27 *Negative Dialektik*, above note 24, at 275; Negative Dialectics, above note 21, at 281.

28 The critique of utopianism by postmodernists takes two forms: those like Lyotard who identify utopian thinking with the rationalist and authoritarian political experiments of the French and Bolshevik revolutions; and those like Derrida, who criticize utopianism less for its politically authoritarian implications, but more for its "essentialist" assumptions about a final end, an unambigious state, a transparency of being – in short, utopian thinking is considered a form of "eschatoteleology." There are different strands of utopian thinking in the Frankfurt School; whereas Marcuse, particularly in *Eros and Civilization*, represents the essentialist tradition, Adorno, following Benjamin, belongs to the tradition of "negative utopianism." Utopia can never be named; it is the gesture of the other, of the Messianic hope which transcends the present. The roots of this mode of utopianism lie less in Greek philosophy than in Christian and Jewish mysticism and Gnosticism. See Scholem, Walter Benjamin, in Über Walter Benjamin 132 (1968); J. Habermas, Bewusstmachende oder rettende Kritik – Die Aktualität Walter Benjamins 1972, in *Kultur und Kritik* 302 (1973).

   In his keynote address to the "Deconstruction and the Possibility of Justice" conference, Derrida cites Levinas. "Levinas speaks of an infinite right: in what he calls 'Jewish humanism,' whose basis is not 'the concept of man,' but rather the other; 'the extent of the right of the other' is a 'practically infinite right' . . ." Derrida, Force of Law: The "Mystical Foundation of Authority," 11 *Cardozo L. Rev.* 919, 959 (1990). It would be fascinating to investigate the influence of the Jewish mystical and utopian tradition on critical theorists like Adorno and Benjamin on the one hand, and Levinas and Derrida on the other. It is, of course, no coincidence that Derrida has extensively drawn on the work of Walter Benjamin. What has not been adequately noted, however, is the extent to which Benjaminesque motifs are present not only in the work of Adorno but also in Habermas's reflections as well. See Critique, Norm, and Utopia, supra note 12, at 327–43.

29 Wellmer, On the Dialectic of Modernism and Postmodernism, 4 *Praxis Int'l* 337–57 (1985).

30 See Epistemologies of Postmodernism, above note 2, at 117 (containing my own critique of Lyotard).

31 Wellmer, above note 29, at 357.

15 CRITICAL THEORY AND POSTMODERNISM: A RESPONSE TO DAVID HOY*

Thomas McCarthy

David Hoy's criticisms of critical theory can be discussed under four principal themes: (1) pragmatism, (2) genealogy, (3) hermeneutics, and (4) pluralism. In what follows, I will comment briefly on each of the complexes of argumentation signified by these headings, that is, on Hoy's arguments against theory, for critical history, for interpretation, and against universalism.

1 PRAGMATISM

One of the disconcerting features of the otherwise welcome renewal of interest in American Pragmatism is the suggestion by some "new pragmatists" that Peirce, James, Dewey, and Mead were actually much closer in spirit to Nietzsche, Heidegger, and the French poststructuralists than to Kant and the German Idealists – whom, unlike the former, they encountered as students and continued to draw inspiration from throughout their lives. In fact, the classical pragmatists were given to theory on a grand scale, and in all the senses decried by neopragmatists, from Peirce's metaphysical realism to Dewey's and Mead's metanarratives of scientific and social progress. Moreover, their thought was marked by the holism, universalism, and utopianism that Hoy rejects in the name of "piecemeal and pragmatic" criticism (p. 107). This is not merely to dispute legitimate ancestry or to reclaim the rhetorical high ground arrogated by Rorty and others. It raises the important question of whether one might not be naturalistic and pragmatic and still aspire to "theory" in one or more of the senses at issue. For, despite the repeated denunciation of all "binary oppositions" and every "critical tribunal," postmodernist discourse actually relies quite heavily on a series of stark "either/or"s to justify a stringent list of "do"s and "don't"s: thou shalt not spin grand historical metanarratives, construct big societal pictures, entertain high utopian ideals, or think deep philosophical thoughts. The supreme opposition, which structures all the rest, is that between *Reason* – that is, foundationalist and absolutist conceptions of reason – and whatever in a given context is identified as *The Other of Reason* – sensibility, imagination, desire, the body, women, nature, history, the non-Western world, language, culture, art, rhetoric, and so on. I argued in *Critical Theory* that these alternatives are not exhaustive. It is only when one accepts an extreme diagnosis of modernity as everywhere corrupted by "ontotheology" or the like, that the extreme remedy of deconstruction seems necessary. Otherwise it is difficult to see why one could not, in a fallibilist, naturalist, and pragmatist spirit, still pursue theory in one or another of the relevant senses.

Which are the relevant senses in the present context? Hoy zeroes in on just the senses that have been central to critical social theory from Marx to Habermas. In the first place, (a) an overarching "metanarrative" of historical development, that is, of large-scale social, economic, political, and cultural changes, which in Marx takes the form of a materialist theory of history and in Habermas that of a theory of social evolution. Then, (b) a "totalizing" account of contemporary society, of its emergence, growth, tensions, and tendencies, of its basic structures and processes, which in Marx takes the form of a critique of political economy and in Habermas that of a critique of system–lifeworld relations. And, finally, (c) a treatment of the conceptual and normative "foundations" (but not in the foundationalist sense) of critical social theory, which in Marx takes the form of a materialist appropriation of Hegelian philosophy by way of a never fully elaborated notion of social *praxis* and in Habermas that of a theory of communicative action.[1] I will address each of these in turn.

(a) Hoy underplays the *critical* orientation and *practical* intention of critical social theory and treats its general accounts of societal transformation simply as "grand metanarratives" of progress, ignoring the *use* to which those developmental schemes are put in the critique of contemporary society. To be sure, there are grounds for this reading within the history of critical theory. The young Marx wanted to distance himself from the philosophy of history, with its pretense to a contemplative view of a whole whose meaning could be rendered in terms of necessary progress. He insisted that the movement of history was not a matter of metaphysical necessity but was contingent in regard to both the empirical conditions of change and the practical engagement of social actors, and that the meaning of history was not a subject for metaphysical hypostatization but for political action. But the mature Marx, in his efforts to distinguish himself from merely philosophical critics and purely utopian socialists, sometimes ascribed to his own conception of history a necessity and scientificity that echoed earlier claims for the philosophy of history. Subsequently, especially in the hands of his "orthodox" followers, the importance of critical self-reflection and emancipatory political practice regularly receded behind the solid, objective necessity of inexorable laws of history. The spectacle of that regression prompted the Frankfurt School's renewed stress on the critical and practical dimensions of Marxism. And yet, as Hoy has indicated, they did not always resist the temptation to treat their own general historical schemes as philosophies of history. I do not think, however, that it is correct to place Habermas's theory of social evolution in the same category. Distinguishing structural patterns from empirical processes under contingent conditions, he attributes neither unilinearity, nor necessity, nor continuity, nor irreversibility to history.[2] But I will not debate Habermas's interpretation here. I want, rather, to emphasize the practical motivation behind critical social theory's interest in "grand metanarratives": their point is to aid in the construction of critical histories of the present. That is to say, the *theoretically generalized narratives* of societal transformation characteristic of this tradition are meant to serve as *interpretive frameworks* for historically oriented, critical analyses of contemporary society. Their underlying purpose is to enhance our understanding of capitalist modernization, with its vast consequences, positive and negative, for traditional social orders. If they are viewed naturalistically and fallibilistically, there is nothing "in principle" impossible about such general schemes. From a pragmatic point of view, the proof of the pudding can only be in the eating, that is, in how well or badly they fare as interpretive frameworks for critical accounts of the contemporary world. As Marx strikingly illustrated in *The Eighteenth Brumaire of Louis Bonaparte*, "metanarratives" of societal change may also serve as narrative foils for the construction of critical histories of particular events, situations, and processes. That use will be discussed in considering Hoy's treatment of genealogy. For now, suffice it to say that claiming "a priori," as it were, that general historical schemes could never be of any use in any context, or that even if they were, it would be wrong to use them, would be a decidedly unpragmatic way of dealing with these issues.

Finally, it should be noted that in the tradition of critical social theory, the historical critiques framed by these general accounts of societal change have typically not been directed at "them" – that is, at other cultures and societies – but at "us" – that is, at our own. The overriding aim has been *self*-criticism, but self-criticism informed by a general sense of how we got where we are and which are the real alternatives and possibilities for change. To be sure, critical theorists from Marx to Habermas have made "invidious comparisons" with traditional societies, both in Europe and elsewhere. But they are mild compared to their trenchant criticisms of the deep pathologies of their own societies. As that is evident, the only issue may be whether social critics should be discouraged from saying or implying anything unflattering about any society – or culture, or group – other than their own. I will discuss the wisdom of that policy under "pluralism."

(b)   What is true of "grand metanarratives" of historical change holds also for "big pictures" of contemporary society. As I argued in *Critical Theory*, there is no need to claim a God's-eye view of the whole; a reflective participant's view will do just fine. The strengths and weaknesses of competing general accounts of contemporary society can certainly be discussed in a naturalistic and fallibilistic spirit. And their usefulness for understanding and explaining particular features of our world surely has to prove itself in practice. Before dismissing them out of hand, it would be well to recall that historically oriented, general accounts of modern society were the stock-in-trade of classical social theorists from Smith and Ferguson, through Marx and Mill, to Durkheim and Weber, and beyond. Is it plausible to assume that we can learn nothing of value from this type of grand theorizing? More likely, without it we would be left with an ever-growing heap of fragmented analyses and interpretations.

One element of Hoy's case against "totalizing" theories of society is the suggestion that they aim at accounting for every detail of every aspect of everything, which would of course be a hopeless task. But if we were to understand the aim of general social theory in the more pragmatic sense of "seeing how things hang together" at a societal level of analysis, it might seem less hopeless. We do, in fact, constantly face questions concerning how what happens in one area of social life or one part of the world or one period of history affects or is affected by what happens in others. If social theorists were to abandon the effort to construct coherent, empirically based accounts of macrohistorical processes and macrosocietal interconnections, then the field would simply be left to the army of journalists, pundits, politicians, and pop-theorists who are always more than willing to supply that need. Furthermore, interpretive practices themselves would be severely limited by the inability, as George Marcus and Michael Fischer have put it, "to represent the embedding of richly described, local, cultural worlds in larger, impersonal systems," for those worlds cannot plausibly be represented as "isolate[s] with outside forces of market and state impinging on [them]." Rather, such forces are "an integral part of the construction and the constitution of the 'inside,' the cultural unit itself, and must be so registered at the most intimate levels of the cultural process."[3]

Another feature of Hoy's attack on "totalizing" social theory is his depiction of it as a continuation of metaphysics by other means, that is, as aiming at the kind of totality and finality that Kant demolished, one would like to say "once and for all," in the "Dialectic" of the *First Critique*. It is important to recall in this connection what was said in *Critical Theory* about the *ongoing* character of such constructions and the *practical* interest of critical social theory. In ongoingly constructing, deconstructing, and reconstructing "big pictures" of basic structures, processes, and interdependencies, no less than in ongoingly fashioning "grand metanarratives" of macrohistorical transformations, the critical social theorist is guided by the aim of enhancing our self-understanding in ways that have implications for practice. Trying to understand, for instance, how investment policies in the industrialized world affect development and underdevelopment in the rest of the world is surely no less a critical activity than trying to understand the self-images of particular cultural units in either, and it is surely of no less practical-political import.

(c)   Critical studies of modernization processes, with their deeply ambivalent record of gains and losses, have, at least since Max Weber, *also* been configured as studies of rationalization processes. Basic social-theoretical concepts and assumptions have been tailored to highlight the rationalizable aspects of social action and to provide a framework for interpreting modernization as rationalization, however ambiguous, one-sided, or distorted. It is here that Habermas's theory of communicative rationality belongs. He understands it as a "metatheoretical framework for action theory," on the same level as and competing with Weber's account of rationality in means–ends terms and its currently influential rational-choice reformulations.[4] He stresses its empirical-theoretical, in contradistinction to ontological or transcendental, character.[5] Hoy's remarks regarding this level of theorizing are ambivalent. On the one hand, he seems to be against any attempt to revive strong theoretical approaches to reason or to continue them by other means. On the other hand, in defending himself against charges of performative self-contradiction, he allows for the possibility of a "metatheory," in contrast to a "first-order theory," of reason (p. 201). But he also suggests that any such metatheory would be too "thin" to support substantive conclusions of any import (pp. 176, 179).

I find this position unconvincing, for a number of reasons. To begin with, neopragmatists like Rorty, genealogists like Foucault, and hermeneuticists like Gadamer have their own theories of reason, truth, objectivity, and the like. To be sure, their accounts are opposed to rationalism at many points. But having a different account – one, say, that stresses history, culture, practice, or power – is not the same as having no account. Nor are these accounts any less general than Habermas's; they are simply different – typically deflationary – general accounts. Nor, finally, do such general, deflationary accounts of reason avoid serving as "critical tribunals" or "cultural arbiters," legislating from on high. They simply proscribe a different list of cultural practices, including most of what theorists have done since Thales. Hoy fits this pattern. On the basis of very general, indeed *universal*, claims about the *unavoidable* historicity, linguisticality, contextuality, and so forth of rational practices, he dismisses many of the cultural practices associated with traditional philosophy or critical social theory. A "metatheory" of reason, on the same general level that philosophy usually occupies, is used as a rationale for legislating against a broad range of practices "a priori," that is, independently of examining their successes and failures in tackling particular problems. If this is so, and if that metatheory is in dispute, it is difficult to see why the refusal to elaborate it should serve the best interests of critical theory and practice.

At one point, Hoy argues that this *cannot* be done, since any attempt to explicate the background as a system of rules or the like is bound to fail (pp. 160–1). As my discussion in *Critical Theory* indicates, I agree on the impossibility of spelling out "complete" systems of rules for our practices; but I do not think this warrants the conclusion that Hoy draws. The issue is not the ontological one of whether we are always "mehr Sein als Bewusstsein," but the pragmatic one of whether it is ever useful to reconstruct, as far as we can, the normative structures embodied in our practices.[6] It is a mistake to suppose that such reconstructions could be useful only if they yielded rules whose application no longer required practical reasoning and judgment. That requirement would make *all* rule systems useless, including the explicit ones that, notwithstanding their "incompleteness" and "imprecision," guide our conduct in so many areas of life from sports fields to law courts. The problem, I think, is once again the all-or-nothing forms of argument that neopragmatists persist in deploying against the philosophical tradition they reject. To borrow a phrase from Arthur Fine, they are locked in a metaphilosophical *pas-de-deux* with that tradition and ignore moves that are not part of their invariant routine: either a Theory of Reason in a foundationalist sense, or no theory of reason at all, in any sense.[7]

Hoy takes a different tack in adopting Foucault's project of showing by historical means that professedly universal conceptions of rationality are merely particular. This approach would replace the traditional search for a grand theory of what reason really is with multiple critical histories of contingent regimes of rationality (p. 146). As I am not in principle against such histories, our disagreement here comes down to whether there is *anything universal at all* to say about reason, truth, objectivity, and the like, or rather anything that would not be too "thin" to be of any use. With regard to thinness, I think one should take the same pragmatic stand as with regard to completeness or exactness: too thin for what purpose? Hoy clearly thinks that his thin "metatheory" of reason's historicity, contextuality, contingency, and so forth is thick enough to defeat the culturally significant claims of traditional philosophy and its successors, to counteract the ethnocentrism of universalist theories, and to point us in the direction of multicultural hermeneutic dialogue. These would be no mean accomplishments. Putting thinness aside, then, the issue remains whether and how a general account of rationality might still be pursued.

In *Critical Theory*, I defended the possibility of a non-foundationalist critique of impure reason. Like grand metanarratives of historical change and big pictures of contemporary society, basic conceptions of reason and rationality can be ongoingly constructed, criticized, and revised in a naturalistic spirit (taking into account their agreement with available evidence and their coherence with other empirical theories), and with a view to the practical purposes for which they are designed (in this case, critical analyses of rationalization processes). As Peirce pointed out long ago, in most practical

contexts some idea of being "true to the facts" will be of decisive importance. The stark opposition between knowledge and interest, which traditionally meant ignoring the latter the better to pursue the former and
recently seems to mean the converse, also has to be superseded by critical
theory.[8] The interests guiding critical theory can be identified at the most
abstract level by those ideas and ideals of reason that Hoy dismisses as
"utopian." He does not inquire why the classical pragmatists felt it important
to invoke similar ideas in their theorizing, such as Peirce's ideas of the "faith,
hope, and charity" that inform rational inquiry or Mead's idea of the "universal discourse" that serves as its normative horizon. Nor does he consider
that the sorts of critique he favors are guided by utopian ideals of one sort or
another, such as Rorty's dream of a "postmodernist liberalism" or Foucault's
hope that "everyone's life [could] become a work of art."[9] Nor, finally, does
he acknowledge that his own hermeneutic conception of a decentered "pluralistic dialogue" is another such ideal. These utopian conceptions are surely
no less "vague" than the ideas and ideals that have guided critical social theory. And like them, they are not meant to replace but to inform critical histories of the present, which like critical theories, may take their normative
orientations from such ideas.[10] Hoy's objections to them are actually objections against their misuse, for example, against the dangerous illusion of a
"thoroughly planned society" (p. 111). It is precisely to head off these mis-
uses that I insisted in *Critical Theory* on the regulative character of such ideas,
and on their negative and critical – as well as their positive and guiding – significance. It is for the same reason that Habermas stresses their formal and
procedural, in contrast to material and substantive, character. The idea of
organizing our lives together on the basis of uncoerced agreements, arrived
at in free and equal exchanges, by considering reasons pro and con, is not
the depiction of any concrete utopia. But neither is it empty: whether individuals and societies are committed to this idea makes an enormous difference. As Hoy notes disapprovingly, Kant proposed that we act as if it were
realizable in some future world and our actions could contribute to that realization (p. 117). Critical theory could do worse than retaining that practical
faith and the utopian impulse that animates it.

2 GENEALOGY

In chapter 5 of *Critical Theory*, Hoy plays Foucault's genealogical approach off
against Habermas's reconstructive approach, much to the latter's disadvantage. His main target there is the theory of social evolution, which makes the
encounter less than ideal, as that is not meant to be the *critical* edge of
Habermas's enterprise. If one compares genealogical histories written with
critical intent to developmental logics set out with reconstructive intent, and
does so from the standpoint of critique, then the outcome is largely prede-

cided. More to the point would be a comparison of genealogy to the sorts of theoretically informed critiques that one finds in Habermas's work from *The Structural Transformation of the Public Sphere* to the *Theory of Communicative Action*. In the latter, for instance, it is clear that developmental-logical considerations are meant in the end to serve the purposes of a critique of contemporary society. Thus the largely reconstructive treatment of rationality in chapter I is followed in chapter II by a discussion of Max Weber's account of the "iron cage" forged by rationalization processes; and the reconstructive chapter III is followed in chapter IV by a discussion of views of rationalization as reification from Lukács to Adorno. This pattern roughly continues until the work culminates in Habermas's well-known diagnosis of the ills of contemporary society in terms of a colonization of the lifeworld by the system. Along the way he indicates quite clearly just how he wants to utilize, for purposes of critique, the reconstructive and developmental considerations he introduces. For example, in his critical appropriation of the Weberian themes of the loss of meaning and freedom, his guiding idea is the *selectivity* of capitalist modernization, the failure of modern societies to actualize and institutionalize in a balanced way *all* the dimensions of reason available in modern cultures.[11] And in developing that idea, he uses his reflections on sociocultural evolution as an interpretive frame. It is this type of use for purposes of social critique that is the proper object of comparison with Foucault's genealogy.

When the comparison is made in this way, the "either/or" divides dominating the topography of Hoy's argument begin to narrow. On the one side, it becomes clear that Habermas too is interested in critically interpreting the present for the sake of identifying possibilities closed off in the past. On the other side, it begins to appear that Foucault too relies on general and abstract "metatheories" and interpretive frames to write his large-scale, critical narratives of the present. The differences between them become matters of which and how rather than whether or not. In what follows I will sketch the bare outlines of such a critical comparison, not because everything turns on "who wins, Habermas or Foucault," but because the issues Hoy raises are so diverse and complex that I couldn't hope to address them except by proposing a different comparative perspective.

Looking at the trajectory of critical social theory since its appropriation of Max Weber, we find that its basic direction is quite similar to Foucault's in an important respect: it aims to understand the ways in which reason and rationality have been socially constructed, as a means of achieving a critical self-understanding with implications for practice. From Lukács through Horkheimer and Adorno to Habermas, there has never been the slightest doubt that rationalization processes are not a story of unmitigated progress but a "dialectic of enlightenment." The real differences with Foucault concern whether there is at all a positive side to the story, an emancipatory dimension of enlightenment. I want to recall here what I argued in *Critical*

Theory concerning the many facets of rationalization that the radical critics of reason take for granted. That applies to Hoy as well. He invokes a distinction between matters for empirical research and the claims of metaphysics; he draws at every turn on the results of nineteenth-century historical enlightenment and twentieth-century anthropological enlightenment; he assumes the possibility and the right to call into question inherited beliefs, values, practices, and identities; he treats as more or less obvious the equal respect due to *all* individuals – to mention only a few of the more obvious aspects of cultural rationalization that he, if sometimes only implicitly, plainly relies upon as positive achievements. On this general issue, then, it is difficult to see how Hoy and Foucault can make sense of their critical enterprises without themselves adopting some version of the dialectic of enlightenment.

As to more specific issues, the opposition between internal and external critique that Hoy frequently invokes seems to me to cut precisely in the opposite direction from what he suggests. No one in this debate claims an extramundane, God's-eye standpoint from which to view the whole of history, society, and culture. So the opposition must turn on distinguishing critical approaches within the world. There are any number of different ways in which the key distinction may be drawn. Some of the more promising, it seems to me, build on a hermeneutic distinction that Hoy adopts: the distinction between talking about people as if they were mere objects of interpretation and talking with them as cosubjects of interpretation. In Habermas's frame of reference, this connects with the question of whether or not the interpreter takes seriously the validity claims raised by those she is trying to understand. Foucault, the genealogist, positions himself at the extreme externalist end of this spectrum. Practices in which participants raise claims to reason, truth, justice, authenticity, and the like are not merely reflectively distanced but represented in an optics of estrangement that wholly undercuts participants' spontaneous understandings of what they are up to. By contrast, Habermas, the reconstructionist, takes seriously such claims to validity and attempts to spell out their internal logics, including their pragmatic presuppositions, and their practical implications. As a critic, however, he combines this with techniques of objectification and estrangement; but, unlike Foucault's, they are never meant to be the last word. And that, it seems to me, is the central issue. Neither genealogy nor critical theory wants to cede to the participants and their traditions the only say about the significance of the practices they engage in. Both see the need for gaining some distance from "insider's" views and adopting some form of "outsider's" perspective; and both believe that historical accounts of how and why purportedly rational practices came to be taken for granted serve this purpose. But whereas the genealogist resolutely brackets the validity claims embedded in practices, the better to objectify them, the critical theorist tries to reconstruct and critically engage those claims. As Hoy himself wants in the end to combine the external perspective peculiar to genealogy with the internal perspective proper to hermeneutics, I will not belabor this point but will turn to his objections specifically against Hegelian-Marxist ways of combining them.

His disagreements with the idea of determinate negation are basically two: he rejects the claims to *necessity* and to *superiority* he sees inherent in it. As to the former, few critical social theorists would today claim any necessity for the historical developments they trace, and Habermas is certainly not among them.[12] As Hoy himself refers to passages in which Habermas explicitly renounces any such claim (p. 158), the real issue must lie elsewhere. If one examines Hoy's objections closely, they seem to target Habermas's claim that there is an underlying *logic* to patterns of sociocultural change, stages of development that have to be passed through *if* a society is to get from one point to another.[13] But that has to do only with *conditional* necessity. In any case, as the line of argument set out in my opening statement depends only on the "weaker" sorts of claim Hoy attributes to MacIntyre (pp. 155–6), it is not committed to necessity in any of the senses Hoy finds objectionable.

The more important disagreement concerns the progressivist implications of developmental claims. Hoy argues for dropping any and all "Whiggish" notions of superiority in favor of the less offensive notion of difference. But this is inconsistent with his larger view of the contemporary situation, as the term "postmodern" suggests. The superiority he claims for his own genealogical hermeneutics rests on taking for granted the "progressive" nature of the fruits of rationalization I mentioned above, and much else besides. It is because he is convinced that we know more and better about the historical variability and cultural diversity of forms of life, about the lin-guistically mediated character of thought and action, about the contingency and contextuality of rational practices, and the like, that he considers tradi-tional metaphysics, classical rationalism, and transcendental philosophy no longer to be viable options for us. It would be impossible for him to get his argument off the ground without assuming that we had *learned* something in those respects. For, after all, the bare-bones schema for learning processes amounts to no more than this: if y is superior to x in some respect, and a cul-ture, group, or individual comes to appreciate that over time, it may be said to have learned something. Neither Hoy nor any other postmodernist critic can wholly reject this notion of learning and still make sense of his critical enterprise. And if that is so, it is surely legitimate, and may well be impor-tant, for critical theorists to think seriously about the nature of sociocultural learning processes.

This Habermas does in his theory of social evolution. As I have explained elsewhere, I have my own reservations concerning that theory.[14] But I do not think that the problems lie where Hoy sees them, and so I shall confine my remarks to refocusing the discussion.[15] As it will turn out, the points at issue are largely of an empirical-theoretical nature and thus cannot be decided by conceptual fiat. To begin with, though Habermas does say that "in a certain way it is only socialized subjects that learn," he immediately adds that "social systems can, by exploiting [individuals'] learning capacities, form new structures."[16] The main aim of his theory is precisely to comprehend how the accomplishments of individual learning processes get more widely disseminated and become part of the shared worldviews of groups in a society, how such advances in cultural knowledge can then figure in social struggles, and how, under certain circumstances, they can be drawn upon to transform the existing institutional order.[17] In a word, the theory of social evolution aims to understand broad cultural and societal developments and *not* the appearance of "higher types of individuals," and particularly not of the "rare genius" (p. 154). Moreover, it focuses only on selected aspects of large-scale changes. Thus, as Hoy notes (p. 159), it does not imply that society as a whole progresses, that life gets better and better. Rather, "progress" takes the more limited form of advances in specific cultural dimensions (e.g., in science and technology, law and morality, or art and art criticism), in the institutionalization of learning processes in those dimensions (e.g., in research laboratories, universities, legal systems, or institutions for the production, dissemination, and criticism of art), and in the exploitation of such cultural advances for social-structural transformations. Hoy does not focus his objections on these developmental claims. Rather, his most sustained criticisms target the idea that we can speak of progress in regard to *self-interpretations* (e.g., p. 202). A distinction has to be made here. Habermas does indeed regard certain epochal shifts in collective identity as advances (e.g., from clan-based through state-centered to more abstract forms of identity); but at any one of these very general "developmental-logical" levels, there is room for an indefinite proliferation of particular collective self-interpretations. To make his point against Habermas's developmental approach, Hoy would have to be willing to argue, for instance, that in-group/out-group self-understandings in terms of religious fundamentalism, ethnic purity, neo-nationalism, and the like are, in general, neither superior nor inferior to the sort of tolerant, live-and-let-live self-understanding he pleads for. And that would be neither theoretically consistent nor practically sound.

What does all this have to do with genealogy or with critical historiography more generally? Habermas is emphatic in rejecting the notion that particular histories could be written as *applications* of general theories, whether theories of social evolution or of contemporary society. He does, however, hold that such theories can serve as *interpretive frameworks* for writing histories.[18] Hoy rejects this in the name of Foucault's (rhetorical) insistence on the local and particular. But Foucault's (actually existing) historical studies usually deal with epochal shifts from one "age," "episteme," "regime," or the like to another, often reaching from the Renaissance to the present, and sometimes, as in the *History of Sexuality*, even spanning the distance to the Ancient World. Perhaps it will be argued that while his genealogies are not "local," they are "specific." Sweeping histories of madness, sickness, punishment, and sexuality, especially when written as keys to the history of reason, truth, subjectivity, and the like, may be more "specific" than general theories of sociocultural development, but it is hard to see that they are more specific than, say, Weber's accounts of the rationalization of religion, law, and administration, or than the Frankfurt School's studies of authority and the family, music and art, mass culture, anti-Semitism, the authoritarian state, law and legal procedure, punishment, and state capitalism, or, for that matter, than Habermas's account of the structural transformation of the public sphere. The point of this line of argument is simply to establish that the differences at issue cannot be captured by the abstract opposition "history versus theory." Critical social theorists from Marx to Habermas have aimed, in the end, at social-theoretically informed critical histories of the present.

There is, to be sure, a difference from Foucault in their explicit elaboration of social-theoretical frames of interpretation. But Foucault's genealogies are hardly theory-free. In the 1970s, for instance, his "metatheory" of the internal relations between power and knowledge served as a general framework within which his critical histories were written. Then, too, there was the vaguely functionalist perspective implicit in his scattered remarks on just why it was that new regimes came to replace the old.[19] Beyond these, there were the (abstract and general) interpretive schemes that Foucault himself proposed from time to time.[20] My point is simply that the notion of "pure" genealogy is a myth. In his historical studies Foucault routinely made use of various general schemes, frames, pictures, perspectives, and the like, which were not so different in level or function from those used in critical social theory. And this should come as no surprise, for what Foucault is after in his genealogies is a "history of reason," of "the forms of rationality and knowledge," and of "the rational subject."[21] He wants to understand how "matters stand with the history of reason, with the ascendency of reason, and with the different forms in which the ascendency operates." And this, as he notes, is "the same question" that drives "the current of thought from Max Weber to Critical Theory . . . from Max Weber to Habermas."[22] They, like him, wanted to show that "the form of rationality presented as dominant, and endowed with the status of the one-and-only reason . . . is only *one* possible form among others."[23] But he, unlike them, holds that reason is "self-created," and so "you cannot assign a point at which reason would have lost sight of its fundamental project."[24] This, I think, is a more helpful situating of his similarities to and differences from the Weberian Marxism of the Frankfurt School. The issue between them is not whether to pursue general histories of rationality or to restrict oneself instead to particular local histories, but rather how best to write general histories. In deciding that issue, we cannot avoid comparatively evaluating the different metatheories and interpretive schemes that inform their approaches to the history of the present. I see no inherent virtue in leaving them largely implicit rather than working them out and assessing them, in both empirical and normative respects. My own view is that Foucault's powerful insights and techniques do not require, and indeed are not even compatible with, either his ontology of power or his totalistic conceptions of society, and that they can be developed more fruitfully as a continuation of, rather than as an alternative to, critical social theory.[25]

3   HERMENEUTICS

This repositioning of Habermas *vis-à-vis* Foucault may serve as well to refocus his differences with Gadamer. As we saw, like Foucault he aspires to a critical history of the present written with the practical-political intent of promoting a different future. But unlike Foucault, he holds that the interpretive frames they both rely upon in practice should be made explicit and subjected to ongoing scrutiny. In his view, the latter include general accounts of reason and rationality, of societal structures and processes, and of major transformations in the history of culture and society. And this view has implications for his relation to hermeneutics as well, for it implies that there is no intrinsic virtue in leaving the background of interpretive activity in pristine indeterminacy. Granted, as Hoy argues, that the background can never be rendered completely determinate (p. 161), we can nevertheless try to articulate some of its key elements and expose them to critical examination. And since very different assumptions on very important matters often do inform the conflicting interpretations of Foucault, Gadamer, Habermas, and other participants in the discourse of modernity, there is every good reason to do so. Our hermeneutic starting point ineluctably figures in our selection of key phenomena, the angle of vision we adopt on them, the categorial frame in which we articulate them, the judgments of significance we make about them, the connections we draw among them, and so on. When it includes broad views of the sorts just discussed, that has consequences for the kind of future we anticipate, the standpoint we adopt on the present, the way we understand our past, and the sense of community – the "we" – that we identify with. Such systematically generalized views are meant, then, not to replace interpretation and narrative but to inform and enrich them. They are *per se* neither too empty nor too thin to make a difference. And they certainly do not restrict the historian to writing "affirmative" narratives; in fact, it was Habermas's insistence on a *critical* historiography that was at the heart of his debate with Gadamer.[26] And Hoy's present efforts to conceive a genealogized hermeneutics might well be taken as an admission of sorts that he was right, that Gadamer's own conception of hermeneutics was conservatively slanted. But I will not pursue these intellectual-historical questions here. I want to focus instead on some of the claims Hoy raises for and about hermeneutics.

"No one," he writes, "should aspire any longer to a social theory that transcends its own socio-historical context and makes universal validity claims . . . [P]hilosophical hermeneutics . . . insists on the context-bounded-ness of understanding and sees theories . . . as contingent social actions themselves" (p. 172). I noted above that contingency is opposed to necessity and not to universality. (Physical theories are no less the product of contingent social actions than social theories, but that does not prevent them from plausibly claiming universal validity.) I also contended that universality should not be confused with infallibility, and that claims to universal validity are especially exposed to criticism and refutation. Finally, I recommended that we distinguish the various types of theoretical knowledge that enter into our interpretive frames from the concrete interpretations they inform. The issue that remains, it seems to me, is whether interpretations or the theories that inform them can and should claim a validity beyond the context in which they are put forward. As I want to focus now on interpretation, I shall simply repeat my contention that neither the necessity nor the desirability of abandoning the type of general social theory associated with the classical tradition has been convincingly argued. If put forward in a self-consciously fallibilistic spirit, the claims of general theories to context-transcending validity are at the same time an invitation to criticism from all sides: they carry only if and insofar as they can stand up to critical discussion. The more general the claim, the broader the invitation to join the discussion, and the greater the burden of justification on the claimant. Given this non-absolutist conception of theory, it is not clear how Hoy and other contextualists could object to any theoretical practice *in advance of*, or independently of, a consideration of its viability and usefullness. In the final section of this response, I shall consider some of Hoy's objections to tying any validity claim to expectations of universal consensus. For the present I will stick to issues of interpretation.

When used to cover everything from what are usually referred to as general theories to attempts at individual self-clarification, the term "interpretation" suffers greatly from indeterminacy. Analogies with "texts" and the "reading of texts" have been broadened to include just about every sort of cultural activity. This may have had some salutary effects in wringing the last gasps of life out of foundationalism, scientism, non-internal realism, ahistorical logocentrism, and the like, but it has also brought on a night in which everything appears an indistinguishable grey. Properly to assess the claims Hoy raises concerning the logic of interpretation – and they are, it should be noted, quite general claims – we would have to distinguish among very different types of interpretation – for instance, those dealing literally with texts from those dealing with various sorts of text analogues, within the former among religious, legal, philosophical, scientific, fictional, etc. texts, within the latter among historical, social, cultural, economic, political, psychological, etc. text analogues, and so on and so forth. And then in each type we would have to distinguish further the different sorts of interpretations constructed in different contexts for different purposes. At present, I shall confine myself to a few remarks on two broad types of interpretation Hoy singles out: critical history and self-understanding. The points I wish to stress are, first, that such interpretations are susceptible to critical-reflective examination and, second, that they can be examined under different aspects.

With regard to the former, the notions of "proliferation" and "multiplicity" that Hoy opposes to the idea of "one right interpretation" should be taken to mean not that "anything goes" but rather that "more than one thing goes" (p. 201). Since he retains the regulative idea of consistency in interpretation (p. 178), he will have to allow for conflicts of interpretation and for critical-reflective discourses dealing with them. If we were to understand those discourses, broadly speaking, in MacIntyre's terms, which Hoy does not rule out (p. 156), the conflicts would be expressed in familiar types of argument concerning the pros and cons of competing interpretations. In the case of historical interpretations, the burdens of such argument are not light, for one of the principal aspects under which historians debate their differences is a concern with truth. Denied the appeal to truth, with its attendant prescriptions concerning a critical use of sources and the like, historiographical discourse would be immensely impoverished, if not rendered simply incoherent.[27] Nevertheless, experience has shown that that appeal often does not suffice to eliminate all but "one right interpretation." And philosophical hermeneutics, with its rich elaborations of effective-historical consciousness, the hermeneutic circle, the interpretive standpoint with its preconceptions and pre-judgments, and the like, has contributed mightily to our understanding of why this should be the case. As for my disagreements with Hoy, they do not turn on denying the possibility, desirability, or even necessity of offering ever-new interpretations of the past from ever-changing points of view in the present and orientations toward the future. They have to do, rather, with the conditions under which this sort of proliferation should transpire. Relatively few historical interpretations manage to stand up to the pressures of critical-reflective examination. And the differences among those that do are often differences of perspective, interest, emphasis, and the like, that is, the sorts of differences that might possibly be reconciled in a more comprehensive interpretation. According to Gadamer, it is some such regulative idea of completeness, of an ideal unity of sense, that structures historiographical discourse.

Hoy allows that such a "critical monism" regarding interpretations might reasonably be held, but he regards its regulative ideas as "empty" and thus prefers to adopt a "critical pluralism" (p. 200). At least in the field of historical interpretation, which he singles out, the ideas of completeness and unity or coherence seem anything but empty. For one thing, they are an important impetus to the proliferation that Hoy espouses. They spur historians ongoingly to examine and re-examine materials from ever-changing points of view and thereby to produce new historical accounts, ongoingly to test the consistency of those accounts against the expanses of historical research regarded as "well established" and to adjust for inconsistencies in one way or another, and ongoingly to construct more comprehensive accounts that integrate novel insights into a coherent sense of the whole. They also serve to instigate the sorts of challenge to claimed unity and completeness characteristic of genealogical and decontructionist historiography. Hegel taught us long ago that the dialectic lives from such claims. Without them, I am afraid, we would likely drift into an uncritical pluralism of "whatever serves your purposes, whatever they may be." The point of stressing the regulative character of these ideas is to turn attention away from metaphysical issues and toward questions of historiographical practice: with what idealizing assumptions do historians normally work and what would their discourses look like if they tried to do without them? Can we write *history* – in contrast, say, to fiction, propaganda, or rationalization – without being oriented to the idea of truth? And can we be so oriented without getting into just the sorts of debates that historians, including critical historians, typically engage in? These are the kinds of questions for which Hoy will have to find convincing answers if he is to persuade us to de-emphasize the idea of truth in favor of that of usefulness, and the idea of coherent unity in favor of that of proliferation. A more dialectical approach might suggest that we should trace the internal relations between such seemingly opposed pairs.

Part of the explanation for Hoy's emphasis on pluralism is the context in which he discusses the idea of a genealogical hermeneutics. The interest that guides him is fundamentally an ethical one: self-understanding as a key to the good life. Unlike Aristotle, he no longer believes that there is, in general, one right path to the good life. The pluralism of forms of social life and the individualism of forms of personal life have rendered that view implausible in the contemporary world. Unlike Gadamer, he is also skeptical of the idea that unbroken traditions might be hermeneutically continued so as to furnish culturally specific, yet normative, conceptions of the good life. He holds instead to the (late-) Foucaultian idea that each individual's life might be a work of art, and from that perspective he rejects the idea of a general self-understanding that is normative for all members of the species or of a culture. I have argued elsewhere that the aesthetics of personal existence is an inadequate ethical-political response to a world in which misery and injustice are rampant.[28] If aspirations to self-invention are to be limited by considerations of justice, we have to ask what kinds of social orders will put such limits into effect and how those limits can be justified to those who are supposed to feel bound by them. To be sure, Hoy is also in favor of an overarching framework of justice; but that then demands its own reflective elaboration. We also have to investigate the social, economic, political, and cultural conditions that perpetuate misery and injustice and render the chances of making one's life into a work of art very different at different societal locations. And for that we need a critical theory of contemporary society at the level of Marx's *Capital* or Habermas's *Theory of Communicative Action*, which enables us to view universal justice and individual goods in complementary rather than oppositional terms. Although Hoy does not address himself to these general levels of practical reasoning, he cannot do without it if he does not want his pluralism to degenerate into a war of all against all.

I have used the – admittedly vague – term "theory" to characterize some of the elements missing from Hoy's approach to critical thinking, because I want to stress that they have in principle to be defended in free and open discussion with any and all interlocutors. That is, the claims to validity of theories of justice or of contemporary society or of social evolution are not context-bound in the way that Hoy insists "social-theoretical interpreta-tions" inevitably are (p. 172). Such theories can legitimately be contested from standpoints outside the context in which they originate, precisely because they claim a general validity on grounds that no competent, well-informed person could reasonably reject. The same cannot be said for the *self*-interpretations that are the crux of Hoy's argument. The self-understand-ings that figure in personal and collective identities are indeed context-bound in ways that general theories are not. *All* intellectual activity is, to be sure "contingent social action" (p. 172) and as such "bound" in some sense to the context in which it is carried out. But it is a fateful *non sequitur* to sup-pose that this ontological condition suffices to show that the meaning and validity of the claims that arise from the various activities are all tied *in the same way* to their contexts of origin – as if there were not important differ-ences between such "contingent" activities as doing mathematics, physics, history, or criticism. We have to attend in each case to the nature of the rea-soning involved, the scope of the audience intended, the sorts of considera-tions that are relevant, the types of criticisms that have to be faced, and so on. In the case of collective self-interpretations, there are specific ways in which deliberation remains context-bound.[29] Public discussion of such mat-ters typically takes place within the horizons of shared histories, traditions, forms of life. The cogency or persuasive power of the considerations offered in support of different views derives in significant measure from those shared backgrounds. The intended audience is the "we" projected in the proposed self-interpretation. And the basic concern is with who "we" are and who "we" want to be. But this does not mean that there are no univer-salizable *aspects* of such discussions.

As Hoy notes, traditions typically comprise conflicts of interpretations; they are ambiguous and often divided legacies that can be taken up and con-tinued in very different ways. And as Gadamer has convincingly argued, the sorts of historical self-understanding involved have practical – ethical and political – implications. The question of who "we" have been is intimately linked with those of who "we" are and who "we" want to be. In Heidegger's parlance, identity is a matter of "thrown projection," in which past, present, and future are inextricably intertwined. That our relation to the past is interpretively mediated does not mean, however, that it has nothing to do with truth claims.[30] At least since historical scholarship became animated with nationalistic aspirations in the last century, debates concerning *"wie es eigentlich gewesen war"* have been part and parcel of collective identity formation. And it has been particularly important to *critical* hermeneutics that public self-understandings can *also* be scrutinized under this aspect. To take a recent example, Habermas's intervention in the German *Historikerstreit* turned importantly on issues of truth in combatting the attempt by conservative politicians and their historian allies to rewrite German history for purposes of "putting the National Socialist past behind us."[31] Questions concerning the causes, nature, and scope of the Holocaust were central to that debate, as were questions concerning the extent of support enjoyed by the National Socialist regime, its main war aims (particularly as regards the Soviet Union), the behavior of the German Army on the Eastern Front in 1944/45, the ways in which the German citizenry did and did not "come to terms with the past" in the 1950s, and so on. It was absolutely crucial to blocking the effort to "normalize" the past for purposes of re-establishing continuity with a superseded political identity that it could be thematized under the aspect of historical truth: did it or did it not measure up to international standards of historical scholarship.

It was also important that the revisionary undertaking could be discussed under context-transcending aspects of right; for the identity the revisionist historians aimed to shore up involved strongly contextualized notions of responsibility. Is it right, for example, to interpret the events of that period from the perspective of daily life, personal experience, local community, and the like, so as to cramp the vision of nationally organized horrors? Is it right to place the sufferings of the Jews on a moral par with that of the Germans? Is it right to put the fascist past behind us now the better to get on with the business of the present? Is it right to project a future centered on German exceptionalism, its "middle-European" geopolitical position, and its "cultural" distance from the "civilization" of the West with its heritage of universal rights and principles? These questions are illustrative of the important role that aspects of moral, legal, and political right can, do, and should play in public processes of collective self-interpretation. Projected group identities can be criticized not only for lies, distortions, and half-truths about the past, but also for the unfairness they show and the harm they do to minorities within and strangers without. The power of the critical interpretations developed in connection with the contemporary politics of identity, it seems to me, also depends crucially on the context-transcending import of these two aspects of self-understanding, truth and rightness.

Though viable group-identities have to respect claims to truth and justice – if for no other reason than to avoid making themselves easy targets in the public conflicts of interpretation that are increasingly typical of ethical-political deliberations in pluralistic and democratic societies – they certainly cannot be derived from them. For identities are as Hoy says irreducibly plural, and that plurality is bound up with the incalculable diversity of individual and group life-histories and forms of life. This is also the case with "truthful" and "righteous" identities, that is, those incorporating a respect for and orientation to truth and justice. These are not the only publicly debatable aspects of self-interpretations. Questions of well-being, self-fulfillment, and authenticity, while not context-transcending in the same way, are no less arguable. The fact that we no longer expect them to have one right answer for everybody, does not render public deliberation about them pointless. Practical reasoning in a particular context is still practical *reasoning*; and insofar as the context is common to the parties to the discussion, the cogency of reasons or their lack of it is an intersubjective matter. While Hoy acknowledges the conflicts of interpretation at the heart of virtually every tradition, he tends, like most contextualists, to treat the recognition of difference as the end of the story rather than as the beginning of discussion and debate, which, as Mill famously reminded us, are the lifeblood of cultural and political affairs in a democratic society. Public disagreements are played out in the public sphere. Members of the "we" assumed or projected in public discussion can enter the fray, contest the ideals and strong evaluations appealed to, argue that a proposed arrangement is not, all things considered, good for "us" in the long run, criticize the conception of who "we" are and want to be that is behind it, unmask the illusions or self-deceptions involved in it, and so on. Thus, in the German historians' debate, in addition to questions of truth and justice, issues of these latter sorts figured prominently. Do we (Germans) really want to re-establish continuity with *those* aspects of our heritage? Or with others? And how? Should German identity center around particularities of German culture and tradition or be oriented more strongly to values and principles shared with other democratic, pluralistic societies? Should the anti-Communism Germans share with the latter be taken as more basic to their identity than commitments to the rule of law, popular sovereignty, or international justice? Should post-War generations spend less time talking about the past and get on with their lives, or should they somehow assume responsibility for it and try to come to terms with it? The notion of responsibility does not figure centrally in the aesthetics of self-making, particularly not that of our responsibilities to others. This is a fatal flaw. Individual identities are formed in and through social relations, group identities are shaped in complex webs of cultural interaction and social interdependency, and local identities are increasingly refracted through global networks. In a world in which larger and larger waves of politically and economically driven migrants press or are pressed against the walls of national identities, eighteenth-century cosmopolitanism seems a better starting point for thinking about collective identity.

4 PLURALISM

It should be evident by now that critical theory of the Habermasian sort is in no way "opposed to pluralism" (p. 200). It simply refuses to equate it with "anything goes" and insists that an acceptable pluralism requires an over-arching framework of justice, so that one group's well-being does not come at the expense of another's. In Hoy's argument, the suggestion that critical social theory is somehow unfriendly to pluralism is tied to Habermas's expli-cation of the meaning of validity in terms of rationally motivated consensus. Once again, it will be important to resituate the issues before addressing them. To begin with, Habermas has consistently restricted the focus of his analysis of justification to *discourse* – critical, reflective, argumentative dia-logue – *about questions of truth and justice*. He does not claim, and in fact explicity denies, that suppositions of like universality attach to critique or textual interpretation, or to discussions of ethics, politics, identity, and the good life. In such matters, differences in context and perspective do influ-ence the form and substance of deliberation in ways that restrict the scope of claims to validity – for instance, to claims about who *we* are and want to be, about what is good *for us* in the long run, or the like.[32] Furthermore, even in those types of discourse which Habermas does see as structured by a suppo-sition of there being one right answer – so that two conflicting views cannot both be correct – he does not treat consensus as *determining* validity.[33] "Social agreement" is not the "arbitrator of validity" (p. 174), nor is validity "founded on consensus" (p. 177). Thus the contrast that Hoy draws between Gadamer's privileging of *die Sache*, what is being talked about, and Habermas's privileging of agreement among those talking is misleading (pp. 189–90). Both *Verständigung* and *die Sache* figure centrally in *both* analy-ses: dialogue and discourse are oriented toward achieving mutual under-standing *concerning* the matter under discussion.

Habermas's discourse theory of validity is not meant to *define* either truth or moral rightness but to offer an account of what is involved in "redeem-ing" or *justifying* truth and rightness claims.[34] Cast in epistemic rather than in ontological terms, it attempts to elucidate the pragmatic presuppositions of the critical-reflective discourses in which such claims are debated. And it is in that context that notions like rational assertability, rational acceptability, and agreement under ideal conditions figure. Hoy asks us to choose between the view that "agreeing to something makes it true" – "truth as the result of agreement" – and the view that "we agree to something because it is true" – "agreement as the result of truth" (p. 189). But there is quite a bit of space between these two poles, and it is there that we will find Habermas. As Hoy himself acknowledges, our only access to the *Sache* and the truth about it is through language. Thus neither can be set over against agreement in language, either the global sorts of agreement that Wittgenstein held to be presuppositions of making sense at all, or the more domain-specific sorts of agreement that we rely on in regard to this or that subject matter. In domains of inquiry in which critical-reflective discourse has been institutionalized, the achievement of agreement rests on an argumentative weighing of reasons pro and con. There, it is not because we agree that we judge a claim to be valid; rather, we agree because we have grounds for granting its validity. It is not the agreement that warrants the claim but the warrants for the claim that ground the agreement. To make his case against Habermas on this point, Hoy would have to explain how truth can produce agreement in a way that is not epistemically mediated through evidence and argument. But that would be inconsistent with his own hermeneutic position.

Where does this leave us? The real issue, it seems to me, is whether critical-reflective discourse about claims to truth and justice rests on the pragmatic presupposition of there being one right answer, to which any reasonable, well-informed person could rationally agree under ideal conditions. Spelling out such conditions is, of course, notoriously problematic.[35] But that is not my concern here, since Hoy objects to the very idea of there being an internal relation between truth or rightness and universal acceptability, no matter under what conditions. I argued in *Critical Theory* that scientific discourse about the objective world is guided by the supposition of there being one truth about the world, and I will not repeat that argument here. The challenge it presents to Hoy is to provide an alternative, more plausible reconstruction of scientific discourse that does not include that supposition. The more difficult cases for my position are truth claims about the *human* world, and many of the difficulties lie parallel to two questions that Hoy analytically distinguishes and then ("contingently") reconnects: (1) whether there is only one right understanding of a sociohistorical "text," and (2) whether sociocultural differences call for a higher community with shared principles (p. 178). I will follow his analytical distinction in my response.

(a)   The key issue in what Hoy calls the "hermeneutical question" is one that divided Habermas and Gadamer in their influential exchange. Habermas aspired to a *theory* of communicative action, by which he meant at least the following: a coherent set of truth claims about the social world, which have to be defended against reasoned criticism from whatever quarter. The latter is part of what is meant by saying that their validity is context-transcending. Does Hoy think we can do without theoretical, context-transcending truth claims altogether? Not entirely. He acknowledges the "paradoxical" nature of the "metatheoretical" claims that make up the core of his reply, for they are themselves context-transcending claims about the nature of truth, mean-

ing, interpretation, historicity, and the like. As we saw, that paradox is typical of contextualist arguments generally. Hoy handles the appearance of
contradiction by distinguishing metatheories from first-order theories or
interpretations. While the former may properly claim context-transcending
validity, the latter may not (p. 201). But this claim itself depends on his
metatheory being the right one, and thus is not the end but the beginning of
disagreement. Moreover, the considerations that Hoy advances in defense of
his metatheory look suspiciously like *substantive* claims about language,
interpretation, and so forth. That should come as no surprise, for there is a
long history of failed attempts to distinguish "meta" from "object" languages. What we in fact have are two competing, substantive accounts of
certain aspects of sociocultural life, each claiming to be not just "true for us"
but "true, period." And if those substantive claims can legitimately aspire to
context-transcending validity, there is no obvious reason why others may
not as well. Nor is Hoy's metatheory neutral with respect to "first-order"
interpretations. It implies, for instance, that any interpretation which fails to
recognize the variability of forms of life or the interpretational nature of
worldviews and self-understanding is inadequate, for it conflicts with central
insights of the (one right) metatheory.

The fact that postmodernist thinkers invariably suppose much of what
they are denying is of particular significance in an argument *about* unavoidable presuppositions. Be that as it may, Hoy might want to argue that whatever presuppositions the genealogical hermeneut does rely upon, they do
not include the expectation of rationally motivated consensus. And here, it
seems to me, we have the nub of his criticism of Habermas. Reasoned discourse about the human world has, since Socrates, been structured around
the assumption that one view of a given matter (*Sache*) is better than competing views, and that argumentation, if carried out properly, will show us
in the long run which it is – which has the preponderance of reasons on its
side. If this supposition were dropped, the nature of discursive activity would
change significantly; and that would have practical consequences, for in
many areas of life there are no clear alternatives to reasoned discourse of the
familiar sorts. At the same time, discussions about the human world often
seem interminable. We have gotten used to living with unresolved disagreements in all the "human sciences," where what Kuhn calls the "preparadig-
matic" stage seems never to be superseded by "normal science," as regularly
happens in the natural sciences. We even have plausible explanations of
why this should be the case, and they turn on the ineliminable interpretive
dimension of social inquiry and the standpoint-bound character of interpretation.[36] Hoy insists on these same features and concludes that we have to
drop the supposition that there is a unique truth about the human world. Is
there no alternative?

I argued above that historical interpretations can and should be critically
examined under the aspect of their truth to the facts.[37] The same holds for

interpretations of the social world generally. Hoy will point out that this is normally not sufficient to eliminate all but one interpretation of a given domain of phenomena, precisely because of the standpoint-boundness or contextuality of interpretive activity. "An interpretation," he notes, "can only illuminate at the cost of shading over or leaving out. . . . [This] does not imply . . . that all interpretations misrepresent what they are about. They capture aspects of the *Sache* correctly, but the *Sache* is more complex than any single interpretation can possibly be" (p. 191). This is true. But if one adds the regulative constraints of consistency and coherence, then the space for an "irreducible plurality" of equally good interpretations considerably narrows: for an interpretation to stand up over time to critical scrutiny, it will have not only to square with the agreed upon facts and the accepted methods for determining them, but will have to be internally consistent and cohere with everything else we think we know about the domain under consideration, or it will have to defend its failure to do so by challenging elements (including purported facts) of the established consensus. The conflict of interpretations in history and the social sciences is normally carried out under just such constraints. They are what structure the conflict as a reasoned discourse, as a debate about which is the best interpretation, all things considered. And yet, the debate frequently fails to end in consensus; there often remains a plurality of viable candidates for "the best interpretation." But the pragmatically important point is not that discourse should always lead to rational agreement, but that it should be carried out *as if* rational agreement about which is the right, or at least the best, interpretation were possible. The pluralism that then remains is not that of self-encapsulated, incommensurable points of view, but of different voices in an ongoing discursive consideration of the reasons for and against competing views. That is to say, it is a critical pluralism closer to what John Stuart Mill espoused than to the cultural archipelagos envisioned by radical contextualists.

(b)   It is not clear to me in which of these directions Hoy wants to go. He expressly recommends a critical pluralism (p. 200). But some of his arguments seem to undercut it, for instance, the suggestion that to claim one's views are right or better than competing views borders on intolerance, disrespect, and ethnocentrism (p. 203). If rational discourse about what is true or morally right presupposes an ideal of uncoerced consensus, and if we believe we have good reasons for our beliefs, then, he argues, we have to suppose that ideally others should agree with us – and that is ethnocentric. But *all* parties come to the discussion thinking they have good reasons for holding the beliefs they do. Respect for opposing views is shown not by granting, prior to any discussion, that they are just as good as one's own but by listening carefully to them, trying honestly to understand them, weighing fairly the grounds on which they are held, and being open to the possibility that they *may* prove superior to one's own. This is what one expects, ideally, from all parties to a rational discourse. It is the sort of respect we show to those we regard as our moral and intellectual equals.[38] Lack of respect is not, then, endemic to the very idea of argumentative discourse, but only to some of the ways it has been put into practice. Hoy's contention that Habermas's way belongs among these rests on attributing to him a principle of charity in interpretation which supposes that "most of our beliefs must be true" (p. 203). But Habermas's position on that is much closer to the one I sketched in Chapter 3 of *Critical Theory*: the interpreter must suppose that the views she wants to understand are by and large held for reasons that make sense in their context. And, as I argued in section 3.4, the question of whether they are reasons that could convince her in the end must be left to critical-reflective dialogue. The "charity" required for understanding others' views requires neither, *pace* Davidson, supposing most of their beliefs to be true (from our perspective) nor, *pace* Hoy's reading of Habermas, supposing most of our own to be true. It means supposing that, like us, they hold their views for reasons that have to be understood, appreciated, and discursively weighed. This model of interpretive understanding leaves open the question of whose views will turn out to be superior in a given respect.

But not entirely open, Hoy might well reply, since the social-evolutionary components of Habermas's interpretive frame ensure that the interpretation of some types of traditional views will represent them from the start as "pre-modern" and hence not up to discursive par (p. 204). Here I can only refer back to what I argued at some length in *Critical Theory*. All the participants in the discourse of modernity, including Hoy, rely on presuppositions that mark their standpoints as post-traditional. There is no getting round that. He is committed, for instance, to regarding putatively timeless, necessary truths as in need of "unmasking" (p. 207). His target is traditional metaphysics and its disguised continuations; but of course a similar "unself-consciousness of contingency" applies to much vaster domains of traditional *and* – hermeneutically and genealogically unenlightened – contemporary thought. He insists that unmasking not be understood as "seeing through illusions" or "showing us how society really is" (p. 207), but he clearly does hold that timelessness and necessity (really) are illusions that have to be dispelled or "deconstructed." And he clearly does believe that critical historiography discloses reality in important ways: "genealogical research will show that self-understandings that are taken as universal, eternal, and necessary [really] have a history with a [real] beginning and therefore, possibly, an end" (p. 207, my additions). In these respects, at least, new interpretations may be better interpretations because, being historically and hermeneutically enlightened, they capture better the way things really are.

I agree with Hoy that "things" should not be understood here to refer to "things in themselves" or even to *Gegenstände* in the sense of the objects of the natural sciences (p. 193). Inquiry in the human sciences has to do with *Sachen* that are always already interpreted; it aims at interpretations of interpretations. As interpretations are always from a point of view, and as interpretive points of view are themselves variable, "no interpretation is ever final (even ideally) . . . new interpretations will always be needed" (p. 190). This holds for our conception of what it is we have to understand no less than for our understanding of it: "the *Sache* is not eternal, but is itself evolving with the history of interpretation" (p. 190). This internal historicity of the objects of the human sciences means that even "the ideal of a complete or final representation" is out of place there (p. 190). As Gadamer has put it, "whereas the object of the natural sciences can be described *idealiter* as what would be known in the perfect, complete knowledge of nature, it is senseless to speak of a perfect or complete knowledge of history . . . [or] of an object in itself toward which research is directed" (quoted on p. 193). Picking up on the same line of thought, Albrecht Wellmer has argued that while the notion of an ideal language of unified science seems to make sense, the notion of a single, ideal language of interpretation does not.[39] Our finitude and historicity mean that we have unendingly to construct new interpretations from ever-changing points of view.

On this point I am in agreement with Hoy. Even if we grant with Habermas the possibility of incorporating general theories and metatheories into our interpretive frames, and thus of reducing to some extent their contextuality, that will not eliminate the need to adopt particular points of view on particular phenomena. A structural description of "post-traditional" modes of consciousness, for example, does not of itself capture the myriad, different, concrete shapes of consciousness compatible with it. Nor can a general model of the basic structures and dynamics of developed capitalist societies itself explain the different historical shapes they take. As a result, there is every reason to expect the conflict of interpretations to be a permanent feature of human studies. But the consequences of this need not be those Hoy envisions. If interpretations can *also* be assessed under the aspects of truth, internal consistency, and coherence with other bodies of knowledge and interpretation, then, this conflict can take the form of critical-reflective discourse. Hoy sets dialogue in opposition to the regulative ideas of universality and consensus; in reality, those ideas are often its driving force. Dialogue in the form of discourse lives from the effort to persuade interlocutors of the validity of one's claims. And if they are claims to truth or rightness *tout court*, the circle of potential interlocutors is in principle without limits. I suggested in *Critical Theory* that this has to be given a pragmatic formulation. The rhetorical occasions for reasoned persuasion are constantly changing, and with them the partners, contexts, and purposes of dialogue. Thus, I argued, we have to see the vindication of universal validity claims through the reasoned agreement of a universal audience as something that is always only ongoingly accomplished, in ever-changing circumstances, and for all practical purposes. At the same time, the discourses that serve as the vehicle for this are guided by ideas of truth and justice, *foci imaginaria*, without which these types of communicative activity would be impossible. Of course, it would be an error or, as Kant would say, a transcendental illusion to take these "subjective necessities" (i.e. pragmatic presuppositions) of discourse to be "objective necessities in things," and then either to affirm or to deny them as such. What is at stake here are the requirements of a certain type of activity.

Hoy sometimes seems to be suggesting that we could do without them. He writes, for instance, that while Habermas's "meta-procedural" ideal of uncoerced consensus may be hard to disagree with, it is too "empty" to be of consequence, and in any case is not "necessary" (p. 176). Against the charge of emptiness and lack of "epistemological or normative import" (p. 179), I will simply reaffirm the (pragmatist) view that the idea of settling cognitive and moral disagreements by reasoned discourse and uncoerced consensus rather than by force, authority, dogma, or the like is perhaps without equal in its consequences for civilization.[40] The fact that this idea has a history seems to indicate that it is not necessary. But what is the sense of necessity at issue here? Neither side is arguing for metaphysical or transcendental necessity. Habermas's claim is that the idea of uncoerced, reasoned agreement is a pragmatic presupposition of certain types of discursive practice which are central to modern forms of life and to which we have no viable alternatives. So what Hoy has to argue is that we could do without practices, like the one in which we engaged, in which claims are advanced on grounds meant to persuade any competent and reasonable judge. I will leave the very considerable burden of that proof to him.

*ACKNOWLEDGMENT

This chapter first appeared as pp. 217–48 of a book written by David Couzens Hoy and myself (*Critical Theory*, Cambridge Mass.: Blackwell, 1994), and is my response to Hoy's critique of critical theory, which he presented in the preceding part of the book. Parenthetical citations to Hoy in the text are to that work.

NOTES

1 The lack of elaborated foundations in Marx explains the repeated attempts by "*praxis* philosophers," beginning with the young – Heideggerian – Marcuse, to flesh out Marx's notion of social practice.

2 See Jürgen Habermas, *Communication and the Evolution of Society*, trans. T. McCarthy (Cambridge, Mass.: MIT Press, 1976), pp. 95–177.

3 George E. Marcus and Michael M. J. Fischer, *Anthropology as Cultural Critique* (Chicago: The University of Chicago Press, 1986), p. 77.

4   *The Theory of Communicative Action*, 2 vols, trans. T. McCarthy (Boston: Beacon Press, 1984, 1987), vol. 1, p. 6.

5   Ibid., pp. 137–40.

6   The German phrase is Gadamer's, from "Rhetorik, Hermeneutik und Ideologiekritik," in K. O. Apel et al., *Hermeneutik und Ideologiekritik* (Frankfurt: Suhrkamp Verlag, 1971), pp. 57–82, here p. 78.

7   Fine applies this image to the realism/anti-realism debates in "And Not Anti-Realism Either," *Nous* 18 (1984): 51–65.

8   See Jürgen Habermas, *Knowledge and Human Interests*, trans. J. J. Shapiro (Boston: Beacon Press, 1971).

9   See Richard Rorty, "Postmodernist Bourgeois Liberalism," in Rorty, *Objectivity, Relativism, and Truth* (Cambridge, UK: Cambridge University Press, 1991), pp. 197–202; and Michel Foucault, "On the Genealogy of Ethics," in P. Rabinow (ed.), *The Foucault Reader* (New York: Pantheon, 1984), p. 350.

10   Cf. Nancy Fraser, "Foucault on Modern Power: Empirical Insights and Normative Confusions," in Fraser, *Unruly Practices* (Minneapolis: University of Minnesota Press, 1989), pp. 17–34. Like postmodernists generally, Hoy implicitly ties his hopes for a better world to "genuine" enlightenment – in his case, genealogical and hermeneutic self-understanding – though in discussing Horkheimer and Adorno he dismisses any such tie as an "utopian illusion" (p. 115).

11   See *The Theory of Communicative Action*, vol. 1, pp. 235–42.

12   Thus in *Communication and the Evolution of Society* he clearly distinguishes developmental logics from learning processes under contingent conditions, on pp. 140ff.

13   Claims of this kind are pervasive in developmental studies of linguistic, cognitive, interpersonal, and moral learning processes. For a naturalist, whether they are justified can only be a matter of which are the best empirical theories of the domains in question – and not a matter for conceptual legislation.

14   See Thomas McCarthy, *Ideals and Illusions* (Cambridge, Mass.: The MIT Press, 1991), chapter 5.

15   One source of our differences is Hoy's focus on Habermas's "Geschichte und Evolution", in J. Habermas, *Zur Rekonstruktion des Historischen Materialismus* (Frankfurt: Suhrkamp Verlag, 1976), pp. 200–59, an essay written to counter Niklas Luhmann's systems-theoretic approach to history. It contains formulations that can be misleading when taken out of that context. There are more straightforward formulations in *Communication and the Evolution of Society* and *The Theory of Communicative Action*.

16   *Communication and the Evolution of Society*, p. 154.

17   For an overview, see Thomas McCarthy, *The Critical Theory of Jürgen Habermas* (Cambridge, Mass.: The MIT Press, 1978), pp. 232–71.

18   That is, the "narrative perspective" of the critical historian may include an "interpretive frame" informed by such theories ("Geschichte und Evolution," pp. 203–7). In an interview with Perry Anderson and Peter Dews, Habermas goes so far as to say that theories of the type that interest him "prove their worth in the end only by contributing to the explanation of concrete historical processes." Peter Dews (ed.), *Habermas: Autonomy and Solidarity* (London: Verso, 1986), p. 167.

19   Cf. Axel Honneth, *The Critique of Power*, trans. K. Baynes (Cambridge, Mass.: The MIT Press, 1991), chapter 6.

20   Some of these are discussed in T. McCarthy, *Ideals and Illusions*, chapter 2.

21   Michel Foucault, "Structuralism and Post-Structuralism: An Interview with Gérard Raulet," *Telos* 55 (1983): 195–211, here pp. 198ff.

22   Ibid., p. 200.

23   Ibid., p. 201.

24   Ibid., p. 202.

25 There are many passages in which Foucault even sounds like a neo-Marxist. For instance, in *Power/Knowledge,* trans. Colin Gordon et al. (New York: Pantheon, 1980), he says that we have to understand how low-level mechanisms of power became "economically advantageous and politically useful" to the "real interests" of the bourgeois "system" and how, "as a natural consequence, all of a sudden they came to be colonized and maintained by global mechanisms and the entire State system. It is only if we grasp these techniques of power and demonstrate the economic advantages or political utility that derives from them in a given context for specific reasons, that we can understand how these mechanisms come to be incorporated into the social whole" (p. 101). Indications of some sort of materialist functionalism can be found in his historical studies as well. See, for instance, *Discipline and Punish,* trans. A. Sheridan (New York: Vintage, 1979), pp. 220–2, where he cites Marx's *Capital.*

26 See Georgia Warnke, *Gadamer: Hermeneutics, Tradition and Reason* (Oxford: Polity, 1987), chap. 4. The passage from Habermas Hoy cites concerning the "affirmative" character of history ("Geschichte und Evolution," p. 245) has to be read in context. That it is not meant to deny the "critical potential" of historical writing becomes evident on the following page, where Habermas discusses "critically oriented history" that aims not to reaffirm an established tradition but to foster a different one, such as "a history of blocked liberalization, of suppressed social struggles, [or] of missed emancipation, a Benjaminian history from the standpoint of the victims" (p. 246).

27 The idea of truth is equally important to *critical* discourse. Removing the appeal to truth from the "weapons of critique" risks delivering up the conflict of interpretation to the balance of power.

28 See *Ideals and Illusions,* pp. 67–75.

29 See Jürgen Habermas, "On the Pragmatic, the Ethical, and the Moral Employments of Practical Reason," in *Justification and Application: Remarks on Discourse Ethics,* trans. Ciaran Cronin (Cambridge, Mass.: MIT Press, 1993), pp. 1–17.

30 On p. 191 Hoy seems to endorse a similar view, when he writes that though interpretations do not "mirror an independent reality" they can "capture aspects of the *Sache* correctly." Since the *Sache* is always linguistically mediated, this amounts, he notes (212, n. 35), to a kind of "internal realism" not unlike the one that Hilary Putnam sketches in *Reason, Truth, and History* (Cambridge: Cambridge University Press, 1981). He does not consider, however, that Putnam explicates the notion of truth basic to his internal realism in terms of "idealized rational acceptability" or "rational acceptability under ideal conditions" (p. 55). This comes very close to Habermas's version of an internal realism tied to rational consensus under ideal conditions.

31 On what follows see chapters 9 and 10 of Jürgen Habermas, *The New Conservatism,* trans. S. Nicholsen (Cambridge, Mass.: The MIT Press, 1989). For a brief overview of the controversy, see Robert Holub, *Jürgen Habermas: Critic in the Public Sphere* (New York: Routledge, 1991), pp. 162–89. For a broader treatment, see Charles Maier, *The Unmasterable Past* (Cambridge, Mass.: Harvard University Press, 1988).

32 By and large, these are the matters that concern Hoy in chapter 6. The difference in focus may account for some of the differences in views. Habermas discusses the varying scope of the different types of critical reflection and the claims that issue from them in *The Theory of Communicative Action,* vol. 1, pp. 20–4, and in *Justification and Application, passim.*

33 Some of his earliest formulations of the discourse theory of truth might be read in that way, especially those in "Wahrheitstheorien," in H. Fahrenbach (ed.), *Wirklichkeit und Reflexion* (Pfullingen: Neske, 1973), pp. 211–66. But his subsequent formulations are clear on this point. See, for instance, *The Theory of Communicative Action,* vol. 1, pp. 316–18.

34 Again, the later formulations are clearer on this point than the earlier. See the previous footnote and Habermas's "Reply," in A. Honneth and H. Joas (eds), *Communicative Action* (Cambridge, Mass.: The MIT Press, 1991), pp. 231ff.

35 Habermas's earliest efforts issued in the notion of an "ideal speech situation," which has been a magnet for criticism ever since. See "Wahrheitstheorien."

36   Cf. the essays collected in *Understanding and Social Inquiry*, F. Dallmayer and T. McCarthy (eds), (Notre Dame: University of Notre Dame Press, 1977); and *The Interpretive Turn*, D. Hiley, J. Bohman and R. Shusterman (eds), (Ithaca: Cornell University Press, 1991).

37   To say that there are no uninterpreted facts is not to say that there are no facts. And to say that factual claims are inherently contestable does not mean that agreement on facts is impossible. These two common errors indicate that we need a new theory of facts.

38   Compare the "politics of mutual respect" discussed by Amy Gutmann and Dennis Thompson, "Moral Conflict and Political Consensus," in R. Douglass, G. Mara, and H. Richardson (eds), *Liberalism and the Good* (New York: Routledge, 1990), pp. 125–47.

39   Albrecht Wellmer, *The Persistence of Modernity* (Cambridge, Mass.: The MIT Press, 1991), pp. 168–82.

40   Cf. C. S. Peirce, "The Fixation Belief," in P. Wiener (ed.), *Charles S. Peirce: Selected Writings* (New York: Dover, 1958), pp. 91–112.

16 PATHOLOGIES OF THE SOCIAL: THE PAST AND PRESENT OF SOCIAL PHILOSOPHY

Axel Honneth
(translated by James Swindal)

Like all areas of theoretical investigation, philosophy has in the last two hundred years undertaken a process of internal division which has led to the development of a number of subdisciplines and specialties. Even though introductory texts today often are categorized by the classic threefold division of theoretical, practical and aesthetic philosophy, new specialties have been worked out in the practice of academic philosophy which barely fit the old pattern. In the realm of practical philosophy – originally a discipline which included only ethics, political philosophy, and the philosophy of law – a new development has led to a multiplicity of disciplines within which the borders between the individual subspecialities are beginning to become more blurred. Today hardly anyone knows exactly where the particular lines of division are drawn between moral philosophy, political philosophy, the philosophy of history, and cultural philosophy.

In this confused terrain, social philosophy in the German-speaking world has increasingly taken on the role of a residual discipline. Indeterminant in its relation to the neighboring fields of study, by default it functions as an overarching organization for all practically oriented subdisciplines, a normative supplement for empirically oriented sociology, and an interpretative undertaking that is time diagnostic.[1] In Anglo-Saxon lands, on the other hand, since the early days of utilitarianism an understanding of social philosophy has emerged that is roughly what in Germany has been conceived as "political philosophy": a study which emphasizes normative questions that are revealed in the places where the reproduction of civil society requires the intervention of the state (the maintenance of property, the apportioning of punishment, healthcare, etc.).[2] Though this selection of undertakings has the advantage of providing social philosophy with a clear task, it inevitably has the disadvantage of causing it a certain loss of identity. Social philosophy consists no longer of an independent object domain or a distinct set of questions, but has become a lesser strain of political philosophy.

If these two independent developments are viewed together, it is not difficult to ascertain that social philosophy finds itself in a precarious situation today. In the Germanic realm by expansion of its domain it is on the verge of developing into a awkward discipline, while in the Anglo-Saxon realm due to the restriction of its domain it threatens to become a subdiscipline of political philosophy that no longer possesses independent features. To counteract both of these dangers, this chapter aims to determine a task for social philosophy which is of rather traditional origin. As my title indicates, it is imperative for social philosophy to find a determination and discussion of those developmental processes of society that can be conceived as processes of decline, distortions, or even as "social pathologies."

In the following analysis, I shall try to specify the claims and tasks of such a social philosophy so as to clarify its relation to its neighboring disciplines. First of all, I shall present a historical reflection on the development of that tradition of thought, in which an understanding of social philosophy emerged that ascribed to it the task of a diagnosis of social deviations. A social philosophical reflection takes its beginning, if not in name at least in subject matter, from Jean-Jacques Rousseau's critique of civilization. Its analysis employs concepts like "bifurcation" and "alienation" for the ethical criteria by which certain modern processes of development can be conceived as pathologies (I). This tradition has undergone a meaningful enrichment in our century, inasmuch as philosophical reflection can now support itself upon the results of the established social sciences. Starting in the thirties and forties, when social philosophy attained a particular importance due to the historical emergence of fascism and Stalinism, a direct path into the present started with the work of Hannah Arendt and continued in the valuable contributions to a determination of social pathologies by authors such as Michel Foucault, Jürgen Habermas, and Charles Taylor (II). The results of this historical reflection finally permit us, in a third step, to outline the theoretical claims and the specific questions of social philosophy. Since its primary task is to diagnose social processes of development, which must be understood as impairments of the possibilities of the "good life" among members of society, it is ordered by ethical criteria. Thus social philosophy, in distinction from both moral philosophy and political philosophy, can be understood as an instance of reflection within which measures for successful forms of social life are discussed (III).

I   FROM ROUSSEAU TO NIETZSCHE: THE EMERGENCE OF SOCIAL-PHILOSOPHICAL INQUIRY

Even if Thomas Hobbes gave the discipline its name in the middle of the seventeenth century,[3] social philosophy came to life in a real sense one hundred years later with the work of Jean-Jacques Rousseau. Under the title "social philosophy," Hobbes had searched for the legal conditions under which the absolutist state could win the measure of stability and authority necessary for the pacification of the religious wars. In the *Leviathan* his proposed solution of the formation of the contract laid out as a guidepost the question of how, under the social conditions of ever present conflict of interests, the clear survival of civil order could be guaranteed. But when Rousseau worked on his *Discourse on the Origin of Inequality* in the middle of the eighteenth century, this viewpoint had almost no interest for him. He was interested less in the presuppositions under which civil society was able to maintain itself than in the factors that led to its degeneration. In the hundred years that transpired between Hobbes and Rousseau, the process of capitalistic modernization had progressed to such an extent that a civil sphere of private autonomy was able to form in the shadow of the absolute state. Within the early bourgeois public sphere, which at that time still had no political influence in France, ways of interacting developed that later would provide the lifeworld framework for both democratic institutions and capitalistic exchange.[4] A form of social life emerged which would have been unrecognizable for Hobbes. Under the growing pressure of economic and social competition, ways of acting and of orienting one's life arose that were grounded upon deception, feigning, and jealousy. With the acute perception of the isolated loner, Rousseau fixed his gaze on the form of life that developed with this way of acting. Above all he was interested in whether or not it still contained all of the practical presuppositions under which men could lead a good and successful life. With Rousseau's change of attitude, modernity's project of social philosophy was put into effect. Unlike political philosophy, social philosophy no longer tried to determine the conditions of a correct or just social order, but set forth the conditions imposed by the new lifeform on human self-realization.

Rousseau had already begun his social-philosophical inquiry in a text published in Geneva five years before *Discourse on Inequality*. His key question, "whether the restoration of the sciences and arts has contributed to the restoration of morals," offered him for the first time the opportunity to sum up succinctly his critical reflections on civilization.[5] Full of passion, but without conclusive argumentation, the text already contained in a rough form all of the observations that later would become the substance of his mature theory: civilization developed in tandem with a process of need refinement that made humans dependent upon artificially formed desires and increasingly robbed them of their original freedom. The removal of mankind's natural security mechanisms led to a decline of public morals, since with the inevitable division of labor the need for reciprocal recognition mounted to such an extent that pride, vanity, and hypocrisy predominated. In this process the arts and sciences eventually took on only the role of increasing authority, since they provided this individualizing tendency new possibilities of expression.[6] But the negative answer that Rousseau reached regarding his primary inquiry contained scarcely a reference to the criteria that were at his disposal for a critical assessment. The text does make unmistakably clear that the ethical quality of the social life should be measured by the condition of its individual freedoms and public morals. But it remains persistently unclear how the ideal forms of both spheres were to be conceived in order to expose a process of "loss" or of "decline" by means of them. When he lamented the decline of public morals Rousseau did recall as a means of comparison the political publicness which many of his contemporaries believed to know to have been present in the ancient polis. But when he criticized the process of need intensification, since to him that was the point at which the loss of individual freedom seemed generally to emerge, he oriented himself to the ideal of a prehistoric state in which man lived in a natural self-sufficiency. This well-defined duality remained in force until he provided a broader and more theoretical concept of civilization critique in *Discourse on Inequality*.[7] Here the tension between historical and anthropological measures of values is resolved in favor of the second option: it is now a determinant, or natural, form of human self-relation that functions as a critical reference point in the diagnosis of the modern way of life.

Even though the academy's new task at this time inquired into fundamental causes that led to the "different conditions among men," Rousseau nevertheless employed it for a critique not only of social injustice, but of an entire form of life. Already the formal construction of his writing makes clear that in the meantime he had cast off a significantly differentiated account of the methodical problems of a critique of civilization. In the first part of his argument he now sketches in powerful strokes, by means of empirical information, an image of the human condition of nature. This serves, in the second part of the text, as the contrasting background before which the pathologies of the modern form of life come clearly into focus. Rousseau draws up his outline of the state of nature from two original human characteristics, both of whose existence can in no way be deduced from it. Even before it matures in the course of socialization away from its natural form of life, the human subject is characterized by an impulse towards survival and the capacity for compassion. This first characteristic, the *amour de soi*, entails barely more than the minimum of narcissistic self-occupation that is demanded for individual survival in a hostile environment. But the second characteristic, *pitié*, designates the natural care with which humans, and in a lesser sense also animals, react as soon as they see their own kind suffer. Rousseau is convinced that both of these impulses are limited reciprocally inasmuch as the struggle for survival in the state of nature can approximate only to a qualified form of a general permissiveness. His objection to Hobbes is that the motive of compassion always imposes moral shackles on the survival impulse, though without entirely suffocating its necessary reproductive function.[8]

Yet it is not this element of an impulse-guided morality that Rousseau holds in ethical consideration as the central characteristic of his state of nature. In his critique of civilization, compassion in fact now plays the same role on an anthropological level, as his often used expression "natural morals" shows, that the ethical common life of the "polis" had taken on a historical level. His social philosophical diagnosis is anchored so solidly in the pre-historical existence of mankind, that even "public morals" have become a fact of nature. But what Rousseau actually places at the core of the state of nature ideal emerges only at the end of his discourse. There in a dramatic and stylistically masterful context the illusion that man has lived "in him- self" before all socialization turns up.[9] This inconspicuous formulation pro- vides the key both for Rousseau's image of the state of nature and for the ethical intent of his critique of civilization. For it outlines the form of the individual self-relation that he saw inverted in the bourgeois society of his time.

When he says that a human life is fulfilled "in itself," Rousseau imagines what emerges directly from his methodological premise of the deepest possi- ble isolation in the state of nature. Since there humans would have lived independently of interaction partners, they would have oriented their action only by motives determined without reference to behavior expectations of other persons. Positively viewed this means that subjects under natural con- ditions act within the security of their own wills. Distracted by no performa- tive orientation, they live out their lives in quiet certainty wanting only what their natural instincts recommend. Here the model of a completely monological self-relation provides the ethical measure that Rousseau lays out as the foundation of his assessment of the process of civilization. Thus one must differentiate the outer level of his critique from its inner social philosophical core. As for the "official" outer level, which carries out the responses to his key questions, Rousseau outlines with the acuteness of an early sociologist the ways in which the abandonment of humans' natural way of life necessarily led to the instantiation of social diversity. But he interprets the same event from a second, rather hidden, level as the begin- ning of a process through which mankind was forced into a relation of self- alienation. In both cases it is the rupture of the monological self-relation that prepared the way for the critical development. But the very status of the event modifies itself according to the point of view under which Rousseau undertook his critical diagnosis.

On the basis of the description that Rousseau gave the state of nature, he naturally allowed its end to coincide with the first steps of socialization. If the natural course of life of humans is characterized by a form of individual self-relation that is free from all intersubjective orientation, it must begin to disappear when elementary communication relations with the family or tribe emerge. But the explanations that Rousseau offers for the origin of such early forms of society, by which he regards the human state of nature as definitively ended, are sadly insufficient. The results that emerge from the changing life contexts for individual behavior are explained to the reader in a train of thought whose negative intensity is not free from personal affect: as soon as subjects have to relate to each other reciprocally, as is the case with the emergence of the first relations of interaction, the orientation of their behavior forcefully shifts to an external point of view; instead of following the guidance of their own instinctual needs, they direct themselves by the expectations that the communication partner imposes on them; the agitation of permanent self-exhibition now replaces the role that the control over their own desires had previously occupied; anxious that intersubjective expectations cannot be fulfilled, each subject is occupied with a presentation of itself that promises more than is actually redeemable; as soon as this stage of socialization is reached, a social dynamic arises whose goal is caught up in the incessant circle of striving for value and possession of prestige. Individuals encounter one another only with the intention of feigning the talents and capacities that can provide them a higher measure of social recognition.

It thus seems a bitter irony that by this conclusion Rousseau simply inverted the scheme of development of Hobbes' teaching. While in Hobbes' state of nature a situation of anger and threat predominates, so here it is the peace of the allowance of autonomy. But it is this autonomy that during the entrance into the state of society first leads to the form of an anxiety-ridden disquiet that Hobbes in fact believed was overcome straightaway through the social contract. In fact the two conceptions cannot be compared at all, since Rousseau investigates a completely different problem than Hobbes wanted to solve by his design of a contract. Hobbes looks in a practical intention for the proper conditions under which the departure from the state of nature can lead to the origin of the stable order of a civil state. But Rousseau is interested in diagnosing the qualitative consequences that result for the individual's course of life from the fact that the state of nature has already been abandoned. Thus the first point of view, under which Rousseau goes into the consequences of the outline of development, is for him probably only of lesser importance. The situation of a universal struggle for prestige, in which the monological self-relation is ruptured, forcefully gave rise to the origin of social diversity. For with the *amour propre*, the artistically sustained need for winning prestige, the pressure to earn private property emerges. The social class structure, however, would prepare the way for this development.

Rousseau is now at the point where he makes the transition to his second viewpoint of critical diagnosis. Here we find the central question regarding what the process of development implies about the chances of humans achieving a fulfilled life. Again Rousseau counts on that process of decline, which he had already advanced in his *Discourse on Science and the Arts*, in order to prove his critical claims empirically. Again the answer, with which he concludes his discussion, possesses the same blunt straightforwardness that his early writings had. But now Rousseau has at his disposal the measure that he had in the meantime secured under the ideal of a monological self-relation in order to focus his critical diagnosis upon a single thesis: if every natural mode of existence of an instinctual course of life is broken up when subjects place themselves in regularized relations of interaction, then they becomes victims of the externalization of their orientation of behavior. For with the viewpoint that henceforth they project from the perspective of their communication partner onto themselves, subjects fall into the permanent compulsion of having to present a false image of themselves. The modern loss of freedom and the growing destruction of morals are for Rousseau two sides of a process that has its origin in the structure of a life ordered from without. With the unrest of self-presentation, individual independence and the original virtue of compassion are steadily eroded. Thus Rousseau can conclude with the thesis that lies at the heart of his critical diagnosis: "The savage lives inside itself, but the man in society is always outside himself and is allowed to live only in the opinion of the other."[10]

By this conclusion Rousseau became, we can say without exaggeration, the founder of modern social philosophy. But it was not from the content of his diagnosis that the new discipline took its departure, but both from his way of posing questions and from his methodological form of answering them. This method brought a new kind of philosophical investigation to life. By his attempt to conceive the social life of his time as having become foreign to man's original existence, Rousseau developed the philosophical idea of "alienation" if not in concept at least in subject matter.[11] This made it possible to investigate a social lifeform no longer only under the aspect of its political-moral legitimacy, but also by questioning the structural limitations that it imposes on the goal of human self-realization.

As Hegel wrote his first works at the beginning of the nineteenth century, he stood no less in the spell of Rousseau's problematic than the young Karl Marx did forty years later. Admittedly the empirical descriptions of the social world, upon which the early Hegel and then Marx fastened their discontent of bourgeois society, had already changed considerably relative to the middle of the previous century. In their theoretical designs both reacted not only to the events and the effects of the French revolution, but above all to the rapid acceleration of industrialization. Rousseau had come to the rudiments of his social philosophy by a series of unfortunate experiences that he must have had in his contact with early bourgeois society in Paris. All that he must have experienced about the pressure of competition, the force of prestige, and the possession of distinction he attributed both to a loss of freedom and to the destruction of morals. But he interpreted these processes with the help of the interpretative models of "reversal" and "alienation" as the necessary consequences of the removal of an anthropologically derived initial situation. But Hegel characterized his contemporary society chiefly by means of a loss of subjective freedom. Unlike Rousseau, what he experienced as pathological in social life was the destructive effect that emerged from the process of a massive increase of individual particularism. The empirical phenomena, which stood vividly before his eyes, were social isolationism, political apathy, and economic impoverishment. But like Rousseau, Hegel held that these historical declines signaled a social danger, because they imposed too many restrictions on the conditions of a good life.

Hegel consistently viewed the central problem of his time as the formation of a social sphere in which citizens related to one another only on the basis of the lifeless bonds of legal regulation. Both his reading of the effects of the French revolution and his view of political relationships in Germany were marked by the conviction that with the legal freeing of the individual subject came the threat of an atomization of the common life. Equipped with the abstract properties of a person bearing rights in a "bourgeois society," the individual now enjoyed a measure of subjective freedom as never before. Its simple negative determination was no longer limited by any social constraint that could extend beyond purely instrumental orientations. Admittedly Hegel turns into a social philosopher in the above sense only when he views the loss of community in this development as more than merely a problem of political guidance. His historical-philosophical conviction allowed him early on to see a crisis in place that would detrimentally affect social life *as a whole.*[12] No less than many of his contemporaries, Hegel was convinced that with the emergence of bourgeois commercial exchange a form of ethical totality, which at one time must have existed under natural conditions or in ancient Greece, had been destroyed.

The ways in which individual life and public mores mutually limited each other had given the individual the chance to know itself as always embedded in an overarching universal as a constitutive element. But as soon as individuals began to relate to each other only under the condition of their newly won freedom, the universal medium in whose horizon they were able to develop a rational identity threatened to dissolve along with the disintegration of social bonds. The social life that Hegel had in mind was marked by a loss of universality, which had pathological consequences both for the subject and for the community. Within the single individual, no longer constitutively included in the public sphere, duty and inclination face each other just as abstractly as the atomized members of society are faced with the institutions that have turned lifeless.

Hegel's use of the expression "bifurcation," which grounds his entire social-philosophical diagnosis, reveals his entire difference from Rousseau. In order to justify his claims, Hegel has to presuppose a condition of social unity that can be divided into opposing parts. According to his interpretation, the fact that what previously had formed a totality is now fallen apart into two halves already takes on the quality of a social pathology. For Rousseau, on the other hand, the ideal initial condition consists not in any form of unity, but in isolated individuals acting independently of one another. Moreover, as soon as the self-referential individual begins to lose its center of gravity through union with others, it begins to decline. This difference in evaluation emerges naturally out of the difference that existed between both thinkers with respect to the social conditions through which they thought a successful human life was possible. For Rousseau it was a condition of the most extreme form of individual self-governing [*Autarkie*] possible, while for Hegel it was the reciprocal duty to one common good, which was valid at any one time, as the condition for a form of society that can make self-development possible for its members. Thus during his entire life Hegel had to look out for a social medium, which Rousseau had investigated only in the *Social Contract*, that could become the source of ethical integration under the conditions of the modern principles of freedom. The various solutions that he developed for this crisis he himself designated were his early idea of a folk religion he borrowed from early Christianity, his short-lived program of aesthetic mythology, his orientation towards the model of the ancient polis, and finally his fruitful concept of a state-regulated ethical life.[13]

The image that the later Hegel drew of the social life of his time was only marginally affected by the phenomena of economic impoverishment. Only with the work of his disciple Marx do economic concerns move into the forefront of social philosophy. In the advancing nations of the West the process of capitalistic industrialization had accelerated so quickly, that the impact on the lifeworld had become immense. The experience of economic misery and social uprooting gave impetus to the development of Marx's theory. But he too perceived the social phenomena that outraged him not simply as consequences of a moral injustice. Like Rousseau and Hegel, he interpreted these tendencies as social developments that opposed the goal of human self-realization. Moreover, the teleological concept of humanity that Marx now set at the base of his reflection contained a kind of degeneration that had been completely foreign to Rousseau and Hegel. Corresponding both to the historical experience that guided his remarks on economic life and to the Romantic influences of his youth, Marx held that the human subject succeeds to self-realization through the process of self-determining work.[14] The critical diagnosis, which he had set as his goal, attempts to identify those presuppositions of capitalism that structurally opposed the development of such a form of work. In his early writings Marx gives this undertaking the form of a critique of social alienation.

Even after Marx abandoned the alienation-theoretic approach of his early writings, nothing changed in the social-philosophical orientation of his critique of capitalism. From his continued study of political economy he realized that the capitalistic mode of production may be criticized only if a structural contradiction can be detected in its laws of movement. And with the increasing thrust toward the methodological model of the sciences, he wanted take a firm position regarding its conviction that the talk of "social alienation" borrowed too much from a speculative concept of capacities of the human species. But the transformation of his approach into a scientific program of a critique of political economy did not lead to anything that would cause him to leave his critique of capitalism without a social-philosophical orientation. Essentially it had to do with more than simply working out the inner lawfulness by which the exploitation logic of capital carries into the economic crisis. Rather he wanted to show that this same process exhibited a social decline because it made a peaceful life among men impossible. In order to reach this goal, Marx replaced the concept of alienation by the representational model of "reification" that, though sparser in anthropological content, was just as powerful in regard to the determination of social pathologies.[15] Marx understood reification as the process through which the exploitative force of capital causes subjects to become bound to a kind of permanent category mistake relative to reality. Relegated to economic pressures and divorced from all non-usable phenomena, subjects cannot help but perceive reality as a whole in accordance with the scheme of reified entities. For Marx this process must be criticized, since even the conditions under which a subject can succeed to an actuality of its own are destroyed. For as soon as their environment is reduced to a correlation between simple entities, humans lack any possibility of securing their own vital power in the medium of an external reality.

As the previous analysis shows, even this new model of critique cannot function without a systematic reference to anthropological determinations. Marx had to make strong assumptions about the structures of human self-realization in order to criticize the process of reification as an obstacle for the good life. Moreover, he had to show in a previously inserted level that an objectivizing view of reality is a kind of category mistake. But Marx can from now on do without the substantial assumptions about the conative structure of man that the concept of alienation had demanded. What his new model of critique presupposed about the details of the structure of human self-realization referred not to its aims or intentions, but only to its necessary conditions of fulfillment. The fact that in our century the reification model of critique has developed a strong and unwavering aura-like force may be explained by its relative paucity of anthropological assumptions. But before it could be generally perceived as a social-philosophical concept, the sixty years between Marx's *Das Kapital* and the early work of Georg Lukács had to elapse. Lukács' *History and Class Consciousness* exposed for the first time the fact that the critique of political economy had also contained a social-philosophical interpretation of capitalism.[16] Marx's economic writings actually were not viewed as a contribution to social philosophy during his lifetime. Inasmuch as the theory had not become already reinterpreted in an objectivistic concept of history, in the ranks of worker movements the interest in his theory validated above all its political, economic, and perhaps even moral-theoretical conclusions. But in addition to the socially oriented crisis, other phenomena like economic misery quickly moved into the foreground of the social experience of crisis.

In the second half of the nineteenth century the first steps of political democratization emerged in several Western nations. Under the moral pressure of worker movements, which were already referred to the far-reaching institutionalization of principles of equality, the liberal rights of freedom were extended to new groups and at the same time were infused with specifically political elements. Connected with the process of urbanization, these egalitizing tendencies quickly set off negative reactions in certain circles of the bourgeoisie. It did not take long before the catchword "de-individualization" [*Vermassung*] was created to place the fears of external threats under a common denominator. As a result, there emerged particularly in Germany a growing unease regarding the consequences the process of industrialization produced in the realm of everyday culture. The social life-world became desolate and devoid of meaning since its every endeavor to attain authentic greatness and originality seemed to fail. Even Tocqueville, at the very time Marx wrote his *Economic and Philosophical Manuscripts*, warned of the dangers of the cultural deprivation that could follow social equalization. Barely thirty years later, John Stuart Mill in *On Liberty* cautioned against the growing tendency of universalizing conformity. But Nietzsche was the first to achieve a theoretical perspective that made all of these phenomena appear as cultural symptoms of a single comprehensive crisis. What his contemporaries either conjured up as the proliferation of egalitarianism or posited as the result of a social de-individualization, he traced back with a brilliant simplicity to the spiritual constellation of modern nihilism.

Admittedly the specific viewpoint under which Nietzsche observed the social world, led both to a meaningful enrichment of and a typical difference from the development hitherto of social philosophy. Unlike Hegel and Marx, Nietzsche was not really interested in the social phenomena of his time. In his writings he interpreted them simply as exemplary instances of a disruption whose origin and focus lay solely in the realm of a cultural orientation of mankind. Through this change in perspective, he gave new impetus to a form of historical interpretation that broke with the premises of both the flourishing historicism of the time and the idealistic concept of progress. From the cultural system of interpretation of the past, he had to bring out the intellectual content that had prepared the ground for the spiritual pathology of the present. By this theoretical path that he forged, Nietzsche invented the genealogical analysis of cultural history. It has remained until today a methodological model for carrying out a social-philosophical diagnosis of the times, as evidenced in Foucault's investigations and in a certain way also in the analyses of Horkheimer and Adorno.

II   BETWEEN ANTHROPOLOGY AND PHILOSOPHY OF HISTORY: SOCIAL PHILOSOPHY AFTER THE DEVELOPMENT OF SOCIOLOGY

While social philosophy in the nineteenth century depended heavily upon Rousseau's critique of culture, in the twentieth century it found itself completely under the spell of the intellectual constellation of Marx and Nietzsche. Rarely do we meet a problem or topic that did not arise out of an attempt to overcome the tension between these two thinkers. But in the meantime the crucial point of this intellectual dispute became detached from its point of origin and shifted to another field. The pathologies of the modern world were theoretically handled no longer in philosophy or in one of its extra-academic confines, but in the newly-emerging academic sociology. As often in its history, social philosophy briefly took on the decisive impulse of an empirical science.

Sociology offered its services for the further refinement of social philosophy, since in contrast to the latter's future-oriented development it oriented itself to ethical problems. The founding fathers of the new science were without exception deeply convinced that modern society was threatened by a moral impotence, which necessarily led to massive disturbances in social reproduction. With the institutional transition from a traditional to a modern social order, so claimed the general diagnosis, the social value structure had lost that ethical power of formation which had up until now allowed the individual to interpret its life as meaningful relative to a social aim. Sociology could now be conceived as an answer to the resulting pathology, since it was conceived unanimously as a completely unspecialized "moral" or "cultural scientific" undertaking.

Within this model of the diagnosis of the times, theoretical influences both from Nietzsche and from Marx found expression in methods that from a modern vantage point are no longer easy to reconstruct. In their youths all of the famous sociologists were permanently marked by Nietzsche's diagnosis of nihilism (with the exception of Durkheim for whom Bergson may have played a similar role). From it they must have inferred the idea that with the destruction of the objective world order every ethical objective upon which the subject could orient its life meaningfully was similarly undermined. The economic theory of Marx also exercised a determinant influence upon this first generation of academic sociologists. By universalizing his critique of capitalism, they learned the ways in which the new economic order led to a form of human relations that rested not upon personal bonds but upon purposive rational expectations. It took very little to combine both idea complexes into a single explanatory model that constituted the thesis that dominated the sociological diagnosis of the times at the threshold of the twentieth century: the institutional causes for the increase of a loss of ethical orientation, and thus of nihilism, was to be found in the achievement of an economy of exchange. In one way or another this claim formed the kernel of the various interpretative schemes that were utilized at that time for the explanation of the transition to the modern social order. Whether it was Simmel speaking of the reification of personal relations, Tönnies considering the dissolution of common social relations, Weber drawing attention to the radical demystification of the world, or Durkheim seeking the origin of organic forms of solidarity, all were concerned with the historical process that together with the establishment of the new economic order had led to a moral impoverishment of the social lifeworld.

Only a few decades separate this culminating point of a sociological diagnosis of the times from the historical moment in which German fascism descended upon European countries. With this event not only the methodological orientation, but also the very subject matter of social philosophy altered fundamentally. Until this powerful transformation, the perceptual field of social philosophy was still determined for the most part by the models of interpretation that the founding fathers of sociology had developed at the turn of the century. In the forefront of the otherwise highly variant diagnoses of the present, if one leaves out thinkers like Helmuth Plessner, as a rule that impairment of human self-realization attributed to the process of capitalistic modernization remains. Whether reification or loss of community, whether cultural impoverishment or increase in aggression, the social reference point of analysis always portrays a one-sided rationalizing force in capitalistic economy. With the National Socialist seizure of power in Germany and the expansion of terror that was gradually becoming evident in the Soviet Union, a far-reaching transformation began in this model of diagnosis of the times. Gradually there moved into the center a convergence that appeared to exist between the fascist power domination and the Stalinist system of power. Soon there was scarcely a theory with social philosophical sensibilities that did not see the core of all social pathologies in the conditions that made totalitarianism possible. The capitalistic form of economy thus receded to the background as a determinant influence, and instead the new world relation as a whole moved to the forefront. But even this sustained alteration of outlook did not lead to a methodological reorientation of social philosophy: both books in which the historical convergence of fascism and Stalinism are investigated probably with greatest intensity – Horkheimer's and Adorno's *Dialectic of Enlightenment* and Hannah Arendt's study of totalitarianism – are based upon either anthropological or historical-philosophical procedures of explanation.

As the Frankfurt *Institute for Social Research* began in the thirties under the leadership of Max Horkheimer, its common framework of orientation was still marked by historical-philosophical openness to progress. Under its formulation by Marx, capitalism was conceived, no differently than it was by Lukács except in empirical attitude, as a relation of social reification that was ended by the revolutionary resistance of the proletariat. The interdisciplinary work of the Institute was dedicated to the confusing question of how against all rational expectations the relation could have come to the social integration of the worker classes. Despite all the differences among its members, scarcely any serious doubt emerged as to the prospect of an emancipatory transformation. Forced by the situation in Germany into exile in America ten years later, the research group found that its historical-philosophical perspective underwent a fundamental change. Under the impression that fascism and Stalinism had in the meantime formed a totalitarian whole, the group believed that all hopes for a revolutionary change had vanished, leaving a cultural-critical pessimism. This new orientation was further voiced in the *Dialectic of Enlightenment*, co-authored by Horkheimer and Adorno. With this book the threshold was reached in the history of social philosophy where the historical roots of totalitarianism became the dominant theme.

How much the spiritual horizon of the thinking of Horkheimer and Adorno had shifted is revealed by their desire to follow the causes of the totalitarian state back to the beginnings of human history. The social pathology revealed in fascist systems of domination is so entrenched that it can be explained only if it is understood as a consequence of a decline of the total process of civilization. Not just by chance do these grounding insights formally resemble the premises upon which Rousseau had already forged his critique of culture. He had been convinced that the actual perceived alienation pointed to a disturbance of human behavior far in the past which had originally motivated the return to the state of nature. Moreover, there is also clear agreement in both approaches with regard to the question of which methodological character the representation of the beginnings of civilization should possess. Just as it remains unclear whether Rousseau's sketch of the state of nature is meant fictively or empirically, Horkheimer and Adorno leave open-ended the way in which they want their excursus into the early history of mankind understood. On the one hand their text contains a series of concealed initial premises about the grounds of ethnic and anthropological research, but on the other hand it is so onesided and exaggerated in its conclusions that in the end the argument seems to be intended fictitiously. If the methodological similarities had been understood up until this point, the factual disagreement between the two approaches emerges all the clearer today. While Rousseau had fastened the beginning of the decline of civilization onto the communication between men, Horkheimer and Adorno fix it at the very first act of a rational possession of nature. In a more direct reversal of the positive interpretation of Marx which until then was dominant, both Horkheimer and Adorno still perceive in human work only the element that serves instrumental domination. The subject forms the capacity of rational control of its natural impulses in the effort of work. Through the activity of work the natural environment is reduced, conversely, to a simple conceptual field of human purpose. Both approaches now provide an interpretation in which the process of civilization can be reduced to a logic of increasing decline no less onesidedly than in Rousseau's critique of culture. The first act of instrumental domination, with which man learns to dominate nature, is followed gradually by the disciplining of his desires, the weakening of his sensible capacities, and the formation of social relations of domination. Whereas with Rousseau at the end of the process of decline the uncontrolled struggle for prestige pits all against all, with Horkheimer and Adorno it leads ultimately to the totalitarian domination of the present. Here the historical spiral of increasing reification reaches its high point, since it creates within society a new form of natural relations in which psychically emptied individuals are delivered over to the purposive-rational large organizations just as defenselessly as earlier they were given over to the invincible power of nature.

The historical-philosophical explanation that Horkheimer and Adorno thus give for the origin of modern totalitarianism stands clearly in the succession of a Marxist appropriation of Weber's rationalization thesis. Even the domination of the totalitarian system of power is still conceived as a social embodiment of the cognitive process that human history from the beginning takes on in the form of a methodical increase in the possession of knowledge. Such a concentration on the developmental logic of instrumental reason entails two limitations in the theoretical field that have a disadvantageous effect on the diagnosis of totalitarianism. For one all those factors that do not stand in a more or less direct relation to the process of technical rationalization remain detached from the historical process of emergence. So much did Horkheimer and Adorno both focus on the development of mass media and psychic behaviour dispositions, that the analysis of these events always takes place under the limiting condition in which can be perceived only broader forms of a reason become totalitarian.

What the task of social philosophy demands, is the second aspect of still greater weight. Since totalitarian domination is viewed as a culmination point of a process of rationalization that reaches back to the early history of the human species, its special role in civilization appeals to grounds taken from that view. No longer the social reality of totalitarianism itself, but the civilization process as a whole represents a form of social pathology. Like Rousseau, Horkheimer and Adorno were caught under the force of an immense broadening of the suspicion of pathologies. As soon as the historical process is conceived only under the form of an increase of an early historical destruction, no progress in the broadening of legal freedoms, in the democratization of political decisions, or in the opening of the space of individual behavior can any longer occur.[17] It is, as it would be, precisely this weak point of the *Dialectic of Enlightenment* that Hannah Arendt had in mind with the conception of her own analysis of totalitarianism. For in that respect the emergence of the totalitarian domination of power was conceived precisely as the consequence of a social pathology that could have formed itself only in the midst of modern society.

Situated in Arendt's analysis of totalitarianism is a type of social philosophy that shares with the diagnosis of the times of the early Hegel the tendency to allow the normative justification of critique to appear extensively only in the veiled form of a historical idealization. Throughout her life Arendt was convinced that distortions of the social world could be recognized as developments that the communicative presuppositions of an open discussion of political import threaten to destroy. But instead of supporting this grounding thought anthropologically, in such a way that it would have been provable by empirical evidence, she tried to justify it in a consistent way only by means of an idealist description of the ancient polis. If all historical reference is later removed from the parts of her work that serve this express purpose, then the anthropological claims emerge upon which she supported her social-philosophical diagnosis: human subjects are ordered according to their whole nature to be perceived and recognized in a public sphere because only in this way can they acquire the measure of psychic stability and self-consciousness that they need for coping with their existential problems and risks. Moreover, the individual subject is in the situation to experience itself as a free being only if it learns to engage itself actively in public discussion of political import. Both presuppositions taken together support the systematic conclusion that Arendt couches at one point in the normatively held description of the ancient polis, and at another point in the philosophical rehabilitation of the Aristotelian concept of praxis: individual freedom and public praxis are so intertwined in humans that only the existence of a social sphere of the political public opens up for them the chance to lead a successful life.

It is the social ideal that follows from this thesis that Arendt then employs as the measure by which to be able to conceive totalitarianism's social system of domination as a social pathology. That is why she proceeds – not in the temporal sense of the succession of her writings, but in the systematic sense of the construction of her social philosophy – on two levels: at one level a universal tendency of alienation from the world is claimed for the industrial society of modernity, and in a second step the system of totalitarian domination is understood as the particular formation and fulfillment of this alienation. In her study entitled *The Human Condition*, she proposes an analysis of social ways of behaving that constitutes the epitome of modern alienation from the world. Under the condition of a progressive industrialization, so goes her thesis, the technical forms of activity of production and of labor achieve social domination so powerfully, that they threaten to suppress completely the freedom-creating praxis of public discussion and communication. But since, as a result, that particular sphere of activity is restricted in which alone it is possible for the individual to develop a relationship of trust to itself, to its fellow humans, and to the world as a whole, the increase of a universal alienation then follows from the triumphal march of technology with a powerful force.[18]

These processes of development are now, as Arendt believes, what prepared the socio-cultural ground for the achievement of totalitarianism. In the dominating power of National Socialism, so she shows in her large-scale study of the "Sources and Elements of Totalitarian Domination," modern human's loss of the world [Weltverlust] was manipulated for the purpose of mobilizing the masses. Cut off from the interaction that establishes meaning by the emaciation of the public spaces, having to fend for themselves, and having their own identities become uncertain, individuals find an adequate form of organization of their interests only in the totalitarian movements. But such mass organizations can gain stability only when they develop a collective ideology that draws out all aggression and then focuses it upon an external enemy in order to create within the heart of each a feeling of common threat and common responsibility. Thus at the end there emerges that fatal and lethal cycle in which the totalitarian movements are able to maintain their domination only by transposing their own ideology step for step into the praxis of mass extermination.

In contrast to the historical-philosophical approach to explanation that Horkheimer and Adorno worked out, Arendt's analysis of totalitarianism is modest in its rational-critical claims, weak in its psychological differentiations, and almost naive in its views of how modern mass media work. But her proposal regarding what makes up the social enabling of totalitarian domination and what its emergence means in the context of a social pathology provides an unequaled interpretative power. Her thesis – that the sphere of freedom-guaranteeing behavior is restricted as a consequence of the extension of technical performance of activity, by which at the same time a destruction of the political public sphere follows so that in the end no more barriers stand in the way of the totalitarian domination – is not only explicitly applied to real historical events as all the reflections one finds in the *Dialectic of Enlightenment* are. Above all, with this thesis the view of a social degeneration was drawn, which should still have retained an explosive nature and actuality for modern societies, as National Socialism was already crushed and the Stalinistic apparatus of domination had further lost its terroristic traits. That is why it cannot surprise us that in the fifties and sixties it was Arendt's theory, and not for instance the *Dialectic of Enlightenment*, from which the most important impulses for social philosophy started. Very few of the authors who happened at that time to attempt to interpret the epoch philosophically were not in some way influenced by her writings. Whether it was the concept of discussion free from domination for Habermas, the idea of revolutionary praxis for Cornelius Castoriadis, or the image of a freedom-guaranteeing public for Charles Taylor, at the beginning of each of their critical analyses is always found the Arendt's diagnosis that the hegemony of the instrumental activity threatens to dissolve the realm of communicative action.

III   GROUNDING FORMS OF A DIAGNOSIS OF SOCIAL PATHOLOGIES: TOWARD THE PRESENT SITUATION OF SOCIAL PHILOSOPHY

As a new form of social philosophy, which owes its essential impetus to the work of Arendt, began to form in the sixties and seventies with the writings of Habermas, Taylor, and Castoriadis, it was not only the political situation that had changed decisively. Because of the growing influence of linguistic analysis on philosophy, the methodological demands that were made on the reasoning of philosophical statements, even in rather obscure areas of inquiry, had grown as well. The discussion within social philosophy did not remain untouched by this development. For a certain time the discussion focused on the question of how statements about social pathologies can be methodically justified. Before the historical account became extended to the present, it had to be first of all conceived in the form of a systematic retrospective on the concept of social philosophy outlined earlier. Only in view of its special cognitive intent can we thus gauge in what the foundational problems of this discipline must consist today.

The historical point of the emergence of that undertaking that we now can call social philosophy suggests it be viewed as the place to deal with a philosophical problem that initially was separated out from modern thought on the basis of methodological considerations. Even Hobbes had already renounced the classical tradition of political philosophy going back to Aristotle, abandoning its excessive claims to knowledge. Instead he concentrated upon a single question: not how a common way of life can guarantee a good and just life of its members, but how it is able to arrange a universal order capable of agreement. By framing the question in this way, the separation of morality from ethics that Kant later officially established for moral philosophy had already emerged in political philosophy. Philosophy need answer only the problems which refer to the justice of social action, while the conditions of the good life remain excluded from its framework since they are much less accessible to a universal determination. But the position that Rousseau supports in his cultural historical writings is that since, at least with reference to common life, the ethical question cannot be simply set aside, it has merely taken on another form under the presuppositions of the scientific enlightenment. Obviously he wants even less to revive, than Hobbes before him and Kant after him, the perspective of the Aristotelian tradition in which the state is understood as the stable goal of human self-realization from the very beginning. But, conversely, he also wants to inquire whether the organization of social life makes possible a successful life among men. Two theoretical modifications made this transformation of the ethical question possible for Rousseau. First, the Aristotelian viewpoint became radically formalized to such an extent that it dealt no longer with the naturally given purposes of human self-realization, but only with the universal conditions of its possibility. Second, what we consult about the presuppositions which are made available for a human course of life is no longer the state, but the society gradually distancing itself from it.

Indeed the structure and function of social philosophy is determined by this view of its conditions of instantiation only in a very rough way. The makeup of the central concerns of the new discipline is fully revealed by accounting for a further salient factor that is already observable in Rousseau's critique of culture, and even more evident in the projects of his followers. Social philosophy never emerges as a positive teaching in Marx, Nietzsche, or Arendt. Instead it functions primarily as the critique of a social condition that is experienced as alienated, meaningless, or reified. How this critical intention is connected with the previously developed perspective of a formally conceived ethics indicates the idea upon which social philosophy is more or less directly characterized from the beginning. A "pathology" of social life can thus be meaningfully spoken of only if certain presuppositions are known about how the conditions for human self-realization are procured.

The concepts of "diagnosis" and "pathology," which are closely linked to the knowledge-interest of social philosophy, both come from the field of medicine. By "diagnosis" is understood first of all the exact comprehension and determination of an illness that strikes the human organism. A clinical representation of health, which for the sake of simplicity is often characterized by the sheer functioning capabilities of the body, serves as the scale from which such abnormal appearances are measured.[19] "Pathology" acts in a complementary way to this idea of "diagnosis." Though initially a pathology indicated only the theory of illnesses, today it refers to the abnormal states themselves.[20] A pathology thus represents the precise organic deviation that is to be discovered or confirmed in the diagnosis. But the application of both concepts to the realm of psychic disturbances presents major difficulties, since clear standards of what is normal for the psychic life of a person until now were barely established in clinical research. A present discussion in medicinal psychology and psychoanalysis addresses the question of how an unambiguous or at least plausible concept of mental health would be formulated.[21] The broadening of both of these concepts into the field of social phenomena is even more difficult due to the fact that the reference point can no longer simply be the individual. In order to speak of a social pathology that is accessible to the medical model of a diagnosis, a model of normality applicable to social life as a whole is required. The breakdown of all the social-scientific approaches, which the functional demands of society wanted to secure only through external observations, had made evident the immense problems attached to such a notion: since what passes as developmental potential or as normality in social contexts is always culturally defined, social functions and their corresponding disturbances are always determined only by hermeneutic reference to the internal self-understanding of societies.[22] In this respect there exists a defensive possibility to speak of social pathologies within a cultural concept of normality. According to it we can limit ourselves only to an empirical description of what a given culture views as a disturbance at any given time. Since that is too restrictive for its purposes, social philosophy from the beginning pursued that other path that points in the direction of a formal ethic. The cultural-independent conditions must then serve as the idea of normality that allows social members an unlimited form of self-realization.

Before further pursuing the difficulties that are raised by this alternative, we must briefly clarify to what extent the direction which the development of social philosophy took after Rousseau is actually determined appropriate by it. The approaches we have presented all were efforts to critique social states, which were experienced as meaningless, reified or entirely dysfunctional. Accordingly, social defects were determined not simply as injuries to the foundations of justice; rather, disturbances came to be criticized that, like psychic limitations, restricted or deformed life possibilities presupposed as "normal" or "healthy." For this aim of social philosophy concepts are used that designate for the levels of social life exactly the same as what is meant by the concept of "pathology" with regard to the individual psyche. In the first phase that we have followed its categories were "bifurcation," "reification," "alienation," and "nihilism." But after the emergence of sociology, strongly empirically imbued concepts arose such as "loss of community," "demystification," "depersonalization," and "commercialization." More recently Sartre made use of the concept of "collective neurosis" for the same goal.[23] If we now try to investigate what the representations of social normality to which all of these concepts indirectly refer have in common, we must choose a very abstract reference point so as to exclude none of them. Not all of the implicitly presupposed ideal conditions are characterized by the existence of an kind of totality: only a few distinguish themselves by a determinant art of naturalness, others appear equipped with a higher measure of social intensity or proximity. However the definitions may be derived in particular details, they are situated on a level of concretion for which no feature can be found that would be typically the same for all of the listed concepts. Such a communality emerges if the reference point is approached not as to the "how" of any ideal state, but as to the "for what" it aims. Without exception the various negative concepts aim indirectly to the social conditions that should thereby be designated, since they provide the individual a life that is fuller and better, or in other words, successful. In this way an ethical representation of social normality, which is derived from the conditions of possibility of self-realization, represents the scale from which social pathologies are measured.

This ethical background conception is formal in the sense that what should be brought out normatively is not the goal of human self-realization itself, but only its social presupposition. In fact there is a certain tendency in the direction of an ethical perfectionism in both Hegel and Marx that represents the human by means of an Aristotelian model of a determinant telos. Nietzsche and Arendt as well are not free from the attempt to conceive very specific goals when they try to outline successful ways of life. But even these opposing tendencies can still be understood with a well-meaning interpretation so that in their unclear form of profession of goals [*Zielvorgaben*] they intend to make only statements about social conditions only on the basis of which humans can succeed to self-realization. Thus for Marx labor free from alienation does not necessarily have to signify an ethical goal for mankind unconditionally, but may rather merely represent the unavoidable presuppositions that allow a person to develop a satisfactory relation to self.[24] This approach allows Arendt, for example, to claim to have distinguished the commitment to the praxis of democratic will formation that is above all ethical, since it helps the individual come to a consciousness of his or her own freedom.

The drawback of such approaches derives not from the fact that they provided certain goals for human life and by this were fettered to an incalculable perfectionism. What crippled them was rather their tendency to view such forms of activity as universal conditions of human self-realization, whose worth often derived only from highly selective and usually temporary life ideals. Since its emergence into an ethical perspective in which only formal claims are linked with regard to an explication of the "good," social philosophy is anchored, if not by its focus on the individual, certainly by its methodological arrangement.

This thesis must account for two further conspicuous features that have emerged from the previous sketch of the development of social philosophy. First, it is not entirely clear how the various approaches can rely on one single ethical ground, since they propose entirely different ideas of social normativity. Our overview of the key concepts of social philosophy has already shown that the spectrum of normative ideals extends from radical individualistic models to communitarian models. While Rousseau and Plessner view as normal a social lifeform that provides the greatest possible distance between the subjects, Hegel, Durkheim, and Arendt uncover the presupposition of social normality in the existence of strong conditions of commonality. In order to comprehend these differences, we need to look closely at the formal construction of social philosophical diagnosis. The social life conditions of individual subjects represent the reference point of all the noted attempts to find a measure for the normality of social relations. The organizational forms of the social that allow to the individual an uncoerced self-actualization of itself are always esteemed as successful, ideal, or "healthy." In a certain way the formal conception of the good, which social philosophy lays out as a critical measure, aims toward the well being of individuals, inasmuch as it lies in the framework of possibility of society. But as for the question of how far these conditions of the social reach, the approaches are distinguished by fundamental differences. To consider how strong the influence that social life imposes in respect to the individual well being is, the envisioned ideal state must assume either an individualistic or collective character. Thus if these alternatives designate the two poles of possible solutions, all further differences measure themselves relative to the concrete presuppositions that are viewed as necessary for the details of self-realization. Here what plays a central role, whether it takes a communitarian form of ethical life or a distance-creating public life, is the unalienated labor or the mimetic interaction with nature through which a successful life is made possible for the individual within society. In sum, we can say that the determination of social pathologies in social philosophy always proceeds with a view to the social conditions that can promote the individual's self-realization.

From this analysis, there emerges a further feature that concerns the methodological problem upon which social philosophy is focused today. If the way in which the social conditions of self-realization are determined in the various approaches is closely examined, it becomes clear that there is a return to two opposing figures of thought: what the human needs from her society for a successful life reveals itself either by looking back to her natural state of emergence or by projecting an ideal based upon her knowledge of an expected future. The first possibility took methodological form with Rousseau and gained an exemplary form in the German tradition of philosophical anthropology. The second possibility was prepared by Hegel and found its paradigmatic form in Lukács' writings. We should note that both of these alternatives obtained the methodological functions, which we still associate with them, only after the "in between" approach of Nietzsche. Both Rousseau through Vico and Hegel through Herder could have been taught something better, but they were so convinced of the similarity of all human cultures that they raised no serious doubt as to the universalistic content of philosophical statements.[25] Thus they presupposed as self-evident that their insights into the conditions of personal freedom must find application for each person without distinction. But after Nietzsche had drawn out the radical consequence of his perspectivism from the actual pluralism of cultures, social philosophy could no longer persist in such a self-certainty. From then on it was methodologically necessary to defend every statement about human character or social regulation against the charge of cultural dependency. Thus the theoretical situation emerged in which anthropologists and philosophers of history undertook the specific task of trying to justify the universalistic claims of social philosophical diagnosis: recourse to the nature of human beings or even to an ideal of their future knowledge can show that individual life is ordered over all cultural limitations precisely to social presuppositions that provide the standard of critique as the perfect example of a social ideal.

From this point on a path of gradual self-radicalizing doubt led to the threshold of the discussion which characterizes the situation of social philosophy today. It was not long until the argumentation of *History and Class Consciousness* was understood as a construction that shares with every form of philosophy of history the starting point of value convictions not grounded in themselves: the historical development can be applied to a single goal only teleologically, because until then a normative perspective had been tacitly assumed under which the heterogenous material led to a meaningful and narratively represented whole.[26] Moreover, what was valid for the philosophy of history could be shown to be foundational for philosophical anthropology as well. Why shouldn't its initial empirical conditions be achieved in the same way that the unreflected value premises of a determinate culture are projected into the natural provisions of human beings? From the exigencies of that question the discussion soon intensified to the methodological problem of whether every social-philosophical diagnosis in the final analysis is not grounded in an ethical judgment about what is valid as a suitable condition for human self-realization. Then, however, no external means could be given by which the search for a determination of social pathologies would be defended from the objection that it is nothing other than any expression of culturally dependent views. But before this last level of problematization was reached, in the sixties social philosophy established itself once again on anthropological foundations. From Arendt it had already been shown that social philosophy supported its critique of the industrial world from premises on the basis of which it was claimed that humans naturally relied on practices of communicative freedom. In this same period Arnold Gehlen developed a conservatively colored diagnosis of the times that built specifically upon the results of his chief anthropological work.[27] Even Habermas ultimately took as his point of departure the empirical determinations of an invariant locus of human interest in order to give his critique of the technizing of the social world a universalistic ground.[28]

Common to these various approaches is the fundamental conviction that a social functioning that belongs to the deeply rooted presuppositions of all human life is threatened by the acceleration of industrial growth. But both the character of the processes viewed as causes of the pathology and their form of appearance change, depending on the way these invariant conditions are interpreted. For Arendt, given the intersubjective praxis of political self-understanding, the ever-increasing expansion of technical action performance necessarily led to the destruction of the subject's very trust in the world and to a kind of alienation from the world. For Gehlen on the other hand, anticipating the conservative culture critique of Daniel Bell, rapid industrialization occurs simultaneously with a growth in a consumer stimulation that overloads persons so much that the life-supporting stability of social institutions is undermined.[29] For Habermas the process of technological development results in the increasing autonomy of purposive rational systems of behavior through which every sphere of communicative agreement, upon which the production of the human species is essentially ordered, is diminished. If the anthropological approaches that were formerly worked out in the continuation of social ontology in the later Lukács, Agnes Heller, and György Márkus are directed to this series of time-diagnostic sketches, then it is possible to speak of a broad consensus during the sixties in respect to the methodological presuppositions of social philosophy.[30] Scarcely any one of the attempts to analyze the social pathologies of the times does not begin in some way with the natural initial conditions of human beings. What must have thus been seen as an even greater challenge was the designing of the social philosophy that began to take form in the writings of Michel Foucault, who shares with Nietzsche not only his concentration on the phenomena of power but also his distaste for anthropological universalism. Even though the methodical justification that Foucault gives his critique of the disciplinary society remains incomprehensible, the arguments that he brings against every generalized unhistorical concept of human beings still appear convincing.

Like Nietzsche, Foucault develops a social philosophy that consists only of historical investigations that lay out the internal consistencies of determinant methods of human knowing, corresponding models of social discipline, and forms of individual courses of life. The more Foucault detaches himself from his scientific historical beginnings, all the more the structure of modern power relations becomes apparent as the main focus of his studies. He is convinced, in a certain similarity with Max Weber on the one hand and with Adorno on the other, that the progressive development of modern society is able to maintain itself only because a narrow net of controlling institutions effects a growing disciplining of the human body. By this discipline the subject is forced to pursue a purposive rationally organized course of life and so nips every form of opposition in the bud. But in this diagnosis it remains unclear to what extent the described processes of power accumulation generally can be treated as forms of social disturbance. For every method of knowing or knowledge must, according to Foucault, be seen in such a close alliance to the given relations of power, that the external perspective no longer is given from which the social events could be determined as a deviation from an ideal. Indeed one can glean from the later writings, which try to outline an aesthetic of existence on the example of ancient life practices, certain references to a transcending concept of human self-realization that can be conceived reflexively as the measure of a diagnosis of modern relations of power.[31] But overall Foucault's normative criteria remain so obscure and so overshadowed by this knowledge-theoretical perspectivism, that the moral direction of his critique of power usually is seen only in its political-journalistic statements, not in the main writings themselves. But it is precisely this perspectivism, whose thesis is that the truth of knowledge claims is solely and exclusively proportionate to the grade of its social achievement, by which Foucault started an entire philosophical movement rolling. From

Richard Rorty to Judith Butler many have come to defend the thesis that in every context-transcendent norm, and all the more in every reference to a nature of human beings, a power-bound construction is directly per-ceivable.[32]

As the problem is presently formulated, if social philosophy in accordance with its knowledge-interest is directed to a universal measure for the nor-mality of social life whose validity can no longer simply be identified by a dislocated anthropology, then its continued existence depends entirely on the foundation of a formal ethic. Starting with Rousseau and continuing through Hegel, Marx, Adorno, and Hannah Arendt, social philosophy has always been marked by anthropological and historical-philosophical modes of thinking. Out of these modes of thinking arose ethical criteria for social pathologies so imperceptibly that they were unrecognizable as such. Prepared by Nietzsche with great consequence and dramatically emphasized by Foucault for our times, this external veneer of social philosophy in the meantime was so completely destroyed that its ethical core was left exposed. In this way the future of social philosophy today depends in large part upon the possibility of justifying ethical judgments about necessary presupposi-tions of human life in convincing ways. Initially three alternatives appear to offer a solution to this problem.

The first way of justifying ethical judgments of the kind that social philos-ophy necessitates consists in the attempt to proceduralize ethics. In his latest writings Habermas urges us to view the clarification of ethical questions as the task of practical discourses, which earlier were held as possible only for questions of justice.[33] What must be viewed as "normal" or "ideal" for a social lifeform emerges first from the extent to which the members of the society themselves attain a consensus in a democratically organized will for-mation about the desirability of social development. Indeed such a method would have to validate specific conditions of validity for ethical discourses, since they are bound to the presuppositions of a limited community of value distinct from those that a conventional method stipulates for practical dis-courses. But in principle it appears not only possible but promising to make the clarification of ethical questions dependent upon such a procedure.[34] The disadvantage of this alternative is that it effectively dissolves social philoso-phy as a theoretical undertaking. Interpretative competence transfers specifi-cally, and only, to those who as members of a concrete society decide what counts as "pathological" in their social lifeform.

There is in the work of Habermas still another grounding strategy that pre-vents this erosion of social philosophy and can be viewed as the second method of justifying ethical judgments. In the *Theory of Communication Action* social theory is entrusted to provide the critical threshold beyond which the pressures of the systems imperatives of the social lifeworld must be viewed as social pathologies. The arguments by which the differences between "nor-mal" and "pathological" are justified originate in the ideals of a weak formal anthropology that are anchored in a universal pragmatics that seeks to prove an originary form of human speech as a necessary presupposition of social reproduction.[35] A second way of grounding ethical claims thus consists in this most modest possible anthropology, which reconstructs few, though fundamental, conditions of human life. Recent examples of this are found in the later writings of Martha Nussbaum,[36] and above all in the broad-ranging investigations of Charles Taylor.[37] Along with the works of Habermas and Foucault, Taylor's studies of the modern world can be conceived as the third important contribution to social philosophy of the present. Although in his philosophical anthropology Taylor offers the thesis that humans are self-interpreting beings whose life forms and existential possibilities are proportioned by a historically given system of interpretation, he wants nevertheless to make ethical judgments of social pathologies independent of historically-given interpretations alone. Rather the possibility to articulate oneself productively and uncoercedly is linked to the presuppositions of a series of social conditions, which can be conceived as the central components of a formal ethic. For Taylor the measure of value that makes a diagnosis of social pathology possible emerges out of a formal anthropology that outlines the universal conditions of an unforced articulation of human life ideals. Admittedly this anthropological alternative already stands in conflict, even in Taylor's work itself, with a further foundational strategy, which can be conceived collectively as a third justification of social philosophy.[38]

In *Sources of the Self* Taylor in a certain sense lays out a historically relativized grounding for ethics.[39] The hermeneutical reflection on ethical values, by which modernity guides its cultural self-understanding, supplies information about which social developments are to be conceived as social pathologies. It is this third kind of grounding that lies nearest to Foucault's. The measure of value, with whose help social philosophy discusses and diagnoses historical disturbances, thus has only a historically limited validity, since it can be applied only in a historical epoch whose preliminary ethical decisions it must forcefully assume. Indeed such a historically relativized form of grounding would not put the project of social philosophy as a whole in question: in the future social philosophy would be conceived under such theoretical presuppositions as an instance of reflection in whose framework social disturbances could be discussed on the basis of historically given values and their corresponding life ideals. But the classic claim of social philosophy would die: the claim of judging certain developments in social life as pathologies by means of context-transcendent claims. That is why the survival of social philosophy, in the form shown here through a historical visualization, depends on the success with which the claims of a weak, formalistic anthropology may be justified in the future.

NOTES

1   See "Sozialphilosophie," in *Philosophie: Fischer-Lexikon*, ed. A. Diemer and I. Frenzel (Frankfurt, 1967), pp. 301ff.

2   See Joel Feinberg, *Social Philosophy* (Englewood Cliffs, New York, 1973); Gordon Graham, *Contemporary Social Philosophy* (Oxford, 1988). In German circles this conceptual determination followed Maximilian Forschner, *Mensch und Gesellschaft: Grundbegriffe der Sozialphilosophie* (Darmstadt, 1989).

3   Thomas Hobbes, *Leviathan*, ed. C. B. Macpherson (Harmondsworth, 1979).

4   See Jürgen Habermas, *The Structural Transformation of the Public Sphere* (Cambridge: MIT Press, 1989), chapter III, §8.

5   Jean Jacques Rousseau, "Abhandlung über die von der Akademie zu Dijon gestellten Frage, ob die Wiederherstellung der Wissenschaften und Künste zur Läuterung der Sitten beigetragen habe," in his *Sozialphilosophie und politische Schriften*, (Munich, 1948), pp. 9ff.

6   See the excellent summary which Robert Spaemann has given by taking in account the Christian and Platonic influences on this text in *Rousseau: Bürger ohne Vaterland* (Munich, 1980), pp. 40ff.

7   Rousseau, "Abhandlung über den Ursprung und die Gundlagen der Ungleichheit unter den Menschen," in *Sozialphilosophie und politische Schriften*, pp. 41ff [*The Discourse of the Origin of Inequality* (Indianapolis: Hackett, 1992)].

8   Rousseau, "Ungleichheit unter den Menschen," p. 83.

9   Ibid., p. 123.

10   Rousseau, "Ungleichheit unter den Menschen," p. 123.

11   See N. J. H. Dent, "Alienation," in *A Rousseau Dictionary* (Oxford, 1992), pp. 27ff.

12   From the copious amount of literature on this subject, I would point to two particularly insightful treatments: Charles Taylor, *Hegel and Modern Society* (Cambridge, 1979), and Michael Theunissen, *Selbstverwirklichung und Allgemeinheit: zur Kritik gegenwärtigen Bewußtseins* (Berlin/New York, 1982).

13   In an extremely interesting article, Sergio Dellavalle developed "three and one half" models which can be found in Hegel's works for a solution to the problem of ethical integration. See his "Hegels dreieinhalb Modelle zum Bürger-Staat-Verhältnis," in *Hegel-Jahrbuch*, 1994.

14   For background on this, see my "Work and Instrumental Action: On the Narrative Basis of Critical Theory," in *The Fragmented World of the Social*, ed. Charles W. Wright (Albany: SUNY Press, 1995), pp. 15–49.

15   See also Georg Lohmann, *Indifferenz und Gesellschaft: Eine kritische Auseinandersetzung mit Marx* (Frankfurt, 1991), ch. 1. Lohmann provides a very precise reconstruction that emphasizes not the concept of "reification," but that of "indifference."

16   See Georg Lukács, "Geschichte und Klassenbewußtsein," in *Werke*, vol. II (Neuwied/Berlin, 1968), pp. 161ff. [*History and Class Consciousness*, tr. R. Livingstone (Cambridge, Mass.: MIT Press, 1971)].

17   See Jürgen Habermas, *The Philosophical Discourse of Modernity* (Cambridge, Mass.: MIT Press, 1987), ch. 5.

18   For an enlightening treatment, see George Kateb, *Hannah Arendt: Politics, Conscience, Evil* (Totowa, New Jersey, 1984) ch. 5, pp. 149ff; for an analysis of totalitarianism, see ch. 2, pp. 52ff.

19   For the history of this idea, see F. Kudlien, "Diagnose," in *Historisches Wörterbuch der Philosophie*, vol. 2, pp. 162ff. For the content of the problem see Georg Lohmann, "Zur Rolle von Stimmungen in Zeitdiagnosen," in *Zur Philosophie der Gefühle*, ed. H. Fink-Eitel and G. Lohmann (Frankfurt, 1993), pp. 266ff.

20   For this history of this concept, see P. Probst, "Pathologie," part IV, in *Historisches Wörterbuch der Philosophie*, vol. 7, pp. 187ff; for the content of the problem, see Jürgen Habermas, "Überlegungen zur Kommunikationspathologie," in *Vorstudien und Ergänzungen zur Theories des kommunikativen Handelns* (Frankfurt: Suhrkamp, 1984), pp. 226ff, especially pp. 226–32.

21   For the philosophical point of view, see Ernst Tugendhat, *Probleme der Ethik* (Stuttgart, 1987), pp. 53ff; for the psychoanalytic point of view, see L. Kubie, "The Fundamental Distinction between Normality and Neurosis," in *Symptom and Neurosis: Selected Papers*, ed. H. J. Schlesinger (New York, 1978).

22   See Jürgen Habermas, "Ein Literaturbericht: Zur Logik der Sozialwissenschaften," in *Zur Logik der Sozialwissenschaften* (Frankfurt, 1982), pp. 89ff, especially pp. 183ff. For the difficulties associated with determining a measure of social pathologies, see Klaus Eder, *Geschichte als Lernprozeß? Zur Pathogenese politischer Modernität in Deutschland* (Frankfurt, 1985), pp. 30ff.

23   Jean-Paul Sartre, *Der Idiot der Familie: Gustave Flaubert 1821–1857*, 5 vols (Reinbek bei Hamburg, 1977), especially vol. 5.

24   See Andreas Wildt, *Die Anthropologie des frühen Marx*, study brief for Fernuniversität Hagen, 1987.

25   For the grounding of the cultural pluralism through Vico and Herder, see Isaiah Berlin, *Vico and Herder: Two Studies in the History of Ideas* (London, 1980).

26   See Arthur C. Danto, *Analytical Philosophy of History* (Cambridge: Cambridge University Press, 1965); Hans Michael Baumgartner, *Kontinuität und Geschichte: Zur Kritik und Metakritik der historischen Vernunft* (Frankfurt, 1972).

27   Arnold Gehlen, *Die Seele im technischen Zeitalter: Sozialpsychologische Probleme in der industriellen Gesellschaft* (Reinbek bei Hambrug, 1957). Gehlen continues this discussion in *Der Mensch: Seine Natur und seine Stellung in der Welt* (Frankfurt, 1971).

28   Habermas, "Technik und Wissenschaft als 'Ideologie'," in *Technik und Wissenschaft als Ideologie* (Frankfurt: Suhrkamp, 1968), pp. 48ff.

29   Daniel Bell, *Die Zukunft der westlichen Welt. Kultur und Technologie im Widerstreit* (Frankfurt, 1976).

30   Agnes Heller, *Everyday Life* (New York: Routledge, 1987); György Markus, "Der Begriff des menschlichen Wesens in der Philosophie des jungen Marx," in *Die neue Linke in Ungarn*, ed. A. Hegedus (Berlin, 1976), vol. 2, pp. 41ff.

31   See Michel Foucault, *Discipline and Punish: The Birth of the Prison* (New York: Random House, 1979); On the relationship of Foucault to Adorno, see my "Foucault and Adorno: Two Forms of Critique of Modernity" in A. Honneth, *The Fragmented World of the Social*, pp. 121–31. On Foucault's relationship to Weber, see my reflection in *Desintegration: Bruchstücke einer soziologischen Zeitdiagnose* (Frankfurt, 1994), pp. 61ff.

32   Richard Rorty, *Objectivism, Relativism, and Truth: Philosophical Papers*, vol. 1 (Cambridge: Cambridge University Press, 1991); Judith Butler, *Gender Trouble* (New York: Routledge, 1990).

33   See Habermas, "On the Pragmatic, the Ethical, and the Moral Employments of Practical Reason," in *Justification and Application*, tr. C. Cronin (Cambridge, Mass.: MIT Press, 1993), pp. 1ff.

34   See as a suggestion, Henry S. Richardson, *Practial Reasoning about Final Ends* (Cambridge, 1994).

35   See Habermas, *Theory of Communicative Action*, tr. T. McCarthy (Boston: Beacon Press, 1984, 1987) vol. 1, ch. 4.

36   See Martha Nussbaum, "Human Action and Social Justice: Toward a Defense of Aristotlean Essentialism," in *Gemeinschaft und Gerechtigkeit*, ed. M. Brumlik and H. Brunkhorst (Frankfurt, 1993), pp. 323ff. For a criticism, see Christiane Scherer, "Das menschliche und das gute menschliche Leben: Martha Nussbaum über Essentialismus und menschliche Fähigkeiten," in *Deutsche Zeitschrift der Philosophie* 5 (1993), pp. 905ff.

37   See Charles Taylor, *The Ethics of Authenticity* (Cambridge, Mass.: Harvard University Press, 1992), and *Sources of the Self: The Making of the Modern Identity* (Cambridge, Mass.: Harvard University Press, 1989).

38   On this division, see Holmer Steinfath, "Authentizität und Anerkennung: Zu Charles Taylors neuen Büchern 'The Ethics of Authenticity' und "The Politics of Recognition,' " in *Deutsche Zeitschrift der Philosophie* 3 (1993), pp. 433ff.

39   See Taylor, *Sources of the Self*.

PART VII

Bibliography

17 A BIBLIOGRAPHY OF CRITICAL THEORY

James Swindal

The following list of books and articles on critical theory is highly selective. Several comprehensive studies on critical theory, in particular those of Jay (1973), Arato and Gebhardt (1978), Held (1980), Wiggershaus (1986), and Kellner and Bronner (1989), already provide extensive bibliographies. Thus I list only the most significant primary works of critical theory and the most recent secondary works. I cite almost exclusively monographs and collections of articles. I have given particular priority to works on critical theory that are either written in or translated into English. English translations of works written in German are listed in brackets.

I   The Primary Writings of the Institute of Social Research

1   The Institute's Publications

1910–30   *Archiv für die Geschichte des Sozialismus und der Arbeiterbewegung* (vols I–XV).
1932–39   *Zeitschrift für Sozialforschung* (vols I–VIII:2).
1939–41   *Studies in Philosophy and Social Science* (vols VIII:3–IX:3).
1955–74   *Frankfurter Beiträge zur Soziologie.*

2   Collected Works of the Institute

1929   Henryk Grossmann. *Das Akkumulations und Zusummenbruchsgesetz des kapitalistischen System*. Leipzig.
1929   Friedrich Pollock. *Die planwirtschaftlichen Versuche in der Sowjetunion 1917–1927.* Leipzig.
1931   Karl August Wittfogel. *Wirtschaft und Gesellschaft Chinas: Versuch der wissenschaftlichen Analyse einer großen asiatischen Agrargesellschaft*, vol. 1. Leipzig.
1934   Franz Borkenau. *Der Übergang vom feudalen zum bürgerlichen Weltbild: Studien zur Geschichte der Philosophie der Manufakturperiode.* Paris.
1936   *Studien über Authorität und Familie.* Paris: Felix Alcan.

3   The Institute's Histories and Research Reports

1925   Gesellschaft für Sozialforschung, eds. *Institut für Sozialforschung an der Universität Frankfurt am Main*. Frankfurt/M.
1934   International Institute of Social Research, American Branch. *International Institute of Social Research: A Short Description of its History and Aims*. New York.
1938   International Institute of Social Research. *International Institute of Social Research: A Report on its History and Activities, 1933–38*. New York.
1944   Institute of Social Research. *Ten Years on Morningside Heights: A Report on the Institute's History 1934–44*.
1952   Institut für Sozialforschung. *Ein Bericht über die Feier seiner Wiedereröffnung, seiner Geschichte, und seine Arbeiten*. Frankfurt/M.
1957   Institut für Sozialforschung. *Zum politischen Bewußtsein ehemaliger Kriegsgefangener*. Hektographierter Forschungsbericht.
1961   Institut für Sozialforschung. *Student und Politik: Eine soziologische Untersuchung zum politischen Bewußtsein Frankfurter Studenten*. Neuwied.
1966   Institut für Sozialforschung. *Totalitäre Tendenzen in der deutschen Presse*. Hektographierter Forschungsbericht.
1968   Institut für Sozialforschung. *Angestellte und Streik: Eine soziologische Untersuchung der Einstellungen organisierter Angestellter zum Dunlop-Streik*. Hektographierter Forschungsbericht.
1970   Institut für Sozialforschung. *Kritische Analyse von Schulbüchern: Zur Darstellung der Probleme der Entwicklungsländer und ihrer Positionen in internationalen Beziehungen*. Hektographierter Forschungsbericht.

4   Work on Individual Members of the Institute

1963   *Zeugnisse: Theodor W. Adorno zum 60. Geburtstag*. Ed. M. Horkheimer. Frankfurt/M.
1992   *Kritik und Utopie im Werk von Herbert Marcuse*. Frankfurt/M: Suhrkamp.

5   Works of Historical Importance for the Institute

1924   Carl Grünberg, "Festrede gehalten zur Einweihung des Instituts für Sozialforschung an der Universität Frankfurt a. M. am 22 Juni 1924," *Frankfurter Universitätsreden*, vol. XX. Frankfurt/M.

II   The Writings of the Principal Figures in Critical Theory

1   Theodor Adorno

For Adorno's collected works, see *Gesammelte Schriften* (23 vols), ed. R. Tiedemann, Frankfurt/M: Suhrkamp, 1970–; *Musicalische Schriften* (6 vols), Frankfurt/M: Suhrkamp, 1978–1984; and *Soziologische Schriften* (2 vols), Frankfurt/M: Suhrkamp, 1972–75. See also *Akte: Theodor Adorno 1924–1968* in the archives of the former philosophy faculty at the University of Frankfurt/M. For a bibliography of Adorno's work, see René Görtzen's "Theodor W. Adorno: Vorläufige Bibliographie seiner Schriften und der Sekundärliteratur," in *Adorno Konferenze 1983*, ed. L. Friedeburg and J. Habermas, Frankfurt/M: Suhrkamp, 1983.

1933 *Kierkegaard: Konstruktion des ästhetischen* [*Kierkegaard: Construction of the Aesthetic*. Minneapolis: University of Minnesota Press, 1989].

1949 *Philosophie der neuen Musik*. Tübingen: Mohr [*Philosophy of Modern Music*. London: Sheed and Ward, 1973].

1950 *The Authoritarian Personality*. Co-authors E. Frenkel-Brunswick, D. Levinson, and R. Nevitt Sanford [2nd edn. New York: Norton, 1969].

1951 *Minima Moralia: Reflexionen aus dem beschädigten Leben*. Frankfurt/M [*Minima Moralia: Reflections from Damaged Life*, 2nd edn. London: New Left Books, 1974].

1955 *Prismen: Kulturkritik und Gesellschaft*. Frankfurt/M [*Prisms*. London: Neville Spearman, 1967].

1956 *Zur Metakritik der Erkenntnistheorie: Studien über Husserl und die phänomenologischen Antinomien*. Stuttgart [*Against Epistemology: A Metacritique*. Cambridge: MIT Press, 1983].

1958 *Noten zur Literature I*. Frankfurt/M: Suhrkamp [*Notes to Literature*, vol. 1. Ed. R. Tiedemann. New York: Columbia University Press, 1991].

1964 *Jargon der Eigentlichkeit*. Frankfurt/M: Suhrkamp [*Jargon of Authenticity*. London: Routledge and Kegan Paul, 1973].

1966 *Negative Dialektik*. Frankfurt/M: Suhrkamp [*Negative Dialectics*. New York: Seabury Press, 1973].

1969 *The Positivist Dispute in German Sociology*. Introduction and two essays by Adorno. London: Heinemann [*Positivismusstreit in der deutschen Soziologie*. Darmstadt: Luchterhand, 1972].

1970 *Ästhetische Theorie*. Eds. G. Adorno and R. Tiedemann. Frankfurt/M: Suhrkamp [*Aesthetic Theory*. London: Routledge and Kegan Paul, 1984].

1974 *Noten zur Literatur II*. Ed. R. Tiedemann. In *Gesammelte Schriften*, vol. 11 [*Notes to Literature*, vol. II. New York: Columbia University Press, 1992].

1975 *Gesellschaftstheorie und Kulturkritik*. Frankfurt/M: Suhrkamp.

1991 *The Culture Industry: Selected Essays on Mass Culture*. London: Routledge.

1993 *Hegel: Three Studies*. Cambridge: MIT Press.

2   Theodor Adorno and Max Horkheimer

1947 *Dialektik der Aufklärung*. Amsterdam: Querido [*Dialectic of Enlightenment*. New York: Herder and Herder, 1972].

1962 *Sociologia*. Frankfurt/M: Europäische Verlagsanstalt.

3   Walter Benjamin

For Benjamin's collected works, see *Gesammelte Schriften* (7 vols), eds. R. Tiedemann and H. Schweppenhäuser, Frankfurt/M: Suhrkamp, 1972–1989. See also *Briefe* (2 vols), eds. G. Scholem and T. Adorno, Frankfurt/M: Suhrkamp, 1966. See also *Habilitationakte Walter Benjamins* in the archives of the former philosophy faculty at the University of Frankfurt. For a bibliography, see Rolf Tiedemann, "Bibliographie der Erstdrucke von Benjamins Schriften," in *Zur Aktualität Walter Benjamins*,

Frankfurt/M: Suhrkamp, 1972, pp. 227–97. See also Bernd Witt, *Walter Benjamin*, Reinbek Bei Hamburg, 1985, pp. 147–54.

1936   *Deutsche Menschen Eine Folge von Briefen.* Written under pseudonym Detlef Holz. Frankfurt/M: Suhrkamp [2nd edn, 1977].

1965   *Zur Kritik der Gewalt und andere Aufsätze.* Frankfurt/M: Suhrkamp.

1966   *Versuche über Brecht.* Ed. R. Tiedemann. Frankfurt/M [*Understanding Brecht.* London: New Left Books, 1973].

1968   *Illuminations. Essays and Reflections.* Ed. H. Arendt. New York: Schocken.

1970   *Berliner Chronik.* Ed. G. Scholem. Frankfurt/M: Suhrkamp.

1974   *Charles Baudelaire: Ein Lyriker im Zeitalter des Hochkapitalismus.* Ed. R. Tiedemann. Frankfurt/M. [*Charles Baudelaire: A Lyric Poet in the Era of High Capitalism.* London: New Left Books, 1971].

1979   *Reflections.* New York: Harcourt, Brace, Jovanovich.

1980   *Moskauer Tagebuch.* Ed. G. Smith. Frankfurt/M: Suhrkamp.

1980   *Walter Benjamin – Gershom Scholem: Briefwechsel 1933–1940.* Ed. G. Scholem. Frankfurt/M.

4   Erich Fromm

For Fromm's collected works, see *Gesamtausgabe* (10 vols), ed. R. Funk, Stuttgart: Deutsche Verlags-Anstalt, 1980–1. A bibliography is found in volume 10. All titles were first published in English. For other references see Adelbert Reif, *Erich Fromm: Materialien zu seinem Werk*, Vienna, 1978.

1941   *Escape From Freedom.* New York: Farrar and Rinehart.

1947   *Man for Himself: An Inquiry into the Psychology of Ethics.* New York: Rinehart.

1955   *The Sane Society.* New York: Rinehart.

1956   *The Art of Loving.* New York: Harper.

1962   *Beyond the Chains of Illusion: My Encounter with Marx and Freud.* New York: Simon and Schuster.

1963   *The Dogma of Christ and Other Essays on Religion, Psychology and Culture.* New York: Holt, Rinehart and Winston.

1964   *The Heart of Man: Its Genius for Good and Evil.* New York: Harper and Row.

1973   *The Anatomy of Human Destructiveness.* New York: Holt, Rinehart, Winston.

1976   *To Have or To Be?* New York: Harper and Row.

1984   *The Working Class in Weimar Germany: A Psychological and Sociological Study.* Cambridge: Harvard University Press.

1992   *The Art of Being.* New York: Continuum.

1993   *On Being Human.* New York: Continuum.

5   Jürgen Habermas

For a complete bibliography, see René Görtzen's *Jürgen Habermas: Eine Bibliographie seiner Schriften und der Sekundärliterature 1952–1981*, Frankfurt/M: Suhrkamp, 1982. A revised version will be forthcoming. See also his shorter version in David Rasmussen's *Reading Habermas*, Cambridge: Blackwell, 1990, pp. 114–40.

1954 *Das Absolute und die Geschichte: von der Zwiespaltigkeit in Schellings Denken.* Dissertation, Universität Bonn.

1962 *Strukturwandel der Öffentlichkeit.* Berlin: Luchterland [*Structural Change of the Public Sphere.* Cambridge, Mass.: MIT Press, 1989].

1968 *Erkenntnis und Interesse.* Frankfurt/M: Suhrkamp [*Knowledge and Human Interests.* Boston: Beacon Press, 1971].

1968 *Technik und Wissenschaft als Ideologie.* Frankfurt/M: Suhrkamp [*Toward a Rational Society.* London: Heinemann, 1971].

1971 *Theorie und Praxis,* 2nd edn. Frankfurt/M: Suhrkamp [*Theory and Practice.* London: Heinemann, 1974].

1971 *Philosophisch-politische Profile.* Frankfurt/M: Suhrkamp [*Philosophical-Political Profiles.* Cambridge, Mass.: MIT Press, 1983].

1973 *Kultur und Kritik: Verstreute Aufsätze.* Frankfurt/M: Suhrkamp.

1973 "Wahrheitstheorien." In *Wirklichkeit und Reflexion: Walter Schulz zum 60. Geburtstag.* Ed. H. Fahrenbach. Pfullingen: Neske, pp. 127–83.

1973 *Legitimationsprobleme im Spätkapitalismus.* Frankfurt/M: Suhrkamp [*Legitimation Crisis.* Boston: Beacon Press, 1975].

1976 *Zur Rekonstruktion des Historischen Materialismus.* Frankfurt/M: Suhrkamp [*Communication and the Evolution of Society.* Boston: Beacon Press, 1979].

1981 *Theorie des kommunikativen Handelns* (2 vols). Frankfurt/M: Suhrkamp, 1981 [*Theory of Communicative Action* (2 vols). Boston: Beacon Press, 1984, 1987].

1982 *Zur Logik der Sozialwissenschaften,* 5th edn. Frankfurt/M: Suhrkamp [*On the Logic of the Social Sciences.* Cambridge, Mass.: MIT Press, 1988].

1983 *Moralbewußtsein und kommunikatives Handeln.* Frankfurt/M: Suhrkamp [*Moral Consciousness and Communicative Action.* Cambridge, Mass.: MIT Press, 1989].

1984 *Vorstudien und Ergänzungen zur Theorie des kommunikativen Handelns.* Frankfurt/M: Suhrkamp.

1985 *Philosophische Diskurs der Moderne.* Frankfurt/M: Suhrkamp, 1985 [*Philosophical Discourse of Modernity.* Cambridge, Mass.: MIT Press, 1987].

1986 *Autonomy and Solidarity: Interviews.* Ed. P. Dews. New York: Verso [2nd edn, 1992].

1987 *Eine Art Schadensabwicklung.* Frankfurt/M: Suhrkamp [*The New Conservatism: Cultural Criticism and the Historians' Debate.* Cambridge, Mass.: MIT Press, 1989].

1987 "Wie ist Legitimität durch Legalität möglich?" In *Kritische Justiz* 20, pp. 1–16.

1988 *Nachmetaphysisches Denken.* Frankfurt/M: Suhrkamp [*Postmetaphysical Thinking.* Cambridge: MIT Press, 1992].

1989 "Towards a Communication-Concept of Rational Collective Will-Formation: A Thought Experiment." In *Ratio Juris* 2, pp. 144–54.

1990 *Texte und Kontexte.* Frankfurt/M: Suhrkamp.

1990 *Die nachholende Revolution.* Frankfurt/M: Suhrkamp.

1990 "Justice and Solidarity: On the Discussion Concerning Stage 6." In *The Moral Domain: Essays in the Ongoing Discussion between Philosophy and the Social Sciences.* Ed. T. Wren. Cambridge, Mass.: MIT Press, pp. 244–51.

1990 "Volkssouveränität als Verfahren: Ein normativer Begriff der Öffentlichkeit." In *Die Moderne: Ein unvollendetes Projekt.* Leipzig: Reclam, pp. 180–212.

1991 *Vergangenheit als Zukunft.* Zurich: Pendo, 1992 [*The Past as Present.* Lincoln: University of Nebraska Press, 1994].

1991   *Erläuterungen zur Diskursethik*. Frankfurt/M: Suhrkamp [*Justification and Application*. Cambridge, Mass.: MIT Press, 1993].

1992   *Faktizität und Geltung*. Frankfurt/M: Suhrkamp [*Between Facts and Norms*. Cambridge: MIT Press, 1996].

1994   "Postscript to *Faktizität und Geltung*." In *Philosophy and Social Criticism* 20:4, pp. 135–50.

1995   "Reconciliation Through the Public Use of Reason." In *Journal of Philosophy* 42:3, pp. 109–31.

6   Max Horkheimer

For Horkheimer's collected works, see *Gesammelte Schriften* (18 vols), eds. G. Schmid Noerr and A. Schmidt, Frankfurt/M: Fischer, 1987–. Most of Horkheimer's essays in the *Zeitschrift für Sozialforschung* are found in *Kritische Theorie: Eine Dokumentation* (2 vols), ed. A. Schmidt, Frankfurt/M: Fischer, 1968. See also *Akte Max Horkheimer: 1922–65* in the archives of the former philosophy faculty at the University of Frankfurt. For a bibliography, see *Horkheimer Heute*, eds. A. Schmidt and N. Altwicker, Frankfurt/M: Fischer, 1986, pp. 372–99.

1931   "Die Gegenwärtige Lage der Sozialphilosophie und die Aufgaben eines Instituts für Sozialforschung." In *Frankfurter Universitätsreden*, vol. XXXVII.

1934   *Dämmerung*. Written under the pseudonym Heinrich Regius. Zurich: Oprecht und Helbling.

1947   *Eclipse of Reason*. New York: Oxford University Press [2nd edn, 1974].

1953   "Zum Begriff der Vernunft." In *Frankfurter Universitätsreden*, vol. 7.

1962   *Um die Freiheit*. Frankfurt/M.

1967   *Zur Kritik der instrumentellen Vernunft*. Frankfurt/M: Suhrkamp [*Critique of Instrumental Reason*. New York: Seabury, 1974].

1968   *Kritische Theorie: Eine Dokumentation* (2 vols). Ed. A. Schmidt. Frankfurt/M: Fischer [*Critical Theory*. New York: Herder and Herder, 1972].

1972   *Sozialphilosophische Studien: Aufsätze, Reden und Vorträge 1942–1970*. Ed. W. Brede. Frankfurt/M.

1972   "Traditional and Critical Theory." In *Critical Theory*. New York: Herder and Herder, pp. 188–243.

1978   *Dawn and Decline: Notes 1926–1931 and 1950–1969*. New York: Seabury.

7   Leo Löwenthal

For his collected works, see *Schriften* (4 vols), ed. H. Dubiel, Frankfurt/M: Suhrkamp, 1980.

1949   *Prophets of Deceit: A Study of the Techniques of the American Agitator*. Palo Alto: Pacific Books [2nd edn, 1970].

1957   *Literature and the Image of Man*. Boston: Beacon Press.

1961   *Literature, Popular Culture, and Society*. Palo Alto: Pacific Books [2nd edn, 1968].

1989   *Critical Theory and Frankfurt Theorists: Lectures, Correspondence, Conversations*. New Brunswick: Transaction Books.

8   Herbert Marcuse

For Marcuse's collected works, see *Gesammelte Schriften* (9 vols), Frankfurt/M: Suhrkamp, 1978–1987. For a complete bibliography of Marcuse's works, see *The Critical Spirit: Essays in Honor of Herbert Marcuse*, eds. K. Wolff and B. Moore, Boston: Beacon Press, 1967.

1932   *Hegel's Ontologie und die Theorie der Geschichtlichkeit*. Frankfurt/M [*Hegel's Ontology and the Theory of Historicity*. Cambridge, Mass.: MIT Press, 1987].
1941   *Reason and Revolution: Hegel and the Rise of Social Theory*. New York: Oxford University Press.
1955   *Eros and Civilization: A Philosophical Inquiry Into Freud*. Boston: Beacon Press.
1958   *Soviet Marxism: A Critical Analysis*. New York.
1964   *One Dimensional Man*. Boston: Beacon Press.
1968   *Negations: Essays in Critical Theory*. Boston: Beacon Press.
1968   *Psychoanalyse und Politik*. Frankfurt/M.
1969   *An Essay on Liberation*. Boston: Beacon Press.
1972   *Counterrevolution and Revolt*. Boston: Beacon Press.
1975   *Zeitmessungen*. Frankfurt/M.
1978   *The Aesthetic Dimension: Towards a Critique of Marxist Aesthetics*. Boston: Beacon Press.

9   Friedrich Pollock

1957   *The Economic and Social Consequences of Automation*. Oxford: Basil Blackwell.
1975   *Stadien des Kaptialismus*. Ed. H. Dubiel. Munich.

III   Selected Secondary Works on Critical Theory

1   General Studies

Agger, Ben. *The Discourse of Domination: From the Frankfurt School to Postmodernism*. Evanston: Northwestern University Press, 1992.
Benhabib, Seyla. *Critique, Norm, and Utopia: A Study of the Foundations of Critical Theory*. New York: Columbia University Press, 1986.
—— and Dallmayr, Fred, eds. *The Communicative Ethics Controversy*. Cambridge, Mass.: MIT Press, 1990.
Andrew Benjamin, ed. *The Problems of Modernity: Adorno and Benjamin*. New York: Routledge, 1989.
Bogner, Artur. *Zivilisation und Rationalisierung: die Zivilisationstheorien Max Webers, Norbert Elias' und der Frankfurter Schule im Vergleich*. Opladen: Westdeutsche, 1989.
Bottomore, Tom. *The Frankfurt School*. New York: Tavistock Publications, 1985.
Brunkhorst, Hauke. "Paradigmatikern und Theoriendynamik der Kritischen Theorie der Gesellschaft." In *Soziale Welt* 3 (1983).
Bubner, Rüdiger. *Essays in Hermeneutics and Critical Theory*. New York: Columbia University Press, 1988.

Cooke, Maeve. *Language and Reason*. Cambridge, Mass.: MIT Press, 1994.

Dallmayr, Fred. *Between Freiburg and Frankfurt: Toward a Critical Ontology*. Amherst: University of Massachusetts Press, 1991.

Dews, Peter. *Logics of Disintegration: Post-Structuralist Thought and the Claims of Critical Theory*. New York: Verso, 1987.

Dubiel, Helmut. *Kritische Theorie der Gesellschaft*. Munich: Juventa, 1988.

Erd, Rainer, et al., eds. *Kritische Theorie und Kultur*. Frankfurt/M: Suhrkamp, 1989.

Gamm, Gerhardt, ed. *Angesichts objektiver Verblendung: Über die Paradoxien Kritischer Theorie*. Tubingen, 1985.

Freenberge, Andrew. *Lukács, Marx, and the Sources of Critical Theory*. New York: Oxford University Press, 1986.

Guess, Raymond. *The Idea of a Critical Theory*. Cambridge: Cambridge University Press, 1981.

Günther, H. et al., eds. *Die Gewalt der Verneinung: Die Kritische Theorie und ihre Folgen*. Stuttgart, 1987.

Held, David. *An Introduction to Critical Theory*. London: Hutchinson, 1980.

Hesse, Heidran. *Vernunft und Selbstbehauptung: Kritische Theorie als Kritik der neuzeitlichen Rationalität*. Frankfurt/M: Fischer Wissenschaft, 1984.

Holub, Robert. *Jürgen Habermas: Critic in the Public Sphere*. New York: Routledge, 1991.

Honneth, Axel and Wolfgang Bonns, eds. *Sozialforschung als Kritik*. Frankfurt a/M: Suhrkamp, 1982.

—— and Albrecht Wellmer, eds. *Die Frankfurter Schule und die Folgen*. New York: Walter de Gruyter, 1986.

Horster, Detlef. *Jürgen Habermas*. Stuttgart: Metzler, 1991.

Ingram, David. *Critical Theory and Philosophy*. New York: Paragon House, 1990.

Jay, Martin. *The Dialectical Imagination: A History of the Frankfurt School and the Institute of Social Research, 1923–1950*. Boston: Little Brown, 1973.

—— *Marxism and Totality: The Adventures of a Concept from Lukács to Habermas*. Berkeley: University of California Press, 1984.

—— *Permanent Exiles: Essays on the Intellectual Migration from Germany to America*. New York: Columbia University Press, 1986.

Kearney, Richard. *Modern Movements in European Philosophy*. Manchester: Manchester University Press, 1987.

Kellner, Douglas. *Critical Theory, Marxism, and Modernity*. Baltimore: Johns Hopkins University Press, 1989.

—— and Stephen Bronner, eds. *Critical Theory and Society: A Reader*. New York: Routledge, 1989.

Kelly, Michael, ed. *Hermeneutics and Critical Theory in Ethics and Politics*. Cambridge, Mass.: MIT Press, 1990.

Lovenich, Friedhelm. *Paradigmenwechsel: über die Dialektik der Aufklärung in der revidierten Kritischen Theories*. Würzburg: Königshausen und Neumann, 1990.

Marcus, Judith and Zoltan Tar, eds. *Foundations of the Frankfurt School of Social Research*. London: Transaction Books, 1984.

Malaga, S. L. et al., eds. *Die Frankfurter Schule: Wie aktuell ist die Kritische Theorie?* Rotterdam: Universitaire Press, 1990.

McCarthy, Thomas. *Ideal and Illusions: On Reconstruction and Deconstruction in Contemporary Critical Theory*. Cambridge, Mass.: MIT Press, 1991.

— and David Couzens Hoy. *Critical Theory*. Cambridge: Blackwell, 1994.

Münkler, Herfried, ed. *Grand Hotel Abgrund: Eine Photobiographie der Kritische Theorie*. Hamburg: Junius, 1988.

Nielsen, Kai. *After the Demise of the Tradition: Rorty, Critical Theory, and the Fate of Philosophy*. Boulder: Westview Press, 1991.

Norris, Christopher. *What's Wrong with Postmodernism: Critical Theory and the Ends of Philosophy*. Baltimore: Johns Hopkins University Press, 1990.

— *Spinoza and the Origins of Modern Critical Theory*. Oxford: Blackwell, 1991.

O'Neill, John, ed. *On Critical Theory*. New York: Seabury Press, 1976.

Outwaite, William. *New Philosophies of Social Science: Realism, Hermeneutics, and Critical Theory*. New York: St. Martin's Press, 1987.

Schmidt, Alfred. *Zur Idee der Kritischen Theorie*. Munich: Hanser, 1974.

Theunissen, Michael. *Kritische Theorie der Gesellschaft: Zwei Studien*. New York: Walter de Gruyter, 1981.

Thompson, John. *Ideology and Modern Culture: Critical Social Theory in the Era of Mass Communication*. Stanford: Stanford University Press, 1990.

Wellmer, Albrecht. *Critical Theory of Society*. New York: Seabury Press, 1974.

Wiggershaus, Rolf. *The Frankfurt School: Its History, Theories, and Political Significance*. Cambridge, Mass.: MIT Press, 1994.

2   Critical Theory and Politics

Agger, Ben. *A Critical Theory of Public Life: Knowledge, Discourse and Politics in an Age of Decline*. London: Falmer, 1991.

Dubiel, Helmut. *Wissenschaftsorganisation und politische Erfahrung: Studien zur frühen Kritische Theories*. Frankfurt/M, 1978 [*Theory and Politics*. Cambridge, Mass.: MIT Press, 1985].

Forester, John, ed. *Critical Theory and Public Life*. Cambridge, Mass.: MIT Press, 1985.

Fraser, Nancy, et al. *Critical Politics: From the Personal to the Global*. Melbourne: Arena, 1994.

Gangl, Manfred. *Politische Ökonomie und Kritische Theorie*. Frankfurt/M: Campus, 1987.

Leonard, Stephen. *Critical Theory in Political Practice*. Princeton: Princeton University Press, 1990.

Linklater, Andrew. *Beyond Realism and Marxism: Critical Theory and International Relations*. Basingstoke: Macmillan, 1990.

Schnädelbach, Herbert. *Vernunft und Geschichte*. Frankfurt a/M: Suhrkamp, 1987.

Sciulli, David. *Theory of Societal Constitutionalism: Foundations of a Non-Marxist Critical Theory*. New York: Cambridge University Press, 1992.

Slater, Phil. *Origin and Significance of the Frankfurt School*. London: Routledge and Kegan Paul, 1977.

Studiner, Hugo. *Die Frankfurter Schule*. Wurzburg, 1982.

Wagner, Hans. "Einiges über die Kritische Theorie der Frankfurter Schule." In *Kritische Philosophie*. Ed. K. Bärthlein and W. Flach. Würzburg: Königshausen and Neumann, 1980, pp. 468–83.

Wellmer, Albrecht. *Critical Theory of Society*. New York: Seabury Press, 1974.

Wolin, Richard. *The Terms of Cultural Criticism: The Frankfurt School, Existentialism, Poststructuralism*. New York: Columbia University Press, 1992.

3 Critical Theory and Psychology

Döbert, Rainer, Gertrud Nunner-Winkler and Jürgen Habermas. *Entwicklung des Ichs*. Cologne, 1977.

Levin, David. *The Listening Self: Personal Growth, Social Change, and the Closure of Metaphysics*. New York: Routledge, 1989.

Lorenzer, Alfred. *Die Wahrheit der psychoanalytischen Erkenntnis: Ein historisch-material-istischer Entwurf*. Frankfurt/M: Imago-Druck, 1974.

Schmid Noerr, Gunzelin. *Das Eingedenken der Natur im Subjekt: zur Dialektik von Vernunft und Natur in der kritischen Theorie Horkheimers, Adornos und Marcuses*. Darmstadt: Wissenschaftliche Buchgesellschaft, 1990.

Whitebook, Joel. *Perversion and Utopia. A Study in Psychoanalysis and Critical Theory*. Cambridge, Mass.: MIT Press, 1994.

Wiegemann, Jutta. *Psychoanalytische Geschichtstheorie: Eine Studie zur Freud-Rezeption W. Benjamins*. Bonn: Bouvier, 1989.

4 Critical Theory and Theology

Ahrens, Edmund, ed. *Habermas und die Theologie*. Dusseldorf, 1989.

Lakeland, Paul. *Theology and Critical Theory*. Nashville: Abingdon Press, 1990.

Peukert, Helmut. *Science, Action, and Fundamental Theology: Towards a Theology of Communicative Action*. Cambridge, Mass.: MIT Press, 1984.

Pannenberg, Wolfhardt. *Wissenschaftstheorie und Theologie*. Frankfurt/M: Suhrkamp, 1973.

Rouner, L. S., ed. *Civil Religion and Political Theology*. Notre Dame: Notre Dame University Press, 1986.

Siebert, Rudolf. *The Critical Theory of Religion and the Frankfurt School: From the Universal Pragmatic to Political Theology*. New York: Mounton, 1985.

—— *From Critical Theory to Communicative Political Theology: Universal Solidarity*. New York: Lang, 1989.

Taylor, Mark. *Tears*. Albany: SUNY Press, 1990.

5 Critical Theory and Feminism

Cocks, Joan. *The Oppositional Imagination: Feminism, Critique, and Political Theory*. New York: Routledge, 1989.

Fraser, Nancy. *Unruly Practices: Power, Discourse, and Gender in Contemporary Social Theory*. Minneapolis: University of Minnesota Press, 1989.

Neumann, Walter. *Das Primat Kognitiver Praxis: Die Kritische Theories der Frankfurter Schule: eine weibliche Idee*. Frankfurt/M: Haag und Herchen, 1990.

6 Critical Theory and Aesthetics

Bermann, Russell. *Modern Culture and Critical Theory: Art, Politics, and the Legacy of the Frankfurt School*. Madison: University of Wisconsin Press, 1988.

Roblin, Ronald, ed. *The Aesthetics of the Critical Theorists: Studies on Benjamin, Adorno, Marcuse, and Habermas*. Lewiston: E. Mellen Press, 1990.

7 Critical Theory and Education

Bühner, Bernd and Achim Birnmeyer. *Ideologie und Diskurs: Zur Theorie von Jürgen Habermas und ihrer Rezeption in der Pädagogik.* Frankfurt/M: Haag und Herchen, 1982.

Young, Robert. *A Critical Theory of Education: Habermas and Our Children's Future.* New York: Teachers College Press, 1990.

8 Works on Specific Authors

(a) Adorno

Buck-Morss, Susan. *The Origin of Negative Dialectics.* New York: Free Press, 1967.

Brunkhorst, Hauke. *Theodor W. Adorno, Dialektik der Moderne.* Munich: Piper, 1990.

Früchtl, Josef. *Mimesis: Konstellation eines Zentralbegriffs bei Adorno.* Würzburg, 1986.

—— and Maria Calloni, eds. *Geist gegen den Zeitgeist: Erinnern an Adorno.* Frankfurt/M: Suhrkamp, 1991.

Gripp, Helga. *Theodor W. Adorno: Erkenntnisdimensionen negative Dialektik.* Munich: Schöningn, 1987.

Habermas, Jürgen and Ludwig von Friedeburg, eds. *Adorno Konferenz 1983.* Frankfurt/M: Suhrkamp, 1983.

Jay, Martin. *Adorno.* Cambridge, Mass.: Harvard University Press, 1984.

Roberts, David. *Art and Enlightenment: Aesthetic Theory after Adorno.* Lincoln: University of Nebraska Press, 1991.

Rose, Gillian. *The Melancholy Science.* London: Macmillan, 1981.

Scheible, Hartmut. *Theodor W. Adorno: mit Selbstzeugnissen und Bilddokumenten.* Reinbek bei Hamburg: Rowohlt, 1989.

Steinert, Hans. *Adorno in Wien: Über die (Un-)Möglichkeit von Kunst, Kultur und Befreiung.* Vienna: Verlag für Gesellschaftkritik, 1989.

van Reijen, Willem. *Adorno zur Einführung.* Hamburg: Junius, 1992.

Wellmer, Albrecht. *Zur Dialektik von Moderne und Postmoderne: Vernunftkritik nach Adorno.* Frankfurt/M: Suhrkamp, 1985.

Wiggershaus, Rolf. *Theodor Adorno.* Munich: Beck, 1987.

Zuidervaart, Lambert. *Adorno's Aesthetic Theory: The Redemption of Illusion.* Cambridge, Mass.: MIT Press, 1991.

(b) Benjamin

Buck-Morss, Susan. *The Dialectics of Seeing: Walter Benjamin and the Arcades Project.* Cambridge, Mass.: MIT Press, 1989.

Bulthaupt, Peter, ed. *Materialien zu Benjamins Thesen ''Über den Begriff der Geschichte'': Beiträge und Interpretation.* Frankfurt/M, 1977.

Fuld, W. *Walter Benjamin Zwischen den Stühlen: Eine Bibliographie.* Munich and Vienna, 1979.

Garber, Klaus. *Zum Bilde W. Benjamins.* Munich: Wilhelm Fink, 1992.

Konersmann, Ralf. *Erstarrte Unruhe: Walter Benjamins Begriff der Geschichte.* Frankfurt/M: Fischer, 1991.

Missac, Pierre. *Passage de Walter Benjamin.* Paris: Editions du Seuil, 1987.

Pensky, Max. *The Politics of Melancholia: Studies in the World of Walter Benjamin.* Amherst: University of Massachusetts Press, 1993.

Roberts, Julian. *Walter Benjamin*. London: Macmillan Press, 1982.

Scheurmann, Ingrid and Scheurmann, Konrad. *Für Walter Benjamin. Dokumente, Essays und ein Entwurf*. Frankfurt/M: Suhrkamp, 1992.

Schmidt, Burghart. *Benjamin*. Hanover: SOAK Verlag, 1984.

Scholem, Gerschom. *The Correspondence of Walter Benjamin and Gerschom Scholem*. Cambridge, Mass.: Harvard University Press, 1992.

Speth, Rudolf. *Wahrheit und Asthetik: Untersuchungen zum Frühwerk W. Benjamins*. Würzburg: Königshausen und Neumann, 1991.

Tiedemann, Rolf. *Studien zur Walter Benjamins*. Frankfurt/M: Suhrkamp, 1973.

Unseld, S., ed. *Zur Aktualität Walter Benjamins*. Frankfurt, 1982.

Wolin, Richard. *Walter Benjamin: An Aesthetic of Redemption*. New York: Columbia University Press, 1982.

(c)   Fromm

Funk, Rainer, *Erich Fromm: The Courage to Be*. New York: Continuum, 1983.

(d)   Habermas

Arato, Andrew and Jean Cohen, eds. *Civil Society and Political Theory*. Cambridge, Mass.: MIT Press, 1992.

Baynes, Kenneth. *The Normative Grounds of Social Criticism: Kant, Rawls, and Habermas*. Albany: SUNY Press, 1992.

—— et. al., eds. *After Philosophy*. Cambridge, Mass.: MIT Press, 1987.

Bernstein, Richard, ed. *Habermas and Modernity*. Cambridge, Mass.: MIT Press, 1985.

Braaten, Jane. *Habermas's Critical Theory of Society*. Albany: SUNY Press, 1991.

Brand, Arie. *The Force of Reason: An Introduction to the Work of Jürgen Habermas*. London: Allen and Unwin, 1989.

Calhoun, Craig, ed. *Habermas and the Public Sphere*. Cambridge, Mass.: MIT Press, 1992.

Dallmayr, Winifried, ed. *Materialen zu Habermas's "Erkenntnis und Interesse"*. Frankfurt/M: Suhrkamp, 1974.

Ferry, Jean-Marc. *Habermas, l'éthique de la communication*. Paris: Presses Universitaires de France, 1987.

Flynn, Bernard. *Political Philosophy at the Closure of Metaphysics*. London: Humanities Press, 1992.

Frank, Manfred. *Die Grenzen der Verständigung: Ein Geistergespräch zwischen Lyotard und Habermas*. Frankfurt/M: Suhrkamp, 1988.

Günther, Klaus. *Der Sinn für Angemessenheit: Answendungsdiskurse in Moral und Recht*. Frankfurt/M: Suhrkamp, 1988.

Held, David and John Thompson, eds. *Habermas: Critical Debates*. Cambridge, Mass.: MIT Press, 1982.

Honneth, Axel. *Kritik der Macht*. Frankfurt/M: Suhrkamp, 1985.

—— and Hans Joas, eds. *Communicative Action: Essays on Jürgen Habermas's Theory of Communicative Action*. Cambridge, Mass.: MIT Press, 1991.

—— et al., eds. *Zwischenbrachtungen im Prozess der Aufklärung*. Frankfurt/M: Suhrkamp, 1989.

Horster, Detlef. *Habermas zur Einführung*. Hanover: SOAK, 1980.

Ingram, David. *Habermas and the Dialectic of Reason*. New Haven: Yale University Press, 1987.

Kuhlmann, Wolfgang, ed. *Moralität und Sittlichkeit: Das Problem Hegels und die Diskursethik*. Frankfurt/M: Suhrkamp, 1986.

McCarthy, Thomas. *The Critical Theory of Jürgen Habermas*. Cambridge, Mass.: MIT Press, 1978.

Mellos, Koula, ed. *Nationalité, Communication, Modernité: Agir Communicationnel et Philosophie Politique chez Habermas*. Ottawa: Presse de L'université d'Ottawa, 1991.

Rasmussen, David. *Reading Habermas*. Oxford: Basil Blackwell, 1990.

—— ed. *Universalism and Communitarianism*. Cambridge, Mass.: MIT Press, 1988.

Rehg, William. *Insight and Solidarity: The Discourse Ethics of Jürgen Habermas*. Berkeley: University of California Press, 1994.

Rockmore, Tom. *Habermas on Historical Materialism*. Bloomington: Indiana University Press, 1989.

Roderick, Rick. *Habermas and the Foundations of Critical Theory*. New York: St. Martin's, 1986.

Schnädelbach, Herbert. *Reflexion und Diskurs*. Frankfurt/M: Suhrkamp, 1977.

Thompson, John. *Critical Hermeneutics. A Study in the Thought of Paul Ricoeur and Jürgen Habermas*. New York: Cambridge University Press, 1981.

van Gelder, Frederick. *Habermas' Begriff des historischen Materialismus*. Frankfurt/M: Peter Lang, 1987.

Wellmer, Albrecht. *Ethik und Dialog*. Frankfurt/M: Suhrkamp, 1986.

White, Stephen. *The Recent Work of Jürgen Habermas: Reason, Justice and Modernity*. Cambridge: Cambridge University Press, 1989.

Zimmermann, Rolf. *Utopie – Rationalität – Politik: Zu Kritik, Reconstruktion und Systematik einer emanzipatorischen Gesellschaftstheorie bei Marx und Habermas*. Freiburg: Karl Alber, 1985.

(e) Horkheimer

Gumnior, Helmut and Rudolf Ringguth. *Horkheimer*. Reinbek bei Hamburg: Rowohlt, 1973.

Hartmann, Frank. *Max Horkheimers materialisticher Skeptizismus*. Frankfurt/M: Campus, 1990.

Küsters, G.W. *Der Kritikbegriff der Kritischen Theorie Max Horkheimers: Historischsystematische Untersuchung zur Theoriegeschichte*. New York, Frankfurt/M, 1980.

Maor, Maimon. *Max Horkheimer*. Berlin, 1981.

Schmidt, Alfred. *Die geistige Physiognomie Max Horkheimer*. Frankfurt, 1974.

—— and Nobert Altwickler, eds. *Max Horkheimer Heute: Werk und Wirkung*. Frankfurt/M: Fischer, 1986.

Scholem, Gerschom. *Walter Benjamin: Die Geschichte einer Freundschaft*. Frankfurt/M, 1975.

Tar, Zoltan. *The Frankfurt School: The Critical Theories of Max Horkheimer and Theodor Adorno*. New York: Wiley, 1977.

Wurger, Wolfgang. *Kritische Theorie und Weltveränderung: Der Praxisbegriff in der Philosophie Max Horkheimers*. Gießen: Focus, 1987.

(f) Works on Löwenthal.

Löwenthal, Leo. *Mitmachen wollte Ich nie: Ein autobiographisches Gespräch mit Helmut Dubiel*. Frankfurt/M, 1980.

(g)   Works on Marcuse.

Claussen, Detlev. *Spuren der Befreiung: Herbert Marcuse*. Darmstadt, 1981.

Flego, Gvozden, and Wolfdietrich Schmied-Kowarzik, eds. *Herbert Marcuse: Eros und Emanzipation*. Gießen: Germinal, 1989.

Görlich, Bernhard. *Die Wette mit Freud: Drei Studien zu Herbert Marcuse*. Frankfurt a/M: Nexus, 1991.

Katz, Barry. *Herbert Marcuse and the Art of Liberation: An Intellectual Biography*. London, 1982.

Kellner, Douglas. *Herbert Marcuse and the Crisis of Marxism*. London, 1984.

Pippin, Robert, ed. *Marcuse: Critical Theory and the Promise of Utopia*. South Hadley: Bergin and Garvey, 1988.

ACKNOWLEDGMENT

I would like to thank Josef Früchtl for his generous and helpful assistance with my preparation of this bibliography.

INDEX

jurisprudence, 181–2
just war theory, 146
justice
 Adorno on, 327
 and deconstruction, 327
 and discourse, 359, 364
 group identity respect for, 358
 Habermas on, 122, 123, 124, 128, 129, 132, 133, 135, 138, 141–4, 153, 174, 230, 359, 393
 Hoy on, 355–6
 postmodernism, 330
 Rawls on, 119, 131, 156, 169, 174–5, 177
 and reason, 138–9, 148–58
 of social action, 386
 and social defects, 388
 and thought, 21
 Walzer on, 138, 141, 144–7
justification, 89, 106, 147–9, 156–8
 burdens of, 353
 Habermas on, 147–8, 229, 359
 Kuhn on, 83
 Popper on, 79, 81–2
 public, 243–5, 247, 251
 and social pathologies, 386
juxtaposition, 328

Kafka, Franz, 50
Kandinsky, Wassily, 330
Kant, Immanuel, 78, 87, 89, 93, 96, 97, 99, 267, 270, 287, 365
 actions, 346
 and Adorno, 307–8, 334, 335
 autonomy, 245, 246, 252–3n
 categorical imperative, 154, 277
 critical theory origins, 11
 determination of art, 312
 dialectic of enlightenment, 24, 152
 Hegel on, 154, 278
 idea of immortality, 315
 intentional subject, 335
 law, 174
 legitimacy concept, 168
 moral ideal, 336
 moral subject, 330
 morality, 26, 68, 70, 119, 125, 154, 174, 386
 natural-law theory, 179
 philosophy of consciousness, 169
 public sphere, 209
 rational self-identity, 327
 reason, 13, 26, 149, 152–3, 154
 subject–object relations, 92
 totality, 343
Kathedersozialisten, 54n
Kautsky, Karl Johann, 15
Kierkegaard, Sören Aaby, 24, 129

Klage, Ludwig, 25
Klee, Paul, 330
Kluge, Alexander, 314
knowledge, 260, 316, 364, 383
 Apel on, 258, 263, 268, 279–80n
 Descartes on, 328–9
 Foucault on, 96, 97, 351, 392
 of the future, 390
 Horkheimer on, 19, 57, 59
 and interest, 31–3, 346
 and interpretation, 353
 and political philosophy, 386
 and power, 23, 351
 and social sciences, 264, 265
 systems-theory, 91–2, 95–6
 tragic, 57–71
knowledge-directing interests theories, 84–90, 102
Kohlberg, Lawrence, 89, 108, 300
Kohut, Heinz, 295
Korsch, Karl, 42, 48, 49
Kracauer, Siegfried, 44, 45, 55n, 307, 308, 311, 315, 316
Kuhn, Thomas S., 83, 95, 97, 102, 109, 361

labor process, 14
Lacan, Jacques, 303–4n
LaCapra, Dominick, 51
Lakatos, Imré, 271, 272
Landauer, Karl, 44
Landes, Joan, 225
language, 258, 332, 333, 335, 360, 361, 364
 Habermas on, 35–6, 170, 177, 236
 and psychoanalysis, 299, 303–4n
 and systems theory, 176
 see also observation language
language games, 92, 123, 258, 261, 267
Lavan, Paul, 44
law, 142–3, 369
 and democracy, 166–85, 206–7, 210
 duality of, 167–9
 Hegel on, 15
 legitimacy of, 168, 178–80, 183, 206–7, 210
 and morality, 168, 174, 179–80
 need for, 172–4
 and power, 174, 180–1, 182–5
Lazarsfeld, Paul, 46, 312
learning processes, 349–50
Lebensnot, 293
Lebensphilosophie, 61, 62
legal institutions, 175, 207–8
legal norms, 125, 128, 130, 132, 143, 178
legality, 221
legitimation, 89, 125, 130
 crisis of, 202
 of the law, 168, 178–80, 183,

206–7, 210
 Rawls' principle of, 244
Lenin, Vladimir Ilyich, 15
lesbian rights, 234–5
Levinas, Emmanuel, 339n
liberalism, 178–80, 183, 184, 191–2, 193–7, 210, 244
 Apel on, 274–5
 human freedom, 288
 Marcuse on, 192, 194, 195, 211–12n
 new respect for, 298, 301
 postmodern, 346
liberation *see* freedom
libido, 294
life, 61
life-histories, 358
life-world
 Apel on, 273–4, 284n
 and consensus, 173
 desolation of, 379
 Habermas on, 102–5, 142–3, 172, 187n, 220, 224, 229, 233, 234, 341, 347
 impact of capitalism, 377
 and system, 103–4, 142–3, 220, 224, 229, 341, 347
linguistic analysis, 386
literary public sphere, 223, 226, 227
Locke, John, 178
logic, 61, 64, 334
logocentrism, 353
logos, 86, 87, 97, 297
Löwenthal, Leo, 17, 45
 and Adorno, 310, 313, 318
 essay on Hamsun, 40
 Frankfurt Lehrhaus, 45, 50
 psychoanalysts, 45, 287
 in US, 47, 307
Luhmann, Niklas
 and the law, 175–7, 181, 188n
 systems-theory, 78–9, 90–7, 100, 101–5, 175–7
Lukács, Georg, 18, 42, 309, 347, 378, 390, 392
 capitalism, 381
 Marxist theory, 48, 49
 working class, 16
Luxemburg, Rosa, 15
Lynd, Robert, 46
Lyotard, Jean François, 58, 92, 335, 339n

MacDonald, Dwight, 47
MacIntyre, Alasdair, 349, 354
MacIver, Robert, 46
madness, 304n
magic, 23, 332
Mahler, Gustav, 309, 311, 320
majority rule, 207, 209
male subjectivity, 334
Mann, Patricia, 226
Marcus, George, 343
Marcuse, Herbert, 17, 61, 298, 313, 314
 and Apel, 259

things, 363
Thomas Aquinas, 169
thought
  and action, 11–15, 61
  and freedom, 13–14, 21
  in history of German
    philosophy, 13
  and social justice, 21
threats, 374
Tillich, Paul, 312
time, 293–5
Tocqueville, Alexis de, 379
Tolstoy, Leo, 306
Tönnies, Ferdinand, 381
totalitarianism, 26, 381, 382,
  383–5
totality
  and civil society, 220
  and democracy, 191–7, 201,
    202, 210, 211n
  ethical, 376
  loss of confidence in, 51
  and modern art, 337
  and postmodernism, 338
  and reason, 151
  and social normality, 388
  and social theory, 341, 343
totalizing reason, 319
Toulmin, Stephen, 51
tradition, 89, 102, 355, 356
traditional societies, 342
traditional theory, 16–21, 31–2,
  34, 59–61, 190, 259–60
tragic knowledge, 57–71
transcendence, 344
transcendental philosophy, 349
transcendental pragmatics,
  258–78
transgressive *imagos*, 301
transience, 293, 294, 295, 296,
  297
transparency, 63, 327
tribal communication, 373
truth
  Adorno on, 317, 319
  and art, 29, 30, 333
  of beliefs, 363
  and critical discourse, 367n
  Habermas's notion of, 152,
    359–60
  historical, 87–8, 354, 355,
    357
  Hoy on, 360, 361, 363, 364
  natural science, 263
  systems-theory, 92, 95, 97
  of theories, 83
truth claims, 169, 170, 262,
  357–8, 360
U principle, 121, 122–5, 126,
  130–1, 132, 135, 206,
  276–7, 285n
U! principle, 276–7, 278, 285n
unconscious, 299, 300, 301
understanding, 84–9, 103,
  236–7, 250, 359
  of actions, 81, 85–6, 106
  Apel on, 260, 262, 279–80n
  communicative, 262, 266,

268, 280n
  sociology of, 102, 104
uniqueness, 251
United States
  legal system, 181–2
  new right politics, 235
  queer politics, 234
unity, 337, 354–5
universal consensus, 353
universal discourse, 346
universal validity, 258, 353, 364
universalism
  of alienation, 384–5
  anthropological, 392
  of conformity, 379
  contingency, 353
  ethics, 119, 120
  Habermas on, 359
  and Hegel's social life, 376
  Hoy on, 360
  pragmatics, 340
  rationality, 345
  social philosophy, 390
  systems-theory, 95
universalization principle *see* U
  principle
university, role of, 40–52
unproveability, 82
urban environment, 328–9
urban influences, 40–52
urbanization, 379
utilitarianism, 369
utopianism, 149, 301–2, 330,
  333, 338, 340, 346
  Adorno on, 154, 293, 336–7,
    339n
  Apel on, 277–8
  and art, 334
  Habermas on, 293
  Marcuse on, 290–1, 293, 294,
    297, 301, 339n
utterances, 122, 250, 262

validity
  Apel on, 258–9, 263, 266
  contextual, 353, 356, 358,
    360–1
  ethics, 119, 120, 121, 122, 124,
    125, 126–7, 130–5, 154, 276
  and facticity, 167–9, 170,
    173, 174, 180
  notion of, 31–6, 169
validity claims, 105, 108, 109,
  157, 173
  Apel on, 152, 267, 271, 272,
    276–7, 284n, 285n
  Habermas on, 151–2, 169,
    170–2, 174, 229, 250, 348,
    359
  Hoy on, 353, 356, 364
value, striving for, 374
value convictions, 391
value judgements, 79, 266
value spheres, 173
values, ethical, 394
vanity, 371
Vico, Giambattista, 390
virtue

and the way of the world,
  11–12
Volkhochschule im Westen, 314
voluntary associations, 220
voting, 166
vulnerability, 231, 236, 237,
  238–9

Wagner, Richard, 320
Waldron, Jeremy, 244
Walzer, Michael, 138, 141,
  144–7, 155, 156–7,
  159–60n
want satisfaction, 246
Weber, Max, 177, 262, 266, 272
  account of modern society,
    343
  anti-modernism, 301
  civilization, 289
  demystification, 381
  dialectic of enlightenment, 24
  disenchantment, 29, 172,
    333
  occidental rationalism, 315
  on politics, 203
  power, 100, 392
  rationality, 351
  rationalization, 29, 35, 40,
    48, 49, 104, 141, 334, 344,
    347, 351, 383
  reason, 22, 205, 351
  validity claims, 284n
  value spheres, 173
Weil, Felix, 16, 42
Weil, Hermann, 16, 42, 43
welfare state, 185, 224
well-being, 358
Wellmer, Albrecht, 124–5, 126,
  127, 131, 132, 315, 337,
  364
will, 131–2
will-formation, 142, 143, 181,
  203, 208, 209, 300, 389
Williams, Bernard, 145
Williams, Raymond, 213n
wisdom, 296
Wittfogel, Karl August, 54n
Wittgenstein, Ludwig Josef
  Johann, 258, 330, 335, 360
women
  in the public sphere, 225–8,
    230
word-presentations, 299
work, activity of, 382
workers' movement, 16, 17,
  21, 378, 379
working class, 16, 17, 49, 225,
  382
world, 92–3
  scientific discourse, 360
world, way of
  and virtue, 11–12

Young, Iris Marion, 231

Die Zeit, 314
Zeitschrift für Sozialforschung,
  55n, 318